Advance Praise for

THE PEACEMAKER

———————◆———————

"A luminous examination of one of the most consequential yet elusive figures in modern US and world history. Years in the making and based on a vast array of sources, *The Peacemaker* is a richly textured work of broad scope and deep analytical power. Critics no less than supporters of Reagan and his foreign policies should read Inboden's provocative, absorbing book."

—Fredrik Logevall, Pulitzer Prize–winning
author of *Embers of War: The Fall of an Empire and the Making of America's Vietnam*

"William Inboden's *The Peacemaker* makes the strongest case yet for Reagan as a successful grand strategist. Clearly written, thoroughly researched, full of fresh information, this comprehensive account will shape all future studies of the role the United States played in ending the Cold War."

—John Lewis Gaddis, Pulitzer Prize–winning
author of *George F. Kennan: An American Life*

"William Inboden has written a remarkable, singular book on Ronald Reagan's foreign policy and, specifically, on his determination from the outset of his presidency to be a peacemaker even as he pursued the collapse of the Soviet Union. Inboden's careful documentation and analysis of how Reagan developed and implemented this dual and seemingly paradoxical strategy will confound both the left and the right today, just as Reagan did while he was president. Inboden makes a compelling case that Reagan—criticized by the left as a warmonger, by the right as too soft, and by most of the foreign policy establishment as naive, unrealistic, and ill-informed—was in fact an extraordinarily successful grand strategist in pursuit of his twin goals. And deeply committed to avoiding a nuclear holocaust. *The Peacemaker* is an important contribution to understanding Reagan's foreign policy and is, at the same time, a great read."

—Robert M. Gates, CIA deputy director 1982–1989, secretary
of defense 2006–2011, and #1 *New York Times* bestselling author
of *Duty: Memoirs of a Secretary at War*

"[A] mesmerizing book . . . so easy to pick up and keep reading, so hard to put down . . . [with an] impressive range of archival, oral, and published sources that buttress every chapter."
   —Paul Kennedy, *New York Times* bestselling
      author of *The Rise and Fall of the Great Powers*

"Ronald Reagan was one of the most consequential presidents in US history. And this is the most consequential book yet written on his foreign policy. There is no better guide than William Inboden to the remarkable turn of events that ended the Cold War—and Reagan's unique role in bringing them about."
   —Hal Brands, author of *The Twilight Struggle: What the Cold War Teaches Us About Great-Power Rivalry Today*

"William Inboden has made a major contribution to our understanding of the Reagan presidency and the twilight of the Cold War era. Meticulously researched, vividly detailed, crisply paced, and judiciously argued, *The Peacemaker* paints a compelling portrait of a president with deep (often religiously grounded) convictions, steadfast purpose, and surprisingly deft diplomatic skills. Inboden's account has persuaded even this initially skeptical reader to rethink Reagan's foreign-policy record and give him his due as a visionary architect of the Cold War's conclusion. A landmark study in the character and consequence of transformative leadership."
   —David M. Kennedy, Pulitzer Prize–winning
      author of *Freedom from Fear: The American People
      in Depression and War, 1929–1945*

"President Reagan's commitment to the negotiated surrender of the Soviet Union entailed turning their strengths into liabilities while revivifying America's economy, military, alliances, and confidence, integrating power and diplomacy. This landmark book provides a long-overdue reconsideration of grand strategy in the Reagan administration, casting light on the degree of difficulty associated with reviving the geopolitical fortunes of the free world. It also reveals the centrality of religious faith in President Reagan's worldview. William Inboden has achieved something wonderful in conjuring the past so skillfully with this excellent book."
   —Kori Schake, author of *Safe Passage: The Transition
      from British to American Hegemony*

"A timely reminder of Ronald Reagan's strategy for advancing peace through strength in a world where, as he famously said: 'A nuclear war cannot be won, and it must never be fought.'"

    —Graham Allison, Douglas Dillon Professor of Government at Harvard University and author of *Destined for War: Can America and China Escape Thucydides's Trap?*

"William Inboden has written *the* book on Ronald Reagan's national security policy. As Americans stare down the possibility of a Beijing-led twenty-first century, we would do well to learn from Ronald Reagan. Taking office during a time of anxiety and doubt not unlike our own, Reagan defeated Soviet communism and enlarged the free world. Reagan navigated hard choices, fierce criticism, political divisions, and the constant threat of nuclear destruction to win the Cold War and leave a legacy that endures today. Like no author before, William Inboden rekindles America's familiar story with deft prose, a gripping narrative, and new insights in every chapter of this definitive account."

    —Senator Ben Sasse

"William Inboden has given us the definitive account of Ronald Reagan's greatest contribution to world history: his strategy to obtain a negotiated surrender from Soviet leadership that would end the Cold War with a decisive American victory. *The Peacemaker* is both gripping and meticulously researched. Inboden has dramatically enhanced our understanding of the president who saved America while bringing freedom to millions worldwide."

    —Representative Mike Gallagher

THE PEACEMAKER

RONALD REAGAN, THE COLD WAR, AND THE WORLD ON THE BRINK

WILLIAM INBODEN

DUTTON

DUTTON

An imprint of Penguin Random House LLC
penguinrandomhouse.com

Copyright © 2022 by William Inboden
Penguin Random House supports copyright. Copyright fuels creativity, encourages
diverse voices, promotes free speech, and creates a vibrant culture. Thank you for buying an
authorized edition of this book and for complying with copyright laws by not reproducing, scanning, or
distributing any part of it in any form without permission. You are supporting writers and allowing
Penguin Random House to continue to publish books for every reader.

DUTTON and the D colophon are registered trademarks of Penguin Random House LLC.

All insert photographs courtesy of the Ronald Reagan Presidential Library, except where indicated.

LIBRARY OF CONGRESS CATALOGING-IN-PUBLICATION DATA

Names: Inboden, William, 1972– author.
Title: The peacemaker: Ronald Reagan, the Cold War, and the world on the brink / William Inboden.
Other titles: Ronald Reagan, the Cold War, and the world on the brink
Description: [New York]: Dutton, [2022] | Includes bibliographical references and index. |
Identifiers: LCCN 2022001710 (print) | LCCN 2022001711 (ebook) |
ISBN 9781524745899 (hardcover) | ISBN 9781524745912 (ebook) |
Subjects: LCSH: United States—Foreign relations—1981–1989. | Reagan, Ronald. | National
security—United States—Decision Making—History—20th century. | United States—Foreign
Relations—Soviet Union. | Soviet Union—Foreign relations—United States. | Cold War.
Classification: LCC E876 .I54 2022 (print) | LCC E876 (ebook) |
DDC 973.927092—dc23/eng/20220201
LC record available at https://lccn.loc.gov/2022001710
LC ebook record available at https://lccn.loc.gov/2022001711

Printed in the United States of America

1st Printing

BOOK DESIGN BY ELKE SIGAL

While the author has made every effort to provide accurate telephone numbers, internet addresses,
and other contact information at the time of publication, neither the publisher nor the author assumes any
responsibility for errors or for changes that occur after publication. Further, the publisher does not have any
control over and does not assume any responsibility for author or third-party websites or their content.

For my parents, Bill and Connie

Blessed are the peacemakers,
for they shall be called sons of God.

—MATTHEW 5:9

CONTENTS

THE PEACEMAKER

INTRODUCTION

I

London. The eighth of June 1982. The Western alliance is being rent asunder by some of the most piercing rifts in three decades. The United States has sanctioned its NATO allies over a disputed oil pipeline from the Soviet Union to Western Europe and plans to deploy nuclear missiles in NATO nations over the fierce resistance of European publics. America and Britain remain mired in economic recession as tax cuts, spending austerity, and tightened monetary supply fail to restore growth and employment. The Soviet Union sits at the apex of its military might, with a nuclear arsenal that outmatches that of the United States and an overwhelming advantage in ships, tanks, and troops. Martial law in Poland enters its sixth month. British forces are fighting and dying in the Falkland Islands. In the east, the United States and China are in a tense standoff over Taiwan, while Washington and Tokyo remain at an impasse over trade. Two days earlier, Israel invaded Lebanon, setting the Middle East aflame.

The American president has just arrived in the United Kingdom for his first visit in office. The Royal Gallery of Westminster Palace swelters with anxious parliamentarians, lords, and ministers. Its walls loom with portraits and memories of orators past. Pitt, Gladstone, Disraeli, Lloyd George, Chamberlain, and the greatest of them all, Churchill, have uttered words from this palace that launched navies, inspired revolutions, defeated tyrants, sparked wars, brokered peace, and altered the landscape of the globe.

1

Ronald Reagan will be the first US president in history to address both houses of Parliament. Prime Minister Margaret Thatcher took no mean risk in inviting her friend to do so. Reagan has been in office less than eighteen months, yet in that time has endured an assassin's bullet, domestic discord, economic travails, foreign policy setbacks, and turmoil within his own feuding staff. In the words of a confidential cable to Thatcher from the British ambassador in Washington, "Reagan stands lower in the opinion polls than Carter did at this period in his presidency" and risks "being written off as a lame-duck president two years before the end of his term."[1] In the UK, he inspires fear and loathing in equal parts. Outside, over one hundred thousand protestors flood Hyde Park denouncing him as a deranged warmonger. Inside Westminster, more than two hundred Labour Party MPs boycott his visit.[2]

As the venerable actor steps to the stage, the crowd in the Royal Gallery turns expectantly toward their guest. Reagan knows the script well, for he wrote much of it himself. As he speaks, his words begin to echo not just through the hall but into the coming decades. He denounces totalitarianism's "barbarous assault on the human spirit" and the Berlin Wall as "that dreadful gray gash across the city." He praises the people of Poland for being "magnificently unreconciled to oppression." He heralds the "democratic revolution" gathering across the globe and calls for a "crusade for freedom" to accelerate it. And he condemns Marxism-Leninism to the "ash-heap of history." To those with ears to hear, he distills what the next six and a half years of his foreign policy will entail. The moral and ideological bankruptcy of communism, and the exhaustion of the decrepit Soviet economy. The integration of force and diplomacy, and a military expansion combined with diplomatic outreach to the Soviet Union. The horror of nuclear weapons and the dream of their ultimate abolition. The promotion of political, religious, and economic liberty around the world as a better way than communism. The arc of history guiding the present moment. And the triumph of freedom and peace.

To Reagan's multiple audiences in London, on the Continent, behind the Iron Curtain, in Moscow, in the developing world, and at home in the United States, the import of the speech will become known only with the passage of years. His Westminster oration unveils a new offensive that in seven short years will bring the Cold War to a victorious, peaceful end.

II

Along with Franklin Roosevelt, Ronald Reagan was one of the two most consequential presidents of the twentieth century. He was reviled and ridiculed by many experts and pundits at the time, but history's unfolding now offers a new window to reassess him, particularly his foreign policy. His critics, who were legion, feared that his presidency would lead to disastrous outcomes such as nuclear apocalypse, "another Vietnam," and America's terminal decline. Instead, with the peaceful end of the Cold War, collapse of the Soviet Union, renewal of the United States, and global expansion of freedom and prosperity, Reagan's grand strategy succeeded beyond even his imagining.

These achievements become all the more remarkable when considered in light of the geopolitical landscape that confronted him upon taking office. With the passage of time and the complacency that the Cold War's pacific resolution induces, we risk forgetting the terror and drama of the day. Communist regimes controlled a vast swath of the Eurasian landmass and used armed revolution and subterfuge to make further advances in Latin America, Africa, and Asia. The Soviet Union targeted upwards of forty thousand nuclear warheads at the United States, on alert to launch at a moment's notice. Many experts believed that the USSR was strong and resilient, matching if not eclipsing the United States as a world power, and would remain America's adversary for the indefinite future.

The United States, meanwhile, appeared to much of the world as a crippled giant, in inexorable decline from economic stagnation, military weakness, political dysfunction, and international ineptitude. At home, a crisis of confidence further eroded America's political will and capability to confront challenges domestic or foreign. Many Americans, and more than a few allied leaders, worried that the presidency itself was broken. Political division, insoluble policy challenges, and the burdens of the office seemed to render it impossible for any president to succeed. Not since Eisenhower two decades earlier had a US president completed two full terms in office. Of the five since, an assassin's bullet had felled John Kennedy; Vietnam had crippled Lyndon Johnson and forced him to eschew reelection; Watergate had driven Richard Nixon to resign ahead of certain impeachment; his unelected successor, Gerald Ford, had lost to Jimmy Carter; Carter had just been defeated by Reagan.[3] Restoring America's standing could not happen without restoring the office of its chief executive.

As a candidate, Reagan believed these trends could be reversed. As president, he set out to do so. He led the American economic recovery, helping spark a global boom. He rebuilt the American military and used it to help repair America's alliances and bring the Soviet Union to heel. He revived his nation's belief in itself, its values, and its role in the world. He recaptured the strength, dynamism, and grandeur of the office of the president. Across the globe, Reagan recognized the emerging information age and democratic wave, and positioned his country to help steer and shape both. In the Cold War, he perceived the Soviet Union's frailty and illegitimacy, and developed a strategy to exploit its weaknesses while also partnering with it to reduce the risk of nuclear apocalypse.

Reagan tried to do all this while preventing the outbreak of war and ridding the world of nuclear weapons. How to resolve these seemingly incompatible goals? How could he try to defeat Soviet communism while at the same time cooperating with the Kremlin to end the arms race? Reagan did this by pursuing the Soviet Union's *negotiated surrender.* "Negotiated" because he favored diplomacy over war and wanted to partner with a Soviet leader to negotiate arms reductions and reduced tensions, leading ultimately to eliminating nuclear weapons. "Surrender" because he loathed Soviet communism as a reprehensible system, a plague on all whom it ruled, and he sought to render it extinct. In many ways these goals were in tension, even at times contradiction. Yet while Reagan sometimes emphasized one and other times the other, he held tenaciously to both.

He built his Cold War strategy on eight pillars. First, restoring the American economy as a foundation of national strength and morale. Second, delegitimizing Soviet communism as a system of government. Third, building up and modernizing America's military. Fourth, supporting anticommunist insurgencies around the world. Fifth, making "mutual assured destruction" (MAD) obsolete through the Strategic Defense Initiative. Sixth, promoting human rights and freedom around the world, especially in the Soviet bloc. Seventh, pressuring the Soviet system into producing a reformist leader with whom Reagan could negotiate. Eighth, reducing the number of nuclear weapons in the world—with the ultimate hope of abolishing nuclear weapons entirely.

Above all, Reagan sought to turn Soviet strengths into liabilities. He believed that the massive Red Army, Warsaw Pact vassals, Soviet support for Third World communist movements, and the Kremlin's control of its own people all displayed the Soviet system's weakness, rather than its power. He sought to break this system apart by finding fissures and driving wedges into every crack. He pursued policies to free the Warsaw Pact satellite nations from Moscow's control, to liberate the Soviet people from the police state, to isolate the Kremlin from the rest of the world, and to impose such unsustainable costs on Soviet communism that it would collapse.

In sum, Reagan pursued a comprehensive Cold War strategy that sought to rebuild America's strengths and pose them against the Soviet Union across virtually every dimension. An alliance system built on choice versus the coerced colonies of the Warsaw Pact. Weapons systems that outmatched their Soviet counterparts. An open society against a closed one. Self-government versus dictatorship. Religious faith against atheism. Prosperity versus penury. Freedom over tyranny.

III

The Cold War was Reagan's central concern but not his only concern. Presidents do not get to choose the crises and challenges that cascade into the Oval Office. Other foreign policy issues consumed much of his time, including trade tensions with Japan, the world economy, terrorism, Middle East wars, Israeli-Palestinian conflicts, famine in Africa, and political and economic transformations in Latin America and Asia. Managing these policies—sometimes successfully, sometimes not—in the midst of waging the Cold War put an unrelenting strain on the Reagan administration. His Cold War strategy cannot be understood without appreciating the complications of the many other issues he confronted. In some of these, especially Asia, the global economy, and the growth of democracies, Reagan would achieve notable successes and leave a significant legacy. In others, such as the Middle East and terrorism, he would struggle.

So while this is a Cold War story—because little in the 1980s escaped the Cold War's shadow—it is also more than a Cold War story. Just as the Cold War had transformed the world, and Reagan took office trying to transform the Cold War, the world itself was undergoing other changes during this time that would transcend the Cold War. Given the multiple shocks of the lost war in Vietnam, the Watergate scandal, the OPEC oil embargo, economic stagnation, the Iran hostage crisis, Third World revolutions, and Soviet ascendancy, America experienced the 1970s as a demoralizing time of national decline. But behind these headlines, and away from policy decisions being made in Washington, DC, there lurked several signs of renewal, unseen waves forming far out at sea, or at least far from Washington, DC, and Moscow.

Some of the most consequential global changes originated in Reagan's home state of California in the 1970s. The historian Francis Gavin points out that in a short window in the mid-1970s, California produced "the sale of the early Apple personal computer, the release of *Star Wars*—the highest grossing motion picture of all time, and the famous 1976 'judgment of Paris' in which previously unknown wines from Napa Valley bested established French wines in a blind taste test." Each of these innovations would soon reverberate across the nation and around the world, as American technology and culture would help catalyze the coming era of globalization. While policymakers in Washington, DC, agonized over America's diminished resources, intractable problems, and declining national power, "the future was being made elsewhere and in different ways than policymakers understood in places like California, where deep and often obscure historical forces were working to transform the US economy, society, technological base, and culture in ways that would have profound effects on American power and world history."[4]

In the global arena, historian Hal Brands describes the 1970s as "a period when several deep structural trends were starting to rework the international landscape in America's favor, even as short-term events made it appear decidedly otherwise." Among these trends, technological innovation, the communications revolution, economic integration, and liberalization all created the possibility of American renewal and global prosperity, while new human rights institutions and activists were poised to expand liberty and democracy around the world.[5]

While such currents provide the possibility of change, they do not mean change is foreordained—or that it will be positive. Few saw these waves at the time, nor was their success inevitable. As a transplanted Californian and native optimist, Reagan perceived such trends sooner than most. When he combined this perception with his confidence in human ingenuity and democratic capitalism, he did not have to work hard to persuade himself that better days for America and the world lay ahead—and that he could lead both there.

IV

_____

This book will unfold as a narrative. The chronological approach gives the reader the vantage point of seeing history as it happened and as it appeared to Reagan and the senior members of his administration. In the words of Secretary of State George Shultz, the "simultaneity of events" beset the White House, as it does every presidency—no issue could be considered on its own, no decision deferred in the fullness of time, because the world does not wait on the White House Situation Room calendar.[6] Readers may on occasion feel a bit of whiplash as the story moves from event to event and issue to issue. This is by design, to capture in part the chaos of policymaking as it felt to Reagan and his team.

Who were not always a team. Amid the deluge of events, the White House found itself plagued by acrimony and infighting. The Reagan administration was weakened by some senior officials who were ill equipped for their roles, riven by other senior officials who were capable yet detested each other, and overseen by a president who despite his strategic vision was a dreadful manager. This book will explore the paradox of how Reagan achieved consequential successes with a notoriously fractious staff, bedeviled by constant leaks, fierce policy differences, and occasional criminality.

Several themes pervade this story. Each is essential for understanding Reagan's foreign policy across all domains, not just the Cold War. The themes are:

Allies and Partners. What Reagan accomplished, he did not do alone. Perhaps more than any other US president, he put alliances at the center of his strategy and formed close personal partnerships with allied leaders such as Britain's Margaret Thatcher, Japan's Yasuhiro Nakasone, West Germany's Helmut Kohl, and Canada's Brian Mulroney. Reagan believed that allies served as force multipliers and a source of national power. In the Cold War, they gave the United States an asymmetric edge over a Soviet bloc bound together more by coercion than choice. In other realms, allies deepened American influence, provided novel conduits of insight, and enhanced American diplomacy, intelligence, and economic power.

All was not always well with the alliances, however. Allies also caused some of Reagan's most consuming problems and painful trials. He and his policies in turn provoked some deep rifts with partner nations. Managing this turbulence would occupy him almost as much as any other realm of statecraft. Yet the centrality of allies can be seen in the fact that with almost every important Reagan administration policy, the allies were nearby, and often at center stage.

History. History looms over every White House. Reagan viewed both the presidency and America's international leadership as stewardships entrusted to him by history, to be preserved and strengthened for the future. In part because of his cinematic past, he saw himself as an actor in the great historical drama of the Cold War. Two historical episodes in particular, World War II and the Vietnam War, shadowed the Reagan White House and shaped the worldviews, values, and operating environment for Reagan and his senior team. The wars and their legacies also conditioned public opinion in Europe, Asia, and the United States in ways that Reagan alternatively sought to appeal to or resist.

World War II served as the formative life experience for most senior members of the Reagan administration. Vice President George H. W. Bush served as one of the youngest naval aviators in the war, surviving being shot down at sea while on a bombing run near Japan. Secretary of State George Shultz, Secretary of Defense Caspar Weinberger, and Secretary of the Treasury and White House Chief of Staff Donald Regan all saw combat in the Pacific theater. Chairman of the Joint Chiefs Jack Vessey earned a battlefield commission at Anzio. CIA director William Casey served behind enemy lines in Europe with the Office of Strategic Services. Poor eyesight disqualified Reagan himself from any combat role, but he served stateside with the Army Air Forces, putting his thespian talents to use making training films. General Colin Powell, who held several senior roles in the administration, later recalled that with Reagan's election, "the World War II generation was back in the saddle. The President's military screen credits may have been modest . . . but the war was a defining experience for him."[7]

Reagan believed that the World War II era demonstrated the dangers of isolationism and the need for American international leadership, especially against totalitarianism. As president he often spoke of how America's trade protectionism and isolationism in the 1930s weakened the West and contributed to the outbreak of war. The war also gave birth to the modern alliance system, and Reagan saw the United States' leadership of the Allies in defeating the Axis powers and establishing the postwar international order as a tradition to continue. America's wartime support for Joseph

Stalin's Soviet Union also helps explain the Reagan administration's support for many authoritarian regimes. In the midst of an existential conflict with a totalitarian foe, painful moral and tactical compromises are sometimes seen as necessary, even if it means backing ghastly dictators who brutalize their own people. Both World War II and the Cold War entailed using morally ambiguous means—and sometimes worse—for the morally unambiguous end of defeating totalitarianism.

Vietnam was a more recent trauma. When Reagan swore the oath of office on January 20, 1981, it was almost eight years to the day since the United States had signed the Paris Peace Accords and ended its combat in Vietnam in ignominious defeat. Several senior Reagan administration officials had fought in Vietnam, including national security advisors Bud Mc-Farlane, John Poindexter, and Colin Powell, as well as Secretary of State Al Haig and Secretary of the Navy James Webb, and numerous influential midtier officials such as the Pentagon's Richard Armitage and Oliver North of the National Security Council (NSC) staff.

While Vietnam reminded the Reagan team of the perils of ill-conceived interventions in far-flung lands, its particular lessons sparked fervent debate. In future conflicts, should the United States equip others to fight for it? Or use overwhelming American force? Or stay out of civil wars altogether? The White House also felt the Vietnam burden in the nation's collective memory. Much of the public wariness and congressional skepticism about Reagan's Central America policies derived from fears of "another Vietnam." In this case, history served as a trap to bind the White House's options. In other times, history would serve as a tool as Reagan appealed to the past in order to shape the future.

Force and Diplomacy. Reagan presents a paradox on the use of force. The American president who launched one of the most expansive military buildups in history, and who used militant rhetoric toward America's adversaries, was in fact extremely reluctant to deploy the military in combat. During his eight years in office, Reagan only ordered ground forces to fight once, in the relatively small-scale Grenada invasion.[8]

Behind this lay Reagan's concept of "peace through strength." Oft-cited but little understood, for Reagan it meant integrating force with diplomacy. Military power would not just deter aggression, it would also fortify negotiations and thus render the need to fight much less likely. Reagan's defense modernization had a *diplomatic* purpose as much as a military purpose. For this reason his military buildup focused on *quality* as much as *quantity* of arms; it was not just the degree but the kind of expansion that leveraged America's technological advantages to both outsmart and overmatch the Soviets. Reagan used this military modernization to force the Soviets into an arms race that they could neither afford nor win, leaving the Kremlin no option but to negotiate from weakness, leading to a negotiated surrender.

Religious Faith and Religious Freedom. For Reagan, the Cold War was a religious war. His personal convictions and the policies of his administration cannot be understood apart from the role of religious faith and religious freedom. Faith provided personal inspiration to Reagan, who believed God had called him to defeat Soviet communism and abolish nuclear weapons. This divine mandate gave Reagan the resolve to pursue his policies in the face of overwhelming criticism and opposition, and also a serenity and equipoise even as the world teetered on the brink of nuclear apocalypse.

Reagan's faith was at once idiosyncratic, elusive, and deeply held. His theological commitments appear to have been a distinctively American amalgam of conventional evangelicalism, prosperity gospel, premillennial dispensationalism, and occasional strains of Catholic mysticism. As eclectic as his beliefs may have been, his faith formed a firm core in his being and defined many of the most consequential elements of his presidency. He also viewed the conflict with the Soviet Union in religious terms, especially given Moscow's pronounced and militant atheism. This is why the White House gave priority to religious freedom in its human rights policy and sought to promote religious freedom as a good in its own right as well as an instrument to undermine and delegitimize communism.

Tragedy. Despite Reagan's congenital optimism, a sense of the tragic pervades his presidency. On one level it stems from the unrelenting staff acrimony, and the human costs of scandal, betrayal, and failure. On another level it is tragedy in the classical sense: No options were free of taint or risk. Many of the Cold War dilemmas Reagan faced were choices between bad and worse, where no matter what action—or inaction—was taken, terrible costs awaited. This dilemma was not unique to Reagan; it is the perpetual challenge of statecraft. Yet it was sharpened in the Reagan years by the accelerating crisis of the Cold War, by Reagan's belief that the conflict could be won and not just managed—and that merely prolonging it would only lead to more misery.

Of perhaps the most infamy, the tragic includes the carnage and suffering wrought by many authoritarian regimes and insurgencies supported by the Reagan White House in the name of anticommunism. Though the

Reagan administration may have had a Cold War justification for supporting such regimes, the oppression and crimes committed with American
support still besmirch the administration's record and must be included in
a full moral and strategic accounting. Reagan, reluctant to admit unpleasant truths, often evaded acknowledging this by denying to himself and others that certain dictators or insurgents—such as Marcos in the Philippines,
Pinochet in Chile, the Nicaraguan contras, and the Afghan mujahideen—
engaged in odious abuses.

As a matter of presidential history, this was unexceptional. Starting
with Franklin Roosevelt's billions of dollars in military and economic aid
to Stalin, every one of Reagan's predecessors had supported ruthless dictators in the cause of anti-totalitarianism, whether anti-Nazism or anticommunism.[9] Reagan's apologists should not deny the terrible abuses that his
policies sometimes enabled, yet nor should Reagan's critics gloss over the
very hard choices that he faced. Considering that communist regimes in the
twentieth century caused death counts estimated at from sixty-five million
to one hundred million people, the alternative had its own grim costs.[10]

Battle of Ideas. Every previous American president saw the Cold War
primarily as a great-power conflict between the United States and Soviet
Union, undergirded by a contest of ideas. Reagan reversed this. He saw the
Cold War primarily as a battle of ideas, overlaid on a great-power competition.[11] As former Reagan NSC staff member Henry Nau describes, "for Reagan, the bedrock force in international affairs was ideas . . . which defined
the identities of nations and motivated the way they behaved in international institutions and what they did with their power."[12] Because the Cold
War was a standoff between American ideals and Marxism-Leninism, between freedom and tyranny, Reagan knew it would only end when one set
of ideas bested the other. This shaped every aspect of Reagan's Cold War
strategy, including his arms buildup, information programs, diplomacy, covert actions, human rights policies, and speeches. Many of Reagan's most
iconic speeches as president, from Notre Dame in 1981 to Moscow in 1988,
can be read in sequence as his sustained argument against the Soviet system, which he saw not just as a nation-state to be defeated but as a worldview to be refuted.

Expansion of Liberty. Beyond showing communism's catastrophes, Reagan
also sought to promote the better model of free societies. He put the expansion of human liberty at the center of his global strategy. Reagan and Shultz
together became apostles for the information age, knowledge economies,

open trade, and democracy as interlocking drivers of prosperity and human flourishing. This was not mere instrumentalism; they believed in democratic capitalism as a good in its own right and promoted it worldwide, among authoritarian friend and communist foe alike. This included urging America's autocratic partners—such as South Korea, the Philippines, Taiwan, Chile, Brazil, and El Salvador—to respect human rights and embrace democracy. Likewise with free trade and market economies; Reagan and Shultz fought protectionism and sought to build an open trading order to spread economic growth as far and wide as possible. This stemmed from more than just market efficiencies. They believed that the trinity of political, economic, and religious liberty provided the better way for the world to live and a vision for the globe beyond the Cold War.

V

One challenge in writing a historical narrative is that most readers already know how the story ends. In the case of this book, it ends with the peaceful denouement of the Cold War. However, the main actors did not know at the time how their story would end—or even how each hard day would end. Reagan and his advisors reacted to events, argued their positions, waged their feuds, and advanced their policies, all with the future unknown. They faced a staggering array of choices that felt overwhelming in their complexity, too constrained in time—and the unrelenting fear that any misstep could destroy the world.

The story that follows tries to recapture that uncertainty. It is a story of men and women under pressure—of flawed human beings with complex motives, limited information, trying to discern the tides of history and chart a course in an uncertain future, in the midst of some of humanity's most perilous days.[13] Appreciating how it looked and felt to decision-makers at the time disabuses us of the inevitability fallacy. This is hindsight bias, the sense that the Cold War ended peacefully because it could not have been otherwise.

But it was not geopolitically foreordained. It came to pass in part from structural factors and trends in the international system, but also from Reagan's deliberate, and often controversial, policy choices—and from the decisions of Soviet leader Mikhail Gorbachev as well. The alchemy of these global trends and individual choices, of shifting tectonic plates and visionary world leaders, produced unexpected outcomes that appeared very unlikely at the time.

At the center of this drama is the person of Ronald Reagan himself. A beguiling, enigmatic figure, he looms large in the American political pantheon and as a defining leader of the twentieth century, yet has confounded many a biographer. His personality was alternately warm and engaging or cold and distant. He showed indifference to many victims of American-supported regimes, yet became empathetic and captivated by the plight of individuals in distress, such as prisoners of conscience or hostages. His mind was alternately inattentive and facile toward policy details, yet brilliant in its photographic memory and strategic vision. He lived in terror of nuclear annihilation, yet maintained a lightness of being that steeled him with the self-confidence and equanimity to weather unfathomable pressures and burdens. He hated communism more than any other American president, yet built a deeper friendship with a Soviet leader than any of his predecessors ever enjoyed. He was not an intellectual, and his simplicity provoked exasperation from his staff and ridicule from his critics. But he possessed a strategic imagination that enabled him to transcend the stale verities of the Cold War, envision a world beyond, free and at peace—and work to bring it about.

This is that story.

CHAPTER 1

EAST OF CALIFORNIA

I

On Tuesday, November 13, 1979, an eager audience gathered in the ballroom of the New York City Hilton to hear the worst-kept secret in politics revealed. Former governor of California Ronald Reagan was going to announce his third attempt at the presidency. His first campaign, in 1968, had been a half-hearted effort soon stymied by his California rival Richard Nixon. His second effort, in 1976, a primary challenge against the incumbent Gerald Ford, had come within a heartbreak of victory, ending only on a sweltering summer night in Kansas City at the Republican convention when Ford's delegate count barely beat Reagan's. It was the last time in American presidential politics when a political convention determined a major party's nominee. Many also expected it was the last time Reagan would seek the White House.

But the ensuing years of the Jimmy Carter presidency witnessed Reagan's new incarnation as a conservative speaker and broadcaster who stayed in the public eye—and kept his own eager eyes on the White House. Now aged sixty-eight, Reagan stood at once as a conservative icon and an old man. His campaign aimed to persuade Republican primary voters to focus on the former and disregard the latter.

Perhaps seeking to recapture the enchantment of his political debut, 1964's "A Time for Choosing," the television speech that launched his political career, Reagan forsook the traditional campaign announcement before a hometown crowd and instead returned to a nationwide broadcast. His campaign purchased airtime on some eighty television stations across the nation to reintroduce viewers to the man who would be president.

Arriving inside the Hilton from Gotham's chill fall air, the two thousand guests encountered the singular blend of Hollywood and Washington, DC, that would define the Reagan presidency. His good friend and fellow actor Jimmy Stewart welcomed the audience and introduced Reagan, who took the stage and began to speak to the gathered crowd—and to a curious nation.[1]

For the man who would devote much of his presidency to waging the Cold War, Ronald Reagan gave but a perfunctory mention to the Soviet Union. Instead, he spent most of his foreign policy attention on North America. Proclaiming, "We live on a continent whose three countries possess the assets to make it the strongest, most prosperous and self-sufficient area on earth," he called for "a developing closeness among Canada, Mexico, and the United States—a North American accord."

Why this focus on North America? Because for Reagan, defeating Soviet communism began with restoring national strength at home. He believed that a free and prosperous North America held the key to the United States' power projection in the world. In contrast to the Soviet Union's position on the Eurasian landmass—a decrepit empire surrounded by coerced vassal states to its west and impoverished and wary neighbors to its south and east—Reagan held that these "three countries with such long-standing heritages of free government" could forge a new hemispheric partnership committed to liberty and prosperity.[2]

Yet before he could get to the White House, Reagan had to win the election. And before he could win the election, he had to win the Republican nomination, which meant winning over many skeptics in his own party. In what would be a recurring theme over the next decade, prominent conservative voices lambasted Reagan's announcement speech for being too soft on Moscow. The weekly magazine *Human Events*, at the time perhaps the nation's most influential conservative periodical, pulled no punches: "Considering the grave peril to this country because of the Soviet worldwide challenge, the foreign policy portion of the Reagan speech had a rather pathetic quality to it." The *Wall Street Journal* editorial page voiced similar displeasure at the speech's anemic foreign policy content, noting caustically, "Perhaps Mr. Reagan will offer more as time goes by. For his own sake, he will have to."[3]

Considering the multiple security crises facing the nation, such caviling was understandable. Just one week earlier, Iranian revolutionaries had stormed the United States embassy in Tehran and seized the American staff—an ordeal that would continue for 444 days with 52 Americans held hostage and the United States subjected to unrelenting global humiliation. The next month, the Red Army would pour across the Friendship Bridge in the Soviet Union's surprise invasion of Afghanistan. These two blows to America's already battered national psyche and international credibility reinforced the sense among many voters that the Carter presidency was weak, and put the United States at more risk in a dangerous world.

II

It was also a different world than the one Reagan had faced fifteen years earlier when he had made his national political debut. His "A Time for Choosing" speech, aired nationwide in support of Barry Goldwater's presidential campaign on October 27, 1964, catapulted Reagan from a forgotten Hollywood actor and corporate pitchman to a conservative political luminary. One abiding concern connected Reagan then with Reagan now: a hatred of communism, and the conviction that the Cold War must not be lost and could be won. He declared in the speech,

> We cannot buy our security, our freedom from the threat of the bomb by committing an immorality so great as saying to a billion now in slavery behind the Iron Curtain, "Give up your dreams of freedom because to save our own skin, we are willing to make a deal with your slave masters." . . . There is no argument over the choice between peace and war, but there is only one guaranteed way you can have peace—and you can have it in the next second—surrender.[4]

Reagan had long worried that the United States' Cold War strategy failed to exploit America's strengths and Soviet communism's weaknesses. In a 1963 speech he complained that American policy was "based on pure conjecture that maybe communism will mellow and recognize that our way is better." Instead, he asked,

If we truly believe that our way of life is best aren't the Russians more likely to recognize that fact and modify their stand if we let their economy come unhinged so that the contrast is apparent? . . . In an all out race our system is stronger, and eventually the enemy gives up the race as a hopeless cause. Then a noble nation believing in peace extends the hand of friendship and says there is room in the world for both of us.[5]

Reagan envisioned how the Cold War would end—more than a quarter century before his presidency would help bring it about.

Among the many Americans who took note of Reagan's speech for Goldwater was former president Dwight Eisenhower. While splitting time between his Gettysburg farm and a winter home in Palm Desert, California, Eisenhower also worked to shape and steer the Republican Party. This mission became an even more critical rebuilding project after Goldwater's landslide loss in 1964. Captivated by Reagan's communication skills, Eisenhower reached out and urged him to register as a Republican (Reagan had only left the Democratic Party two years earlier) and consider running for office.[6] Over the ensuing four years, particularly after Reagan won the California governorship in 1966, Eisenhower became Reagan's first foreign policy mentor, conducting a series of discussions on statecraft, world affairs, and lessons of World War II and Korea. In one meeting Eisenhower told Reagan that the most successful use of military force was to win a victory without firing a shot. If an enemy battalion controls a hill, the aging general said, "give me a division and I will take it without a fight."[7] Eisenhower's message shaped Reagan's emerging worldview on force and statecraft: Be cautious about going to war, but if you do, then go all in. And be sure the employment of military power is connected to a strategic policy goal.

Their final meeting on March 9, 1968, a round of golf in Palm Desert followed by lunch, covered the relationship between the economy and national power. Reflecting on his generalship during World War II, Eisenhower declaimed, "It was the American economy, the arsenal of democracy, that really won the war." Mindful of the need for a strategic focus in Pentagon spending, the former president, who had balanced several budgets while maintaining a strong military, also admonished Reagan to "limit defense spending" and "expand the economy," saying, "Sooner or later, that's how we'll win [the Cold War]."[8] The next month Eisenhower suffered a heart attack, and he died less than a year later. Even in death he left his mark, and he would become the single most influential of Reagan's predecessors in shaping the fortieth president's time in office.

III

Interestingly, in this mentorship Eisenhower also revealed his preference for Reagan over another prominent California Republican, Richard Nixon. This was all the more remarkable because Nixon had served as Eisenhower's vice president for eight years, and Eisenhower knew him much better than he knew Reagan. Yet perhaps it was knowing Nixon so well that led to Eisenhower's disdain. During their White House years, Eisenhower had held his vice president in low regard, cutting him out of major policy decisions, and he had done little to help Nixon's 1960 presidential campaign.

As perspicacious as Eisenhower was in spotting Reagan's talent, he misjudged Nixon, who would soon mount one of the singular comebacks in American political history and twice win election to the presidency. Along the way, Nixon and Reagan developed a relationship of tortured complexity. Both bitter rivals and uneasy allies, the two Californians alternately worked against each other and with each other, while together dominating Republican presidential politics for nearly a half century.[9]

Nixon and Reagan shared much in common. Both had family roots in the Midwest. Both had survived troubled, sometimes abusive fathers; both in turn had found comfort in their pious, nurturing mothers. Both came from families of little means and low social standing. Both found California a land of opportunity and upward mobility, for Nixon first in the practice of law and then in politics, for Reagan in the movie industry, then as corporate pitchman for General Electric, and finally also in politics.

Yet they could not have been more different in outlook, temperament, character, and convictions.

They differed especially over foreign policy. For example, in Asia the two Californians envisioned different priorities. Nixon saw China as the strategic key to the region; Reagan believed instead that Japan was the strategic cornerstone of America's Asia posture. Nixon used international economic policy as a mere instrument subordinate to geopolitics, whereas Reagan believed open trade to be a fundamental principle in its own right and a key pillar of the free societies he sought to promote. Nixon disdained promotion of human rights and democracy as distractions from America's core interests, while Reagan put political and religious liberty at the center of his strategic priorities. In short, Nixon saw the world as it was and tried to align American policy with the way things were. Reagan envisioned the world as it could be and directed American policy toward creating that new reality.

Their biggest difference came over America's main enemy, the USSR. When Nixon and his national security advisor Henry Kissinger took office in 1969, they beheld an ascendant Soviet Union and a weakened United States mired in the Vietnam War. They developed the policy of détente to reduce tensions with Moscow through arms control agreements and other conciliatory measures, while pursuing a negotiated exit from Vietnam. They also expanded the global chessboard by bringing China into alignment with the United States as a counterweight to the USSR. For a time détente worked. But then it mutated from a temporary tactic that had advanced American interests in a particular geopolitical moment into a permanent posture that advantaged the Kremlin. It rested on several assumptions: that the Soviet Union was motivated by rational interests rather than communist ideology; that its government and economy were strong and durable; that moderated American policies could change Moscow's international conduct; and that the Kremlin's torment of its own citizens could not be changed. As historian John Lewis Gaddis notes, détente invited the critique "that Nixon, Ford, and Kissinger . . . acquiesced in the emergence, for the first time since World War II, of a serious rival to the United States in virtually all categories of military competition."[10]

Détente also conceded Soviet-sponsored gains in the developing world. In the 1970s alone, communists seized power in South Vietnam, Laos, Cambodia, Angola, Ethiopia, Mozambique, South Yemen, Afghanistan, Nicaragua, and Grenada.[11] In the pungent summary of Tom Reed, a senior Pentagon official in the Nixon and Ford administrations who later joined the Reagan NSC staff, détente meant "losing as slowly as possible."[12] And losing at any rate was still losing. Détente was becoming a self-fulfilling prophecy of Soviet strength and American weakness.

Reagan emerged as détente's most prominent critic. He rejected its assumptions and prescriptions, and in 1976 tried to defeat its main proponents, Ford and Kissinger, in the Republican primary. Reagan did not believe American decline was inexorable, or that the Soviet Union would surrender its ambitions. He lamented that détente only fueled Moscow's malign intentions, dismissing it as "a one-way street that simply gives the

Soviets what they want with nothing in return."[13] He frequently described détente as "what a farmer has with his turkey—until Thanksgiving Day."[14] This line was pithy, simplistic, even corny. But it exposed détente's pretensions in a way that any American could understand—and that Nixon, Ford, and Kissinger found hard to rebut.

Reagan's sustained campaign against the Nixon-Ford-Kissinger foreign policy became a defining moment in the history of the Republican Party, and in Reagan's own political career. The national security debate marked Reagan as a new kind of Republican who simultaneously sought to bring his party back to the principles of Eisenhower while updating them for a new era and adding a few unique elements of his own. Yet for those who assumed that a Reagan presidency would make a clean break with Nixon, some surprises lurked—as Nixon would later resurface as a quiet but influential voice in the Reagan White House.

IV

Notwithstanding his New York City announcement speech, Reagan's 1980 presidential campaign had actually begun over three years earlier in Kansas City when he conceded the 1976 GOP nomination to incumbent president Gerald Ford. On August 18, 1976, the convention delegates voted for Ford by the agonizingly close margin of 1,187 to 1,070. At the time, it seemed like a career-ending defeat for the sixty-five-year-old former California governor, who had now failed twice to secure his party's support for the presidency.

But Reagan's camp had already put its imprint on the party through platform planks that praised Soviet dissident Aleksandr Solzhenitsyn (whom President Ford had refused to meet with in the White House) and called for "morality in foreign policy"—a clear repudiation of Nixon, Ford, and Kissinger's more transactional approach to the Soviet Union.[15] Reagan himself had electrified the convention hall audience with his concession speech. He asked the audience to imagine putting a letter in a time capsule to be opened a hundred years hence. Reagan spoke of writing the letter about the challenge closest to his heart:

That we live in a world in which the great powers have poised and aimed at each other horrible missiles of destruction that can, in a matter of minutes, arrive in each other's country and destroy virtually the civilized world.

And suddenly it dawned on me.

Those who would read this letter a hundred years from now will know whether those missiles were fired. They will know whether we met our challenge. Whether they have the freedoms that we have known up until now will depend on what we do here.

When Reagan concluded, the convention center erupted in adulation. As Reagan biographer Edmund Morris recalled, "there was a palpable sense in the hall that [they'd] nominated the wrong man."[16] The nomination may have gone to Ford, but in Kansas City, Reagan captured the GOP's heart, its mind, and its future.

As a congenital optimist and fierce competitor, Reagan salved the disappointment of his 1976 loss by turning almost immediately to the next presidential election cycle. He used the ensuing years to prepare for the White House by traveling the world, giving speeches and radio addresses, campaigning for Republican candidates, and expanding his policy team.

Richard "Dick" Allen became one of the first experts to join Reagan for what would become the next campaign. Though Allen had helped draft the Reagan-inspired foreign policy planks for the 1976 GOP convention, he did not know the man well. The week after Jimmy Carter's inauguration in January 1977, Allen flew to California to see Reagan. Meeting in Reagan's home, the two spent the morning discussing foreign policy. Then over a casual sandwich lunch at the kitchen table, Reagan made a statement that would change history. "A lot of very complex things are very simple if you think them through. . . . My theory of the Cold War is we win and they lose."[17]

Almost no one thought that way in 1977, let alone said it out loud. For most foreign policy experts, the Cold War was a permanent reality in world affairs, and the Soviet Union a strong and stable rival that could at best only be managed, not defeated. For most Americans, the Cold War was entering its fourth decade as the normal state of things, with the fear of nuclear annihilation lurking as a simmering terror, and fresh traumas such as Vietnam and economic stagnation reminding them that their nation's best days were in the past. The notion of an American victory in the Cold War seemed laughable, even a perilous delusion. Yet it was a goal that Reagan would herald as a candidate and then pursue as president.

Just over two weeks after Carter's inaugural address, Reagan arrived in

Washington, DC, to deliver a speech of his own. Taking the stage on February 6, 1977, at the annual Conservative Political Action Conference (CPAC), Reagan cited Carter's hopeful inaugural assertion that "the passion for freedom is on the rise." To which Reagan responded tartly, "If it is true, then it is the most unrequited passion in human history." Instead, Reagan painted a grim global picture, with communist tyranny ascendant and an enervated United States in retreat. He worried that the Carter administration and too many other Americans disregarded the severity of the threat. In a historical parallel he would return to often, Reagan compared the present moment to "Europe in the late Nineteen Thirties when so many refused to believe and thought if we don't look the threat will go away." Yet he made clear that "above all we want peace. And to have that, the United States has to immediately reexamine its entire view of the world and develop a strategy of freedom."[18] In this quest, Reagan would spend the next three years waging a battle of ideas on two fronts: against the Carter administration on one side and against a sizable cohort of his fellow Republicans on the other.

On June 9, 1977, he arrived at the Waldorf-Astoria hotel in New York City to skewer both camps. Speaking before a foreign policy conference, Reagan first took aim at President Carter's recent pronouncements elevating human rights as a first-tier priority. While affirming the value of human rights, Reagan complained that Carter followed a "double standard" of criticizing nations aligned with the United States, such as Chile, Argentina, Brazil, and South Africa, while ignoring the far worse repression of America's communist adversaries, such as Cambodia, Vietnam, Cuba, and the USSR.[19]

Reagan then turned to the Soviet Union's growing influence, particularly through its support for communist forces in places such as Indochina, Angola, and Ethiopia. He blamed this in part on détente, which "may actually have improved the climate for Soviet promotion of proxy wars and skirmishes." This he believed was also a bitter fruit of Nixon and Ford policies. Reagan quoted a British intelligence report citing Soviet premier Leonid Brezhnev's remarks to Eastern European Communist Party leaders in 1973: "Trust us, comrades, for by 1985 as a consequence of what we are now achieving with détente, we will have achieved most of our objectives in Western Europe. We will have consolidated our position. We will have improved our economy. And a decisive shift in the correlation of forces will be such that, come 1985, we will be able to exert our will wherever we need to."[20]

With these two speeches, Reagan unknowingly set a trap for himself.

He did not seem to appreciate the tension—even contradiction—between his call in his CPAC speech for a global "strategy of freedom" and his New York criticism of the Carter administration for badgering authoritarian American allies to respect human rights. In Reagan's mind, he probably believed he was just affirming two distinct policy principles: promoting liberty and keeping faith with allies. Yet what to do when those principles collide, when an anticommunist ally is also an autocratic thug? This was the reality in nations such as South Korea, Taiwan, the Philippines, Chile, Haiti, El Salvador, South Africa, and others. On the campaign trail, Reagan could afford to dodge this contradiction. But once he took office, his words and competing principles would confront him with hard choices, as freedom activists and repressive rulers both appealed for American support.

V

Reagan possessed a showman's instinct for detecting issues with audience appeal. Such was the Carter administration's plan to return the Panama Canal to the government of Panama. In the 1970s the proposed Panama Canal treaties, two linked agreements to grant Panama control of the canal and preserve its neutrality, fueled heated debates across the United States. Reagan made opposition to the treaties one of his signature forays into foreign policy and used it to elevate his national profile. The issue wed political benefit with his genuine convictions.

In treaties first negotiated under President Theodore Roosevelt at the turn of the century, the United States had supported Panama's independence from Colombia while securing the right to build the Panama Canal and control the surrounding territory. By the 1960s, amid the global wave of decolonization and independence movements, American ownership of the canal began inspiring violent protests in Panama. This prompted the Lyndon B. Johnson administration to enter into protracted discussions with the Panamanian government about returning the canal to Panama; the Nixon and then Ford administrations continued these negotiations in fits and starts, amid ongoing Panamanian unrest.

Reagan had first seized on the canal issue during his 1976 primary challenge to Ford (who supported the treaties), when Reagan developed his signature line "We built it, we paid for it, it's ours and we are going to keep it!" For many Americans the canal issue fueled feelings of national humiliation following the Vietnam War, worry about losing an important resource during an economic recession, and a general fear that the United States was losing ground even in its own hemisphere.

The issue did not fall completely along partisan lines. As a presidential candidate in 1976, Jimmy Carter had blasted Ford for the treaties and promised, "I would never give up full control of the Panama Canal" (upon becoming president, Carter reversed his position), while prominent conservatives such as William F. Buckley Jr., George Will, Barry Goldwater, and even John Wayne all supported returning the canal to Panama.

Despite Reagan's many radio addresses, newspaper columns, and speeches, in 1978 the US Senate narrowly ratified the treaties and finalized the canal's return to Panamanian sovereignty. For Reagan this policy loss was a political win. He had bolstered his name on a galvanizing issue, burnished his credibility with the emerging New Right political movement, built a national fundraising infrastructure, and helped lead what author Craig Shirley describes as "one of the most impressive populist uprisings in American history."[21]

Yet in one of the ironies of politics, once Reagan became president, he would benefit from Carter's decision. In returning the canal to Panama, Carter lanced a boil of resentment toward the United States felt by many Latin Americans, who perceived the canal as a fifty-mile-long symbol of Yankee imperialism. While the Reagan administration would face many controversies in the region, the Panama Canal would not be among them.

VI

Reagan used these wilderness years to speak out on many other issues. His daily radio commentaries, broadcast nationwide, and his syndicated newspaper column provided regular venues to test, refine, and promote his ideas with the American public.

Beyond urging increased defense spending, Reagan focused on particular weapons systems that he believed would give America a strategic edge over Moscow. In a 1978 radio address, he excoriated Carter for canceling the B-1 bomber. Reagan described how the B-1 could penetrate Soviet air defenses guided by terrain-hugging radar and deliver nuclear-tipped cruise missiles to targets deep inside the USSR. Foreshadowing his strategy of using a strengthened military based on advanced technologies to bankrupt the Kremlin, Reagan concluded, "We know the Soviets will have to spend more than the B-1's cost to develop a defense against them and what's wrong with that?"[22] In other addresses he extolled the importance of the navy for American security in the Pacific theater, and defended the CIA against congressional investigations and Carter's personnel and budget cuts.[23]

Reagan also embarked on extensive foreign travel. Journeys abroad are helpful for any political leader, but they were especially so for Reagan, who learned in part by intuition and experience. In addition to his reading, Reagan formed his insights and convictions based on firsthand encounters— with international leaders, foreign cultures, and the people of other lands. The two regions where he would achieve the most policy successes as president, Europe and Asia, were also the two continents that he visited most often, both before and during his presidency.

In 1978 he undertook two international trips. First, in April, he circumnavigated the globe. He began his journey in Asia with visits to Tokyo, Taipei, and Hong Kong, continued on to Iran, and then proceeded to London and homeward to California. The first leg reinforced his conviction that Japan anchored America's interests in Asia. This was not a popular opinion in the United States at the time. Most Americans perceived Japan as an economic competitor, even predator, rather than a strategic ally. Trade tensions ran hot, especially over Japan's combination of import barriers and cascading exports to the United States, both hurting American manufacturing jobs. A rising public chorus supported increasing tariffs and other measures to restrict Japanese imports. Americans who focused on defense policy had become frustrated with Japan for free-riding under the American security umbrella while Tokyo spent paltry amounts on its own military, despite having the world's third-largest economy.

In Tokyo, to his surprise, Reagan found himself impressed with Ambassador Mike Mansfield. Though a Democrat appointed by Carter, Mansfield held views closer to Reagan's on the primacy of the United States–Japan relationship. Reagan also met with several Japanese officials, including Prime Minister Fukuda and one of the Diet's leading policy experts, Yasuhiro Nakasone, who in 1982 would become prime minister and one of Reagan's closest friends and allies. Speaking to a group of senior Japanese business and political leaders, Reagan extolled the United States–Japan alliance as "the key ingredient for peace, stability and economic development in the entire Pacific basin" and warned against "the forces of blind protectionism, which could severely damage our alliance."[24]

From Tokyo, Reagan traveled to Taipei, where he encountered a nation racked with worry over President Carter's rumored plans to switch diplomatic recognition from the Republic of China (Taiwan) to the People's Republic of China (PRC). For Carter, such a move would be the culmination of Nixon and Kissinger's opening six years earlier and would solidify Beijing as a strategic partner in countering the Soviet Union. Reagan saw it instead as a betrayal of Taiwan, America's ally of three decades. In Taipei he praised the island's economic prosperity and religious freedom (while saying nothing critical of Taiwan's hereditary dictator Chiang Ching-kuo) and fulminated against the potential recognition of mainland China. In a strategic context he described "South Korea, Japan, and the Republic of China—all in alliance with the United States—forming a security shield in the western Pacific."[25]

Then westward to Iran. Landing in Tehran early in the morning, Reagan arrived at a fraught time in the United States–Iran relationship—though neither he nor anyone else knew just how much more fraught it would soon become. The shah had ruled Iran for a quarter century with a combination of an iron fist to repress any dissent and an aggressive modernization agenda to improve his country's livelihood, all while aligned with the United States. Washington in these years had provided robust support to Iran's anticommunist ruler while taking advantage of Iran's border with the Soviet Union for intelligence cooperation. Now many Iranians, fed up with the shah's corruption and repression, were beginning to agitate against him. Meanwhile the Carter White House vacillated between supporting the shah, pressuring him to reform, engaging with his opposition, and worrying his government would collapse.

Reporting on his visit to his radio audience, Reagan gushed about how "ancient Persia is becoming as modern as tomorrow" and praised "the great effort the government is making to upgrade the standard of living and to eliminate poverty." Reagan continued, "Above all we should know that Iran has been and is a staunch friend and ally of the US . . . [and] has a clear understanding of the Soviet threat to the free world."[26] His praise for the shah showed his reflexive instinct to stand with American allies—even when those allies were weak, corrupt, and prone to brutalizing their own people. He also sought to bolster support for the shah in the face of growing media criticism and the Carter administration's waffling. Neither Reagan nor Carter could envision how Iranian vexations would soon enough plague both of their presidencies.

Reagan's hawkishness may have energized his conservative base, but he and his advisors knew that elections are not won on the base alone. He faced the additional risk that his hard-line positions could frighten centrist voters. And scared voters can become motivated voters—motivated, that is, to support your opponent. Allen distilled these concerns in a memo to Reagan in August 1978. Noting Reagan's desire to promote a "strategy for peace," Allen raised "the problem of how you are perceived by a wide stratum of the public" as "a 'saber-rattler,' a 'button-pusher,' or as 'too willing to send in the Marines.'" Moreover, bemoaned Allen, "this false image is happily amplified by the media," which caricatured Reagan as eager to use "nuclear weapons to support reactionary and fascist dictatorships against hapless subjugated nonwhite majorities." Allen then summarized recent polling that revealed the American people's ambivalence on Cold War policy: "The public seems to want to conclude arms limitation agreements with a rival power of which it is becoming increasingly distrustful and suspicious." Notably, on the balance of international power, the memo described accelerating trends in public opinion, to the point where 42 percent of Americans now believed the United States was weaker than the Soviet Union, while only 12 percent saw the US as stronger than the USSR.[27]

In sum, Reagan faced several challenges with public opinion. He had to convince the American people that the United States could reverse course and become stronger than the Soviet Union; that both the Carter and the Nixon-Ford-Kissinger approaches toward the USSR would not work; that Reagan's alternative strategy combining confrontation with negotiation *would* work; and that Reagan could be trusted to bring world peace rather than World War III.

In November Reagan returned to Europe. He visited Germany, France, and the United Kingdom. On this trip he had several encounters that would anticipate pivotal themes in his presidency. Reagan began in London, where he called on Margaret Thatcher, then the leader of the Conservative opposition. The two had first met three years earlier, when they discovered an easy rapport and shared policy convictions on free enterprise and anticommunism. As the historian Richard Aldous observes, they also bonded over "the shared religious sensibility that helped reinforce their mission."[28] In their London meeting, Thatcher and Reagan primarily discussed economic concerns and "the Soviet threat and the SS-20s that were pointed at all the capitals of Europe, which had a very strong effect on Reagan," as aide Peter Hannaford recalled.[29] The Kremlin's deployment of the SS-20 two years earlier had exemplified the USSR's growing strength and assertiveness. An intermediate-range ballistic missile, the SS-20 included a multiple independently targetable reentry vehicle (MIRV) that contained three nuclear warheads, each able to hit a separate target.

The SS-20 changed the strategic equation in three ways, all to the Kremlin's advantage. First, from its launch sites in the western Soviet Union, the SS-20 could hit almost any city or NATO military base in Europe within a mere seven to ten minutes. This meant certain destruction for those targets and did not allow time for NATO to retaliate. Second, because it was solid fueled, the SS-20 could be launched instantaneously on command, without the laborious fueling process required of older liquid-fueled missiles. This precluded NATO spy satellites from being able to detect the missiles' being gassed up and provide advance warning of a potential launch. Third, the SS-20s were based on mobile launchers that could travel easily across many terrains. Because they were not housed in fixed locations, it would be nigh impossible for NATO forces to locate and destroy them either in a preemptive attack or in a retaliatory strike. The missiles also enhanced the Kremlin's diplomatic leverage, since even the mere threat of a launch could blackmail the Western alliance into major concessions.

Taken together, the SS-20s' three advantages of no response time, no warning, and no fixed bases struck new terror into Western Europe and posed a new dilemma for the United States and its allies. The doctrine of mutual assured destruction had long meant that America would retaliate if the Soviets launched a nuclear attack against Washington, DC, or Los Angeles, and this fear had preserved the Cold War's perverse stability. But the SS-20 sharpened an uncomfortable question that had long lingered within the alliance: Would America engage in a nuclear war if the Soviets instead struck Bonn, Paris, or London? It was a dilemma that would cause some of the worst tensions in the transatlantic alliance and provoke some of the most agonizing decisions Reagan faced as president, yet ultimately produce one of his greatest diplomatic triumphs.

From London, Reagan traveled first to Paris, where his meetings with French leaders seemed only to produce mutual disregard. Then on to Germany, for Reagan's first visit to the divided country that occupied much of the central stage in the Cold War. On a cold, gray winter morning in West Berlin, Reagan beheld the Berlin Wall for the first time and saw where the body of a desperate young East German man had lain after he was shot and killed while trying to flee over the wall. Escorted by US consulate officials, the Reagan group then crossed through "Checkpoint Charlie" into East

Berlin—his first time setting foot inside a communist nation. While his errand into East Berlin lasted but a few hours, Reagan witnessed an encounter that would stay with him for the rest of his life. Standing outside a department store, he watched East German police detain a young man otherwise innocently carrying a shopping bag and demand that the frightened youth show his papers. Such surveillance was the daily lived reality for millions of citizens behind the Iron Curtain, but as Hannaford later wrote, Reagan "saw it as an example of authoritarian oppression in action"; it was "an event he would mention many times upon his return to the United States."[30]

As he would the Berlin Wall itself. In his syndicated column the following week, Reagan described the wall's fiendishly elaborate construction: "Before a person reaches the wall itself he must go over small ones on the east side; cross a run guarded by attack dogs; come under the glare of searchlights, brave automatically fired machine guns, barbed wire and other obstacles and—in many cases—swim in the River Spree. . . . At one section of the Berlin Wall . . . there is one huge spray-painted graffito that reads: 'Those beyond this wall live in a concentration camp.'"[31] With that grim image, Reagan reminded his readers how the wall represented a Soviet derivation of Germany's Nazi past.

VII

A few weeks earlier, a white puff of smoke over the Vatican heralded the selection of archbishop of Kraków Karol Wojtyla as the new Pope, who took the name John Paul II. His election caused alarm throughout the Soviet bloc. The Polish secret police (SB) sent an analysis to the KGB that captured their panic: "Wojtyla holds extreme anti-communist views." In June 1979, this first Polish Pope in the two millennia of church history returned to his homeland for a visit that enraptured his countrymen, captivated the world, and further aggravated the Kremlin. Brezhnev had anticipated the worst, warning Polish communist leader Edward Gierek against approving the trip. When Gierek protested that he had no choice, a resigned (and unusually prophetic) Brezhnev replied, "Do as you wish. But be careful you don't regret it later." Despite extensive joint efforts by the SB, the East German Stasi, and the KGB to discourage Polish audiences and undermine the visit, during his nine-day sojourn John Paul II spoke to an estimated eleven million people (one-third of the total population). Though his homilies avoided politics and instead focused on human dignity, the sacrifice of Christ, and the love of God, the Soviet Politburo warned—not inaccurately—that the Pope had launched "an ideological struggle against the Socialist countries."[32]

Reagan also appreciated the significance of the visit, devoting two of his radio addresses to the papal homecoming. Though not himself Catholic, Reagan remembered his father's Catholic faith, and as an ecumenical Protestant, Reagan still held the Catholic Church in high regard. Reminding his listeners that "atheism is as much a part of Communism as is the Gulag," Reagan described the overwhelming crowds who embraced John Paul II in contrast to the four decades of suffering that the Polish people had endured under Nazism and then communism. Reagan knew the Pope had opened a new front in the Cold War: "Now with the eyes of all the world on them they have looked past those menacing weapons and listened to the voice of one man who has told them there is a God and it is their inalienable right to freely worship that God." Reagan concluded, "Things may never be quite the same behind the Iron Curtain."[33]

Another spiritual standoff that year also drew Reagan's attention: the plight of the Siberian Seven, a small group of Russian Pentecostal Christians who had suffered decades of persecution and imprisonment in their Siberian hometown of Chernogorsk. Eight members of the Vashchenko and the Chmykhalov families had rushed through the gates of the US embassy in Moscow in June 1978. Seven of them made it inside to safety, while one was seized by Soviet police, gruesomely beaten outside the embassy walls, and never seen again. The acting head of the embassy, Jack Matlock, made the decision to grant the Pentecostals refuge. There ensued a prolonged diplomatic standoff, with the Siberian Seven demanding the right to emigrate yet refusing to leave the embassy due to fear of persecution, while the Soviet authorities insisted that the United States eject them from the embassy yet offered no guarantees of their safety.

Reagan became captivated by their straits. In a radio address, he criticized the embassy leadership for preventing them from speaking out and confining them to "a 20 by 12 ft. room the Marine guards call the dungeon." He concluded that this marked yet another failure of détente. "Détente is supposed to be a 2 way street. Our wheat, and technology can get into Russia—why can't the Vashchenko and [Chmykhalov families] get out?"[34]

VIII

The arms control agreements that the Nixon, Ford, and Carter administrations negotiated with the Soviets frequently drew Reagan's ire. He had criticized the Strategic Arms Limitation Talks (SALT) under Nixon and Kissinger as part of détente's distraction from ongoing Soviet aggression and castigated the Anti-Ballistic Missile (ABM) Treaty's severe restrictions on America's ability to develop and deploy defenses against ICBM attack. When Carter signed the SALT II agreement in 1979, Reagan found it even worse than its predecessor, because its terms reinforced Soviet strengths and American deficiencies in the arms race. Reagan's jeremiads against these agreements gave the American public and many foreign leaders the impression of a bellicose warmonger who had never met a nuclear weapon he did not like. Yet this missed a profound truth about Reagan that was hidden in plain sight: He was terrified of nuclear war and wanted to abolish all nuclear weapons.

In 1979, Reagan and his aide Martin Anderson visited the North American Air Defense Command (NORAD), bunkered beneath Colorado's Cheyenne Mountain. The commander, General James Hill, showed them the facility's futuristic capabilities to detect, monitor, and follow any projectiles approaching the North American landmass—whether they be Soviet bombers, ICBMs, or even St. Nicholas, as with NORAD's whimsical tracking of the journey of Santa and his airborne sleigh every Christmas Eve. Anderson punctured this aura of American technological prowess with a deceptively simple question: What would happen if just one SS-18, the USSR's largest ICBM, hit the mountain? "It would blow us away," replied General Hill. To a follow-up question of what NORAD would do if the Soviets launched just one missile at an American city, the general responded, "Well, we would pick it up right after it was launched, but by the time the officials of the city could be alerted that a nuclear bomb would hit them, there would be only ten or fifteen minutes left. That's all we can do. We can't stop it."

This struck Reagan as perverse. Not only would NORAD's hardened bunker and every American city be rendered helpless in the case of a nuclear attack, the commander in chief would be as well. As a somber and troubled Reagan reflected to Anderson on the flight back to California that evening: "We have spent all that money and have all that equipment, and there is nothing we can do to prevent a nuclear missile from hitting us. . . .

The only option a president would have would be to press the button or do nothing. They're both bad. We should have some way of defending ourselves against nuclear missiles."[35]

Over the previous years, brilliant strategists had developed and refined the "mutual assured destruction" (MAD) theory of nuclear deterrence, in which the reciprocal fear of annihilation in the Soviet Union and United States dissuaded each from attacking the other and preserved a stable stalemate in the Cold War. At first glance, MAD appeared to have worked for the past three decades. After all, neither side had ever launched nuclear strikes, despite some agonizingly tense standoffs, such as the Cuban Missile Crisis and multiple crises over Berlin. Yet Reagan had grown skeptical of this mutual vulnerability, especially as the Soviet nuclear arsenal had eclipsed America's and several Soviet officials had voiced the belief that the USSR could survive—and win—a nuclear exchange.[36] There in the dark bunker on Cheyenne Mountain, as Reagan contemplated his imminent White House campaign, he confronted MAD not as an abstraction of game theory but as the chilling reality of what it would mean in practice: a terrified president, with heart pounding and fingers trembling, in a cold sweat, with a quivering voice, reading the launch codes over the secure phone to order the annihilation of millions of Russian civilians—just minutes before the incoming Soviet missiles killed millions of Americans. It was a choice he vowed to do all he could to avoid.

Even as Reagan privately agonized over this dilemma, he publicly campaigned against Senate ratification of the SALT II agreement that President Carter had signed the month prior. Reagan had long been skeptical of the SALT process. In a 1979 speech to a GOP convention in San Diego, Reagan framed his concerns by first recalling the days of his mentor. "The great legacy of the Eisenhower years," he declared, "when the US created the strategic superiority that maintained world peace and served as a counterbalance to the conventional military superiority of the Soviet Union—has vanished." In contrast, Reagan averred, when the Nixon administration signed the SALT I agreements, "the Soviets began their exploitation of our naïve desire to believe" and launched a massive military buildup coupled with aggressive support for communist expansion in the Third World.

Yet Reagan then took his critique in a direction his Republican audience likely did not expect: "SALT II is not Strategic Arms Limitation, it is Strategic Arms Buildup with the Soviets adding a minimum of 3,000 nuclear warheads to their inventory and the US embarking on a $35 billion catchup which won't be achieved until 1990, if then." In short, having read the fine print on the treaty, Reagan knew that SALT II merely slowed the rate of growth in the arms race—and did so by conceding a permanent advantage to the Soviet arsenal. Instead, Reagan called for a strategic shift in two directions. First, "our task is to restore the security of the US" by reviving weapons programs that the Carter administration had slowed or canceled, such as the B-1 bomber and the MX missile. Second, he said, "Let us assure the Soviet Union we will join in any arms limitation agreement that legitimately reduces nuclear armaments to the point that neither country represents a threat to the other."[37] He repeated these attacks on SALT II in numerous radio addresses and speeches.

Perceptive listeners heard the emerging framework of what would become his strategy in the White House: building up American power to exploit Soviet weaknesses and force Moscow to negotiate major reductions in nuclear arms, leading to the Cold War's end.

IX

Nineteen seventy-nine brought another development closer to home that accelerated the appearance of Soviet advances and American decline. It would also vex Reagan's presidency. In July in Nicaragua, leftist Sandinista forces overthrew the corrupt and repressive Anastasio Somoza dictatorship. While the United States had supported Somoza for years, upon his defenestration the Carter administration made a goodwill gesture to the Sandinistas of $90 million in aid for the new regime. Carter trusted that such generosity would induce the Sandinistas to embrace democracy and resist Soviet and Cuban blandishments.

Where Carter saw hope, the Reagan team saw a problem. From the outset Reagan's advisors regarded the Sandinistas as the vanguard of Marxism coopting Nicaragua and menacing the region. Roger Fontaine, a Latin America expert with the Reagan campaign, wrote an eleven-page memo just two weeks after the Sandinistas seized power. Fontaine made a remarkably accurate prediction of the looming Sandinista alignment with the Soviet bloc—and also foreshadowed the strategic framework through which the Reagan White House would view Latin America.

Fontaine identified the Sandinista victory as "the first of its kind in the Americas in two decades," since Fidel Castro had led the communist takeover of Cuba in 1959. In the ensuing years, several other communist revolutions had been squelched, been overthrown, or otherwise failed in Venezuela, Peru, Bolivia, Brazil, Argentina, Uruguay, and Chile. Fontaine now worried that Nicaragua portended a decisive shift to further communist advances throughout Latin America. The Sandinistas had not acted alone. The "most important friend" of the Sandinistas was a newly emboldened Castro. Behind the Sandinista revolution stood Cuba, and behind Havana stood Moscow.

Fontaine made two predictions. First, despite feigning to rule as a coalition that included both democratic and communist elements, the new Sandinista regime would soon give up the pretense of pluralism and embrace its Marxist and "fundamentally anti-American" nature. Second, "the danger is hardly confined to Nicaragua," as Managua would soon begin supporting communist insurgencies in neighboring nations, such as El Salvador, Guatemala, and Honduras. Mindful that America's Vietnam misadventure had ended just a few years earlier, Fontaine explicitly disavowed the "domino theory" that a communist takeover in one nation would inevitably lead to the fall of bordering nations, since the Central American countries would "not drop easily or automatically." But he stated, "They are, however, in danger." He concluded, "The next president will have to move quickly and decisively to save what is left in our own neighborhood."

In this memo Fontaine outlined what would become the Reagan White House's Latin America strategy: Stand with anticommunist governments. Support anticommunist insurgents in communist nations. These pillars were clear, simple, realistic about the threat communism posed to the region, and aligned with what would become the administration's overall Cold War strategy. They also ensured the Reagan administration would sponsor some odious regimes engaged in horrific abuses. Such were the tragic choices of the Cold War.

Of course, for Reagan and his team, the quickest way to end human rights abuses was to defeat communism. Yet Fontaine's failure to mention any support for democracy and human rights in the region ultimately represented a failure in his diagnosis. It was a gap that foretold what would become sharp divisions within the Reagan administration, until Reagan would decide that defeating communism in Latin America depended on supporting governments that answered to their citizens rather than abusing them.[38]

X

_____

As Reagan finished his New York City speech announcing his campaign and basked in the applause of his gathered supporters, they and millions of others viewing it on television heard Reagan's peroration: "A troubled and afflicted mankind looks to us, pleading for us to keep our rendezvous with destiny; that we will uphold the principles of self-reliance, self-discipline, morality, and—above all—responsible liberty for every individual, that we will become that shining city on a hill."[39]

But at the time his hopes sounded discordant to Americans distraught over their nation's travails. The week prior, the evening news had broadcast terrifying scenes of Iranian radicals storming the United States embassy in Tehran and seizing over fifty American hostages. Meanwhile, the same day that Reagan launched his campaign, the Kremlin was secretly planning its surprise invasion of Afghanistan. When the Soviet Fortieth Army crossed into Afghanistan on Christmas Day the next month, it delivered a further blow to American credibility.

Humiliated abroad and demoralized at home, the United States stumbled to the end of the 1970s with many Americans wondering if things could get any bleaker. The decade had begun with America's first lost war and ignominious withdrawal from Vietnam, followed by the traumas of Watergate, the geopolitical humiliation of the OPEC oil embargo and economic pain of the energy shock and recession, communist advances across the developing world, and the Soviet Union's growing military and nuclear superiority. Would the next decade be worse?

XI

_____

Almost as soon as Reagan's campaign launched, it began to fall apart. Although he started in the pole position, he faced several credible rivals for the GOP nomination, especially John Connally, a former Treasury secretary and Texas governor, and George H. W. Bush, former CIA director and ambassador to the UN.

Those opponents posed less of a threat to Reagan than his own team did. His campaign manager John Sears, widely regarded as a political genius, was also widely detested by the other staff. Sears requited their sentiments.

Staff feuding became vicious even by the low standards of politics, to the point that Reagan's closest longtime advisors, such as Michael Deaver, Lyn Nofziger, and Martin Anderson all either quit or were fired by Sears within weeks of the campaign commencement.

The staff acrimony anticipated the internecine warfare and misman-agement that would bedevil his presidency. It also almost prevented him from reaching the White House in the first place. Bush started with a sur-prise victory in the Iowa caucuses. In addition to raising nettlesome ques-tions about whether Reagan's age rendered him too weak for the rigors of the presidency, the Iowa win catapulted Bush into the front-runner's seat. An electoral showdown with Reagan in New Hampshire loomed next.

The campaign tailspin also prompted Ed Meese, Nancy Reagan, and a few other advisors to stage an intervention that would have profound con-sequences not just for the election but for the American intelligence com-munity and Reagan's national security policy. Seeking to expunge Sears, they quietly approached the New York lawyer William "Bill" Casey to gauge his interest in taking over the campaign. When Casey signaled his willing-ness, Reagan—stung by the Iowa loss, fretting about his plummeting poll numbers, and fed up with Sears—offered Casey the job. Under Casey's lead-ership, the Reagan campaign reeled off a string of primary victories on the way to capturing the Republican nomination.

Who was this new campaign manager? He was a man easy to carica-ture, easy to underestimate, and hard to understand. One of the more color-ful and enigmatic figures in American history, Casey embodied several paradoxes. A devout Catholic who repeatedly cut ethical corners. An orga-nizational genius whose personal habits and attire were invariably described as "slovenly." An Office of Strategic Services (OSS) veteran from World War II who otherwise had not worked in national security for over three de-cades, except for a brief stint in the Nixon State Department handling eco-nomic policy. Above all, he embodied the outsider-become-insider, an Irish Catholic and Fordham graduate who penetrated the WASP and Ivy League establishments of the intelligence community and Wall Street. In the words of his biographer, "he was a bundle of contrasts," for behind "the washed-out eyes, the slumped posture, the pouched, gray face, something lurked, some-thing in the brusque manner, the machine-gun speech, the palpable ego, that bespoke an unspent energy."[40] Among these contradictions, the ultimate one was this: A famously disorganized Casey exercised a remarkable organiza-tional turnaround of the Reagan campaign and would go on to become the most powerful director of central intelligence since Allen Dulles almost three decades earlier.

XII

For the United States, the end of 1979 went from bad to worse. Norman Podhoretz captured the perilous moment in an influential essay for the March 1980 issue of *Commentary* magazine titled "The Present Danger." With the takeover of the US embassy in Iran, he declaimed, "One period in American history ended; and less than two months later, on December 25, when Soviet troops invaded Afghanistan, another period began."[41] Podhoretz articulated what many Americans felt was a frightening new reality: The United States was a crippled giant. Reagan, who had been sounding such warnings for years, now felt vindicated by world events and genuinely angered by what he saw as Carter's hapless responses. He faced the challenge of how to capitalize on these foreign policy crises while reassuring voters that as president he would have a steady hand and not a loose trigger finger.

Reagan attempted to thread this needle with a major speech. On March 17, 1980, he spoke to the Chicago Council on Foreign Relations, the Midwest's most venerable foreign policy organization. Following his standard critique of Carter's weakness, Reagan pivoted to his willingness to negotiate with the Soviets—but from a position of strength:

> We cannot negotiate arms control agreements that will slow down the Soviet military build-up, as long as we let the Soviets move ahead of us in every category of armaments. Once we clearly demonstrate to the Soviet leadership that we are determined to compete, arms control negotiations will again have a chance. On such a basis, I would be prepared to negotiate vigorously for verifiable reductions in armaments.

Reagan's speech had the intended effect. *The Washington Post* headlined it "Reagan Is Conciliatory in Foreign Policy Statement," and the article noted that amid his boilerplate demands for a military buildup, "what was new today was Reagan's stress on the arms negotiations he said must arise from this buildup."[42] Of course to those who had listened to Reagan over the years, his call for negotiations to reduce nuclear arsenals was not new at all.

Even while reassuring voters of his desire for diplomacy with Moscow, Reagan continued to press his belief that the Soviet Union was uniquely strong *and* brittle. In a lengthy profile published by *The New Yorker* on March 24, reporter Elizabeth Drew asked Reagan if he believed the United States could "regain military superiority over the Soviet Union." Reagan replied:

> Yes, I think the Soviet Union is probably at the very limit of its military output. It has already had to keep its people from having so many consumer goods. Instead, they're devoting it all to this military build-up. . . . I think it tops what Hitler did. . . . Now, what I think the Russians would fear more than anything else is a United States that all of a sudden would hitch up our belt and say "O.K., Buster, we've tried this other way. We are now going to build what is necessary to surpass you." And this is the last thing they want from us, an arms race, because they are already running as fast as they can and we haven't started running.

This quote is classic Reagan: corny ("O.K., Buster"), shaped by World War II, confident in America, perceptive of Soviet weaknesses. He believed that while in the near term the Kremlin posed a threat of a magnitude not seen since the Third Reich, the USSR's military expansion and totalitarian system made it fragile and vulnerable—and America could renew its strength and force Moscow into an unwinnable competition.[43]

XIII

As his candidacy gathered momentum, Reagan also began expanding his foreign policy team. Foreign policy advisors serve four overlapping functions on presidential campaigns. First, and most obviously, they advise the candidate on the issues, through briefing papers and meetings, and also by writing the candidate's position papers, talking points, and speech drafts. Second, they act as surrogates for the campaign, defending the candidate's positions in the media, debating experts from other campaigns, and using any other means to promote the candidate's views in the public square.

Third, they help validate the candidate. Particularly if the advisor is a person of some eminence, their public support can provide a welcome political boost and enhanced credibility for the candidate. Fourth, they form a government-in-waiting; in the fortunate scenario of a victory, today's campaign advisors become tomorrow's senior officials.

Mindful of these purposes, the Reagan campaign's outreach aimed at multiple camps, including scholars, Republican experts from past administrations, young rising stars, and even—especially—Democrats. Reagan recruited one such Democrat when he read the article "Dictatorships and Double Standards" in the November 1979 issue of *Commentary*. The author, Georgetown professor Jeane Kirkpatrick, eviscerated the Carter administration's foreign policy as a "failure" that subjected America's allies to harsher treatment than America's enemies. Focusing on the recent revolutions in Iran and Nicaragua, she identified the core problem as the Carter administration's refusal to distinguish between right-wing authoritarian regimes and left-wing revolutionary regimes. The former were more reliable as anticommunist partners and more prone to reform and democratization, while the latter often descended into totalitarianism. As a result, Kirkpatrick wrote, "everywhere our friends will have noted that the US cannot be counted on in times of difficulty and our enemies will have observed that American support provides no security against the forward march of history."[44]

An impressed Reagan wrote to Kirkpatrick that her article "had a great impact" on him and invited her to meet "to discuss some of the points" she had raised. Reagan appreciated her argument in part because he had made similar criticisms in his New York speech two and a half years earlier.[45] As a former Democrat, Reagan had no qualms about reaching out across party lines to solicit national security wisdom, but Kirkpatrick still felt loyal to her party and wary of Reagan's supplications. She was not alone in her angst. The slow-motion political earthquake that tore through the United States during the 1970s fractured both major parties from within. Just as the Reagan camp engaged in a years-long battle with the Ford-Kissinger wing for the soul of the GOP, the Democrats fell into their own internal rifts over national security. Hawkish Democrats found their lodestar in two-time presidential candidate Senator Henry "Scoop" Jackson of Washington, a fierce critic of détente whose sponsorship of the Jackson-Vanik Amendment restricted Soviet exports to the United States unless Moscow agreed to permit free emigration—especially allowing Soviet Jews to move to Israel. What began as an obscure trade provision soon became perhaps the most influential human rights movement of the Cold War.

In an effort to staunch their party's foreign policy bleeding, in January 1980, several former Jackson staff and supporters, including Kirkpatrick and Elliott Abrams, met with Carter at the White House to appeal for a stronger anti-Soviet line. It did not go well. Peevish and beleaguered, Carter lectured rather than listened, including a bizarre appeal for help on his Uruguay policy. In a mere thirty minutes, Carter consummated the alienation of his fellow Democrats. He also increased the ranks of Reagan supporters. Exiting the White House, Kirkpatrick exclaimed, "I am not going to support *that* man." Instead, she endorsed Reagan.[46] Kirkpatrick was not the only Democrat to switch her allegiance. With anguished hearts but clean consciences, others soon followed, including Abrams, Podhoretz, Richard Perle of Jackson's staff, former Johnson administration official Eugene Rostow, Paul Wolfowitz of the Carter Pentagon, and Paul Nitze, a Cold War icon whose policy career traced across several presidencies, back to the Truman State Department.

In addition to poaching disillusioned Democrats, Reagan kept adding Republican national security experts to his campaign. He landed an early recruit in Fred Iklé, who combined the mien of a scholar with the ferocity of a Cold Warrior. The Swiss-born Iklé had first migrated to the United States for doctoral study at the University of Chicago, writing his dissertation on the tragic effects of Allied bombing on cities in Germany and Japan and the need to protect civilian populations from direct targeting in warfare. This struck at the heart of the doctrine of mutual assured destruction, of which Iklé had written, "It is a tragic paradox of our age that the highly humane objective of preventing nuclear war is served by a military doctrine and engines of destruction whose very purpose is to inflict genocide."[47] He shared Reagan's loathing of MAD as strategically unstable and morally repellent.

Other intellectuals soon followed. Of the forty-one names announced on Reagan's foreign policy team that spring, thirty-three held doctorates, and most of them served on the faculty at universities such as Stanford, Yale, Harvard, Georgetown, and Johns Hopkins.[48] Because Reagan saw the Cold War as a battle of ideas, he and conservative scholars developed a mutual attraction.

XIV

On Monday morning, July 14, 1980, Reagan boarded a private jet in Los Angeles to fly to Detroit for the Republican National Convention. Beyond Michigan's electoral appeal as a swing state, foreign policy considerations had also influenced the GOP's selection of Detroit as host city. The "Motor City," for decades home of the nation's top automobile manufacturers, embodied one of America's acute international challenges: the competition from Japan's booming carmakers. The decline of the American auto industry—including a 30 percent unemployment rate, stagnant wages, poor quality, diminished output, and falling sales—seemed to exemplify the decline of the nation as a whole. Reagan saw Detroit as ground zero in his vision of restoring America's economy, confidence, strength, and global standing. The small group traveling on Reagan's plane included longtime advisor Stuart Spencer. During the flight, Spencer asked Reagan a deceptively simple question: "Why do you want to be president?"

To which Reagan answered, "To end the Cold War."

A startled Spencer followed up with the obvious: "How do you plan to do that?"

Reagan's reply came humble and honest: "I'm not sure, but there has got to be a way."

From there, he detailed the weaknesses in the Soviet economy, the sclerosis in its corrupt and repressive political system, the stale verities of détente, and his personal aversion to nuclear weapons.[49]

It was a bold vision. But how to square Reagan's desire to "end" the Cold War with his claim to Allen three years earlier that he wanted the United States to "win" the Cold War? These two comments provide both the bookends and the puzzle for the Cold War policy that Reagan would pursue as president: Did he seek victory in the Cold War or just its peaceful end? While the two outcomes are not mutually exclusive—victory implies a finish, after all—they can, and often did, exist in tension with each other throughout the Reagan presidency.

Reagan held clear end goals: the expansion of liberty in the world, the end of Soviet communism, the abolition of nuclear weapons, peace between the American and Russian people, and a world free of the Cold War. But how all those fit together, and how they could be achieved, posed the strategic puzzle. Did he desire to inflict a crushing defeat on the Soviet Union or to negotiate a peaceful truce? It was a question that would cause bitter feuds among his senior team.[50] Once in office, Reagan would resolve the puzzle by fusing it together: He would pursue the Soviet Union's *negotiated surrender*.

When he arrived at the convention in Detroit, Reagan's top priorities were to select a running mate and launch his general election campaign. The former task prompted one of the more bizarre episodes in American political history. The next afternoon, Reagan paid a visit to the hotel suite of former president Gerald Ford—and invited Ford to serve as his running mate. On one level, the gambit made political sense. Though conservative in his principles, Reagan was a ruthless competitor, hungry to win. He also possessed a pragmatic streak, often willing to compromise on policies and work with those who did not share his political convictions. Having Ford as his running mate held undeniable political appeal. It would help unify the GOP's moderate and conservative wings, reassure the electorate of Reagan's broad-mindedness, and add a steady hand of experience that would mollify any voters concerned about Reagan's fitness for leading the nation.

On another level, it was political malpractice that bordered on lunacy. Having challenged Ford in the 1976 GOP primary campaign, having defined his foreign policy as the antithesis of the Ford-Kissinger approach, having made the case that he was ready to be commander in chief, Reagan now teetered on a head-smacking reversal. Adding Ford to the ticket would undercut Reagan's credibility, cheapen his foreign policy convictions, and— with two men both known as "Mr. President" working simultaneously in the West Wing—sow confusion as to who was in charge. After a brief flirtation, Reagan and Ford both recognized it as the bad idea it was. Instead, Reagan invited George H. W. Bush to join his ticket. Bush brought most of Ford's advantages with few of the liabilities. As a moderate, he would help unify the GOP and broaden Reagan's appeal in the general election. As a former congressman, ambassador to the UN, envoy to China, and CIA director, his national security experience rivaled and perhaps even exceeded that of Ford. And the grateful Bush would be a loyal lieutenant to Reagan.

The next night, the rapturous convention crowd ushered Reagan to the podium on a cascade of applause. Every eye in the sweltering hall, and millions more watching on television, waited for what Reagan would say in accepting the nomination. He focused most of his speech on domestic issues, specifically America's dismal economy, joblessness, and energy crisis. This made political sense; Reagan could not win the White House without addressing the immediate concerns and needs of American voters. He also knew, and often said, that renewing America's standing abroad began with restoring its economy and self-confidence at home.

However, Reagan connected the nation's domestic ennui with its international enervation and bemoaned that as America lost its belief in itself, its allies were also losing faith in the United States:

> Who does not feel a growing sense of unease as our allies, facing repeated instances of an amateurish and confused administration, reluctantly conclude that America is unwilling or unable to fulfill its obligations as the leader of the free world? . . .
>
> No American should vote until he or she has asked, is the United States stronger and more respected now than it was three-and-a-half years ago? Is the world today a safer place in which to live?

He then grounded his vision of "peace through strength" in history:

> Four times in my lifetime America has gone to war, bleeding the lives of its young men into the sands of beachheads, the fields of Europe and the jungles and rice paddies of Asia. We know only too well that war comes not when the forces of freedom are strong, but when they are weak. . . . The United States has an obligation to its citizens and to the people of the world never to let those who would destroy freedom dictate the future course of human life on this planet. I would regard my election as proof that we have renewed our resolve to preserve world peace and freedom.

Just as the audience thought the speech was ending, Reagan surprised them—and perhaps even himself—with a closing comment that was not in his prepared remarks:

> Can we doubt that only a Divine Providence placed this land, this island of freedom, here as a refuge for all those people in the world who yearn to breathe freely: Jews and Christians enduring persecution behind the Iron Curtain, the boat people of Southeast Asia, of Cuba and of Haiti, the victims of drought and famine in Africa, the freedom fighters of Afghanistan and our own countrymen held in savage captivity.

I'll confess that I've been a little afraid to suggest what I'm going to suggest—I'm more afraid not to— Can we begin our crusade joined together in a moment of silent prayer.[51]

At that, Reagan bowed his head, and a quiet descended in the convention hall as thousands of other heads bowed with him. With this benediction, Reagan voiced his belief in a divine purpose for America as a beacon of religious freedom and human dignity, and a personal faith reliant on prayer. Cynics can dismiss Reagan's plea as a shameless use of piety for political gain, and no doubt it played well with many in the convention hall. To dismiss it, however, is to miss a foundational dimension of Reagan. His diaries and private correspondence regularly reveal the sincere Christian devotion of this otherwise private and inscrutable man. He believed in forgiveness of sins and salvation through Jesus Christ's death and resurrection, the divine inspiration of the Bible, and the power of prayer. Spiritual sincerity did not mean consistency, of course. Reagan was an infrequent churchgoer, enjoyed ribald humor, and sometimes deviated from Christian orthodoxy. Yet he believed in a providential plan for his life and for America, and this sense of divine sovereignty helped give Reagan the equipoise that would confound his critics and supporters alike.

XV

Coming out of Detroit, Reagan enjoyed a commanding lead in the polls. His advantage came more from voters disillusioned with Carter than those attracted to Reagan. By early August, Carter's approval rating plumbed the depths at 21 percent, among the lowest recorded in presidential history. But then Reagan committed a series of gaffes and missteps that decimated his lead and renewed voter doubts about his judgment. In biographer Steven Hayward's description, Reagan "experienced perhaps the worst first 10 days of campaigning of any modern candidate."[52] Two of his costliest mistakes concerned national security.

The first came on August 16, when Reagan and Bush held a press conference on the eve of Bush's upcoming trip to China and Japan. Asked about his position on Taiwan, Reagan urged an "official governmental relationship" between the United States and the Republic of China. His effort to explain what he meant only bollixed things further.[53] At best he came across as befuddled and ill informed; at worst he seemed to advocate a reversal of America's official diplomatic recognition of Beijing and defiance of the Taiwan Relations Act. Both had been adopted the year before as the carefully negotiated framework governing the United States–China–Taiwan triangle. China reacted with predictable umbrage. It took Bush's traveling to Beijing to endure a tongue-lashing from Deng Xiaoping, followed by Reagan reluctantly reading a statement reaffirming America's diplomatic recognition of the PRC, to calm the transpacific furor. One benefit emerged from the episode. Bush's combination of public loyalty to Reagan and deft private diplomacy with Beijing, which drew on Bush's deep China experience, created trust between the two men and confirmed Reagan's choice of running mate.[54]

In the midst of Reagan's self-induced Taiwan crisis, he stumbled over another tripwire in Chicago. Once again it pertained to America's fraught recent history in Asia. The Veterans of Foreign Wars invited Reagan to speak at their annual conference on August 18 and honored him as the first presidential candidate to be endorsed in the history of the VFW. Reagan and his team saw this as the perfect venue to deliver, in Peter Hannaford's words, "a measured exposition of his views on the state of US security, our need to rebuild our defenses, and to seek genuine arms reductions with the Soviet Union."[55]

When read in full, Reagan's speech did just that. Yet Reagan insisted on adding some strong words on the Vietnam War:

> For too long, we have lived with the "Vietnam Syndrome." . . . It is time we recognized that ours was, in truth, a noble cause. . . . We dishonor the memory of 50,000 young Americans who died in that cause when we give way to feelings of guilt as if we were doing something shameful. . . .
>
> There is a lesson for all of us in Vietnam; if a war does come, we must have the means and the determination to prevail or we will not have what it takes to secure the peace. And while we are at it, let us tell those who fought in that war that we will never again ask young men to fight and possibly die in a war our government is afraid to let them win.

The problem with Reagan's words was not that they were all wrong. North Vietnam was a brutal communist regime, American troops who fought honorably in the war had answered their nation's call, and Reagan's principles for the deployment of force were sound. As he had been saying for several years, his nation should not let the traumas of Vietnam forever cripple its foreign policy. However, for an America still deeply divided and scarred by the war, and still coming to terms with its losses, hubris, mistakes, and even crimes, the words *noble cause* stung as ill timed and ill chosen. They also eclipsed the rest of Reagan's speech themes and detonated another round of negative media coverage. As a *Washington Post* writer summarized, Reagan's comments "cast doubt on his fitness as a leader, if not, by implication, on his sanity." The campaign's internal polling showed as much, with a majority of Americans expressing disapproval.[56]

XVI

As the race tightened into the fall, the Reagan campaign fretted that Carter would pull off an "October surprise" by securing—or appearing to secure—the release of the American hostages in Iran on the eve of the election. Throughout his campaign, Reagan faced the political and moral challenge of how to exploit Carter's perceived mishandling of the hostage crisis without seeming to wish ill on his nation in general or the hostages in particular. Iklé wrote a memo to Meese and Allen that distilled the campaign's dilemma. As a first principle, he said, "We want the soonest possible release of all the American hostages," by which Iklé made clear that the Reagan team welcomed the release of the hostages even if it took place prior to Election Day and benefited the Carter campaign. On the other hand, Iklé took a very cynical view of Carter, warning, "Our opponent will try to maximize his election advantage in a most cold-blooded fashion. Almost any form of deception or costs to the broader national interest will be acceptable to him as long as it seems useful for the next seven weeks."[57] Such was the pervasive distrust between the camps.[58]

Meanwhile, the national mood and polls continued to fluctuate throughout October, with many surveys showing Carter starting to pull ahead. The Reagan team realized that with voter doubts about Reagan lingering, setting the campaign cruise control on "not Carter" would be insufficient to win. They needed to regain the lead and reassure voters that the old Hollywood star could handle the acute strains and big stage of the White House.

So in addition to scheduling a debate with Carter, on the night of Sunday, October 19, Reagan delivered a nationwide televised address titled "A Strategy of Peace for the '80s." As one Reagan advisor put it, they scheduled the speech to respond to voter concerns on "the war issue and the competency issue." Carter himself had been fueling those questions, goading Reagan with the inflammatory charge that the election would decide "whether we will have war or peace" and accusing Reagan of wanting a "shootout at the O.K. Corral" with the Kremlin.[59] Political ploy though it was, the speech also reflected Reagan's genuine convictions.

He began by assuring viewers that his "primary goal" was the "establishment of lasting world peace." In an incantation one would expect more from John Lennon or the Maharishi Mahesh Yogi than a Republican presidential candidate, Reagan repeated the word *peace* forty-one times throughout the speech, more than once every forty-four seconds.[60] He tried to walk a tightrope in persuading the public that his policies of military expansion, arming anticommunist forces, and launching a rhetorical offensive against Moscow would not provoke war but rather provide the surest path to peace— or, as Reagan's mantra went, "peace through strength."

Just over a week later, Reagan arrived in Cleveland for his only debate with Carter. A television audience of over one hundred million Americans tuned in, the largest debate viewership in history. Carter, a skilled debater, landed many rhetorical punches on Reagan over the ninety minutes. But Reagan's closing appeal—as much about America's imperiled national security as it was about the electorate's pocketbook worries—sealed Carter's fate: "Are you better off than you were four years ago? . . . Is America as respected throughout the world as it was? Do you feel your security is safe, that we're as strong as we were four years ago?"[61]

Seven days later, American voters answered Reagan's questions by electing him president in a landslide. He carried 44 states with 489 electoral votes to just 49 for Carter.

Foreign governments the world over, especially in the Kremlin, marveled at the scale of Reagan's victory. They realized that, whatever else they might have thought of this peculiar new American president, he would take office with a popular mandate. Such things matter in national security. Other world leaders would gauge his strength not just by the size of the American economy or the lethality of the American military, but also by how much support he enjoyed from the American people.

XVII

National security proved a significant factor in Reagan's victory. An overwhelming 82 percent of voters disapproved of Carter's foreign policy and believed America had become weaker, less respected, and more vulnerable under Carter.[62] As an overall verdict on Carter's presidency, this was a valid judgment. But in fairness to Carter, in his final eighteen months in office, he had executed a quiet turnabout in his foreign and defense policies that collectively handed the incoming Reagan team a stronger hand than would otherwise have been the case.

Carter withdrew the SALT II treaty from Senate consideration, increased the defense budget, and restored new weapons systems, such as the MX missile. As a career CIA officer, Bob Gates served on the Carter NSC staff and recalls that "Carter began numerous covert actions to counter Soviet advances in the Third World. Well before the invasion of Afghanistan, he approved intelligence findings aimed at countering the Soviets and/or Cubans in Grenada, Jamaica, Nicaragua, El Salvador, Yemen, and even Afghanistan."[63] Following the Soviet invasion, Carter expanded this covert action to include arming the mujahideen resistance fighters, in addition to the Carter Doctrine's declaration of resolve against further Soviet expansion in the Persian Gulf.

In political terms these changes amounted to too little too late for Carter's public image and reelection prospects. But collectively these measures meant that when Reagan took office, he inherited some policies and programs on which to build.

XVIII

For all of his aspirations to lead a global transformation, the morning after Election Day, Reagan woke up to face a more immediate challenge: Having at last won in his long quest for the White House, how to make it work?

Reagan knew that the answer to this question started with the chief of staff. The morning after the election, Reagan surprised many of his team by inviting James Baker to the Century Plaza Hotel and offering him the job. Baker was Bush's former campaign manager and best friend. Though he had joined the Reagan campaign when Bush became the running mate and done an able job with debate negotiations and preparations, Baker was otherwise still little known to Reagan. An accomplished lawyer from a patrician Texas family, the shrewd and savvy Baker was also a nonpareil political operator. He brought to the job discipline, organization, polish, media acumen, street smarts, and a ruthless streak. Picking him over loyalists such as Ed Meese revealed Reagan's pragmatism. He wanted his presidency to succeed.[64]

For one of Reagan's first steps, he assembled the seventeen-person Interim Foreign Policy Advisory Board, chaired by Bill Casey and headlined by former president Ford, and including luminaries such as Kissinger, George Shultz, and Bill Clements, the Texas governor and former deputy secretary of defense. The advisory group's foremost purpose was to send a message of political unity, especially given Ford and Kissinger's pronounced differences with Reagan on policy.[65] While Casey pined to lead the State Department, Reagan instead picked him for CIA director, a more fitting role for the old OSS veteran. Reagan also continued his deliberate outreach to Democrats. Kirkpatrick, whom Reagan would soon appoint as ambassador to the United Nations with cabinet rank (the first UN ambassador thus elevated), became the first of numerous Democrats to take senior policy positions in the Reagan administration. Others included Elliott Abrams, Eugene Rostow, Max Kampelman, Richard Perle, Paul Nitze, and Paul Wolfowitz. To little surprise, Reagan selected Dick Allen as national security advisor (NSA).[66]

There are approximately two and a half months between Election Day and Inauguration Day, an impossibly short time for the new president-elect to plan his administration, fill thousands of positions, and prepare to lead the free world. Every presidential transition produces a flood of policy memos from the president-elect's "transition team" of campaign staff, elder statesmen, eager volunteers, donors, and assorted grifters and hangers-on, all jockeying to shape US policy—and not infrequently to advance their own careers. Most of these get discarded or filed away unread. Not so with an eleven-page memo from New York City that Reagan read with interest. Its author was Richard Nixon. Describing himself as "one who has been there and who seeks or wants absolutely nothing except your success in office," Nixon went on to offer Reagan detailed, unvarnished advice on politics and personnel.

This letter continued a transformation in Reagan's relationship with Nixon. At the time, Nixon was one of just three men alive who knew what it was to be president of the United States—including the unfathomable pressures, the unrelenting scrutiny, the impossible decisions, the elixir of power, and the lonely burdens of the Oval Office. That fact, coupled with Nixon's foreign policy acumen and political skills, made Reagan willing to overlook their past rivalry and continuing policy differences and at least listen to Nixon's counsel. Perhaps to the surprise of both men, over the next eight years Nixon would become a valued advisor and sounding board for Reagan.

Nixon urged Reagan to focus first on the economy, noting, "Unless you are able to shape up our home base it will be almost impossible to conduct an effective foreign policy." This advice reinforced Reagan's own instincts and those of his senior team; it was the course he would follow. Nixon then offered specific recommendations for every cabinet position and guidance on subcabinet roles as well. He began with the State Department: "Whoever is appointed as Secretary of State must have a thorough understanding not only of Europe, but of the Soviet Union, China, Japan, the Mideast, Africa and Latin America. He must also share your general views with regard to the Soviet threat and foreign policy generally. These requirements pretty much limit those who could be considered. Haig is your guy." A four-star army general who had just retired as supreme allied commander in Europe, Alexander Haig had previously served in the Nixon administration as Kissinger's deputy national security advisor and then as White House chief of staff. Knowing of Haig's many detractors, Nixon then tried to preempt his critics in the Reagan camp: "Those who oppose him because they think he is 'soft' are either ignorant or stupid. . . . He would be personally loyal to you and would not back-bite you on or off the record."

Nixon proved almost comically wrong in assuring Reagan of Haig's personal loyalty. Nor did Haig, a Kissinger protégé, share Reagan's strategic convictions on the Kremlin's vulnerability to an ideological offensive. Turning to other potential candidates for State, Nixon dismissed George Shultz, writing, "I do not believe that he has the depth of understanding of world issues generally and the Soviet Union in particular that is needed for this period." To his everlasting regret, Reagan followed Nixon's advice. He selected Haig, though not before having Meese, Baker, and Allen quietly discuss with the general the need to disavow his own presidential ambitions and devote himself to serving Reagan's agenda. Haig gave the needful assurances—and then almost immediately proved to be a calamitous choice.[67]

For other positions, Nixon's suggestions proved more sound. He recommended William French Smith for attorney general and Casey for CIA director (a.k.a. director of central intelligence, or DCI). For secretary of defense, Nixon praised Caspar Weinberger as "intelligent . . . wise, and totally loyal." Reagan would select Weinberger, whose virtues included his close relationship with Reagan and his facility with budgets from his past service as Office of Management and Budget director in the Nixon White House. Nixon closed with a request: "The opportunity to provide advice in areas where I have special experience to you and to members of your Cabinet and the White House staff where you deem it appropriate," adding, "President Eisenhower said to me when I visited him at Walter Reed Hospital after the election of 1968, 'I am yours to command.' I now say the same to you."[68]

During the transition the departing president usually leaves most important policy decisions for his successor to decide. Policy crises that cannot be postponed lead to delicate discussions between the outgoing and incoming White House staffs. One of these policy crises sat on death row in Seoul. South Korea in 1980 was an American treaty ally, a reliable anticommunist partner in the Cold War, a booming market economy—and a military dictatorship. President Chun Doo-Hwan had taken power in a coup the year before, imposed martial law, and on September 17 sentenced to death the country's leading dissident, the democracy activist and devout Catholic Kim Dae Jung. Carter and his senior team had remonstrated fervently with Chun to spare Kim's life. They had limited leverage, given the resentment that South Korean leaders felt toward Carter over his effort earlier in his presidency to withdraw all US troops from South Korea. His election loss rendered Carter's hand weaker still. By mid-November, many news reports and foreign diplomats indicated that the Chun regime planned to put Kim to death any day.[69]

Giving American allies a free pass to execute peaceful dissidents was not what Reagan had envisioned when he criticized Carter's human rights policy on the campaign trail. Mindful that he was not yet sworn in as president, Reagan nonetheless wanted to save Kim.

At Reagan's behest, and in coordination with Carter's NSA Zbigniew Brzezinski, Allen quietly enticed Seoul with a deal: In exchange for sparing Kim's life and lifting martial law, Reagan would invite Chun to the White House as one of the first foreign leaders to visit in his new presidency. An eager Chun accepted the offer. Both sides kept the arrangement quiet until, in a careful choreography, on January 21 the new Reagan White House announced Chun's upcoming visit, and three days later Seoul announced the lifting of martial law and the commutation of Kim's sentence.[70] The doughty dissident eventually went into exile in the United States.

During the interregnum, Allen also met twice with Soviet ambassador Anatoly Dobrynin. The dean of the Washington diplomatic corps, the suave and crafty Dobrynin had served in the post since 1962 and known every American president since Kennedy. He thought he had seen it all in American politics—until Reagan won the election. Dobrynin recalls that Kremlin anxieties focused on two aspects of Reagan's convictions: "One was his apparent determination to regain military superiority; the other, his determination to launch an ideological offensive against the Soviet Union and foment trouble inside the country and among Soviet allies." On November 17, Moscow directed Dobrynin to reach out to Reagan's inner circle during the transition to see what he could divine about how this new president would govern.[71] In response to Dobrynin's overture, Allen and policy advisor Henry Nau met with the Soviet emissary twice for lunch. Concerned over what to expect from Reagan, Dobrynin stressed Moscow's preference for Nixon and Kissinger's détente framework and use of quiet "back channel" diplomacy with the Soviets (not least because Dobrynin himself had been one of the main conduits for that back channel). Allen and Nau responded warily and reiterated Reagan's warning against a possible Soviet invasion of Poland to crush the burgeoning Solidarity movement, especially given recent Red Army exercises on the Polish border. Dobrynin reacted sharply, protesting that "the Soviet government has been very restrained" and "we don't want to be threatened" by the Americans.[72]

Reagan used the transition period to return to a theme from his campaign announcement speech over a year earlier: deepening America's ties with its continental neighbors. On January 5, he flew from California to El Paso and then walked across the Bridge of Friendship, where he greeted Mexican president José López Portillo, followed by a meeting on the Mexican side in Ciudad Juárez. As the first American president-elect to visit Mexico, Reagan embraced his southern neighbor as a cherished, albeit nettlesome, friend and the gateway to Central and South America.[73] Mexico stood as the United States' third-largest trading partner, behind only Canada and Japan.

In the next two weeks, the Iran hostage negotiations entered the final crucible as the Carter administration finalized a complex arrangement to return to Tehran billions of dollars in frozen assets in exchange for the release of the hostages. Reagan and his senior team watched in anxiety and ambivalence. Allen sent Reagan a memo on January 16 summarizing the latest developments and worried that a desperate Carter might concede too much to the Iranians while setting precedents on asset retrieval and compensation claims that would shackle the Reagan administration. "On the plus side," Allen wrote, if Carter's negotiations succeeded, "the hostage problem would be essentially over. . . . The Iranians would no longer hold the leverage over the United States that the hostages gave them."[74] Allen was correct, and four days later, when the hostages were freed, Reagan would inherit a fresh start and freer hand on foreign policy. Meanwhile, Reagan prepared for a few days hence, when he would take the oath of office as commander in chief, diplomat in chief, and leader of the free world.

CHAPTER 2

TAKING THE STAGE

I

I t may have been the most awkward drive in presidential history. January 20, 1981, dawned bright and clear in Washington, DC, as a recent cold snap gave way to a warming day. Just before noon, President Jimmy Carter and President-Elect Ronald Reagan embarked on one of the more ticklish rituals in American politics, the outgoing and incoming presidents riding together in the presidential limousine from the White House to the Capitol for the inauguration ceremony.

The campaign had illuminated their contrasts in personality, style, and conviction. Those were rendered all the more stark this morning. Carter had been awake for forty-eight hours straight in a desperate gambit to se-cure the release of the Iran hostages, and he looked the part. Haggard, pale, and exhausted not just from the past two days but from the past four years, the outgoing president remained bitter at his election loss and regarded his successor with contempt. Reagan, on the other hand, was hale, fresh, con-fident, and eager to take the oath.

In the car, the two men barely spoke to each other.

Carter probably felt relieved when the car phone's ring punctured the painful silence. National Security Agency director Admiral Bobby Ray In-man was on the line. Inman informed Carter that Iran had just released the American hostages and allowed them to board a departure flight at the Tehran airport. But, Inman continued, Ayatollah Khomeini would not per-mit the plane to take off until Reagan took the oath of office and Carter officially became ex-president. It was Tehran's final humiliation of the thirty-ninth president.[1]

Their motorcade arrived at the Capitol. The assembled crowd waited eagerly at the West Front, where Reagan would soon become the first president in history to hold his inauguration on that side rather than the traditional East Front. The location was by design. The view west from the Capitol steps represented Reagan's idea of his presidency. Pointing his audience to the presidential memorials and Arlington National Cemetery stretching before him, Reagan spoke of the weight of history they together inherited: "At the end of this open mall are those shrines to the giants on whose shoulders we stand."

He delivered a workmanlike inaugural address. Dispensing with soaring prose, Reagan spoke plainly to the nation's economic pain, loss of spirit, and hope for renewal. Of foreign policy he said little, with no mention of the Soviet Union or Cold War. Instead, he again assured his nation, and its friends and foes beyond, "Peace is the highest aspiration of the American people. We will negotiate for it, sacrifice for it; we will not surrender for it, now or ever."[2]

Later that afternoon, as Ed Meese reclined in his new West Wing office chatting with James Baker and Michael Deaver, Haig burst in holding a paper that he insisted the president sign. It was a draft Haig had written of National Security Decision Directive 1. One of the most important national security orders every president issues, it establishes the authorities and responsibilities of each senior official in the National Security Council. It is where bureaucracy and power meet. Haig knew this better than most. As a veteran of the Nixon White House, he had observed his mentor Kissinger's consolidation of power to the point of holding the jobs of both national security advisor and secretary of state concurrently for two years. Haig's draft document for Reagan had almost the same effect. It gave the secretary of state control of the entire National Security Council, subordinating the secretary of defense and CIA director to State, and relegating the NSA to a mere clerk.

Haig had previewed his demands in a private meeting with Reagan two weeks earlier, when Haig proposed that "the Secretary of State be your Vicar for the community of Departments having an interest in the several dimensions of foreign policy." He further insisted that the NSC staff have no contact with the media or any foreign officials outside the State Department.[3] Haig claims in his memoir that Reagan "nodded after each point and agreed."[4]

More likely Reagan, averse to both conflict and details, had simply nodded his acknowledgment of Haig's demands. The conniving Haig took the
president-elect's silence as assent.

Baker and Meese knew otherwise. The chief of staff later said of Haig's
Inauguration Day gambit, "Talk about bad timing. We were still in formal
attire. We hadn't even unpacked our briefcases. And here was Al Haig, not
yet confirmed by the Senate, with a twenty-page document no one—
including the president—had yet seen."[5] Meese took Haig's draft and placed
it in his briefcase, never to be seen again. Over the next few weeks, Baker
and Meese consulted with Weinberger, Casey, and Allen, and produced
an organizational framework for national security that, in the words of a
White House memo, "melds greater Cabinet (particularly State) responsibility with continuing assurance of a Presidential perspective." Ominously
forecasting the next eight years, the memo also warned, "Our start-up problems with NSC, State, and Defense (over national security jurisdiction) . . .
are, in my view, harbingers of the future."[6]

The irony of Haig's power grab was how unnecessary it was. During the
transition, Reagan had made clear his intention to restore the prominence
of the secretary of state and reduce the authority of the NSA by having Allen report through the "troika" of Baker, Deaver, and Meese instead of directly to the president. As Bob Gates recalls, "Symbolic of this was [Allen's]
ouster from the large, bright corner office on the first floor of the West Wing
of the White House—which Kissinger had acquired over a decade earlier
and Brzezinski had kept—to a basement office just outside of the Situation
Room."[7] Regardless of Reagan's intentions, these organizational chart and
real estate changes emasculated the NSA position in the eyes of the other
departments represented on the National Security Council, such as State,
Defense, and CIA (collectively known in Washington-speak as the "interagency"). It also doomed Allen from the start.

As for Haig, in grasping for more, he ended up with less. He provoked
humiliating headlines—*The Washington Post* titled its story "Organization
Table for Foreign Policy Limits Haig's Role"—and in the process created
several enemies in the White House and cabinet.

Reagan also continued filling out the top ranks of his national security
team. For deputy secretary of state, he selected his former gubernatorial
chief of staff Bill Clark. An affable rancher and California supreme court
justice, Clark had previously studied for the Catholic priesthood before
turning to politics and the law. He lacked any foreign policy experience but

possessed two qualities the president valued: conservative convictions and Reagan's trust. Haig seemed to have little of either, and Reagan's inner circle made clear their hope that Clark would keep watch on his ostensible boss at Foggy Bottom.

Reagan persuaded Inman to take the role of CIA deputy director. A native of the small East Texas town of Rhonesboro, over a three-decade naval career Inman had distinguished himself with a near-photographic memory, a keen analytic mind, organizational skill, and political savvy. As the tandem overseeing the intelligence community, Inman's management experience, focus on intelligence analysis, and close ties to Capitol Hill seemed on paper a perfect complement to Casey's entrepreneurial zeal and focus on spying and covert action. In practice they would soon become bitter rivals, barely on speaking terms.

II

On January 29, Reagan held his first press conference as president. Walking into the Old Executive Office Building's fourth-floor auditorium, he made brief opening remarks focused on the economy. The press questions soon turned to foreign policy. Sam Donaldson of ABC News asked: "Mr. President, what do you see as the long-range intentions of the Soviet Union? Do you think, for instance, the Kremlin is bent on world domination that might lead to a continuation of the Cold War, or do you think that under other circumstances détente is possible?"

Reagan's reply sent shock waves around the world:

> Well, so far détente's been a one-way street that the Soviet Union has used to pursue its own aims. I don't have to think of an answer as to what I think their intentions are; they have repeated it. I know of no leader of the Soviet Union since the revolution, and including the present leadership, that has not more than once repeated . . . that their goal must be the promotion of world revolution and a one-world Socialist or Communist state, whichever word you want to use.
>
> Now, as long as they do that and as long as they, at the same time, have openly and publicly declared that the only morality they recognize is what will further their cause, meaning they reserve

unto themselves the right to commit any crime, to lie, to cheat, in order to attain that, and that is moral, not immoral, and we operate on a different set of standards, I think when you do business with them, even at a détente, you keep that in mind.[8]

Rarely if ever had an American president uttered such an unvarnished condemnation of Soviet communism. This was not just political posturing. Reagan spoke from his convictions. He wrote in his diary a few days later, "We need to take a new look at the whole matter of strategy. Trade was supposed to make Soviets moderate, instead it has allowed them to build armaments instead of consumer products. Their socialism is an ec[onomic] failure. Wouldn't we be doing more for their people if we let their system fail instead of constantly bailing it out?"[9]

At the time the Kremlin reciprocated Reagan's sentiments. A KGB assessment shortly after Reagan's election disparaged him as embodying "the most conservative, chauvinist, and bellicose part of American politics . . . pressing for the restoration of American world leadership after the defeat in Vietnam." In the words of Cambridge historian Christopher Andrew and former KGB officer Vasili Mitrokhin, "Probably no American policymaker at any time during the Cold War inspired quite as much fear and loathing in Moscow as Ronald Reagan during his first term as president."[10]

Whenever a new American president takes office, the world watches to see which foreign leader will make the first White House visit. The invitation symbolizes much about the new administration's foreign policy priorities. It came as no small surprise when on January 28, Reagan welcomed the prime minister of . . . Jamaica. Edward Seaga had just won election three months earlier, defeating an incumbent who had aligned Jamaica more closely with Cuba and the USSR. Though strategically insignificant by itself, Jamaica sent a message about Reagan's support for democratic capitalism against communist inroads in the Western Hemisphere. Reagan wrote in his diary that evening, "[Seaga] won a terrific election victory over a Cuban backed pro-communist. I think we can help him and gradually take back the Caribbean which was becoming a 'Red' lake."[11]

Five days after hosting Seaga, Reagan fulfilled his quiet deal with South Korea by welcoming President Chun Doo-Hwan to the White House. Reagan used the Chun visit, in the words of an NSC briefing memo, as his "first signal to the region . . . of the vital interests of the Free World in Asia, and that consistent American strength and support are necessary if we are to make the Pacific Basin a stable and secure area."[12] A week before the meeting, Chun made a goodwill gesture by lifting martial law. Nonetheless, Reagan hosted him with little enthusiasm. As NSC staffer Don Gregg recalls, the Reagan team "had a low opinion of the draconian Chun . . . [and] downplay[ed] Chun's visit in every way possible," including hosting merely a lunch rather than a state dinner.[13]

Greeting Chun in the Oval Office, Reagan reassured him that, contrary to Carter's early efforts to withdraw all American troops, Reagan would maintain the substantial US military forces in South Korea. After Chun offered some hollow platitudes on human rights, Reagan gave the dictator further absolution, saying, "Together the ROK and the United States must consider the question of human rights in the proper manner," and lamenting, "In the past it has seemed the United States has ignored the greatest violators of human rights, most of whom are to be found behind the bamboo and iron curtains."[14]

It was a missed opportunity. By not pressing Chun to respect human rights, Reagan indulged double standards of his own that winked at South Korea's brutal repression, failed to follow up on the success of protecting Kim Dae Jung's life, and undermined American credibility. Little did Reagan anticipate that within six years he and his administration would help usher Chun from power and support South Korea's transition to democracy.

In 1981 there was only one democracy in Asia. It happened to be one of America's most important allies *and* one of its knottiest foreign policy challenges: Japan.

Many Americans viewed Japan less as a strategic partner than as an economic predator, flooding the United States with Sony and Toshiba electronics and Toyota and Datsun vehicles that may have been enjoyed by American consumers but hurt American manufacturers and put many American workers out of jobs. A protectionist Congress channeled these public attitudes with regular threats to pass legislation imposing tariffs and import quotas on Japan. The Reagan administration faced the challenge of confronting Japan over trade imbalances while also cooperating on strategic concerns.

Six days after Reagan took office, Ambassador Mike Mansfield sent a cable from Tokyo that set the contours of the administration's Japan policy—because of its clarity and insight, and because it reinforced the president's own convictions. Reagan described the cable in his diary as "a very scholarly and thorough analysis of our relations with Japan."[15] Recalling fondly their first meeting in Tokyo in 1978, Reagan had asked Mansfield to stay in the post as ambassador to Japan, even though the envoy was a Democrat appointed by Carter. Mansfield made three main points in his cable: "[America's] alliance and partnership with Japan is the most important bilateral relationship that we have in the world," the United States should address its policy frictions with Japan in this overall strategic context, and Washington should encourage Tokyo to play a more active global role as a fellow industrialized democracy.[16]

Mansfield was correct to describe the United States–Japan relationship as "the most important" in the world. America's other allies, such as the United Kingdom, held great value, but London sat alongside Paris and Bonn as one of three European capitals on which transatlantic relations depended, whereas Japan stood apart as the world's third-largest economy and the United States' largest trading partner, most important technology supplier, host of vital military bases, and only democratic ally in Asia.[17] Senior Pentagon official Rich Armitage described the Reagan administration's strategic interest in Japan in real estate terms: "Location, location, location . . . the naval bases and the air bases . . . [were] central to our ability to project power [in the Asia-Pacific]."[18] America's entire posture in Asia—especially countering the Soviet Union, with its three thousand miles of Pacific coastline—depended on Japan.

This is not to say that the United Kingdom did not matter. It was America's most important European ally, and British prime minister Margaret Thatcher would become Reagan's closest friend among allied leaders. On February 26, he welcomed her to the White House as the first European leader to visit since his inauguration.

She landed in Washington in the midst of a trial. Allen told Reagan, "Mrs. Thatcher comes here at an exceptionally difficult moment so far as her domestic position is concerned"; she was beset by Britain's economic woes and her emboldened political opposition. *Time* magazine irked Thatcher with an article previewing her visit titled "Embattled but Unbowed" (she thought *embattled* gave her political adversaries too much credit).[19]

Reagan and Thatcher both knew that the "special relationship" between their countries needed renewal. Not since the early 1950s, when Eisenhower and Churchill led their nations, had the United States and United Kingdom both enjoyed leaders with such shared values and mutual commitment to the alliance. One of Thatcher's briefing memos described Reagan as the first "strong" American president since Eisenhower and lauded his commitment to addressing "the most serious problem of United States external policy, the growing discrepancy between commitments and resources."[20] More crass, but no less appreciative, Reagan told his staff, "[Thatcher is] the only European leader I know with balls."[21]

One mark of the depth of a president's relationship with another world leader is the breadth of issues they discuss. Heads of state who only discuss their own nation's concerns may get some transactional benefits for their homeland but will not influence the most powerful man in the world on other global issues. In contrast, those leaders whom Reagan would become closest to knew he valued their counsel and insights on the broad range of global issues he confronted.

Such was Thatcher. Over the course of three days, including a White House state dinner and reciprocal black-tie dinner at the British embassy, she and Reagan discussed the Middle East, southern Africa, Latin America, economic and defense policy, and of course the Soviet Union. Just a few days earlier, Brezhnev had given a speech proposing to meet with Reagan concerning the arms race. Thatcher asked Reagan his assessment of the Soviet leader's proposal and cautioned that "when you sup with the devil you must have a long spoon. In fact you had better have a whole lot of long spoons." Reagan assured her his response would be "not a no, not a yes" and said, "We're considering it very carefully." He also stated that any negotiations with the Soviets should not be confined to arms control. "We will want to discuss a whole lot of other things too, for example, Soviet backing of Cuban subversion."[22]

Most important, they solidified their personal bond as two conservative leaders trying at home to promote free markets while abroad expanding liberty and countering Soviet communism. Thatcher even lent a lobbying hand on Reagan's tax-cut proposal when she visited Capitol Hill and, as the grateful president wrote in his diary, "was literally an advocate for our ec[onomic] program. Some of the Sen[ators] tried to give her a bad time. She put them down firmly and with typical British courtesy."[23]

III

At initial glance, Caspar Weinberger appeared an unusual pick for secretary of defense. Like Casey, he had hoped to be secretary of state, so Reagan's request that he helm the Pentagon came as a consolation prize. Though Weinberger had served in World War II on General MacArthur's army staff, he otherwise had little background on defense policy. What he did have was a close relationship with Reagan dating back to his time on the California gubernatorial staff; federal budget acumen from having been OMB director and secretary of health, education, and welfare in the Nixon and Ford administrations; and considerable management ability. A dapper and gracious man, Weinberger's winsome personality masked an adamantine resolve that his admirers revered and his opponents found infuriating. Once Weinberger developed a policy position, like a Rottweiler with a rib eye in his mouth, he would not let it go—sometimes even when Reagan overruled him.

Weinberger arrived at the Pentagon with a sense of history—both the lessons of the past and the gravity of the present. As with many of his administration colleagues, World War II and Vietnam had instilled the most potent catechesis. From boyhood, he had been a devoted reader of Winston Churchill's books, and Weinberger recalled following, as a student at Harvard in the late 1930s, "the unfolding drama of Churchill's lonely fight in the House of Commons for greater preparedness and his fury at the appeasement of Munich." In September 1941, Weinberger enlisted in the US Army. Three months before Japan's attack on Pearl Harbor brought America into the war, new buck private Weinberger became disgusted at the army's poor training, shoddy matériel, and abysmal morale, which together amounted to its "total lack of preparedness for war." He wrote that this lesson from World War II would stay with him the rest of his life: "It is an extremely risky and dangerous business for any country to allow itself to become unarmed and unready for war." Some three decades later, Weinberger would draw another conviction from America's misadventure in Vietnam: "It was a very terrible mistake for a government to commit soldiers to battle without any intention of supporting them sufficiently to enable them to win, and indeed without any intention to win."[24]

From his new office in the Pentagon's E-Ring looking across the Potomac River, Weinberger worried that the military he'd inherited suffered from both historical afflictions: poor preparedness reminiscent of the 1930s, and diminished public support with an uncertain mission reminiscent of Vietnam. America's Cold War foe was exploiting these problems. Weinberger recalled classified briefings during the transition: "The Soviet expansion had been taking place at a very rapid rate, and they were actually ahead of us in practically every category. . . . The gap was growing because we had been taking the basic idea of détente very seriously and had cut back. They took the idea of détente seriously and expanded."[25]

The Soviet buildup had concentrated on Europe, the geographic epicenter of the Cold War. When the Reagan team took office, the Soviet and Warsaw Pact forces that looked menacingly across the Iron Curtain overmatched their NATO adversaries in virtually every military metric. A classified NATO assessment found that the Warsaw Pact outnumbered NATO forces by two or even three to one in artillery, personnel carriers, weapon launchers, attack helicopters, and overall troop strength.[26] Tank aficionados have debated for years whether the American M1A1 Abrams or Soviet T-72 was superior in quality and lethality. Quantity, however, was beyond debate. The Red Army and its Warsaw Pact allies possessed over seventy thousand tanks, compared to just thirty thousand in the United States and NATO arsenal.[27] When combined with the USSR's intermediate-range nuclear missiles and geographic advantages of internal supply and communication lines (the Soviet Union bordered Europe, whereas American forces had to cross the ocean), Moscow's strategic advantage and ability to mount a surprise attack on Western Europe appeared formidable.

The USSR had also leapt ahead in the nuclear arms race and posed the gravest threat to the United States itself since the Soviets withdrew their missiles from Cuba in 1962. Senator John Tower, the chairman of the Armed Services Committee, wrote a confidential memo to Weinberger just a few days before the inauguration, warning, "At every level of the force spectrum . . . we face vulnerabilities of potentially catastrophic proportion." Specifically, worried Tower, "Within two years if not sooner, the survivability of our ICBM force will have been so eroded as to make us incapable of supporting a rational military strategy, with all that implies for our susceptibility to coercion—to losing—in a political confrontation with the Soviet Union."[28]

In plain English, Tower meant that the Soviets could win without fighting. The American strategic nuclear arsenal consisted of the triad of intercontinental ballistic missiles (ICBMs), submarine-launched ballistic missiles (SLBMs), and long-range bombers carrying nuclear bombs and cruise missiles. In 1981, the Soviet Union possessed roughly one-third more ICBMs, SLBMs, and strategic bombers than the United States—a gap projected to continue growing unless the Americans reversed course.[29]

Critics of the arms race often pointed out that the United States already possessed enough nuclear weapons to destroy the world many times over. They were right. But their faith that mutual vulnerability would prevent the Soviets from ever launching a first strike disregarded two critical facts. First, some senior Kremlin officials had begun saying that the USSR could absorb millions of casualties and still win a nuclear war, especially as its larger arsenal could survive an American retaliatory strike. Second, Moscow hoped to use its growing military superiority to gain diplomatic advantage over Washington and induce further American retreat in the face of communist advances around the world. The Reagan administration's grand strategy sought to turn this calculation against the Soviets, by outpacing them in an arms buildup that would empower the United States to engage in its own coercive diplomacy. Such was the ultimate goal of "peace through strength"—not to start a hot war, but to win the Cold War without firing a shot.

IV

Weinberger, meanwhile, moved with dispatch to assemble his Pentagon team. Though General David Jones had been appointed by Carter as chairman of the Joint Chiefs of Staff (CJCS), Weinberger and Reagan overcame their concern that Jones had been too close to Carter and agreed to keep him in the role, for continuity and to buffer the military from partisanship and the political calendar. For deputy secretary, Weinberger selected Frank Carlucci, whose government career had included the Foreign Service, several positions in the Nixon administration, and most recently CIA deputy director in the Carter administration. Carlucci was a moderate Republican whose managerial skills and budget acumen made him invaluable in overseeing the defense buildup. He also had a gimlet eye for talent and selected an impressive army brigadier general named Colin Powell as his military assistant, which would catalyze Powell's meteoric rise over the next eight years. Fred Iklé became under secretary of defense for policy, the Pentagon's third-ranking position.

Weinberger tapped former naval aviator John Lehman as secretary of the navy. From this perch, Lehman would oversee a massive shipbuilding program and the assertive deployment of the US fleet in power projection against the Soviets. From Senator Scoop Jackson's staff came Richard Perle, who as the Pentagon's lead arms control official combined encyclopedic policy knowledge and strategic creativity with a yen for starting bureau-cratic knife fights—and an aptitude for winning them.

The department's Asia and Middle East policy would be handled by Richard Armitage. Built like a fire hydrant topped with a bald dome, he had culminated five combat tours in Vietnam by single-handedly leading the evacuation of over twenty thousand South Vietnamese refugees on a thirty-ship armada as Saigon fell in 1975. Armitage thought that America's troop withdrawal had betrayed its South Vietnamese allies. He described it as "akin to getting a lady pregnant and leaving town," and said, "I thought we were a runaway dad."[30] He brought to the Pentagon a fidelity to America's allies and a resolve not to abandon them again. His gravelly voice switched easily from telling coarse jokes to dispensing strategic insights and steam-rolling recalcitrant bureaucrats. Belying his midlevel rank, one scholar called him "arguably the most influential man in the Pentagon" given his close relationship with Weinberger.[31] Diverse in background, temperament, and ideology, this group shared a devotion to Weinberger and a commit-ment to rebuilding the military and reasserting American power in the world.

As Weinberger prepared the White House's first Pentagon budget, he realized that he owed some gratitude to the Carter administration. Carter's hawkish pivot in his last months in office included a 13 percent increase in defense spending. It was not near enough to fix America's atrophied mili-tary, but it gave the Reagan administration a running start. In Weinberger's first week on the job he testified before the Senate Armed Services Commit-tee and noted appreciatively the "comparatively large FY 1981 defense bud-get" from Carter. He also confronted the additional cost that the nation's dismal economy imposed on the Pentagon in the form of inflation, which dampened the purchasing power of the recent budget increase.[32]

Reagan's program to revive the American economy consisted of tax cuts, domestic spending cuts, regulatory relief, and supporting the Federal Reserve's high interest rates to curb inflation. The contradiction with his increased defense spending seemed obvious; how could he do that while cutting other government programs and reducing tax revenues? Reagan himself recognized this tension. While chairing an NSC meeting in March, Reagan confessed, "I am afflicted with two allergies: the allergy of wanting to control government spending and the allergy of wanting to increase our national security posture."[33]

Yet there was less of a contradiction than Reagan's critics claimed. He believed that the government's primary constitutional responsibility was to "provide for the common defense," but that much domestic spending was unwarranted and wasteful. Because his economic philosophy emphasized enterprise, innovation, and growth, he hoped that a revitalized economy would not only provide more revenue to fund the defense expansion but also generate new technologies for advanced weaponry. This is why the Reagan defense program did not just consist of massive budget increases. At its core were cutting-edge weapons systems based on unique technologies that could outmatch anything the Kremlin wielded, no matter how much more the Soviets spent and built.

The Reagan team would find help for this effort from a small, secretive Pentagon office led by a monkish intellectual. Andrew Marshall had been brought into the Defense Department by Secretary James Schlesinger in the Nixon administration, and he and his Office of Net Assessment (ONA) had labored creatively across successive presidencies to understand Soviet strengths and weaknesses and to develop American defense policies in response. Marshall's office assessed that the USSR had a gross national product (GNP) only about 25 percent the size of the United States' GNP, and that the Soviet military was consuming between 30 and 40 percent of the nation's economy. These estimates challenged the conventional views of the policy community, reinforced by CIA analyses, that the Soviet economy was at least half the size of the United States' and only 10 to 20 percent of it was spent on defense.[34] Yet even if over the long term the Soviet system appeared unsustainable, in the near term the Kremlin was ahead. As one highly classified NSC strategy review found, the United States confronted a "predicament" in "the general quantitative superiority, and, in many areas, at least qualitative equivalence, that the forces of the Soviet Union possess."[35]

More important, ONA's assessments mirrored Reagan's own intuitions of the Soviet economy's fragility and vulnerability to American pressure. Given this alignment of views, Weinberger oddly ignored Marshall at first. Impatient with scholars, the defense secretary disregarded Marshall's treatises as too long and too dense to read. Fortunately, Marshall found an eager audience in fellow intellectual Iklé, who recognized at once that ONA's analysis and prescriptions for the Cold War reinforced Reagan's intuitions. Together, Iklé and Marshall pressed the military services to build budget plans around "exploiting opportunities to impose disproportionate costs on the USSR over the long term." This was Marshall's concept of "competitive strategies," which "depended on identifying areas of comparative US advantage and using them to exploit areas of comparative Soviet weakness or disadvantage."[36]

For example, even though the Soviet navy boasted three times as many submarines as the US Navy, American submarines possessed edges in quieting technology and sensory capabilities that enabled them to both detect and evade Soviet submarines. This advantage in undersea hide-and-seek meant that no matter how many more submarines Moscow built, it could rarely beat the Americans in the great game of the deep. To exploit the Soviet Union's lack of warm-water ports and aircraft carriers, the Reagan administration planned to expand the US Navy's fleet to seventeen aircraft carriers. To counter the Soviet Union's thicket of surface-to-air missiles and radar arrayed against high-altitude strategic bombers, the United States designed the B-1 bomber with ground-hugging avionics for low-altitude penetration beneath Soviet defenses—followed by the B-2 stealth bomber, invisible to radar altogether. America's new strategic bombers would force the Kremlin to throw countless rubles at new air defenses in an unsustainable race it could not win.[37] To counter the Warsaw Pact's massive tank arsenal, the United States developed tank-killer aircraft like the A-10 Thunderbolt II jet and AH-64 Apache helicopter. Other new technologies based on America's edge in information-processing microchips, including global positioning and precision-guidance systems, and advanced command-and-control communications, all gave the Pentagon a multitude of innovations to offset, outmatch, and outsmart traditional Soviet strengths.

In addition to rebuilding the American military's might, Reagan sought to restore its morale. A month into his presidency, a unique opportunity emerged. Roy Benavidez, a Green Beret, had just been recognized with the Congressional Medal of Honor for his battlefield valor thirteen years earlier in saving several fellow soldiers trapped behind enemy lines during a Vietnam War operation. On February 24, the thousands who gathered at the Pentagon for the ceremony heard Reagan describe Benavidez's heroism—as the first president in history to read a Medal of Honor citation. Reagan also took another swipe at the "Vietnam syndrome." American soldiers, he said, "came home without a victory not because they were defeated, but because they were denied permission to win."[38] General Colin Powell, who had helped bring Benavidez's case to the White House's attention, described the significance of Reagan's gesture: "Even more than inauguration day, that afternoon marked the changing of the guard for the armed forces. We no longer had to hide in civvies. A hero received a hero's due. The military services had been restored to a place of honor."[39]

Reagan did not want the nation to forget the Vietnam War, just to remember it differently: not as a disgraceful defeat but as a valiant cause fought by troops undermined by pusillanimous politicians and a divided home front. The timing was no coincidence; that same month Reagan faced growing outcry about "another Vietnam" in Central America.

V

Reagan viewed the Western Hemisphere as of such importance that he devoted his first National Security Council meeting to Central America. Other national security issues—the Soviet Union, transatlantic relations, the Pentagon budget, the global economy, terrorism, and all other manner of challenges—demanded presidential attention, but none felt more urgent to Reagan than the crisis in America's backyard. He viewed the region as foundational to his effort to turn around American foreign policy.

The NSC consisted of the top officials in the administration responsible for national security, including Vice President Bush, Haig, Weinberger, Casey, General Jones, Secretary of the Treasury Don Regan, and Allen. The NSC staff, housed at the White House and overseen by the NSA, provided support for NSC meetings and subcommittees, and also served as the president's personal staff on foreign and defense policy. The NSC usually met in either the White House Cabinet Room or the smaller but more secure Situation Room. The latter was located off the White House basement underneath the old swimming pool and known informally as the "Sit Room." Newcomers often found its cramped quarters, bland wood paneling, and seats so tight that dignified knees bumped the table and each other to be discordant with the power wielded by those assembled and the gravity of the decisions they faced.[40]

Sitting at the head of the table, Reagan put Central America in hemispheric context. He worried that the United States was "way behind, perhaps decades, in establishing good relations with the two Americas." He continued, "We must change the attitude of our diplomatic corps so that we don't bring down governments in the name of human rights. None of them is as guilty of human rights violations as are Cuba and the USSR. We don't throw out our friends just because they can't pass the 'saliva test' on human rights." Reagan's reflexive rejection of Carter's policies may have been a necessary recalibration; communism posed the greater threat to the United States, and as Reagan noted, communism's depredations included tens of millions of dead. Reagan would soon realize, however, that embracing right-wing dictators carried its own political, strategic, and moral costs.

Reagan saw El Salvador as the hinge to stop communism's advance and restore American credibility in the region. "El Salvador is a good starting point. A victory there could set a good example," he told his team, and repeated as he concluded the meeting, "We can't afford a defeat."[41] El Salvador's embattled president, José Napoleon Duarte, faced growing insurrections from the Left and the Right while his fragile centrist government seemed to be crumbling from within. The communist insurgency known as the Farabundo Martí National Liberation Front (FMLN) enjoyed support from the Soviet bloc in its campaign to overthrow Duarte and take over the country. From the other side, he faced pressure from far-right elements led by former military officer and sadistic killer Roberto d'Aubuisson. In the scholar Russell Crandall's description, "Duarte's dilemma . . . was that the oligarchy and military distrusted him for being a communist, and the revolutionary left accused him of being a rightist."[42]

The FMLN and right-wing militias both committed ghastly atrocities—against each other, Duarte supporters, and civilians guilty of nothing but being in their way. Catholic clerics suffered some of the worst crimes. On March 24, 1980, as Archbishop Óscar Romero celebrated mass, an assassin acting at d'Aubuisson's behest killed him with a single rifle bullet to the heart. Just over eight months later, on December 2, 1980, Salvadoran National Guardsmen raped and summarily executed four American Maryknoll nuns who had been working with refugees displaced by the civil war.[43] An outraged President Carter, weeks from leaving office, suspended all United States aid to El Salvador. Yet at the same moment, an emboldened FMLN appeared to be on the verge of overthrowing the government and establishing a communist state. Days later, Carter reversed himself and resumed economic aid, and then just before he left office, he increased military assistance to the Salvadoran government.

The policy dilemma that confronted Reagan was tragic in the theological sense: No option was untainted by human suffering. The choices he confronted ranged from bad to awful. In practical terms, the White House faced the double challenge of helping neutralize the communist insurgency while tipping the internal balance toward Duarte and away from d'Aubuisson's thugs. A frustrated Reagan confided to his diary on February 11, "We have absolute proof of Soviet and Cuban activity in delivering arms to rebels in El Salvador—Also their worldwide propaganda campaign which has succeeded in raising riots and demonstrations in Europe and the US Intelligence reports say [Fidel Castro] is very worried about me. I'm very worried that we can't come up with something to justify his worrying."[44]

Reagan likely had in mind a secret intelligence assessment he had received a few days earlier. It drew on sensitive Cuban sources to describe Havana's hope that increased support for communist insurgents "in El Salvador will eventually spread to Guatemala and Honduras, confronting the US with a 'Vietnam-type situation' in Central America."[45] The Vietnam concerns resurfaced in another NSC meeting a few days later. Haig worried that "the American people won't support another Vietnam situation where US troops are stationed in Central America." Weinberger cautioned against even sending military advisors to El Salvador in case they came under fire: "There is the temptation to send in more men to protect them and we get into a Vietnam situation."[46]

For his part, Reagan agonized from insisting El Salvador wasn't another Vietnam, trying to avoid letting it become a Vietnam, and pursuing victory in part so that the United States would overcome Vietnam. A February 18 NSC meeting brought the Vietnam concerns full circle. John McMahon, the head of the CIA's clandestine service, began with a briefing on the other Soviet-aligned nations and actors shipping arms to the communist guerillas in El Salvador, including Cuba, Ethiopia, Libya, even the Palestine Liberation Organization (PLO)—and Vietnam. The irony was painful. The communist government in Hanoi, having defeated the United States several years earlier, had now joined a menagerie of fellow Marxists and other mischief-makers, such as Muammar Qadhafi and Yasser Arafat, trying to inflict similar setbacks on America in its own hemisphere.[47] Haig called this a "global Marxist grand strategy" that had targeted El Salvador for its next takeover and had to be stopped.

Overwrought though Haig may have been, he also highlighted a truth that the Reagan administration's critics often failed to appreciate: Communist regimes around the world had chosen Central America as a priority front. The Kremlin said as much. Soviet foreign minister Andrei Gromyko observed happily, "This entire region is today boiling like a cauldron." His Kremlin colleagues salivated at the chance to foment revolution in Central

America, which they called the "strategic rear" and "soft underbelly" of the United States.[48]

Even knowing this, Reagan was conflicted. He worried about overextension and provoking further resentments in the region. "I'm concerned that whatever we do, we do not do it in a heavy-handed way. I fear a negative reaction in Latin America," he told the NSC. He repeated this ambivalence at the end of the meeting: "We do have to win in Central America, but we don't want to get bogged down in that old Yankee interventionist question."[49] The United States' troubled history in the hemisphere, from military deployments to occupy Latin American countries in the 1920s and '30s, to the Guatemala coup in 1954 and the ouster of Salvador Allende in Chile in 1973, plagued Reagan's options. Even American economic assistance sometimes carried a paternalistic stench. Reagan told Thatcher, "Too many of these programs were undertaken without enough sensitivity for the feelings of the people living there, so many of whom felt intimidated by the Colossus of the North. . . . The United States wants to try a new approach. We want to bind these two continents together in a love of freedom."[50]

Mindful of balancing such concerns, on February 27 Reagan decided to send to El Salvador a relatively small assistance package of $25 million and twenty additional military advisors "in a strictly training capacity" with "specific prohibitions against any combat advisory role."[51] The symbolism mattered more than the size. With this decision, Reagan took the first step in what would become not just a larger aid program for El Salvador but an eight-year immersion in Central America's Cold War.

Because of the Catholic Church's opposition to communism and strong presence in Latin America, the White House sought to collaborate with the Vatican. John Paul II worried in particular about the regional inroads made by liberation theology, which he viewed as a sacralized form of Marxism that corroded Christian orthodoxy while providing spiritual cover for communist mischief, or even revolution. In a meeting in early May, the Pope told Haig that "if the US had not done what it did in El Salvador, another totalitarian state like Nicaragua would have been installed."[52] One indicator of the severity of the Vatican's concern was its willingness to back the Reagan administration's military support for the Salvadoran government even after the murders of Romero and the Maryknoll nuns. John Paul II later commenced the sainthood process for Romero, and the Vatican eventually canonized him in 2018.

The Vatican's quiet backing of American policy contrasted with the vocal opposition from liberal Protestant leaders in the United States. Reagan noted the irony that on Good Friday, April 17, "while representatives of the Nat[ional] Co[uncil] of Churches [NCC] paraded (carrying the cross) in front of the W[hite] H[ouse] protesting our effort to help El Salvador, Cardinal Cook of N.Y. came to visit us in the W[hite] H[ouse]." The NCC in particular became a persistent critic of America's anticommunist policies under Reagan, who made an acid confession to his diary: "Sometimes I think (forgive me) the [NCC] believes God can be reached through Moscow."[53] It is not clear whether Reagan's apology was directed to his diary, the NCC, or God, but in one sense the Kremlin may have shared his assessment of the NCC. Throughout the Cold War, the KGB targeted liberal church bodies such as the NCC's global sister organization the World Council of Churches as useful albeit unwitting front groups for disseminating Moscow's disinformation and propaganda.[54]

VI

Though Reagan focused on America's economic woes during his first months in office, European wailing and gnashing of teeth over the United States' high interest rates soon reminded him that foreign policy offered no escape from domestic policy. In some ways European umbrage at Reagan was unfair because the independent Federal Reserve, not the president, set interest rates. However, the president has authority to select the Federal Reserve chairman, and Reagan had chosen to keep Paul Volcker in the job despite his being a Carter appointee. Reagan's support for Volcker provided political cover for the Fed even while creating political risk for Reagan. For example, when asked about the high interest rates at his first press conference, Reagan responded:

I've met with Mr. Volcker, and not with the intention of trying to dictate, because it is an independent agency, and I respect that. But I think that we have to face the fact that interest rates are not in themselves a cause of inflation; they're a consequence. And when you have, as we have had, double-digit inflation back to back for 2 solid years now . . . there is no question that interest rates are going to have to go up and follow that inflation rate. . . . The answer to the interest rates is going to be our program of reducing government

spending, tied to the reduction of the tax rates that we've spoken of
to bring down inflation, and you'll find that interest rates come
down.[55]

The Europeans did not find this persuasive. West German chancellor
Helmut Schmidt repeatedly complained to Reagan that America's 20 percent interest rates were hurting the German economy by "suck[ing] into
New York City all the liquidity in the world," as German investors pursued
higher returns across the Atlantic rather than deploying capital in their
home country. The anxious German worried that American economic policies could even cost Schmidt his job, pleading to Reagan, "Please remember
that what you do has consequences. There can be political destabilization
as a result." Newly elected French president François Mitterrand shared
Schmidt's concerns. His foreign minister lamented to Reagan that the strong
US dollar "amounted to a 'third-oil shock,'" since Europe used dollars to
buy oil; and he echoed Germany's worry that American interest rates
"forced Europeans to raise their own rates, making it difficult to generate
the investment necessary to fight unemployment."[56]

While European leaders badgered Reagan about American economic
policies, Reagan began badgering Japanese leaders about Tokyo's economic
policies. During Reagan's first year in office, he met with officials from Japan more often than with those of any other nation. In the first three and a
half months alone, he hosted separate meetings with Japan's foreign minister, ambassador, and former prime minister, and in May he welcomed
Prime Minister Zenkō Suzuki to the White House for a state visit.

Reagan delivered the same message in each meeting: Japan needed to
reduce its automobile exports to the United States and increase its defense
budget. On the former, Reagan warned of Congress's appetite to impose
mandatory curbs on Japanese cars; on the latter, he warned of the Soviet
appetite for Japanese territory. With his commitment to free enterprise, as
a matter of principle Reagan resisted tariffs, and instead urged Tokyo to
reduce *voluntarily* the number of automobiles it sold in the United States
each year. This, he hoped, would ameliorate the competitive pain hurting
the American auto industry while avoiding a costly trade war.

The specter of the 1930s also haunted the discussions, as both a caution
against protectionism and a spur to the democracies to stand fast against
tyranny. This burden weighed heavily on the Japanese leaders, given their
nation's troubled past. Former prime minister Fukuda, for example, told the

president that he appreciated Reagan's reminder to Congress not to repeat 1930s-style protectionism because a half century earlier "political problems had not been handled well, and . . . World War II had resulted."[57]

Reagan wore a broad grin as Prime Minister Suzuki's motorcade pulled around the South Lawn for his White House arrival ceremony on the morning of May 7. Suzuki's government had just announced that Japan would reduce its car and truck exports to the United States, handing Reagan a policy success on the eve of the visit. They met first in the Oval Office, accompanied only by their interpreters. In words that would have caused heartburn for Margaret Thatcher, Reagan assured Suzuki that Japan was "the most important ally that the US has." An appreciative Suzuki described Japan's toughened stance toward the Soviet Union following the Afghanistan invasion.

The two leaders then walked to the Cabinet Room, where they were joined by their respective national security teams. Their discussion ranged across the Indo-Pacific region. Reagan expressed his hope "that as the United States continues to project its forces into the Indian Ocean, Japan's assistance in the Northwest Pacific will make it easier for the United States to carry this additional burden" of countering the Soviets in maritime South Asia. Suzuki thanked Reagan for keeping American troops stationed in South Korea because they "contribute significantly to maintaining peace on the peninsula." Suzuki then promised to continue improving Japan's relationship with its other longtime rival, China, because if Beijing "should lose faith in the West and tilt toward the Soviet Union this would disturb the balance of power in Asia." Continuing their discussion the next day, Suzuki pledged to increase Japan's defense spending, and Reagan urged him to extend Japan's naval patrol perimeter farther out to counter Soviet encroachments (and lighten the burden on the US Navy). Reagan concluded by enlisting Japan in the global battle of ideas, telling Suzuki, "In dealing with the Third World we should use our examples of high living standards and respect for human rights to demonstrate that we and Japan are the models to follow, not the Soviet Union."[58]

The warm glow of Suzuki's Washington visit began to chill as soon as he boarded his flight home. Speaking at the National Press Club shortly before his departure, Suzuki was asked about the joint communiqué he had just issued with Reagan, which in Weinberger's description affirmed "for the *first time* in the postwar era" that the United States and Japan would share "defense responsibilities in the Pacific." Suzuki showed courage in signing it but clumsiness in explaining it. He fumbled through a description of how his country's "alliance" with the United States would include expanded military cooperation and Japan's commitment to defend its territory and sea lanes out to one thousand miles. Such talk was taboo in the officially pacifist nation. Outrage erupted in the Japanese media and public. The embarrassed prime minister then scapegoated the Foreign Ministry, prompting Foreign Minister Ito to resign in disgrace.[59]

Yet Ito's loss was America's gain. As scholar Michael Green observes,

> Alliance managers in both Washington and Tokyo seized on the commitment as a benchmark for Japan to acquire real capability in air defense and antisubmarine warfare in order to bottle up Soviet air and naval forces in the Far East. Japan was poised to form the "shield" as the United States developed the "spear" in the navy's emerging Maritime Strategy against Soviet forces in the Far East.[60]

Suzuki's travails and Ito's demise nevertheless reminded the Reagan team that their Japanese counterparts did not protest in vain. They faced massive resistance among the Japanese public to increasing military spending and closer security cooperation with the United States. Overcoming these constraints would take a Japanese leader with Reaganesque charisma and a deft political touch. The cautious and clumsy Suzuki was not that man; his successor would be.

Inside the White House, a quiet revolution was taking place in the United States' strategic posture in Asia. Reagan's three predecessors—Nixon, Ford, and Carter—had all pursued a "China first" policy, believing that America's interests in Asia began with Beijing. Reagan reversed this, shifting to a "Japan first" policy that viewed Tokyo as the supreme partner in the region.

However, Reagan did not neglect China. On March 19, he met with two senior Chinese diplomats, Ambassador Chai Zemin and Ji Chaozhu. Reagan told them he had just approved the export to China of eleven items of "sensitive electronic equipment" that were "not available to the Soviet Union." Returning the goodwill, Ji informed the group that China under Deng had rejected Mao's previous stance of using force to conquer Taiwan and said, "Our policy is to resolve the Taiwan question peacefully." Appealing to their shared interest in countering the Soviets, Ji said that "the polar bear from the north" had inspired this policy shift. Continuing, Ji noted that "the US, China, Taiwan and Japan are all threatened by the southward expansion of the polar bear, and that together we would better be able to resist Soviet expansionism." China's apparently softened stance did not mean that Beijing had given up its claim on Taiwan, however. Ji and Chai then launched into a long harangue against America's arms sales to Taiwan. Reagan bristled and reminded them that the United States would stand by its friends, especially given its obligations under the Taiwan Relations Act to provide for the island's defense.[61]

VII

While Reagan talked to the Chinese about new ways to poke the "polar bear from the north," he also sought to feed the bear's subjects. Carter had imposed an embargo on grain sales to the Soviet Union after the invasion of Afghanistan. This loss of access to the Russian market brought considerable hardship to American farmers, and during the campaign, Reagan had promised to lift the embargo, believing that it caused more pain to Americans than to the Kremlin. While chairing an NSC meeting on March 26 on the simmering crisis in Poland, Reagan asked "whether some quiet indication that the United States might be willing to lift the embargo if the Soviet Union exercised restraint with respect to Poland might help the situation."[62] This suggestion provoked a unanimous response from Reagan's national security team: They all opposed it. Weinberger, Haig, and Casey each warned that even a hint about ending the embargo would send the wrong message to Moscow at a time when the United States sought to deter a Soviet crackdown on Poland.

Reagan and his team deliberated on the grain embargo amid what felt like unrelenting waves of global challenges. At this same NSC meeting, in just sixty minutes they also tackled whether to evacuate American personnel from Nicaragua over fears of Sandinista mob violence after the termination of US aid (Reagan had discontinued the Carter administration's financial assistance to the Sandinista government), discussed ways to quietly support the rebel leader Jonas Savimbi in his fight against the communist government and Cuban soldiers in Angola, wrestled with how to press South Africa to withdraw its forces from occupying Namibia, and as an afterthought considered changes to US assistance to El Salvador and Pakistan. Other NSC gatherings during the administration's first months were similarly sprawling. A February 18 meeting addressed in one session the US strategy for the Caribbean basin, support for El Salvador, the sale of F-15 fighter jets to Saudi Arabia and Israel, and Israel's arms sales to Central America. A February 27 meeting revisited those issues plus the Poland crisis. Allen's opening comments for the April 1 NSC meeting are the ne plus ultra:

> There are at least six items on today's agenda. Secretary Haig's upcoming visit to the Middle East; the proposed AWACS [airborne warning and control systems] sale to Saudi Arabia; Israel's request for further financial aid; the strategic petroleum reserve; terminating economic assistance to Nicaragua; reprogramming economic assistance to El Salvador and Liberia; and the Secretary of State's recommendations to the President concerning Libyan activities in Chad.[63]

The fact that Allen said "six items" and then proceeded to list *seven* shows just how befuddling the cascade of issues had become even for the NSA himself.

This was no way to run a superpower. Some of these issues could have been handled at subcabinet levels; others were consequential and complex enough that they merited their own dedicated NSC meeting, rather than being crammed into a five-minute discussion sandwiched by other unrelated topics. The Reagan NSC was trying to do too much at once—even allowing for the many decisions that demanded presidential attention, the complexity and interconnectedness of the issues, the new administration's need to establish its policies, and crises that could not be ignored.

The chaotic NSC process mirrored growing discord among Reagan's team. Late March brought a new eruption. Not surprisingly, Haig was the volcano at the center. Seething over his stature ever since he had failed in his Inauguration Day power play, Haig's ego took another blow when he learned that Reagan and Baker had selected Vice President Bush over him to chair the White House's crisis management group. A furious Haig complained to Reagan that he planned to resign. Despite reassuring Haig of his continued support, Reagan expressed considerable annoyance in his diary, writing on multiple days that Haig has "something of a complex about this," is "seeing things that aren't there," and "has half the cabinet teed off."[64] No doubt mindful that the secretary of state he had recommended was floundering, Nixon wrote to Reagan that "the major mark of a big man is his ability and willingness to enlist and tolerate other big men on his team."[65]

Nixon's support notwithstanding, what Haig in his vainglory failed to appreciate is that he derived his authority not from the former president but from the current one. Reagan, otherwise patient to a fault with the peccadillos, vanities, and petty feuds that afflicted his team, found himself wearying of Haig after just two months.

VIII

The Kremlin did not wait for the administration to get its act together. Seizing the initiative to test the new president, in early March Brezhnev wrote a long letter to Reagan. It combined equal parts splenetic bluster and diplomatic outreach. Contrary to the past decade of the Kremlin's military expansion, Brezhnev insisted, "The Soviet Union has not sought and does not seek military superiority." He then took a preemptive shot against Reagan's strategy: "But neither will we permit such superiority to be established over us. Such attempts, as well as attempts to talk to us from a position of strength, are absolutely futile." From there he suggested a number of issues that the Kremlin sought to negotiate with the United States, of course on terms favorable to Moscow.[66] Reagan's advisors spent the next three weeks feuding over how to answer the letter, bickering over various draft responses.[67]

While Washington argued with itself, in Moscow on March 25, 1981, KGB director Yuri Andropov took the podium at a KGB caucus meeting to give the assembled chekists—the top ranks of Soviet security and intelligence operatives—their marching orders. The Communist Party's Twenty-Sixth Congress had concluded three weeks earlier. The roomful of hardened spies were accustomed to striking terror at home and abroad, but on this day they heard their leader sound an unfamiliar note of fear.

After disgorging a litany of Marxist agitprop, Andropov inadvertently echoed Reagan's assessment that détente had been advantageous to the Kremlin as he wistfully traced the advances that the USSR had enjoyed during the decade of détente, when "the ranks of the world communist movement widened even further." But now "the most reactionary circles of the West . . . have yet again resorted to the policy 'from the position of strength.'

They brought to the forefront an ardent anticommunist—the American president R[onald] Reagan, and an ardent anti-Sovietist—the English prime minister M[argaret] Thatcher."

Andropov then made an assertion that likely stunned the room: "The imperialists are waging an arms race on an unprecedented scale, and are expediting preparations for war. . . . One of the crucial elements of nuclear strategy is to strike in such a way that one strike disables as many vital installations of the enemy as possible." This gave new urgency to the KGB's intelligence mission, as Andropov exhorted his officers to look aggressively for America's "preparations for a nuclear strike," telling them, "We must know about the brewing military schemes of the United States, its NATO allies, and its Peking hegemonists, in detail, ahead of time and at the earliest possible stages."[68]

Andropov's speech offers a chilling window into Soviet paranoia and the Cold War's precarious balance of terror: The Kremlin's top leadership genuinely believed that Reagan was preparing to launch a surprise nuclear attack on the USSR. This misperception made the Soviets prone to misinterpret other American actions—and more inclined to order a preemptive strike of their own. For the next three years, the Cold War would descend into its most dangerous phase since the Cuban Missile Crisis.

Five days after Andropov's speech, the man who provoked Soviet fears lay on the operating table barely clinging to life. As Reagan had exited the Washington Hilton after a speech, a deranged gunman named John Hinckley had shot him. The most serious damage came from a .22-caliber bullet that ricocheted off the presidential limousine's armor and entered near his heart. Rushed to the George Washington University Hospital, Reagan immediately underwent emergency surgery.

His diary entry for that day bears witness to his Christian faith. Reagan described his thoughts as he struggled to breathe in the emergency room: "I focused on that tiled ceiling and prayed. But I realized I couldn't ask for God's help while at the same time I felt hatred for the mixed-up young man who had shot me. Isn't that the meaning of the lost sheep? We are all God's children and therefore equally beloved by him. I began to pray for his soul and that he would find his way back to the fold."[69]

As frenzied doctors worked at the hospital to save Reagan's life, chaos consumed the White House. Were there other gunmen afoot? Was the shooting part of a broader attack on the nation? Was the KGB or a terrorist group behind it? And with Reagan unconscious on the operating table, and Vice

President Bush in flight from Texas on Air Force Two, who was in charge of the United States government?

Upon hearing initial reports of the shooting, Haig and Weinberger both rushed to the White House, joining Allen and other senior staff in the Situation Room. Their minds raced, terrified over the president's condition and anxious about the two Soviet nuclear submarines that lurked underwater just miles off the Atlantic seaboard. CJCS General Jones called Weinberger on the secure phone and told him that because the Soviet submarines had moved closer to American shores than their normal patrol patterns, their nuclear missiles could hit Washington, DC, in "ten minutes, forty-seven seconds." Allen and Weinberger worried that the Soviets might have assassinated Reagan as a prelude to launching a surprise nuclear attack. Weinberger told Jones to raise the alert level of the Strategic Air Command, readying America's B-52 bomber fleet for potential retaliatory strikes.[70]

Such was the unrelenting terror of the Cold War in 1981. The United States and USSR mistrusted and feared each other so much that within a five-day period in March, the head of the KGB warned his officers that the United States was preparing a preemptive nuclear strike, while the top echelons of the American government suspected the Kremlin had tried to assassinate their president and intended to launch nuclear missiles at their capital.

Meanwhile, White House counsel Fred Fielding told the senior staff in the Situation Room that he was preparing paperwork for Reagan to transfer presidential authority temporarily to Bush under the terms of the Twenty-Fifth Amendment. Knowing that the vice president was still airborne with limited communications, Haig asserted to anyone listening, "So the helm is right here. And that means right here, in this chair for now, constitutionally, until the vice president gets here." Haig's claim to be the acting president stunned the room. Even worse than grandiose, it was wrong. The Constitution put the Speaker of the House and president pro tempore of the Senate both ahead of the secretary of state in the line of presidential succession.

No one corrected Haig, but all soon wished they had. Upstairs in the press room, White House deputy press secretary Larry Speakes flailed about in a growing panic. Inundated with media questions on live national television, Speakes refused to confirm or deny any reports, let alone provide any details, on Reagan's condition—or on who wielded the authority of the presidency. The senior officials in the Situation Room watched Speakes's meltdown on a video feed. All were alarmed, but only Haig decided to rush upstairs and remedy it. Bursting into the press room, the flushed and sweaty secretary of state grabbed the podium and told the room—and the watching world—"As of now, I am in control here, in the White House, pending return of the vice president."[71]

With this episode Haig made himself a figure of ridicule for the rest of his life. He may have intended to reassure the nation that the American government remained intact. This was a legitimate concern amid the chaos. Yet to his colleagues who had suffered his venom and self-regard for the previous two months, the grasping, unhinged figure at the White House lectern confirmed their suspicions of the real man, now revealed to the world in all his hubris and presidential pretensions. Though Haig would last another fifteen months as secretary of state, his reputation would never recover.

Reagan survived the surgery and began to heal. As with many who escape death, he came away a changed man. Americans noticed. Biographer Lou Cannon observed that Reagan's grit and good humor in the aftermath of the shooting "cemented a bond with the American people that never dissolved. And that's because they saw a genuine person that day. They began to feel for him the way they would feel for a friend or someone close to them, not just some politician."[72] For Reagan, his survival deepened his faith and sense of divine calling. He wrote in his diary, "Whatever happens now, I owe my life to God and will try to serve him in every way I can."[73]

Back at the White House, Reagan spent weeks recuperating, often sitting in robe and pajamas in the rooftop solarium to bask in the sun and regain his strength. There he reflected, "Perhaps having come so close to death made me feel I should do whatever I could in the years God had given me to reduce the threat of nuclear war; perhaps there was a reason I had been spared."[74]

With this sense of divine mandate to bring the Cold War to a peaceful end, Reagan decided to respond to Brezhnev's letter from early March. Since his fractious aides remained deadlocked over the language, Reagan decided to write the letter himself. He sent his handwritten draft to the NSC staff and State Department for review, and noted two days later, "I should know today whether my letter to Brezhnev has passed inspection by the striped pants set."[75] It did not. Despite his reputation as a hard-liner, Reagan's initial stab at outreach to Brezhnev irked the professional diplomats, who considered it too soft. One senior State official called Reagan's conciliatory draft "atrocious"; Richard Pipes of the NSC staff dismissed it as "mawkish . . . written in a Christian turn-the-other-cheek spirit, sympathetic to the point of apology."[76] The State and NSC staff then wrote an alternate draft that criticized the USSR's military expansion and global aggression, and said that the right conditions did not yet exist for a Reagan-Brezhnev summit meeting.

Reagan made some edits to soften the new draft, yet he also handwrote *another* letter to Brezhnev. Reagan included the draft of this new letter in his diary. It focused on human rights and religious freedom, and particularly the plights of imprisoned Jewish dissident Anatoly Shcharansky and the Siberian Pentecostals sequestered in the US embassy basement. Noting that he had recently met with Shcharansky's wife, Avital, Reagan's letter implored Brezhnev to allow both Shcharansky and the Siberian Pentecostals to emigrate to the United States. Reagan promised, "This is between the two of us and I will not reveal that I made any such request. I'm sure however you understand that such actions on your part would lessen my problems in future negotiations between our countries."[77]

Reagan does not seem to have sent this letter to Brezhnev, though it is unclear why. That he wrote it and included it in his diary shows his concern for human rights and religious freedom, especially the individual prisoners who captivated and troubled him. Meanwhile, having reluctantly agreed to send the State Department's version of the response, Reagan then decided to handwrite a *third* letter to Brezhnev, drawing in part on the first draft he had penned a week earlier. This one he did send, as a cover note to the State Department missive. On April 25, a befuddled Kremlin thus received two letters—one handwritten, the other typed, both signed by Reagan.

In his personal note, Reagan recalled his first encounter with Brezhnev a decade earlier at President Nixon's home in San Clemente, California, and reminded the Soviet leader that then as now, "the hopes and aspirations of millions and millions of people throughout the world" depended on decisions made by the leaders of the US and USSR. In a direct shot at the Soviet system, Reagan asked, "If [the people of the world] are incapable, as some would have us believe, of self government, then where among them do we find any who are capable of governing others?" He then proclaimed America's innocence of any threat to the Soviet Union or "imperialistic designs" on the rest of the world and invoked World War II's aftermath to support his case. "Our military might was at its peak—and we alone had the ultimate weapon, the nuclear weapon. . . . If we had sought world domination then, who could have opposed us? But the United States followed a different course—one unique in all the history of mankind. We used our power and wealth to rebuild the war-ravaged economies of the world, including those nations who had been our enemies."

Reagan concluded with a conciliatory gesture, telling Brezhnev, "In the spirit of helping the people of both our nations . . . I have lifted the grain embargo."[78] Reagan hoped this would show the Soviets his willingness to negotiate. He also had other audiences in mind, beyond American farmers and Kremlin leaders. As he told Japanese prime minister Suzuki, America's European allies "began to get ideas from 'my firm language' that the US was not willing to engage in arms control talks with the Soviet Union. . . . The lifting of the embargo was done actually as a 'gesture' on the part of the US towards its allies in Europe."[79] Reagan recorded a similar sentiment in his diary: "I'm reluctant about [lifting the embargo] but think it will reassure our allies that while we're hard nosed about the Russians we aren't refusing to talk."[80]

Brezhnev was unpersuaded. He wrote back with what Reagan described as an "icy reply" that conceded nothing, "blamed the United States for starting and perpetuating the Cold War, and then said we had no business telling the Soviets what they could or could not do anywhere in the world." A resigned Reagan concluded, "So much for my first attempt at personal diplomacy."[81] Soviet ambassador Anatoly Dobrynin, more perceptive than his boss, appreciated the significance that "while lying wounded, Reagan for the first time in his life addressed a personal letter to the leader of the Soviet Union and its Communist Party in his own hand." However, Dobrynin concluded "the time was not yet ripe" for the American president and Soviet premier to connect.[82]

The time would not ripen for over four years. Yet Reagan's letters to Brezhnev and lifting of the grain embargo reveal how from the start he blended confrontation and conciliation toward Moscow. Even at this early juncture, Reagan showed the approach that he would continue over the next eight years. He would extend one hand in friendship to the Soviet Union while using the other hand to try to bring it down.

CHAPTER 3

⟫⟪

THE GLOBAL CHESSBOARD

I
————

It was a grim spring of assassination attempts. On May 13, a Turkish gunman—likely sponsored by the KGB—shot Pope John Paul II in St. Peter's Square. The bishop of Rome was rushed to the hospital, his condition so grave that a fellow priest administered last rites. He would recover, but John Paul II came as near death as had Reagan six weeks earlier.[1] That they both survived bonded them in a sort of providential kinship. Reagan wrote to the Pope, "Happily, few leaders in the world today have the dubious distinction of knowing with some precision the kind of event you have just experienced."[2] Bill Clark later reflected that "both men took shots in the chest by would-be assassins only . . . weeks apart. With a smile they decided that was God's wake-up call that they had to work even faster in bringing down the Soviet empire."[3]

Four days after the Pope was shot, Reagan flew to South Bend, Indiana, to give the commencement address at the University of Notre Dame. Four years earlier, President Jimmy Carter had delivered his first major foreign policy address at Notre Dame's graduation ceremony, where he downplayed Soviet malevolence and proclaimed, "We are now free of that inordinate fear of communism."[4] Now Reagan chose the same venue to deliver a different message. To the assembled graduates, he praised the virtues of the free society and prophesied, "The West won't contain communism, it will transcend communism . . . it will dismiss it as some bizarre chapter in human history whose last pages are even now being written."[5]

Back at CIA headquarters, Bill Casey sat in his office salivating to get into the fight. A man who combined subtle intelligence with a doctrinaire worldview where, in his biographer's words, "issues were not black and white; they were red and white," Casey brought to CIA the street smarts of a blue-collar kid from Long Island, the anticommunism of a devout Catholic, and the flexible ethics of a New York lawyer.[6] Reagan's campaign against communism would be a full-spectrum military, political, economic, and intelligence effort, and Casey was an eager general for the latter—and an occasional interloper in the other domains too.

At first many in the CIA workforce found themselves befuddled by their new director, whose last work in intelligence had ended in 1945 and whose background and manner were unlike anything they had seen before in the seventh-floor director's suite. Bob Gates, a career analyst who would hold several leadership positions at the CIA in the Reagan administration, including as Casey's chief of staff, recalls his first encounter with Casey:

> The old man, nearly bald, tall but slightly hunched, yanked open his office door and called out to no one in particular, "Two vodka martinis!" Without waiting for a response, he slammed the door shut. It was February 11, 1981, and this was the first time I had seen the new DCI since his appointment. Casey, in the job less than three weeks, was having lunch with John McCone, his predecessor under President Kennedy. Panic in the outer office. The DCI's suite had been dry under Admiral Turner and there was no liquor. Finally, a bottle was produced—no doubt from someone's desk drawer—and a vague semblance of a martini was carried in to the thirsty pair. . . . Years later I would think about the martini episode and realize that, however trivial, it foreshadowed how Casey would approach CIA on consequential matters. He would demand something be done immediately which the Agency no longer had the capability to do. He would fire instructions at the closest person regardless of whether that person had anything to do with the matter at hand. And he would not wait around even for confirmation that anyone heard him.[7]

Those who did hear Casey often could not understand him. A blow to his trachea in a boxing match during his teenage years had left him with a lifelong struggle to speak clearly. To this he seems to have added the artifice of intentional mumbling when he did not want certain audiences—such as congressional oversight committees or skeptical journalists—to understand him. Reagan, already hard of hearing, often found Casey unintelligible during NSC meetings.

For all of his trouble speaking, Casey possessed a skilled pen and preferred communicating by letter with the president. On May 6, Casey wrote a long missive to Reagan describing his challenges at CIA. "The Analytical and Operations units are most in need of improvement and rebuilding. The analysis has been academic, soft, not sufficiently relevant and realistic." Casey also wanted to revitalize the Directorate of Operations (DO), the CIA's elite clandestine service, which had been gutted of experienced officers under Carter and his CIA director Stansfield Turner. He concluded the letter by reminding Reagan of what they faced from their main foe: "We are working . . . to build up the elements needed to cope with a Soviet service which outnumbers us by three to one around the world." Reagan scribbled "ok" and initialed his concurrence.[8]

Even with his president's support, Casey found himself regularly sparring with the other two branches of government. That summer, a federal judge in New York ruled that a decade earlier Casey had misled investors in one of his companies. The Senate Select Committee on Intelligence (SSCI) immediately opened an investigation. Casey had done himself no favors with his dismissive posture toward legislative oversight. As Gates put it, "Casey was guilty of contempt of Congress from the day he was sworn in as DCI."[9] Congress soon reciprocated the sentiment. The next week SSCI chairman and conservative icon Barry Goldwater, fed up with what he saw as Casey's prevarications, called on him to resign. Several other influential GOP senators, including Majority Leader Howard Baker and Majority Whip Ted Stevens, supported Goldwater. Goldwater's opposition left Casey's job on virtual life support and produced what Newsweek called "the first political crisis" of the Reagan presidency.[10]

As the White House began quietly preparing a list of candidates to replace Casey, the embattled DCI fought back. He enlisted support from his old OSS colleagues and GOP luminaries such as George Shultz. Inman reluctantly lent his considerable credibility to Casey by appearing on Ted Koppel's influential ABC News program Nightline and voicing confidence in the director—a double irony considering that the two were already at odds over several intelligence matters, and Goldwater wanted Reagan to appoint Inman to replace Casey.

Amid this public campaign, Casey turned over many more documents and endured hours of further grilling from the SSCI, which a few days later determined there was insufficient evidence to remove him from office. Casey's attorney then demanded that the SSCI pronounce Casey "fit to serve." SSCI vice-chairman Daniel Patrick Moynihan, who relished a good linguistic fight, countered with the grudging formulation that Casey was "not unfit." In a compromise, the final SSCI statement declared, "No basis has been found for concluding Mr. Casey is unfit to serve as DCI."[11]

Casey returned to Langley both chastened and defiant. Soon many CIA officers, especially in the DO, found themselves inspired and emboldened by their peculiar DCI. They came to see him the same way an OSS lieutenant had described him four decades earlier: "Bill had a healthy contempt for bureaucracy, for form and protocol. He was like a breath of fresh air. Suddenly everybody wanted to work for Casey. He was a feet-on-the-desk, get-the-job-done-I-don't-care-how-you-do-it executive. I was under his spell."[12] Casey saw Nazis and communists as vultures of the same feather. After Nazi Germany's surrender, Casey had visited the Dachau concentration camp and called it his "most devastating experience of the war." His service in Europe also exposed him to Soviet barbarity, not to mention Moscow's treachery in refusing to reciprocate OSS intelligence cooperation. The main difference he saw between Hitler and Stalin was merely that "the Nazis are finished. But the Communists are still unbeaten."[13] Four decades later they remained unbeaten, and as Gates recalled, "Casey came to CIA primarily to wage war against the Soviet Union."[14]

In this spirit, Casey and his administration colleagues soon found at least one Carter program worth embracing. During his last year in office, Carter had signed a finding authorizing the covert provision of arms to the Afghan mujahideen fighting against the Soviet occupation of their country. When the DO briefed Casey on the program, the new DCI erupted in enthusiasm. "This is the kind of thing we should be doing—only more. I want to see one place on this globe, one spot where we can checkmate them and roll them back. We've got to make the Communists feel the heat. Otherwise we'll never get them to the negotiating table." He dismissed critics who caviled about the costs and risks of the program by appealing to his last war. "We've got to make these people understand what we learned in World War II. When we supported organized resistance against Hitler, it saved lives in the long run. It's the same thing in Afghanistan." With Reagan's support, Casey continued the CIA's aid to the Afghan rebels.[15]

II
―――――――

Several miles down the George Washington Memorial Parkway, Weinberger sat in his suite in the E-Ring at the Pentagon trying to rebuild a Defense Department that seemed broken in body and spirit. Unlike Casey, at least he had Capitol Hill behind him. Perhaps the most revealing indicator of the woeful state of the American military in 1981 was the congressional unity in supporting Reagan's defense expansion. In May, the Senate voted 92 to 1 in favor of a substantial defense budget increase, and two months later the House passed it by 354 to 63. The cover of *Time* coupled a photo of Weinberger with the words "How to Spend a Trillion" and described the White House's ambitious goal of allocating $1.5 trillion to the military over the next five years. By 1985 the defense budget would be 50 percent larger than in 1980.[16]

Not that Congress agreed on precisely where this money should be spent. A heated argument emerged over the MX missile. Intended to counter the Soviet Union's fearsome SS-18, the longest-range and largest-payload ICBM the world had ever known, the United States responded by developing the MX Peacekeeper. With its pinpoint accuracy and ten nuclear warheads on a MIRV platform, once launched, the MX could inflict unfathomable destruction on Soviet targets. The problem was getting it launched. One of the perverse paradoxes of the arms race was that such uniquely powerful ICBMs were also uniquely vulnerable. Once in flight they were impossible to stop, yet while sitting inert in their silos they were difficult to protect and made an enticing target for a Soviet surprise attack. Thus the problem: The MX's capability provided a strong counter to the SS-18, but if the MX could not be stored securely, it risked making the United States even more vulnerable by tempting the Soviets to strike first.

The Carter administration had advanced development of the MX but left the unsolved quandary of how to base it—a puzzle that would bedevil the Reagan administration for its first few years. The many ideas and opponents the MX basing controversy generated display a nuclear kaleidoscope of American politics, culture, ingenuity, and occasional lunacy. The Carter team had originally planned to build the "Racetrack" system, a giant subterranean railway underneath a vast swath of Nevada and Utah that would house two hundred MXs on hundreds of miles of tracks able to carry the missiles to a range of launch sites beyond Soviet detection. Considering that the land needed was the same size as New Jersey, the Nevada and Utah political leadership strongly resisted relinquishing so much acreage—not to mention putting a bull's-eye on their states for Soviet missiles. The Race-track suffered its final death knell when the Mormon Church leadership, with large membership in both states, issued a statement in May 1981 that they were "most gravely concerned" over the planned deployment, saying, "We plead with our national leaders to marshal the genius of the nation to find viable alternatives."[17] Another idea, known as "Big Bird," involved car-rying the MX aloft in a massive cargo plane and then launching the missile from the air. Perhaps the most outlandish proposal was "Dense Pack," which posited basing all the Peacekeepers closely together in adjoining silos that would—so the theory went—cause the wave of incoming Soviet mis-siles to detonate each other in a fratricidal self-destruction. All told, there were at least thirty-five different MX basing schemes floated before Con-gress, which refused to fund the missile without a feasible plan.[18]

III

In the midst of pressuring Congress to pass his military budget and his tax-cut package to stimulate the American economy, Reagan traveled to Ottawa for his first Group of Seven summit. Known informally as the G7, the an-nual gathering of the world's leading industrial democracies brought to-gether America's most important allies: Japan, the United Kingdom, West Germany, France, Italy, and Canada. In their summit at the historic forest resort Château Montebello, Reagan met the new French president, François Mitterrand, for the first time. Many observers expected them to clash, since the crafty French socialist and affable California capitalist would seem to have little in common. Instead, they built a genial rapport.

Like many other European socialists, Mitterrand detested commu-nism. He was eager to partner with Reagan against the Soviet Union. In their private meeting, Mitterrand shared a secret: The French intelligence service was running an agent deep inside the KGB. Code-named "Farewell" by the French, KGB colonel Vladimir Vetrov worked at the Yasenevo head-quarters building in Moscow evaluating the intelligence collected by Direc-torate T, Line X, a massive Soviet espionage campaign to steal Western technology. Moscow had exploited the many US-USSR scientific and com-mercial exchanges set up in the 1970s under détente, taking advantage of

American and European openness to purloin untold billions of dollars' worth of Western technology. The real costs were measured not in dollars but in Soviet knowledge of the Pentagon's capabilities and Moscow's corresponding advances in weapons systems and communications technology— often giving the Kremlin disproportionate advantages over the United States. As former secretary of the air force and senior Reagan NSC official Thomas Reed recalled, "Given the massive transfer of technology in radars, computers, machine tools, and semiconductors from the US to the USSR, the Pentagon had been in an arms race with itself."[19] Line X's penetration had gone undetected for a decade, until Vetrov became disillusioned with Soviet communism and offered his services to French intelligence early in 1981.

Upon learning of Vetrov from Mitterrand, Reagan put Vice President Bush in charge of the sensitive follow-up. Five years earlier, while serving as CIA director, Bush had built a trusted relationship with his counterpart in French counterintelligence, Marcel Chalet, whose agency now oversaw the handling of Vetrov. A few weeks later Chalet traveled to Washington, DC, and gave Bush a detailed briefing on their singular source, including a thick file of intelligence collected from Vetrov that became known as the Farewell Dossier. The next day Bush convened a meeting with a select group of senior intelligence leaders, including Casey and Inman. He handed them the Farewell Dossier and directed them to develop a plan to exploit the revelations from this new French connection.[20]

IV

In the late afternoon of Sunday, June 7, 1981, eight Israeli Air Force (IAF) F-16 fighter jets took off from a base in a desolate corner of the Sinai Peninsula. Flying just one hundred feet above the ground and below radar, they flew over the Gulf of Aqaba, skirted the edge of Jordan, traversed the vast desert of Saudi Arabia, and crossed into Iraq. Their target was the Osirak nuclear reactor, scheduled to become operational within months. Each plane carried two two-thousand-pound bombs, and seven of the pilots scored direct hits on the reactor dome. The bombing obliterated Osirak, thwarting Iraq's quest for a nuclear weapon. It was a triumph for Israel, a humiliation for Iraqi dictator Saddam Hussein, a shock to the world, and a crisis for the Reagan administration.[21]

Reagan's first reaction was apocalyptic—in the literal sense. On hearing of the attack, he confessed to his diary, "I swear I believe Armageddon is near."[22] Channeling his fascination with the Book of Revelation and horror at nuclear weapons, Reagan worried that his first year in office might also be the last year of planet Earth's existence. Otherwise it was not clear what to do. As a matter of policy, the White House supported Israel, opposed nuclear proliferation, and disdained Saddam Hussein—all factors that would argue for endorsing the attack. Yet the White House's other policy priorities included deepening ties with Saudi Arabia, tilting toward Iraq over Iran in the ongoing war between the two, and promoting peace and stability in the Middle East—all factors that pointed toward condemning the attack.

Reagan had long backed Israel. Two months earlier he had written in his diary, "The Jewish community . . . [has] never had a better friend of Israel in the W[hite]H[ouse] than they have now."[23] His fidelity to the Jewish state stemmed in part from his hatred of anti-Semitism. While making training films for the Army Air Forces during World War II, Reagan had seen raw film footage of Nazi concentration camps liberated by American forces. Horrified at these early images of the Holocaust, Reagan kept a copy of the film for himself because, as he later told George Shultz, he worried that "some people would later deny that it could have been so bad—or that it had taken place at all." This exposure to anti-Semitism at its most demonic seared in Reagan a lifelong commitment to supporting Jewish rights and the state of Israel.[24] It also helped inspire his advocacy for Soviet Jews.

So Reagan was surprised to find his White House in a series of rifts with the Jewish state throughout 1981 that put US-Israel relations under severe strain. Besides Osirak, two other crises descended on Reagan's desk in the summer of 1981: the sale of airborne warning and control systems (AWACS) planes to Saudi Arabia, and possible war in Lebanon. Renewed threats from Libya provided an additional regional challenge. The Reagan team had come into office primarily viewing the Middle East through a Cold War lens, which entailed supporting Israel and opposing any further Soviet inroads in the region. The White House soon found that the Middle East had complexities and demands that went well beyond Israel and the Cold War alone.

Lebanon had begun simmering just over a month prior to the Osirak attack. Syrian forces, which had occupied Lebanon since 1976, began deploying SA-6 missiles inside Lebanon. The Soviet-built surface-to-air batteries would pose a significant threat to the IAF. Israel began planning to strike the SA-6 sites, which risked escalating into a full-scale war in Lebanon. On May 5, Reagan met with Israeli ambassador Ephraim Evron, who warned that "Syria had crossed a threshold" with the missile deployment and "time is short" to respond. Reagan urged Israel not to attack Lebanon so that the United States could try to "bring about a settlement" and noted that he "had just dispatched Ambassador Philip Habib" to the region. Reagan had called Habib, an iconic career Foreign Service officer of Lebanese Christian descent by way of a childhood in a Jewish neighborhood in Brooklyn, out of retirement for this special mission.[25]

In the midst of Habib's shuttle diplomacy, Israel's attack on Osirak took the White House by surprise as much as it did the Iraqis. Adding to the embarrassment, the United States had sold the F-16s to Israel just a year earlier. This led many Arab nations to assume that Washington had partnered with Israel in destroying the reactor. Further, the American terms of the sale stipulated that Israel could only use the jets for "defensive purposes"—a definition strained by the preventive strike on Osirak. Another complication: France, America's NATO ally, had helped build and maintain the reactor in exchange for reduced rates on Iraqi oil, and those killed in the bombing included a young French nuclear technician. Israel's action risked causing a rupture between the United States and some of its most important allies in both the Middle East and Europe.

As an immediate step, Reagan suspended any further sale of F-16s to Israel, even though additional planes were scheduled for delivery later that week. On June 11, Reagan met with a cohort of Arab ambassadors representing Saudi Arabia, Jordan, Morocco, Sudan, and Bahrain. He then welcomed Israeli ambassador Evron, which likely created an awkward encounter in the small West Wing reception room as the Arab ambassadors departed while Evron arrived. The Arab delegation warned Reagan of "the embarrassing situation that your friends in the Arab world—particularly Jordan and Saudi Arabia—are in as a result of this action by Israel." Reagan defended Israel as a small nation "outnumbered by a hundred to one, and many of these countries . . . will never rest until Israel no longer exists." Next, in his meeting with Evron, Reagan complained of being "caught by surprise" by Israel's strike and refused the ambassador's entreaties to lift the suspension of F-16 deliveries. Reiterating his support for Israel, Reagan nonetheless admonished Evron, "Please keep in mind our primary objective to influence moderate Arab states in the peace effort," and stressed in particular his worry about war in Lebanon.[26]

This Oval Office shuttle diplomacy reflected Reagan's personal ambivalence. He mused that in ordering the attack, Israeli prime minister Menachem Begin "took wrong option," writing, "He should have told us and the French, we could have done something to remove the threat." However, two days later, Reagan fulminated to his diary, "The Arab indignation on behalf of Iraq is a waste. Saddam Hussein is a 'no good nut' and I think he was trying to build a nuclear weapon. He has called for the destruction of Israel and he wants to be the leader of the Arab world—that's why he invaded Iran."[27]

In the end, the Reagan administration, split internally, also split the difference in its response. Weinberger, much disposed toward the Arab states, argued for terminating all US assistance to Israel.[28] The White House officially denounced the attack, and Ambassador Kirkpatrick at the UN refused to veto a Security Council resolution condemning Israel. However, soon after suspending the F-16 sales, Reagan reversed course and allowed them to resume, while many senior officials applauded Israel unofficially. Elliott Abrams, serving at the time as assistant secretary of state for international organizations, recalls, "The official administration position was we condemned it, but we didn't mean it."[29]

Viewing the Middle East through a Cold War prism was not wrong, just insufficient. A secret CIA assessment three weeks after Osirak concluded, "Washington's ability to promote Arab cooperation against a Soviet threat or to bring the Arabs and Israelis to the bargaining table has been struck a hard blow. . . . In the absence of US restraint on Israel, Arab leaders will intensify their search for alternative ways to boost their security and protect their interests; this presents opportunities for the USSR."[30] The Soviets continually looked for ways to increase their leverage, or at least play a spoiler role and undermine American interests in the Middle East. While the USSR's regional influence had diminished after President Anwar Sadat had expelled Soviet military advisors from Egypt in 1972, the Kremlin remained a patron to mischief-makers such as Libya, Syria, and Iraq, and Moscow continued to harbor designs on the Persian Gulf's hydrocarbon reserves.

Habib wielded his diplomatic wizardry and in late July succeeded in negotiating a precarious cease-fire in Lebanon. Returning to Washington a few days later, Habib met with Reagan and gave the president a positive assessment of Begin's commitment "to bring peace" to the region. Habib also stressed that "the Saudi role . . . had been indispensable" in forging the Lebanon agreement, especially in putting quiet pressure on Syria and the

PLO to reduce their rocket attacks on Israel. Riyadh's inducements had included giving the PLO $20 million to agree to the cease-fire.[31]

Reagan appreciated such Saudi support because he was spending considerable political capital on the kingdom's behalf. He had inherited from the Carter administration a commitment to sell an arms package featuring enhanced avionics for F-15 fighters and five E-3A AWACS jets to Saudi Arabia. With an advanced radar platform able to monitor airspace at all altitudes for a vast radius, the AWACS jets would give the Saudis an "eye in the sky" of unparalleled vision. The only other nations the United States sold the plane to were NATO members, so sharing it with the Saudis would give Riyadh a qualitative edge in the Middle East's military balance.[32] This provoked fierce opposition from Israel and Israel's supporters in the US Congress. Saudi Arabia remained hostile toward the Jewish state, and Israel feared that the AWACS planes would give the kingdom and its Arab allies air superiority. The IAF in particular would be hindered from mounting any future radar-evading raids like Osirak.

The Reagan administration had several motives for selling the arms package to Saudi Arabia. These included honoring commitments to a partner nation; implicitly compensating for the humiliation of Israel's Osirak raid; generating revenue and jobs for the American defense industry; preserving the Saudis as reliable petroleum suppliers; deepening collaboration with the Saudis against Soviet communism; and helping the House of Saud maintain its hold on power amid growing threats from Islamist revolutionary movements. Reagan later recalled of the AWACS sale, "I didn't want Saudi Arabia to become another Iran." He also "wanted to send a signal to our allies and to Moscow that the United States supported its friends and intended to exert an influence in the Middle East not just limited to our support for Israel."[33] In so doing, Reagan continued another Carter legacy, by reinforcing the Carter Doctrine of opposing Soviet encroachment on the Persian Gulf region.

V

Reagan also faced renewed acrimony among his advisors over China and Taiwan. Once again Haig stood at the center of the storm. In early summer Reagan had decided to sell arms to Beijing, as part of a strategy to deepen cooperation with China against the Soviets while trying to ameliorate the

PRC's opposition to American arms sales to Taiwan. The White House decided to keep its decision secret until later in the fall, to allow time for consultation with allies such as Japan and Taiwan. Haig, who shared his mentor Kissinger's affinity for Beijing and disregard for Taiwan, objected to the delay. The next week, on a trip to Beijing, Haig abruptly announced at a press conference that the United States would be selling weapons to China. The journalist Jim Mann recalls that "even Haig's aides at the State Department were stunned at the disclosure." Also stunned were NSC staff member Jim Lilley and Pentagon official Rich Armitage, who had accompanied Haig on the trip in part due to White House concerns that the secretary catered too much to Beijing—concerns that Haig's reckless comments vindicated. Lilley was a career CIA officer who had been the first American intelligence professional to serve in the PRC, in the US liaison office headed by his old Yale classmate George Bush.[34]

To curb Haig's freelancing, Lilley turned some of his intelligence tradecraft against the State Department. During his previous tour of duty at the US embassy, he had secretly established a secure communications link with CIA headquarters and the NSC, bypassing the State Department. Lilley and Armitage now used this channel to send urgent messages to Allen and Weinberger, unbeknownst to Haig. Allen then alerted Reagan. The irked president told a press conference in Washington that same day, "I have not changed my feelings about Taiwan," and reaffirmed his support for weapons sales to the island. Reagan's words detonated in Beijing, aggravating the Chinese leadership and humiliating Haig. In retaliation, Haig tried to throw Lilley and Armitage off the trip and make them take commercial flights home, only relenting when they threatened to tell the press about his petulance.[35]

To show the White House its displeasure, that summer Beijing invited a series of former senior Carter administration officials to China. These visitors included Carter himself, who, after being fêted by Deng Xiaoping, told a Chinese television interviewer that the Taiwan issue should be settled by the Chinese people "without interference from my country."[36] For a former president to undercut his own government while overseas represented a remarkable breach of protocol. It revealed the enmity that Carter still felt toward his successor—a bitterness that Beijing relished exploiting.

The transpacific dustup forced the White House to resolve the issue of arms sales to China. Lilley and Armitage worked with the State Department to forge an agreed position, which culminated in a rare joint memo from

Haig and Weinberger to Reagan recommending selling arms to China as long as allies were consulted, and the weapons did not threaten Taiwan and could not be used against the United States.[37] Reagan approved; in doing so he aligned himself with every predecessor since Nixon who had sought to deepen United States–China ties.

His decision also completed a remarkable turnabout from just two years earlier when Reagan had railed against America's diplomatic recognition of Beijing. Why the change? Once in office, Reagan realized that it was in America's interest to maintain productive relationships with *both* China and Taiwan—and that he needed as many partners as possible in his main priority: defeating the Soviet Union and bringing the Cold War to a peaceful end.

VI

That summer, the Kremlin confronted Reagan with three urgent questions. First, how would he address the Soviet deployment of intermediate-range nuclear missiles targeting Western Europe? Second, how would he respond to the plans by several Western European nations to partner with the USSR on a massive pipeline project supplying oil and gas from the Soviet Union to Europe—and enriching Moscow with much-needed hard currency? Third, did he want to support the growing movement in Poland resisting Soviet control of its largest Warsaw Pact satellite?

Each issue by itself was vexing; taken together they reminded Reagan that he had not yet developed a strategy to guide his administration in the Cold War. Yes, he had long-held convictions about exploiting Soviet vulnerabilities, renewing American power, waging a war of ideas, and negotiating from a position of strength. But Reagan and his staff had not yet built those principles into a coherent strategy that aligned ideas with resources, established priorities and goals, and provided a blueprint for his national security team to implement. Meanwhile, Moscow did not wait for them to do so.

The Soviets had changed the strategic balance a few years earlier by deploying several missile systems known variously as theater nuclear forces (TNF) or intermediate-range nuclear forces (INF) targeting Western Europe, including the SS-20, bristling with three warheads. NATO had responded in December 1979 with the "dual-track" decision to deploy its own missiles while also negotiating with the Soviets over reducing the INF threat. The Reagan administration inherited this NATO policy but now had to figure out how to implement it. Specifically, the White House had to decide the knotty sequencing of whether and when to start negotiations with the Soviets, whether and when to reassure anxious Europeans by *announcing* those negotiations with the Soviets, and how to deploy Pershing II intermediate-range ballistic missiles and ground-launched cruise missiles (GLCMs) without provoking an overwhelming backlash from European publics who did not want nuclear weapons in their own backyards—and who threatened to vote out their leaders who permitted the missiles.

Arms control would incite some of the most acrimonious divisions among Reagan's advisors during his eight years in office, and the INF debate was no exception. Haig argued strongly for assuaging the Europeans by announcing a specific date to start negotiations with the Soviets. Weinberger, joined by Allen and Casey, resisted, preferring instead to study the Soviet threat and American capabilities before committing to any discussions with the Kremlin. Reagan, ever averse to conflict, said he "did not see much difference between [the] State and DOD positions" and suggested a compromise statement that the US "hope[d]" to begin negotiations with the Soviets by the end of the year.[38]

The pipeline project originated in a simple economic reality: Western Europe had growing energy needs, and the Soviet Union had some of the world's largest hydrocarbon reserves. Moscow had long relied on oil exports to bring in hard currency and sustain its economy, but a 1981 CIA assessment observed, "The Soviet oil industry is in serious trouble," and it faced likely production declines in the coming decade due to diminishing reserves and growing drilling costs in its current fields. So the Kremlin decided to shift to natural gas, which it possessed in abundance. It salivated after Western Europe as its primary export market and economic lifeline. The CIA believed that "the USSR is counting heavily on hard currency earnings from these gas sales to compensate for a decline in oil export revenues, which accounted for nearly half of Soviet hard currency earnings in 1979." The Soviet need for foreign currency revealed its economic fragility and the costs of its global ambitions. As Richard Pipes put it in an NSC memo opposing the pipeline, "The less hard cash the USSR has, the less mischief it can cause us and our friends."[39]

Some of those friends, however, had other priorities. America's allies had much at stake beyond meeting their natural gas demands. Japan joined several European countries in pushing for the pipeline because they all had banks that sought to finance it, energy and construction companies that sought to build and maintain it, and voters whose jobs depended on it. The CIA concluded US efforts to stop the pipeline "would probably have a low yield and a high cost," noting, "The Allies have already decided that the project is in their interest and will not voluntarily halt their participation. . . . US pressure could thus pose major risks for US-Allied relations."[40]

Jettisoning the CIA director's traditional role as provider of intelligence but not policy advice, Casey deviated from the analysts who worked for him and advocated a hard line on the pipeline. He told Reagan and the other NSC principals that pressuring Europe to halt it "is our greatest opportunity ever to force the Soviets to divert resources from military programs," since Moscow would need to fund and build the pipeline on its own. Kirkpatrick added the worry that the pipeline would increase Western Europe's dependence on the USSR—which could blackmail the Europeans by shutting down the gas flows—and invoked an aphorism from Lenin about capitalist greed, warning, "We don't want to increase the tendency towards the Finlandization of Europe. We don't want to help the Soviets. We don't want to sell them the rope to hang us!"[41]

Haig pointed out that European leaders felt frustration at alleged American hypocrisy in lifting the US grain embargo on Moscow while trying to prevent European-Soviet cooperation on energy. He reminded Reagan, "Our European allies are in a blue funk about their economic situation. They blame us in part for their problems . . . because of our interest rates."[42] Reagan agonized for months over the pipeline. At one point he lamented to his diary that it was "the most profound decision I've ever had to make."[43] He decided that preserving cooperation with America's allies mattered more than squeezing the Soviet economy. For now, he chose to tell his European counterparts of his objections to the pipeline but dispense with any stronger actions.

The Polish crisis had been simmering since the summer of 1980, when Soviet forces had mobilized on the Polish border and threatened to quash the burgeoning Solidarity movement of Gdańsk shipyard workers. Led by the charismatic Lech Walesa, the Solidarity workers formed the first independent labor union in communist Poland and pressed for more political rights. Poland's prime minister Wojciech Jaruzelski, torn between his Kremlin overlords, his communist faith, and his Polish nationalism, tried at first to curtail Solidarity while also resisting Moscow's pressure to crack down harder. Soviet fears escalated when the Solidarity leaders issued a public letter greeting "the workers of Albania, Bulgaria, Czechoslovakia, the GDR [East Germany], Hungary, Romania, and all the peoples of the USSR" and proclaiming, "We support those among you who have decided to enter the difficult path of struggle for a free trade union movement."[44] Brezhnev feared that Solidarity could infect the entire Soviet bloc, especially since the movement received considerable support—organizational, financial, and spiritual—from the Vatican and many Polish clerics. Into the summer of 1981, Poland's travails worsened, as its economy shrunk by some 10–15 percent and the government imposed severe food rationing. Reagan had to decide whether the United States and its allies should throw Warsaw an economic lifeline. Doing so could strengthen Solidarity and draw Poland closer to the West—or could provoke a Soviet crackdown. Not doing so could mean strangling the Solidarity movement and abandoning Poland to the Kremlin's control. An NSC memo spelled out the "high-stakes decision" he faced:

> Either to risk, by inaction, the economic undermining of Poland's challenge to Moscow or to undertake a prolonged, costly, and inherently speculative multilateral aid program to shore up Poland's capacity to preserve its independence. The strategic and political rewards for success could be the neutralization of the second largest military force in the Warsaw Pact and the loosening of Soviet control of all of Eastern Europe. Success cannot, however, be assured.[45]

Poland's plight weighed on Reagan, especially as he struggled with his own country's stagnant economy. He unburdened himself to his diary: "[Poland's] economy is going bust. Here is the 1st major break in the Red dike—Poland's disenchantment with Soviet communism. Can we afford to let Poland collapse? But in the state of our present economy can we afford to help in a meaningful way?"[46]

History again loomed over the Reagan team's deliberations. Haig argued for aiding Warsaw, warning that "the failure of Poland's challenge to Moscow for lack of Western assistance would be the modern equivalent of Yalta, a historic act of indifference." These debates over Eastern Europe showed Haig at his best. Distrusted and disliked though he was by his colleagues, none could deny Haig's expertise and strategic acumen, especially when the former supreme commander of allied forces in Europe held forth on transatlantic issues. Everyone around the table appreciated his reference to the 1945 conference when Churchill and a dying Franklin Roosevelt had conceded Poland to Stalin's sphere of influence—and replaced Nazi tyranny with Soviet tyranny over the long-suffering Poles. Though Reagan admired Roosevelt, he realized that he now faced the consequences of Roosevelt's weakness. He decided that the United States would provide $50 million in emergency food aid to Poland, channeled primarily through charities affiliated with the Catholic Church. He hoped that by feeding the Polish people, he could also starve their Soviet overlords of support.[47]

VII

Presidential vacations are something of a myth. Even when away from the White House, a president never stops being president. Daily intelligence briefings, a regular stream of phone calls and staff memos demanding decisions, unrelenting media coverage, and inexorable national and global crises all command the president's time and attention—no matter where he is. Even if a president does enjoy a brief mental break from the office, the omnipresent Secret Service and military aide carrying the briefcase with the nuclear launch codes all remind him that he cannot escape his singular responsibilities. As Reagan once bemoaned to his diary, "Presidents don't have vacations—they just have a change of scenery."[48]

On the afternoon of August 6, Reagan departed the White House for his California ranch, eager for a few weeks away from Washington, DC. At the end of a rugged dirt road high in the Santa Ynez Mountains, Rancho del Cielo had become Reagan's most beloved place on earth since he and Nancy had purchased it six years earlier. Visitors invariably found it surprisingly remote and rustic. The spartan homestead sat like a pebble in the shadow of the mountain. The Reagans stayed in a small adobe ranch house, parts of which Reagan had built himself, in a bedroom with rumpled twin beds bound together with wire, off a cramped kitchen with an ancient stove. A bookshelf with many of Reagan's favorite volumes and a worn couch and chairs completed the living room. Outside, a wood fence he built rimmed the house, and the front porch looked out on a tranquil pond. Steep hills covered with solemn oak trees and pierced with dirt paths converged on an open meadow at the summit capped by a wild grass field. There, on his daily

horseback ride, Reagan could behold a western vista where, befitting the
ranch's name, the light azure sky met and melted into the darker blue of
the Pacific.[49]

Though he could not escape the duties of office, Reagan still found the
ranch a place of mental and physical respite, the latter an acute need as he
continued to recover from the assassination attempt. Two crises loomed
over his time in California, both testing his credibility before a watching
world. The first had erupted three days earlier when the Professional Air
Traffic Controllers Organization (PATCO) called a nationwide strike. The
majority of the nation's air traffic controllers walked off the job, choking
flights at many airports and leaving many travelers stranded during the
height of vacation season. The PATCO leadership believed they held the
upper hand on Reagan because they had endorsed him during the 1980
campaign, one of the only labor unions in the nation to support the Republican candidate.[50]

Reagan did not blink. The morning the strike began, he called a press
conference and read a statement he had drafted himself. He recalled in his
diary, "I . . . announced that they would have 48 hours in which to return
and if they don't they are separated from the service."[51] Two days later Reagan did just that and fired the striking air traffic controllers.

The PATCO strike may have appeared at first only a domestic issue, but
it quickly became international. The Soviet news agency TASS denounced
Reagan for his "brutal repression" of the strikers. World leaders watched to
see how this new president would handle the crisis. Reagan held firm. He
deployed military air traffic controllers to keep airports operating while his
Justice Department arrested PATCO leaders and imposed punitive fines
that soon depleted the union's coffers. A short time later PATCO capitulated
and dissolved as a union.[52] Many around the world took notice. George
Shultz later reflected, with just small exaggeration, that firing the PATCO
strikers "was the most important foreign policy decision Ronald Reagan
ever made."[53]

The other crisis was fomented earlier in the summer by the maniacal
Libyan dictator Muammar Qadhafi. His transgressions were many. Qadhafi
was the world's most extensive sponsor of terrorism; supplied weapons to
the PLO, Irish Republican Army, and Sandinistas; frequently tried to assassinate disfavored foreign leaders and political opponents; had close ties with
the Soviet Union; and in December 1980 had invaded the neighboring country of Chad. Qadhafi escalated his confrontation with the United States

when he declared the Gulf of Sidra in the Mediterranean Sea to be his exclusive territory. Extending out north from Libya's coast, the gulf had long been recognized as international waters, and the US Navy held regular exercises there.

Reagan decided to defy Qadhafi's claim. In an NSC meeting on July 30 he approved the Pentagon's recommendation to send two aircraft carrier battle groups into the gulf "to assert freedom of navigation"—to sail over the line that Qadhafi had drawn in the water. Reagan authorized the navy to return fire if fired upon, and said that if Libyan jets attacked and then tried to hide in Libyan airspace, "we would chase them right into the hangar."[54]

The navy scheduled its exercise for August 18–19. While Reagan was in California, the fleet sailed into the Gulf of Sidra and began launching air patrols by F-14 Tomcats, the navy's most advanced air superiority fighter. Two Libyan Su-22s, a modern Soviet-made fighter jet, intercepted two of the American planes. One Su-22 fired a missile at a Tomcat while the other Libyan fighter locked its radar on the other F-14. The American jets retaliated with Sidewinder heat-seeking missiles that destroyed both Su-22s.

The shootdown of Qadhafi's jets marked the first use of force on Reagan's watch, and the first combat by the US military since Carter's calamitous Desert One hostage rescue mission the year prior. If the images of the burning US aircraft in the Iranian desert had epitomized America's weakness, the Reagan White House hoped that the destruction of the two Libyan jets showed the world a new picture of American strength. Weinberger later boasted that the navy's action "did more to reassure our allies than any budget amounts we were committed to spend, or any amount of rhetoric."[55]

The navy stayed busy in August. While the Sixth Fleet confronted Qadhafi in the Mediterranean Sea, farther to the north the Second Fleet sailed an aircraft carrier battle group into the Barents Sea, on the Soviet Union's Arctic doorstep. F-14s launched from the carrier decks probed even farther, to the edge of Soviet air defenses. Before leaving for his California ranch, Reagan had approved Ocean Venture '81, described by Secretary of the Navy Lehman as "the largest and most aggressive US and NATO at-sea exercise within memory." It mobilized fifteen NATO nations, over one thousand aircraft, and two hundred fifty ships to show America's ability and willingness to project power globally.[56] Monitoring Moscow's reactions from CIA headquarters, Inman observed that the exercise "scared the hell out of the Soviets."[57] Reagan and his team hoped that this Arctic armada would expand the Cold War chessboard and strengthen America's hand at the negotiating table. As Lehman later wrote, "diplomatic power was the shadow cast by military and naval power."[58] The White House meant to lengthen that shadow.

VIII

Reagan returned to Washington on September 3. He was welcomed back by fierce opposition to the AWACS sale from some of his normal national security allies in Congress, such as Scoop Jackson, who along with Republican Bob Packwood led the bipartisan campaign in the Senate to defeat the deal. Jackson lacerated Saudi Arabia as a "nondemocratic, potentially unstable nation," hostile to Israel and indifferent to American interests. Earlier that summer he had marshaled fifty-five senators—a voting majority—to write to Reagan opposing the sale.[59] Reagan faced the prospect of a humiliating defeat.

Even worse, he found himself in the uncomfortable position of fighting Israel's efforts to scupper the deal. This included Prime Minister Begin himself. Reagan welcomed the Israeli leader to the White House in early September for a state visit. Despite their differences, Reagan thought the visit went well—until, as he wrote in his diary, "[I] was annoyed to learn that P.M. Begin had gone to the hill and had lobbied against the sale after leading me to believe he wouldn't."[60] Though it remains unclear how much Begin actually did to kill the deal, Reagan's belief that the Israeli misled him fueled a growing mistrust between the two.

In the midst of the AWACS fight, America lost an important friend elsewhere in the Middle East. On the morning of October 6, Haig awakened Reagan with the news from Cairo that Egyptian leader Anwar Sadat had just been assassinated by Islamic militants. It furthered Reagan's fear of Islamic revolutionary forces destabilizing America's Arab allies. The next day he redoubled his efforts on the AWACS vote. Deploying his canny chief of staff, James Baker, as the lead lobbyist and vote counter, Reagan made a remarkable personal investment in winning the Senate. Unlike the campaign for his economic package earlier in the summer, where Reagan had barnstormed the country and taken his case directly to the American people, on this he played strictly an inside game. Most Americans knew little about Saudi Arabia, and what they did know they did not like, especially considering Riyadh's leadership of the OPEC oil embargo that had caused high prices and long lines of misery at gas stations several years earlier. So instead of persuading the public, Reagan focused on persuading just fifty-one senators. Over the course of a few weeks he invited dozens of senators to the White House for individual meetings in which Reagan appealed to each for his vote. The whole world seemed to be watching. As *Time* magazine observed, "In European as well as Middle Eastern capitals, US allies awaited the vote as a test of Reagan's credibility in defining American policy." His combination of arm-twisting, reasoned national security arguments, and Oval Office blandishments for Senate egos proved enough, barely. On October 28, the Senate voted fifty-two to forty-eight to approve the AWACS sale.[61]

<h2 style="text-align:center">IX</h2>

Meanwhile, up at the United Nations, Kirkpatrick had emerged as a lonely voice crying in the wilderness of Turtle Bay. She found the institutional hypocrisy most galling, decrying the UN as "the glass house where everyone throws stones." She also lambasted the institution for its skewed priorities, complaining in a speech to the General Assembly that while it habitually singled out Israel for condemnation, the UN remained "silent while 3 million Cambodians died in Pol Pot's murderous utopia . . . while a quarter million Ugandans died at the hands of Idi Amin . . . and while thousands of Soviet citizens are denied equal rights, equal protection of the law; denied the right to think, write, publish, work freely, or emigrate."[62] In launching these fusillades, Kirkpatrick enjoyed Reagan's full support. With his devotion to America's allies, he was a committed multilateralist, but Reagan had grown to detest what he saw as the UN's distorted moral equivalency between tyrannies and free societies, and its habitual opposition to the United States and Israel. He also wanted to reclaim a measure of American sovereignty and freedom of action as part of his agenda of renewing the nation's strength.

Kirkpatrick was a lonely voice in other ways. At the UN she was the only woman representing a major nation, while on her frequent trips back to Washington, DC, she found herself the only woman in Reagan's cabinet and national security team. Though she downplayed it in public, privately she felt herself at the margins, especially given the sexist contempt she endured from Haig and some of the other men in the cabinet. As her biographer recalls, during a meeting in the Situation Room with Reagan and the rest of the NSC, Kirkpatrick "saw a mouse scurry across the floor and thought to herself that it was no more surprising that such a creature should be there than that she, a woman, should be."[63]

Kirkpatrick's broadsides against the UN's double standards nonetheless raised hard questions about whether the Reagan administration had its own double standards. Specifically, did the White House see human rights merely as an instrument to bash communist regimes or as a universal good, to be promoted in adversary and allied nations alike? Reagan's team was divided, and he seemed himself unsure.

Reagan's initial determination to be the antithesis of Carter and to support anticommunist partners meant downplaying and even disregarding how such governments abused their own people. This sometimes amounted to providing a blank check to oppressive regimes. For example, in March Reagan and Haig hosted in the Oval Office General Roberto Viola, a leader of the military junta ruling Argentina that tortured, murdered, or otherwise "disappeared" thousands of its political opponents. The CIA briefing for Reagan on Viola noted that "the change in emphasis in US human rights policy has been warmly received by Argentine leaders." In the meeting, Reagan and Haig assured Viola that "there would be no public scoldings and lectures" on human rights; Viola cynically replied that he "hoped there would be no private scoldings either."[64] In another case that tarnished the White House's moral standing, in December a Salvadoran militia that had been trained and equipped by American military advisors murdered hundreds of civilians, including women and children, in the village of El Mozote. The Reagan administration disbelieved and denied the initial reports of the massacre, which only made it appear even more complicit in the eyes of critics of its El Salvador policy.[65]

However, Reagan's hatred of communism, sympathy for individual cases of human suffering, and hope to promote liberty around the world also led to meaningful human rights gestures in his first year. Religious freedom held special purchase for him, especially the persecution of Jews and Christians in the Soviet Union. One particular dissident in the gulag's Perm 35 prison camp soon captured his attention. In 1978 the Soviets had sentenced Anatoly Shcharansky to thirteen years' imprisonment because of his Jewish faith and his opposition to the Kremlin. On May 28, 1981, Reagan welcomed to the White House Shcharansky's wife, Avital, and another Soviet Jewish activist, Yosef Mendelevich, who had served eleven years in prison. Avital combined pure-eyed innocence with fierce advocacy for her husband. Moved by their appeal and Shcharansky's plight, Reagan denounced the Kremlin in his diary that evening in visceral terms: "D--n those inhuman monsters. He is said to be down to 100 pounds and very ill. I promised I'd do everything I could to obtain his release and I will."[66]

That fall, two senior Reagan appointees at the State Department, Elliott Abrams and Paul Wolfowitz, grew concerned at their administration's growing credibility gap on human rights. Abrams and Wolfowitz had much in common: Both were former Democrats, both were Jewish, both were neoconservatives (in the term's original sense of hawkish Democrats who moved right on foreign policy), and both were intellectuals. Both also saw strategic and moral problems with the Reagan administration's inconstant human rights policy. Abrams recalls, "It is not an accident that people like the [South African apartheid regime], [Philippine dictator Ferdinand] Marcos, and [Chilean dictator Augusto] Pinochet were all delighted when Reagan won."[67] In October 1981, Abrams and Wolfowitz broke with Kirkpatrick, Haig, Weinberger, and Casey in arguing for the White House to make a consistent commitment to human rights and democracy.

As director of the Policy Planning Staff, the State Department's iconic strategy office, Wolfowitz coauthored a memo with Assistant Secretary Larry Eagleburger to both Haig and the White House. They argued that the administration's indifference on human rights was undermining its credibility with Congress, jeopardizing important aid programs such as the one for El Salvador, and amounted to unilateral disarmament in the Cold War: "'Human rights'—a somewhat narrow name for our values—gives us the best opportunity to convey what is ultimately at issue in our contest with the Soviet bloc." However, they cautioned, "a human rights policy cannot be credible if it has impact only on pro-Soviet countries" and instead urged that the United States be "a positive force for freedom and decency" with friend and foe alike.[68] Three weeks later, Abrams drafted a memo to Haig in tandem with Deputy Secretary Bill Clark that made a similar appeal for moral consistency while connecting human rights to America's core identity. "'Human rights' isn't something we add on to our foreign policy, but is its very purpose: the defense and promotion of liberty in the world," they averred.[69] In trying to close the gap between Reagan's rhetoric about freedom and the inconsistent reality of his policies, Wolfowitz and Abrams also hoped to seize the initiative in the Cold War. They knew, as did Reagan, that the Kremlin's greatest vulnerability was not its economy or its overstretched military but its abuse of its own people.

The two memos marked the beginnings of a shift by the Reagan administration to more principled support for human dignity and liberty, and to integrating human rights into its overall Cold War strategy against the Soviet Union. The Abrams and Clark memo also anticipated new jobs for both. Abrams, frustrated that his role as assistant secretary for international organizations trapped him in constant bureaucratic tension between Haig and Kirkpatrick, believed he would be more effective as assistant secretary of state for human rights and humanitarian affairs. A few weeks later Reagan appointed Abrams to that position—and also asked Clark to take on a new role.

X
_____

The fall also confronted Reagan with a series of decisions on America's nuclear forces. In short order he had to decide what new weapons to acquire, where to target them, and how to negotiate about them with the Soviets. Reagan addressed the first two questions with National Security Decision Directives (NSDD), highly classified memoranda issued only to his top officials. He answered the third question in a speech at the National Press Club, delivered for all the world to hear—especially the Kremlin.

Reagan agonized about these issues in his diary, writing that determining what to do with nuclear arms "may be the most momentous decision any Pres[ident] has had to make."[70] He felt particularly conflicted because he faced the tension between his loathing of Soviet communism and his hatred of nuclear weapons. In the arms race, America's nuclear arsenal had fallen behind the Soviets in quality and quantity, and Reagan had campaigned on restoring America's strength and strategic advantage. He did so not because he wanted to launch a nuclear war (despite the accusations from some of his more hysterical critics) but because he wanted to negotiate with the Soviets for the reduction and eventual elimination of nuclear arms. This is what he meant by "peace through strength."

On October 1, Reagan signed NSDD-12. It ordered an upgrade in all three legs of the triad, the American arsenal of strategic nuclear weapons. NSDD-12 directed the construction of one hundred MX missiles, the development of both the B-1 Lancer bomber and what would become the B-2 stealth bomber, and the replacement of older missiles on Trident nuclear submarines with the advanced D5 SLBM. Less visible but no less important, NSDD-12 also declared that "the highest priority element in the program" is the creation of "command and communications systems for our strategic forces that can survive and endure before, during, and after a nuclear attack."[71] In the perverse logic of the nuclear age, the vulnerability of America's arsenal could induce the Soviets to launch a surprise nuclear attack. The Reagan administration believed that building a secure communications system that could guarantee America's ability to retaliate would deter Moscow from any preemptive strikes.

Three weeks later, Reagan issued NSDD-13, with its grim dictates on where US nuclear forces would be aimed. Not declassified until 2017, this directive gave priority to destroying the Soviet nuclear arsenal and command-and-control structures, known as "counterforce" targeting. It committed the United States to "limit[ing] collateral damage" where possible. This nod to minimizing civilian casualties also implicitly acknowledged the unfathomable destructive power of nuclear weapons. NSDD-13 then described the unpredictability of the balance of terror: "While it will remain our policy not to rely on launching our nuclear forces in an irrevocable manner upon warning that a Soviet missile attack has begun, we must leave Soviet planners with strong uncertainty as to how we might actually respond to such warning."[72] When reviewing this section of his policy, Reagan probably thought back to his visit to NORAD two years earlier, when he had learned that if American radar detected incoming Soviet missiles, the US president had no options other than launching a retaliatory strike. That choice terrified him—but so did the alternative of doing nothing as his nation faced annihilation.

Reagan again connected his nuclear arms buildup with pressure on the Soviets to reduce arsenals. He described this in a secret message to Thatcher on his nuclear modernization decisions: "Without this program there would be no incentive for the Soviets seriously to negotiate meaningful and substantial arms reductions, a course to which my government remains fully committed."[73] It was a deceptively simple plan: The US would build up its nuclear arsenal so that the Americans and Soviets could then agree to tear their weapons down.

A few weeks later, Reagan saw what his world might look like in a nuclear war. On Sunday, November 15, he finished a turkey-hunting trip in the Texas Hill Country and flew back to Washington, DC, on a secret version of Air Force One called the "Doomsday plane." This specially modified Boeing 747, designed to withstand an electromagnetic pulse from a nuclear blast, could carry up to 114 crew and staff and would serve as the president's command post—and home—for up to three airborne days in the midst of a nuclear attack. Reagan's terse diary entry about the flight—"Was briefed on its capabilities. It's like being in a submarine—no windows"—offered a spare image for the darkness and distance he would feel from the people he was sworn to protect—many of whom would be perishing in a nuclear wasteland below, while the commander in chief circled above.[74] Around this same time, Reagan chaired an NSC meeting on how the United States would fare in a nuclear attack, and learned of the Pentagon's estimate that "Right now in a nuclear war we'd lose 150 mil[lion] people. The Soviets could hold their loss down to less than were killed in W.W. II," about 15 million people.[75] That month the Pentagon also gave him a briefing on the "Single Integrated Operational Plan," the anodyne name for the terrifying process for Reagan to order nuclear strikes that would incinerate the Soviet Union.[76] Taken together, these experiences deepened Reagan's resolve to free the world, and himself, from the nightmare of nuclear weapons.

Three days after his maiden Doomsday flight, Reagan walked up to the lectern at the National Press Club and called for eliminating all intermediate-range nuclear missiles in Europe. With the actor's gift for connecting with his audience, Reagan began the speech with a personal touch. Reading long excerpts from the letter he had written to Brezhnev seven months earlier, Reagan tried to take the moral high ground while reminding the world that global security often comes down to the bonds between individual leaders. He then turned to history, recalling, "Twice in my lifetime, I have seen the peoples of Europe plunged into the tragedy of war," and pointed out that only the postwar creation of the Atlantic Alliance had prevented a third world war while creating a prosperous and free Western Europe.

Then Reagan came to the heart of his proposal: "The United States is prepared to cancel its deployment of Pershing II and ground-launch cruise missiles if the Soviets will dismantle their SS-20, SS-4, and SS-5 missiles." "Zero-zero," or the "zero option," as it came to be known, seized the strategic initiative for the United States. America had not yet deployed its missiles in Europe, whereas the USSR wielded several hundred operational missiles targeted at NATO capitals. Reagan's proposal held the political appeal of ensuring a European continent free of intermediate-range nuclear missiles and the strategic appeal of, as *Newsweek* put it, "something for nothing":

The Soviets would have to eliminate their existing missiles while the United States would merely refrain from deploying new ones.[77]

The zero option had initially been proposed by Weinberger and his brilliant assistant secretary of defense Richard Perle. Weinberger and Perle, both skeptics of arms control, seem to have crafted the idea as a measure to wrong-foot the Soviets and stymie any pressures on the United States to reduce its arsenal, since they could point to the Kremlin's refusal to eliminate its missiles as justification for American inaction. Haig and most of his top State Department advisors opposed the zero option, fearing that the Soviets would reject it out of hand and the NATO allies would dismiss it as unserious. In an NSC meeting on the eve of his speech, Reagan chose to embrace it—not because he shared Weinberger and Perle's deviousness, but because, in his words, "we can begin negotiations with the hope that we can eliminate all of these missiles totally, verifiably, and globally. Then, in good faith, we can with regard to other nuclear weapons, look to a realistic reduction."[78]

The White House broadcast the speech, the first major foreign policy address of his presidency, to some fifty nations and two hundred million people worldwide. Reagan had to persuade multiple audiences with different concerns. He needed to assure the American people that he would keep them safe, the leaders of Europe that he was committed to the alliance, the people of Europe that he was committed to peace, and the Kremlin that he was serious about arms control talks.

The American response was positive. Media outlets normally not friendly to Reagan applauded the speech. *Newsweek* called it "a 22-minute virtuoso performance," and *The Washington Post* described it as "a masterful performance that took the high ground."[79] West German chancellor Schmidt phoned Reagan, just before Schmidt was to meet with Brezhnev, to "express my gratitude" and said the speech "just came in time." Reagan asked Schmidt to assure the Soviet leader of Reagan's sincerity in proposing the zero option. Reagan also reminded the West German that Brezhnev had "some problems on his side with the economy in his country and the hunger of his people, that he might be more amenable now to not spending so much on [the] military."[80] For its part, the official Soviet media dismissed Reagan's proposal as "sheer demagoguery" and "propaganda."[81]

Reagan's gambit was unprecedented in the annals of the Cold War. Arms control for the previous two decades had focused on slowing the growth of the American and Soviet arsenals—not reducing, let alone eliminating, an entire class of offensive weapons. But that was not all that Reagan had in mind. In a little-noticed section tacked on to the end of his speech, Reagan spelled out his broader strategic goal: "The American concept of peace goes well beyond the absence of war. We foresee a flowering of economic growth and individual liberty in a world at peace." After all, he continued, "terms like 'peace' and 'security' . . . have little meaning for the oppressed and the destitute. They also mean little to the individual whose state has stripped him of human freedom and dignity. . . . We must recognize that progress in the pursuit of liberty is a necessary complement to military security."[82]

Reagan did not seek merely to delegitimize Soviet communism, but to show a positive alternative of democratic capitalism, of free societies and free markets, prosperity and peace, throughout the world. He believed in a trinity of religious freedom, political freedom, and economic freedom. For the latter, earlier that fall he had entered the staid precincts of the World Bank and International Monetary Fund to launch his global campaign for free enterprise. The postwar creation of the World Bank and IMF, he declared, "rested upon a belief that the key to national development and human progress is individual freedom—both political and economic." Continuing, he contended, "We cannot have prosperity and successful development without economic freedom; nor can we preserve our personal and political freedoms without economic freedom." For this reason "my own government is committed to policies of free trade, unrestricted investment, and open capital markets."[83]

The Soviet Union was the world's largest nonmarket economy. It was also in serious trouble—but just how much trouble was much debated. While many Western experts, including the CIA, had in the 1970s consistently overestimated Soviet economic strength, the CIA issued a secret assessment in October that began to detect Moscow's economic travails. "The [Soviet] economy has turned sour," it declared. "Slower economic growth will present President Brezhnev and his colleagues with some increasingly tough and politically painful choices regarding resource allocation and economic management." When sending the report to Reagan, Casey's cover letter noted, "The Soviets now face serious problems in almost every sector of their economy."[84]

Meanwhile, Reagan opened another front in the war of ideas. On September 9, he launched "Project Truth," a worldwide campaign spearheaded by the United States Information Agency (USIA). It involved offense and defense. Project Truth would project "an accurate image of the United

States and its foreign policy," refute "misleading Soviet propaganda and dis-information," show "the Soviet threat to the stability and security in various areas of the world," and "underline the common values—*moral, spiritual, cultural*—that bind us to our allies."[85] Under the leadership of the irrepress-ible USIA director Charles Wick—a business executive and longtime Rea-gan friend from California who made up for in zeal what he lacked in experience—the Reagan team joined the fight with fervor.

XI

In late November, a despondent Richard Allen walked out of the White House for the last time as national security advisor. Technically, he was on administrative leave, but his dismissal would soon become permanent, making him the shortest-serving NSA in history.[86] The public story was that he resigned over a bizarre episode involving a $1,000 cash gift from Japanese journalists, for a photo session with the First Lady, that Allen had forgotten in a White House safe. The real story was that he had never fit the role and got pushed out when virtually everyone, including Reagan, lost confidence in him. After just ten months in the job, he had never developed a rapport with Reagan; alienated Baker, Deaver, and the First Lady; failed to build the confidence of Bush, Weinberger, and Casey; exasperated the patient Meese; and never overcame Haig's unrelenting hostility. His early exit fu-eled the constant stories of an administration at war with itself.

Allen's departure also meant that in December the Reagan White House faced its biggest foreign policy crisis yet without a national security advisor (Allen's deputy James "Bud" Nance filled the role in an acting capacity). On Sunday, December 13, at six A.M. in Warsaw, Prime Minister Jaruzelski commandeered Polish national television and declared, "The State Council has imposed martial law all over the country." He imprisoned over six thou-sand Solidarity members, banned public gatherings, imposed a nationwide curfew, closed the borders, and cut all telephone lines within Poland and to the outside world.[87] Jaruzelski was tightening the Iron Curtain on his own country and using it to strangle Solidarity in the process.

Martial law shocked the White House. Up until late October, the CIA had been collecting intelligence on the communist regime's intentions from Polish army colonel Ryszard Kuklinski, one of Langley's most valued agents. Kuklinski's reporting came to an abrupt halt when fears he was about to be arrested prompted Inman to order the CIA to exfiltrate him in a fraught clandestine operation on November 7. It saved the spy's life, but the loss of Kuklinski's intelligence closed the Reagan administration's best window into Poland.[88]

Now Reagan needed to decide what to do. He saw the hand of the Kremlin behind martial law and wanted to respond in ways that would punish both Jaruzelski and the Soviets while still leaving room for a negotiated solution, and not derailing the arms control talks getting under way in Geneva. For his part, Brezhnev phoned Jaruzelski on December 13 with congratulations on the crackdown and the promise of further Soviet economic assistance. The Kremlin also appealed to communist nations around the world to send aid to Poland, including Czechoslovakia, Hungary, East Germany, Cuba, Mongolia, Vietnam, and Laos.[89] Moscow and its satellites saw Poland as a central front in the survival of the communist bloc.

Not all of America's allies saw it that way, however. On December 19, Reagan sent impassioned letters to Thatcher, Mitterrand, and Schmidt warning of possible Soviet intervention in Poland, calling for strong measures and "alliance unity," and concluding, "This may well be a watershed moment in the political history of mankind—a challenge to tyranny from within." A contemptuous Thatcher told her foreign minister, Lord Peter Carrington, "[Reagan's message] was so vague I didn't even think it was worth reading last night." Thatcher dismissed the Polish crisis as "simply an internal situation," doubted any Soviet role, and disparaged Reagan's call to punish Moscow, saying, "It seems a bit absurd if the Russians aren't actually in the front line of it to take it out on them when they're not." She concluded that "there is nothing we can do to help the wretched people" of Poland beyond "say nasty things" about martial law.[90] Mitterrand and Schmidt were equally reluctant to get involved.

Fortunately for Reagan, another European leader did want to get involved. Pope John Paul II grieved over his home country. Reagan phoned him on December 14 to assure the Pope of America's support for Solidarity. The next day Reagan welcomed the Vatican secretary of state Agostino Cardinal Casaroli to the White house.[91] During their ninety-minute lunch, Reagan pivoted to the larger question of whether the Polish unrest revealed Soviet vulnerabilities. He wondered if "in our emphasis on the impressive buildup of Soviet military power . . . we had failed to appreciate how tenuous was the Soviet hold on the people in its empire." The power of religious faith to undermine communism particularly captivated Reagan. He commented that "the Pope's visit to Poland had showed the terrible hunger for God in Eastern Europe" and noted "reports of the fervor of the underground Church in the Soviet Union itself," saying, "[I have] heard stories of Bibles being distributed page by page among the believers."

Turning to the arms race, Reagan told Casaroli, "[We] could threaten the Soviets with our ability to outbuild them, which the Soviets knew we could do if we chose. Once we had established this, we could invite the Soviets to join us in lowering the level of weapons on both sides."[92] Reagan had just described several features of the Cold War strategy he would pursue for the next seven years: Use a weapons buildup to pressure the Soviet economy and force Moscow to negotiate major arms reductions, while supporting political and spiritual dissidents behind the Iron Curtain who would undermine the Kremlin from within.

But first there was the Poland crisis. On December 19, the Polish ambassador to the United States, Romuald Spasowski, defected to America. Three days later Reagan and Bush welcomed him to the Oval Office, where Spasowski's emotional pleas for a strong response to martial law further stiffened Reagan's resolve. Spasowski appealed to Reagan to continue Radio Free Europe's broadcasts: "Please, sir, do not ever underestimate how many millions of people still listen to that channel behind the Iron Curtain."[93] Over the next week Reagan convened several NSC meetings on Poland. In one meeting, the impassioned president exclaimed: "This is the first time in 60 years we have had this kind of opportunity. There may not be another in our lifetime. Can we afford not to go all out? . . . It is like the opening lines in our declaration of independence. 'When in the course of human events.' This is exactly what the Poles are doing now." Reagan then called for "a complete quarantine of the Soviet Union," saying, "Tell the allies that if they don't go along with us, we let them know . . . that we may have to review our alliances." He compared the moment to the eve of World War II, when Roosevelt "asked the free world to join in a quarantine of Germany. On that request his brains were kicked out all over." Undaunted by the opposition FDR had encountered, Reagan demanded "an absolute quarantine of all trade as President Roosevelt had proposed in 1938."[94]

Even as Reagan fulminated against the Kremlin, he did not seek to break off all contact. He made clear that the United States would continue the INF talks with the USSR in Geneva and would not consider suspending diplomatic relations by closing the Moscow embassy. Reagan rejected the latter in part because "we would have to give back the seven Christians that are there" in the embassy basement.[95] The Siberian Pentecostals were never far from his mind.

Frustrated though he was with the NATO allies, Reagan recognized a new set of allies emerging from the Poland crisis: the Polish people, especially Solidarity. In lauding their historic valor and persistence, Reagan saw anew how some of America's most valiant partners against Soviet communism were the everyday citizens living behind the Iron Curtain. He paid tribute to them in a televised address from the White House on December 23. Lamenting that "this Christmas brings little joy to the courageous Polish people," Reagan announced a series of sanctions against the Polish regime, including some economic restrictions, suspending landing rights for the Polish national airline, and forbidding Polish fishing fleets from operating in American territorial waters.[96]

Reagan's appeal was heartfelt, but the measures he imposed were modest. He still lacked support from his European allies and still hoped to persuade the Kremlin and Jaruzelski to reverse course. He wrote an unsparing private letter to Brezhnev the same day as his speech. "Your country has repeatedly intervened in Polish affairs during the months preceding the recent tragic events," accused Reagan as he warned of further consequences.[97] Brezhnev's reply arrived two days later on Christmas. Over five pages blistering with indignation, the Soviet leader remonstrated that the United States was guilty of "gross interference in the internal affairs of Poland." Annoyed at Brezhnev's effort to turn the tables, Reagan wrote a note to himself distilling what he saw as the difference between the American and Soviet positions: "It seems to me that we are supporting the right of the Polish people to vote on the government they'd like to have. Mr. B. is supporting the right of the government to deny the Polish people a voice in their government."[98]

Brezhnev's broadside disabused Reagan of any hopes for resolving the crisis. On December 29, the White House unloaded a barrage of new sanctions against the USSR. These included suspending all Aeroflot flights to the United States, banning many US exports to the Soviet Union, and, crucially, restricting licenses for American and European firms to sell oil and gas equipment to Moscow. Though aimed at the Kremlin, some of these sanctions threatened America's NATO allies, particularly those with companies involved in the Siberian pipeline project.[99] Realizing this risk, Reagan wrote to Pope John Paul II the next day requesting "your assistance in using your own suasion throughout the West in an attempt to achieve unity on these needed measures." Pipes captured the import of these new steps. "The sanctions, which we imposed on the Soviet Union in December 1981 had a significance beyond economics in that they broke with the Yalta syndrome that had tacitly acknowledged Poland as lying within the Soviet sphere of influence. They represented a direct challenge to the legitimacy of the Communist bloc."[100] The unrest in Poland also added a new pillar to Reagan's emerging Cold War strategy. He already sought to exploit the Soviet Union's internal vulnerabilities in its economy and repression of its own people, and support anticommunist forces resisting Soviet proxies in the Third World. Now the administration would also increase pressure on the Kremlin in its border regions and Warsaw Pact satellites. Reagan would be targeting Soviet communism around its periphery, in its near abroad, and at its core.

As the year drew to a close, Reagan and his White House had survived. That was no small success. The trials of 1981 included deepening economic recession, multiple fights with Congress, tensions with allies, a Middle East close to war, the murder of Sadat and near-murder of the Pope, Reagan's own brush with death from an assassin's bullet, and now a tense standoff with the Soviet Union. The next year would not be any easier.

CHAPTER 4

THE BATTLE IS JOINED

I

On the morning of Tuesday, January 5, 1982, the least-qualified national security advisor in history walked into the West Wing for the first day of his new job. As of just eleven months earlier, Bill Clark had not worked a day in his life in foreign or defense policy, beyond a brief stint in the army three decades ago. A California native, Clark had previously dropped out of seminary after studying for the priesthood, dropped out of Stanford University without completing his bachelor's degree, and dropped out of Loyola University law school without finishing his law degree. In 1966 he volunteered for Reagan's gubernatorial campaign, and after the election, he joined the governor's office, rising to become chief of staff, until Reagan appointed him as a justice on the California supreme court. The laconic and self-effacing Clark was a rancher, devout Catholic, and resolute conservative who shared with Reagan a love of horseback riding and a hatred of communism.

The year before, when Reagan had nominated him to be deputy secretary of state, Clark had suffered through a torturous Senate Foreign Relations Committee confirmation hearing. He confessed that his sole foreign policy experience came from spending "72 hours in Santiago" in 1967, while fumbling basic questions on world affairs. Notwithstanding this humiliation, the Senate confirmed Clark for the post, but the damage endured. Much of official Washington, DC, and many foreign capitals dismissed him as an ignorant naïf.[1]

Over the ensuing ten months, Clark had served quietly and faithfully as deputy secretary, learning much about foreign policy. In December, partly at the urging of Casey and Weinberger, Reagan reached out to Clark to gauge his interest in replacing Allen. They sealed the deal over the New Year's holiday. Reagan agreed to restore the practice of having the national security advisor report directly to him, meaning Clark now could send memos straight to Reagan, meet with Reagan without any other minders present, and have "walk-in privileges" to enter the Oval Office anytime he wanted.[2]

Reagan also restored the status of the position as equal to the other cabinet officers. The NSA's authority derives entirely from the president. Unlike the secretary of state, who oversees hundreds of ambassadors and thousands of Foreign Service officers, or the secretary of defense, who commands over a million uniformed service members and hundreds of billions of dollars, or the director of central intelligence, who controls thousands of case officers and analysts and vast sums of money, the NSA has a small staff and almost no budget. What it does wield is the power of the presidency. Now Clark could sit at the head of the table in the White House Situation Room and look Haig, Weinberger, Casey, and other officials in the eye as a peer. When Clark spoke, those listening would know he spoke for Reagan.

What Clark lacked in credentials or expertise, he made up for with two essential qualities. First, as one of Reagan's few close friends, he enjoyed the full trust and backing of the commander in chief. Second, Clark knew how to organize, inspire, and lead a team. Contrary to the expectations of elite and (im)polite opinion, in short order he would become the most influential of Reagan's national security advisors and one of the most important— albeit least remembered—national security advisors in history.

As Clark moved into his new office and sorted through a deluge of goodwill letters and unsolicited advice memos, one lengthy missive from New York City caught his eye. It was twelve pages of counsel from Richard Nixon. Now that Reagan had passed his economic platform through Congress, Nixon urged making foreign policy his priority in 1982. To do so, Clark would need "a very substantial strengthening" of the NSC staff, which Nixon found lacking in competence. Replacing the laggards would not be easy, however. In Nixon's acerbic words, "The problem that all conservative administrations face is that those who are loyal are not bright, and those who are bright are not loyal." He closed with an admonition that resonated with Reagan's own aspirations: "This year I think it is very important for the President to be seen at home and abroad as a peacemaker." Nixon then drew a comparison from his own long-ago vice presidency: "During the Eisenhower years, Dulles played the role of the hawk and allowed Eisenhower, who was just as tough as Dulles, to be the great conciliator." He urged Clark to have Reagan imitate this model, letting Haig and Weinberger display their talons while Reagan extended the olive branch of peace.[3] What Nixon failed to appreciate, but Clark knew, is that over the next seven years Reagan intended to play the roles of both hawk and dove himself.

Sharing Nixon's concern for the quality of the NSC staff, Clark overhauled his team. He replaced Deputy National Security Advisor Nance with Robert "Bud" McFarlane, a marine who had seen combat in Vietnam and whose policy experience included the NSC staff under Kissinger, the Senate Foreign Relations Committee, and most recently service as a counselor at the State Department. Among Clark's other new hires, the most notable was Tom Reed. Reed had designed nuclear warheads at Lawrence Livermore National Laboratory, helped manage both of Reagan's gubernatorial campaigns and his 1968 presidential gambit, pioneered a new business model in the California wine industry, founded a superconductor company, developed the Breckenridge Ski Resort in Colorado, run Bill Clements's 1978 insurgent campaign to become the first Republican governor of Texas since Reconstruction, and held multiple senior roles at the Pentagon under Nixon and Ford, including secretary of the air force. He was a longtime friend of both Reagan and Clark, who would soon give him some of the NSC's most sensitive and important assignments.

A final irony of Reagan's selection of the rock-ribbed conservative Clark as NSA is that the appointment came just as right-wing frustration with Reagan reached one of its periodic crescendos. At the end of 1981, the Heritage Foundation issued a scathing 150-page report on the administration's national security policies that bemoaned that Reagan's foreign and defense agenda thus far bore "little resemblance" to the recommendations Heritage had presented a year earlier during the transition.[4] A widely circulated conservative newsletter in January 1982 wailed, "After one year, conservative momentum is stalled, or, at least, slowed to a creep, and 1982 presently offers little hope for traction," and warned, "On the right, there is already a near-mutiny."[5] Forty-three Republican members of Congress wrote Reagan in February complaining, "In too many cases it appears as though career bureaucrats or Carter Administration hold-overs are being appointed to sensitive positions and are determining policy in ways contrary to the principles that were the bedrock of your 1980 campaign."[6] A few months later Norman

Podhoretz penned a lengthy screed for *The New York Times Magazine* titled "The Neo-Conservative Anguish over Reagan's Foreign Policy" that described "sinking into a state of near political despair" over the White House's alleged failures.[7]

In these conservative brickbats, Reagan's iniquities included failing to confront the Kremlin with sufficient ardor, failing to increase the Pentagon budget with sufficient alacrity, failing to roll back communist advances in Central America with sufficient assertiveness, failing to support Israel with sufficient zeal, and failing to appoint senior officials with sufficient conservative credentials. Regardless of the merits or consistency of these criticisms, such public grousing reminded the embattled White House that as 1982 unfolded, Reagan was vilified by the Left and distrusted by the Right.

II

A few days before Clark started his new job, Augustina Vashchenko and her daughter Lidiya stopped eating. As two of the seven Siberian Pentecostals living in the basement of Embassy Moscow, their desperation after almost four years in diplomatic limbo led them to launch a hunger strike. By mid-January their physical condition had deteriorated to the point of alarm. A distressed Reagan wrote a secret letter to Brezhnev appealing for him to "intervene personally" and allow the Pentecostals to emigrate. Brezhnev responded the next week with a diatribe denying Reagan's request, asserting that "the entire responsibility for the existing situation rests with the US side" and accusing America of "detain[ing] those people within the walls of its Embassy."[8]

After a month the two resumed taking liquid nourishment, but by then Lidiya veered so close to death that Reagan approved Ambassador Art Hartman's request to rush her to the hospital, even at the risk of rearrest and imprisonment once she left the embassy compound. An appalled Reagan noted that "the Soviets refused to send an ambulance," so Hartman dispatched an embassy car to take her.[9] After she recovered in the Moscow hospital, in a small gesture the Kremlin permitted Lidiya to return to her Siberian hometown of Chernogorsk, though she was still barred from leaving the Soviet Union. Her six fellow believers remained in the embassy basement.

That same month Reagan played a new card against the Kremlin. In

January Bill Casey came to him with a secret proposal based on the Farewell Dossier that Mitterrand had shared the previous summer. At Casey's behest, NSC staff member Gus Weiss had worked with a team of CIA technology experts to develop a devilish plan. Since the Farewell Dossier revealed Soviet penetration of Western technology companies and pilfering of Western expertise, Weiss had proposed to Casey, "Why not help the Soviets with their shopping? Now that we know what they want, we can help them get it." Tom Reed recalls, "There would be just one catch: the CIA would add 'extra ingredients' to the software and hardware on the KGB's shopping list," hidden modifications designed to sabotage the products being stolen by the Soviets.[10]

This was just the sort of tradecraft that Casey and Reagan loved. It leveraged American ingenuity and exploited Soviet treachery. In Weiss's recollection, with the quiet cooperation of American industry, "contrived computer chips found their way into Soviet military equipment, flawed turbines were installed on a gas pipeline, and defective plans disrupted the output of chemical plants and a tractor factory. The Pentagon introduced misleading information pertinent to stealth aircraft, space defense, and tactical aircraft. . . . The program had great success, and it was never detected."[11]

In January, the CIA issued two reports highlighting "the Soviet economy's distress." Langley estimated that Soviet economic growth fell from 4 percent per year throughout the 1970s to just 1.5 percent per year in 1980 and 1981, even while Moscow's subsidies to its Warsaw Pact satellites increased "from nearly $5 billion in 1975 to more than $18 billion in 1980." As NSC staff member Norman Bailey put it in a memo to Reagan and Clark, the Soviets were learning that "empire is costly." Moreover, the CIA discovered that the Kremlin was hemorrhaging its cash reserves as "skyrocketing imports from the West—especially grain—and a soft world market for Soviet oil are major factors in the Soviet hard currency squeeze."[12]

Reagan salivated to exploit these Soviet vulnerabilities, but his efforts to persuade the allies to help left him gnashing his teeth. Poland and the Siberian pipeline continued to be the main transatlantic frictions, along with the perennial chestnut of America's high interest rates. The year seemed to start off well enough when Reagan hosted West German chancellor Helmut Schmidt for a visit. The German leader had spent the prior week on vacation in Florida. Watching American television news and reading newspapers had left him shocked by the fact that the US media and public viewed him as supine in the face of the Polish crisis and considered West Germany an impediment to stronger action. A chagrined Schmidt assured Reagan that he held the Soviets responsible for martial law and that his nation would not try to undermine any of the US measures in response. True to form, Schmidt then complained again about America's high interest rates, fretting that they could cause the "worldwide recession" to turn into a "worldwide depression."[13]

Reagan responded by assuring Schmidt of his commitment to consult with the allies on any further steps on Poland, and that the United States would not suspend its Geneva arms control talks with the Soviets over martial law. An ebullient Schmidt phoned Thatcher after his White House meetings to report that they had "gone extremely well." The surprised German also confessed to Thatcher, "I have come really to like [Reagan]."[14]

Poland also sparked another round of conservative kvetching. On January 15, *The Washington Post*'s front page reported on the White House's internal divisions over martial law, with Weinberger and Kirkpatrick featured for dissenting from what they saw as Reagan's insipid response and excessive deference to the allies. Weinberger and Kirkpatrick had urged Reagan to declare Poland in default on its external debt, which would have forced the many European banks that had lent to Poland to demand repayment or seize its assets. This would crush the Polish economy—but also potentially collapse Western Europe's economy with it. Such a move might also bring down the Jaruzelski regime—or bring Poland back even more tightly under Moscow's control. Uncomfortable with such a high-risk gambit, with the only certain outcome being rupturing the Western alliance, Reagan sided with the State and Treasury Departments against the declaration of default.

Two weeks later Thatcher delivered another broadside at the White House. The British leader had learned that a frustrated Reagan was reconsidering another round of tougher sanctions on Poland, including the dreaded declaration of debt default. At Thatcher's request, Haig rerouted his return trip from the Middle East and Geneva to stop in London. She gave the exhausted secretary of state an earful. On his flight home over the Atlantic, Haig cabled Reagan:

> [Thatcher] raised two concerns with unusual vehemence. The extraterritorial reach of the sanctions we have already imposed and rumors she has heard of consideration by us of additional extreme measures including possibility we might call Poland into default

on its debts. She pointed out that . . . the cost of the sanctions imposed thus far are greater to Europe than to the US.[15]

Thatcher reiterated these points in a long letter she wrote to Reagan as soon as Haig departed. "We must not allow the Soviet crisis in Poland to bring about a crisis in the Western alliance which would suit only Soviet purposes," she warned. She closed with an appeal for perspective. "The crisis in Poland looks like being a prolonged one. We risk losing the prize if we act hastily or out of step."[16]

Thatcher's warnings resonated with Reagan. He explained to his diary the next night, "Our choice—to go it alone with harsher steps against Poland and risk split in the alliance or meet with E[uropean] alliance on things we can do together. The latter is my choice. The plain truth is we can't—alone—hurt the Soviets that much."[17] None of this caused him to change his fundamental course of trying to push aggressive policies on Poland without getting too far out in front of the allies. To do so he was willing to play the long game. As Clark recalled, Reagan believed "that if Poland started to unravel, the whole Soviet Empire would come down."[18]

Meanwhile, a group of Polish college students who formed a human rights organization smuggled a letter to Reagan via the US consulate in Kraków. "We have been deeply moved by . . . your words of support for the Polish nation fighting for man's basic right to freedom and dignity," wrote the students, and they thanked Reagan "for solidarity with us, for your condemnation of the disgraceful action of the regime in Poland." Touched by this appeal, Reagan told Clark he wanted to keep a copy of it in his office.[19] Such appeals would have influence far beyond Poland. The letter reminded Reagan of the multiple audiences for his orations. His listeners included not just American citizens and foreign governments but ordinary people, and extraordinary dissidents, around the world. It was an insight he would remember in crafting many of his future speeches.

III

Poland was not Reagan's only preoccupation in the new year. He also faced a contentious decision on arms sales to Taiwan, simmering tensions with Israel as the Levant threatened to erupt in more violence, and growing challenges in Central America.

The question Reagan faced on Taiwan was deceptively simple: Should the United States sell it an advanced fighter jet known as the FX? Yet whatever Reagan decided about Taiwan would not stay in Taiwan. It would affect America's relations with China, its posture in Asia, and even the strategic stakes in the Cold War. One of Reagan's briefing memos reminded him, "The Polish situation makes US-PRC relations a matter of additional concern and sensitivity," while West German chancellor Schmidt worried to Reagan about "reverse ping-pong" in the US-China relationship. By this, Schmidt meant that the Taiwan question was pushing the United States and China apart, in contrast to how the visits of table tennis teams had brought the two nations together in "Ping-Pong diplomacy" in 1971, anticipating Nixon's historic visit the next year.[20]

For Reagan, achieving the right balance would prove tantamount to walking a tightrope as one side (China) kept shaking the pole, while the supporters of the other side (Taiwan) in Congress hurled cantaloupes at the tightrope artist. Even worse, before Reagan could balance between China and Taiwan, he needed to bridge the divide within his own administration, which was growing almost as wide as the Taiwan Strait itself. Haig had continued trying to maneuver Reagan into a more pro-Beijing posture, while the NSC staff, led primarily by NSAs Allen and Clark along with Jim Lilley, continued to resist. As Lilley pointed out to Reagan, for Haig, "resolving" the Taiwan issue meant capitulating to Beijing's demands. And those demands kept escalating. In October 1981, Beijing had pocketed Haig's concession that future US arms sales to Taiwan would be reduced in "quality and quantity." Then Foreign Minister Huang Hua insisted that the United States declare a future date by which its arms sales to Taiwan would end altogether. A few weeks later Huang met with Reagan in the White House Cabinet Room and upped the ante again. Speaking on behalf of Deng Xiaoping, Huang intoned that America must end all arms sales to Taiwan, period.[21]

Lilley wrote afterward, "Deng believes that if he makes the cost high enough, a pragmatic US President will accommodate the Chinese." No doubt with Haig in mind, Lilley continued, "The Chinese believe they have a strong constituency in the US Government, in the press, among academics who will support the strategic relationship with Peking at the expense of Taiwan."[22] That same month Reagan appointed Lilley the director of the American Institute in Taiwan, the de facto US ambassador. Under the convoluted terms negotiated by the Carter administration for America's diplomatic recognition of the People's Republic of China, the United States could maintain an "unofficial" presence in Taiwan that was elaborately circum-scribed. In the bemused Lilley's description, "We were officially consultants under contract to the State Department working in an unofficial capacity at a nonembassy to advance America's interests in Taiwan." Diplomatic con-tortions aside, Lilley arrived in Taipei with something more important than an ambassadorial title. He had the backing of the commander in chief. Be-fore his departure, Reagan invited Lilley and his family into the Oval Of-fice for photos and a farewell greeting. The president pulled Lilley aside and reminded the emissary of Reagan's strong personal commitment to Taiwan.[23]

Meanwhile, in his first week on the job, Clark helped engineer a sur-prising consensus in two NSC meetings to sell Taiwan less-advanced fighter jets, the F-5E and F-104. A conflicted Reagan approved this compromise. He resented the constant pressure from elite opinion and his own State Depart-ment to jettison Taipei for Beijing. Yet he knew that China was a more po-tent strategic partner against the Soviet Union. As Foreign Minister Huang had reminded Weinberger, Chinese forces "pin[ned] down" one million Red Army troops on the Sino-Soviet border, detaining those Soviet forces far away from Western Europe.[24] Though it pleased no one, Reagan's decision mitigated the worst outcomes and bandaged the China-Taiwan issue for the time being.

Until Haig tore off the bandage the next month. The secretary of state suggested publicly that the United States would keep its arms sales to Tai-wan below the levels of Carter's final year in office, which had been mini-mal. In Taipei, Lilley received an earful of anger and confusion from Taiwan officials, forcing him to ask the White House for clarification. In response, the State Department composed a pro forma statement that reiterated America's commitments to the Taiwan Relations Act, and Reagan added a handwritten note: "We keep our promises to Taiwan—period."[25] Reagan complained to his diary, "[Haig] wants to make concessions which in my view betray our pledge to Taiwan. . . . I'm convinced the Chinese will re-spect us more if we politely tell them we have an obligation to the people [of] Taiwan and no one is going to keep us from meeting it."[26] Reagan wor-ried that Haig's approach turned the United States into a supplicant seeking China's permission rather than a superpower acting in its own interests and keeping faith with its allies. Yet Reagan bore some blame for Haig's conces-sions. The president's earlier inattention to the details and refusal to corral his own team had given Beijing an opening to exploit.

IV

Reagan had taken office intending to focus his national security energies on the Cold War. But the Middle East refused to be ignored and kept pulling him back in. Whether it was Libyan assassination plots against Reagan and his senior team, Israel's tensions with Syria and the PLO over Lebanon, the high-maintenance Saudis, the troubled implementation of the Camp David Accords and Sinai disengagement, the Iran-Iraq War, or other crises, not a month went by without some new—or ancient—Middle East issue demanding presidential attention.

Part of the problem Reagan inherited was a fractured regional security order. In previous decades, the United States had relied on its "two pillars" strategy of supporting Saudi Arabia and Iran as joint partners to deter the Soviets and preserve stability in the region, but Iran's 1979 revolution had torn down one pillar. As Reagan said to the Egyptian defense minister in a March meeting on Iran's regional mischief, "I sure miss the Shah."[27] Reagan looked in part to Egypt, but even more to Israel to take over Iran's previous role as regional security partner. Amid the acute tensions with Israel throughout 1981, the Reagan administration still elevated the US-Israel relationship to a formal defense partnership. The United States–Israel Memorandum of Understanding (MOU) deepened military cooperation between the two nations, including expanded support for procurement and sales of advanced weapons systems, and deeper consultation on defense issues in the region. State Department official Dennis Ross helped craft the MOU; he later described its significance as "for the first time put[ting] the relationship with Israel on a basis not just of shared values but of shared interests as well."[28] For Israel, the benefits included a solidified partnership with a global superpower and, Begin hoped, greater freedom to act in the region without worrying that any controversies would rupture its relationship with the United States.

Begin immediately put those shared interests to the test. Two weeks after finalizing the agreement, the prime minister announced that Israel would apply its law to the Golan Heights. It was a technical matter that landed in the Middle East and Washington, DC, like a nuclear blast. Captured by Israel from Syria fourteen years earlier during the Six-Day War, the Golan Heights remained under Israeli military control, but this was disputed by Syria and unresolved by the United Nations. Coming so soon after the MOU, Begin's announcement amounted to a poke in the eye to the Arab states and a slap in the face to Reagan. The furious president suspended implementation of the defense agreement. US ambassador to Israel Samuel Lewis called on Begin, recovering at home from a broken hip, to deliver Reagan's message. The bedridden Israeli castigated Lewis and the United States for seventy-five minutes, complaining, "Do you think Israel is a vassal state of the United States? Are we just another 'banana republic'?"

Begin's anger was not just for show. Immediately after blowtorching Lewis, he chaired a cabinet meeting in which he announced his support for Defense Minister Ariel Sharon's plan to invade Lebanon. Fed up with the PLO's use of southern Lebanon as a safe haven from which to launch attacks on Israel, Begin and Sharon intended to eradicate Yasser Arafat and his terrorist organization once and for all. They also hoped to push back Syria's foothold in Lebanon.[29] As the White House monitored Israel's preparations to invade Lebanon, Reagan noted to his diary, "We are trying to persuade them they must not move unless there is a provocation of such a nature— the world will recognize Israel's right to retaliate. Right now Israel has lost a lot of world sympathy."[30]

V

Al Haig continued to seethe. Disdained by his administration colleagues and increasingly disregarded by Reagan, the secretary of state vented his frustrations to Clark in a tense West Wing meeting. Clark followed up with a terse note:

Al:

Today you expressed several points that concern me:

1. the President "lacks trust and confidence" in you
2. the President has "backed away from his commitment to the PRC"
3. the President has "made a grave mistake on his MX decision"
4. the President has failed to follow your advice on Salvador

Al, if you truly believe all the above, we have a problem. Bill[31]

Clark found such confrontations with Haig especially distasteful because in his prior role as Haig's deputy, Clark had learned the craft of foreign policy under him. Now they were peers in rank, and it pained the protégé to see his erstwhile mentor self-destructing in slow motion.

One of Haig's many gripes concerned Central America, which continued to bedevil the White House. The previous November, Reagan had deepened American involvement in the region when he authorized, in his words, "a plan of covert actions etc. to block the Cuban aid to Nicaragua and El Salvador."[32] At the NSC meeting where he approved these operations, Reagan voiced his misgivings: "What worries me most is this. If the people won't support the leader and the cause then there will be failure. It is clear the press would like to accuse us of getting into another Vietnam. How can we solve this problem with Congress and the public opinions being what they are? . . . How do we deal with the image in Latin America of the Yankee colossus?"[33] Now, as 1982 unfolded, many of those concerns came to pass.

Despite Reagan's reservations, other hemispheric leaders implored him to staunch communist advances. In a White House meeting, Venezuelan president Luis Herrera Campíns warned that El Salvador "has become a neuralgic point for world Communism and Communist forces have set a victory in Salvador as a point of honor for them," and "the defeat of Communism in Salvador will have worldwide significance."[34] A few months later Reagan welcomed President Luis Alberto Monge of Costa Rica to the Oval Office. Monge reported that he and other Latin American leaders saw their region "caught in pincers, with economic crisis on the one hand, and Marxist-Leninist-sponsored subversion on the other."[35]

Reagan's strategic goals in Central America were clear: Halt the spread of communism, curtail Soviet and Cuban influence, and promote democratic governments with market economies. Much harder was how to achieve those goals. The lack of good partners posed the most acute challenge. The El Salvador government was divided, plagued with ineptitude, and pocked with war criminals. The contras in Nicaragua suffered similar maladies as a beleaguered rebel force that controlled little territory. The military government in Guatemala, confronting a Marxist insurgency, became so barbaric in slaughtering its own people that the Reagan administration maintained only token support.

Statecraft often means choosing from options that range from bad to dreadful. Such is what confronted Reagan in Central America. To do nothing meant ceding the region to the Soviets and Cubans, who continued to pour money, matériel, training, and personnel into Nicaragua and El Salvador while promoting brutal oppression. Reagan at times exaggerated the fear of communism swamping the region, but it was a real prospect that reflected Moscow's and Havana's ambitions.

Persuading the American people, and Congress, to back his policies was another matter. Well-publicized atrocities by United States–supported proxy forces eroded public support. The traumas of Vietnam loomed; some American opponents of Reagan's policy put on their cars a bumper sticker reading, "El Salvador is Spanish for Vietnam."[36] A February *Newsweek* poll found that 74 percent of Americans believed El Salvador "could turn into a situation like Vietnam" and 54 percent believed the United States should have no involvement in El Salvador. Luminaries of the anti–Vietnam War movement, such as Reverend William Sloane Coffin, Father Daniel Berrigan, and Chicago Seven member David Dellinger, reincarnated themselves as activists against US involvement in El Salvador—and perversely urged support for the communist rebels instead.[37]

Faced with this growing opposition, Reagan needed to try to win over public opinion. He decided to give a speech laying out a positive vision for the region, his continuing dream of a "hemisphere of liberty." Two weeks later, he appeared before the Organization of American States and announced the Caribbean Basin Initiative. In a nod to the burdens of history, Reagan said, "At times we have behaved arrogantly and impatiently toward our neighbors," and "Our very size may have made it seem that we were exercising a kind of paternalism." Yet he proclaimed, "In the commitment to freedom and independence, the peoples of this hemisphere are one . . . we are all Americans." He then proposed three economic initiatives: lowering tariff barriers to imports of regional goods, an increase of $350 million in US aid to Central American countries, and a package to increase investment in the region.[38] *Time* magazine, not prone to cheerleading for Reagan, applauded his speech as "thoughtful and moderate."[39]

Reagan's positive economic message took a hit three weeks later when *The Washington Post* ran a story by Bob Woodward (of Watergate fame) revealing the covert action finding that Reagan had signed in November providing $19 million for a five-hundred-member opposition force in Nicaragua.[40] The money appropriated was small in sum but large in meaning. It marked the birth of Reagan's support for the contras, the expansion of the fight in Central America—and the seeds of what would become his administration's biggest scandal.

Senate Intelligence Committee chairman Barry Goldwater, who had been briefed on the program, confirmed "everything in the *Post* story was true."[41] The original finding focused the contra efforts on stopping the Sandinistas from shipping arms across Honduras to the FMLN rebels in El Salvador. Within a few months, under Duane "Dewey" Clarridge, the buccaneering new head of the CIA's Latin American Division, the contra force ballooned to eleven hundred members and began operating out of Costa Rica as well, on Nicaragua's southern border.

One thing on which the Reagan administration and its fiercest critics agreed was that the United States should not send combat troops to Nicaragua or El Salvador. The White House, under congressional pressure, capped the number of American military advisors deployed in El Salvador at a paltry fifty-five. Despite the Vietnam comparisons that Reagan's critics invoked, American involvement in El Salvador was of a different nature altogether. Rather than doing the fighting itself, the United States helped its friends do the fighting.

The White House also helped its friends do the voting. As part of his strategy to promote democracy as an alternative to communism, Reagan urged El Salvador to hold a national election. Duarte agreed to do so in March. The White House hoped that a successful election would solidify Duarte's legitimacy, discredit the FMLN, and marginalize the militant right wing. On March 28, over 80 percent of eligible Salvadorans went to the polls and delivered the first two goals, but not the third. Duarte's Christian Democrats won the most assembly seats and 40 percent of the vote. The overwhelming voter turnout, which the Catholic Church had urged but the FMLN had threatened to block, revealed the guerillas to be antidemocratic and lacking in popular support. However, a coalition of rightist parties, led by the Nationalist Republican Alliance (ARENA), captured a majority of the vote. This coalition tried to install the vicious Roberto d'Aubuisson as president. The State Department and CIA maneuvered behind the scenes with centrist Salvadoran leaders to block d'Aubuisson, including threatening to terminate US economic aid. A month later the assembly reached a compromise that selected Álvaro Magaña as president.[42] However, d'Aubuisson received the consolation prize of heading the assembly, and ARENA ensured that death squad violence would continue.

In elections, the conduct of the losers matters even more than the conduct of the winners. Duarte agreed to step down and turn the presidency over to Magaña, setting an important precedent for Salvadoran democracy.

US senator Nancy Landon Kassebaum led a congressional delegation to observe the elections. Afterward they visited the White House and, in Reagan's words, "told the most inspiring stories about the people standing in line 10 to 12 hours in order to vote." Frustrated at the American media's critical coverage of his El Salvador policies, Reagan also noted, "I liked it best when they said the people chanted at the press (our press) 'Tell the Truth.'"[43]

The Salvadoran election's unexpected impact landed in the Oval Office. It furthered Reagan's growing realization that right-wing authoritarians often made bad partners, and encouraged his belief in promoting democracy and human rights with friend and foe alike.

VI

Bill Clark knew that the White House could not keep reacting to each emergency as it erupted. The challenges were relentless. The first few weeks of the job alone had deluged his inbox with different crises with Poland, Israel, Lebanon, Syria, Cuba, China, Taiwan, El Salvador, and Nicaragua. Not to mention the perpetual tensions with the allies, and the threat of nuclear apocalypse from the Soviet Union that loomed every day at the White House and every night at home when he collapsed into bed. The Reagan administration needed a blueprint for what it wanted to do in the world, a road map to guide its ways, means, and strategic end goals. When Clark accepted the job, he had insisted on the authority for the NSC to conduct strategy studies involving every department and agency.[44] The unassuming Clark made no pretense of being a grand strategist. But he worked for one. In the words of Yale historian John Lewis Gaddis, Reagan was "his own chief strategist."[45] Clark planned to take Reagan's strategic vision and turn it into presidential directives that would ensure each department and agency understood what to do in specific policy areas and how its work fit into the overall strategy.

The process of producing these directives mattered almost as much as the final text. The NSC staff would draft a National Security Study Directive (NSSD) to be issued by Reagan ordering the study and setting out the terms of reference. Clark and his NSC staff would then convene officials from the Defense Department, State Department, intelligence community, and economic policy departments and agencies for a series of discussions and working groups, culminating in a draft report. Clark would present the draft to Reagan for his input before returning it to the interagency team for further edits. Reagan would then convene an NSC meeting where he and his cabinet principals would debate and resolve any remaining issues. Reagan would approve the final version, known as a National Security Decision Directive (NSDD), and distribute it to senior interagency officials as a presidential statement of US policy.

During Clark's twenty-two months in the job, the NSC would issue seventy-two NSDDs. The two most consequential would be NSDD-32, "US National Security Strategy," and NSDD-75, the strategy toward the Soviet Union. The Reagan NSC developed NSDD-32 and NSDD-75 simultaneously, though on separate tracks. At Clark's direction, Tom Reed took charge of NSDD-32, while Senior Director for Soviet Affairs Richard Pipes (on leave from Harvard, where he was an eminent scholar of Russian history) led the drafting of NSDD-75.

To start the process, Reed met with Reagan to seek the "commander's intent." In the Oval Office, Reagan brought up a favorite book that he and Reed had read years earlier. Written in 1952 by Whittaker Chambers, *Witness* tells of the author's life as an American communist spying for the KGB in the 1930s, before losing faith in communism, embracing Christianity, and eventually exposing the ring of his fellow American communist spies, including senior State Department official Alger Hiss. It is a searching book, eloquent and melancholic, a formative text in the canon of American conservatism and the Cold War. Reed recalls,

> We're . . . talking about the Cold War and why we need to end it and how, [and Reagan] recited key words from Whittaker Chambers' letter to his children in *Witness*. And he was really focused on the lines about why did Chambers quit being a Communist and why his friends quit being Communists. And his friend put the word that's in Chambers' book, because they heard the screams. And Reagan and I recited to each other that Communism has wonderful ideals, but to make it work you need terror, and that leads to the screams of people in the prisons, political prisoners on the trains headed off into Siberia.[46]

This recounting revealed why Reagan so loathed communism. For Reagan the "screams" showed more than just the moral bankruptcy of the Soviet system. They also unveiled its weakness. A system dependent on tormenting its people did not enjoy their devotion. Dictators that kept seven

Siberian Pentecostals detained in an embassy basement for four years feared their own citizens. Reagan believed that offering American support to the Soviet people would help them bring down the system that oppressed them. He had mused back in 1976, "We could have an unexpected ally if citizen Ivan is becoming discontented enough to start talking back."[47]

Reed then asked the president what he envisioned as the "end goal" for the Cold War itself. Reagan repeated to Reed what he had told Allen several years earlier: "We win, they lose."[48] With that presidential mandate, over the next four months, Clark and Reed led an intense process that convened dozens of interagency meetings with scores of officials, produced thousands of pages of draft studies, and formed consensus positions as well as identified issues needing presidential decisions. Every week, Clark and Reed would give Reagan a progress update, request his review of draft chapters, and seek his guidance on disputed questions. They would then take Reagan's input back to their working groups and continue the process.

Reagan oversaw the crafting of NSDD-32 mindful of his place in Cold War history. He had read the original Cold War strategy issued by President Truman in 1950, NSC-68, when it had been declassified in 1975. At the time Reagan had written a radio script that summarized NSC-68's main points: "Russia is determined to impose its authority over the world; . . . we are the principle obstacle they would have to overcome, and if their expansionism wasn't checked or contained soon *no possible combination of the remaining free nations could assemble sufficient strength to stop them short of their goal.*"[49] Yet while Truman and NSC-68 had emphasized the Soviet Union's strength, now, as president, Reagan focused as well on the Soviet Union's weakness. Over three decades into the Cold War and over six decades since the Bolshevik Revolution, Reagan believed that the Soviet system was breathing its last. The ideological bankruptcy of Marxism-Leninism, the economic sclerosis of a command economy, the unsustainable military spending, the fragility of the Soviet empire, and the moral rot of totalitarianism had all combined to make the Soviet Union a decrepit colossus. Reagan built his strategy to exploit these many vulnerabilities.

While Reagan's national security team believed the Soviet regime was brittle, they differed on just how brittle it was. A key debate concerned how much of the Soviet economy was devoted to military spending. In one NSC meeting, several senior officials expressed the conventional view that the USSR was spending about 16 percent of its GDP on the military—a large share but potentially sustainable. Reagan asked, "Why can't we just push the Soviets over, backwards?" From one of the back seats, the chairman of the National Intelligence Council, Henry Rowen, broke in: "Yes, you can, Mr. President. Actually, they're spending about fifty percent of the GDP on defense and they're going broke."[50]

Knowing the precise amounts was impossible then and remains so now. The USSR's expenditures on its military and the overall size of its economy were notoriously hard to calculate, for reasons including Kremlin secrecy, the challenge of converting Soviet rubles into hard currency like US dollars, Soviet manipulation of economic production statistics, and the opacity and paranoia that afflict a totalitarian society. Kremlin internal distrust was so endemic that the Soviet leaders themselves may not have known their own economic and defense figures. But whatever the exact number, Reagan's insight remained: The USSR was cannibalizing itself to fund its military on a much larger scale than most Western estimates, including most CIA assessments. By comparison, the United States spent roughly 5 percent of its GDP on defense during the Reagan years. The Soviet levels, whether three or five or ten times that, could not be sustained.[51]

It is important to recall just how heterodox Reagan's views were at the time. Most elite opinion saw the Soviet Union as stable and resilient. The famed former Kennedy White House advisor Arthur Schlesinger Jr. visited Moscow in 1982 and declared, "Those in the US who think the Soviet Union is on the verge of economic and social collapse, ready with one small push to go over the brink, are . . . only kidding themselves."[52] Two of America's leading scholars on the Soviet Union, Columbia University's Seweryn Bialer and Smith College's Joan Afferica, wrote a sneering analysis of Reagan's Soviet policies in *Foreign Affairs* at the end of 1982. Reflecting widespread academic opinion, they denounced Reagan's "shrill, incendiary rhetoric," dismissed his belief in the Kremlin's vulnerability as "profoundly erroneous," and condemned his strategy as doomed to fail: "Even were the West able to impose extreme economic choices on the Soviet Union, the system would not crumble, the political structures would not disintegrate, the economy would not go bankrupt, the elites and leadership would not lose their will and power to rule internally and to aspire externally to the status of a global power."[53]

Such were the expert tides Reagan swam against.

In the midst of debating the Soviet economy's vulnerabilities, Reagan participated in an exercise that showed his own country's vulnerability to a Soviet nuclear attack. Reed's special projects included a highly classified effort to overhaul America's nuclear command-and-control system to ensure that the American government could survive a Soviet first strike. As part of this, Reed engineered the "Ivy League" continuity of government exercise, a three-day simulation of what the top echelons of the United States government would do and where they would go—and who would survive to lead the country—in a thermonuclear war. It involved over one thousand US officials, helicopter evacuations to top secret underground bunkers such as Raven Rock in Pennsylvania and Mount Weather in Virginia's Blue Ridge Mountains, and displays in the White House Situation Room using red dots to show Soviet launches and nuclear detonations on a map of the United States.

Reagan became the first president since Eisenhower to participate in such an exercise. He probably wished he had not done so. Sitting in the Situation Room on the morning of Monday, March 1, Reagan watched the screen showing the first Soviet missiles incinerating Washington, DC; the dead included the US president. As Reed recalls, "While he looked on in stunned disbelief . . . for the next half hour more red dots wiped out the survivors and filled in the few holes in the sea of red. In less than an hour President Reagan had seen the United States of America disappear."[54]

Ivy League terrified Reagan. It also stiffened his resolve to end the threat of nuclear weapons. On April 16, he convened a National Security Council meeting in the Cabinet Room to discuss the latest draft of NSDD-32. Reed opened with a bracing statement of how the world looked to the White House in early 1982:

We are at a time of greatest danger to our national security since World War II. It is highly likely that, over the course of this decade, fundamental changes in East-West relations will occur . . . we call for active measures to counter Soviet expansionism, to encourage the liberalizing tendencies in the Soviet bloc, and to force the Soviet Union to bear the brunt of its economic mismanagement. *The bottom line is we are helping encourage the dissolution of the Soviet empire.*

This was not stray bluster; Reed voiced the strategic principles that he and Reagan shared. His prediction of profound change within the decade would also prove prophetic.[55]

This blend of fear and hope contained the paradox that confronted the

White House. The Soviet Union was militarily more powerful than ever, yet its economy and political system were weaker than ever. The Kremlin had the military force to threaten the very existence of the United States—and the insecurity and vulnerability that might make it want to do so. This made the Kremlin uniquely dangerous—a bear, yes, but a wounded and angry one. Reagan's strategy sought to overmatch the Soviet Union's strengths while exploiting its weaknesses. Even in this meeting dedicated to planning the demise of the Soviet empire, Reagan reiterated his desire to negotiate with the Kremlin: "A vigorous defense build-up will also be a great help at arms control talks. The Soviets do not believe that they can keep up with us."

The discussion turned to several themes in the strategy. It highlighted the Reagan administration's predicament with allies. In Reed's words, "Allies are indispensable; we cannot go it alone. But we need more help from the Allies than in the past, and this makes us more vulnerable to Allied behavior." Weinberger focused on another aspect of the Reagan military expansion: providing American weapons and training to other countries. "Security assistance is the cheapest and best way of defending the United States," he contended. In a later meeting, Casey echoed Weinberger. The CIA director highlighted eleven countries "threatened by Soviet actions and the actions of Soviet proxies" and said, "The threatened countries are not capable of defending themselves. . . . They need light weapons and communications gear. We must remember that a little gets a lot done when it comes to security assistance."[56]

These points, codified in NSDD-32, captured other purposes of Reagan's military buildup. He also intended his defense expansion to strengthen America's alliances with security assistance and to induce US allies to spend more on their own defense by assuring them that the United States was a reliable partner. Finally, anticipating what would become the Reagan Doctrine, the military buildup would help strengthen America's allies and partner forces to fight Soviet proxies—and in the case of Afghanistan, the Red Army itself.

NSDD-32 emphasized the importance of allies perhaps more than any other national strategy document in American presidential history. In this it reflected Reagan's own convictions. The United States had built its alliance system in the decade after World War II. Reagan's strategy, by putting allies in a central role, represented the maturation of the system. Reagan would rely on allies more than any previous Cold War president, would devote more time and effort to them, and would demand more of them. He believed that allies helped compensate for America's weaknesses and multiplied America's strengths, and provided the United States an asymmetric advantage over the Soviets—whose only "allies" were its coerced satellites in the Warsaw Pact. "Given the loss of US strategic superiority and the overwhelming growth of Soviet conventional forces capabilities, together with the increased political and economic strength of the industrial democracies . . . [there was] no other alternative" to deepening cooperation with allies, NSDD-32 declared. NSDD-32 also singled out NATO members and Japan in particular as needing to increase their military spending—and their willingness to deploy their forces.

NSDD-32 turned Reagan's convictions into official US policy. No longer just trying to contain Soviet expansion as past administrations had done, with NSDD-32 Reagan announced the new strategic goal of "forcing the USSR to bear the brunt of its economic shortcomings, and to encourage long-term liberalizing and nationalist tendencies within the Soviet Union."[57] Pipes elaborated on one theme of NSDD-32 in his own work on Reagan's Soviet strategy: "We turn Soviet energies from expansion to internal reform."[58] In the fashion of the Harvard professor that he was, Pipes crafted a paper explaining the "theoretical rationale" of Reagan's Soviet policy that ran over seventy pages. In the fashion of the US government, the interagency bureaucracy resisted his paper, with the State Department finding it too "ideological" and then-NSA Allen rejecting it as too long. Though verbose and controversial, Pipes's paper contained the pillars of Reagan's emerging Soviet policy. Pipes understood Reagan's strategic convictions well and combined those with his own exhaustive knowledge of Russian history and Marxist-Leninist ideology. Pipes summarized the main propositions as:

- Communism is inherently expansionist: its expansionism will subside only when the system either collapses or, at the very least, is thoroughly reformed.
- The Stalinist model on which Soviet Communism, the linchpin of worldwide Communism, is based, confronts at present a profound crisis caused by persistent economic failures and difficulties brought about by overexpansion.
- The successors of Brezhnev and his Stalinist associates are likely in time to split into "conservative" and "reformist" factions, the latter of which will press for modest economic and political democratization.

- It is in the interest of the United States to promote the reformist tendencies in the USSR by a *double-pronged* strategy: *encouraging pro-reform forces inside the USSR* and *raising for the Soviet Union the costs of its imperialism.*

Reagan read a "shorter" (though at twenty-five pages, not short) version of the Pipes paper and wrote on it, "Very sound." It mirrored his own thinking.[59]

The last proposition is of profound importance. From his presidency's outset, Reagan had hoped the Kremlin would choose a path of reform. But hope is not a policy. Reagan's Cold War strategy entailed pressuring the Soviet system on every front—military, economic, ideological, diplomatic—not only to exploit its weaknesses, but to produce a reformist leader. A leader whom Reagan could negotiate with, and partner with, to end Soviet imperialism and end the Cold War. He would spend the rest of his first term looking for such a Soviet reformer. In his second term, he would find one.

For all of NSDD-32's ambitions, it was a global strategy setting America's overall posture in the world yet did not detail just how the United States would confront the Kremlin. Seeing that need, Pipes proposed to Clark and Reagan that the White House produce a new NSDD dedicated to Soviet policy. Part of the need, Pipes contended, came from confused allies. He cited a recent plea from a senior French official: "You are asking us to go with you on a journey but you are not telling us where you are heading and where we will end up." Pipes sharpened this question in his terms of reference for the study: Did the United States seek to "stabilize" or "destabilize" the Soviet bloc?[60]

Clark agreed and put Pipes in charge of the process. The irascible professor did not win many friends at Foggy Bottom with his controversial views and abrasive manner. He told Clark, "The basic difference between State and myself is philosophical. State believes that we should be content with an attempt to influence Soviet *behavior*. . . . Following what I sense to be the President's belief, I, by contrast, argue that behavior is the consequence of the *system* and that our policies . . . aim at modifying the system as prerequisite of changed behavior."[61]

Once the State Department realized that Reagan and Clark wanted the NSDD produced, they began cooperating on the process.[62] The NSC finalized the strategy just as Pipes's government sojourn ended and he returned to Harvard. Reagan signed and issued it in January 1983. NSDD-75 declared, "US policy toward the Soviet Union will consist of three elements: external resistance to Soviet imperialism; internal pressure on the USSR to weaken the sources of Soviet imperialism; and negotiations to eliminate, on the basis of strict reciprocity, outstanding disagreements." The "internal pressure" on the Kremlin included encouraging a reformist leader to emerge by promoting "the process of change in the Soviet Union toward a more pluralistic political and economic system." It then laid out a comprehensive set of military, economic, diplomatic, and political lines of action, to be undertaken in concert with the allies.[63]

Reagan's strategy of targeting the Soviet system itself may seem obvious in hindsight. But at the time it was risky, controversial, ridiculed by many, seen as revolutionary by others. No previous president had tried it. Each preceding US president had sought in different ways to contain Soviet expansion from without. None until Reagan had sought to erode the Kremlin from within.[64]

Reagan's strategy answered many questions, but it also raised hard new ones. Could you negotiate with the Soviets while also trying to defeat them? Did he seek to win the Cold War or to end it?[65] This puzzle lies at the core of Reagan's strategy. His own team and closest advisors would answer it in different ways over the next six years, each emphasizing different elements of pressure or diplomacy, often with much acrimony. Reagan always believed in both pressure and negotiations, together in service of the larger strategic goal. In short, he resolved these strategic paradoxes by embracing them. He believed the USSR was both strong and weak. He believed that, partly from US pressure, a Kremlin reformer could emerge and be encouraged to take actions that would dissolve the Soviet empire. By pushing to end Kremlin control of Eastern Europe and the Soviet republics, the United States would win the Cold War *and* end it.

Reagan's fascination with World War II helps explain this puzzle. In America's last fight against totalitarianism, President Franklin Roosevelt had demanded the *unconditional surrender* of both Nazi Germany and imperial Japan. In the context of total war, against implacable dictators such as Adolf Hitler and Hideki Tojo, Roosevelt's insistence on unconditional surrender made strategic sense. Such a demand did not fit the Cold War. Much as Reagan looked to Roosevelt and World War II as a model for how the free world should confront dictatorships in thrall to evil ideologies, in the case of the Cold War and the Soviet Union, calling for "unconditional surrender" from Moscow would have been delusional and foolhardy—especially since Reagan remained desperate to prevent the Cold War from turning hot and ending in nuclear apocalypse. Instead, combining pressure with diplomacy, working against the Soviet system while working with Soviet leaders, Reagan sought to bring the Kremlin to a *negotiated surrender.*

The terms of a negotiated surrender would mean tough demands of Moscow: Lift the Iron Curtain and end Soviet control of its satellite states in Eastern Europe. Quit inflicting communist revolutions on the Third World. Stop tyrannizing its own people. Cease threatening the United States with nuclear destruction. Reagan would pursue these terms through a combination of coercion and persuasion, improvisation and adaptation, engagement and cost imposition, shifting back and forth from hard line to soft touch—all tactical adjustments in the service of a strategic vision.

VII

Though Reagan's strategy prioritized cooperation with allies, the allies did not always reciprocate—nor did the United States always make an easy partner. Transatlantic tensions soon boiled anew over the White House's economic warfare against the Soviet Union—which threatened much collateral damage in Western Europe. The Siberian pipeline once again lay at the center of the dispute. When he imposed the Poland sanctions at the end of 1981, Reagan had suspended a decision on "extraterritoriality," specifically whether the prohibition on American companies' providing pipeline equipment also applied to European subsidiaries and licensees—many of whom held the bulk of the pipeline construction contracts. If the United States wanted to block the pipeline, its sanctions would only scratch American companies while seriously wounding European companies.

It was time to talk. In March, Reagan dispatched a delegation to Europe led by Under Secretary of State James Buckley (a former US senator, and brother of the conservative icon William F. Buckley Jr.). They hoped to negotiate a common position with West Germany, France, Italy, and the United Kingdom on increasing economic pressure on the Soviet Union. Reagan instructed the delegation to downplay the pipeline dispute and instead try to curtail European economic engagement with the Kremlin going forward. Specifically, he said the Buckley mission should focus on "ensuring that no additional medium- or long-term official or officially-guaranteed credits will be granted to the Soviet Union" and "discourage their firms from entering new prime contracts with the Soviet Union."[66]

The credits in particular rankled the Reagan team. The White House believed that Western European governments providing generous loans at below-market rates to Moscow only strengthened the Kremlin and freed up more rubles to spend on the Red Army. As Roger Robinson, the NSC's senior director for international economic affairs, recalls, "In 1982 the Soviets had an empire stretching from Hanoi to Havana, but their hard currency revenue totaled only about $32 billion a year. . . . They were spending about $16 billion more annually than they were making, with the funding gap— the USSR's life support—being financed by Western governments and banks."[67]

Still plagued by recession and high unemployment, Western European countries feared a double risk from curtailing credits to the Soviet Union. Over the past decade their banks had lent about $80 billion to Soviet bloc countries, and ending credits now could jeopardize repayment of those loans. Additionally, in 1982 alone, European credit guarantees would finance $4 billion in steel and machine tool exports to the Soviet bloc—and the thousands of Western European jobs that helped produce those goods.[68]

Buckley was blunt in describing his trip's goal: "To show the idiocy of subsidizing the Soviet arms buildup through credits." He was equally blunt on the result: "We failed." The French and Germans in particular refused to curtail their business with Moscow. Buckley reported that the Europeans admitted that their policies over the past decade (encouraged by détente) of "extending huge amounts of credits to Eastern European countries and the Soviet Union were fundamentally misguided." But having dug themselves into that hole, their economies could not now afford the cost of digging out.

Hearing Buckley's report, Reagan veered from frustration to resignation. Ever the optimist, he ended the meeting on a hopeful note:

Let me raise a question from the world of fantasy. . . . [The Soviets] are still in Afghanistan, they are still supplying Cuba, they are still preventing Jews and Christians from emigrating. Is there a right time for the West to cooperate? The Europeans do not understand. Can we foresee a time when [the Soviets] are in a desperate plight, when the military deprives the people of food, and we might be able to say to them: "Have you learned your lesson? If you rejoin the civilized world we will help you bring wonderful things to your people. But you must get out of Afghanistan, deal realistically in Geneva. No one wants to attack you."[69]

Reagan's ruminations captured a fundamental difference between him and the Western European leaders. The Europeans looked at the Soviet Union as it was and asked how they had to deal with it. Reagan envisioned a Soviet Union transformed and asked how he could bring it about—to the point where Soviet communism gave way to a better system.

VIII

America's allies in Asia also needed attention. Reagan continued his practice of meeting with almost every senior Japanese official who came to Washington, DC—a level of presidential attention that no other country received. In January he met with the minister of international trade and industry, in February with the special trade representative, and in March with the foreign minister. Each time, Reagan reaffirmed the value he placed on the United States–Japan relationship and pressed the same two points: Japan needed to increase its defense spending and open its markets to American goods.

Repeating these points without much headway tested Reagan's patience. Much as he treasured Japan as an ally, it also caused some of his biggest political headaches. As his meeting with Special Trade Representative Masumi Esaki ended, the normally decorous president told a bizarre story about a man trying to sell a stubborn horse, who clubbed the poor animal between the eyes with a two-by-four plank because "that's how you get his attention." This provoked much consternation and confusion among the Japanese delegation and media, who puzzled over what the unfortunate equine represented in Reagan's parable: Was it Congress, or the media, or the bureaucracy, or . . . ? At a reception that evening, it fell to an NSC staff member to sheepishly inform a Japanese reporter that the president saw Japan as the horse.[70]

In the spring Reagan dispatched both Bush and Weinberger on separate trips across the Pacific to tend to relations with Japan and South Korea. Upon arriving in Tokyo, Weinberger pressed Prime Minister Suzuki to implement his commitment of the previous May to extend Japan's defensive perimeter out one thousand nautical miles. The Soviet navy's Pacific Fleet constituted its largest force at 720 ships—more than the entire United States Navy. America needed Japan's help to contain this growing Soviet presence. In a speech at the Japan Press Center, Weinberger appealed to Japan to "complement" the American military buildup and forward deployments: "If these Japanese and American elements are supplemented by US Sea Control and Projection forces in the Southwest Pacific and Indian Oceans, the vital arteries of free commerce in the Pacific would be strengthened." The Japanese leadership responded to such appeals because Reagan and Weinberger were not just engaged in yen-counting on military spending but rather building a genuine partnership. As Michael Green points out, "The Reagan administration sought specifically to elevate Japan to NATO levels of decision making and to agree on a division of roles and missions and integration of defense strategies with Japan."[71]

From Tokyo, Weinberger flew to Seoul. During a ceremonial luncheon for the secretary, President Chun Doo-Hwan described South Korea as an "unsinkable aircraft carrier" available to its US ally for power projection in northeast Asia. Chun's bluster masked a deeper vulnerability. A few months earlier, US ambassador Dixie Walker had sent a cable to Washington, DC, describing Chun's dictatorial rule and crackdowns on the many political and religious dissidents calling for democracy. Walker concluded that while Chun might hold power for a time, "eventually the incongruity between the economically and socially modern society which is emerging and the traditional form of government, could threaten serious instability."[72] Geographically the South Korean landmass may have been an aircraft carrier, but its political ferment threatened to sink its repressive government.

The shadow of a recent event four thousand miles away clouded the view that Reagan and his senior team had of Korea. The Iranian Revolution three years earlier had cautioned the White House on how popular discontent against an American-backed authoritarian regime could turn into a radical revolution. Yet there were many dissimilarities between Iran and South Korea. Soon the Reagan administration realized that the main question was not who the Korean dissidents were protesting against but what they were advocating for. Unlike the Islamic revolutionaries in Iran, the Korean activists were pushing for democratic self-governance.

A month after Weinberger's visit, Bush arrived in Seoul determined to send quiet but strong signals of support for freedom in South Korea. NSC staff member Don Gregg accompanied Bush on the trip. A CIA officer with almost three decades of experience in Asia, Gregg's service had included chief of station in Seoul in the 1970s. He maintained close ties with his Korean intelligence counterparts, who cautioned him that President Chun had become even more repressive than his brutal predecessor Park Chung Hee.[73] Bush defied Chun's objections and spoke to the National Assembly on "the importance of political diversity as a source of strength, not weakness." His appearance before the legislature highlighted its role as a potential check on Chun's dictatorial authority. More provocatively, Bush hosted a breakfast meeting at the US embassy with a group of South Korean political dissidents, including Protestant and Catholic church leaders critical of the Chun dictatorship—and of American support for Chun. Even *The New York Times* ran an editorial applauding Bush's "important signal" for human rights.[74]

Bush's stop in Singapore highlighted the importance that smaller Asian nations placed on America's alliance with Tokyo—and the suspicion with which they regarded Beijing. In their meeting, Singapore's iconic prime minister Lee Kuan Yew admonished Bush, "It's all right for you to be the sheriff of the Pacific. But just be sure that your posse is Japanese, not Chinese."[75] Lee's message was clear: Other Asian countries regarded Japan as a more trustworthy regional power than China.

Ironically, while Singapore urged America to favor Japan over China, Japan urged America to repair its relations with China. In March, China and Japan had held confidential talks. The Chinese delegation appealed to Japan to impress upon the Americans that while China would show some flexibility on Taiwan arms sales, Beijing would downgrade ties if the United States did not compromise. A worried Prime Minister Suzuki wrote to Reagan of his "concern [that United States–China relations might] suffer from a setback" over Taiwan. Then Ambassador Mansfield wrote to Reagan, "The Japanese are more anxious than we have ever seen them over the possibility that US-PRC relations may deteriorate. Over the last decade, for the first time this century, Japan, China, and the US have developed mutually good relations which . . . have given the Japanese a greater sense of security."[76]

Bush's original itinerary did not include China, but while the vice president was in New Zealand for the last stop on his trip, with Deng Xiaoping's agreement Reagan asked Bush to circle back to Beijing before returning to Washington, DC. The vice president arrived in China bearing a letter from Reagan to Deng expressing confidence "that a means can be found to resolve current differences and deepen our bilateral and strategic cooperation." This followed two other letters Reagan had sent to Deng and Chinese premier Zhao Ziyang three weeks earlier. The PRC whipsawed Bush with a "good cop, bad cop" routine. Foreign Minister Huang Hua berated the vice president for two hours, complaining about US arms sales to Taiwan. Yet the next morning Deng charmed Bush with a congenial discussion over two and a half hours that did not resolve the issues but at least improved the tone.[77]

Bush's visit to Beijing, and the State Department's subsequent release of Reagan's three letters, caused a furor in Taipei. Taiwan's vice foreign minister lambasted Lilley, complaining, "Why three letters? Why the need to grovel?" Lilley himself had been blindsided by the release of Reagan's three epistles. Seeking to repair the United States–Taiwan relationship and recover his own standing with his host government, Lilley requested that Reagan send a private message that he could deliver to President Chiang Ching-kuo. Reagan did, enabling Lilley to provide Chiang with Reagan's specific reassurances that the United States would not set a date for ending arms sales and would not pressure Taiwan to negotiate with Beijing.[78]

Reagan and Bush's reassurances had calmed Beijing, Taipei, and Tokyo for the moment. But much of Asia, and much of Reagan's own government, still watched and wondered how he would resolve the Taiwan issue.

IX

In the predawn dark of April 2, one thousand Argentine troops floated in ships offshore from a barren, windswept pair of islands in the South Atlantic. Around four thirty A.M. their first landing craft motored through the waves to the island coast and unloaded a unit of navy commandos for an amphibious assault. Other landing craft and helicopters soon deployed the rest of the invasion force. A small garrison of British Royal Marines fired only token shots of resistance, killing a few Argentine servicemen. Within a few hours, the Argentine forces took control of the territory and raised Argentina's flag over the capitol building.[79]

The islands, known to Argentina as the Malvinas and to the United Kingdom as the Falklands, soon provoked a crisis on three continents and confronted Reagan with the problem of what to do when two friends go to war with each other over disputed islands of which most of the world has never heard. Argentine military dictator General Leopoldo Galtieri had taken power a few months earlier. He had inherited a populace resentful of the junta's repression and an economy falling apart from mismanagement and a ballooning debt crisis. To bolster his domestic standing, unite his divided country, and distract his critics, he decided to start a war.

Reagan had tried to stop the invasion. Knowing of America's close ties with Argentina, Thatcher had appealed to Reagan to urge Galtieri against the use of force. Reagan phoned Galtieri on the evening of April 1 and spoke for fifty minutes. An NSC staffer who took notes on the call wrote that Galtieri "sounds like a thug" with "broken mafioso-type English" and lamented, "None of [Reagan's] eloquent delivery cuts any ice with the junta leader." Galtieri's intransigence was in part liquid fueled. Clark recalled that the dictator "had obviously been drinking, and this habit may have influenced his actions."[80] Indeed, the invasion force was already in motion.

Bereft of natural resources and military significance, inhabited by more sheep than people, the Falklands were hardly a strategic asset. The coming battle resembled, in the acid description of Peruvian writer Mario Vargas Llosa, "two bald men arguing over a comb." *Washington Post* correspondent Don Oberdorfer called it "a cross between a 19th century melodrama and a Peter Sellers farce." But now that comedy was turning into a crisis.[81] Thatcher had already mobilized a naval armada to sail to the South Atlantic and retake the islands—just as Reagan had warned Galtieri she would do.

The Falklands mattered because Galtieri and Thatcher decided they mattered—and because the Argentine and British publics decided they mattered. At that point the issues became, in the words of British scholar Sir Lawrence Freedman, "international reputation and the principles of nonaggression, self-determination, and loyalty among allies."[82]

Loyalty to *which* allies was the question that divided the Reagan White House. On the surface it may have seemed an easy choice to favor the British. The United Kingdom was a NATO treaty ally, a nuclear power, a democracy, and America's most important European partner. Thatcher was Reagan's closest friend among world leaders, and her nation was acting in self-defense. Argentina, on the other hand, was a dictatorship, led by a buffoon, with a bankrupt economy and a third-rate military. It was also the aggressor.

But that was not the whole story. Reagan valued Argentina as a hemispheric partner against communism. The junta resisted Argentina's being taken over by communists and quietly supported the anti-Sandinista forces in Nicaragua with training, matériel, and manpower. The White House also inherited the Monroe Doctrine's resistance to European meddling in the

Western Hemisphere, and America's historic aversion to European colonialism. In this light, Britain's efforts to retain its imperial territories eight thousand miles from London did not garner much American sympathy. Further, Reagan knew that all of Central and South America would watch to see what he would do, and he did not want to incite further resentments in the region.

As the British task force sailed south on its three-week journey to recapture the Falklands, the Reagan administration tried to figure out where it stood. Jeane Kirkpatrick emerged as a forceful voice for Buenos Aires. Her affinity for Argentina dated to graduate school, when she wrote her dissertation on Argentine politics, and now her strategic priorities focused on countering communism in the Western Hemisphere and keeping the Argentine junta in power.[83] Haig, torn between his transatlantic loyalties and hemispheric proclivities, favored a posture of neutrality. He also favored placing himself in the limelight as the chief mediator brokering a diplomatic resolution to the crisis. Weinberger, a lifelong Anglophile, firmly supported the British. As did Inman, who substituted for the traveling Casey at multiple National Security Planning Group (NSPG) and NSC meetings on the Falklands crisis.[84]

Reagan at first seemed to support Haig and Kirkpatrick. He dispatched the secretary of state on several rounds of shuttle diplomacy between Buenos Aires and London; told the media, "We're friends of both sides"; and did not speak to Thatcher for the first week of the crisis.[85] Meanwhile, Weinberger and Inman began at once providing the British with sensitive intelligence and made the American military base on Ascension Island (in the mid-Atlantic, roughly halfway between the UK and the Falklands) available as a resupply point for the British armada. Weinberger and Inman did this surreptitiously, under existing intelligence and military cooperation agreements between the United States and UK. Weinberger also personally granted every British request for weapons, including state-of-the-art Sidewinder heat-seeking missiles, which British Harrier jets would use to decimate the Argentine Air Force.[86]

Reagan had a jocular line to describe the confusion and infighting in his White House: "In my administration, sometimes our right hand doesn't know what our far-right hand is doing."[87] It was worse in the Falklands crisis: The two hands actively worked against each other. While Weinberger engineered the munitions resupply and intelligence-sharing operation to support the British, Haig pursued a diplomatic deal that in effect favored

Argentina. Once *The Washington Post* disclosed Weinberger's secret efforts, a distressed Haig sought to recapture the posture of neutrality and pressed in vain to end American intelligence and logistics support for the British armada. This further incensed Thatcher.[88]

By the end of April, Haig's negotiations had failed. He had presented several versions of sweetheart terms to the Argentines that he described as "a camouflaged transfer of sovereignty" which in time would have given the Falklands to Argentina, but the vainglorious Galtieri rejected each deal because it did not let him claim immediate victory. Reagan began feeling more pressure to side with London. The US Senate overwhelmingly approved a resolution demanding Argentina's withdrawal from the Falklands.[89] On April 30, Reagan decided to shift the American position from neutrality to explicit support for the British. He did this with some ambivalence and still hoped for a "future role for the US as a mediator."[90]

Reagan's pivot toward the UK did not pacify Thatcher. Tensions between the two leaders only worsened. Thatcher took umbrage at Reagan's continued efforts to dissuade her from the use of force, especially as the crisis turned into a war. On May 2, the British submarine *Conqueror* torpedoed the Argentine cruiser *General Belgrano,* sinking it and killing 321 Argentine sailors. Two days later an Argentine fighter jet sank the British destroyer HMS *Sheffield* with an antiship missile. Most of the crew survived, although 20 perished with the ship. A CIA assessment described this turn in the conflict as going from the "comic opera stage into the grim business of killing."[91]

Reagan still hoped that a settlement could end further bloodshed. On May 13, at Kirkpatrick's behest, he phoned Thatcher to urge her to "hold off military action" and cooperate with United Nations peace negotiations. An irked Thatcher responded, "[The Argentines] attacked our ships yesterday, so they're not holding off on military action." Reagan pleaded that America's support for the UK was exacting "a price on what we've been trying to accomplish in creating a better relationship with the Latin states, the South American countries," and warned Thatcher that the Argentines were succeeding in "creating a kind of David-Goliath image now, in which you're Goliath." Thatcher retorted, "I can hardly be Goliath when I have to go eight thousand miles." She also reminded Reagan that the Falkland residents themselves wanted to "live under democracy" and not Argentine dictatorship, and admonished the president, "You wouldn't like to put any of your people . . . under a military junta. . . . I can't put mine under that either."[92] Nonetheless, Thatcher relented a bit and agreed to submit a peace proposal that offered significant concessions to Buenos Aires. Which the junta summarily rejected. Thatcher then ordered the invasion to retake the islands. British troops landed ashore on May 21. While they slowly advanced in fierce fighting, Reagan called Thatcher again on May 31. This time he tried to persuade the prime minister to impose a cease-fire and allow an international "contact group" of peacekeeping troops to superintend the islands. Thatcher would have none of it. Growing livid at Reagan, she protested, "I didn't lose some of my finest ships and some of my finest lives, to leave quietly under a cease fire without the Argentines withdrawing." Each time Reagan tried to interject, Thatcher browbeat him with fusillades of indignation and argument, leaving the president to stammer, "Margaret, I . . . well . . . yes, well . . ."[93]

Thatcher soon quieted her fury, especially knowing that she would be meeting with Reagan in four days at the Versailles G7 summit and hosting him in London right afterward. She also took heart from the steady advance of British troops, who completed their conquest and raised the Union Jack triumphantly over the islands on June 14.

Argentina's surrender and humiliation led to Galtieri and his junta compatriots' being toppled from power by their own citizens. To Reagan's pleasant surprise, what came next in Buenos Aires was not a revolutionary leftist government but a transition to democracy. The aftermath of the Falklands War may have provided another lesson for the Reagan administration, or at least a nudge to question its support of right-wing autocrats. Military dictatorships could be aggressive abroad and brittle at home, and less stable as allies than democracies. Reagan would spell out this insight in London that same month—with Thatcher sitting before him.

CHAPTER 5

—✦—

SUMMER OF FREEDOM

I

As Air Force One taxied down the runway at Andrews Air Force Base on the morning of June 2, 1982, Reagan looked forward to his first trip outside North America as president. He would need every measure of his congenital optimism. He left a United States still mired in recession, where only 45 percent of Americans approved of his job performance, Congress continued feuding with him over his budget, and his administration was rife with rivalry and leaks.

What awaited him across the Atlantic was no better.

He would soon be landing in a Europe that regarded him with wariness at best, if not outright hostility. Most European publics worried that, as *Time* magazine put it, "the leadership of the Western alliance is in the uncertain hands of a trigger-happy cowboy." Hundreds of thousands of protestors would demonstrate for nuclear disarmament (and against Reagan) during his stops in Bonn and London.[1]

To till the soil for his Europe sojourn, three weeks earlier Reagan had traveled to Eureka College in Illinois. The president returned to his alma mater as the commencement speaker on the fiftieth anniversary of his graduation. His trip hearkened back to the worst his country had endured in his lifetime. Remembering his alma mater during the Great Depression, when "we [students] were totally without funds, our families destitute victims," Reagan alluded to the isolationism of the era when the United States turned away from its fellow democracies and failed to confront the threats of Nazi

Germany and imperial Japan. He compared the present moment to the 1930s as "a crucial juncture in history."

This time he resolved that America would not retreat to its 1930s cave, but instead would bear the mantle of global leadership that history had thrust upon it. Mindful of his upcoming transatlantic journey, he declared, "Our own nation's fate is directly linked to that of our sister democracies in Western Europe." He then came to the core of his speech: a proposal for new negotiations with the Soviets, the Strategic Arms Reduction Talks (START). Its goal would be "to reduce significantly the most destabilizing systems, the ballistic missiles, the number of warheads they carry, and their overall destructive potential."[2] It was a shrewd maneuver. At once he signaled to skeptical Europeans that he was serious about arms control, seized the initiative again in proposing genuine cuts (just as he had several months earlier in calling for scrapping all intermediate-range nuclear missiles), and targeted the Soviet advantage in ballistic missiles. The Soviet ICBM and SLBM force exceeded the American arsenal by almost 50 percent, so the START reductions would fall disproportionately on the Kremlin's arsenal.[3]

Reagan paired his arms control outreach to the Kremlin with a separate outreach to the Kremlin's biggest critics. The next day, back at the White House, he hosted a luncheon with eight Soviet dissidents exiled from their home country. The idea for the lunch had originated with the most famous Soviet dissident, who ultimately refused to attend: Aleksandr Solzhenitsyn. Over the past year, numerous members of Congress had urged Reagan to invite the Nobel laureate in literature to the White House. NSC staffer Richard Pipes, however, had counseled against the invitation, primarily because of his concern over Solzhenitsyn's "often anti-Western and anti-democratic" attitudes.[4]

A combination of media leaks, White House staff ineptitude in mishandling the invitation, and Solzhenitsyn's vanity led him to decline the meeting with Reagan. Solzhenitsyn then made his refusal public, causing further embarrassment for the White House, though the imperious writer did offer to host Reagan at his farm in Vermont "when you will no longer . . . be president and will have full freedom of action."[5] Meanwhile, the White House had invited eight other dissidents, who embraced the chance to dine with the president. They represented diverse religious commitments, including Orthodox, Baptist, Jewish, and Muslim, and ethnicities including Ukrainian, Tatar, and Russian. What united them was a shared opposition to Soviet tyranny and the common experience of suffering. Pipes noted, "All of them have given proof of their courage and most have spent long years in Soviet prisons and psychiatric wards."[6]

The dissidents seldom missed a chance to take a stand on principle. Walking into the White House dining room, the Baptist pastor Georgi Vins saw wine on the table and proclaimed his refusal to eat at a meal where alcohol would be served. The staff removed the libations, Vins's abstemious conscience was salved, and Reagan welcomed his guests by remembering the many prisoners of conscience still incarcerated in the Soviet Union.[7] The president told of his hope for the prisoners: "Someday, they may wake up knowing there will be no more persecution, no more pain, just because they love the truth, strive for a greater good, and believe in God."[8]

American media coverage of the meeting focused on the snub by Solzhenitsyn. The more important audience was in the Kremlin, however. Moscow Radio fulminated, "Perhaps Reagan finds pleasure in meeting people who, for American dollars, slander their former homeland."[9] Knowing that his support for human rights struck a nerve in Moscow, the meeting fueled Reagan's determination to make it central to his Cold War strategy.

II

On June 2, Air Force One landed just before midnight in Paris, where Reagan enjoyed two days of ceremonial meals and bilateral meetings. From there he journeyed to Versailles for the G7 summit. The palace evoked memories of its eponymous treaty at the end of World War I, which had deepened splits in the Western alliance and failed to resolve the European security issues that would lead two decades later to World War II. For Reagan, this summit would also disappoint.

The leaders of the other G7 countries—Canada, France, Italy, Japan, the United Kingdom, and West Germany—all arrived at Versailles bearing frustrations with Reagan, and with each other. All of their nations save Japan were suffering recessions, which they continued to blame on America's high interest rates. All of their nations, including Japan, felt threatened by Reagan's economic warfare on the Soviet Union, especially the potential pipeline sanctions and crackdown on credit to Warsaw Pact states. All of them save Thatcher worried that Reagan's confrontational posture toward the Kremlin put their countries at greater risk of nuclear war.

While Reagan stood alone in his opposition to the Siberian pipeline, in his effort to curtail export credits to the Soviet bloc, he enjoyed vocal support from Thatcher and quiet support from Japanese prime minister Suzuki and Italian prime minister Giovanni Spadolini. Mitterrand, Schmidt, and Trudeau all resisted. Much wrangling ensued over whether the summit's communiqué would commit to "limiting" export credits. The final compromise called for "commercial prudence in limiting export credits." Its ambiguity confused everyone and satisfied no one.[10] One problem was most European leaders did not share Reagan's belief in Moscow's economic vulnerability. French foreign minister Claude Cheysson channeled European skepticism when he told a reporter, "Don't forget that we are dealing with a totalitarian state. They are in a position to impose, I would say, anything on their people. So we can't bring the Soviets to kneel because they don't have the money. I think we may be out of breath before they are."[11]

As the Versailles gathering concluded, a new war erupted in the Middle East when Israeli tanks rolled across the border into Lebanon. Three days earlier in London, Palestinian terrorists had attempted to assassinate the Israeli ambassador to the United Kingdom, leaving him crippled for life from gunshot wounds. This prompted Prime Minister Begin and Defense Minister Ariel Sharon, after months of rumors and warnings, to follow through on their threats to invade southern Lebanon and eradicate the PLO forces that targeted Israel with rockets and other terrorist attacks. The war would lead to one of the biggest crises of Reagan's presidency, but for now Haig and Clark kept him updated on Lebanon while he focused on the remainder of his Europe trip.

From France, Reagan journeyed to Rome for his first meeting with Pope John Paul II. Sitting beneath Perugino's masterpiece painting *Resurrection*, the president and the Pope bonded over their shared survival of assassinations the previous year and their common sense of divine destiny. In their public remarks together, Reagan expressed solidarity with "the martyred nation of Poland—[the Pope's] own homeland," and reaffirmed his commitment "to help bring a real, lasting peace throughout the world." The Pope in turn prayed, "May America step forward in this crucial moment in history to consolidate her rightful place at the service of world peace."[12]

Turning words into deeds, on this visit Reagan and John Paul II also solidified a unique intelligence-sharing arrangement. Casey, Clark, and Special Envoy Vernon Walters would continue providing sensitive intelligence to the Vatican on Poland and other countries of interest from America's signals intercepts and human sources. The Vatican, in turn, would provide the Reagan administration with confidential insights from its own intelligence sources—its singular network of clergy and laity behind the Iron Curtain.[13] Not since Harry Truman collaborated with Pius XII against communism in Europe at the outset of the Cold War had an American president and a bishop of Rome forged such a partnership.

Once in the UK, an exuberant Reagan described his London visit as "a fairy tale experience."[14] Perhaps it was taking a horseback ride with the queen, or the black-tie and white-tie dinners she hosted for him on two consecutive nights at Windsor Castle, or perhaps it was the warm welcome from his friend Thatcher, eager to put aside their rift over the Falklands.

Or perhaps it was delivering the greatest speech of his presidency.

Few expected it, certainly not the British government. In a confidential cable to Thatcher previewing the visit, her US ambassador Nicholas Henderson described Reagan's weakening political standing at home: "Public confidence in his policies is eroding as month after month goes by without the promised economic turnaround." Reagan, he said, would be "walking another tightrope" as he navigated his unpopularity on both sides of the Atlantic and would use his Westminster speech, Henderson predicted, "to project himself as . . . a peacemaker and not a warmonger."[15]

Reagan devoted considerable time to crafting the address in the weeks before his trip. The White House speechwriter who produced the initial drafts, Tony Dolan, was a devout Catholic, gifted stylist, and fierce Cold Warrior who, like Reagan, saw the conflict as a battle between good and evil. A Yale man, before joining the White House Dolan had been mentored by William F. Buckley Jr., won a Pulitzer Prize as a reporter, and recorded an album as a conservative folk singer (yes, such a creature did exist, for one album at least). This rhetorical pugilist was quick to draw his pen against any perceived threats or ideological deviations, especially among the rest of the White House staff. He shared the view expressed by one of his colleagues: "The speechwriters were a band of brothers. . . . Our enemies were the Soviets, liberal Democrats, and the White House senior staff, although, come to think of it, I just listed them in the wrong order."[16]

Reagan worked closely with Dolan on the speech. Dolan based his initial draft on his research into Reagan's critiques of communism over the past twenty years. Pipes provided some of the intellectual framework in the analysis of Marxism-Leninism and exposure of the Soviet system's vulnerabilities.

Columnist George Will provided input as well. Clark helped shepherd the process. But all knew that it was Reagan's speech. Two scholars who analyzed every draft found Reagan personally wrote at least 60 percent of the final speech text.[17] Biographer Steven Hayward notes how Reagan placed his remarks in the historical stream originating four decades earlier: "There is an obvious symmetry to this speech: its debt to Churchill's 1946 'Iron Curtain' speech at Westminster College in Missouri . . . is evident. Churchill's speech might be said to have been the official announcement of the beginning of the Cold War. Here, at another location named Westminster, Reagan began to lay out an understanding of how it might end."[18] As Robert Zoellick points out, Reagan "would be speaking to three audiences—Americans, Europeans, and Soviets—who ranged from worried and doubtful to hostile."[19] Though Reagan knew he needed to hearten Americans, reassure Europeans, and scare the Soviets, he also resolved to give a speech that transcended the precarious political moment. Reagan would describe his ambition to bring the Soviet Union to a negotiated surrender—and the world he envisioned in its wake.

That vision entailed recognizing some emerging trends. Historian Hal Brands observes that by the late 1970s, the world was "undergoing an epochal political awakening in which demands for democracy and individual rights were ever-harder to ignore." Crucially, this trend was enveloping nations ruled by both communist regimes and right-wing autocrats.[20] It was not apparent to many at the time, however. Just three years earlier, the Iranian and Nicaraguan revolutions had seemed to embody a very different wave of the future when they brought radical authoritarians to power, not democracies. Reagan, though fearful of any more Iranian- or Nicaraguan-style revolutions, saw the democratic wave forming earlier than most leaders and sought to encourage it. The task of statecraft is to spot trends when they begin to simmer, embrace the good and mitigate the bad, and develop policies that steer these trends in the right direction.[21]

Stepping to the podium, Reagan felt history's weight from the surrounding statues and paintings displaying great moments in the British past. Now before him sat a legion of British leaders, polite but skeptical, casting a doubtful gaze at this American who just weeks earlier had been an uncertain ally in the Falklands and who they feared put their island at risk of nuclear annihilation.

Then Reagan's voice began to fill the hall. Beginning with a tribute to democracy's English roots, he traced its present progress. "Democracy is proving itself to be a not-at-all-fragile flower. From Stettin on the Baltic to Varna on the Black Sea, the regimes planted by totalitarianism have had more than 30 years to establish their legitimacy. But none—not one regime—has yet been able to risk free elections. Regimes planted by bayonets do not take root." In a prophetic note, he decried the Berlin Wall as "that dreadful gray gash across the city . . . in its third decade" and praised Poland as "being magnificently unreconciled to oppression."

But it was the ideology behind that wall that most exercised Reagan. He conscripted communism's philosopher king for his own prediction:

> In an ironic sense Karl Marx was right. We are witnessing today a great revolutionary crisis, a crisis where the demands of the economic order are conflicting directly with those of the political order. But the crisis is happening not in the free, non-Marxist West, but in the home of Marxist-Leninism, the Soviet Union. It is the Soviet Union that runs against the tide of history by denying human freedom and human dignity to its citizens.

From philosophy, Reagan turned to the reality of life behind the Iron Curtain and how the people behind it voted with their feet:

> One of the simple but overwhelming facts of our time is this: Of all the millions of refugees we've seen in the modern world, their flight is always away from, not toward the Communist world. Today on the NATO line, our military forces face east to prevent a possible invasion. On the other side of the line, the Soviet forces also face east to prevent their people from leaving.

Then he pointed to hope. "Beyond the troublespots lies a deeper, more positive pattern. Around the world today, the democratic revolution is gathering new strength." Yet, "If the rest of this century is to witness the gradual growth of freedom and democratic ideals, we must take actions to assist the campaign for democracy . . . [fostering] the infrastructure of democracy, the system . . . which allows a people to choose their own way to develop their own culture, to reconcile their own differences through peaceful means. This is not cultural imperialism, it is providing the means for genuine self-determination and protection for diversity."

He concluded with a prophecy, and a way to hasten it: "What I am

describing now is a plan and a hope for the long term—the march of freedom and democracy which will leave Marxism-Leninism on the ash-heap of
history."[22]

In hindsight it may look obvious; at the time, Reagan's imprecation
seemed radical, even delusional. His speech generated predictable gnashing
of teeth among the Soviet leadership, which accused him of being "the
gravedigger of the ideas of détente.'" *The Washington Post*'s Moscow correspondent wrote that the Kremlin "no longer sees Reagan as a simplistic
cowboy shooting from the hip with ill-conceived statements. Instead, he
now appears to be seen here as a far more dangerous politician out to inflict
maximum damage on the Soviets."[23]

The British and American media reaction was not as negative as the Kremlin's, but not much less so. A column in *The Guardian* disdained the speech
as "unmemorable" and sardonically invoked Lincoln's Gettysburg Address
to predict that "the world will little note nor long remember what we say
here." NBC News anchor Tom Brokaw dismissed the speech as "naïve."[24] A
New York Times editorial complained that "characteristically, [Reagan] failed
to point the way from here to there, or to give the Russians a plausible range
of policy choices. Soviet society has always endured great hardship to resist
and arm against danger. If it responds at all, it will not be to alien appeals
for democratic capitalism."[25] Even some conservatives piled on. Columnist
Robert Novak lambasted Reagan's trip as "an abysmal failure" and lacerated
the policies in the speech as "in some ways . . . softer than Jimmy Carter."[26]

These disparate critics shared a common concern about the unreal-
ism of Reagan's proposals to reduce nuclear arms and expand democracy.
Whether from the Left or the Right, they shared a default commitment to
the Cold War status quo of two nuclear-armed blocs and a stagnant number
of democracies. Reagan challenged these verities and envisioned a new world
beyond the Cold War. Commenting on Reagan's foresight, Dolan believed it
came in part from his background as an actor. "He sees that life is a drama
in which a lot of scenes still haven't been written," Dolan once told two of his
fellow speechwriters. "Reagan can imagine a post-Soviet world—he can really *see* it. So he tossed out the old script to write a new script of his own."[27]
He believed that showing communism's manifest failures would make the
case for democracy and free markets better than any abstract arguments.
And he now knew that his call for political, economic, and religious freedom
must apply universally—including to America's authoritarian allies. Reagan
did not just seek to defend the free world; he sought to enlarge it.

The day after his speech, Reagan met with Thatcher again. The UK's unfolding victory in the Falklands put her in a magnanimous mood. Absolving the president of her earlier frustrations, she thanked Reagan "for his magnificent support of the United Kingdom's position" and regretted that she "could not specify in public the extent of that support." They closed by previewing their trip to Bonn that afternoon for the NATO summit. Speaking of the need to support Eastern European countries trying to extricate themselves from the Kremlin's vise grip, Reagan told Thatcher, "Our aim should be to teach the emerging countries the nuts and bolts of democracy."[28] That comment contained the seeds of what would become a major initiative birthed by his Westminster speech: the National Endowment for Democracy.

In Bonn, some three hundred thousand demonstrators greeted Reagan with a massive protest against his defense policies. The protestors had more in common with the president than they realized. Speaking to the Bundestag, Reagan reflected, "The nuclear threat is a terrible beast. Perhaps the banner carried in one of the nuclear demonstrations here in Germany said it best. The sign read 'I am afraid.'" Continuing, he spoke to the protestors: "To those who march for peace, my heart is with you. I would be at the head of your parade if I believed marching alone could bring about a more secure world." Instead, in the words of The Washington Post, "Reagan won his loudest applause when he pledged his support to the Western alliance that was forged in the aftermath of Germany's defeat in World War II."[29]

He made his final stop in West Berlin. Visiting Checkpoint Charlie and the Berlin Wall, Reagan saw again the physical symbols of communism's depredations and a divided continent. Asked by a reporter what he thought of the wall, Reagan replied, "It's as ugly as the idea behind it." When another asked if he thought Berlin would ever be reunited, the president responded, "Yes." He spoke at Tempelhof Airport to thousands of US troops stationed in West Berlin—a visceral reminder of America's security commitment to the lonely city surrounded by communist East Germany.[30]

III

Though his Europe trip somewhat reassured the allies, it made no progress on the pipeline dispute. Back at the White House, Reagan convened an NSC meeting on June 18 to resolve the extraterritoriality question of whether US sanctions would apply to European companies. Clark's briefing memo reminded the president, "Last Sunday commemorated the six-month benchmark of martial law in Poland, where the situation remains basically unchanged if not worse." Cataloging the interagency positions, Clark noted that State and Commerce favored lifting the sanctions, while the Pentagon, CIA, and US Mission to the UN (namely Kirkpatrick) favored extending the sanctions.[31]

Reagan had tipped his hand the day before in a speech to the United Nations General Assembly. He had invoked his favorite predecessor:

> As President Eisenhower once said . . . "We are for peace first, last, and always for very simple reasons." . . . He said to those who challenge the truth of those words, let me point out, at the end of World War II, we were the only undamaged industrial power in the world. Our military supremacy was unquestioned. We had harnessed the atom and had the ability to unleash its destructive force anywhere in the world. In short, we could have achieved world domination, but that was contrary to the character of our people. Instead, we wrote a new chapter in the history of mankind.

Reagan contrasted America's conduct at the end of the war with the Kremlin's, then and since:

> Since World War II, the record of tyranny has included Soviet violation of the Yalta agreements leading to domination of Eastern Europe, symbolized by the Berlin Wall—a grim, gray monument to repression that I visited just a week ago. It includes the takeovers of Czechoslovakia, Hungary, and Afghanistan; and the ruthless repression of the proud people of Poland.[32]

He then detailed four decades of Soviet intransigence on arms control. Reagan was in no mood to compromise.

He carried that resolve into the NSC meeting. Under Secretary of State Larry Eagleburger sat in for the absent Haig, who had stayed in New York to meet with Soviet foreign minister Andrei Gromyko. After hearing his advisors air their conflicting views, Reagan unleashed his frustrations. He recalled how at Versailles he had admonished the allies, "The Soviet Union is more vulnerable than ever, especially economically because of their military outlays and foreign adventures. They are literally starving their people to keep this up." "But I got no support," Reagan complained. The allies stayed quiet or criticized him, while Moscow remained intransigent. "The Soviet Union has given us nothing but words to show that they will abandon the global Marxist state. . . . The time has come for someone to stand on principle. . . . We cannot retain credibility with our Allies who will say that we are all rhetoric and no action." Reagan's conclusion jolted the table. "So unless the Soviet Union takes action and shows us, then they can build their damn pipeline without our help."[33] Still seething that night, the president wrote in his diary: "Cabinet very divided. I ruled we would *not* remove sanctions. There hadn't been the slightest move on the Soviets', part to change their evil ways."[34]

But that was only part of the story. In this same NSC meeting where Reagan threw down the gauntlet, he also offered the Kremlin a quiet off-ramp to save face. "We can use quiet diplomacy," he told the room. "We must not issue an ultimatum which will make it impossible for them to give in." He had Clark remove the language describing Soviet obstinance on Poland from the White House statement announcing the new sanctions. Reagan, worried, said, "The specific references as to what they have not done in Poland means that they cannot give in. . . . If we mention what should be done, we almost foreclose the possibility of it being done."[35] Showing an essential attribute of statecraft—the ability to see through the eyes of your counterparts—Reagan sought to preserve space for negotiations with the Soviets and to give Moscow room to make quiet concessions without appearing to capitulate to American demands. Though Reagan wanted to bring the Soviet Union to a negotiated surrender, he did not seek a public surrender ceremony.

IV

There would be no more NSC meetings for Al Haig. On the Europe trip, he had made a series of vainglorious stumbles that left his days numbered. He whined about not being included on Reagan's helicopter from Heathrow Airport to Windsor Castle, stood at the head of the president's receiving line at 10 Downing Street (moving only when Thatcher told him he was standing in Reagan's spot), and erupted into a shouting match with Clark at Windsor Castle over a UNSC resolution on Lebanon. Clark had told Haig to review the resolution with Reagan first, while Haig insisted on devising the US position without consulting the president. *Washington Post* reporter Lou Cannon witnessed the Clark-Haig kerfuffle and wrote that it "marked the end of any accommodation of the secretary of state."[36]

Now back in Washington, Haig felt outraged anew that Reagan had extended the pipeline sanctions without even consulting him. On June 24, the embittered secretary met with the president and presented a bill of particulars detailing his many grievances and demands. Reagan read the document and the next day told a surprised Haig that he accepted his resignation—even though the secretary had not formally offered it. Reagan had had enough. He went out to the press pool and read a terse statement announcing Haig's departure. Later that day a humiliated Haig wrote and issued his resignation letter, and ascribed his exit to disagreements over policy. Reagan wrote that night in his diary, "Actually the only disagreement was over whether I made policy or the Sec[retary] of State did."[37]

The tragedy of Haig is that it did not need to be so. He was a man of enormous talent, fervent work ethic, singular accomplishment, courage, and grit; his gifts nonetheless kneeled to his ego. His marginalization was not ideological. Moderate figures in the administration, such as Baker and Deaver, found Haig just as insufferable as did conservatives, such as Kirkpatrick, Weinberger, Casey, and Clark. On some issues, like his hard line toward Cuba and his zeal for Israel, Haig arguably stood to the right of Reagan; on others, like his affinity for China and his sympathy toward détente with the Soviets, he was to Reagan's left. Regarding personality, temperament, and chain of command, he was always out of step.

Reagan knew that in Haig he had gotten his most important cabinet choice wrong. This time he would get the choice right. At Reagan's direction, Clark tracked down George Shultz in London, where he was on a business trip. Clark asked Shultz to make haste to the US embassy so that Reagan could talk to him on a secure line.

The president got to the point:

"Al Haig has resigned, and I want you to be my secretary of state."

Shultz clarified, "Mr. President, are you asking me to accept this job now, over the phone?"

Reagan said he was. Shultz replied, "Mr. President, I'm on board."[38]

It was an inspired choice. Shultz was one of the most accomplished men in the annals of American statecraft. A Princeton football player and marine who saw combat for two years in the Pacific theater in World War II, Shultz then earned a doctorate from MIT in economics; became dean of the University of Chicago's business school; served in the Nixon administration as director of the Office of Management and Budget, secretary of labor, and secretary of the Treasury; and then became president of Bechtel, one of the world's largest construction companies. More important, Shultz's strengths complemented Reagan's and compensated for the president's weaknesses. Analytical where Reagan was intuitive, attentive to detail where Reagan saw the big picture, and a skilled manager where Reagan neglected organization, the two could have clashed. Instead they would develop into one of the most effective president–secretary of state tandems in American history, and Shultz would become—in this author's estimation—the greatest secretary of state since Dean Acheson.

Shultz shared Reagan's moral assessment of the Cold War. During his confirmation hearing before the Senate Foreign Relations Committee, liberal California senator Alan Cranston asked Shultz: "Can you tell us what the United States, for its part, has done to contribute to the tension that exists between the United States and the Soviet Union?"

Replied Shultz: "Nothing."[39]

Shultz also shared many other convictions with Reagan, including the vulnerability of the Soviet Union and the need to combine force with diplomacy; the priority of expanding political, religious, and economic freedom; the primacy of allies; and the advantages of open societies in harnessing the emerging globalization trends for good. They also both understood something Haig had failed to grasp: Reagan was president, and the secretary of state served at his behest. Shultz knew that his effectiveness would depend on his closeness to Reagan, so that his foreign counterparts around the world and the State Department officials serving under him all saw him as a surrogate for the president.

Shultz was not without faults. His self-confidence could blur into arrogance, his judgments were not infallible, and since he did not suffer fools gladly, he too often regarded as "fools" any who disagreed with him. But unlike the frenetic Haig, Shultz camouflaged his self-regard with a quiet dignity and congenial warmth. The career diplomats at the State Department quickly embraced their new chieftain.

V

On Friday, July 16, Shultz arrived at the White House to be sworn in. There was no time for champagne toasts; as soon as the ceremony ended, Reagan and his new secretary walked down the cramped stairway to the Situation Room for an NSC meeting on the rift within the transatlantic alliance over the pipeline sanctions. It was just one of the several crises he faced.[40]

Afterward Shultz's motorcade made the short drive back to the State Department. An overflowing inbox greeted him in his seventh-floor suite. Everything was important; few items make it to the secretary of state's desk that are not. Rather, Shultz needed to determine what problems were most urgent and demanded his immediate attention. Lebanon and Taiwan jumped out.

The Middle East had consumed much of Shultz's confirmation hearings before the Senate Foreign Relations Committee. Several senators worried that due to his extensive Bechtel work in Arab countries, Shultz would be hostile to Israel (a concern that would turn out to be groundless). He disputed with Senator John Glenn over sending marines to Lebanon as part of a multinational peacekeeping force. Like Shultz, Glenn was a marine combat veteran of World War II who had flown many missions in the Pacific theater.

To Glenn's query, Shultz answered, "I favor the use of US forces if it can be done properly and safely" to help remove the PLO fighters and preserve a peace settlement. Glenn retorted, "If it can be done safely, we do not need the Marines. And if it cannot be done safely, then we are going to be attending some funerals over in Arlington with Marines coming back in body bags one of these days."[41]

It was a prescient exchange.

The Lebanon crisis had escalated when Israeli troops advanced all the way to the outskirts of Beirut, violating Begin's earlier indications that the IDF would halt its invasion just a few miles over the Israel-Lebanon border. Begin and Defense Minister Ariel Sharon harbored grandiose ambitions to kill Yasser Arafat, destroy the PLO once and for all, and transform Lebanon by installing Israel's ally Maronite Christian Phalangist leader Bashir Gemayel as president. Sharon hid most of these designs from the Israeli cabinet, which had approved only a limited incursion into Lebanon. Reagan and Shultz feared that Sharon's dream might instead destroy Lebanon and set the entire Middle East aflame. As soon as Israeli tanks had breached the border, Reagan dispatched Phil Habib back to the region for yet another effort to forge a cease-fire, if not a peace settlement.[42]

Seeking some creative ideas and regional insights, during his first afternoon in the office, Shultz phoned several colleagues and friends and asked them to join him for a strategy session the next day. Among them was Henry Kissinger, who flew down from New York City. Shultz and Kissinger often disagreed, but Shultz held his predecessor in high regard. Shultz also invited CIA officer Robert Ames to the Saturday meeting. Ames, the CIA's premier Arabist, had served for two decades in various Middle Eastern countries. For over ten years he had maintained a covert back channel with the PLO.[43]

Shultz valued Ames's expertise but distrusted his employer. Three days after the State Department gathering, Ames met again with a PLO representative, which Shultz complained was done "against my instructions but with CIA Director Bill Casey's approval." Moreover, the intelligence that Ames relayed from his PLO liaison turned out to be inaccurate. Wrote Shultz, "I saw then that Bill Casey and the CIA acted independently and provided information on which I could not necessarily rely." It marked the start of Shultz's frictions with Casey and skepticism toward the CIA.[44] Ames largely escaped the secretary's disdain, as Shultz would continue to rely on his insights and involve him in emerging diplomatic initiatives.

The Reagan administration's goals in Lebanon were simple but not easy: Get Israel, Syria, and the PLO out of the country, and hold Lebanon together. Those tasks were hard enough. But from the outset, the White House also sought to use the crisis to advance the stalled Israeli-Palestinian peace process. As Clark wrote to Reagan in a June 14 briefing memo, the United States should exploit its leverage over Israel "by linking our Lebanese peace efforts with major concessions from Begin on the question of autonomy and Israeli policy towards the Palestinians on the West Bank."[45]

Escalating violence in Lebanon eclipsed any notions of Israeli-Palestinian peace and forced Reagan and his team to focus on the fracturing country. In early August, Israeli forces launched an assault on Beirut in hopes of crushing the PLO. Foreign Minister Yitzhak Shamir visited Washington that same week. On August 2, Reagan met with Shamir at the White House and delivered an unvarnished warning. An Israeli invasion of Beirut "would have grievous consequences for US-Israeli relations," the president cautioned, and "the slaughter of innocent civilians must stop."

Shamir played the Soviet card in response. If the United States supported Israel's campaign to remove the PLO, he promised, then the United States would have "the most important position in the region," and it would be "as if the Soviet Union does not exist." Reagan did not buy this ploy. He retorted that "in reality Russia has profited the most" from the Lebanon crisis. The angry president continued, "The television is showing the human results of the use of phosphorous bombs: burned babies. . . . This benefits the Soviet Union."[46] Reagan's mounting fury toward Israel coincided with his growing realization that the Middle East could not be seen only through the lens of the Cold War. But how it should be viewed was a murkier question.

As the Israeli assault escalated, Shultz and his team stayed up all night on August 3 in the State Department's Operations Center, on a constant telephone circuit with Habib in Lebanon, Shamir at his hotel in Washington, and Begin and Sharon in Israel, all in a vain effort to stop Israel's bombardment of Beirut.[47] At seven fifteen A.M. the next morning, a sleepless Shultz rushed over to the White House, where Reagan called an emergency NSC meeting. The meeting went over four hours, with Reagan and others shuttling in and out as they fielded new reports and tried frantically to negotiate a cease-fire. The president alternated between anger at the PLO and anger at Israel. When Kirkpatrick interjected, "The PLO is not a bunch of agrarian reformers. They are international terrorists who are working against US interests and committing acts of violence throughout the world supported by the Soviet Union," Reagan agreed with her and asserted the need to expel the PLO from Lebanon. Then Reagan rewrote a draft letter to Begin and read it to his team. His missive blamed Israel's aggression for the latest impasse and concluded with a threat shorn of the usual diplomatic finesse: "The relationship between our two countries is at stake." Recalling a newspaper photo of an infant injured by Israeli bombing, Reagan ended the meeting in disgust: "I'm getting extremely tired of a war whose symbol has become a burn[ed] baby with no arms."[48]

World War II loomed over Reagan and Begin's exchanges. In one tense phone call, Reagan told Begin that Israel's bombardment was "causing a holocaust in Beirut." This infuriated Begin, whose parents and brother were murdered in the Holocaust. He responded, "Don't teach me about holocausts. I and my people know very well what 'holocaust' means." Soon afterward Begin wrote to Reagan, hinting at Israel's intention to kill Arafat, saying, "I have sent an army to Berlin to wipe out Hitler in the bunker."[49]

The combination of Israeli force, American pressure and diplomacy, and PLO desperation finally led to a deal for the PLO's exit and Israel's restraint. Habib's negotiations had taken an unexpected turn when almost every Arab state refused to accept the PLO fighters, and Habib realized that his challenge was not just to persuade the PLO to leave Lebanon but also to persuade other countries to take them. Arab leaders' braying support for the PLO masked the uncomfortable fact that those same leaders privately regarded Arafat and his cohort as troublemakers unwelcome in their countries. Habib and other US ambassadors twisted enough arms in the region that a reluctant Tunisia agreed to take Arafat and most of his forces, with other PLO members dispersing to South Yemen or Syria.[50] On August 22, the PLO began to leave Lebanon. The day after their departure, the Lebanese parliament elected Christian Phalangist Bashir Gemayel as president, furthering Begin and Sharon's plan to have an Israeli friend running Lebanon. Two days later, Reagan sent eight hundred US marines to Lebanon to join French and Italian troops in a multinational peacekeeping force.[51]

With the PLO out and the marines in Lebanon, Reagan and Shultz decided to use this new leverage to resume their hopes for Arab-Israeli peace. Shultz had developed a peace plan in secrecy with Reagan and just a few close advisors over the past several weeks. Having lost trust in Begin, he did not consult him or any other Israeli officials on the terms. Instead, Ambassador Lewis briefed Begin on the details on August 31, the day before Reagan announced the plan to the world in a major speech.

The Reagan Plan had enough to upset everybody. Its call for Israel to freeze settlements in the West Bank and grant the Palestinians "self-government" in association with Jordan outraged Begin, as did the Americans' blindsiding him with the plan. Its denial of an independent state to the Palestinians and its refusal to press Israel to return to pre-1967 borders angered many Arab leaders. Nonetheless, as Shultz wrote, "President Reagan's new initiative now commanded the high ground. . . . By having an agenda out there, we at least had everyone's attention."[52] The value of that attention was another matter. State Department official Dennis Ross concluded, "The Reagan Plan would gain us nothing with the Arabs, but would not mark the low point in US-Israel relations."[53]

That low point came just a few weeks later.

On September 14, a Syrian intelligence operative planted a bomb in the Phalangist party headquarters that killed President Gemayel and twenty-six others. The next day, the Israeli army seized control of west Beirut, ostensibly to restore order. Two days later, Phalangist militias, fueled by drugs and bloodlust, entered the Sabra and Shatila refugee camps and massacred hundreds, perhaps thousands, of Palestinian refugees, most of them women and children. At Sharon's direction, Israeli forces stood by, giving tacit permission for the Phalangist slaughter.[54]

An outraged Reagan called an emergency NSC meeting on Sunday. He had not imagined that Sharon was capable of such barbarism—nor that Lebanon's fragile progress could crumble so quickly. He told his diary, "I finally told [the NSC] we should go for broke." Reagan had withdrawn the marines two weeks earlier when stability seemed to be restored; now he redeployed them again to join French and Italian troops as part of the Multi-National Force (MNF) peacekeepers. He described his goals: "We are asking the Israelis to leave Beirut. We are asking Arabs to intervene and persuade Syrians to leave Lebanon. . . . In the meantime Lebanon will establish a government and the capability of defending itself. No more half way gestures, clear the whole situation while the M.N.F. is on hand to assure order." Reagan also believed that his team stood unified behind him. "George S[hultz] and Jeane K[irkpatrick] were enthusiastic about the idea and apparently there was no disagreement."[55]

Reagan's optimism would not avail. His administration was in fact divided, with Weinberger and the Joint Chiefs in particular opposed to sending the marines back. After a tense meeting with the military leadership on the Lebanon mission, Clark pointed out to Reagan, "There seems to be a distinct difference between your perspective and that of the JCS on the value of using US military power for specific peacetime roles in the Middle East."[56] Reagan and Shultz believed in the diplomatic and deterrent value of displays of force; Weinberger and the Joint Chiefs focused on the costs and risks. The result was a dangerous muddle. In Shultz's words, Weinberger used "a standard Pentagon tactic: when you don't want to do something, agree to do it—but then with such an impossible set of conditions . . . that the outcome will be to do nothing."[57] These White House divisions produced a compromise with the worst possible elements: deploying the marines with tight operational restrictions, limited resources, and an unclear mission into the midst of a civil war. It also caused tensions with the allies. Weinberger's comment that the marines would be "lightly armed" provoked complaints from the French that the strict American rules of engagement, constrained weapons, and vague mission of "presence" would render them ineffective.[58]

The Middle East confounded all of Reagan's customary values and instincts. In other strategic regions of the world, such as Europe and Asia, he employed some basic principles to guide his policymaking: Stay committed to allies, build rapport with key heads of state, oppose communist inroads, align power and diplomacy, and promote democracy and free markets. None of those verities applied in the Middle East. The United States had a special but complicated relationship with Israel, and no treaty allies in the region. Reagan never built close personal ties with any Middle Eastern leaders. While the Soviets had client states such as Syria and Iraq, there were no communist regimes in the region except destitute South Yemen. Nor were any Arab states receptive to appeals to democracy and free enterprise. Adding to these challenges, Reagan never once set foot in the region as president and never developed an instinctual feel for navigating its politics, as he would in Asia and Europe. When he looked at the Middle East, it appeared as disorienting as a haboob on a moonless night. Feeling unsure and conflicted, he would struggle to resolve the fierce feuds that would divide his national security team and bedevil American policy.

VI

Support for small, isolated nations in hostile regions is a unique feature of American foreign policy. In the midst of the Reagan team's struggles with Israel, they also navigated troubled waters with Taiwan. Many influential members of Congress weighed in with Reagan throughout the summer urging expanded arms sales to the island, while China issued escalating threats if Reagan did not cater to Beijing's demands. During the three-week interregnum between Haig's departure and Shultz's arrival, most of the State Department's Asia hands also pushed for terms favorable to China.

Though Reagan often paid little heed to policy details, on occasion he delved in depth on issues that were personal priorities, such as relations with the Soviet Union. And Taiwan. In early July, the State Department sent Reagan a fourteen-page memo, dense with legal and diplomatic minutiae, proposing a settlement with China on Taiwan arms sales. It reflected the terms Haig had negotiated before getting fired. Reagan read it with care, making marginal notes in every paragraph and rewriting the language in several places. He struck out the sentence committing the United States to the "ultimate objective" of ending arms sales to Taiwan. This was the president's most important edit. Reagan did not trust China's intentions and did not want to leave Taiwan vulnerable in the future. Otherwise, he made clear, the United States would continue providing weapons to Taiwan—no matter Beijing's remonstrances.[59]

Deng Xiaoping tried in vain for a few more weeks to extract further American concessions, until conceding in mid-August that China would sign the agreement, known as the Joint Communiqué or Third Communiqué. It stated that the United States "does not seek to carry out a long-term policy of arms sales to Taiwan" and "intends to reduce gradually its sales of arms to Taiwan, leading over a period of time to a final resolution."[60] Even with the amendments he had made to the communiqué, Reagan still feared that over time Beijing's pressure might abrade American support for Taiwan. It was in part a problem of his own making. Over the previous year Reagan had allowed Haig and others at the State Department to concede much more to Beijing than he had intended. To remedy this, Reagan made two additional gestures, the first to reassure Taiwan, and the second to buttress his own government.

First, Reagan directed Jim Lilley in Taipei to meet with President Chiang Ching-kuo and give the Taiwanese president "six assurances." These commitments, which Lilley helped craft, reaffirmed America's commitment to the Taiwan Relations Act and promise not to pressure Taiwan into negotiations with Beijing.[61] Then, the same day that he signed the Joint Communiqué, Reagan drafted a secret memo to Weinberger and Shultz delivering presidential guidance on how to interpret the Joint Communiqué. Reagan's memo declared, "The US willingness to reduce its arms sales to Taiwan is conditioned absolutely on the continued commitment of China to the peaceful solution of the Taiwan-PRC differences." It also ordered that "the quality and quantity of the arms provided Taiwan be conditioned entirely on the threat posed by the PRC."[62]

Reagan's memo is one of the most unusual documents in the annals of American diplomacy. With one hand he had signed the Joint Communiqué, satisfying most of Beijing's demands, while with the other hand he had drafted a codicil that vitiated the communiqué in terms that Beijing would never have accepted. It could have led to a disastrous confrontation between the United States and China. But instead, thanks to careful implementation and deft diplomacy over the coming years, Reagan's two steps solidified and rebalanced the settlement with Beijing and Taipei, and helped preserve peace across the Taiwan Strait for the next four decades. In Michael Green's summary, "The communique reestablished the link between arms sales and the Chinese threat to Taiwan—at least for the American side—and the Six Assurances put in place a straightforward formula for protecting American interests in the security of Taiwan independent of developments in US-China relations."[63] Shultz affirmed this framework and set about implementing it.

It came at a cost, however. Notwithstanding Reagan's assurances to Taiwan, Beijing signed the communiqué because Deng Xiaoping still got much of what he wanted. When the agreement was announced publicly, many media reports portrayed it as a victory for Beijing. Reagan, in part because of his secret memo and promises to Taiwan, consoled himself in his diary: "[The] truth is we are standing with Taiwan and the P.R.C. made all the concessions."[64] But this was not entirely true. As Jim Mann recalls, over the previous year "the administration had repeatedly yielded ground in the talks with China, only to have Beijing ask for more. American objectives, such as obtaining a concrete pledge from China not to use force against Taiwan, were progressively weakened."[65]

Still, in resolving the Third Communiqué in this way, Reagan rejected the zero-sum approach that both Beijing and Taipei had adopted. In their minds, any US concession to one side of the Taiwan Strait meant a proportionate loss for the other side. Reagan avoided this trap. He wanted the United States to maintain constructive relations with both nations and determined to adopt policies to do just that. Setting that paradigm for the US-China-Taiwan triangle may have been Reagan's most important legacy for cross-strait relations.

VII

On July 16, in the forest outside Geneva, Paul Nitze went for a walk. This was not a normal stroll for the septuagenarian and chief US negotiator for the INF talks. Nitze was accompanied by Soviet diplomat Yuli Kvitsinsky, and they had work to do, such that their ambulation in the Swiss woods would soon become the most famous walk in arms control history.

If the American establishment had an icon, it would be the silver-maned Nitze. To the manner born in 1907, he went from Harvard to the army to Wall Street and would continue revolving through the door between government and finance for the next four decades. A longtime Democrat and lifelong hawk, in the 1970s Nitze had grown disenchanted with his party's softened stance toward the Soviets and been among the many Democrats who supported Reagan. His career bookended the Cold War. In 1950 he had authored NSC-68 as America's strategy at the outset of the Cold War, and now, at age seventy-four, Nitze had returned to service in the Reagan administration to help negotiate the conflict's end.

The INF negotiations took place in Geneva, a city that combined natural beauty with Cold War neutrality. After a year of little progress, Nitze sought escape from the stalemate. Washington and Moscow both remained wary of being the first to offer a concession, out of the fear that the other side would sense weakness and demand more. Nitze spent weeks cloistered away, crafting a plan that he hoped would enable both sides to slip this negotiating trap. He then invited Kvitsinsky on a hike.

The two envoys strolled along a logging road until they came to "a pile of felled trees" and sat down side by side. Nitze pulled out of his jacket four papers and handed them to the Soviet one by one. The papers detailed Nitze's proposal, which amounted to an "integrated package" in which the US would only deploy seventy-five GLCMs, the Soviets would reduce their arsenal to seventy-five SS-20s, and both sides would limit their total European deployments to two hundred twenty-five nuclear warheads each. An intrigued but noncommittal Kvitsinsky agreed to consult his superiors in Moscow on the proposal; Nitze said he would do the same in Washington.[66]

There was one problem. Reagan had not authorized Nitze's gambit. Nor had Shultz, who took office as secretary on the same day as Nitze and Kvitsinsky's walk. Nitze, a wily bureaucratic operator, took advantage of the three-week interregnum at the State Department to spring his proposal with no oversight. Creative and bold though it was, it contradicted Reagan's "zero-zero" position. Nitze's biographer (and grandson) Nicholas Thompson calls the initiative "one of the most astonishing acts of insubordination in US-Soviet history."[67]

Nitze returned to Washington ten days later to start sharing the outlines of his proposal with senior officials such as Clark, Shultz, and Weinberger. While all were willing to hear him out, misgivings quickly emerged. One NSC staff member who sat in on Nitze's briefing wrote to Clark, "We are now faced with potentially very severe bureaucratic and substantive problems. Mr. Nitze has strayed way off the reservation. . . . [He] may have undercut the future of the Administration's 'zero option' with the Soviets by dealing informally with the Soviets on a 'non-zero' approach."[68] The State Department's Richard Burt, not normally a hard-liner, objected that Nitze had undermined America's credibility with its NATO allies, many of whom had taken considerable risks both with their publics and with the Soviets in backing the Pershing II and additional GLCM deployments that Nitze now proposed jettisoning.

Ironically, one of Nitze's fellow Democrats and erstwhile protégés took the lead in euthanizing his proposal. Richard Perle, the assistant secretary of defense and originator of the zero option, had learned the arms control field at Nitze's feet over a decade earlier. Perle was attending a conference in Aspen, Colorado, when frantic messages from his staff alerted him to Nitze's freelancing. With no access to a secure telephone line, it took several cryptic messages and calls from pay phones for his staff to inform Perle, "Our white-haired gentleman . . . has made a far-reaching proposal without any instructions." An outraged Perle returned to Washington ready to do battle. Working with Weinberger and some Pentagon and NSC staff, Perle mobilized people and arguments against Nitze. One point that gained purchase with Reagan was that Nitze's proposal conceded the "fast-flyer" SS-20s to the Soviets while allowing only the "slow-flyer" GLCMs to the United States. Reagan did not see why the Soviets should retain ballistic missiles that were denied to the Americans.[69]

Matters came to a head on September 13, when Reagan convened a meeting in the Situation Room on the INF negotiations. When Nitze protested that Reagan's zero-zero position demanded that the Soviets trade their deployed missiles for mere American aspirations to deploy, the president responded, "Well, Paul, you just tell the Soviets that you're working for one tough son of a bitch."[70] However, while Reagan held firm on zero-zero, he remained hopeful about negotiations with the Soviets and authorized Nitze to keep open the private channel to Moscow via Kvitsinsky.[71] Any other American official who engaged in such maverick diplomacy would have been fired with dispatch. Nitze's survival testified to his singular stature.

Perle's maneuvering and Reagan's reluctance killed the proposal at the US end. But it was a gratuitous death, since the Kremlin had killed it in Moscow already. When Kvitsinsky met again with Nitze three months after their walk, the Soviet admitted that as soon as he had returned to Moscow bearing Nitze's proposal, Foreign Minister Gromyko and senior Red Army and KGB officials had all rejected it out of hand without even showing it to Brezhnev. The Soviets feared that the proposal was too hard on them in limiting SS-20s and too soft on the Americans in permitting the GLCM deployment.[72]

The Walk in the Woods mattered because of, not despite, its failure. The Kremlin's summary rejection of its terms, even though they were quite favorable to Moscow, revealed Soviet suspicion of the United States and solidified Reagan's commitment to zero-zero. The episode also reinforced Reagan and Shultz's conviction that power strengthens diplomacy, and deepened their resolve to deploy the Pershing IIs and GLCMs the next year. They realized that absent a show of force by the United States to alter the strategic balance in Europe, the Kremlin would not budge.

Meanwhile, a growing terror beset many in the West that the arms race itself—and not the Soviet Union—posed the greatest threat to world peace. Activists coalesced behind the "nuclear freeze" movement, which called for the United States and Soviet Union—especially the former—to halt any further production of nuclear weapons. In June, some 750,000 protestors marched in New York City against nuclear arms. This largest gathering in the city's history brought together, in the words of *The New York Times,* "pacifists and anarchists, children and Buddhist monks, Roman Catholic bishops and Communist Party leaders, university students and union members."[73]

The communists and Catholics posed a particular problem for the Reagan White House. The communist activism represented a new front in Moscow's covert activities, whereas the Catholics represented the possible loss of an important ally. On the former, the KGB increased its surreptitious sponsorship of antinuclear and peace activities. A secret US intelligence assessment in 1982 found that the USSR was "invigorating the peace movement" with extensive financial and organizational support across many European countries and a particular focus on inciting public opposition to the upcoming INF deployment.[74] Most of the antinuclear protestors protested from sincere convictions. But as two scholars conclude based on extensive KGB records, "The constant stream of Soviet peace propaganda, reinforced by KGB active measures, encouraged—even if it did not cause—the overconcentration by most Western peace activists on the nuclear menace posed by Reagan and his NATO allies rather than on that from the Soviet Union."[75]

Even as Reagan deepened his anticommunist alliance with the Vatican and populated his administration with devout Catholics such as Casey, Clark, Dolan, and Chief of Naval Operations Admiral James Watkins, he faced opposition from other corners of Catholicism. The National Conference of Catholic Bishops (NCCB) began preparing a "pastoral letter"—really a book-length manifesto—on nuclear weapons. Clare Boothe Luce—the writer, ambassador to Italy under Eisenhower, former Republican member of Congress, member of the President's Foreign Intelligence Advisory Board, devout Catholic convert, and all-around iconoclast—alerted Clark that an early draft of the NCCB letter took aim at Reagan's nuclear weapons policy.

As a former seminarian keen on maintaining Catholic support for the White House, Clark read the seventy-page draft and wrote back to Luce with a detailed critique that he intended her to share with the NCCB. Clark identified "two major concerns" with the letter. First, it showed a "fundamental misunderstanding" about US deterrence policy, specifically in its call for the United States to declare a "no first use" policy. Clark objected that this disregarded the threat from the Red Army's massive conventional forces, which could only be deterred by the possibility of nuclear retaliation. Otherwise, a no-first-use pledge could "lead the Soviets to believe that Western Europe was open to conventional aggression." Second, Clark complained that the draft ignored Reagan's "very far-reaching efforts" to negotiate significant reductions in nuclear arsenals with the Soviets.[76] The draft letter alarmed the White House so much that it mounted a sustained effort to get the bishops, or the Vatican itself, to cease and desist. A few months later Shultz met at the Vatican with the Pope and Vatican secretary of state Casaroli. Shultz called the draft letter "a matter of tremendous importance" to him and Reagan and told Casaroli, "It is an illusion to think that the moral values we hold dear can be defended by unilateral disarmament."[77]

What the protestors, Catholic bishops, and other critics failed to appreciate is that Reagan feared and detested nuclear weapons as much as they did. They did not realize that the nuclear abolitionist-in-chief resided in the White House. It is just that Reagan detested Soviet communism even more, and remained determined to build up America's nuclear arsenal in order to bring down both the Soviet Union and the world's most destructive weapons.

VIII

Deluged by crises and policy fights over Lebanon, Taiwan, INF, and much else, Reagan needed a break. In August, he returned to the repose of Rancho del Cielo. Not yet twenty months since swearing his inaugural oath, he was already on his second national security advisor and his second secretary of state, and his "team" continued to be riven by infighting and leaking. Recession still afflicted the economy, and a *New York Times* headline blared, "Approval Rating for Reagan Is Lowest Ever," citing his decline to 41 percent in the Gallup poll.[78] His briefing materials for his flight to California included a memo from his White House political staff on the latest polling data and public opinion assessments. It made for grim reading. "The President's image as a leader has declined considerably. . . . It appears to many that the Reagan Administration may have commenced its demise."[79]

Reagan also carried a personal burden to the ranch. Nancy's beloved father, Loyal Davis, an avowed atheist, lay dying in Arizona. Reagan handwrote a four-page letter trying to persuade his father-in-law of the Christian Gospel message. Describing biblical prophecies and the life and death of Christ, and then quoting John 3:16, Reagan concluded, "All we have to do is ask God in Jesus' name to help. . . . A greater life, a greater glory awaits us . . . all that is required is that you believe and tell God you put yourself in his hands." Ten days later Loyal Davis died, but not before seeking out the hospital chaplain for a desperate conversation and prayer.[80] Reagan would share a similar message with a Soviet leader six years later.

IX

Reagan returned from California to a transatlantic storm in Washington. Barely two months after he imposed the pipeline sanctions, the European allies waged an open revolt. The British firm John Brown, with thousands of employees, verged on bankruptcy due to lost contracts for gas turbines it made for the pipeline. In an extraordinary public rebuke, Thatcher told a BBC television interviewer on September 1 that America's actions made her and her country feel "deeply wounded by a friend."[81]

Reagan also began to see how sanctions could function as a cluster bomb rather than a rifle shot and inadvertently hurt his allies with friendly fire. On September 22, he convened the NSC to review the situation. Upon learning that the sanctions were preventing the construction of a pipeline in Australia that had no connection with the Soviet Union, Reagan asked, "We want to hurt the Soviets. Are we stopping the Australian pipeline?" He had intended to inflict pain on Moscow, not Melbourne. Yet even those who opposed the pipeline sanctions had grown frustrated with the allies. Shultz groused, "The Europeans are out of their minds to put themselves in the position of reliance on Soviet energy."[82]

The allies' objection to the sanctions should not be dismissed as typical European squishiness. At the core of European concern, repeated ad nauseam in their meetings with Americans, was the disparity in costs, burdens, and risks. It seemed to European leaders that in demanding that their nations stop helping build the pipeline, the United States insisted that European companies bear the financial costs of lost contracts, that European publics bear the burden of higher gas prices, and that European nations bear the risks of Soviet wrath—especially since they lived in the shadow of the Iron Curtain. Whereas the United States stood five thousand miles away behind an ocean buffer and enjoyed relatively secure energy supplies, and, in a point that European leaders repeatedly invoked, Washington remained unwilling to reimpose its grain embargo on the Soviets because of the cost to American farmers.

Like Haig, Shultz opposed the pipeline sanctions. Unlike Haig, he knew how to relate to Reagan, to gain his trust while respecting his authority as president. The economist in Shultz believed the sanctions would not work; the diplomat in him feared they risked harming alliances beyond repair. He felt particular concern to keep the allies on board for the upcoming deployment of INF missiles, especially since the five European countries that would host the missile bases (Great Britain, West Germany, Italy, the Netherlands, and Belgium) all had major equities with the pipeline.

Shultz believed that Reagan would be receptive to these arguments and knew that Reagan needed an off-ramp to avoid the sanctions' rift becoming a permanent rupture. While Reagan's strategic insight that the Soviet Union was vulnerable to being starved of hard currency and Western technology was sound, the pipeline sanctions were not the best way to prey on that vulnerability. Shultz persuaded Reagan to let him explore alternatives and then spent much of October and November negotiating with his European counterparts to resolve the impasse. The agreement Shultz reached had the United States lift the sanctions in exchange for the allies' agreeing to eschew any new gas contracts with the Soviets and to tighten restrictions on technology exports and loans to Moscow. Shultz's deft diplomacy lanced a painful boil in the transatlantic relationship.[83]

The sanctions reversal did not mark the end of Reagan's economic warfare on the Soviet Union. Building on Shultz's diplomacy, the NSC issued NSDD-66, codifying various measures with the allies to maintain economic pressure on the Soviets. Nor did American efforts to sabotage the pipeline abate. The covert program to slip defective devices and infected software into the KGB's Line X pilfering continued its quiet work, damaging the pipeline and baffling the Soviets.[84] NSC staff member Roger Robinson summarized the collective results. When the pipeline "finally came online it was roughly two and a half years late, resulting in the loss of roughly $25 billion in anticipated hard currency earnings. The second [pipeline] strand never came online (estimated to have earned Moscow some $12–15 billion a year)."[85]

Reagan and his team also turned to other Soviet vulnerabilities, such as Eastern Europe. On paper the countries of the Warsaw Pact and the countries of NATO stood as two rival blocs, each bound together in mutual defense treaties in a tense face-off across the Iron Curtain. In reality there was a profound difference. NATO member states had joined the alliance of their free will, while the citizens in the Warsaw Pact were shackled involuntarily by the Soviet Union. This is why Reagan saw the Warsaw Pact as a liability for Moscow. Maintaining control of its satellites consumed money, manpower, and diplomatic energy, while draining the Kremlin of moral capital and generating resentments among the occupied. This insight was not new to Reagan. George Kennan had distilled it at the Cold War's outset when, channeling his reading of Edward Gibbon's analysis of the fall of the Roman Empire, Kennan described "the unnatural task of holding in submission distant peoples."[86] Reagan agreed. He would enlist the peoples of Eastern Europe as allies against the Soviet foe, and use Eastern Europe to create fissures in the Soviet bloc.

Clark and the NSC staff had already put together an Eastern Europe strategy for Reagan's review. Reagan issued it on September 2. NSDD-54 declared, "The primary long-term US goal in Eastern Europe is to loosen the Soviet hold on the region and thereby facilitate its eventual reintegration into the European community of nations."[87] NSDD-54 admitted that the policy itself was not new, since "differentiation toward Eastern Europe . . . has been US policy for nearly 20 years." What was new were the measures Reagan would employ to advance it.

Bill Casey soon brought him an option. As Poland suffered under martial law, Solidarity continued its peaceful resistance. That summer, Clark had directed Casey to explore what could be done, including covert action, to support Solidarity. The CIA put together an ambitious proposal. On November 4, as Seth Jones describes, "Reagan agreed to sign a presidential

finding to provide money and nonlethal equipment to moderate Polish opposition groups through surrogate third parties, hiding the US government's hand. The finding also authorized the CIA to conduct clandestine
radio broadcasting into Poland."[88] This program, code-named QRHELP-
FUL, would help change the course of the Cold War.

In the same spirit, Reagan moved to implement his Westminster call
for a "crusade for freedom." Even before the June speech, the White House
had been working on what *U.S. News & World Report* reporter Sara Fritz
described as a project "to establish a quasi-governmental program to promote democracy in the third world by financing political parties, Labor
unions and newspapers." In a note to her editors, Fritz added the snark, "I
can't help noting the irony in the Reagan administration wanting to fund
Labor unions."[89] But Fritz overlooked that Reagan had once been a union
leader himself, as head of the Screen Actors Guild, and that in his anticommunist coalition he saw labor unions as allies—starting with Solidarity.

With this presidential mandate, Clark moved to institutionalize support
for human freedom. He designated NSC staff member Walter Raymond to
lead Project Democracy, which gave birth the next year to the National
Endowment for Democracy (NED). Former Kirkpatrick staff member Carl
Gershman became its inaugural president.[90] Under Gershman's able leadership over the coming decades, the NED would become the most influential
democracy-promotion organization in the world.

Reagan made it a personal priority. On November 4, he walked into the
White House East Room to greet, as he wrote in his diary, "delegates from
all over the *free* world here for the Conference on elections." He noted, "This
grew out of my speech to Parliament last summer in London—start of a
program to sell democracy to the world."[91] In his remarks to the assembled
leaders from democratic nations in Latin America, Asia, Africa, and Europe, the president quoted Eisenhower's words just after World War II: "Our
most effective security step is to develop in every country where there is any
chance or opportunity a democratic form of government." To this Reagan
added, "I do not underestimate the capabilities for repression of dictatorships of either the left or the right or the devastating effect of terrorism. But
the imperishable democratic ideal and the democratic movement—these
are stronger."[92] He saw the beginnings of a global democratic wave—and
sought to coax it along.

Freedom's advance depended on not just conferences, programs, and
dollars but also—especially—the courage of individual dissidents. While

Reagan hosted the White House luncheon, Anatoly Shcharansky lay starving in a cell at the remote Chistopol Prison some five hundred miles east of Moscow. He had launched a hunger strike over a month earlier. Reagan, worried that Shcharansky might die, wrote to Brezhnev on October 20 urging his "release from prison and permission to join his family in Israel."

By this point the Soviet Union was feeling Reagan's pressure on all fronts—economic, military, ideological, human rights—and Brezhnev was in a surly mood. He complained to East German leader Erich Honecker, "There has never been such an unbridled and aggressive administration in the USA as that of Reagan." Replying to Reagan's letter, the truculent Soviet huffed that because Shcharansky had been "sentenced for espionage and other grave anti-Soviet crimes . . . there are neither legal nor other grounds for resolving it in the manner you would wish."[93]

It would be the last correspondence between the two leaders. Less than two weeks later, on November 11, the ring of Reagan's secure bedside phone in the White House residence woke him at three thirty A.M. The caller was Bill Clark, informing the president that Brezhnev had just died.[94]

A few days later, the president and First Lady rode with Clark up Sixteenth Street to the Soviet embassy. Walking inside, they signed the condolence book for the dead leader. Then Reagan smiled at Clark and asked, "Do you think they'd mind if we just said a little prayer for the man?" The three bowed their heads and Reagan invoked God's blessings on the late Brezhnev and his atheist nation.[95]

X
———

The Soviet Politburo replaced one geriatric hard-liner with another. Two days after Brezhnev's death, the Kremlin announced KGB director Yuri Andropov as the new general secretary of the Communist Party. Andropov became the first KGB director to attain the supreme Soviet leadership position. He shared Brezhnev's suspicion of the United States and continued to fear that it planned to launch a surprise nuclear attack. He had put his warnings into action with Operation RYAN, a worldwide endeavor to gather intelligence on America's purported intention to strike first.

Now that he commanded the Kremlin, Andropov upped the ante on Operation RYAN. He ordered every KGB *rezidentura* (station) around the world to work "systematically to uncover any plans in preparation by the main adversary [the United States] . . . to use nuclear weapons against the USSR or immediate preparations being made for a nuclear-missile attack." Andropov's directive specified a list of warning signs to watch for in NATO countries that encompassed almost every dimension of human activity, including lights on in buildings, cars in government parking lots, cattle in slaughterhouses, and even supply levels at blood banks. For a paranoid leader, almost anything could indicate an impending attack. In another time, it would have been the stuff of parody, of bureaucracy and conspiracism run amok. At the height of the Cold War, it was terrifying. A misperception by either side could mean the end of the world.

Late in 1982, a senior KGB officer in London dutifully shared Andropov's Operation RYAN directive with his team—and then passed it on to his MI6 handler as well. Oleg Gordievsky had risen through the ranks of Soviet intelligence while spying for the British. Each week he met surreptitiously at a Bayswater safe house with a small MI6 team to share documents, microfilm, and insights from the KGB's inner workings. MI6 in turn began sharing some of this intelligence with its CIA counterparts.[96] The intelligence windfall provided by Gordievsky reinforced the value that Reagan placed on allies. Notably, of the three most important Soviet human intelligence sources for the United States in the 1980s (Vladimir Vetrov, who provided the Farewell Dossier; Adolf Tolkachev, a radar technician in Moscow run by the CIA; and Gordievsky), two of the three came from allied intelligence services.

Not all was grim in Moscow. Amid his fears and hostility toward the United States, Andropov held some hope of improved relations between the rival superpowers. Bush and Shultz flew to Moscow for Brezhnev's funeral, and a chance to size up his successor. Historian Simon Miles observes that "Andropov's briefing papers for this meeting described the future of East-West relations with striking optimism. The United States had made its intention to improve relations sufficiently clear, as had the Kremlin." In his meeting with Bush and Shultz, Andropov downplayed the public criticisms each country made of the other and instead pledged Moscow's interest in improved bilateral relations "since this would be in the interests of not only our two countries, but in fact of all mankind."[97]

Andropov had one condition, however. He wanted the United States to stop hectoring the Kremlin about its abuse of its own people. Andropov told Shultz that Reagan's "interference" on human rights irritated the Politburo and hurt relations between Moscow and Washington.[98] Andropov's complaints had the opposite effect. They reinforced for Reagan and Shultz the Kremlin's vulnerability to dissent and sense of its own illegitimacy. It was a point they would relentlessly press going forward.

XI

Andropov was not the only new leader to debut on the world stage. In the next two months, America's World War II enemies elected heads of government who would become two of Reagan's closest friends and most valued partners. In October, West German voters welcomed Helmut Kohl as their new chancellor, and the next month, Japan selected Yasuhiro Nakasone as prime minister. Now from Tokyo to London to Bonn, the most powerful countries of the Western alliance had center-right leaders committed to free enterprise and anticommunism.

Kohl visited the White House on November 15. He and Reagan had first met in 1978 when both aspired to their nation's top roles; now they greeted each other as president and chancellor. Kohl assured Reagan that no matter what transpired, he should "proceed on the assumption that [West Germany] will stand by the United States." The German leader also reinforced his commitment to the scheduled deployment of GLCMs and Pershing IIs the next year, promising that Germany would install the missiles "even if I have to do it all by myself."

Their discussion ranged wide across the world economy, the need for West Germany to increase its defense spending, how to deal with Mitterrand, Sino-Soviet relations, KGB support for "peace movements," the importance of Solidarity in Poland, whether Marxist ideology or Russian historical paranoia drove Soviet behavior (answer: both), and what to make of Andropov. Both felt skeptical of the new Soviet leader, with Reagan seeing Andropov as a "tough adversary" who would not bring "great changes in Soviet policy." Reagan assured Kohl, however, that he continued to reach out to the Soviet Union "on a human basis" and had "been recently pursuing quiet diplomacy with the Soviets." Specifically, Reagan said he had asked the Kremlin to release the Siberian Pentecostals garrisoned in the US embassy as a "gesture" of goodwill. He had promised Moscow that if the Pentecostals were released, "the US would not publicize it, but would reciprocate with an appropriate response."[99] The meeting cemented an enduring partnership.

So did Reagan's call to Tokyo two weeks later. Reagan phoned Prime Minister Nakasone to congratulate him on his election and invited him to visit the White House in January.[100] Unbeknownst to Nakasone, a month earlier Reagan had issued NSDD-62, on United States–Japan relations. Combining new NSC staff member Gaston Sigur's encyclopedic knowledge of Japan with Reagan, Weinberger, and Shultz's strategic intuitions, the directive affirmed treating Japan as on par with NATO allies while pressing Tokyo on the perennial needs to expand its defense commitments and further open its economy.[101] Nakasone would prove a willing partner on these priorities.

XII

For his final international journey of the year, Reagan traveled south to Latin America. He made democracy the focus of his trip. The four countries on his itinerary, Brazil, Colombia, Costa Rica, and Honduras, had each held elections in the previous year. Reagan and Shultz hoped a presidential visit would encourage further democratic progress throughout the region. What was planned in private matched what was said in public. While Reagan's trip remarks and White House publicity materials, such as a glossy twenty-page booklet titled *A Hemisphere of Democracy,* trumpeted the democracy theme, Reagan issued the top secret NSDD-71, affirming "the development of stable and democratic political systems and institutions which promote respect for basic human rights" in Latin America as a policy priority.[102]

NSDD-71 also set a goal of supporting "a region free of Soviet-dominated or hostile governments." Reagan fixed on the fear of Soviet inroads in part because he continued to hear it voiced by the region's leaders. In the months before his trip, he met at the White House with President Roberto Suazo Córdova of Honduras, who called Nicaragua "practically Marxist-Leninist . . . a cancer . . . [that] could metastasize throughout the region and destroy Honduras' tranquility," and with Panama's president Ricardo de la Espriella, who warned Reagan that "the Soviets were behind much of the trouble" in the region and urged him to "warn the Soviets bluntly to keep their hands off," saying, "The people of the region want liberty and to work towards democracy."[103]

Landing first in Brazil, Reagan found an immediate rapport with President João Figueiredo. They visited the Brazilian's ranch and bonded over their shared equestrian interests; Figueiredo let Reagan ride one of his champion stallions. In São Paulo, Reagan returned to a favorite theme and asked Figueiredo for help on "how we could realize my dream of an accord between the nations of South America and North America."[104] Reagan repeated this call in his speech to a Brazilian audience, where he also hailed the "strong democratic tide running in the Americas." In Costa Rica, he told a national television audience that the United States and Costa Rica both "live the peaceful revolution of democracy, secure under the rule of law, and prospering under economic freedom." But elsewhere, Central America was ensnared in "a struggle of ideas between the violence of false revolutionaries and the reaction of false conservatives."[105]

Reagan pointed toward democratic capitalism as the middle path between the communist and right-wing authoritarian governments that afflicted the region. Yet he had to reckon with his administration's support of the latter. Just before his speech in Costa Rica, he met with President Magaña of El Salvador and pressed Magaña to improve "human rights so [the United States] could continue to help." Other instances were less defensible. The next day, in Honduras, Reagan met with the newest Guatemalan dictator, Efraín Ríos Montt, who had taken power in a coup a few months earlier. Reagan wrote in his diary that evening: "[Ríos Montt's regime is] getting a bad press rap as a mil[itary] government, which makes it hard for us to help even though they are under constant terrorist attacks."[106] Reagan was wrong. Ríos Montt may have been an anticommunist, but he was a brutal thug, responsible for the deaths of tens of thousands of innocent civilians. He would be deposed in yet another coup the next year.

XIII

Congress ended the year delivering two gut punches to Reagan. First, the House and the Senate both voted in December to terminate funding for the MX missile until the White House came up with a viable basing plan. Reagan thought he had resolved the issue two weeks earlier when he had issued a formal decision to deploy the first one hundred MXs in a "dense pack" of hardened silos spaced closely together at Warren Air Force Base in Wyoming. A majority in both houses of Congress, including many Republicans, found the basing plan outlandish and scuttled it, despite weeks of arm-twisting and cajoling by Reagan. He worried that not deploying the MX weakened his diplomacy with the Soviets. He wrote in his diary, "I shudder to think what it will do to our arms reduction negotiations in Geneva."[107] One reporter commented that Reagan "is very down, almost depressed" over the vote and "regards the MX defeat as the biggest setback of his presidency."[108]

The second blow came on December 9, when Representative Edward Boland, chairman of the House Permanent Select Committee on Intelligence (HPSCI), persuaded the House to pass unanimously his amendment banning the use of any funds "for the purpose of overthrowing the Government of Nicaragua." The HPSCI had oversight and funding responsibility for CIA covert action programs. Former State Department official Robert Kagan highlighted the ambiguity in the Boland Amendment: "The Reagan administration could aid the contras, who sought to overthrow the Sandinista government, so long as it was not the Reagan administration's intent to overthrow the Sandinistas."[109] In truth, many administration officials, including Reagan himself, would not have minded if the Sandinista regime were removed from power. But the relatively paltry funding the White House provided was far from sufficient for a regime-change insurgency—which the contras were incapable of marshaling anyway.

Dewey Clarridge, the Latin America Division chief in the CIA Directorate of Operations, who ran the contra aid program, later confessed, "In truth, no one in the Agency was going to shed any tears if Daniel Ortega, Tomás Borge, and the rest of the Sandinista ruling directorate found unemployment as a result of our efforts. However, with permission to work with a disorganized, small band of insurgents on the Honduras/Nicaragua border, no one knew better than I how far from that possibility we really were."[110] Much of the acrimony over Nicaragua policy was not about Nicaragua. Rather the debate revolved around the fitting historical analogy and the perceived threat of Soviet communism. Congressional Democrats who opposed contra aid saw Nicaragua as "another Vietnam" and argued the United States should not intervene in a civil war, especially against a Sandinista government of agrarian reformers who resented Yankee imperialism. These voices regarded Soviet influence in Central America as an overhyped irritant but not a threat, and saw Managua's nods toward Moscow as more rhetorical than real. Whereas contra supporters saw Nicaragua as "another Cuba" whose Sandinista government sought to impose Castro-style tyranny on its own people while offering itself as a Soviet intelligence outpost and military base, and supporting communist insurgencies in neighboring countries such as El Salvador. Judging by the Kremlin's actions, Moscow seemed intent on creating a new Cuba. A CIA assessment found that the Soviet Union grew its military aid to Nicaragua from $6 million in 1981 to $53 million in 1982, including tanks and mobile rocket launchers, in addition to $163 million in development and technical assistance.[111]

Beleaguered, demoralized, diminished, the Reagan presidency stumbled to the end of the year. If he could not even win negotiations with his own Congress, how could he negotiate successfully with the Soviets? To many pundits and pollsters, Reagan's presidency appeared to be failing. Appearances can conceal more than they reveal, however. Hidden beyond the headlines of economic woes and political defeats, Reagan had built a foundation for American renewal, the global expansion of freedom, and a decisive shift in the Cold War's balance of power.

CHAPTER 6

RAISING THE STAKES

I

Bill Clark looked with dread to the new year. Twelve months into the NSA job, he had enjoyed much success. He had channeled Reagan's ideas and principles into several concrete strategies, recruited able new staff to the NSC, and helped mobilize the vast machinery of the US government behind the president's vision. But this came at a great cost. Clark felt exhausted, pummeled by unceasing crises, demoralized by staff feuding, and drained by constant leaks. Everything from frictions with allies, to smackdowns from Congress, to incessant skirmishing with the press, all pervaded by the daily dread of nuclear war, afflicted him with unrelenting stress.

Clark informed Reagan on January 7, 1983, that he was considering resigning. The worried president told his diary that he "didn't try to talk him out of it" because of concern over the strain on Clark, but added, "Lord knows I want him to stay." Clark eventually told Reagan he would only stay for one more year.[1] For good and ill, that year would be the most consequential of Reagan's presidency.

Reagan began 1983 in the lowest trough of his political standing. His approval rating plumbed the depths at 35 percent. As an unpopular president and, at the time, the oldest ever to hold the office, he caused many in the media and even his own staff to doubt he would run for reelection.

When presidents are strong, they act with confidence. When they are weak, they form commissions. With his political capital on its last reserves after his congressional losses on the MX, the defense budget, and Central

America, Reagan resorted to two commissions. First, he established the Commission on Strategic Forces to recommend new basing options for the MX. A few months later he announced the Commission on Central America. He asked the former national security advisors for his erstwhile rival President Ford to chair one each. Brent Scowcroft would lead the strategic forces commission, while Henry Kissinger would preside over the Central America commission. Reagan chose them in part for their expertise and availability, but also as a political outreach to the moderate wing of the GOP, which had opposed him on the MX and Nicaragua votes. For similar reasons he enlisted prominent Democrats such as former Carter Pentagon official Bill Perry and labor union leader John Lyons for the strategic forces commission, and Lane Kirkland and Bob Strauss for the Central America commission. Bill Clements, the former deputy secretary of defense, and investment banker Nicholas Brady were the only two men appointed to both.

The new year brought more personnel turmoil when Reagan fired Arms Control and Disarmament Agency director Eugene Rostow on January 12. One of the original hawkish Democrats to support Reagan, Rostow had alienated many in the administration and among conservative Republicans in Congress with his sharp elbows and suspect views. He burned his final bridge when he continued to advocate for Nitze's Walk in the Woods formula abandoning the zero option, long after Reagan had decided otherwise. In his stead, Reagan nominated Ken Adelman, a young intellectual then serving with Kirkpatrick at the UN, whose past escapades included being Muhammad Ali's translator during the "Rumble in the Jungle" match in Zaire against George Foreman in 1974. Adelman had also worked in the Ford Pentagon and on the 1980 Reagan campaign, and viewed the arms control establishment with a jaundiced eye. Earlier he had written that "perhaps nowhere in life is the disparity greater between exalted expectations and a dismal track record than in arms control."[2] Such heresies provoked the opposition of many Democratic senators and a few liberal Republicans as well. The Senate only confirmed him after a long fight and close vote, secured by Reagan's personal appeals to several senators.

A few days later Reagan issued NSDD-75, making official his strategy of combining pressure with diplomatic outreach to crack open the Kremlin. As part of this strategy, Reagan continued his rhetorical and spiritual outreach to the Russian people. On January 31 he spoke to four thousand preachers with the National Religious Broadcasters, one of the most influential

Protestant groups in the country, whose collective radio and television programs reached tens of millions of listeners each week. Reagan announced
that he had ordered the USIA to expand its religious broadcasts behind the
Iron Curtain, and then spoke in a direct and personal way of his commitment to religious freedom:

> To those who would crush religious freedom, our message is plain:
> You may jail your believers. You may close their churches, confis-
> cate their Bibles, and harass their rabbis and priests, but you will
> never destroy the love of God and freedom that burns in their
> hearts. They will triumph over you. . . .
>
> [The Soviets have] the most awesome military machine in his-
> tory, but it is no match for that one, single man, hero, strong yet
> tender, Prince of Peace . . . Jesus.[3]

Reverend Billy Graham, the world's most prominent evangelist, phoned
Reagan afterward and told him his speech "was the greatest declaration for
the Lord any Pres[ident] has ever made."[4] Even discounting Graham's flat-
tery, Reagan's remarks combined his personal faith with his view of the Cold
War as a religious conflict.

II

As Prime Minister Yasuhiro Nakasone's motorcade drove through the
White House gates, he knew that the man he was about to greet would do
much to determine whether Nakasone's government would succeed or fail.
A waiting Reagan also knew that the Japanese leader would have similar
sway over his presidency. The United States was still in an economic slump,
which many voters blamed on Japan. The night before, Reagan had written
in his diary, "This Nakasone meeting is going to be a make or break one."[5]
Reagan had prepared extensively for the summit, including multiple meetings with American business leaders about, in Reagan's words, "Japan's
gimmicks to pretend free trade but practice protectionism."[6] On the strategic level, Reagan and Shultz sought to bring Japan into the free world's
varsity ranks, where Japan could help uphold and defend the international
order from which it had so benefited. The two nations together accounted
for 35 percent of the globe's economic output. Reagan and Nakasone both

knew that if they could temper their economic rivalry and elevate their strategic partnership, the United States–Japan alliance would pose a formidable counterweight to the Soviet bloc.

Before traveling to Washington, DC, Nakasone took four actions to address Reagan's concerns. He visited Seoul to help repair relations between Japan and South Korea; he boosted Japan's defense spending by 6.5 percent; he lifted restrictions on the export of sensitive military technology to the United States; and he reduced or eliminated import tariffs on many agricultural and industrial goods.[7] To the White House, these gestures were a welcome start, though not enough. Describing the protectionist pressures erupting from Capitol Hill, Reagan warned Nakasone that unless they cooperated to lower trade barriers, "the collapse in the free trade system might result in conditions worse than the Great Depression." After they moved into the Cabinet Room to include their policy teams, Nakasone said that he agreed with Reagan's concern about protectionism and the specter of the 1930s.[8] It was a potent comparison for both nations, considering that decade had led to Pearl Harbor and Hiroshima.

Earlier that day, in a breakfast with reporters, Nakasone had described Japan as America's "unsinkable aircraft carrier." (This metaphor was a favorite of America's Asian allies; President Chun had used it two years prior to describe South Korea, as had General Douglas MacArthur to describe Taiwan decades earlier.) For Nakasone, it was more than rhetoric. He invited Reagan to deploy nuclear-capable F-16s at Misawa Air Base in northern Japan—less than a one-hour flight to the Soviet border—from where they would bolster Japan's defenses against Soviet Backfire bombers and remind the Kremlin that America could project power into its airspace.[9]

Nakasone also told Reagan that the United States and Japan should cooperate on maintaining the Sino-Soviet rift. Nakasone found common cause with China, which may have historically been Japan's regional rival but now saw the Kremlin as a greater threat. With American encouragement, Japan began sharing intelligence on the USSR with China. Beijing in turn welcomed Tokyo's defense expansion.[10]

For the past two years, Reagan had been increasing military pressure on the Soviet Union's western flank, especially with the forthcoming missile deployments in Europe. Now, in Japan, he had an ally to squeeze Moscow from the east too. Feeling this pressure, the Soviet news agency TASS reacted hysterically to Nakasone's comments by threatening a nuclear strike against Japan that "could spell a national disaster more serious than the one that befell it 37 years ago [at Hiroshima and Nagasaki]." Not surprisingly, such ghoulish threats only further solidified Japan's aversion to the USSR and embrace of the United States.[11]

The two things Reagan valued most in his foreign counterparts were conviction and chemistry. Nakasone had both. The Japanese leader shared Reagan's commitments to free markets, democracy, and anticommunism, and his affable manner and easy rapport. They quickly moved to a first-name basis of "Ron" and "Yasu." They did not fix all of the problems between their nations. Rather, they built a new relationship that elevated what their countries had in common over what divided them. Reagan and Nakasone also built a framework to address their differences—and to keep those differences from poisoning what the White House still regarded as "the most important bilateral relationship in the world."[12] For these reasons, when Reagan urged Japan to take a chair at the high table of international politics, Nakasone readily agreed.

III

A few days later, Shultz flew to Asia. The region had long fascinated him. Four decades earlier, as a Princeton undergraduate, he had taken a senior seminar on American strategy in the Pacific. Then as a young marine, he had fought against the Japanese on several islands in the Pacific theater, where he "learned to view the Japanese fighting ability with great respect."[13] From this background he would become, in the words of Michael Green, "the most effective secretary of state on Asia and the Pacific in the history of the republic."[14]

Because Shultz saw Japan as the centerpiece of America's posture in the region, he made sure to visit Tokyo before continuing on to China, Hong Kong, and South Korea—and then stopped again in Japan on his return leg to brief them on what transpired in the other countries. It helped that the week prior in Washington, Shultz had hit it off with his counterpart, Foreign Minister Shintaro Abe. In a region that values symbolism, no one missed the signal that Shultz sent by stopping in Japan first and last.

By this juncture the Reagan administration's Asia strategy had come into focus. Developed largely by Shultz and Sigur based on Reagan's convictions, it was built on five strategic triangles, with the United States forming a point of every one. A strategic triangle consists of three nations whose interests are defined in relation with each other—whether as friends or foes or something in between. Each triangle had its own internal logic and challenges; each also intersected with the other triangles.

The first was the triangle of values. It consisted of Japan, Australia, and the United States, the region's three main democracies. Reagan had described it to Australian prime minister Malcolm Fraser in 1981, when the president said the "triangular relationship between Japan, the United States, and Australia" provided an anchor "to bring all of the nations of the Pacific along to greater prosperity and security."[15] The second was the triangle of allies, formed by Japan, South Korea, and the United States. It framed America's forward presence in northeast Asia to contain Soviet expansion. The third was the triangle of power: Japan, China, and the United States, the Asia-Pacific's three largest militaries. In this triangle the United States sought to balance its relations with the region's two most formidable countries— who happened to be historic rivals of each other yet also shared an adversary in the Soviet Union. The fourth was the triangle of the Taiwan Strait. Comprised of China, Taiwan, and the United States, this triangle delivered more headaches than benefits, as the United States navigated the tensions between Beijing and Taipei while trying to maintain stable relations with both. Fifth was the strategic triangle: the United States, China, and the Soviet Union. This triangle consisted of the three main antagonists in the Cold War.[16] For the first two decades of the conflict, the Soviets and China had aligned against the United States, but the triangle's balance had shifted when Nixon and Kissinger's opening to Beijing aligned it with the United States, an alignment that Reagan sought to both deepen and recalibrate. Paul Wolfowitz, then the new assistant secretary of state for East Asia, recalls, "The best way to rebalance relations with China [was] to make them realize that Japan [was] number one and [we wouldn't] give away anything more on Taiwan."[17]

For all his strategic insight, Wolfowitz was a novice at travel to Asia. When Shultz's plane landed in Tokyo, his Japanese hosts ushered him and his delegation straight into a ceremonial meal. Exhausted and jet-lagged, Wolfowitz fell asleep at the table during Shultz's toast. Roused awake, an embarrassed Wolfowitz asked a seasoned colleague how to avoid transpacific fatigue. "I have been sitting on my fork," came the reply.[18]

Over the next two days, Nakasone and his cabinet devoted much of their time with Shultz to discussing the Soviet threat and arms control. The Japanese supported Reagan's "position of negotiating from strength" but feared that any INF agreement would "merely shift [more] Soviet SS-20s from Europe to Asia," where the missiles menaced Japan (and China) from bases in the Russian Far East. Shultz assured Nakasone that he and Reagan would hold firm on eliminating all INF missiles, not just those targeting Europe. The secretary also reminded Nakasone of Reagan's massive boost in defense spending and urged Japan to do the same.[19] Reagan and Shultz believed that leading by example obtained more progress with allies than public hectoring.

Shultz then flew to Beijing, his first time in China. US ambassador to China Arthur Hummel wrote Shultz before his arrival, describing Beijing's "sharp disappointments caused by inflated expectations ... that the [United States] ought to give China highly preferential treatment." Fortunately, Hummel continued, the Chinese government "[is] becoming more realistic" about the United States and "putting relations on a firmer, more rational basis."[20] Beijing realized that gone were the days of Nixon, Kissinger, Carter, and Brzezinski, when China dominated the American strategic imagination. Reagan and Shultz were not so bedazzled by China's glow as the debutante of 1970s geopolitics. Twenty-first-century readers mindful of China's recent ascent to world power should recall that in 1983 it was still weak and impoverished. Its economy was smaller than Canada's and less than one-fifth the size of Japan's, and its military, though large, was primitive and incapable of projecting power beyond China's borders.

Many of America and China's shared interests stemmed from their common foe in Moscow. In practice this included partnering to support anti-Soviet insurgencies in Afghanistan and Cambodia (known at the time as Kampuchea). Beijing viewed the Soviet presence in both countries as part of the Kremlin's hostile encirclement of China, from Afghanistan on its far western border to Cambodia to its south, along with Soviet troops deployed along the northern border China shared with the USSR. Vietnamese forces sponsored by the Kremlin occupied Cambodia. A pastiche of Cambodian opposition groups had united to fight the Vietnamese, ranging from nationalists under former head of state Prince Sihanouk to the diabolical Khmer Rouge. The latter were maniacal Maoists who had murdered 1.8 million Cambodians during their reign of terror from 1975 to 1979, until Vietnam's invasion of Cambodia displaced them from power. As part of Mao's loathsome legacy, China had long supported the Khmer Rouge, now including its guerilla campaign against the Vietnamese occupiers.

The United States detested the Khmer Rouge. However, the Reagan administration also feared that the growing Soviet footprint in Vietnam and Cambodia threatened the rest of Southeast Asia, especially Thailand, an American ally. Though the United States and China differed over the Khmer Rouge, they agreed on coordinating "approaches aimed at driving out [the] Vietnamese and restoring peace."[21] The Association of Southeast Asian Nations, the main regional organization, shared these goals and worked with the United States to negotiate Vietnam's withdrawal and the resumption of self-rule in Cambodia by anyone but the Khmer Rouge.

America's collaboration with China to eject Vietnam from Cambodia was another policy that Carter had initiated and then Reagan expanded. Beginning in 1982, Reagan approved a covert action proposed by Casey for the CIA to provide $5 million annually to the noncommunist Cambodian resistance groups who allied with the Khmer Rouge.[22] Reagan prohibited any aid going to the Khmer Rouge, and the administration consistently opposed letting the genocidal fanatics play any role in a future Cambodian government. Modest though the amount of funding was, it opened another front in the White House's counteroffensive against the Soviet Union. Yet this support to the opposition groups also entailed, in the words of Reagan administration official Peter Rodman, "a Faustian bargain . . . for it left [the United States] indirectly in bed with the hated Khmer Rouge."[23]

Shultz had similar complications in mind as Deng Xiaoping ceremoniously welcomed him to the Great Hall of the People. This head of a brutal dictatorship was also a reformer seeking to improve the lives of his people, and a recipient of growing amounts of American military, technological, and intelligence assistance. Seated in the cavernous room, enveloped by the ghosts of history, the two men conversed on the gamut of geopolitics. Deng did most of the talking. As Shultz recalled, over the next three hours the Chinese leader veered from "moderate, pleasant, and jocular tones" to "a seemingly endless, scathing diatribe" against anyone who doubted China's power. Not surprisingly, Shultz made little headway with Deng on human rights. Deng dismissed Shultz's advocacy for greater liberty, responding with a contemptuous reference to China's vast population: "You support the right to emigrate? We'll give you 10 million people today! Would you like 20 million?"[24]

One of Shultz's most notable exchanges took place before an American audience. He gave a speech to leaders of the American business community at a Beijing hotel. Given his background as a business school dean, former secretary of the Treasury, and former president of a multinational construction company, the audience expected he would share their priorities. He did not.

Shultz and the business leaders both knew the PRC's intelligence services had bugged the room, so each was mindful of the electronic audience listening in. To a question from one business leader about loosening export controls on sensitive technologies, Shultz scolded American companies that "sign a contract when they know it falls outside the guidelines" and then demand that the US government approve it. "Buddy, that's your problem when you do that," retorted Shultz, "don't complain to the government."

Another executive griped that Japanese and European governments approved licenses faster than the United States. "Why don't you move to Japan or Western Europe?" replied the secretary.

The next questioner asked for loosened controls on nuclear power. By now Shultz's patriotic dander was up. He shot back, "The question carries the implication, as most of your questions do, that there is something wrong with the United States." Shultz then described the grave risks of nuclear proliferation and concluded, "The question suggests in a rather cavalier fashion that you brush it off. I don't brush it off."

The final question pleaded for more US export subsidies for American businesses. To which Shultz dismissed export subsidies as "nothing more than a form of protectionism" and warned that with the "emergence of a gigantic export subsidy world, we will all be the losers."[25]

Critics of Reagan often derided him as a lackey for commercial interests, but Shultz's Beijing scuffle showed rather that the administration focused on protecting national security and promoting genuine free markets. Both principles were difficult to balance—witness the pipeline sanctions debate—but both were anathema to corporate welfare.

Back in the United States, Shultz gave a speech in San Francisco recounting his trip. He distilled how history shaped his view of the region and how Asia's dynamism encapsulated the global future. In his words, "two simple facts" governed the Reagan administration's outlook on Asia: "We trade more today with the nations of East Asia and the Pacific than with any other region on earth, including western Europe," and "we have fought three wars in the Pacific in the last forty years. We do not want to fight another."[26] When Shultz spoke these words, he did so mindful that the 1980s were the first decade since the 1930s that American troops were not fighting and dying in wars in Asia. The Reagan administration aimed to turn the Asia-Pacific from a region of conflict to a region of commerce and liberty, all while resisting the encroachments of Soviet communism.

IV

Shultz flew from Asia back to a Washington, DC, stymied by a massive snowstorm. This led to an unexpected dinner invitation, and a diplomatic breakthrough. The blizzard prevented the Reagans from making their customary weekend stay at Camp David. On Saturday, February 12, the home-bound First Lady phoned Shultz to see if he and his wife, Obie, would be free to join the Reagans for an impromptu dinner at the White House that night. Over a candlelit table, the couples had a wide-ranging discussion on Shultz's recent Asia trip, and diplomacy and relations with the Soviet Union.

Reagan spoke again of his desire to negotiate with the Kremlin. Karen Tumulty writes, "Nancy had planned [the dinner] so that Shultz would begin to understand something important about her husband. . . . 'I'm sitting there,' [Shultz recalled] 'and it's dawning on me: This man has never had a real conversation with a big-time communist leader, and is dying to have one.'"[27]

The secretary seized the moment. "I will be meeting with Dobrynin again late Tuesday afternoon," he told Reagan. "What would you think about my bringing Dobrynin over to the White House for a private chat?"

Reagan responded enthusiastically. He wanted to meet with the Soviet ambassador.

What Shultz did not realize is that NSA Bill Clark had prepared the way the week prior by writing a long memo to Reagan recommending starting a private dialogue with the Soviets. Clark even suggested that Reagan have Shultz bring Dobrynin into the White House Map Room for a secret meeting. Belying his image as a hard-liner opposed to diplomacy, Clark's memo cautioned that this dialogue "holds some risks" and would "engender criticism from the right." But "it would be worthwhile because it would make clear that you are not ideologically against solving problems with the Soviet Union."[28]

Though they do not seem to have consulted with each other, Clark and Shultz both encouraged Reagan to take a step that the president already wanted to take. Two years after his inauguration, it would be his first encounter as president with a Soviet official.

A few days later Reagan welcomed Dobrynin to the White House residence for what turned into a two-hour meeting. The discussion grew testy; "Sometimes we got pretty nose to nose," said Reagan.[29] They covered arms control, regional conflicts, bilateral economic issues, and human rights. This initial meeting set the template for the future, as these four issue areas would become the framework for US-Soviet negotiations for the rest of Reagan's presidency.[30]

As the time drew late, Reagan looked for a diplomatic opening. He closed with an earnest pitch to the Soviet ambassador about the Siberian Pentecostals, now in their fifth year of basement exile in the US embassy. "If you can do something about the Pentecostals . . . we will simply be delighted and will not embarrass you by undue publicity, by claims of credit for ourselves, or by 'crowing.'"[31]

The imperious Dobrynin reported back to Moscow "recommending that we continue working patiently to bridle Reagan's extremist views." The Kremlin was baffled by his appeal for the Pentecostals. To the Soviets, "Reagan's request looked extremely odd, even suspicious," observed Dobrynin. No one in the Politburo could fathom why this president regarded the plight of the Pentecostals "as if it were the most important issue between" the two countries.[32]

It was a singular moment in the annals of the Cold War. In his debut negotiation with the Soviets, Reagan asked not for a concession on nuclear arms, or troop levels in Europe, or trade, or other high matters of state. Rather he asked that a few stubborn Pentecostals be given exit visas. The decades-long clash and mutual test of credibility between two superpowers now rested on the fates of six renegade, pious, long-suffering Siberian Christians cloistered in the US embassy basement.

To Reagan it made perfect sense. He saw the Cold War as a spiritual conflict. He believed that supporting the religious freedom of Russian Christians could undermine the idolatrous claims of Soviet communism and weaken the Kremlin's grip on its people. He also had a practical reason for his request. The old Hollywood labor negotiator knew that successful bargaining begins with small steps to build trust. Granting exit visas to the Pentecostals should have been an easy gesture for the Kremlin to make, and staying quiet about it would not be hard for Reagan. If both sides honored the deal, trust could be built, preparing the way to tackle bigger issues.

Two weeks later, the Soviets sent an oblique reply that hinted at flexibility on the fate of the Pentecostals. Over the next five months, Shultz and

Dobrynin engaged in a delicate choreography, using a combination of diplomatic finesse, semantic obfuscation, trusted intermediaries, and sheer doggedness to craft a solution. Meanwhile, Reagan and Shultz also enlisted Max Kampelman to open an additional human rights channel with the Soviets. Reagan had designated Kampelman, another Democrat serving a senior role in the administration, to lead the American negotiations in Madrid at the Conference on Security and Cooperation in Europe meetings on implementation of the Helsinki Accords, a set of territorial, security, and human rights agreements signed by the United States, European nations, and the USSR in 1975. In Madrid, Kampelman developed a quiet rapport with the KGB general who oversaw the Soviet delegation. Reagan gave Kampelman a list of imprisoned Jewish refuseniks whom he wanted to see freed, and Kampelman in turn pressed his KGB contact for the release of both the Pentecostals and the Jewish dissidents.[33]

Together these efforts led first to Lidiya Vashchenko's permission to depart the USSR from her home in Chernogorsk, followed by the release from the embassy and subsequent emigration of the remaining six Pentecostals, who settled in St. Louis, Missouri. The Kremlin permitted several other Christian and Jewish dissidents to depart the Soviet Union in this same window. A thrilled Reagan kept his promise of silence. Shultz described the liberation of the Siberian Seven as "the first successful negotiation with the Soviets in the Reagan administration."[34]

Back home, Shultz continued putting his imprint on the State Department. He did so with a soft touch. Though devoted to Reagan's agenda, Shultz empowered the career Foreign Service officers (FSOs) and drew on their expertise in foreign languages, cultures, and diplomacy. Many FSOs would come to regard Shultz as the greatest secretary under whom they served. Shultz never let them forget who they worked for, however. Mindful of the temptations of "clientitis," where diplomats come to advocate more for the interests of the country of their posting rather than the United States, Shultz developed an inoculation. Before sending a new ambassador out to their post, Shultz would hold a farewell meeting in his office. At the end of their discussion, he would tell the diplomat, "You have one more test." Shultz would then spin the globe in his office and tell the new ambassador, "Point out your country." Invariably the puzzled envoy would put their finger on their country of destination. To which Shultz would reply: "Wrong—*your* country is the United States. Don't ever forget it."[35]

Shultz excelled in managing his staff at State and his relations with his foreign counterparts, but he did not play well with his peers in the administration. Especially those, such as Bill Clark, whom he did not regard as a peer. Shultz's memoir drips with condescension toward Clark, saying he "simply didn't comprehend the subtleties or the nuances" of foreign policy and accusing him of "standing in the way" of Reagan's policies.[36] The two men had started off on a collegial note, but their relationship soon deteriorated over differences in style and policy and disputes about bureaucratic turf. For his part, Clark resented, and resisted, Shultz's efforts to cut him and other senior officials out of important policy discussions. Ultimately the fault lay with Reagan himself; the conflict-averse president refused to enforce discipline with his fractious team.

Over his six and a half years as secretary, Shultz would have tensions and sometimes outright feuds with every national security advisor, secretary of defense, and CIA director, and Vice President Bush to boot. He would not build close ties with any other national security principals. Except the one who mattered most: the president.

V

The Cold War's centers of gravity sat in world capitals like Washington, DC; Moscow; London; and Berlin. But sometimes the events of most consequence took place in the mountains of the Hindu Kush, or the shipyards of Gdańsk, or the gulag of the Siberian steppe. Or a hotel conference room in Orlando, Florida.

The thousands of delegates gathered on March 8, 1983, in the Sheraton convention center for the National Association of Evangelicals' annual convention applauded Reagan as he took the stage. His speech, most of which he had written himself, began with domestic issues such as abortion and school prayer. He confessed America's "legacy of evil" in slavery and ongoing racism. Reagan then turned to foreign policy, beginning with the growing number of Catholics and evangelical Protestants embracing the nuclear freeze movement. Even the iconic Billy Graham had participated in a Soviet-sponsored nuclear propaganda conference in Moscow the year before.[37] Reagan closed with an impassioned appeal to his fellow Christians, and what would become his most controversial indictment of the Soviet Union:

The truth is that a freeze now would be a very dangerous fraud, for that is merely the illusion of peace. The reality is that we must find peace through strength. I would agree to a freeze if only we could freeze the Soviets' global desires. . . .

Let us pray for the salvation of all of those who live in that totalitarian darkness—pray they will discover the joy of knowing God. But until they do, let us be aware that while they preach the supremacy of the state, declare its omnipotence over individual man, and predict its eventual domination of all peoples on the Earth, they are the focus of evil in the modern world. . . .

I urge you to beware the temptation of pride—the temptation of blithely declaring yourselves above it all and label both sides equally at fault, to ignore the facts of history and the aggressive impulses of an evil empire, to simply call the arms race a giant misunderstanding and thereby remove yourself from the struggle between right and wrong and good and evil. . . .

I believe we shall rise to the challenge. I believe that communism is another sad, bizarre chapter in human history whose last pages even now are being written.[38]

Ignoring Reagan's commitment to negotiations with the Soviets, his confession of his own nation's sin, and his call for abolishing all nuclear weapons, his critics seized on his condemnation of the "evil empire." *New York Times* columnist Anthony Lewis lambasted the speech as "outrageous" and "primitive." In *The Washington Post,* Richard Cohen dismissed Reagan as a "religious bigot." The venerable historian Henry Steele Commager sneered, "It was the worst presidential speech in American history, and I've read them all."[39]

The Soviets agreed. The Kremlin's news agency TASS inveighed against Reagan's "bellicose, lunatic anti-Communism," and a senior Soviet official denounced his "hypocritical talk" and "outright medievalism."[40] It may have been Reagan's use of the word *empire,* even more than *evil,* that most incited Moscow. Reagan had long criticized the USSR for subjugating the nations of Eastern Europe like colonial properties, and for how its support for communism in the Third World treated developing nations like vassal states. In one writer's words, the Soviet Union was just "the Russian empire operating under an assumed name."[41] This stung Moscow because it turned on its head the standard Marxist-Leninist critique of the United States as "imperialist." When Reagan labeled the Soviet Union an empire, he hit the Kremlin in its most vulnerable ideological spot.

That which offended American liberals and outraged the Kremlin inspired the victims of Soviet tyranny. Sitting in his prison cell some weeks later, Anatoly Shcharansky was given a Soviet newspaper article condemning Reagan's use of the phrase *evil empire*. The dissident was overjoyed. He tapped on his cell wall a coded message to his fellow inmates reporting what the American president had dared say. As word spread through the prison population, shouts of joy erupted. Sharansky recalls, "That moment made it impossible for anyone in the West to continue closing their eyes to the real nature of the Soviet Union. It was one of the most important, freedom-affirming declarations, and we all instantly knew it. For us, that was the moment that really marked the end for them, and the beginning for us."[42]

Reagan was not done with his provocations. Two weeks after recasting the moral terms of the Cold War, he gave another speech reframing its strategic balance. On the evening of March 23, he called for "a program to counter the awesome Soviet missile threat with measures that are defensive."

This announcement came from a combination of Reagan's longstanding convictions and last-minute improvisations. Protecting the nation from nuclear missiles had been a preoccupation of his going back to his 1979 visit to NORAD, and his desire to abolish nuclear weapons went back even farther. As president, he had begun exploring policies for missile defense the previous year when the physicist Edward Teller visited him in the White House. The visionary architect of the hydrogen bomb, Teller had since become something of a rogue in the scientific community, distrusted by many of his colleagues for his anticommunism and his occasionally outlandish ideas. Reagan did not mind. When White House scientific advisor Jay Keyworth endorsed Teller's proposal to research directed energy defenses against nuclear missiles, Reagan scrawled a note to Clark: "We should take this seriously and have a real look. Remember our country once turned down the submarine."[43]

A few weeks prior to his speech, Reagan hosted the Joint Chiefs of Staff for lunch to discuss the MX basing problems. Led by Chief of Naval Operations Admiral James Watkins, a devout Catholic who shared Reagan's abhorrence of the massive civilian deaths a nuclear war would produce, the lunch discussion ranged into more fundamental questions of the arms race and mutual vulnerability in which the United States and USSR both lived under the constant terror of nuclear annihilation. That night, Reagan told his diary that "a super idea" had emerged at the table: "So far the only policy worldwide on nuclear weapons is to have a deterrent. What if we tell the world we want to protect our people not avenge them; that we're going to embark on a program of research to come up with a defensive weapon that could make nuclear weapons obsolete?"[44]

The president may have wanted to "tell the world" this message, but he neglected to tell his secretaries of state or defense. The process of crafting what would become the Strategic Defense Initiative (SDI) was interagency malpractice. Knowing that Weinberger and Shultz would oppose it, Reagan did not inform them of his plans, let alone invite their input. Instead he worked in secret with Clark, McFarlane, and the Joint Chiefs, and wrote the most important parts of the speech himself. Shultz and Weinberger only learned that Reagan would be announcing one of the most consequential decisions of his presidency two days before the speech. Then, as NSC official John Poindexter recalls, "all hell broke loose."[45] Though the secretaries of state and defense rarely aligned on policy questions, both agreed that the SDI announcement would overturn decades of strategic doctrine, rattle the allies with fears that America was retracting its nuclear umbrella, and violate the Anti-Ballistic Missile Treaty. Shultz importuned Reagan to amend the speech, while Pentagon officials Fred Iklé, Richard Perle, and Ron Lehman scrambled to kill the proposal outright. They demanded that Clark and McFarlane inform Reagan of their "most extreme concern" and warned that SDI would "create a furor from which we will never recover."[46]

Reagan incorporated some of Shultz's edits, aiming to mollify the allies and comply with the ABM Treaty, but otherwise disregarded the caterwauling of his staff. He resolved to present his vision for a world rid of the Soviet menace and free of nuclear weapons.

The night of March 23, a nationwide television audience tuned in to see Reagan sitting at his desk in the Oval Office. The bipartisan consensus of two years earlier supporting a boost in defense spending had dissipated. Many congressional Democrats and some Republicans now resisted any further increases in the Pentagon budget. For the first twenty-two minutes of his remarks, Reagan sought to rally the public behind his defense program and against congressional cuts by detailing the Soviet threat across the globe.

Then Reagan paused. He began to speak not as the most powerful man in the world, but as one frightened human being to another—to millions of others, in fact:

> I've become more and more deeply convinced that the human spirit must be capable of rising above dealing with other nations and human beings by threatening their existence. . . . If the Soviet Union will join with us in our effort to achieve major arms reduction, we will have succeeded in stabilizing the nuclear balance. Nevertheless, it will still be necessary to rely on the specter of retaliation, on mutual threat. And that's a sad commentary on the human condition. Wouldn't it be better to save lives than to avenge them?

Then he asked:

> What if free people could live secure in the knowledge that their security did not rest upon the threat of instant US retaliation to deter a Soviet attack, that we could intercept and destroy strategic ballistic missiles before they reached our own soil or that of our allies? . . . I call upon the scientific community in our country, those who gave us nuclear weapons, to turn their great talents now to the cause of mankind and world peace, to give us the means of rendering these nuclear weapons impotent and obsolete. . . .
>
> I am directing a comprehensive and intensive effort to define a long-term research and development program to begin to achieve our ultimate goal of eliminating the threat posed by strategic nuclear missiles. This could pave the way for arms control measures to eliminate the weapons themselves.[47]

The United States and Soviet Union had lived under the balance of terror for over three decades. Reagan sought to render this mutual vulnerability extinct. While presiding over a modernization and expansion of America's nuclear arsenal, he wanted to make those same weapons obsolete.

Neither America's allies nor its enemies shared Reagan's faith. Many NATO nations worried that SDI could mean the United States' folding up the nuclear umbrella that sheltered them under extended deterrence. A secret British Defense Ministry assessment complained that Reagan's announcement "presents particular difficulties for the United Kingdom."[48] If the British were anxious, the Soviets were apoplectic. Andropov issued a blistering statement accusing Reagan of searching for "the best ways of unleashing nuclear war in the hope of winning it," saying, "Engaging in this is not just irresponsible, it is insane."[49]

Reagan threw another curveball a few days later when he suggested that once the United States developed missile defense technology, a future president could "offer to give that same defensive weapon to [the Soviets] to prove to them that there was no longer any need for keeping these missiles. Or with that defense, he could then say to them, 'I am willing to do away with all my missiles. You do away with all of yours.'"[50]

Here was Reagan's second stunning departure from strategic convention in less than a week. He knew that if the United States could build an operational missile defense system, it would upset the delicate balance by enabling the United States to strike the Soviet Union without fear of Soviet retaliation. So Reagan offered to share SDI with Moscow. This would reassure the Kremlin of America's benign intentions and perhaps enable both countries to abolish their nuclear missiles. There was no precedent in the Cold War, perhaps no precedent in human history, for one state sharing its most advanced military technology with its mortal adversary. But precedent mattered little to Reagan, especially if a strategic revolution was within his grasp.

American critics of SDI, who were many and loud, fell into two main camps. The first was much of the scientific community, who decried SDI as technologically infeasible. This included the physicist and defense expert Ash Carter, who wrote a report for the Congressional Office of Technology Assessment dismissing the chances of SDI becoming operational as "so remote that it should not serve as the basis of public expectation or national policy."[51] Seizing on such critiques, Senator Ted Kennedy dismissed Reagan's proposal as "a reckless 'Star Wars' scheme," invoking the popular science fiction movie to treat SDI as fantastical. The term soon took hold in popular media. The second camp were the apostles of arms control, who had developed a theological faith in mutual assured destruction as a guarantor of stability and who feared that SDI would disrupt this delicate balance. In short, the scientists thought that SDI would not work, the arms controllers thought it *would* work, and both of them hated it.

In one sense, both camps were correct. SDI did not become operational by the end of the century despite billions of dollars in research and testing. Yet the mere concept of it disrobed MAD's pretensions to providing stability and peace. Both groups of critics missed the strategic point. For the same reasons they despised SDI, Reagan embraced it. It put the Soviets on the defensive, fueling the Kremlin's perennial fear of America's technological prowess. It envisioned an escape from the trap of MAD, replacing a fragile stability based on mutual terror with peace based on mutual security. And it changed the landscape of the Cold War, as the United States regained the strategic initiative. Shultz soon recognized this and turned from skeptic to enthusiast.

SDI was also the apotheosis of the Reagan defense buildup. It culminated his strategy to grow the military not just in mass but—crucially—in capability to overmatch the Kremlin's quantitative edge in troops, tanks, aircraft, missiles, and ships. Otherwise, Moscow's numeric advantages appeared to stretch far into the future. The Pentagon estimated in early 1983 that the "Soviet investment in future military capabilities," including weapons, bases, research, and development, continued to be "nearly double" that of the United States.[52] The Reagan Pentagon sought to counter those Soviet advantages while recasting the arms race, which had been a contest of quantity, as a contest of quality. As Weinberger had written a few months earlier, the United States was modernizing its military "in such a way that will force the Soviets into an expensive program of research, development and deployment to overcome it."[53]

Stealth aircraft. Precision-strike munitions. Highly accurate, radar-evading cruise missiles. Undiscoverable submarines. Tank-killing aircraft. Advanced guidance, control, and communications systems. And now SDI, a program to shoot Soviet ballistic missiles out of the sky. With these new systems either deployed or under development, Reagan and Weinberger designed their military expansion to neutralize Soviet weapons capabilities, bedevil Soviet planners, impose costs on the Soviet economy, pressure the Soviet system, and strengthen Reagan and Shultz's hands at diplomacy. Reagan sought to outsmart the Soviets as much as outspend them.

Yet as he built out the pieces of his strategy, he faced growing divisions among his team. He lamented to his diary that Shultz and Clark continued to feud, and complained, "Some of the NSC staff are too hard line and don't think any approach should be made to the Soviets. I think I'm hard line and will never appease but I do want to try and let them see there is a better world if they'll show *by deed* they want to get along with the free world."[54]

Moscow was not amused. The day after Reagan's meeting with reporters, *The New York Times* published an article by foreign policy eminence

Leslie Gelb on his recent trip to the Soviet Union. Following ten days of discussions with senior officials, Gelb described the Kremlin's "outright hostility" to the United States and noted "the mood has clearly worsened" since Reagan's SDI speech. Andropov made clear that he had no interest in a summit meeting with Reagan. Gelb's headline summed it up: "Moscow Angrily Settles Back to Await End of Reagan Era."[55]

VI

Reagan and Weinberger wanted to use the formidable military they were building. Not in combat—their strategy sought to deter a shooting war, and both were reluctant to employ force—but through displays of strength that would deter and unnerve the Soviets, such as massive military exercises. Besides rattling Moscow, exercises offered several other advantages. They provided training to military personnel; tested and refined new weapons platforms; strengthened alliances through joint exercises with allied forces and by reassuring allied leaders of American capabilities; and produced valuable intelligence when they prompted the Soviets to respond, thus revealing the Kremlin's detection abilities and tactics.

Calibrating these exercises was not easy. The Pentagon sought to poke the Soviet bear without provoking it to bite back.

Two days after Reagan's SDI speech, the aircraft carrier *Enterprise* set sail from Japan into the northwestern Pacific, where it joined the carriers *Midway* and *Coral Sea* for the Pacific Fleet's largest exercise since World War II. The maneuvers, named Fleetex 83-1, would be a Pacific version of Ocean Venture from eighteen months earlier, continuing navy secretary John Lehman's strategy of "aggressive defense."

The Kuril Islands chain stretches between the Soviet Union's Kamchatka Peninsula and Japan's northernmost island of Hokkaido. Claimed by both Tokyo and Moscow, the Kurils had been occupied by Soviet forces since World War II. Officially, the United States took no side in the territorial dispute. Unofficially, the US Navy decided to show that it did not recognize the Kremlin's claim. In the words of a top secret National Security Agency history, the exercise "served notice that Allied naval forces would intrude into what the Soviets had come to regard as their own private lakes.... These actions were calculated to induce paranoia, and they did."[56]

On April 4, the *Midway* switched into stealth mode, slipped away from the armada, and sailed toward the Kurils. It launched six F-14 Tomcat fighters, which flew at high speed and low altitude over a Soviet naval base on Zeleny Island, catching the Russians by surprise. A Soviet air force squadron based on nearby Sakhalin Island did not scramble in time to intercept the Tomcats. An embarrassed Kremlin lodged a diplomatic protest with the State Department—and sent two Soviet nuclear-capable bombers on an overflight of Alaska a week later, the first intrusion into US airspace by Soviet bombers since 1969.[57]

Moscow also ordered an investigation into its Sakhalin Island air defense lapse. One of the Soviet pilots later recalled, "A commission flew out to the regiment and gave us a dressing down. They really berated us."[58] The Soviet air force determined to be more aggressive against any future aircraft incursions into northeast Asia. It would be a fateful resolution.

The US Navy leadership regarded Fleetex 83-1 as a successful training operation and show of American resolve. They puzzled, however, over the lack of intelligence gleaned on Soviet capabilities. The Soviet navy in particular seemed oddly quiescent; its normally active surface ship surveillance had been "nearly non-existent," wrote one US Navy commander. The Soviets did not need to watch the exercise from the outside because they could view it from the inside. Jerry Whitworth, a radioman on the *Enterprise,* had been spying for the KGB for years as part of a spy ring run by former navy officer John Walker. Whitworth pilfered millions of pages revealing the navy's secure communications codes, countersurveillance tactics, and fleet operations, and passed them on to the KGB via Walker. Two years later, a KGB defector testified that the Walker and Whitworth ring was "the most important operation in the KGB's history."[59]

VII

Provocative exercises were just one use to which Reagan put his military expansion. He also wanted to put American weapons in the hands of other anticommunist fighters. The term "Reagan Doctrine" would not be coined by columnist Charles Krauthammer for another two years, but by 1983 it was already taking shape. From Central America to Central Asia, the United States equipped militaries and insurgent groups to fight communism. These efforts drew a direct lesson from the Vietnam War: Don't send American troops when you can support local forces to fight.

CIA director Casey became the main implementer of this strategy. The previous year he had traveled through Africa, the Middle East, and South Asia. In Pakistan, President Muhammad Zia-ul-Haq laid out for Casey a map of the region showing how the Soviet occupation of Afghanistan put the Kremlin within striking distance of the Strait of Hormuz and control of the Persian Gulf's oil supply lines. Casey also worried that Soviet-backed regimes in Ethiopia and South Yemen could give Moscow control of access to the Red Sea—and thus a veto over Suez Canal traffic.

On his return, Casey wrote a memo to Reagan describing his alarm at how "the Soviets have mounted subversion and insurgency threats to countries which control the most strategic choke points in the world." To counter this, Casey urged Reagan to increase support for anticommunist forces, including "light arms, transport, and communications" equipment.[60] Casey made this case to the public the next year. In April 1983, he wrote a *Wall Street Journal* op-ed describing the Third World—a term originally coined for Cold War regions that were part of neither the Western bloc ("First World") or the Soviet bloc ("Second World")—as "the principal US-Soviet battleground for many years to come." Casey detailed communist takeovers in the past decade in Vietnam, Ethiopia, Angola, Afghanistan, Nicaragua, Grenada, and Suriname, and urged the United States "to help our friends defend themselves" with training and weapons for anticommunist forces.[61] Next to Reagan himself, Casey was the administration official most attuned to the battle of ideas in the Cold War. He saw signs that the tide was turning. The CIA briefed State Department official Peter Rodman in 1983 on a classified study showing that, while for decades most insurgencies around the world had been communist-backed, all of a sudden "almost all the guerilla wars going on in the world were rebellions *against* Communist regimes. It was an extraordinary reversal of fortune."[62] Marxist revolutionary fervor seemed to be running on fumes, while the Kremlin was running out of funds to bankroll new insurgencies.

Afghanistan became the vanguard of this turnaround. While Reagan and Casey had decided two years earlier to continue the CIA covert action inherited from Carter providing $60 million per year in matériel to the Afghan insurgents, by early 1983 the program had stagnated. Influential officials at the CIA and the State Department voiced skepticism about the fighting ability of the mujahideen.[63] Some more cynical observers, noting that the limited American weapons supply would not give the rebels a battlefield advantage over the superior Red Army, said that the United States seemed "willing to fight to the last Afghan."[64]

Even more important, Pakistani president Zia had resisted a major expansion of aid, because he feared it could trigger Soviet retaliation against Pakistan. Since the American and Saudi support for the rebels flowed through Pakistan, Zia held an effective veto on the levels and recipients of the aid. Instead, he told Casey in April 1982 that the United States should "keep the pot boiling, but not boil over," in Afghanistan. However, Zia did urge the provision of more sophisticated matériel, especially ground-to-air weapons that could shoot down Soviet aircraft.[65] He and the CIA agreed that the weapons should be of Soviet bloc origin rather than American manufacture, to obscure the US role as the supplier.

By 1983, this caution began to give way. Two meetings deepened Reagan's personal interest in the Afghan campaign and laid the foundation for expanded US support. The first came in December 1982, when Reagan hosted Zia at the White House for a state visit. Over the thirty-five years since Pakistan's nativity, its relationship with the United States had been fraught and extraordinarily complex. The two nations had been treaty allies with a close intelligence collaboration, partners in Nixon and Kissinger's diplomatic opening to China, and adversaries at odds over Pakistan's nuclear weapons program and destabilizing wars with India—sometimes at the same time. Meeting with Zia privately in the Oval Office, Reagan voiced the obligatory concern over Pakistan's nuclear aspirations and later noted, "Zia gave me his word they were not building [a nuclear weapon]." Zia lied to Reagan. But the president did not press on this prevarication, turning instead to their shared interests in Afghanistan as they moved into the Cabinet Room for an expanded meeting. Zia described the Soviet occupation of Afghanistan and efforts to "intimidate Pakistan" as stemming from the Kremlin's hostility to religion, especially Islam. Between the Iranian Revolution and Islamic movements in Afghanistan and Pakistan, Moscow feared further unrest in "the soft underbelly" of the Soviet Union's own Muslim regions, restive under the oppressive yoke of communist rule. In a recent meeting with Andropov, Zia had realized that the Soviet leader knew his forces were bogged down and sought a way out. Zia and Reagan both saw an opening to impose more costs on the Soviet occupiers.[66]

Zia's analysis resonated with Reagan's own view of the Cold War's religious dimension and of Soviet vulnerabilities in Afghanistan. On top of

Reagan's efforts to aid Christians and Jews behind the Iron Curtain, he would support Zia's Islamic fighters in their holy war against the godless Soviets. That night at the state dinner, Zia toasted Reagan as "a man of God" and predicted that history "[will] remember you . . . [as] Reagan the Peacemaker."[67]

Two months later came the second pivotal meeting. On February 2, 1983, Reagan hosted six Afghan rebels in the Oval Office. Accompanied by CIA officer Gust Avrakotos, the Afghans, including one woman, described their fight against the Soviets and the Red Army's atrocities. One of the Afghans lifted his shirt and showed Reagan the burn marks on his skin from a Soviet chemical weapons attack. The meeting greatly affected Reagan. He wrote of it at length in his diary, describing the "freedom fighters" who suffered under the "inhumanity of the Soviets," including "a village where the Russians had burned 105 people alive with gasoline and chemicals in an irrigation tunnel."[68] This personal connection with the Afghanistan insurgency deepened Reagan's commitment to help.

The mujahideen soon gained an unlikely new ally in Washington, DC. Congressman Charlie Wilson, an East Texas Democrat, had recently traveled to Pakistan and become captivated by the Afghan resistance. A lecherous alcoholic and swashbuckling bon vivant, Wilson was also a tenacious and cunning lawmaker. Following his trip, he engaged in months of legislative legerdemain to increase the congressional appropriation supporting the resistance to $100 million. This 67 percent increase included more lethal antiaircraft guns to target Soviet helicopter gunships. Wilson capitalized on the desire of many of his Democratic colleagues, starting with House Speaker Tip O'Neill, to demonstrate their support for anticommunist forces in Afghanistan in part as political cover for their opposition to Reagan's Central America anticommunist policies on human rights grounds.[69] Such support was ironic given that the mujahideen were hardly democratic and many engaged in serial war crimes. Few were immune to selective morality in the Cold War.

VIII

The struggle over Central America intensified, both in the region itself and in Washington. In January, NSC staff member Alfonso Sapia-Bosch warned Clark of "an increasingly difficult time keeping [the United States'] Central

American program on course in the coming months." Sapia-Bosch detailed growing congressional resistance to the White House's Nicaragua and El Salvador aid and warned that John Paul II's upcoming Central America trip "will be an overall minus from our standpoint," because papal meetings will "legitimize" radical rulers and the Pope will refuse to denounce "leftist priests."[70]

Sapia-Bosch got Congress right and the Pope wrong. In early March, John Paul II visited eight Central American nations in seven days. His trip was pastoral and his main message was spiritual. Consistent with Catholic social thought, the Pope also called for "a climate of true democracy for the promotion of the common good" (words that Reagan quoted a few days later).[71] For John Paul II, this entailed speaking out against communists and liberation theology on the Left, and oligarchs and authoritarians on the Right.

Nicaragua witnessed the trip's most consequential event. The Sandinista regime engineered massive disruptions of the Pope's open-air mass in Managua. Sandinista mischief included loudspeakers drowning out the Pope's words, a bused-in mob, and Daniel Ortega himself leading the Sandinista rulers yelling, "People's power," during the Holy Father's homily. The Pope persisted with the service, at one point yelling, "*Silencio!*" to the mob. The Sandinista stunts backfired, spectacularly. Live television broadcast the mass throughout Central America, leaving millions of viewers, in papal biographer George Weigel's words, "shocked at the vulgarity of Sandinista misbehavior. . . . The Sandinista myth began, slowly, to erode."[72]

A month prior, Jeane Kirkpatrick had traveled to Central America. She and Casey shared the belief that the region was a central front in the Cold War, and they worked together to shape what became the Reagan Doctrine. Kirkpatrick also appreciated that Casey "treated me as an equal," unlike some of her other male peers in the administration. She recalled, "Bill was more interested in my views on Nicaragua than my sex."[73] So was Reagan, who regarded her as one of his most important advisors on Latin America.

Assistant Secretary of State for Latin America Tom Enders and US ambassador to El Salvador Deane Hinton both opposed Kirkpatrick's trip. Enders even sent a secret nine-page cable to the US embassies in each country on her itinerary, instructing them to disregard her views. His skullduggery failed. American and local officials both had the good sense to disregard Enders and welcome the higher-ranking Kirkpatrick. She met with all the US officials and regional leaders she wanted, including a late-night discussion with Duarte in San Salvador, where he impressed upon her the importance of free elections to his country's future.

What Kirkpatrick saw and heard on her trip increased her alarm. Many Central American leaders described growing Soviet, Cuban, and Nicaraguan inroads in the region. She grew to fear that Mexico itself might be ripe for subversion.[74] No slouch at bureaucratic infighting, Kirkpatrick exacted revenge when she briefed Reagan on her trip and persuaded him to fire Enders and Hinton. The president vented to his diary, "I'm now really mad. . . . I'm determined heads will roll beginning with Ambas. Hinton."[75] Both Enders and Hinton favored a power-sharing agreement between the Salvadoran government and the FMLN rebels. Reagan, Casey, Kirkpatrick, Clark, and Shultz all opposed such a settlement, which they feared would enable the FMLN to bypass the election process and even give it an opening to take over the country.[76] Shultz did not mind dismissing Enders and Hinton since he did not want them undermining the administration's policy. To lead the Latin America bureau, he appointed Langhorne "Tony" Motley, then serving as ambassador to Brazil, and replaced Hinton with Thomas Pickering, among the most capable diplomats in the Foreign Service.

Reagan faced growing congressional opposition to his Central America policies, led by Speaker Tip O'Neill himself. For O'Neill it was a spiritual fight, as the Cold War fault lines cut through the Catholic Church. His beloved ninety-one-year-old aunt was a Maryknoll nun, and he described the Maryknoll priests and nuns ministering in Central America as the "special source" of his "passion" for the region. He claimed that these men and women religious sent him an unequivocal message: "I haven't met one of them who isn't completely opposed to our policy." Further, the Speaker feared that Reagan planned to invade Nicaragua and described such a prospect as his "greatest fear about Reagan's foreign policy" (even though Reagan showed no intention of doing so). Nonetheless, O'Neill tried to block all of the White House's efforts to aid those anticommunist forces already fighting in El Salvador and Nicaragua.[77]

Most of the activists and members of Congress who joined O'Neill in mobilizing against Reagan's Central America policies did so from genuine conviction. They feared another Vietnam, lamented America's troubled history in the region, and detested the brutal repression that some Central American anticommunists employed. Few of these activists realized that the KGB supported their efforts. In 1980 the Soviet and Cuban intelligence services launched a covert campaign to fuel popular opposition in the United States to the Salvadoran and contra aid programs. For example, the KGB helped organize and fund the Committee in Solidarity with the People of El Salvador, cofounded by Sandy Pollack of the Communist Party USA, to coordinate activism against US aid to El Salvador. One internal KGB document described this campaign: "Influence was exerted on US public opinion: about 150 committees were created in the United States which spoke out against US interference in El Salvador, and contacts were made with US Senators."[78] The effects of these KGB efforts are hard to measure and should not be overstated, but at a minimum they contributed to eroding support for the White House's policies.

Reagan undertook a campaign to bolster public opinion and secure more backing from Congress. In March and April he and his team poured forth a cavalcade of speeches, interviews, and op-eds to explain their strategy— including an address by Reagan to a joint session of Congress, and even a *Wall Street Journal* op-ed by Richard Nixon titled "Don't Let El Salvador Become Another Vietnam" (by which Nixon meant letting it fall to communism).[79] The White House's messaging featured two main points. First, communist toeholds in Central America threatened "the entire Western hemisphere," including Mexico and even the United States, especially if the Panama Canal were to fall under hostile control. As Reagan wrote to Nixon in a letter thanking him for his op-ed, Soviet bloc advances in the region would herald "the beginning of the conflict for communist control of the United States itself."[80] Second, Reagan's strategy in the region entailed not just stopping communism but promoting democracy.

Reagan highlighted this in his April 25 address to Congress. As with most of his major speeches, he drafted a good portion of it himself.[81] "In response to decades of inequity and indifference," he said, "we will support democracy, reform, and human freedom." For Reagan, democracy was a middle way between the authoritarian, oligarchic Right and the revolutionary Left. He then invoked the Truman Doctrine, also delivered to a joint session of Congress almost four decades earlier, to place his Central America policy in a bipartisan context of Cold War history. He channeled the spirit of Truman's warnings about the global consequences of communist advances: "If Central America were to fall, what would the consequences be for our position in Asia, Europe, and for alliances such as NATO? If the United States cannot respond to a threat near our own borders, why should

Europeans or Asians believe that we're seriously concerned about threats to them?"[82]

Reagan's warnings about how European and Asian allies viewed the United States' credibility in Central America were exaggerated. Numerous European leaders in particular, under pressure from their own inflamed publics, preferred that the United States curtail its military aid programs in the region. Reagan often bristled at these objections, responding that Europeans had the luxury of opining on Central America without facing the risks that the United States did of instability and communist advances on its southern doorstep.

He knew that his appeals for democracy would ring hollow if the Salvadoran government did not protect innocent civilians. He also knew that Congress would not approve any further aid without improvements in human rights. In an April 5 phone call, Reagan urged President Magaña to take specific steps, including releasing political prisoners, investigating the 1980 murders of the Maryknoll nuns, and prosecuting the war criminals in the military.[83] Casey reinforced the message in person soon thereafter. On a secret trip to the region, he had dinner with Magaña in San Salvador and delivered a blunt warning: "Stop the death squads. I'm not going to lecture you about morality—you can worry about your own souls. But I'm telling you this: if you expect the United States to save you from a Salvadoran Castro, cut it out."[84]

Magaña readily agreed to these demands from Reagan and Casey. Whether he could deliver was another matter. Solving the Salvador challenge was hard enough when sober. The weak president, flummoxed by his legislature, fearful of his rogue military, leading a country aflame in civil war, took to the bottle. In a lunch meeting with a visiting American congressman, Hinton recalls that Magaña arrived "unusually late . . . dead drunk. After a bad half an hour, I convinced an aide to take him home."[85]

The White House struggled with its own hangover from Vietnam. On the one hand, Reagan emphatically rejected the comparison. He told reporters, "There is no parallel whatsoever with Vietnam."[86] He repeatedly disavowed any thought of sending American combat troops to El Salvador or even to "Americanize the war with a lot of US combat advisors," as he explained in one speech.[87] On the other hand, Reagan's incessant warnings about American credibility and communist threats to other nations in the region sounded much like the credibility and domino theory arguments that past American leaders had used to justify intervention in Vietnam.

Ironically, Reagan's strategy in El Salvador and Nicaragua did incorporate lessons from the Vietnam experience—so much that he deliberately took the opposite approach. Instead of sending American troops to fight, Reagan supported local forces to do the fighting. Yet for many Americans, Vietnam's lesson was not about how best to support anticommunist forces in a civil war, but rather not to get involved in civil wars at all.

IX

Late on Friday night, April 8, 1983, Clark and a small team of CIA, NSC, and Pentagon officials boarded a presidential airplane at Andrews Air Force Base and flew in secret to South America. Their weekend mission was to reverse communist inroads in a Latin American nation that most Americans had never heard of: Suriname. Its Marxist leader Dési Bouterse had taken power in a coup in 1980. Soon after, he began murdering his political opponents, building ties with the Soviets and Cubans, and welcoming arms shipments from Libya.

Suriname's small size belied its importance in the minds of Reagan and Clark. They feared its becoming the first South American state to slip into the Soviet orbit. As Clark warned Reagan, a Soviet toehold in Suriname would provide a base for maritime surveillance aircraft to track American submarines entering the southern Atlantic and give the Kremlin "the potential to control the Southern Caribbean and endanger shipping lanes," including petroleum transiting from Venezuela to America's Gulf Coast refineries.[88]

Back in early January, Reagan had convened an NSPG meeting on Suriname. His diary entry that night reflected his concern and his limited options. "Press is neglecting this place possibly because the blood thirsty dictator is on the left. He had about 30 labor leaders, academics and civic leaders executed and is seeking alliance with Cuba. This must not be allowed. We have to find a way to stop him. The Marines could do it but we'd lose all we've gained with the other Latin Am[erican] countries."[89] Reagan's fear of a regional backlash to an American military intervention led him to search for other options.

He found one with the Clark mission. It would be an elaborate bluff. In Clark's description, "it was a war plan, a false one but looking very real on paper . . . [to] invade Suriname." Clark and his team first landed in Caracas.

They met with President Campins and threatened that if Venezuela did not halt Bouterse's embrace of Havana and Moscow, the United States would attack Suriname. As Clark recalls, Campins "turned pale" but demurred, protesting that his political troubles prevented him from doing anything. From there the Clark delegation flew on to Brasília. They delivered the same warning to Brazilian president Figueiredo and his staff. Figueiredo, who disliked the notion of a communist outpost on Brazil's northern border, agreed to take care of the problem. "Brazil moved in with a carrot and stick to Bouterse," as Clark described, providing $25 million in development aid while also deploying Brazilian troops to the Suriname border. Bouterse soon distanced his country from Havana and Moscow. Clark's gambit had succeeded. He and Reagan had not sought a change in regime, just a change in behavior.[90]

X
___

Beyond America's backyard, Reagan also looked to the other side of the globe. In 1983 he began spending more time on Africa. That year alone, he hosted separate White House visits by the leaders of Zambia, Ivory Coast, Zaire, Senegal, Zimbabwe, Liberia, Cape Verde, Togo, and Sudan, in addition to Bishop Desmond Tutu of South Africa. While these meetings covered issues particular to each country, every discussion also included the common concerns of Libya's misbehavior, Soviet and Cuban encroachments, and southern Africa's tangle of the odious white supremacist regime in South Africa, its occupation of neighboring Namibia, and the Cuban forces propping up the communist regime in Angola.

Any consideration of Reagan's policies toward South African apartheid becomes entwined with Reagan's record on race and civil rights in the United States. It is a complex subject. Virtually everyone who knew Reagan agreed that he abhorred racism. As a football player at Eureka College in 1931, on a team road trip he had refused to sleep in a hotel that barred two of his Black teammates and instead welcomed them to stay with him overnight in his home.[91] As a baseball radio announcer in the 1930s, he spoke out against the sport's segregation. As president in 1981, he hired Middle East expert Dr. Raymond Tanter as one of the first Black members of the NSC policy staff, and in his second term would select General Colin Powell as the first Black national security advisor in history. Reagan took personal offense at racist behavior. In 1982, he had been appalled to read in *The Washington Post* of the Ku Klux Klan burning a cross on the front lawn of a Black family in Maryland. The horrified president cleared his schedule that afternoon so that he and the First Lady could visit the family at their home and offer consolation and encouragement. That night he lamented to his diary, "There is no place in this land for the hate-mongers and bigots."[92]

However, his background also includes some disturbing episodes. In 1971, following the United Nations' decision to eject Taiwan and welcome the People's Republic of China to membership, then-governor Reagan phoned President Nixon to complain about the support of many African nations for the move. Reagan fulminated, "To see those, those monkeys from those African countries—damn them, they're still uncomfortable wearing shoes!"[93] His language is ugly and indefensible. It also seems to be the only instance in the public record of Reagan's life where he used racist language. Another troubling moment came in his 1980 campaign when he gave a speech in Mississippi extolling "states' rights"—even though the nearby town of Philadelphia had been the site in 1964 of the murders of three civil rights workers by white supremacists. Historian Rick Perlstein describes Reagan as reluctant to give the speech, persuading himself that he had no racist intent even if the audience heard otherwise. Perhaps out of penitence, the next day he visited Black leader Vernon Jordan, recovering from an assassination attempt by a white supremacist, in the hospital, and gave an address to the Urban League.[94]

As Lou Cannon, the journalist who covered Reagan for over two decades, concludes, "Any fair-minded look at Mr. Reagan's biography and record demonstrates that he was not a bigot."[95] Reagan believed in racial equality but was not above occasional displays of racial insensitivity and did not make combating racism his top policy priority.

Instead, Reagan viewed Africa primarily through the lens of the Cold War. As did the Soviets. The previous decade had been good for the Kremlin in Africa. The communist People's Movement for the Liberation of Angola (MPLA) had seized power in Angola with support from Moscow and Havana, while communist dictator Mengistu Haile Mariam brought Ethiopia into the Soviet orbit. Brezhnev bestowed over $1 billion worth of weaponry on the Mengistu regime and deployed over seven thousand Soviet military and civilian advisors in the country, giving the USSR an influential perch on the Red Sea and its channel to the Suez Canal. As historian Odd Arne Westad observes, such victories "gave rise to unprecedented optimism in Soviet Third World policy." The emboldened Kremlin believed, as a senior Soviet official put it, "the world was turning in our direction."[96]

To tackle these problems, Reagan had appointed one of the most capable assistant secretaries in the State Department, Chester Crocker. A Georgetown professor who had previously served on the NSC staff in the Nixon White House, Crocker combined the mind of a scholar with a mastery of bureaucratic knife fighting learned at Kissinger's knee. When Reagan nominated him in 1981 to lead the Africa bureau, Senator Jesse Helms, a close collaborator with South Africa's white supremacist government, blocked Crocker's confirmation for six months because the nominee opposed the apartheid regime in Pretoria. Reagan and Haig stood steadfast behind Crocker, and eventually Helms relented.[97]

With Reagan's support, Crocker developed a strategy for southern Africa predicated on removing foreign forces and bringing peace to the troubled region. The challenges were almost infinitely complex. Angola had become mired in civil war as anticommunist rebels under the National Union for the Total Independence of Angola (UNITA) banner, supported by South Africa and led by Jonas Savimbi, fought the communist MPLA and its Cuban and Soviet backers. The Angolan regime and its Soviet allies in turn supported the African National Congress, the main antiapartheid organization targeting the white minority regime in South Africa.[98] Both Angola and South Africa treated Namibia as their proxy, with Angolan-sponsored insurgents warring against the occupying South African troops.

Reagan and Crocker's strategy linked three goals: ending South Africa's occupation and securing independence for Namibia; removing the fifty thousand Cuban troops from Angola; and ending apartheid in South Africa. Each goal was integrated and sequenced in a complex diplomatic dance; each goal also addressed the fears of the other parties. The South African regime worried that withdrawing from Namibia would allow it to become a base for communist guerilla attacks sponsored by Angola. The Angolan regime worried that losing its Cuban and Soviet backers would lead to its defeat at the hands of UNITA. Reagan, Shultz, and Crocker in turn feared that destabilization in South Africa could lead to the tyranny of apartheid being replaced by the tyranny of communism—and give the Soviets another foothold on the resource-rich southern tip of the continent. Instead they developed a policy of "constructive engagement" that combined protecting Pretoria from communism while pressing Prime Minister P. W. Botha to end the white minority's power monopoly and oppression of the Black population. As Reagan told his diary, "We detest apartheid but believe we can do better with S[outh] Africa by persuasion."[99] While some of Reagan's critics dismissed "constructive engagement" as too soft, Botha himself feared it as a serious threat to apartheid because, in US ambassador Herman Nickel's words, "it appealed to those elements in South African society who wanted change and who saw, as one of the benefits of such change, a better relationship with the United States."[100]

Unlike the White House's use of military aid in Central America and Afghanistan, persuasion was the main weapon that Reagan and Crocker had for the entire region. Congress had passed the Clark Amendment in 1975, banning military assistance to Angola. The removal of that instrument from the US toolkit increased American dependence on the Pretoria government as its main anticommunist proxy in the region. With South African arms and Savimbi's battlefield brilliance, in 1983 UNITA rebels advanced on Luanda itself. This terrified the USSR and Cuba. A CIA analysis found that their client's losses "prompted Moscow and Havana to increase significantly their support for the besieged Angolan regime," including "a major increase in the quality and quantity of arms delivered to" the MPLA.[101] Meanwhile the Reagan administration resorted to a combination of diplomacy and economic development aid to try to roll back communist inroads and bring peace to Africa's troubled southern cone.

XI

Ersatz vehicles and erratic driving were common on the war-ravaged streets of Beirut. Few Lebanese or Americans took much notice when just after noon on April 18, a black GMC pickup truck, its springs groaning with a heavy payload, began creeping toward the US embassy. At 1:04 P.M., its young Shia driver swerved into the embassy driveway, smashed through the glass-windowed lobby, and detonated one ton of high explosives in the truck bed. Bob Ames, visiting for the week from Langley, had just finished a contentious meeting inside the secure vault housing the CIA station. The blast wrenched the seven-story building from its pillars, ripped off its front, and caused its floors to collapse on each other like a deadly accordion. Sixty-three people were killed, including seventeen Americans, eight of them CIA employees. Among the dead was Bob Ames.[102]

The loss of his top Middle East expert shook Casey. In a headquarters ceremony, as eight new stars were inscribed on the CIA's memorial wall, the director paid tribute to Ames as "the closest thing to an irreplaceable man." Soon after, Casey personally recruited veteran officer William Buckley to deploy to Lebanon as chief of station to rebuild the CIA presence in the country.[103] It was a request that would turn into a death warrant.

The bombing heralded a grim new era for the region and America's role in it. It was planned and executed by a new organization, sponsored by Iran, that would soon be known to the world as Hezbollah.[104] It pioneered a new method, suicide bombing, that would wreak havoc for decades to come. It marked a surge in Shia militancy that included an accelerating spate of kidnappings of American hostages in Lebanon. It was terrorism's first major blow to America during Reagan's presidency. It would not be the last.

As smoke still wafted from the embassy ruins, Shultz embarked on a round of shuttle diplomacy. He worried that the bombing might cause a series of further explosions, literal and metaphorical, in the region. Traversing Jerusalem, Beirut, Amman, Jeddah, and Damascus, within a few weeks he brokered the May 17 Agreement, signed by Israel and Lebanon. Under its terms Israel agreed to withdraw its troops from Lebanon, and Lebanon agreed to prevent its southern border region from being used for attacks on Israel.

Syria began to sabotage the deal before its ink had dried. Damascus did so in part to press its own advantage and in part to please its Soviet patrons. The previous year, the Israelis had decimated the Soviet-equipped Syrian military in combat in Lebanon. The Kremlin, wanting to bolster its ally and also bedevil the United States, had launched an emergency airlift to rebuild the Syrian military with $2 billion in weapons and aid.[105] Prince Bandar, the Saudi ambassador to the United States, met with President Hafez al-Assad in Damascus and then returned to Washington to warn Reagan, "The Soviets have increased their influence to a disturbing proportion. . . . Assad kept reading me a list of what the Soviets are doing for him—giving him arms, manning their air defense, providing direct telephone links with Moscow."[106]

Reagan continued to view Middle East and Cold War events in apocalyptic terms. He fretted to his diary, "Syria is poisoning the well and the possibility of an Israeli-Syrian (plus Soviet) confrontation can not be ruled out. Armageddon in the prophecies begins with the gates of Damascus being assailed."[107] Such fears affected Reagan in two paradoxical ways. They deepened his commitment to making peace in a troubled region at the center of history. Yet they also deepened his uncertainty about what policy to choose and which advisors to favor—especially if the end of the world might hang in the balance.

By reinforcing Assad's murderous rule, the Soviets increased their ability to foil American goals in the region. Now, with the May 17 Agreement, which one author described as "stillborn" because it depended on Syrian cooperation, Assad saw his chance.[108] In partnership with Iran, Syria began stepping up its aggression in Lebanon. The Lebanese government became increasingly imperiled. Israel suspended its withdrawal plans. Clark sent Reagan a grim report: "Ratification of the Lebanon-Israel agreement has led the Syrians to make good on earlier threats to destabilize the Gemayel Government. Behind all this activity in the region, the Soviets continue to inveigh against the agreement and our role in negotiating it."[109]

Assad also declared Phil Habib to be persona non grata, barring the envoy from Syria and neutering his effectiveness. Exhausted and frustrated, Habib decided to resign. Clark replaced him with Deputy National Security Advisor Bud McFarlane.[110] McFarlane had two prerequisites for success: He was capable, and he had White House support. But he lacked experience and deep knowledge of the region, and he lacked support from Shultz, who resented this latest NSC intrusion on State's domain.

The American mission in Lebanon became even more muddled. The NSC rather than State had the lead on diplomacy. The State Department advocated for continuing the marine deployment, while the Pentagon opposed it—and opposed McFarlane's role as well. The CIA presence was shattered. In the midst of this acrimony, Reagan could not resolve the differences within his own government—nor could he repair the rift with Israel. Instead, with his administration divided, diplomacy flailing, and the marines left exposed on the front lines with their hands tied and mission unclear, worse trouble awaited.

XII

It was a sign of the times that spring in Washington, DC, witnessed the perennial bloom of the cherry blossoms enveloping the Jefferson Memorial—and the publication of two landmark reports on nuclear weapons. On April

6, the Scowcroft Commission issued its recommendations on the MX missile basing dilemma, and on May 3 the US Conference of Catholic Bishops (USCCB) released its pastoral letter on nuclear weapons.

Both generated national headlines, though the two documents could not be less alike. The Scowcroft Commission report, written in the muscular prose of nuclear strategy, supported the White House's nuclear modernization. Warning that "deterrence is not, and cannot be, bluff," among other measures it urged deploying one hundred MX missiles in hardened Minuteman silos and developing a new, more mobile single-warhead ballistic missile.[111]

The importance of the Scowcroft Report lay not as much in what it said as who said it. Its recommendations largely mirrored the Reagan administration's own emerging plans. But its bipartisan membership of moderate Republicans and Democrats created political cover for fence-sitting members of Congress to reverse their previous opposition. Reagan capitalized on this. Throughout May he threw himself into a lobbying campaign, phoning or meeting personally with over one hundred senators and representatives, to secure their support. It worked. Both the House and Senate, including ninety House Democrats, voted to fund the MX. The Peacekeeper missiles would be deployed in silos in Wyoming. Though never to be launched in anger, their impact would be felt at the negotiating table in Geneva.

If the Scowcroft Report provided political support, the White House feared that the USCCB letter imposed political shackles. Titled *The Challenge of Peace: God's Promise and Our Response,* the densely argued epistle of forty-five thousand words combined Jesuitical casuistry with florid eloquence. It was also widely seen as an inquisition against Reagan's nuclear posture. The USCCB condemned the arms race as "one of the greatest curses on the human race" and demanded that the United States and NATO adopt a "no first use" nuclear policy.[112] Such visible Catholic criticism undermined Reagan's effort to marshal a united religious front against Soviet communism. It could have been worse. The USCCB had revised earlier drafts in response to the concerns voiced by Clark and other Catholic conservatives. Their entreaties persuaded the USCCB to remove its call for a nuclear freeze and amend its accusations that the US nuclear posture directly targeted civilian populations.[113]

Reagan had followed the document closely. He unburdened himself in a letter to a Catholic priest in Ohio who wrote to the White House of his own misgivings with the USCCB's position. Responded Reagan:

I'm sure the bishops supporting the "freeze" and unilateral disarmament are sincere and believe they are furthering the cause of
peace. I'm equally sure they are tragically mistaken. What they
urge would bring us closer to a choice of surrender or die. Surrender of course would mean slavery under a system that would ban-
ish God. I believe there is another way, the way we call peace
through strength.[114]

Yet scrupulous readers of the Scowcroft Commission report and the
USCCB letter would have noticed some surprising areas of convergence.
The Scowcroft Commission concluded with its hope for arms control agreements that would reduce the risk of war and reduce the size of Soviet and
American arsenals, while *The Challenge of Peace* gave a qualified acceptance
of nuclear deterrence. What few readers, let alone the authors of either report, appreciated is how Reagan himself took both goals even further. He
wanted to build up the American arsenal to sufficient strength to force the
Soviets into negotiating—not just to reduce nuclear arms but to abolish
them altogether.

XIII

In the late seventeenth century, the Williamsburg settlement became the
capital of colonial Virginia and one of the birthplaces of democracy. Three
centuries later came the United States' turn to host the G7 summit, and
Reagan chose Williamsburg for this symbolism. He hosted most of the
meetings at the Williamsburg Inn, which creaked with the ghosts of allies
past. Exactly four decades earlier, in May 1943, the combined British and
American joint chiefs of staff had repaired to the Williamsburg Inn while
planning the campaign to liberate Europe from Nazi tyranny. Now, in May
1983, Reagan and his allies gathered there to plan how to liberate the world
from Soviet tyranny.

Reagan welcomed Japanese prime minister Nakasone to the White
House before the G7 gathering. This visit cemented their personal relation-
ship. It also advanced Reagan's "effort to establish a new Pacific emphasis in
US foreign policy," as Clark wrote.[115] Nakasone had earned this return
White House invitation by taking tough political steps back in Tokyo. He
had secured his legislature's approval for several defense measures and, as

important, persuaded a critical mass of the Japanese public to support a stronger military and deepened security cooperation with the United States. Nakasone had sent Reagan a lengthy letter in April outlining these steps, including increased defense spending, lifting the ban on exporting advanced military technology to the United States, and committing Japan to defending its territorial waters and any US forces in the region under attack.[116] Against the view that structural forces alone shape international politics, Nakasone was showing how individual leaders can make a decisive difference. He was engineering a revolution in Japan's strategic posture that none of his predecessors could even envision.

During their White House lunch, Nakasone indulged his penchant for metaphors resonant with American ears. Regarding their strategy at Williamsburg, he told Reagan, "You be the pitcher, and I'll be the catcher." Of course, Nakasone added, sometimes the catcher calls the pitches.[117] It was an apt description of their partnership beyond the weekend summit, through the next four years. An appreciative Reagan wrote that night of Nakasone, "He impresses me more every time I see him."[118] Nakasone proved as good as his word behind Reagan's back. Ahead of the summit he privately told Thatcher that he "wished Williamsburg to demonstrate Western solidarity so that President Reagan felt that all his allies were behind him in the [nuclear arms control] negotiations."[119]

Reagan looked forward to welcoming his counterparts to Williamsburg. Several he now counted as friends, especially Thatcher, Kohl, and Nakasone. He even enjoyed a bonhomie with Mitterrand, despite their political differences. Mitterrand would later commend Reagan's resolve as "primal: like a rock in the Morvan, like plain truth."[120] The one leader Reagan still found grating was Canadian prime minister Pierre Trudeau.

By this point Reagan's economic policies had led to reductions in inflation and interest rates (from 18 percent to 9 percent) as the American economy revived. In Williamsburg he would be spared European complaints about interest rates that had plagued previous meetings. Instead his counterparts had a new gripe: the United States' growing budget deficits. Thatcher and Kohl in particular feared American deficits could provoke inflation's vengeful return and tempt more capital flight from their countries to finance American borrowing.[121]

In Williamsburg, Reagan parried these criticisms by agreeing to vague language in the conference economic declaration committing all member nations to reducing deficits. In turn Reagan secured, with support from

Thatcher and Kohl, strong statements supporting free markets, opposing protectionism, and committing to a new round of General Agreement on Tariffs and Trade (GATT) negotiations. Together they began laying the foundation for expanding free trade and economic growth around the world. It embodied Reagan's vision of displaying the free world's prosperity as an attractive contrast to the penury of the communist bloc.

The scheduled American missile deployment in Europe loomed that fall. European public opinion continued to resist the missiles, even while most European leaders supported them. Before the summit began, Reagan asked Thatcher to suggest a G7 statement endorsing the deployment. Once Thatcher put the idea on the table over dinner, Reagan led the negotiations and even took the notes that would be turned into the statement.[122]

Mitterrand and Trudeau worked to block it. The bombastic Frenchman tried to storm out of the room until physically restrained by the much larger Kohl. Returning to the table, Mitterrand complained on procedural grounds that the INF issue was a NATO rather than G7 concern.[123] Nakasone, however, had a firsthand interest in the INF question. The Soviets had deployed SS-20s in their far east, targeting Japan. Nakasone knew that any hope of removing that threat depended on the diplomatic leverage that American missiles in Europe would provide.

Reagan pulled Mitterrand and Nakasone aside and spoke to Mitterrand on the Japanese leader's behalf: "You've got to understand: Nakasone's side doesn't have any democratic neighbors in Asia. He's got to be part of our democratic community if he's going to be supported effectively as a democratic country." Mitterrand found Reagan's appeal persuasive. When the full group reconvened at the table, Mitterrand spoke up in favor of an INF statement.[124] To reinforce the point, Nakasone took the dramatic step of inserting language in the statement linking Japan's security to Europe's security—a connection no other postwar Japanese leader had ever made in public.

Trudeau posed a bigger problem. The haughty Canadian dismissed the INF deployment as "utterly and tragically wrong" and proposed instead expressing "mutual trust" with the Kremlin because "the Soviet people want peace." The other leaders found those banalities naïve and irksome. Then tempers erupted when Trudeau went a step further and said that Canada, though a NATO member, should not be bound by the INF decision because he had not been in office when NATO first announced it in 1979.[125] Such a sentiment struck at the heart of the alliance's credibility and

integrity, which should not be captive to the whims of an individual premier. Reagan confessed that he "got angry," while Thatcher became down-
right incensed, especially after Trudeau shouted, "We should be busting our
asses for peace!" An amused Reagan told his diary, "I thought at one point
Margaret was going to order Pierre to go stand in a corner."[126] Trudeau relented in the face of this alliance wrath. The other leaders finished crafting
the declaration and dispatched Shultz to read it to the assembled media. The
statement also warned Moscow about the KGB's disinformation campaign
and fomenting of antinuclear protests in NATO countries: "Attempts to
avoid serious negotiation by seeking to influence public opinion in our
countries will fail."[127]

Reagan and his team returned to Washington, DC, feeling triumphant.
Even the *Washington Post* editorial page, not normally supportive, gushed
that "Mr. Reagan personally acted very much the leader of the alliance."[128]

XIV

If Reagan led the Western alliance, John Paul II served as its chaplain.
NATO leaders watched anxiously as the Pope landed in Warsaw on June 16
for his first return to Poland since martial law. A nervous General Jaruzelski
acceded to the Vatican's insistence that the Pope meet with Lech Walesa.
This bolstered the Solidarity leader's spirits and injected the movement with
new vitality. (The CIA's ongoing covert support also helped.) Over seven
days the Pope visited several cities and drew flocks numbering up to two
million of the Polish faithful. In George Weigel's description, the papal visit
"restored hope to a people who had begun to lose hope."[129] A few weeks later
West German foreign minister Hans-Dietrich Genscher visited Washington and told Reagan and Shultz that the Pope's Poland trip would "make the
Soviets think twice" and "effectively answered the question of how many
divisions he has" (a reference to Stalin's derisive comment "How many divisions does the Pope have?").[130]

One month after the Pope's departure, a beleaguered Jaruzelski lifted
martial law. Poland was far from free. But it was a step closer.[131]

Reagan continued to wrestle with the most effective ways to secure
freedom for Soviet dissidents. In May, he had presided over a Rose Garden
ceremony to sign a bill establishing "Andrei Sakharov Day" as an annual
remembrance of the dissident physicist and Nobel Peace laureate, then under

house arrest in the Soviet Union. That night, Reagan confided his ambivalence to his diary: "I'm kind of sorry about the whole thing. We've been working behind the scenes to get him released—quiet diplomacy. This kind of public demand puts the Soviet politicos in a corner where they lose face if they give in."[132]

As he waged his freedom offensive against the Kremlin, Reagan remained mindful of how Moscow perceived it. He continually tried to see the world through Soviet eyes, even as he tried to pressure the Soviet system into producing a reformist leader he could look at directly across the negotiating table.

CHAPTER 7

---◆---

THE MAELSTROM

I
_____

At 2:42 A.M., Soviet air force pilot Gennady Osipovich took off from a base on the Kamchatka Peninsula and throttled his Su-15 interceptor into the night sky. The base commander had ordered him to track an unfamiliar aircraft that had drifted into Soviet airspace. His plane, among the Soviet air force's most advanced fighter jets, was armed with a twenty-millimeter cannon and R-98 air-to-air missiles.

Osipovich soon located the intruder. It was a Boeing 747, one of the world's most widely used civilian passenger jets. With its iconic silhouette and navigation lights on, it would normally have been recognizable, but in the darkness Osipovich could not be sure.

He remembered being upbraided by his superiors five months earlier when the US Navy F-14s had flown over Zeleny Island undetected. He had resolved not to let it happen again.

Osipovich tried to contact the plane over the Soviet military's radio identification system. No response. He fired warning shots from his cannon, but the rounds did not include tracer bullets and were unseen by the 747 pilots. His commander then ordered him to shoot down the aircraft. Osipovich locked in his radar and fired two missiles. One struck the 747.

"The target is destroyed," radioed Osipovich.

But the jet did not immediately explode. Instead, a five-foot hole torn in its fuselage, the 747 began to climb in an awkward ascent.

Its bewildered pilots struggled to control the crippled air giant.

"What's happened?"

"Retard throttles."

"Altitude is going up."

A computer alert sounded in the cockpit: "Attention: emergency descent! Attention: emergency descent!"

The panicked first officer: "This is not working. This is not working."

The captain: "Manually."

"Cannot do manually."

"Is it power compression?"

"Is that right?"

"Rapid decompression descend to one zero thousand!"

The passengers heard the public address system intone over and over, in Korean, English, and Japanese: "Put out your cigarette. This is an emergency descent."

Oxygen masks dropped from the ceiling.

The PA repeated: "Put the mask over your nose and mouth and adjust the headband."

Then the 747 began to descend, first gradually and then in a rapidly accelerating death spiral.

The plane was Korean Air Lines flight 007, en route from New York City to Seoul. Because of a navigation error, it had drifted off course into Soviet airspace. Its 269 civilian passengers and crew spent their last moments in the slow-motion horror of feeling their aircraft plummet from the sky. Twelve terrifying minutes after the missile hit, their plane disintegrated as it crashed into the sea. All aboard died instantly from "blunt force trauma" in the clinical words of the coroner's report. Most of the passengers were South Korean citizens; sixty were Americans.[1]

When news broke of the KAL 007 shoot-down, Senator Henry "Scoop" Jackson called a press conference in Seattle to excoriate the Soviets for their brutal massacre. Hours later he suffered a massive heart attack and died.

Jackson's death deprived Reagan of a friend and a valued ally in the Senate who lent a bipartisan foundation to his Cold War policies. The mournful president wrote in his diary that it was "a real loss."[2]

It would soon get much worse. The next three months would bring the largest loss of life for the American military since Vietnam, the departure of his most trusted member of his national security team, and a new nadir in the US-Soviet relationship. The world would also come to the edge of nuclear war.

II

Earlier in the summer, Reagan and Shultz had renewed their outreach to the Kremlin. They sent the American delegation back to Geneva on June 8 to resume the Strategic Arms Reduction Talks (START) with the Soviets. They also probed for an opening with Andropov.

Reagan received conflicting reports on the economic conditions facing the new Soviet leader. The CIA and the State Department's Bureau of Intelligence and Research, somewhat revising their earlier assessments of economic distress, issued multiple analyses throughout 1983 describing the Soviet Union as on "a slow-growth track" and forecasting a modest GDP increase of 2 to 3 percent. They depicted a stagnant economy, with a few bright spots overshadowed by systemic inefficiency, that could nonetheless keep muddling along and faced little prospect of collapse.[3]

Frustrated by how the intelligence community seemed to accept Soviet official statistics, Andrew Marshall at the Pentagon's Office of Net Assessment commissioned an outside study by a group of Soviet émigré economists based in Maryland. The émigrés combined academic expertise and firsthand familiarity with their home country's pathologies. Their report, circulated widely at the NSC, detailed how the CIA and most other American economists failed to "recognize the extent of the badness" of the Soviet economy. The émigrés described it instead as "desperate" and on the brink of "economic disaster."[4] Their assessment reinforced Reagan's convictions and his strategy to increase pressure on Soviet vulnerabilities.

This strategy could include a summit with Andropov. Reagan and his team deliberated over how to propose such a meeting with the Soviet leader. To replace Pipes after his return to Harvard, Clark had recruited Foreign Service Officer Jack Matlock to the NSC staff as senior director for Soviet affairs. Beyond his policy expertise and Russian linguistic skill, Matlock maintained a good relationship with Shultz and other State officials, which Clark hoped might help ease the persistent NSC-State tensions. Clark and Matlock contended that America's military expansion, allied unity, and impending INF deployment, combined with the "myriad of problems" besetting Andropov, meant "our negotiating strength is stronger than it has been for many years." Shultz agreed. However, all counseled to proceed with caution and "use the summit issue in a manner which enhances our leverage rather than weakening it." They worried that the Kremlin's insecurity and refusal to make concessions could cripple a summit as mere talk with few results.[5]

Reagan decided to explore it with a letter. Andropov had sent Reagan a polite but perfunctory note of holiday wishes on July 4. The next week Reagan handwrote his response. Reiterating his commitment to "elimination of the nuclear threat," Reagan appealed for negotiations across the full spectrum of issues in the US-Soviet relationship, including Eastern Europe, Afghanistan, Central America, arms control, and trade.[6]

It was the second time that Reagan wrote by hand to a Soviet leader suggesting a diplomatic opening, following his missive to Brezhnev two years earlier. The result would be much the same. The two leaders exchanged three more letters over the following month. Andropov focused on the looming basing of American missiles in Europe. The Soviet leader hinted he might reduce the number of Soviet medium-range missiles, but only if the United States halted its planned deployment. In doing so, Andropov inadvertently revealed just how much the Kremlin feared the American missiles—and how much strategic leverage they provided the United States. Andropov demurred on discussing the other issues Reagan raised. This epistolary dialogue, already strained, ended altogether with the shoot-down of KAL 007.[7]

III

As the world grew more turbulent, so did the strains within Reagan's team. The amiable Clark found himself, surprisingly, at the center of the acrimony. From the outside, Clark's star appeared ascendant in the summer of 1983. *Time* magazine put him on its cover, and *The New York Times Magazine* featured him in a story as "the most influential foreign-policy figure in the Reagan Administration."[8] But in his White House basement office, he found himself being squeezed by a three-way vise. The strangulating pressures came from Shultz at the State Department, James Baker and Michael Deaver upstairs in the West Wing, and, most fatally, the First Lady in the East Wing.

Shultz fretted, not without cause, that Clark and the NSC staff were intruding on the State Department's prerogatives and keeping Shultz in the dark—especially on Middle East and Central America policy. After belatedly learning of a major US military exercise near Nicaragua and a Middle

East trip by McFarlane, on July 25 the furious secretary demanded a meeting with Reagan, Bush, Clark, Baker, and Meese. Shultz complained of being sidelined, told Reagan that he should get a new secretary of state, and acidly suggested, "Bill Clark seems to want the job, because he is trying to run everything."[9]

Reagan rejected Shultz's threat to resign and reassured the secretary of his full faith and confidence. This mollified Shultz for but a moment. Four days later he erupted again when the *Time* story appeared, featuring Clark leading the White House's "big stick" approach in Central America and described Shultz's "disappearing act" at the State Department, which further chafed Shultz's fragile ego. As did a *New York Times Magazine* cover story portraying Clark as an influential anti-Soviet hard-liner. Such coverage also irritated the First Lady, who took umbrage at any staff who seemed to eclipse her husband. She phoned Shultz and told him she wanted to see Clark fired. Shultz recalled, not unhappily, "Clark was getting heavy publicity, but I knew his days were numbered."[10]

The next month, on September 14, Reagan was having lunch with Bush and Shultz when Baker burst into the private dining room. The chief of staff, normally unflappable, was irate. He brandished a letter that Reagan had signed earlier in the day authorizing the attorney general to subject any senior official—including the chief of staff, cabinet secretaries, and vice president—to lie detector tests in a leak investigation.

The day prior, *The Washington Post* had published an article on Reagan's Lebanon policy that included leaked information about McFarlane's regional travel that exposed the envoy to danger. An enraged Clark and Meese went to Reagan and persuaded him that only polygraphs could smoke out the culprit and smother the leak fires consuming the White House. They did not consult Baker because they suspected him as the source of the story.

Standing at the lunch table, Baker protested to Reagan that the polygraphs would be ineffective, foolish, and bad for staff morale. Shultz huffed that he would only take a lie detector once (his second resignation threat in less than two months). A flustered Reagan summoned all parties to the Oval Office. Clark and Baker traded angry accusations, while Reagan compromised by ordering an FBI investigation into the leak but eschewing strapping his team to polygraphs.[11]

It was no coincidence that much of this acrimony centered on Middle East policy. Through the summer, the administration had struggled with the deteriorating situation in Lebanon and its regional fallout, all while the

White House's own policy rifts resembled Middle East sectarian strife. The NSC, led by Clark and McFarlane, and State under Shultz supported the marine deployment, to preserve order and negotiate a peace settlement. Though the NSC and State agreed on the mission, they disagreed on tactics—and differed even more on who should be in charge, with each jockeying for the lead role. Meanwhile the Pentagon's civilian and military leadership, under Weinberger and CJCS Jack Vessey, disliked partnering with Israel, saw no national interests at stake in Lebanon, and opposed the marine deployment. America's recent military misadventures shaped their skepticism; one NSC staffer derided Weinberger and Vessey as "charter members of the 'Vietnam never again club.'"[12] In an NSC meeting, Reagan plaintively asked for "innovative ideas on how we might untie this Gordian Knot in Lebanon."[13] His fractious team differed over not just which strand to pull but whether to try to unravel it at all.[14]

With September, conditions worsened. Mortar attacks killed four marines over four days. When Reagan made condolence calls to their families, one father asked the president "if they were in Lebanon for anything that was worth his son's life." Such questions haunted Reagan. He admitted to his diary, "[Lebanon's] Civil War is running wild," and agonized over the "choice of getting out or enlarging our mission."[15] King Hassan of Morocco, one of the region's savviest leaders, privately warned Reagan that Lebanon was a "Syrian trap" to tie down American forces and urged the president to withdraw the marines.[16]

As troubled as that mission was, hindsight is easy and unfair. Reagan's options ran the gamut from bad to worse. Withdrawal and disengagement, as Weinberger and Vessey urged, would have abandoned Lebanon to civil war and massive civilian suffering, handed Syria a vassal state, emboldened terrorism, strengthened the Soviet hand, alienated regional partners, and damaged American credibility. Faced with that alternative, Reagan made the fateful choice to side with his NSC and State Department and doubled down on the mission. The problem was that this choice incurred many of the same grim risks as withdrawal, and others besides.

IV

When Clark phoned Reagan at his ranch with the news of the KAL 007 shoot-down, the president cut short his trip and flew back to Washington.

He could not yet know that ahead lay the most perilous, tragic, and bloody three months of his presidency.

On Saturday, September 2, he chaired an emergency NSPG meeting. He and his advisors, their initial shock turning to sustained outrage, wrestled with how to respond. Several facts complicated the picture. Shortly before KAL 007 had approached the Kamchatka Peninsula, a US Air Force RC-135 spy plane flew a surveillance loop in the vicinity, trying to monitor a rumored Soviet missile test. The RC-135 stayed in international airspace but still irked the Soviets, who dispatched several fighter jets to intercept and track it. When KAL 007 crossed the RC-135's flight path and drifted by accident into Soviet territory, the Soviet radar operators seemed to confuse KAL 007 with the RC-135, as did their interceptor pilots. The Soviet air force, still rattled from the US Navy F-14 intrusion five months earlier, erred on the side of incaution in deciding to shoot down the plane.

It was still inexcusable. Weighed against the mitigating factors were these: Neither the Soviet ground commander nor his interceptor pilots ever made a positive identification of the civilian plane, despite having shadowed it for two and a half hours. Nor did KAL 007 show any hostile intent; the jetliner was actually exiting Soviet airspace when Osipovich received the order to fire on it. The Kremlin's response only reinforced the worldwide impression of its guilt. Rather than showing contrition, Moscow stonewalled: It blocked Japanese and Korean search-and-rescue ships from the area, refused to cooperate in an international investigation, fulminated that KAL 007 had "rudely violated the state border and intruded deliberately into the Soviet Union's airspace," and dismissed international outrage as a "hullabaloo."[17]

Reagan, Clark, and Shultz soon settled on a two-track approach. First, the United States would take the lead in marshaling world opinion against the Soviets and marginalizing Moscow. Clark wrote to Reagan, "[The shootdown] presents us with the opportunity to reverse the false moral and political 'peacemaker' image that the Soviets have been cultivating."[18] Second, Reagan would still pursue his diplomatic endeavors with the Kremlin. Most immediately, Shultz would keep his planned meeting with Soviet foreign minister Andrei Gromyko in Madrid that week, resisting many calls to cancel it.

On September 5, Reagan delivered an address to the nation. Dissatisfied with two different drafts that the White House speechwriters and State Department had sent him, he rewrote most of his remarks himself. Speaking with controlled fury about Soviet atrocities, he drew a line from the shoot-down to the Soviet system itself: "It was an act of barbarism born of a society which wantonly disregards individual rights and the value of human life and seeks constantly to expand and dominate other nations." He announced a series of sanctions, including multinational restrictions on the Soviet state airline Aeroflot.[19]

Jeane Kirkpatrick followed up with a masterful performance at Turtle Bay. Leading a special UN Security Council session, she captivated the room—and the watching world—by playing audio intercepts of the Soviet commander's exchange with Osipovich that closed with the Soviet pilot's cold, clinical reply, "Target is destroyed." To the Kremlin excuse that KAL 007 had violated Soviet airspace, Kirkpatrick's response was withering: "Straying off course is not recognized as a capital crime by civilized nations."[20]

V

Three weeks later, Reagan continued his outreach to Moscow from the podium at the UN General Assembly. Declaring, "I've come today to renew my nation's commitment to peace," he announced several new concessions being offered to the Soviets in the START negotiations and quoted Eisenhower in describing his hope "to meet at the conference table with the understanding that the era of armaments has ended and the human race must conform its actions to this truth or die." He also repeated his vow that "a nuclear war cannot be won, and it must never be fought."[21]

An hour after Reagan finished his speech, Red Army lieutenant colonel Stanislav Petrov walked through the gate at the Serpukhov-15 early warning base south of Moscow to begin his twelve-hour command shift. The Kremlin recently had deployed a new satellite surveillance system known as Oko ("eye") that from outer space could detect any American ICBM launches as soon as they left their silos, ten to twelve minutes before Soviet radar would pick up the missiles as they traversed the Arctic Circle.

The arms race was not just about building bigger, faster, stealthier, and more accurate weapons. It was also about building bigger, better, farther-reaching, and more accurate detection systems. The sooner the Soviets or Americans could learn of their adversary's planned or impending attack, the sooner they could take protective, defensive, and retaliation measures, including scrambling aircraft, moving mobile missiles, deploying subma-rines, preparing launch sequences—and sheltering their leadership. Both sides invested continually in improved detection and alert systems, espe-cially radar, to give their leaders decision advantage.[22]

An engineer, Petrov had helped design and program the new satellite system. He knew that when Oko worked, it gave the Kremlin a view it had never before enjoyed of America's missile bases. He also knew that Oko did not always work.

A few minutes past midnight on September 26 at Serpukhov-15, the red letters "LAUNCH" lit up an alert panel. An alarm siren began to wail. Petrov ordered his operators to double-check their systems for problems or glitches. They reported that all was in order. He thought it must be a false alarm.

Then, as he was on the phone with the duty officer, the screen burst with lights showing at least five American ICBMs incoming, possibly many more. "MISSILE ATTACK," flashed the warning panel. Terrified, Petrov knew that standing orders dictated alerting the Soviet high command so they could launch retaliatory strikes before the American missiles impacted. That deci-sion window was closing in minutes, even seconds.

But something did not seem right. Petrov had not heard Reagan's speech earlier in the day, but he did not need to—he already did not believe Amer-ica would launch a preemptive strike. He did not want to be responsible for a nuclear war. He did not yet see any detection of the missiles by ground-based radar. He did not trust Oko. He made a gut decision and told the duty officer it was a false alarm. He waited, knowing that his career—and the fate of his nation, even the world—rested in the balance.

Petrov was right. As the minutes ticked by and no American missiles descended, he realized another Oko glitch had caused the false alert. (An investigation would reveal that reflections from high clouds over US missile bases in Wyoming had triggered the system.)[23]

Petrov's quiet heroism in preventing a nuclear war would not come to light until a decade hence. The United States knew nothing of it at the time.

Three days later, Reagan welcomed Margaret Thatcher back to the White House. Her recent reelection victory had also reinforced British pub-lic support for basing American nuclear missiles on their soil. She affirmed Reagan's measured response to the KAL 007 shoot-down, particularly his efforts to keep dialogue open with the Kremlin. Reagan reiterated the con-tours of his strategy: "The Soviets are only at the negotiating table because the US is rebuilding its defense posture," he told her. "[The Kremlin] recognizes . . . that they cannot compete . . . the Soviets are at the limit of their military buildup—they can't afford another round in the arms race."[24] Reagan wrote in his diary that night, "I don't think US-UK relations have ever been better."[25] That would change the next month.

Two weeks after her visit, Reagan sat at Camp David and watched the screen in front of him in horror as Soviet ICBMs detonated over Lawrence, Kansas, incinerating the city under a series of mushroom clouds.

It was only a movie. But it terrified Reagan. He was watching an advance screening of *The Day After,* which would air nationwide on ABC a month later and become the most-watched television movie in history. Millions of viewers would share Reagan's trauma. He confessed to his diary, "[The movie] left me greatly depressed. . . . My own reaction was one of our having to do all we can to have a deterrent and to see there is never a nuclear war."[26]

This was not the first movie to frighten Reagan about nuclear war. Earlier that summer he had screened *WarGames* at Camp David. Its tale of a teenage hacker who penetrates NORAD's computer systems and almost triggers a nuclear exchange with the Soviets so tormented Reagan that a few days later he shared his worries at an NSC meeting. CJCS Vessey then ordered a Defense Department review that confirmed the president's fears about the Pentagon's cybersecurity vulnerabilities. This prompted the Reagan administration to issue NSDD-145 the next year—America's first presidential directive on protecting computer and electronic communications systems from hostile actors.[27]

VI

The Lebanon leak and polygraph debacle solidified for Clark what he had planned since January: It was time to leave. In early October he informed Reagan that he was resigning. The unrelenting demands of the job combined with the feuding and acrimony had ground Clark down, leaving him despondent and spent. He still had Reagan's trust, but with Baker, Deaver, Shultz, and the First Lady united against him, Clark knew he could no longer serve effectively. At Clark's request, Reagan made him secretary of the interior, where the lifelong outdoorsman could preside over public lands safe from the White House's daily knife fights.

Reagan should have had a plan to replace him, especially since he had

known for almost a year of Clark's desire to resign. Yet the president's inattention to management fueled instead what Edmund Morris describes as "a
White House power struggle of Lebanese intricacy."[28]

Having shivved Clark, James Baker and Michael Deaver concocted a
scheme for the former to replace him as NSA and the latter to slide up to
chief of staff. They pitched it to Reagan, who agreed without much thought
or consultation. An alarmed Clark learned of this plan on his last day, just
before the president was about to announce the new appointments. Clark
implored Reagan to wait. Clark then marshaled his allies Weinberger, Casey,
and Meese, who together appealed to Reagan to appoint Kirkpatrick as NSA
instead of Baker. The president, about to depart for Camp David, agreed to
think on it over the weekend. Their plot foiled, Baker and Deaver then enlisted Shultz to join them in vetoing Kirkpatrick to Reagan.

The discomfited president settled instead on Deputy National Security
Advisor Robert "Bud" McFarlane as the choice least objectionable to the
feuding factions. It was hardly a ringing endorsement for one of the most
important national security jobs serving the leader of the free world.

Clark's departure brought a cascade of affection and even some tears
from the NSC staff. Several wrote him heartfelt letters pleading that he reconsider. They saw in Clark a leader who had empowered their work, shielded
them from West Wing crossfire, maintained their integrity, and developed
the interlocking pieces of Reagan's Cold War strategy. His legacy would be
felt for the next five years as those many strategy directives continued to
guide the administration.

McFarlane brought to his new role a fierce work ethic, knowledge of
government and policy, and loyalty to the president's agenda. He also suffered torments and insecurities that in time would bring him near to
death—and the administration near to ruin.

VII

It was a rough way to start a new job. McFarlane's very first week as NSA
brought the proverbial "three A.M. phone call" on two consecutive nights.
While accompanying Reagan on a golf weekend with Shultz at Augusta
National in Georgia, at three o'clock in the morning on Saturday, October
22, 1983, McFarlane received a call from Eugenia Charles, prime minister of
Dominica and chair of the Organisation of Eastern Caribbean States

(OECS). She appealed to the United States to intervene on the neighboring island of Grenada. The White House had long been concerned about the growing Cuban military presence on the island, including the construction of a massive military airstrip. The crisis had escalated a few days prior when Prime Minister Maurice Bishop, a communist who had taken power in a coup, was in turn deposed and executed in another coup by his even more radical deputy Bernard Coard.[29] Earlier in the year, the Grenada communists had sponsored a failed effort to overthrow Prime Minister Charles too. She and other OECS nations feared that the new regime would accelerate its efforts to export Marxist revolution in their neighborhood.

The appeal from Charles had been anticipated, but the call still proved a bracing introduction to McFarlane of his new responsibilities. He, Reagan, and Shultz convened in the cottage living room, and Reagan gave the order for Operation Urgent Fury to launch three days hence on October 25.

After trying for a couple hours more sleep, when dawn broke Reagan and Shultz played a round of golf, careful not to give any hint to the traveling press pool of the impending invasion.

The next night McFarlane received another call at two A.M., unanticipated and gut-wrenching. The White House Situation Room informed him that a suicide bomber had destroyed the US marine barracks in Lebanon. The marine deaths shook McFarlane, himself a marine veteran who had fought in Vietnam. As Middle East envoy he had spent two and a half months in Beirut and come to know many of the marines personally— including those now buried in the rubble.

For the second night in a row, McFarlane had to wake the president and inform him of a national security crisis.[30]

Reagan was devastated. He had received many warnings about the risks to the marines and had felt his own growing disquiet. Earlier that month, the intelligence community had issued a special national intelligence estimate expressing the unanimous view that the Lebanon mission was hopeless and the marines in great peril.[31] Two days before the bombing, Weinberger had argued to Shultz that the marines should be redeployed to ships offshore because of the risks they faced in Beirut.[32] That same week Reagan himself wrote in his diary of wrestling with "how to . . . avoid murder of our Marines."[33] Now 241 of them were dead—on a mission he had ordered. A separate, coordinated terrorist bombing killed another 58 French soldiers participating in the Multi-National Force.

Reagan's grief mixed with anger. McFarlane noticed on the president's face "an expression of hatred and wish for revenge that I never saw in him before or since."

"Those sons of bitches," swore Reagan. "Let's find a way to go after them."[34]

He meant it in the moment. But it was a promise he would fail to keep.

Reagan cut short his golf trip and flew back to Washington to confront two crises erupting at once. Six thousand miles from each other, Grenada and Beirut both converged in the White House Situation Room. One crisis was public, the other top secret. The Beirut bombing sparked a media frenzy, while Reagan tried to protect the Grenada operation from disclosure until the troops deployed ashore.

As soon as he landed, that Sunday afternoon Reagan convened a series of NSC meetings. He wrestled with whether to call off the Grenada operation because of Lebanon but at seven o'clock that night gave the order to continue. The invasion fleet kept sailing south.

Since his campaign, Reagan had been eyeing Grenada with growing alarm. Coard's coup sent his fears into overdrive. Some six hundred Americans were enrolled in medical school on the island, and Reagan worried they could be taken hostage. Just over eighteen months since the end of the Iran hostage crisis, it was not an unwarranted concern—especially after Coard's militia rebuffed State Department requests to let the students evacuate by chartered flight or ship.[35]

The administration put together the invasion in haste. Just four days earlier, on October 19, Shultz and Assistant Secretary of State Tony Motley had persuaded Reagan that force might be needed. The State Department, with Motley in the lead, coordinated the planning process along with NSC staff members Constantine Menges and Oliver North. The Pentagon, though reluctant about the use of force, followed orders to begin drawing up war plans that same day.[36] Operation Urgent Fury may well be the most rapidly planned invasion in American military history.

Monday night, October 24, as the troopships sailed into position off the Grenada coast, Reagan summoned the congressional leadership to the White House to inform them of the impending landings. In the midst of his meeting, Margaret Thatcher phoned. It was one A.M. in London, and she was calling in response to two cables Reagan had sent in the past few hours. The first had informed her of his concerns about the island and requested— disingenuously—her "thoughts on the matter." The letter also promised to "inform you in advance" of any military action. Because Grenada was a British commonwealth nation, Thatcher had a personal stake. Before she could reply, a second cable from Reagan arrived informing her that he had decided to launch the invasion—though it did not say when.[37]

Reagan described their call in his diary that night: "She's upset and doesn't think we should do it. I couldn't tell her it had started. This was one secret we really managed to keep."[38] Reagan feared that if given more notice, Thatcher would object and try to block the invasion. He was correct about her views, but his deception damaged his relationship with the British leader. It was a rare moment when Reagan broke faith with an ally. Thatcher found it especially painful because it came just weeks before the American nuclear missiles would be deployed in the UK, which she had spent much political capital to support. To Thatcher this felt more like a personal betrayal than a policy difference.

Just before dawn on Tuesday, October 25, a combined assault force of eight thousand marines, navy SEALs, army rangers, and the Eighty-Second Airborne Division landed on Grenada by sea and air. Though stiff resistance by Cuban troops and several interservice communication fiascos slowed their advance, within a few days the Americans took control of the island, rescuing the medical students and other American citizens. Nineteen American servicemen were killed in action.

Early on the first morning of Urgent Fury, Prime Minister Charles flew to Washington, DC, to join Reagan for a press conference and briefings to Congress. On behalf of her fellow Caribbean leaders, she spoke forcefully about the regional fears that Coard's junta would help the Cubans and Soviets inflict revolutionary violence on other island states.

One reporter asked whether "the United States has the right to invade another country to change its government."

Responded Charles: "But I don't think it's an invasion. . . . This is a question of our asking for support. We are one region. Grenada is part and parcel of us . . . and we don't have the capacity, ourselves, to see to it that Grenadians get the freedom that they're required to have to choose their own government."[39]

Though she was too defensive over the term *invasion* (which it was), her larger point stood: She and her fellow Caribbean leaders wanted to protect their nations from aggression and restore the democracy in Grenada that had been overthrown by the communist coups. Charles later recalled that if Reagan had not invaded, "all of the islands would have gone the way of Grenada," saying, "We must remember that the Communists already had cells in each island."[40]

Thatcher continued to fume over Reagan's duplicity. Reagan phoned her on October 26 to apologize, while fighting still raged. Summoning all of his Hollywood charm, the president began, "If I were there, Margaret, I'd throw my hat in the door before I came in." In between a meandering account of the invasion, Reagan twice expressed remorse "for any embarrassment that we caused you." It would be another two months before she forgave Reagan, and she never forgot it.[41]

Many congressional Democrats and media outlets denounced the operation. Typical was *The New York Times'* editorial philippic: "The cost is the loss of the moral high ground: a reverberating demonstration to the world that America has no more respect for laws and borders, for the codes of civilization, than the Soviet Union." Much of this outrage dissipated a few days later when US Air Force planes flew the rescued students home and national news broadcasts showed several kneeling down and kissing the airport tarmac in relief.[42] As one student told *The New York Times,* "I'm not a big fan of American foreign policy and never have been, but if ever there was a need for intervention it was this country."[43]

The invasion unearthed a hive of Soviet bloc personnel active on Grenada. American forces captured and repatriated almost eight hundred Cuban troops, forty-nine Soviet advisors, fifteen North Koreans, ten East Germans, and three Bulgarians, along with seventeen Libyans.[44] A CIA assessment of a Grenadian document cache concluded the "Soviet Union, Cuba, and North Korea had embarked on major military assistance programs to Grenada," including agreements by the Soviets and North Koreans to supply almost $40 million worth of weaponry.[45] Within a few days the US military turned over power to a transitional government led by the British governor-general; an election restored full democracy the next year.

By military standards, Urgent Fury was a small operation, but its importance transcended its scale. It marked America's first use of ground troops in combat since Vietnam and the first fighting by the all-volunteer force since the end of the draft in 1973. It demonstrated to a watching world Reagan's willingness to use force. As Shultz reflected, the invasion "was a big message to the Soviets. . . . It raised the credibility of the US" and "had an impact around the world" because it showed that Vietnam's legacy no longer crippled America's willingness to fight.[46]

Reagan and Shultz both believed that the credible threat of force strengthened diplomacy—and effective diplomacy made the need to use force much less likely. Though the invasion fueled the alarms of Reagan's critics that he was trigger-happy to send American troops into combat in El Salvador, Nicaragua, or any number of other trouble spots, Grenada would be the first, last, and only time Reagan deployed American ground troops in combat during his eight years in office.

His grief over the Beirut bombing tempered any triumph he felt about Grenada. If Grenada restored American military credibility, then Lebanon displayed America's vulnerability to the world. France was America's closest partner in Lebanon, a former French protectorate. Mitterrand flew to Beirut immediately after the terrorist attacks. He and Reagan spoke on the phone on October 24, following Mitterrand's return to Paris. Reagan told the French president, "If we can find and locate the perpetrators, I'm sure that we are together in wanting retaliation for it. I want you also to know our position is firm. We are not going to let this terrorist attack drive us out of Lebanon." Mitterrand agreed.[47] That same day, Morocco's King Hassan sent Reagan a message confirming that Syria and Iran had jointly sponsored the bombings. Hassan warned, "The Syrians and the Soviets think the USA will become a paper tiger, and once forced to leave Beirut US prestige will sink."[48]

Later that week, Reagan issued NSDD-111, with the discordantly optimistic title "Next Steps Toward Progress in Lebanon and the Middle East." Largely crafted by McFarlane and the NSC staff, it ordered, "Subject to reasonable confirmation of the locations of suitable targets used by elements responsible for the October 23 bombing, attack those targets decisively, if possible in coordination with the French."[49] Shultz and McFarlane believed, not unreasonably, that this provided clear presidential guidance to the Pentagon to prepare retaliatory strikes. Weinberger and Vessey, however, would exploit the caveat about confirming targets as a loophole.

The barracks bombing exemplified the problems bedeviling the American mission in Lebanon. The Pentagon's feud with the NSC and State Department, and Reagan's refusal to resolve it and set a clear policy, meant gridlock in Washington, DC, and grave peril in Beirut. In recent weeks, McFarlane and Shultz had nudged the marines toward protecting the Lebanese army while maintaining an official posture of neutrality. Weinberger continued to resist providing more forces or loosening the rules of engagement.

This had created the worst of all worlds: The Druze, Shia, and Syrian militias fighting the Lebanese army viewed the marines as adversary combatants, yet the marines had their hands tied with peacekeeper cuffs. The suicide bomber had barreled his truck with ten tons of TNT past marine guards holding unloaded rifles, as per standing orders for the peacekeeping mission, who watched helplessly as the truck drove into the building and detonated.

A new terrorist organization named Islamic Amal, a precursor to Hezbollah, carried out the attacks, funded and directed by Iran and aided by Syria. Ayatollah Khomeini likely approved the mission himself. He had many incentives to do so. He wanted to increase Iran's influence in Lebanon by driving out the MNF peacekeepers, deepen his partnership with Syria, harm Israel's interests, weaken the Lebanese army, and—especially—hurt the United States. The Reagan administration had recently begun providing quiet intelligence support to Iraq in its war with Iran, which further fueled the ayatollah's animus.[50]

Reagan's firm words glossed over some hard facts and hard questions. Combined with the April embassy bombing, terrorists sponsored by Iran and Syria had now destroyed both the symbols and substance of America's diplomatic, intelligence, and military presence in Lebanon—and killed over 250 Americans. The available policy options for Lebanon were now even less appealing.

For McFarlane, the baptism into the flames of the national security advisor role extended well beyond the Grenada and Lebanon crises. Each week, the various senior directors on the NSC staff would send him a weekly report summarizing the major issues in their respective policy areas and often requesting decisions from McFarlane. Just a glance through the reports for his first week of October 21 shows the cascade of other policy issues and challenges that confronted him.

These included: resisting congressional efforts to restrict funding and personnel at the United States Information Agency; pushing for political reform by the Ferdinand Marcos regime in the Philippines and overcoming congressional resistance to admitting refugees from Southeast Asia; managing an interagency dispute over funding for the Strategic Defense Initiative; pressing Japan for import concessions in advance of Reagan's upcoming trip; preparing a strategy for trade policy at the London Economic Summit; managing conflicts with NATO allies over armaments cooperation while being buffeted by antinuclear protests in Europe; managing a fight with the

Pentagon over alleged Soviet violations of the Strategic Arms Limitation Treaty; maintaining congressional funding for the B-1 bomber and MX missile; and remedying the sloppy performance by White House staff of a presidential award ceremony for former director of central intelligence Richard Helms.[51]

Every subsequent week on the job would bring a similar litany. The daily demands McFarlane faced were not unique to him; every other NSA, in every presidency before and since, confronted a similar deluge. Scholars and journalists may be able to focus in depth only on one or two issues, but senior policymakers have no such luxury.

VIII

Even though the United States suffered a hard blow in Lebanon, the global view from the Kremlin did not look good. The Grenada operation caught the Soviets by surprise and snuffed Moscow's hopes for another Caribbean foothold. The American missiles would begin arriving in Europe on November 15, countering the Soviet INF advantage. Moscow still suffered global opprobrium for the KAL 007 massacre two months earlier. And the geriatric Andropov, not seen in public since August, hospitalized in declining health, connected more to his dialysis machine than to the Politburo, left unclear who was in charge at the Kremlin.[52]

The White House worried that a weakened Kremlin was a dangerous Kremlin. On November 5, Matlock warned McFarlane that despite Reagan's recent outreach, Moscow's "current policy is to stonewall negotiations and make threatening gestures." Moreover, the recent "blow[s] to Soviet prestige . . . will incline them to seek relatively risk free ways to embarrass us."[53]

But in the Cold War standoff between nuclear powers, nothing was "risk free."

Each fall, NATO conducted a joint military exercise testing its response to a Soviet invasion. For November 2–11, 1983, this exercise would be known as "Able Archer 83." The scenario—which had been crafted in the Pentagon well before the Beirut bombing but now felt even more realistic—began with conflict in the Middle East as Soviet proxies such as Syria increased their hostilities against the United States and its regional partners. Soon it escalated to Europe, with Soviet attacks on NATO countries. Overwhelmed

NATO forces would retaliate with nuclear weapons against the Soviet invaders; the Cold War would turn hot.[54] It was a grim contemplation.

Able Archer 83 involved a combined NATO force of over one hundred thousand troops, the bulk of them American. It included nuclear submarines and, for the first time, nuclear-capable B-52 bombers. It would also take place during the tensest period in US-Soviet relations in over two decades.[55] Soviet and other Warsaw Pact intelligence services monitored Able Archer closely, as they did all NATO exercises. This time, however, in Fred Kaplan's words, "the Soviets . . . reacted in ways that they never had during any previous exercise—in ways similar to how they might have acted if the US were gearing up for a real attack."[56] The Kremlin put its nuclear-capable jets on high alert and moved its SS-20 mobile launchers from their shelters forward to camouflaged positions—undetected by NATO surveillance, able to launch on command within two and a half minutes and to incinerate Western European capitals within ten minutes.

The war footing worried spies on both sides. In London, Oleg Gordievsky saw his KGB and GRU colleagues scrambling under Moscow's orders to detect whether the United States was preparing a preemptive nuclear strike. He warned MI6 that the Kremlin, already conspiratorial from its Operation RYAN monitoring, might be misreading the exercise as a real attack.[57] In Brussels, Rainer Rupp, a NATO civilian employee spying for East German intelligence, sent his handler an urgent coded reassurance: Able Archer was just an exercise.[58] The Gordievsky and Rupp reports helped ease tensions. As Steven Hayward observes, "The avoidance of war in November 1983 may have come down to the actions of two double agents."[59]

Able Archer 83 has attained almost mythical status in Cold War lore. Many scholars contend that it marked the conflict's final brink, a turning point when a paranoid Kremlin almost launched a nuclear war and a terrified Reagan reversed his hard-line approach in favor of conciliation toward the Soviets. The military, intelligence officers, and diplomats involved on both sides felt the tension. Almost four decades later, many still recall their genuine terror that a nuclear war was imminent.

However, more recent scholarship that draws on declassified Soviet and Warsaw Pact records reveals a different picture. Historian Simon Miles shows that the top Soviet and Warsaw Pact leadership knew all along that Able Archer 83 was just an exercise. As Miles writes, "The Kremlin did not take seriously the idea that a surprise nuclear attack was coming. . . . Far from being shocked by what they learned about Able Archer 83 and contemplating a preemptive strike, Soviet policy-makers paid it no heed."[60]

Instead the Kremlin and Red Army leadership used the NATO war games as an excuse to mobilize, test, and terrify its own troops and intelligence officers. The Soviet bloc rank and file along the Iron Curtain were led to believe that NATO may well have been preparing nuclear strikes—and Moscow wanted to see how they would respond. As one senior Kremlin official recalled, "We scared our own people."[61]

IX

When Reagan and his senior team searched the past for inspiration, they often fixed on Winston Churchill. Weinberger and Casey in particular revered the British statesman. The defense secretary had begun reading Churchill's books as a twelve-year-old, found Churchill's prime ministerial speeches so inspiring that as a Harvard student he tried to join the Royal Air Force in 1940 (poor eyesight kept him out), and then, as a US Army officer in the Pacific theater, followed Churchill's every utterance throughout the war.[62] Casey had lived and worked under Churchill's leadership while based in London with the OSS during World War II.

Such affinities led Weinberger and Casey to make pilgrimages to Fulton, Missouri, in 1983. This small town hosted Westminster College, where Churchill delivered his "Iron Curtain" address of 1946. Weinberger and Casey each delivered a speech in the same campus lecture series as Churchill. They hoped to wrap the Reagan administration's policies in a Churchillian cloak and forge a visible connection between World War II and the Cold War.

Clare Boothe Luce introduced Casey for his October speech. She extolled him as "the kind of character a great novelist might dream of inventing," "the American Superspook," and the "hottest of Cold War warriors." Tickled at such acclaim from the glamorous grande dame, Casey took the stage to lay out his view of the Cold War. He described the Soviet Union as both ruthless and vulnerable. "The Soviet Union is crippled . . . in having only a military dimension," he pronounced. "It has not been able to deliver economic, political or cultural benefits abroad. Without exception, the economic record of the countries which have come under Soviet influence has ranged from poor to very poor. . . . The Soviet Union cannot compete in these areas." In contrast to the stagnation of the communist bloc, Casey took hope in the growth of self-government and market economies. "Around the world today, the democratic revolution is gathering new strength, in Asia, in Africa, in our own hemisphere. In Latin America, 18 of 34 countries have freely-elected governments and 6 are working toward democratization, altogether representing 70% of the people of that continent." The United States should support liberty's spread, he believed, because the Cold War "is a conflict deeply rooted in ideas . . . a contest between two elemental and historically opposed ideas of the relationship between the individual and the state."[63]

Back at CIA, Herbert Meyer, the vice-chairman of the National Intelligence Council, elaborated on Casey's arguments in an assessment titled "Why Is the World So Dangerous?" Casey had hired Meyer two years earlier from a journalism career to provide a fresh perspective in the CIA's most elite analytic office.

Meyer did not disappoint. He believed the global spasms of violence in recent months signaled "the beginning of a new stage in the global struggle between the Free World and the Soviet Union . . . that present US policies have fundamentally changed the course of history in a direction favorable to the interests and security of ourselves and our allies." Describing the manifest challenges facing the Soviet Union, including economic "calamity," technology shortfalls, population decline, restive ethnic minorities, dissension within the Warsaw Pact, and anti-Soviet insurgencies in Nicaragua, Mozambique, Angola, Cambodia, and Afghanistan, Meyer argued this left Moscow with a dilemma: "Kremlin leaders could boost their country's economic growth rate only by slashing the defense budget or by enacting massive economic reforms. Either remedy would threaten the Communist Party's grip on power." He concluded, "If present trends continue, we're going to win the Cold War."[64] Casey found Meyer's analysis so compelling that he forwarded it to Reagan.

Others at the CIA disagreed. Reflecting the views of many of his colleagues, senior analyst Hal Ford wrote a rebuttal to Meyer. Against the Soviet weaknesses that Meyer highlighted, Ford described several Soviet strengths and contended the USSR "is going to be with us for years to come." He predicted, "The US-Soviet cold war may still be confronting our grandchildren . . . [and] the Soviet challenge will not disappear as a result either of its own folly or of the brilliance of this or that Republican/Democratic policy initiatives." Mindful that Reagan had read Meyer's analysis,

Ford concluded with his worry that "senior policymakers . . . [would] subscribe to many of the views Herb's memo advances."[65]

X

In the midst of crises in Europe, Latin America, and the Middle East, Reagan flew to Asia. It was his first presidential trip to the region. Earlier in the summer, Clark had told Reagan that his visit could "usher in a new era in US foreign policy in which we elevate the priority of Asia and the Pacific Basin," especially since the Far East "is already more important to us (in economic terms) than Europe." Clark even suggested that Asia would "provide the setting for the 'Reagan Doctrine.'"[66] That nomenclature would later be applied to Reagan's support for Third World anticommunist insurgencies, but the fact that the White House envisioned it for Asia shows just how important Reagan and his team considered the region for his current strategy and future legacy.

Reagan wanted to prioritize America's allies and so deferred a visit to China for the next year. This trip instead focused on the alliance triangle with Japan and South Korea. He could afford to skip China in part because Weinberger had enjoyed a successful visit there in September and ensured that Beijing stayed more favorably disposed toward Washington than toward Moscow. Reagan also hosted Chinese foreign minister Wu Xueqian at the White House a few weeks before his Asia trip. Wu reiterated China's support for the zero option on INF. The 108 Soviet SS-20s deployed in the Russian Far East threatened China as well as Japan, and the missiles' mobility enabled the Kremlin to move them easily between Europe and Asia. Wu told Reagan, "During our talks with the Soviet Union we demanded that these missiles be cut down and dismantled on the spot."[67] Reagan's diplomacy ensured that every major Western European and East Asian nation shared the American position: All Soviet INF missiles should be eliminated.

Reagan's Japan trip approached as he and his friend Nakasone both confronted looming campaigns. Elected leaders share an ineffable bond. They have experienced what neither their closest advisors nor their dictator counterparts can feel: the democratic crucible of running for office, of persuading voters to support them and their party—and of answering to those voters at reelection time. In the United States, Election Day was twelve months away, while the Japanese leader would face the voters in parliamentary elections just six weeks after Reagan's visit. In both nations, voters would render their verdicts in part on their economies and the state of United States–Japan relations. Each leader faced political pressure to take measures that could help their public but hurt the other nation's economy. In this sense, Reagan's and Nakasone's electoral fates were intertwined but not aligned.

The weeks before the trip brought a flurry of emissaries crisscrossing the Pacific to pre-negotiate the nettlesome economic issues. Reagan dispatched Gaston Sigur and US trade representative Bill Brock to Tokyo, while Nakasone sent a personal envoy to Washington. The stakes were substantial. NSC staffer Charles Tyson wrote, somewhat histrionically, that failure to reduce the United States–Japan trade deficit would result in the "destruction of US-Japan strategic, economic, and security relations."[68] A more sanguine Reagan simply noted in his diary, "Japan is still holding stubbornly to trade practices that are unfair. I'll have to really lean on P.M. Nakasone."[69]

When structural forces produce friction in international politics, personal relationships can provide the lubricant that prevents conflict. In Tokyo, Nakasone told Ambassador Mansfield, Brock, and Sigur of his deep affection for Reagan and said, "When a friend is in trouble, you have to stand close by and help, and you know that your friend will do the same for you." However, the prime minister leavened this pledge with his own plea. He reminded the Americans that his own elections were less than two months away and asked for "priority attention" first to his political situation. Nakasone believed this constrained him from opening the Japanese market to imports of American beef and citrus. Drawing on their decades-long friendship, Sigur then met one-on-one with Nakasone. The NSC official "laid it on the line" to Nakasone that America's continued revival depended on Reagan's reelection—and that reelection depended on progress in United States–Japan trade issues. Nakasone reassured Sigur that he and Reagan could "work out any difficulty," saying, "We will and we must."[70]

As Air Force One approached Tokyo, Reagan remained resolved not to let economic tensions hijack the strategic partnership. He began his meeting with Nakasone by reaffirming that the United States–Japan relationship was the most important bilateral pairing in the world for promoting peace and prosperity. Befitting this strategic framework binding the world's two wealthiest democracies, Reagan and Nakasone spent most of their time together discussing the rest of the globe. They covered the Asia triangles, including Japan's much-improved relationships with both China and South Korea; the growing instability in the Philippines under the Marcos dictatorship; arms control and the Soviet Union; and extensive discussion on the Middle East, especially Lebanon, Syria, and the Iran-Iraq War. Japan had an acute interest in the region due to its reliance on Persian Gulf oil, and Nakasone described his efforts to "exert ameliorating influence on both" Iran and Iraq.[71]

Japan's concern with the Middle East showed the connectedness of the Cold War world. Tokyo's ability to increase its military spending and defense commitments depended on a strong economy. Its economy depended on reliable energy supply chains from the Middle East. Reliable Middle East oil supply depended on regional stability. And that stability depended on American policy and presence in the region.

Nakasone honored Reagan by making him the first American president to address the Japanese Diet. Reagan's speech itself was a rather pedestrian effort. He paid homage to the shared values between the nations, criticized Soviet aggression, and warned against trade protectionism. Much more notable was the moment it represented. As a young Hollywood actor, Reagan had first called for the abolition of atomic weapons in August 1945, immediately after the United States destroyed Hiroshima and Nagasaki under mushroom clouds.[72] Now, almost forty years later, Reagan stood before the Japanese government as the leader of its most vital ally and heralded "the day when nuclear weapons will be banished from the face of the earth." He repeated his pledge that "a nuclear war can never be won and must never be fought."[73]

Memories of Japanese aggression in World War II still haunted the region. This history also highlighted how the US alliance reassured other nations. Shultz recalls, "Everywhere I went in the Asia Pacific, the idea of a rearmed Japan was opposed," whereas "the idea of a Japan with a strategic relationship with the United States, including the presence of American troops on Japanese soil, was welcomed."[74] The rest of Asia knew America's tight embrace of Tokyo prevented any renewed Japanese militarism.

From Asia, Reagan recorded his weekly radio address, which he used to warn Congress and the American people against protectionism and to extol the virtues of the free market. Calling trade barriers "defensive and dangerous," he spoke in blunt terms:

Let's recognize Japanese and Korean efficiency for what it is. If their products are better made and less expensive, then Americans who buy them benefit by receiving quality and value. And that's what the magic of the marketplace is all about. The best course for us to take is to take the offensive and create new jobs through trade, lasting jobs tied to the products and technology of tomorrow. I'm confident American products can compete in world markets if they can enter foreign markets as easily as foreign products can enter ours. Currently they can't.

The president then described his pressure on Japan and South Korea to lower their import barriers.[75]

Reagan's broadcast faced a disagreeable American public. Opinion polls consistently showed 60–70 percent of Americans favored imposing tariffs on countries such as Japan with high trade barriers.[76] Politically, defending free trade was not a winning hand for Reagan. But he spoke from his convictions—about the free market and the singular importance of the United States–Japan alliance. He tried to shape and lead public opinion, not pander to it.

Just three weeks after the Beirut bombing, Reagan landed on November 12 in a South Korea grieving from two recent traumas of its own. The KAL 007 shoot-down in September had killed over one hundred Korean citizens. A month later, on October 9, in Rangoon, Burma, North Korean agents had planted bombs targeting the visiting South Korean delegation led by President Chun. A timing glitch spared Chun, but the explosions killed sixteen senior Korean officials, including the foreign minister and other cabinet members.

Many in the South Korean public and military demanded retaliation against Pyongyang, but Chun knew that a counterattack could spark a new war on the Korean Peninsula. With American encouragement, he stayed the hand of vengeance. He and Reagan could also relate to each other on life's fragility: Both had survived assassination attempts.

Reagan's two priorities in South Korea were to demonstrate America's security commitment and to continue pressing the Chun regime toward democracy. The year before, the Reagan administration had quietly negotiated the release from prison of South Korea's leading dissident, Kim Dae Jung (after having secured the commutation of his death sentence in

December 1980), and given Kim sanctuary in the United States. In their private meeting, Reagan told Chun that "the soul of democracy is freedom under law. Those people who are elected to office are our servants, not our masters." He reminded Chun of how President Richard Nixon had resigned and allowed a peaceful transfer of power to Gerald Ford, rather than trying to cling to office through a coup. Reagan and Shultz both urged Chun to reaffirm his previous pledge to step down and allow free elections to be held in 1988. Chun agreed to do so.[77]

Reagan ensured that the Korean people knew of America's support for democracy. Speaking before the National Assembly, which had relatively little power but represented the first seeds of representative government, Reagan affirmed "the continuing development of democratic institutions." He also put the United States on record as saying, "We welcome President Chun's far-sighted plans for a constitutional transfer of power in 1988"— and put the dictator on public notice.[78] South Korea's spiritual fervor struck Reagan. He marveled at the growth of Christianity in the country. Having learned of the leadership of Korean Catholics and Protestants in the democracy movement, Reagan afterward told Vatican secretary of state Casaroli that he "felt a close identification with their quest for freedom."[79]

Even in South Korea, Reagan remained mindful of his dilemma over responding to the marine barracks bombing. He told Chun he appreciated his restraint after the Rangoon attack, despite the desire for revenge. Reagan then said, "I had the same feeling regarding the Beirut situation, yet to do what some wanted us to do would have meant war."[80] Here Reagan revealed a new reason for his hesitation to retaliate: fear of an escalation spiral that would trap the United States in war in the Middle East.

XI

Reagan landed back in Washington from Asia at noon on November 14. He went straight to the White House for an NSPG meeting on whether to retaliate for the terrorist attack on the marine barracks. What happened in that meeting, and a follow-up meeting two days after, still remains disputed four decades later.

While Reagan was in Asia, the NSC staff worked with the State Department and Pentagon military planners to put together a strike package for his review upon his return. It included a draft White House statement announcing the strikes, messages to allied leaders, notifications to US embassies, and war plans for aircraft from the USS *Eisenhower* to bomb Islamic Amal training camps in the Bekaa Valley, which the CIA and French intelligence had identified as the base where the bombing was planned.[81] In the meeting, General Vessey presented the attack options to Reagan but also described the risk of American planes being shot down and of further retaliation against the remaining marines.[82]

McFarlane, also just off the plane from Asia, claims that in the meeting, Reagan "gave his approval for a retaliatory strike to be conducted on November 16. It was a direct, unambiguous decision." The bombing raids would be conducted jointly with French aircraft from the carrier *Clemenceau,* whose commander helicoptered over to the *Eisenhower* to coordinate planning with his American counterpart. Yet McFarlane recounts an early morning phone call two days later with Weinberger, who reported that he had turned down the theater commander's request to strike due to Weinberger's uncertainty about the mission. In his memoir, McFarlane's anger remains palpable: "It was outrageous. Weinberger had directly violated a presidential order."[83]

Weinberger emphatically denied McFarlane's account. In his own memoir, Weinberger avers, "The NSC staff people, always eager for combat at all times, circulated a report that I had been 'ordered' to participate with the French in a joint attack . . . but I had refused at the last minute to carry out that order. This is, of course, absurd; because on the face of it, if I had been ordered by the President to do anything and had refused, I would not have been around for several more years." Weinberger claims that he had not heard anything about a potential attack until receiving a call from the French defense minister the morning of November 16 informing him of France's imminent strike, but "I had received no orders or notifications from the President or anyone prior to that phone call from Paris."[84]

Adding to the confusion is that both McFarlane and Weinberger in their memoirs get the date wrong, citing November 16 as the date of the French strikes. The French strikes took place the next day, November 17—following a second NSPG meeting on November 16 that McFarlane also fails to mention.

Reagan's own diary shows his state of mind at the time but also leaves some ambiguity. On November 14, the date that McFarlane insists Reagan gave the order for a retaliatory strike, Reagan records: "At 2 P.M. a meeting re the same Beirut problem we'd discussed before the trip. We have some additional intelligence but still not enough to order a strike." Two days later, on November 16, Reagan held a second NSPG meeting to discuss options. He wrote in his diary of the meeting, "We've contacted French about a joint operation in Beirut re the car bombings."[85]

What Reagan meant is unclear. "Contacting" the French could have been a consultation to consider a possible strike or a decision to carry it out. Most likely Reagan thought the former, since if he had given a clear order to bomb, he would have written as much. Weinberger's diary entry from the same meeting says, "Concluded we should get more intelligence," which reinforces this view.[86] Deputy National Security Advisor John Poindexter, though no fan of Weinberger, later agreed that the president did not issue an "execute order" directing the military to retaliate.[87]

Early the next morning, November 17, the French defense minister phoned Weinberger to see if the US planes would be participating in the imminent strike. Weinberger's notes from the conversation indicate he replied, "The president has not made a decision; he is still considering it." The secretary then wished the French well in their operation.[88] That same day Reagan's diary notes, "Surprise call from France—they were going ahead without us and bombing our other target in Lebanon. They took it out completely."[89]

Reagan was wrong. The French air raid was a fiasco; their rockets and bombs missed the targets entirely. It embarrassed Mitterrand and fueled French resentment toward the United States for not joining, especially given the superior capabilities of American navy pilots and jets. French bitterness would linger and later prove costly. They "never forgave us for not backing them in the attack," recalled Poindexter.[90] An angry McFarlane confronted Reagan over what he saw as Weinberger's defiance. McFarlane recalls that an "evasive" Reagan expressed disappointment but refused to remonstrate with the defense secretary.[91]

How to explain this sorry episode? While much remains unknown, two conclusions seem warranted. First, when Reagan was unsure about an issue and faced a divided staff, the president sometimes would speak in broad, ambiguous terms that left his team members hearing what they wanted to hear. Reagan may well have said in both the November 14 and 16 meetings that he wanted to strike, but also expressed hesitation about intelligence uncertainty and escalation risks. McFarlane seized on the desire to act, and Weinberger on the reservations. Second, Reagan's comments to Chun in Korea as well as his diary entries reveal his growing misgivings about retaliation. Given those doubts, and the lack of any written record indicating a presidential order to bomb, Weinberger's account seems more accurate.

This does not mean that McFarlane's anger was unjustified. Reagan should have retaliated. His failure to do so damaged American credibility, hurt relations with an important ally, and invited further terrorist attacks.[92]

XII

Though Reagan repeatedly had offered the zero option to the Soviets as an off-ramp for the INF impasse, the Kremlin continued to refuse the deal. This only reinforced Reagan's belief that diplomacy works best when backed by strength. On the eve of the American missile deployment, Reagan met with his ambassador to the Soviet Union, Arthur Hartman. The president wrote in his diary, "[Hartman] confirms what I believe: the Soviets won't really negotiate on arms reduction until we deploy the Pershing II's and go forward with MX."[93]

The US sent 108 Pershing IIs and 464 GLCMs to Europe. West Germany hosted the Pershing IIs, while it joined the United Kingdom, Belgium, the Netherlands, and Italy in basing the GLCMs, also known as Gryphons. This geography dispersed the strategic risk—by spreading the targets behind various groves, hamlets, and secure facilities across Western Europe—and the political risk, as the NATO governments stuck together against public protests.

These missiles frightened the Kremlin even more than large American ICBMs such as the Minuteman or the MX. The Pershing IIs could fly at Mach 8 and hit Moscow within ten minutes of launch, while the terrain-hugging Gryphons could penetrate Soviet airspace undetected by radar. Paired together, they neutralized the Soviet nuclear monopoly in Europe and changed the global strategic landscape.

On his return from Asia, Reagan began receiving a trickle of intelligence revealing the Soviet forces' heightened alerts during Able Archer 83. This coincided with the nationwide broadcast of *The Day After*. Reagan vented to his diary:

I feel the Soviets are so defense minded, so paranoid about being attacked that without being in any way soft on them we ought to tell them no one here has any intention of doing anything like that. What the h---l have they got that anyone would want. George [Shultz] is going on ABC right after its big Nuclear bomb film Sunday night. We know it's "anti-nuke" propaganda but we're going to take it over and say it shows why we must keep on doing what we're doing.[94]

A week after Reagan wrote those words, the Pershing IIs arrived in West Germany, and a message arrived at the White House from Andropov. "Since by its actions the United States has torpedoed the possibility of reaching a mutually acceptable accord at the talks on questions of limiting nuclear arms in Europe . . . the Soviet Union considers its further participation in these talks impossible."[95] Two weeks later the Kremlin refused to engage in the START negotiations as well.

The Soviets had abandoned the negotiations in Geneva. As fruitless as the talks had been, they were also the main mechanism that the two Cold War rivals had to maintain a dialogue. For the first time since 1969, the United States and the Soviets had no arms control talks of any type under way.[96] Now Reagan, as eager as ever to find an opening to negotiate with the Kremlin, watched another door close.

He turned to history for hope. Speaking to reporters on the day the Soviets terminated all talks, Reagan invoked his favorite predecessor:

It was just 30 years ago today, on December 8th, 1953, that President Dwight Eisenhower made a speech on this very subject of nuclear weapons. And in that speech, he said, "To the making of these fateful decisions, the United States pledges before you . . . its determination to help solve the fearful atomic dilemma—to devote its entire heart and mind to find the way by which the miraculous inventiveness of man shall not be dedicated to his death, but consecrated to his life."[97]

The next week, Reagan reiterated to the press, "We're still determined on the reduction, particularly of nuclear weapons, and I am determined that once you start down that path, we must come to the realization that those weapons should be outlawed worldwide forever."[98]

XIII

On December 15, Reagan welcomed his least favorite allied leader back to the White House. Pierre Trudeau arrived to pitch Reagan on his plan to travel to Moscow and play the intermediary between the United States and USSR. Trudeau told Reagan that he appreciated the president's recent arms control initiatives and Tokyo speech calling for reducing nuclear weapons but cautioned that "Reaganism" was "perceived so poorly in the world arena" due to Reagan's military buildup and bellicose rhetoric. With undisguised condescension, the Canadian offered to explain American policies to the Kremlin, while urging Reagan to return to "détente and moderation in global politics."

Reagan responded with a "spirited defense" of SDI and explained to Trudeau that he did not just want to reduce the risk of nuclear war; rather he wanted to escape the MAD trap, eliminate offensive missiles, and end the West's "dependence on the tyranny of these nuclear weapons." For all of his own dreaminess, Trudeau did not seem to grasp Reagan's vision of abolishing nuclear weapons and instead tut-tutted that such a missile defense system "would be destabilizing."

The president replied by describing what he saw as a split between the Soviet system and the Russian people. The Kremlin remained intent on spreading communist revolution worldwide, and by giving so much authority to its military leadership, it had "created a Frankenstein with [its] large military establishment." Soviet citizens, in contrast, "do not want war," especially because of their collective memory of past suffering under the Napoleonic and world wars. Neither did Reagan want war, he told Trudeau, and neither did the American people.[99]

As Reagan spoke these words, he was already planning to take that message directly to the Russian people in the new year.

CHAPTER 8

TOIL AND TROUBLE

I

A joke circulating, furtively, in Moscow went as follows:

> Two KGB officers are talking at the office and one notes that he just received a frantic phone call from a Soviet citizen. The caller indicated that he "had just lost his parrot, but wanted them to know that he didn't necessarily share its views."

Another popular joke among Muscovites:

> The Soviet Union is having problems with the new stamp that was issued with Andropov's picture on it. Apparently, the citizens were encountering difficulties in getting the stamp to stick to the envelope. A lengthy investigation revealed the source of the problems—the people were spitting on the wrong side of the stamp.

Reagan relished these jokes too. The president asked his NSC staff and Embassy Moscow diplomats to regularly collect the latest humor from the Soviet people.[1] Though the old actor loved to disarm his audiences with a good laugh, he also had a more serious purpose. Part of his Cold War strategy involved driving a wedge between average Soviet citizens and the Kremlin. The Russian people and their culture fascinated him; he saw them as allies in his campaign against Soviet communism. He believed that their jokes—told on street corners, in bread lines, at family dinners—provided a window into their collective soul, and also revealed, as only humor can do, the vulnerabilities in the Soviet system, which provoked in its people equal parts fear, revulsion, and contempt.

Time's January 2, 1984, cover featured Reagan and Andropov together as "Men of the Year." The editors chose the two leaders because the standoff between their nations held the fate of the planet in the balance. *Time* painted a bleak picture of the impasse. Describing Reagan's speeches over the first three years of his presidency, the article noted, "To Soviet ears, [Reagan] seems not only to be denying the USSR's coveted claim to equal status with the US as a superpower, but even challenging its right to exist as a legitimate state."[2]

If Kremlin officials read the interview with Reagan in the same issue, they would have heard him make a peace offering. Asked about his imprecation of the Soviet Union as the world's "focus of evil" nine months earlier, Reagan replied, "I would not say things like that again." It is not that he no longer believed it. Reagan had made clear he viewed the Soviet system as wicked but also knew that he had to deal with Moscow—even as he hoped to transform it. He continued, "I would like to convince the Soviets that no one in the world has aggressive intentions toward them. Certainly we don't. . . . I would like to make them see that it is to their best interest to join us in reducing arms . . . [to] join the family of nations."

Reagan concluded with his dream of nuclear abolition. "And if we start down that road of reducing, for heaven's sake, why don't we rid the world of these weapons? Why do we keep them? Here's a world today whose principal armaments would wipe out civilians in the tens and hundreds of millions. Let's get back to being civilized."[3]

Reagan's abhorrence of nuclear weapons did not mean he failed to see their use. In a meeting the next month with British Labour Party leader Neil Kinnock, Reagan said he disagreed with the Labour platform calling for unilateral disarmament. He told Kinnock that nuclear weapons had helped preserve global peace since World War II and continued to be a "key factor in maintaining global stability and preventing war."[4] Reagan needed a formidable US nuclear arsenal to strengthen his hand in confronting the Soviets—and he needed a Soviet negotiating partner to work with him to abolish the nuclear arsenals of both nations. Reagan sought to resolve the puzzle in sequence: He would first use the American buildup as part of his

multipronged pressure to weaken the Kremlin. Once the Soviet system began to crack and produce a reformer, Reagan would have a negotiating partner to join in reducing and then eliminating nuclear weapons.

On January 16, Reagan delivered a speech from the White House East
Room that stretched the olive branch further toward the Kremlin. His address targeted multiple audiences: the Soviet leadership and people, of
course, and also the NATO allies, who sought reassurance that the missiles
based in their countries did not mean the United States had abandoned the
diplomatic track. He also spoke to the American people. In less than eleven
months he faced reelection. While the growing economy helped his electoral prospects, roughly half of Americans still expressed misgivings about
his handling of national security. Reagan strove to remind them—just as he
had four years earlier during the 1980 campaign—that he aimed for peace,
and that he did so with a steady hand.[5] Or as he put it to his diary, he crafted
the speech "to be a level headed approach to peace to reassure the eggheads
and our European friends I don't plan to blow up the world."[6]

He reiterated how America's defense buildup and economic recovery
had restored its deterrent and put the United States in its strongest position
in years to establish a constructive and realistic working relationship with
the Soviet Union. He restated his desire to negotiate with the Kremlin for
significant reductions in nuclear arms, progress in human rights, and above
all, peace. Reagan then closed with a passage he wrote himself. Channeling
the humanity of ordinary Americans, he made his most direct appeal yet to
the Soviet people:

> Just suppose with me for a moment that an Ivan and an Anya could
> find themselves, oh, say, in a waiting room, or sharing a shelter from
> the rain or a storm with a Jim and Sally, and there was no language
> barrier to keep them from getting acquainted. Would they then
> debate the differences between their respective governments? Or
> would they find themselves comparing notes about their children
> and what each other did for a living?
>
> Before they parted company, they would probably have touched
> on ambitions and hobbies and what they wanted for their children
> and problems of making ends meet. And as they went their sepa-
> rate ways, maybe Anya would be saying to Ivan, "Wasn't she nice?
> She also teaches music." Or Jim would be telling Sally what Ivan
> did or didn't like about his boss. They might even have decided

they were all going to get together for dinner some evening soon. Above all, they would have proven that people don't make wars. . . .

If the Soviet Government wants peace, then there will be peace. Together we can strengthen peace, reduce the level of arms, and know in doing so that we have helped fulfill the hopes and dreams of those we represent and, indeed, of people everywhere. Let us begin now.[7]

Reagan's concluding vignette reflected his faith that the Russian people were victims of the Soviet system and that their common humanity could help bring the Cold War to a peaceful end. It struck some on his own team as too maudlin. On seeing the "Ivan and Anya" addition to the speech draft, one White House staff member asked aloud, "Who wrote this shit?"[8]

The Kremlin did not care for it either. A few days later *Pravda* published a lacerating satire in which an impoverished Jim and Sally take Ivan and Anya to a soup kitchen to eat, suffer constant FBI surveillance, and complain of being exploited by the Reagan White House.[9]

II

The morning after Reagan's speech, an anxious Suzanne Massie sat in Bud McFarlane's White House basement office. The diminutive writer was about to advise the most powerful man in the world on the Soviet Union and journey to Moscow as his personal emissary.

Massie had visited the USSR many times and cultivated friendships with many Russians while becoming expert on their art, history, and literature. Four years earlier, she had published *Land of the Firebird: The Beauty of Old Russia*, a book about the millennium of Russian history before the Bolshevik Revolution. Thanks to a series of connections first set in motion by her friend Helen Jackson, recent widow of Scoop, as well as by Admiral Bob Inman, Massie had been introduced two months earlier to McFarlane. He found her insights impressive, a new realm of culture beyond the standard political and economic fare dispensed by the State Department and CIA. McFarlane knew Reagan would enjoy meeting with her too.

Walking upstairs to the Oval Office, Massie expected a short conversation with just Reagan and McFarlane. Her trepidation leapt when she walked in and, half-blinded by the light streaming through the office windows, was greeted by Reagan—and also by Bush, Baker, Deaver, and several other senior staff, all men. To the self-conscious Massie, they appeared as "an intimidating masculine phalanx." Reagan ushered her to a chair next to him, put her at ease, and began with a question: "How much do they [Soviet leaders] believe in communism?"

Massie responded, "Mr. President, of course I can't tell you how all Russians think, but I can tell you what many of them say. They call them [the communist leaders] 'the big bottoms' and say 'they only love their chairs.'"

This, and their ensuing conversation about the fervent Orthodox Christian faith that many ordinary Russians still held, confirmed Reagan's intuition of the growing chasm between the Soviet people and the Kremlin. The former were devout, open to the United States, and distrustful of their rulers. The latter was militantly secular, sclerotic, a parasite on its own society.

As their meeting closed, Massie asked Reagan if he meant what he had said in the prior day's speech about improving relations between the two superpowers. She wanted to carry this message to Moscow. Replied the president, "Yes. If they want peace, they can have it."[10]

For all of the intelligence and policy briefings at his disposal from the US government's legions of Soviet experts, Reagan still felt he lacked a window into the hearts, minds, and—especially—souls of the Russian people. Massie helped fill that gap. The president wrote appreciatively of their meeting in his diary that night, adding the wry note that she "has no truck with the government types."[11] Just as Reagan sought to understand the Russian people, he also tried to see the world through the Kremlin's eyes. His growing knowledge of Russian history led him to appreciate that its insecurities stemmed in part from its past. He often remarked how centuries of invasions such as those by Napoleon and Hitler had given Moscow an understandable paranoia about foreign encirclement.[12]

In January, Shultz traveled to Stockholm for a Helsinki Accords conference. Soviet foreign minister Andrei Gromyko also attended. His speech to the assembly amounted to a snarling bite at Reagan's outstretched hand. Gromyko accused the United States of exporting "militarism, enmity, and war hysteria" to Europe, having a "pathological obsession" with preparing for war against the Soviet Union, "sowing death and destruction" in Lebanon, committing a "piratical act of terrorism" in Grenada, "hurling gangs of mercenaries and terrorists against Nicaragua," "propping up the murderous antipopular regime in El Salvador," and for good measure being "the main threat to peace" in the world.[13]

This was not the reckless invective of a renegade apparatchik. Gromyko stood as one of the two or three most powerful members of the Politburo. Following this diatribe, an outraged Shultz met privately with Gromyko for five hours. Shultz protested Gromyko's slanders against the United States and pressed the obstreperous Soviet on a full range of issues, including human rights, SS-20 deployments, the American mission in Lebanon, and other points of contention. Gromyko yielded little.

Yet as their marathon session drew to a close, Shultz took heart from the fact that he and Gromyko had had a frank exchange of views; the mere act of talking seemed to be progress. Shultz, like Reagan, felt a certain empathy for his Soviet counterpart. The secretary later reflected that he saw Gromyko "as a symbol of communism's tragic flaw. He was a man of dignity and intelligence . . . [but] he lived a life of irreconcilable objectives. He believed the Marxist dogma he preached . . . he believed in the cause of peace, but a peace that could come only when all the world turned communist. That was clearly not happening."[14]

Reagan's outreach did not mean he had abandoned his strategy to bring the Soviet Union to a negotiated surrender. Many scholars and journalists contend that the multiple Cold War crises of 1983 prompted a "Reagan reversal." In this view, the escalated tensions, nuclear war scares, and collapse in the Geneva talks prompted Reagan to abandon his confrontational policies and instead seek conciliation with the Kremlin for the next five years.

He did not. Rather, from the beginning Reagan pursued a dual track of pressure on the Soviets combined with diplomatic outreach. The INF deployment, military expansion, economic warfare, covert support to Solidarity and overt broadcasting, human rights campaign, and support for anticommunist insurgencies all embodied the pressure track. Just as Reagan's repeated letters to Soviet leaders, offers to negotiate arms reductions, refusal to downgrade relations after crises such as KAL 007, vision of abolishing nuclear weapons, and search for a Soviet reformer all embodied the outreach track.

As 1984 unfolded, Reagan did not reverse his two-pronged strategy. Instead he rebalanced it, with a tilt toward diplomacy.

III
———

On January 10, Reagan opened diplomatic relations between the United States and the world's tiniest state: the Vatican. Though Vatican City had no military, a minuscule population, and territory spanning just one hundred acres (one-eighth the size of Manhattan's Central Park), the Holy See wielded the spiritual power of almost one billion Catholics, many living in strategic areas of Eastern Europe, Asia, and Latin America.

Technically Reagan's move was a "restoration" of diplomatic relations with the Vatican, which Congress, in a spate of anti-Catholicism, had defunded back in 1867. Several subsequent US presidents had dispatched special envoys and personal emissaries to Rome, but Harry Truman's bid in 1951 to upgrade the relationship to ambassadorial level had ignited outrage among American Protestants and been rejected by Congress. Now times were different. As Assistant Secretary of State Elliott Abrams had advocated to Clark, Vatican recognition was "an idea whose time has come."[15] A more pluralistic United States valued the Vatican as an anticommunist ally, and Reagan and John Paul II had forged a personal partnership.

Over the past two years, Reagan had worked with eager members of Congress to restore funding for a diplomatic mission to the Vatican. The president also used his personal credibility with evangelical Protestants, including quiet help from Billy Graham, to gauge and in some cases alleviate opposition.[16] Not all agreed. Following the announcement, a flock of prominent evangelical leaders descended on the White House. The group—including Jerry Falwell, Pat Robertson, Tim LaHaye, Oral Roberts, Jimmy Swaggart, and Bill Bright—met with McFarlane and other senior White House staff to voice their displeasure at what they viewed as inappropriate favor to Catholicism.[17] They and their followers formed a vital part of Reagan's political base. His willingness to incur their disfavor ten months before the election shows the priority that he put on Vatican relations. It did not hurt that American Catholics, also an important voting bloc, overwhelmingly supported the move.

Though the White House and Vatican had consummated their union, they did not enjoy a honeymoon. The upgraded diplomatic relations coincided with an increase in policy tensions between the Reagan administration and Holy See. Two issues had become irritants: Poland and Lebanon.

Reagan continued to favor squeezing the Jaruzelski regime with sanctions, while the Pope worried that the sanctions hurt ordinary Poles more than they helped undermine the communist government. A few months earlier, the Nobel Committee had bestowed the Peace Prize on Lech Walesa. Jaruzelski barred the Solidarity leader from traveling to Oslo for the award ceremony. An apoplectic Andropov wrote to Jaruzelski blaming the Vatican for "reawakening the cult of Walesa," saying, "The Church is creating a new kind of confrontation with the Party. In this situation, the most important thing is not to make concessions." Urged on by the Kremlin, Jaruzelski increased the torment of Solidarity. The Polish secret police arrested and tortured many Solidarity activists, and beat at least one to death.[18]

This oppression made Reagan reluctant to ease the pressure on Warsaw, but the Pope worried it was missing the mark. In a February meeting with Bush at the Vatican, John Paul II complained to the vice president that "the people are getting hurt" by the American sanctions and said, "This must be changed." He contrasted Russia's history of czarist and Soviet totalitarianism with Poland's "tradition of freedom." Of the Polish people—his people—he reminded Bush, "Many times in the past they have defended themselves against oppression." The Pope believed that their resistance to dictatorship remained vibrant and a source of Kremlin vulnerability. He appealed for the United States to lift the punitive measures and instead channel more support directly to ordinary Polish citizens.[19]

The next week, Reagan responded in a letter informing the Pope that the United States would ease some sanctions.[20] The White House also worked with Congress, the Vatican, and European allies to allocate $28 million in direct aid to Polish farmers, bypassing the regime. Reagan kept most other sanctions in place, however. Some leading Polish dissidents urged them as a sign of Western resolve, even if their actual impact was dubious. QRHELPFUL continued to keep Solidarity's literature flowing and continued rattling the communist rulers. To outward appearances the Poland crisis remained a grim stalemate, but small tears began to fray the Iron Curtain.[21]

IV

Lebanon remained another friction point between the administration and the Vatican. John Paul II's interest in the country was humanitarian, pastoral, and strategic. He grieved the suffering wrought by the war, felt special responsibility to the Maronites in communion with the Catholic Church, and hoped Lebanon could restore its model of peaceful coexistence of Muslims and Christians for the rest of the region. For these reasons, when Reagan announced on February 7, 1984, the "redeployment" of the marines from Beirut to ships offshore, the Pope wrote to Reagan of his worry that Lebanon could soon descend into an orgy of bloodletting.[22]

It was the first step in what would soon become a complete American withdrawal. Perhaps the person most surprised at Reagan's decision to withdraw was Reagan himself. For the three months since the marine barracks bombing, he had continued to insist, in public and in private, on maintaining the mission. He had also redoubled diplomatic efforts toward a peace settlement. Reagan appointed Donald Rumsfeld, a former (and future) secretary of defense, to replace McFarlane in the special envoy role. Rumsfeld and Shultz both led the diplomatic campaign, with its goals of withdrawing Syrian and Israeli forces and strengthening a pluralist Lebanese government that could impose order despite the terrorists and militias plaguing the country.

Shultz and Rumsfeld stood alone on Reagan's team in wanting to maintain the MNF as leverage for a diplomatic settlement. Weinberger and Vessey continued to press for getting out of Lebanon. They now were joined by Bush and McFarlane. Over the course of November and December 1983, the vice president and NSA both shifted from supporting the MNF mission to favoring withdrawal. McFarlane had changed his posture after an American naval bombing attack on Syrian targets in December resulted in two US planes shot down, with one pilot killed and another captured. A few weeks later, Assad released the imprisoned pilot only after a high-profile visit from the Reverend Jesse Jackson. This embarrassed the White House and emboldened Assad. McFarlane saw little prospect for his divided government to develop an effective policy and decided it was time to exit Lebanon.

Reagan still believed in the mission. In his January 25, 1984, State of the Union address, he proclaimed, "There is hope for a free, independent, and sovereign Lebanon.... We must not be driven from our objectives for peace in Lebanon by state-sponsored terrorism."[23] The next week in his radio address, Reagan conceded the challenges in Lebanon but then declared, "That is no reason to turn our backs on friends and to cut and run. If we do, we'll be sending one signal to terrorists everywhere: They can gain by waging war against innocent people."[24]

Two days later Reagan decided to remove the marines from Beirut.

Before revealing this to the public, he informed Thatcher. His letter to her obfuscated both the decision and its ramifications. Reagan wrote that he had ordered a "phased redeployment" of the marines that "will be balanced by even stronger support for the Lebanese Army."[25] Thatcher was annoyed and not fooled. She had committed British troops to the MNF because she believed in the mission and in keeping faith with her American, French, and Italian allies. Now she knew that with the American retreat, the mission had no hope. The next day she announced the pullout of British forces as well. Coming three months after her row with Reagan over the Grenada invasion, this furthered her frustration with him over coordination on the use of force. Reagan's withdrawal also provoked outrage in Paris. He neglected to consult with Mitterrand before announcing the pullout, which further embittered Franco-American relations.[26]

Why did Reagan reverse course? Because the Lebanese army collapsed. Scholars Alexandra Evans and A. Bradley Potter point out that Reagan's policy had relied on building the Lebanese army (LAF) into a viable force able to protect the nation on its own. Over the previous months the LAF had instead become factionalized and ineffective. Then in the fateful first week of February, a coalition of Shia and Druze militias launched an offensive against LAF positions in Beirut. The LAF did not just retreat; it dissolved. In Evans and Potter's words, "As the militias advanced, desertion rates skyrocketed. Within a week, the Lebanese army was shattered." Without the LAF to rely on, Reagan's resolve dissipated. With success elusive and with his reelection campaign looming, he decided to cut US losses and exit.[27]

Many Americans applauded his decision. Yet the Reagan administration's botched explanations for when and how the marines would depart dissipated much of this goodwill. The next day, Deputy Secretary of State Ken Dam's briefing to Congress led to loud "groans and hisses" from many members—and those were the Republicans. Representative Trent Lott rebuked Dam, saying, "You people are not in touch with reality." *Washington Post* diplomatic correspondent Don Oberdorfer described the "US debacle in Lebanon" as "the most serious defeat for American foreign policy" since the Iranian Revolution.[28] A demoralized Dam confessed to his diary, "We have no Middle East policy that we can describe."[29]

Nor did the marine withdrawal mean the end of danger to Americans. Over the next four months, Shia terrorists in Beirut kidnapped four Americans in succession. The hostages included an engineering professor, a CNN journalist, a Presbyterian minister—and CIA chief of station William Buckley.[30] Reagan may have exited Lebanon. But Lebanon would not let him go.

V

Fast spins the world. While pundits digested Reagan's Beirut withdrawal, two days later Andropov died in Moscow. Global attention lurched back to the Cold War and the new Soviet leader, Konstantin Chernenko. Reagan learned of Andropov's death while at his California ranch. He felt no sadness at the news. The president, supported by Shultz, rejected McFarlane and Matlock's suggestion that he attend the funeral. "I don't want to honor that prick," Reagan scoffed.[31]

Behind his obscenity was a strategy. Though Reagan remained as eager as ever to talk with a Soviet leader, he believed that the value of a summit depended on both sides' committing to addressing substantive issues and convening on neutral ground. Andropov's funeral in Moscow deviated from those terms. Meeting with Chernenko in Red Square would place ceremony over substance, conceding the prestige of a summit without any Soviet concessions in return. Especially while the Kremlin still stonewalled the arms control negotiations in Geneva.

Reagan now faced the third Soviet leader in the three years since he had become president. A protégé of Brezhnev, the seventy-two-year-old Chernenko took office beset by physical infirmities, encroaching senility—and putrescence in the Soviet empire. On top of these challenges, he would fail to consolidate his grip on the Politburo; Foreign Minister Gromyko still held sway on Soviet foreign policy.

Nonetheless, Reagan's quest continued to pressure the Soviet system to produce a reformer. He still yearned to make a personal connection with a Soviet leader and see if he could lure the Kremlin in from the cold. He confided to his diary, "I have a gut feeling I'd like to talk to [Chernenko] about our problems man to man and see if I could convince him there would be a material benefit to the Soviets if they'd join the family of nations etc."[32] Though not optimistic, Reagan decided at least to test whether the USSR's new chieftain might surprise him as a negotiating partner. It began, as always, with a letter.

Bush happened to be in Europe on a diplomatic mission when Andropov died. Reagan asked his vice president to detour to Moscow to represent the United States at the funeral. He dispatched Matlock to join Bush, bearing a letter from Reagan to Chernenko. In it Reagan wrote of his hope to "proceed with [a dialogue] as soon as your government is ready to do so" and reaffirmed his desire to reduce nuclear arsenals as well as make progress on other issues.[33]

Joining Bush for the funeral would be Thatcher, Kohl, Sandro Pertini of Italy, and other European heads of government. The NATO leaders flew to Moscow backed by a strong tailwind of political unity. The alliance frictions

from the failed Lebanon mission had not hurt their shared anti-Soviet resolve. The three leading European countries that had welcomed the INF
missiles—the UK, West Germany, and Italy—had each held elections in
1983 won by leaders who supported the deployments. This popular ratification chastened the Kremlin. The Soviet disinformation campaign had failed
to fracture the alliance. It was not happenstance. For the past eighteen
months, Reagan, Bush, and Shultz had devoted much energy and political
capital to alliance management. They had cultivated, cajoled, commiser-
ated, and compromised with NATO leaders and engaged in extensive outreach to NATO publics, all to preserve alliance unity.

In Moscow, Bush met with Chernenko for thirty minutes. The Soviet
did most of the talking. He maintained a positive tone and affirmed his
desire for better bilateral relations but stuck to Kremlin boilerplate and put
the onus on the United States to take specific policy steps. Bush handed him
Reagan's letter and reinforced the outreach themes in Reagan's January 16
speech and hope for a summit. Bush also stressed the importance of human
rights, especially the cause of imprisoned dissidents Anatoly Shcharansky,
Andrei Sakharov, and Yuri Orlov.[34]

From aboard Air Force Two, Bush sent Reagan his first impressions of
the new Soviet leader. Chernenko "seemed alert, in good health, with a
sparkle in his eye," reported the vice president. "He gave the clear impression that there is somebody at home in the Kremlin with whom we can do
business."[35] Bush could not have been more wrong on Chernenko. But his
optimism showed the White House's eagerness to find a Soviet partner for
peace.

By this point, Reagan had developed high regard for his vice president.
It had not always been so. Even after overcoming his campaign suspicions
of Bush and selecting his rival as his running mate, it had taken time in office for the two men—who differed in temperament, style, and ideology—to
build chemistry and mutual trust. Bush knew his role to be the faithful
lieutenant and honored Reagan's convictions rather than pushing his own
agenda. The vice president said little in NSC meetings. Rather, in other settings, such as meetings with heads of state, reports from his world travels,
and especially his private weekly lunches with Reagan, Bush shared his counsel. The vice president also stayed closely aligned with his best friend, Chief
of Staff James Baker, forming a quiet but formidable power axis in a White
House beset by dueling fiefdoms.

Andropov's funeral prompted Reagan to wonder anew whether atheism might be the Soviet system's downfall. He wrote to Massie: "Watching the scenes of the funeral on TV, I wondered what thoughts people must have at such a time when their belief in no God or immortality is faced with death. Like you, I continue to believe that hunger for religion may yet be a major factor in bringing about a change in the present situation."[36]

Two weeks later, Reagan invited Massie back to the White House for a private lunch with him, McFarlane, and Deaver. The president wanted to hear about her recent trip to Moscow and her views on how the Soviet Union might fare under Chernenko. While her Soviet interlocutors showed little interest in addressing big issues, they had agreed to resume cultural exchanges with the United States, a small but symbolic step. Of more interest to Reagan, Massie's depiction of the people she encountered reinforced his sense of a growing divide between the Russian people and the Soviet state. As Massie put it, citizens of Moscow and Leningrad described Russians as "we" or "us" but dismissed Soviets as "they" or "them." With such insights, Massie cemented her role as Reagan's most valued outside advisor. In James Mann's description, she "began to serve as Reagan's window on the Soviet Union."[37]

The CIA still overestimated the health of the Soviet economy. In April, the CIA predicted it would continue to grow about 2 percent per year for the rest of the decade, a "sluggish" pace but not the endemic crisis that the USSR actually faced. Langley did better in spotting Kremlin leadership trends. Casey gave a speech two months after Andropov's death noting that Chernenko would prove the last commissar of the Stalinist era. "The whole Soviet leadership structure is undergoing a major generational shift," Casey declared, and predicted the next Soviet ruler would be more open-minded and cosmopolitan.[38]

Meanwhile, Chernenko replied to Reagan's letter with a cordial but noncommittal response, parroting Soviet boilerplate. There ensued a series of letters between the two leaders throughout the spring, with both sides sending lengthy missives that broke no new ground. In one letter Reagan added a handwritten postscript paying tribute to "the tragedy and scale of Soviet losses" in World War II and acknowledging how that legacy shaped the Kremlin's fears in the contemporary moment. He again reassured Chernenko, "Neither I nor the American people hold any offensive intentions toward you or the Soviet people."[39]

Reagan's goodwill pleas fell on deaf ears. A doctrinaire Marxist, Chernenko could not free himself from the Soviet system's endemic paranoia, insecurity, and hostility to the United States. For the moment, in both Moscow and Washington, politics trumped geopolitics. The cautious Chernenko had neither the vision, audacity, or authority to break with the wary Politburo and return to the negotiating table with the Americans. Reagan, meanwhile, grew more risk-averse as his reelection approached. He remained open to possible overtures from Chernenko but hesitant to propose any more bold measures while he focused on his campaign.

Through the spring, Reagan's approval ratings began to strengthen, benefiting from the economy climbing up and the Democrats veering left in their primary campaign. Senator Gary Hart and former vice president Walter Mondale competed as the two front-runners for the Democratic nomination. Their contest sparked some colorful observations from Richard Nixon, who wrote McFarlane with advice on politics and policy, which the NSA shared with Reagan.

Nixon chortled, "I never thought the day would come when we would see a candidate more dovish than Walter Mondale. But the new wunderkind, scary Gary, has finally topped him." The former president drew on his first election defeat to warn against complacency at the Democrats' fratricide, however. "As Johnson and Kennedy demonstrated in 1960, Democrats who appear to be fighting each other during a primary have a love fest at a convention. It is like hearing a couple of cats screeching on the back fence in the middle of the night. You think that they are fighting. But in a few weeks you have a dozen more kittens."

Nixon worried more about the Soviets than the Democrats. Given Moscow's hope to see Reagan defeated, he warned that the Kremlin "might try to stir up some trouble someplace in the world hoping that it would lead to the President's defeat."[40] Instead the Kremlin ran a disinformation effort inside the United States against Reagan's reelection. As scholar Seth Jones describes, using a combination of front organizations and unwitting journalists and campaign staff, "the KGB active measures campaign alleged that Reagan discriminated against minorities, that his administration was corrupt, and that he was too closely tied to the military-industrial complex."[41] The KGB promoted the slogan "Reagan Means War!," offered quiet support to Reagan's political opponents, and enticed credulous media outlets to caricature Reagan as a capitalist militarist intent on oppressing developing nations.[42] The KGB had fueled similar gambits the year before to try to defeat Thatcher in the UK and Kohl in the West German elections. Those had failed; so would its campaign to deny Reagan a second term.

VI

The Beirut bombing and subsequent spate of hostage-taking confronted the White House with the need for a terrorism policy. It was a vexing puzzle. While Reagan had been thinking about and opposing communism for forty years, terrorism befuddled him. It was a new challenge and did not fit with the main pillars of his Cold War strategy. The buildup of conventional and nuclear might, economic revival, restored national confidence, support for anticommunist forces, ideological offensive, and diplomacy with foreign leaders all offered little help against terrorism. Unlike Reagan's clarity and foresight on the Cold War, when he looked at terrorism, it felt like he was wearing kaleidoscope glasses in a hall of mirrors.

The Middle East was terrorism's operational core, but its tactics irradiated every continent. Its acolytes included state actors like North Korea; state sponsors such as Cuba, Iran, Libya, Syria, and the Soviet Union; nonstate actors seeking statehood, such as the Irish Republican Army (IRA) and Palestine Liberation Organization (PLO); and nonstate actors trying to overthrow the nation-state system altogether. Its tactics included assassination, suicide bombing, torture, kidnapping, piracy, and the occasional negotiation. Its targets encompassed airliners, barracks, cruise ships, discotheques, embassies, and the remaining alphabet of civilian prey. It attracted adherents from Catholicism, Islamism, communism, nationalism, nihilism, and just about every other "ism." It posed a growing threat—and yet just what it was, and how to stop it, remained maddeningly elusive.

On March 2, 1984, Reagan convened an NSPG meeting on terrorism. Foreshadowing the same debates American leaders would have two decades later in the September 11 era, he and his national security team wrestled with how to define and combat terrorism. The meeting focused on a draft NSDD, composed largely by Oliver North of the NSC staff.

Shultz and Casey, not often aligned, took the most aggressive posture in the meeting. Shultz demanded "that when we know where terrorists are, we will act against them" with preventive force even if the evidence is not "conclusive enough to 'win a Supreme Court case.'" Casey agreed. The CIA was already engaged in "pre-emptive action," he told the table. "We have caused a number of terrorist activities to be aborted." Both stressed that the United States needed more cooperation from its partners, especially in NATO and the Middle East. "Penetration of terrorist organizations is done well by the Israelis, Jordanians, and Egyptians," reported Casey, but he said these liaison relationships needed to be improved. He also urged "diplomatic measures that can be taken to cause others not to support terrorism." In other words, tearing out terrorism at its root causes.

Attorney General William French Smith advocated a very different approach. He argued that "terrorism in the US is a law enforcement function" and should be free from any intelligence, military, or diplomatic involvement. An angry Shultz objected that terrorism knows no borders: "It makes no sense simply to look overseas. . . . To do otherwise would be the same as trying to say that domestic trade and international trade have nothing to do with each other."[43] Reagan and the others agreed to a few technical tweaks to assuage French's concerns; four weeks later the president signed the directive. With NSDD-138, Reagan in effect declared war on terrorism. He directed the Pentagon and CIA to use preventive force against terrorist groups and targeted killings of terrorist leaders. NSDD-138 aimed at both terrorists and the governments that supported them, warning, "The US will hold sponsors accountable."[44]

While Washington deliberated on NSDD-138, in Beirut on the morning of March 16, William Buckley stepped out of his apartment on his way to work. It would be his last morning as a free man. Hezbollah terrorists captured him at gunpoint and threw him in the back of a car, hooded and stunned. Buckley's world went dark. He would soon descend into a hell on earth.

His kidnappers were Hezbollah terrorists, directed by Iran. They targeted him by design. As one account notes, Buckley had become the CIA's "point man in the war against terrorism."[45] Three weeks after the last marine had departed Lebanon, Hezbollah sought to show they now controlled Beirut—and no American was safe. Hezbollah also grabbed Buckley as a bargaining chip. Four months earlier, Shia terrorists had bombed several civilian targets in Kuwait, including the American and French embassies. Kuwaiti authorities arrested and imprisoned seventeen of the terrorists, known as the "Dawa prisoners" after the name of their cell. Hezbollah sought to use Buckley and other Western hostages as leverage to get their Dawa comrades released.[46]

Back in Washington, Oliver North convened the Terrorist Incident Working Group (TIWG) to coordinate efforts to find—and hopefully rescue—Buckley. Intended to implement the White House's upgraded counterterrorism policy, the TIWG included representatives from the State

Department, intelligence community, and military, all led by North in a joint endeavor. It did not start well. North complained to Poindexter after an early TIWG meeting, "There is growing concern that this is not a team effort and that we could well be doing more."[47]

Hidden somewhere in a lonely room in Lebanon, Hezbollah henchmen tormented Buckley. As a former Green Beret awarded a Silver Star for combat valor in Vietnam, Buckley was tough. But no man could endure what he suffered. Two months after his abduction, his captors sent a videotape to the US embassy in Athens, which forwarded it to CIA headquarters. Casey, already racked with guilt over having sent Buckley to Beirut, described his reaction on viewing it: "I was close to tears. It was the most obscene thing I had ever witnessed. Bill was barely recognizable as the man I had known for years. They had done more than ruin his body. His eyes made it clear his mind had been played with. It was horrific, mediaeval and barbarous."[48] At some later point—probably over a year later, after more prolonged torture and psychotropic drugs had wrung out whatever secrets remained in his unraveling mind, his captors executed him.

The Hezbollah leader who engineered Buckley's kidnapping (and who may have personally killed him) was Imad Mughniyeh, a Lebanese Shia. He had also planned the bombings of the US embassy and the marine barracks the previous year, making him singly responsible for the most American deaths during the Reagan era. He eluded many American capture efforts.[49] The wily Mughniyeh would continue his murderous campaign for another quarter century, until a joint Mossad-CIA operation assassinated him in Damascus in 2008.[50]

Meanwhile, Shultz delivered a series of speeches over the course of the year, laying out an assertive counterterrorism doctrine. He also sought to escape the shadow of the Vietnam War. Responding to those who invoked Vietnam against any military deployment that was not overwhelming in scale and public support, Shultz called for using force against terrorists where "a discrete assertion of power is needed or appropriate for limited purposes." He also called for active defense "through appropriate preventive or preemptive actions against terrorists before they strike," and warned, "We cannot allow ourselves to become the Hamlet of nations, worrying endlessly over whether and how to respond."[51]

Not all on Reagan's team believed that terrorism could be defeated, or even was worth the effort. Bush, Weinberger, and Vessey worried that the use of force would create an escalation spiral of more terrorism counterattacks—not to mention distract from the main priority of waging the Cold War. These divisions among Reagan's team derailed his new counterterrorism strategy. Declaring war on terrorism was one thing; waging it was another matter. Hal Brands recounts that NSDD-138's plans "soon unraveled . . . amid internal opposition and fears that such operations could spiral out of control . . . the Pentagon continued to oppose military options, and even more hawkish advisors struggled to identify opportunities to use force effectively and without intolerable risk. . . . [The US] was stuck in a worst-of-both-worlds policy that involved tough talk and very little action."[52]

VII

A White House divided on terrorism found itself surprisingly united on an even more distasteful issue: supporting Iraq in its war with Iran. In 1980, Saddam Hussein had launched a surprise invasion of Iran. Over eight years of gruesome combat and unrelenting atrocities by both sides, the war would claim as many as one million dead, transforming large swaths of desert into vast charnel houses. By 1982, after Iraq's early advances stalled, Iranian counteroffensives gave Tehran the upper hand. As Iranian forces approached Basra, Iraq's second-largest city, and appeared poised to win the war, the Reagan administration decided it had no choice but to support Iraq.

The prospect of an Iranian victory seemed catastrophic. It would accelerate Shia radicalism, embolden terrorism, place up to one-quarter of the world's petroleum reserves under Ayatollah Khomeini's direct control, put Persian Gulf shipping channels and another quarter of global oil supplies at risk, and imperil American partners such as Saudi Arabia, Israel, Kuwait, and Jordan. Once again, Reagan's options ran the narrow gamut from bad to awful. Disengagement could bring calamity. America's European and Asian allies depended on reliable petroleum supplies from the Persian Gulf. Allowing a hostile Iran to win the war and control those energy flows could cripple the economies of Japan, South Korea, West Germany, Great Britain, Italy, and France, and disembowel them from the anti-Soviet coalition. At the G7 summit in London that year, virtually every leader pleaded with Reagan for the United States to do whatever it could to preserve the flow of Persian Gulf oil to their countries. Reagan, ever mindful of solidarity with the allies, agreed.[53] Now that the US withdrawal from Lebanon had ceded the Levant to greater Iranian influence, Reagan and Thatcher also saw the war as a new front to hurt Iran and block its regional expansion.

Not that Iraq was much better. Reagan held no illusions about the vile Saddam Hussein. When Iranian forces had counterattacked into Iraq in 1982, a panicked Saddam bombarded the Iranians with chemical weapons to stall their advance. What started as an emergency measure soon turned into a perverse habit, as Saddam began deploying mustard and nerve gas against Iranian troops and civilians regularly over the next six years.

The State Department responded to these war crimes with a favorite tool: the sternly worded démarche. A midlevel American diplomat told a midlevel Iraqi official that the United States "takes very seriously" the reports of chemical weapons and warned, "This damages Iraq's international image." This anemic scolding triggered a ritual denial from Iraq—and continued use of poison gas at levels not seen since World War I.[54] Mindful of the Iraqi leader's barbarity, State Department diplomat Barbara Bodine put the choice in stark terms: "If you don't like Saddam, we have Khomeini."[55]

The White House viewed a victory by either Iran or Iraq as catastrophic. In the blunt words of the Pentagon's Rich Armitage, "It's a pity the war could not have lasted forever."[56] Reagan pursued unadulterated realpolitik with the morbid immediate goal of stalemate—and the ultimate goal of a truce that would leave both belligerents weakened and less able to destabilize the region, let alone the globe. The logic of this stalemate strategy dictated helping whichever side was losing. Starting in 1982, this meant a tilt toward Iraq. The increased American support included a regular stream of signals intelligence on Iranian troop positions and vulnerabilities, several hundred million dollars in export-import credits, nonlethal equipment such as trucks and helicopters, removing Iraq from the state sponsor of terrorism blacklist, and in 1984 restoring full diplomatic relations with Baghdad.[57]

Meanwhile the White House designated Iran a state sponsor of terrorism, coupled with Operation Staunch, a global campaign to prevent other nations from supplying Iran with weapons. Operation Staunch's diplomacy succeeded in persuading nine European nations to stop selling arms to Iran and cut by 80 percent the matériel flowing to Tehran.

The White House also sought to counter Iran by deepening its support for Saudi Arabia and Kuwait. Reagan chaired an NSPG meeting on March 30 where Special Envoy Rumsfeld, just returned from the region, reported "lots of talk" among the Persian Gulf nations doubting American credibility after the fall of the shah and the marine withdrawal from Lebanon. Many of these Sunni governments also feared being toppled by Iran-sponsored terrorism. Rumsfeld urged regime change in Tehran: "If you want to kill a snake you go for the head. We need to change governments in the countries that practice state-sponsored terrorism." That was a step too far for Reagan and Shultz, who changed the subject. Rumsfeld closed the meeting by reminding the room, "Oil is not the most important thing. Most important is to prevent Soviet involvement in the Gulf."[58] In the coming months, the Soviets further rattled Washington with increased arms sales to Jordan, Kuwait, and Syria. Reagan responded with more arms sales to Saudi Arabia and deployed US Air Force tankers to provide refueling for Saudi fighter jets.[59] The tankers joined American AWACS planes already based in the kingdom, growing the presence of American forces—an irritant in the conservative Islamic theocracy.

This increased commitment to Persian Gulf security, essentially a Reagan Corollary to the Carter Doctrine, would define American policy into the twenty-first century. Its strategic rationale was clear: keeping other hostile powers out of the region while preserving the stable energy supplies on which the United States and its allies depended. It also brought with it a new set of challenges. Shultz and Weinberger coauthored a memo to Reagan that endorsed the policy while warning of the "twin dilemmas" it posed: "trying to defend countries which are reluctant to be seen as cooperating with us and attempting to *unilaterally* protect resources which are vital to the entire Western world."[60] The gulf monarchies wanted more American help but wanted it hidden, while NATO members and Japan wanted the benefits of secure oil without paying the costs. Reagan faced a similar challenge in other regions: Allies were hard to live with but harder to live without.

VIII

In late April, Reagan made his long-awaited trip to China. He found the Far East a welcome reprieve from the tribulations of the Middle East. In Asia, Reagan's strategy of curtailing Soviet encroachments by restoring the alliances with Japan and South Korea, reassuring Taiwan, and reengaging with China had begun to bear fruit. As he and the First Lady stepped down from Air Force One onto the Beijing airport tarmac, it was his first time as president to set foot in a communist country (and his second time ever, after his brief sojourn in East Berlin in 1978).

Reagan arrived in China at an auspicious time. In preparation for the trip, his pollster Richard Wirthlin described China as the only place in the world "where more Americans now feel relations have become better, rather than worse, since the President took office."[61] James Mann describes the era between 1983 and 1988 as "the golden years" in the United States–China relationship, when "the Reagan Administration forged a closer, more extensive working relationship with China's Communist regime than the two governments had before or have had since."[62]

This came about in part from lowered expectations. Both countries shed the illusory hopes each had cultivated in the previous decade, whether Beijing's dream that the United States would jettison Taiwan entirely, or Washington's ambition that a United States–China partnership would by itself transform the region. Instead, Reagan and Shultz had first secured America's commitment to Taiwan and affirmed the primacy of Japan in their Asia strategy. Only then did they turn to fortifying the China leg of those respective strategic triangles. Internal developments in China also helped much. Deng was into his fifth year of leading China into a new era of economic reform, modernization, and international engagement.

China also added a new prong to Reagan's strategy of pressure and diplomacy with the Soviets. His trip came in the midst of his renewed outreach to the Kremlin in Chernenko's early months. Reagan knew that his arrival in Beijing caused fretting in Moscow. By solidifying relations with China, Reagan ensured that when Moscow looked west it saw a united NATO and fissures opening in Poland; to the south it saw Red Army soldiers dying in the Afghanistan quagmire; and to the east it now saw both Japan and China firmly in the American camp. Reagan hoped the Kremlin, surrounded by such a daunting strategic landscape, would turn for relief to the negotiating table with America.

Upon their arrival in Beijing, Deng welcomed the Reagans with the forbidding gauntlet of a twelve-course dinner of quivering delicacies of indeterminate origin. The Reagans knew that any misstep, misbite, or other faux pas could provoke an international embarrassment. Reagan relied on guidance from a seasoned predecessor: "We heeded Dick Nixon's advice and didn't ask what things were—we just swallowed them."[63]

Reagan's strategic partnership with the Chinese government did not thwart his determination to deliver a message of freedom to the Chinese people—which the Chinese government in turn sought to stymie. In Beijing, he contrasted China's Communist Revolution and the American Revolution when he told an audience at the Great Hall of the People:

> [The United States draws] tremendous power from two great forces: faith and freedom. America was founded by people who sought freedom to worship God and to trust in Him to guide them in their daily lives. . . . Our passion for freedom led to the American Revolution, the first great uprising for human rights and independence against colonial rule. We knew each of us could not enjoy liberty for ourselves unless we were willing to share it with everyone else.[64]

Ever the evangelist for America, Reagan reinforced this message in Shanghai in a speech to students at Fudan University:

> We believe "that all men are created equal, that they are endowed by their Creator with certain unalienable Rights, that among those are Life, Liberty and the pursuit of Happiness." . . . We elect our government by the vote of the people. . . .
>
> Religion and faith are very important to us. We're a nation of many religions. But most Americans derive their religious belief from the Bible of Moses, who delivered a people from slavery; the Bible of Jesus Christ, who told us to love thy neighbor as thyself.[65]

The PRC authorities had committed to broadcasting both speeches in full on television, but government censors blocked out the passages about faith and freedom in his Beijing address and did not provide translation for the Shanghai speech, rendering it unintelligible to all except the very few Shanghainese who spoke English.[66]

Even if Chinese leaders blocked Reagan's paeans to freedom, they heard his private appeals. In their meetings with Deng and other senior officials, Reagan and Shultz discussed the importance of liberty to China's future. At the Pope's request, they urged Chinese leaders to grant more religious liberty for Chinese Catholics, including releasing five imprisoned Catholic priests.[67]

Reagan used these private meetings to advance another sensitive issue: cooperating with China to support the anti-Soviet insurgency in Afghanistan. This included the CIA's purchasing huge caches of weapons from China and thousands of Chinese mules—yes, mules—to carry the matériel across the forbidding landscape of western China and the Hindu Kush to supply the mujahideen. Chinese cargo ships carried other weapons by sea from Shanghai to Karachi. The scale was vast; over eight years, the CIA would spend close to $2 billion buying weapons from China, a significant share of the overall Afghanistan program.[68]

Other agreements that the visit produced included increased American weapons sales to China, provision of civilian-use nuclear technology, enlarged cultural exchanges, and agreements for deepened trade across multiple sectors.[69] *The Washington Post* called Reagan's trip "a resounding success."[70] In solidifying the United States–China partnership, Reagan completed the work that his three main political rivals of the past decade—Nixon, Ford, and Carter—had all started.

Of most consequence, the China visit advanced the strategy that Reagan and Shultz developed for the Asia-Pacific region. Reagan had evolved. He still viewed Asia through the lens of the Cold War but also envisioned an Asia beyond the Cold War. As a candidate, he had lacerated the Carter administration for recognizing Beijing; now, as president, Reagan deepened cooperation between the two governments on intelligence, arms sales, and trade. Reagan still favored Japan as America's most important global ally but now also built close ties with Japan's historic adversary. His heart still inclined toward Taiwan, but his head knew that China's greater geopolitical heft offered more benefit to the United States—even as he did not shrink from urging the PRC toward freedom. Though China would not democratize, in a few years several other Asian nations would. Reagan knew that strategy was not always a zero-sum game.

While Reagan worked to open China up to deeper cooperation with the United States, across the strait in Taipei, Jim Lilley worked to open Taiwan up to itself. Reagan's assurances that the United States remained committed to Taiwan's security gave president-cum-dictator Chiang Ching-kuo the confidence to take steps toward political reform and freedom. As the top American official on the island, with Reagan's support, Lilley urged Chiang to release imprisoned dissidents and ease restrictions on civil liberties and the press. Lilley also quietly nudged Chiang to replace his hard-line vice president with the more democratic-minded Lee Teng-hui, knowing that as vice president, Lee would be the ailing Chiang's heir apparent. Meanwhile, Lilley built close ties with leading opposition figure Chiu Len-hui through regular scuba diving trips on the island's southern coast. Through such efforts, Reagan, Shultz, and envoys such as Lilley engaged in an almost unprecedented policy experiment: Could the United States push its authoritarian allies to democracy without losing them as partners against communism?[71]

Reagan and his team viewed the Carter presidency as a cautionary tale. Carter took office when Nicaragua and Iran were ruled by anticommunist dictators aligned with the United States, only to see both of them toppled by the revolutions of 1979 and turned into adversaries. Reagan and Shultz believed they needed to avoid two errors. The first was unblinking support, which besmirched America's moral credibility, fueled resentments in repressed populations, and could also blind dictators to the domestic voices opposing them until it was too late. The second error was pressuring the autocrat to reform too much too soon, which could leave his country vulnerable to revolutionary ferment and, even worse, tyranny under communist rule.

IX

El Salvador embodied these concerns. Reagan sought to push the fragile government to reform and respect human rights while also supporting it enough to keep the communist FMLN insurgents at bay. A turning point came in December 1983. After a series of FMLN offensives had left the Salvadoran army bloodied and reeling, the White House worried that the military would respond with even more attacks on civilians. Reagan needed to deliver a tough message that further American support depended on the military fighting like professional soldiers, not amateur war criminals.

Vice President Bush's trip to Buenos Aires for the presidential inauguration of Raúl Alfonsín (who led Argentina's democratic transition after years of military dictatorship) presented an opportunity. While flying back to Washington, Bush took a secret detour to San Salvador. He had only one purpose: to get the Salvadoran military to stop its atrocities.

At a welcome dinner with President Magaña and other senior officials, when it came time for his toast, Bush abandoned diplomatic niceties. Raising his glass, he denounced the death squads as "a cowardly group of common criminals and murderers" who "are the best friends the Soviets, the Cubans, and the comandantes and the Salvadoran guerillas have." In private, Bush and Ambassador Pickering went further. They gave Magaña a letter from Reagan as well as a list of six senior officers whom American intelligence identified as the death squad ringleaders. They told Magaña that he needed to transfer all six outside the country to toothless diplomatic posts. Magaña complied.

Bush then met privately with a group of twenty other senior Salvadoran officers. He delivered a blunt message: The Salvadoran military must immediately cease terrorism, extrajudicial killing, and other death squad activity, or Reagan would terminate all American aid. When one officer protested that his father and son had been murdered by the FMLN and only a "kill-or-be-killed" approach worked, Bush responded, "If you fight them with the same methods they employ against you, how are you different from them?" The Salvadoran military cleaned up its act, the death squads began to wither, and the number of killings declined substantially.[72]

Into this ferment, the Kissinger Commission had issued its report in January 1984. As with the Scowcroft Commission report the previous year, the Kissinger Commission report was less notable for what it said than for who said it. Its bipartisan participants included Democratic eminences such as Bob Strauss, Henry Cisneros, Lloyd Bentsen, Daniel Inouye, and labor leader Lane Kirkland, alongside Republican luminaries such as Bill Clements, Jack Kemp, and Kissinger himself. The report delivered a bracing message: Central America was in "crisis," it warned over and over, and the United States needed to act with dispatch and boldness: "Unless the externally-supported insurgencies are checked and the violence curbed, progress on those other fronts will be elusive and would be fragile." The commission fingered the "hostile outside forces" fomenting the violence as "Cuba, backed by the Soviet Union and now operating through Nicaragua," and warned against letting the Soviet bloc establish a continental foothold in the Americas beyond its Havana outpost.[73] Congress balked at the report's recommendation of $8 billion in economic aid. Nonetheless, Reagan cajoled Capitol Hill to increase its appropriations to development aid in Central America, even if not on the scale that the commission urged. The report did persuade a number of moderate Republicans and Democrats to reconsider their opposition to military aid to anticommunist forces in the region.[74]

El Salvador's elections delivered an even stronger message. On March 25, an overwhelming 78 percent of eligible voters went to the polls in a peaceful and credible process, with a plurality backing José Napoleon Duarte for president. Duarte benefited from some $2 million in covert CIA funding that Reagan had authorized to support his candidacy, which helped offset the comparable amounts that Salvadoran oligarchs lavished on the campaign of the rightist ARENA party. Its leader, Roberto d'Aubuisson, had campaigned against Reagan's pressure on human rights by invoking the vulgarity that America "makes poor El Salvador grovel while the US 'sodomizes' the only country fighting the communists."[75] Meanwhile the communist-backed FMLN boycotted the elections and tried to derail the vote by burning ballots and destroying voter identification cards. Such subterfuge failed to deter the Salvadoran people.[76]

The Salvadoran elections also boosted the White House's credibility with Congress. House Democratic majority leader Jim Wright (generally an opponent of Reagan's Central America policy) and Republican senator Bill Roth led the congressional election observers. They returned to Washington the next day and went straight to the White House to brief Reagan and his senior team. Deputy Secretary Dam described the delegation as "unbelievably enthusiastic about what they had seen in El Salvador. They felt that the election was an unqualified victory for democracy." Reagan summarized the results in his diary succinctly: "The people of El Salvador want Democracy and we should help them."[77]

Duarte's victory in the El Salvador elections gave the Reagan administration a resounding policy success. It showed that a strategy combining military aid with diplomacy and political reform could produce progress toward a stable democracy. The Salvadoran elections also sparked a delinking of El Salvador and Nicaragua, at least in Congress. Led by Wright, a coalition of Democrats shifted to supporting increased economic and military aid to the Salvadoran government.

By backing Duarte, Reagan took as much heat from his own Right as from the Left. Senator Jesse Helms, a vocal backer of d'Aubuisson and ARENA, denounced Reagan's support for the Christian Democrats and fulminated that State and the CIA had "bought Mr. Duarte lock, stock, and barrel." D'Aubuisson's treachery included sponsoring a plot to assassinate US ambassador Thomas Pickering as he accompanied Duarte on a postelection visit to Washington, DC. American intelligence discovered the assassination plans and protected the envoy from harm. A defiant Helms denied d'Aubuisson's involvement, unpersuasively.[78] Both the conservative and liberal critics of Reagan's policies overlooked the emerging democracy wave. Mired in the binary 1970s paradigm of reactionary rightists against revolutionary leftists, they failed to see a third way of democracy emerging, exemplified by Duarte and the Christian Democrats.

Three days after Duarte won the Salvadoran presidential election,

Reagan gave an address to the nation from the Oval Office, urging more economic support for Central America, especially El Salvador and the contras. He heralded freedom's growth in the region, noting, "26 of 33 Latin American countries are democracies or striving to become democracies." "But," he warned, "they are vulnerable." This was especially true with the Soviet bloc providing $4.9 billion in aid to Cuba and Nicaragua and their efforts to spread communism in the region. Reagan targeted his appeal to Democrats, with quotes from Harry Truman and John F. Kennedy, and tributes to Franklin Roosevelt and Scoop Jackson.[79]

With the Salvadoran election, the White House took two steps forward in its Central America strategy—then stepped on a political land mine in Nicaragua. Even worse, it was a mine planted by the CIA. On April 6, *The Wall Street Journal* published a story revealing that over the past few months, the CIA had been mining Nicaraguan harbors in a campaign targeting merchant ships. Dewey Clarridge, the crafty Latin America Division chief of operations, had devised the program a few months earlier. Clarridge intended it as economic warfare. He and his operatives designed the "firecracker mines" to make loud, flashy explosions but cause little damage. In Clarridge's words, "No one wanted to blow up any ships; we wanted to stop the ships from coming into the harbor." His plan was to scare shipping companies and drive their maritime insurance rates to prohibitive levels. It would squeeze the Sandinistas from both directions: Inbound tankers would refuse to bring much-needed petroleum imports, and outbound ships would refuse to carry Nicaragua's exports of coffee, cotton, and textiles to international markets. It was the sort of madcap scheme that Casey loved. Assistant Secretary of State Tony Motley vetted and endorsed the program, and when an NSPG meeting approved it, Reagan signed a covert action finding putting it in motion.[80]

Its operational logic had a twist of genius, but in political and strategic terms it was ham-handed malpractice. Motley recalls sardonically, "It was a great idea until it went public; then it became a terrible idea."[81] From Reagan on down, its architects failed to ask the classic question: How will this look on the front page of a national newspaper?

The answer was that it looked like a combination of war crimes, recklessness, and ineptitude. Targeting civilian shipping violated the laws of war. The mines hit a Soviet oil tanker, exploded against the hulls of merchant ships from Japan and the United Kingdom, and detonated near several Mexican ships. These amounted to, inter alia, an act of war against a nuclear-armed adversary and attacks on America's two most important allies, and jeopardized relations with America's southern neighbor. The mines did far more damage to America's global reputation than to the Sandinista economy.

Capitol Hill generated the biggest uproar. On the evening of April 5, Senator Goldwater, as chairman of the Intelligence Committee, was leading the effort on the Senate floor to pass the legislation authorizing another $21 million in contra aid. His colleague Senator Joseph Biden noticed the fine print of a CIA report describing the agency's role in planting the mines and sent a query about it that reached Goldwater at his Senate floor desk. The chairman, a frequent tippler who was much into his cups amid the nighttime flow of legislative business, erupted. Believing that the CIA had concealed the mining program from him, an outraged Goldwater began reading the report on it into the Senate public record, until his staff stopped him from further disclosing the classified program. But the word was out; the *Wall Street Journal* reporter drew on Goldwater's disclosures in publishing the article the next day.

Goldwater felt burned. For years he had supported the CIA as its chief patron and protector on Capitol Hill. He complained to his staff, "I've pulled Casey's nuts out of the fire on so many occasions. I feel like such a fool. I feel betrayed." He shot an angry letter to Casey—and a copy to *The Washington Post,* ensuring the whole world knew of his displeasure.[82] Yet Goldwater fired without looking first. The CIA, including Casey himself, *had* previously disclosed the mining operation to Goldwater and the Senate and House intelligence committees on multiple occasions. The SSCI chairman and his colleagues, blinded by the daily deluge of information they received, just had not paid careful heed.[83] Casey and other senior officials spent the next few weeks mollifying bruised congressional egos with an endless round of apologies.

Such penance did not undo the damage. Perhaps more than any other factor, the mining debacle disemboweled congressional support for the contras. Congress immediately passed a law forbidding any future mining operations, and House Majority Leader Wright led ten congressional Democrats in writing a fawning letter to Ortega. Addressed to "Dear Comandante," the letter lamented that "better relations do not exist between the United States and your country" and, in a not-so-veiled reference to Reagan, criticized "those responsible for supporting violence against your government."[84]

Congress followed up a few months later with a third Boland Amendment. This was the most restrictive yet: It declared that "no funds available to the Central Intelligence Agency, the Department of Defense, or any other agency or entity of the United States involved in intelligence activities" could be provided to the contras.[85] On June 25, Reagan convened an NSPG meeting on how to support anti-Sandinista forces even if Congress terminated all assistance. By this point Reagan and his senior team appear to have abandoned any notions of overthrowing the Sandinista government. Rather, Reagan's goal had shifted to using the contras to pressure Ortega into a negotiated settlement that would wean Managua from the Soviet and Cuban orbit.

In this he enjoyed considerable support in the region. A year earlier, Mexico, Venezuela, Colombia, and Panama had launched the "Contadora Group," aimed at restoring peace to Nicaragua. With the encouragement of the United States, the Contadora process soon added the five additional Central American countries (Costa Rica, El Salvador, Honduras, Guatemala, Nicaragua), all of whom save Nicaragua favored ending Soviet and Cuban arms supplies and promoting democracy. Cumbersome though it was, the Contadora process showed regional alignment with US policy goals and provided a diplomatic structure in which to work.

Reagan and Shultz both believed that maintaining pressure on the Sandinistas, especially the military threat from the contras, induced Managua to negotiate. Shultz told Mexican president Miguel de la Madrid, "When [the Sandinistas] are against a tough security situation, they are willing to talk and their rhetoric changes. When that is not so, they stiffen up."[86] Reagan drew a comparison with his nuclear arms buildup and diplomatic outreach to the Soviets, and told his national security team, "The Contra funding is like the MX spending. It is what will keep the pressure on Nicaragua, and the only way we are going to get a good Contadora treaty is if we keep the pressure on." Shultz believed it worked the other way as well. Any dwindling hopes for congressional funding depended on showing Capitol Hill skeptics a diplomatic process with Managua. He reminded the room, "It is essential to have [Sandinista negotiations] going on or else our support on the Hill goes down."[87] Reagan and Shultz envisioned a three-way cycle: American negotiations with the Sandinistas would generate more support in Congress for the contras; congressional support for the contras would keep the military pressure on Managua; the pressure would squeeze the Sandinistas back to the Contadora negotiating table.

Sandinista leader Daniel Ortega tried to escape that squeeze via Moscow. Emboldened by congressional plans to terminate aid to the contras, in mid-June he traveled to the USSR to seek more support from his Kremlin patrons. The Soviets agreed to keep their generous economic and military aid flowing but disappointed Ortega by hedging on their earlier promise to deliver MiG-21 fighter jets to Nicaragua. Shultz had warned Gromyko that the United States would attack and destroy any MiG-21s sent to Nicaragua. This seems to have deterred the cautious Chernenko from such an escalation.[88]

In part because they perceived Ortega as hopelessly enmeshed in the Soviet bloc, Weinberger, Casey, McFarlane, and Kirkpatrick all opposed Shultz's diplomacy with the Sandinistas. Shultz himself remained pessimistic and told the NSPG that he gave only a "two-in-ten" chance that negotiations would succeed. But even a failed negotiation could produce good results of emboldening America's regional partners and isolating the Sandinistas. "If it doesn't succeed," Shultz continued, "it needs to be clear where the responsibility is, and that we have tried to help our Contadora friends obtain a positive outcome." Reagan supported Shultz's negotiations—and ultimately his was the only vote that mattered.

The NSPG meeting also discussed contingency plans for how to keep the contras afloat if Congress did terminate all funding. Casey, Weinberger, and Bush advocated the "third-party" option: urging other friendly nations to support the contras. Shultz strongly opposed this, warning that Chief of Staff Jim Baker said, "If we go out and try to get money from third countries, it is an impeachable offense," because of the legislation restricting aid to the contras. Casey responded that the covert action finding Reagan had issued explicitly allowed for soliciting other countries, and that when briefed on the finding the congressional oversight committees had raised no objections. McFarlane warned the room, "I certainly hope none of this discussion will be made public in any way." To which Reagan retorted, "If such a story gets out, we'll all be hanging by our thumbs in front of the White House until we find out who did it."[89]

Unbeknownst to the others at the table, a few weeks earlier, McFarlane had already approached a third party. In a meeting with Saudi ambassador Prince Bandar, McFarlane had suggested that Saudi Arabia help the contras. Bandar arranged for his kingdom to start providing $1 million a month to the anti-Sandinista fighters. It was the small first step toward what would become the biggest scandal of Reagan's presidency.

In the midst of the Nicaraguan mining eruption, Reagan simultaneously confronted another Latin America crisis. Just four months after restoring its democracy, Argentina fell into an inflation and debt spiral that threatened to bankrupt the country, topple the government, and spread economic contagion throughout the hemisphere. Reagan led his counterparts in Colombia, Mexico, Brazil, and Venezuela in putting together a $600 million rescue package for Argentina. He told a grateful President Alfonsín, "From the Tierra del Fuego to the North Pole, we are all Americans."[90] A bailout for Argentina was a far cry from his vision of a hemisphere-wide trade alliance. But as a gesture to protect a fragile democracy and forge multilateral economic cooperation, it was a start.

CHAPTER 9

MORNING IN AMERICA, TWILIGHT IN THE COLD WAR?

I

Ever since his inauguration, Reagan had been looking forward to the 1984 Summer Olympics. The former college athlete and lifelong sports fan in him loved to watch the events, the statesman in him wanted to display America's renewed vibrancy to the world, the Californian in him delighted that Los Angeles would host the games, and the politician in him knew that a successful Olympiad three months before the election would boost his campaign.

The Kremlin knew this as well. Still smarting over Carter's boycott of the 1980 Moscow Olympics, the USSR exacted revenge on May 8 when it announced its boycott of the Los Angeles Olympics. The Soviet news agency TASS's statement blamed the Reagan White House for "using the games for its political aims," saying, "Chauvinistic sentiments and an anti-Soviet hysteria are being whipped up in the country."[1] Over the next two weeks, thirteen additional Soviet bloc countries announced their boycotts as well. Moscow's belligerence further eroded any hopes Reagan still held for meaningful talks with the Soviets that year. Ivan and Anya would not be meeting Jim and Sally in Los Angeles.

The Kremlin then escalated with one of its most brazen disinformation campaigns. The KGB *rezidentura* at the Soviet embassy in Washington, DC, mailed fabricated letters to the Olympic Committees of many African countries. Purporting to be from the Ku Klux Klan, the letters warned:

THE OLYMPICS—FOR THE WHITES ONLY!

African Monkeys!

A grand reception awaits you in Los Angeles!

We are preparing for the Olympic games by shooting at black moving targets.

In Los Angeles our own Olympic flames are ready to incinerate you. The highest award for a true American patriot would be the lynching of an African monkey.

The letters were a vile and crude effort to exploit America's history of racism. They were also ineffective. The FBI detected the forgeries, and Attorney General William French Smith publicly exposed the KGB campaign.[2] The African countries still sent their athletes to Los Angeles, and the Olympics—with Reagan becoming the first US president in history to preside over the opening ceremonies—were a runaway success.

The KGB did succeed in an even more devilish operation it had initiated the prior year. In July 1983, the *Patriot,* an Indian newspaper covertly sponsored by the Kremlin, published a front-page headline describing AIDS as a "mystery disease caused by US lab experiments." The article claimed that the Pentagon created AIDS as part of its biological weapons program and then tested it on unsuspecting civilians. Over the next four years the KGB and other Soviet bloc intelligence services spread this slander throughout the Middle East, Africa, and Asia, where many publics came to believe it. The Sandinista media perpetrated it in Central America with particular relish. The myth also appeared in numerous European and American media outlets, and Dan Rather even parroted it on *CBS Evening News.*[3] The damage it did to America's global reputation is impossible to measure but substantial.[4]

As the summer began, Reagan prepared to travel to Europe for the G7 summit in London and the fortieth anniversary of the D-Day landings in Normandy. With controversies such as the pipeline sanctions and INF deployments behind him, the American and European economies recovering, and Reagan's outreach to the Kremlin soothing European anxieties, transatlantic relations stood on the best footing of his presidency.

Reagan had recently hosted Kohl and Mitterrand for state visits and spent much of his time with each leader discussing the USSR. Their conversations show Reagan thinking through the Soviet challenge from several angles, reevaluating his assumptions while trying to detect any changes occurring behind the Iron Curtain—or even behind the opaque walls of the Kremlin. Reagan told Kohl that the Politburo had become a corrupt oligarchy, which he found historically ironic: "The Soviets seem to have created an aristocracy such as the one they overthrew" in 1917. Reagan also remarked on the "turn to religion among the young" in the Soviet bloc. Kohl agreed that spirituality seemed to be displacing faith in communism and that the Soviets did not have time on their side. "While the Soviet regime will not collapse overnight, it is brittle," observed the German.[5]

In his visit with Mitterrand, Reagan wondered "if the Soviets had now abandoned ideology and the bureaucracy was simply determined to preserve itself." Yet he also noted that "the Soviets were still pursuing international blackmail and aggression," and recalled Lenin's doctrine of fomenting communist revolutions in Asia and Latin America. Mitterrand agreed. The Russians "wanted to soften the Western coalition," he observed, but hoped to avoid war, largely because of the "leadership's desire to maintain their privileged place in society." The Soviets also "remained fearful of encirclement" and worried that "any setback would start a chain reaction like dominoes." The French leader illustrated Soviet paranoia by telling the kind of clever story that Reagan relished: "A madman thought he was a grain of wheat, and went to the psychiatrist and was cured. Upon leaving the hospital, he saw a chicken and went running back. The psychiatrist reminded him that he was cured and that he no longer thought he was a grain of wheat. The madman responded that he knew that, but did the chicken?"

The Kremlin saw hungry chickens everywhere, or at least behind every American policy. Given such pathologies in Moscow's worldview, Mitterrand counseled Reagan to focus on building a positive alternative model of free societies at peace with each other. "The more the US could create a climate that demonstrated the attractiveness of its system, the more the Soviets would be susceptible to modifying their behavior," suggested Mitterrand. This reinforced Reagan's own convictions. He knew that while Soviet communism was beginning to unravel, to prevail in the Cold War, the United States still needed to show the world a better way of freedom, prosperity, and peace. Reagan and Mitterrand also feared that a corroding Kremlin could be a reckless Kremlin. The French leader warned, "The USSR might be more dangerous now, more prone to react strongly to provocation."[6]

A decaying, insecure Kremlin became more menacing to its own people too. Perhaps sensing their eroding legitimacy and hold on power, the Soviet leadership escalated their persecution of dissidents. Reagan responded by dispatching retired diplomat Walter Stoessel and then Max Kampelman on two successive presidential missions to Europe to maintain multilateral support for human rights and pressure on the Kremlin. Reagan gave Stoessel letters to deliver to European heads of government, warning that human rights in the USSR had "deteriorated badly," that it indicated a Soviet "decision to further restrict the already minimal ties between the Soviet people and the free world," and that the repression violated Soviet commitments to the Helsinki Accords.[7]

The Kremlin targeted Jews in particular. Reagan directed the US embassy in Moscow to deploy American diplomats outside the local synagogue every Friday night to deter the KGB from harassing Soviet Jews trying to attend Shabbat services. Frustrated that the United States was the only nation doing so, the personal letters Reagan had Kampelman deliver to several European leaders urged their respective Moscow embassy staffs to join the Americans in their Friday-night vigils outside the synagogue. Soon a multinational coalition of Western diplomats began protecting the synagogue.[8]

Word of Reagan's solidarity filtered back to imprisoned dissidents in the Soviet Union. Anatoly Shcharansky joined a Christian fellow prisoner named Volodia Poresh in surreptitious Scripture lessons using Poresh's contraband Bible. Recalls Shcharansky,

> We called our sessions "Reaganite readings," first, because President Reagan had declared . . . the Year of the Bible, and second, because we realized that even the slightest improvement in our situation could be related only to a firm position on human rights by the West, especially by America, and we mentally urged Reagan to demonstrate such resolve.[9]

Reagan also supported dissidents by cracking the Kremlin's information monopoly. He increased funding by hundreds of millions of dollars for international broadcasting efforts such as Voice of America, Radio Liberty, and Radio Free Europe to penetrate the Iron Curtain, and recorded a number of broadcasts himself, taking his message directly to the peoples of the Soviet bloc.

II

Shortly before departing for Europe, Reagan welcomed the annual NATO summit to Washington, DC. He brought the NATO foreign ministers to the White House for a discussion of the Cold War. British foreign secretary Geoffrey Howe described the Soviet Union "as running on autopilot. It was an autopilot designed by Peter the Great, modernized by Joseph Stalin, and administered by the present regime." In response Reagan asked "whether it was possible that we were concentrating on the wrong issues, when we analyzed the theories of Marx and Lenin." He continued, "The Soviets have created their own aristocracy, and are primarily interested in maintaining the power of that aristocracy."[10]

The president who saw the Cold War as a battle of ideas now wondered whether his adversaries were losing faith in their own ideas. Some Soviet leaders, such as Chernenko and Gromyko, still believed in the old-time communist dogma. Others in the Kremlin were abandoning belief and merely clinging to power. Reagan realized that the Soviet Union now combined three things in one nation: a Marxist-Leninist revolutionary movement, a gangster kleptocracy, and a paranoid Russian state. The challenge that he faced was how to accelerate the crisis of faith in Marxism, expose and exploit the kleptocracy, and prevent the nationalist paranoia from leading to nuclear war.

Flying to Europe, Reagan landed first in Ireland. He delivered a speech to the Irish Parliament that reaffirmed his quest for peace but still urged victory in the Cold War's battle of ideas: "The struggle between freedom and totalitarianism today is not ultimately a test of arms or missiles, but a test of faith and spirit. . . . As Lech Walesa said: 'Our souls contain exactly the contrary of what they wanted. They wanted us not to believe in God, and our churches are full.'" Reagan heralded these ideas enveloping the globe: "Those truths of the heart—human freedom under God—are on the march everywhere in the world. All across the world today—in the shipyards of Gdansk, the hills of Nicaragua, the rice paddies of Kampuchea, the mountains of Afghanistan—the cry again is liberty."[11]

When he arrived in London for the G7 gathering, Reagan met privately with Nakasone. The Japanese elections a few months earlier had bruised the prime minister, but his coalition had survived and now had more latitude to deepen the alliance with the United States. Nakasone followed through on his promise to Reagan to exceed the "magic figure" of 1 percent of GDP in defense spending. Limiting the defense budget to less than 1 percent of GDP had taken on quasi-sacred status in Japan. Nakasone believed that once he broke through that "psychological barrier," he could persuade his public to accept even higher increases and shoulder more of the security burden in the Pacific.[12]

Nakasone had also delivered for Reagan on the nettlesome economic front. Going into his own reelection cycle, Reagan and his political team knew that the single most important factor to voters would be the economy— and one of the biggest factors shaping the American economy was Japan. Over the previous five months, Bush had led negotiations to try to wring concessions from Japan on its closed markets. In April, when Japanese economic nationalists defied Nakasone to stymie any reforms, it appeared that the talks might collapse and the prime minister could be voted out. Many Japan skeptics in Washington, including some in the White House, such as McFarlane, thought Reagan should distance himself from Tokyo. Instead, Bush and Shultz urged Reagan to "maintain our perspective and not precipitate a public breakdown in negotiations," pointing out, "Our overall relationship with Japan is the best that it has ever been as far as our broad, global interests are concerned."[13]

Reagan agreed. He approved Bush's request to fly to Tokyo in a show of support for the Japanese leader. A grateful Nakasone overrode his obstinate finance minister and resistant bureaucracy. His package included a series of measures to open capital markets and internationalize the yen, tariff cuts across several key sectors, and a doubling of imports of American beef and citrus—the latter a priority for ranchers and farmers in vote-rich states like California, Texas, and Florida. Rib eye steaks and orange juice may not seem worthy of high statecraft, but of such things can alliances fray and elections be won or lost.[14]

III

Reagan's most memorable stop took place on the other side of the English Channel. On June 6, under a gray sky, he stood, in his words, "on a lonely, windswept point on the northern shore of France." It was Pointe du Hoc,

Normandy. Behind him, sheer hundred-foot-high cliffs plunged into the waters of the English Channel. Beneath him stood a Nazi artillery casement buffered by ten feet of reinforced concrete, from which Wehrmacht cannons had defended Hitler's Fortress Europe. Before him sat several European monarchs, international dignitaries—and sixty-two aging American veterans of the Second Ranger Battalion, returned to the site of their ordeal and their triumph.

All had gathered to commemorate the fortieth anniversary of the D-Day landings. Describing the rangers' fortitude in scaling the seawalls amid a fusillade of Nazi fire, Reagan recalled, "One by one, the Rangers pulled themselves over the top, and in seizing the firm land at the top of these cliffs, they began to seize back the continent of Europe."

Looking at the men, he spoke them again into history:

These are the boys of Pointe du Hoc.
These are the men who took the cliffs.
These are the champions who helped free a continent.
These are the heroes who helped end a war.

Reagan then turned from World War II remembrance to Cold War call to arms. He heralded the history that followed Europe's liberation and what it meant for the United States:

Soviet troops that came to the center of this continent did not leave when peace came. They're still there, uninvited, unwanted, unyielding, almost 40 years after the war. Because of this, allied forces still stand on this continent. . . .

We in America have learned bitter lessons from two World Wars: It is better to be here ready to protect the peace, than to take blind shelter across the sea, rushing to respond only after freedom is lost. We've learned that isolationism never was and never will be an acceptable response to tyrannical governments with an expansionist intent.

Though no Soviet leader attended the ceremony, Reagan knew that the Kremlin was listening. He appealed to Soviet history and offered his vision for a better future: "It's fitting to remember here the great losses also suffered by the Russian people during World War II: 20 million perished, a terrible price that testifies to all the world the necessity of ending war. . . . We are ready to seize that beachhead. We look for some sign from the Soviet Union that they are willing to move forward."[15]

The major television networks broadcast Reagan's speech live across the United States. In Boston, a group of coworkers gathered around the office television to watch. One of them later recalled of the moment Reagan paid his solemn tribute to the Ranger veterans, "I started crying. When I looked around the room, I realized that I wasn't the only one."

The office was the campaign headquarters for Walter Mondale, Carter's vice president, who would soon secure the Democratic presidential nomination to challenge Reagan. The teary Mondale campaign staffer was Bill Galston. While viewing the speech by the president he was trying to defeat, despite his loyalty to Mondale, Galston thought, "This isn't a fair fight. . . . The man we're working against represents the memory of America at its best."[16]

Back in Europe, Reagan felt torn between his commitment to the allies and his frustration with them. Like every other president since Truman, he hectored European governments to spend more on defense. He raised this concern regularly in his private meetings with his NATO counterparts, reminding them that America led by example with its own increased military budgets.

In contrast to Reagan's carrots, an ornery Congress preferred a club. As soon as Reagan returned from Europe, he confronted a NATO crisis on Capitol Hill. Senator Sam Nunn, a Georgia Democrat and leading defense hawk, introduced an amendment to withdraw one-third of US troops from Europe unless the NATO countries raised their military spending to 3 percent of GDP. Nunn intended it as a bluff. He told US ambassador to NATO David Abshire that he doubted the amendment would pass but hoped it would "frighten the Europeans into finally meeting their commitments to fund conventional forces." Nunn underestimated its appeal. His amendment soon attracted a veto-proof majority of seventy-five senators. Only concerted appeals by Reagan to Nunn and other senators, coupled with savvy dealmaking by Senators John Tower and Bill Cohen, succeeded in turning enough votes to defeat the amendment. The combined effect worked. By the next year, many NATO governments began further increasing their defense spending.[17]

IV

Reagan knew that his Strategic Defense Initiative (SDI) sent tremors through the Kremlin. But he did not realize just how much SDI spooked the Soviets until late June, when Moscow surprised the White House by proposing that American and Soviet negotiators meeting in Vienna discuss "the militarization of space." This was Kremlin-speak for SDI. The Soviet leadership probably expected Reagan to reject their proposal and hoped to gain a public relations advantage by advertising their willingness to resume negotiations eight months after walking out of the Geneva arms control talks.

The president returned the volley by accepting the Kremlin's invitation—as long as the Soviets would also negotiate over other arms control issues, such as offensive weapons. Chernenko demurred, unwilling even to discuss reductions in nuclear arsenals. Two leaders of Reagan's arms control efforts, Paul Nitze and Ed Rowny, both detected that the Soviets were doing all they could to "derail SDI" while protecting their edge in ICBMs.[18] These negotiations about negotiations masked an underlying strategic shift. Merely by announcing a research initiative that was years away from becoming operational, if it ever would be, Reagan had created new leverage that transformed the arms race, and thus the Cold War.

SDI did not just scare the Soviets; it rattled the allies too. Several NATO nations feared that if the United States built its own missile shield, America might fold up its strategic umbrella over Europe. If the United States could protect itself from ballistic missile attack, they reasoned, it would no longer feel bound to retaliate against a nuclear strike on Europe—and thus fail to deter Soviet aggression, leaving Western Europe at Moscow's mercy. NATO leaders regularly voiced this concern. In an Oval Office visit, West German foreign minister Hans-Dietrich Genscher worried "that SDI would decouple Europe from America."[19] Thatcher asked Reagan, "Are you really going to build a bubble over the United States, and if so, what does that mean about your willingness to use nuclear weapons, which has been your strategy since 1963?" She shared Genscher's apprehension that SDI could mark America's strategic retreat from Europe.[20]

Thatcher also told McFarlane that British scientists unanimously believed that SDI was technically infeasible and could never be built—a skepticism shared by many American scientists. The Soviet leadership, in contrast, believed it just might work. The Kremlin felt both awed and menaced by America's technological prowess. Soviet ambassador Dobrynin recalls that with Reagan's SDI announcement, "[Soviet] leadership was convinced that the great technical potential of the United States had scored again and treated Reagan's statement as a real threat."[21] CIA director Casey told Reagan that the USSR was increasing its research spending fivefold "to counter SDI," thus adding further strain on Moscow's crumbling economy.[22] The Kremlin fretted that SDI could neutralize the USSR's biggest advantage in the arms race: its overwhelming edge in ICBMs.

Having seized Moscow's attention with SDI, Reagan continued his outreach. Gromyko planned to visit New York in September for the UN General Assembly. Reagan invited him to Washington for a White House meeting on September 28. Gromyko accepted. The Soviet foreign minister had last been to Washington in 1978, when he met with President Carter—the most recent time any senior Kremlin leader had set foot in the White House.

Much had transpired in the six years since. Gromyko remained wary of Reagan's intentions. He knew that earlier in the year, Jimmy Carter had met with Dobrynin to warn the Soviets about Reagan. The ex-president expressed his opposition to Reagan's arms buildup and dismissed Reagan's peace overtures as insincere. Carter told Dobrynin he was "utterly convinced" that Reagan would never conclude a single arms control agreement with the Soviets.[23]

The visit with Gromyko would be Reagan's first meeting as president with a Politburo member, and he prepared accordingly. The State Department, Pentagon, and NSC staff all drafted extensive background memos and suggested talking points. Richard Nixon sent his own memo of guidance. Drawing on Gromyko's remarkable longevity in the snake pit of Kremlin intrigue, the former president warned, "He will break no new ground, because he has not survived Stalin, Bulganin, Khrushchev, Brezhnev, and Andropov by taking bold new positions."[24]

After reading these reams of material, Reagan decided to write his own script. Over the weekend at Camp David, he filled four legal pad pages with notes on what he would say to Gromyko. A few days later Reagan welcomed the Soviet with the ceremonial adornments usually reserved for heads of state, including a formal luncheon and extended photo session with a media throng pulsating in successive waves through the Oval Office. Then down to business. Reagan opened the meeting with the thoughts he had written out and had been longing to say to a Soviet leader: "The rest of the world knows that the fate of all mankind is in our hands; that a war between us could literally wipe out all humankind. Mr. Minister, the United States will never start such a war."

Reagan then turned to how the United States viewed the Soviets. "Yes we are rebuilding our depleted strength now because your own massive military buildup, the greatest in world history, is far beyond any defense needs and we feel it is a threat to us." However, Reagan continued, he also understood Moscow's fears of encirclement and invasion grounded in Russian history, and he assured Gromyko that the United States harbored no violent designs toward the USSR. "Would not arms reductions be an easier problem to solve if we could prove to each other that neither of us has any aggressive intent?"

Reagan concluded his opening remarks with an appeal for human rights. He acknowledged Soviet annoyance at this subject and assured Gromyko of his commitment to quiet diplomacy. "But let me point out why we are concerned," he continued. "Ours is a nation of immigrants. We are made up of the bloodlines of all the world, and our people retain a loyalty to the countries of their origin." Reagan saw his country's diversity as a strength, a source of its idealism and concern for the welfare of those outside its borders. He invoked the political demands for human rights from American ethnic groups to allow the Kremlin to save face by making concessions on humanitarian grounds without appearing to capitulate to White House demands.[25]

True to form, Gromyko disagreed. Describing their meeting as a "confrontation," the Soviet foreign minister—a true believer in Marxism-Leninism—retorted, "Certainly we take the view that the capitalist order will be replaced by the socialist order—we believe this in the way people believe the sun will rise tomorrow morning—but this process will occur quite naturally, as a result of historical development. . . . Socialism will win because it is the superior system."[26] Gromyko meant this to reassure Reagan that the Kremlin did not need to foment armed revolution, since the world was inevitably turning to communism anyway. Yet the tone-deaf Bolshevik misread his audience. To Reagan and his team, Gromyko's monologue confirmed their suspicions that the USSR really did envision the global triumph of communism. Here was the Cold War in a nutshell: Gromyko and Reagan each believed that the other's system was destined to fail.

The discussion went on for some two hours. It achieved no breakthroughs, but it gave both sides the chance to say their piece. As the gathering broke for lunch, Reagan, as suggested by Nixon, held Gromyko back for a private moment. Reminding him that their nations possessed the power to destroy the globe, "My dream," said Reagan, "is for a world without nuclear weapons." Gromyko responded with a circumlocution: "That is the question of all questions."[27]

The group repaired to the State Dining Room for a formal luncheon. The First Lady appeared. Gromyko raised his glass in a spontaneous toast to Nancy Reagan and mischievously urged her to whisper the word *peace* in her husband's ear every night at bedtime. Deploying her wit and charm, the First Lady smiled and told Gromyko that she wished to whisper the word *peace* in his ear as well.[28]

Devoid of wit or charm was the official Soviet news organ TASS, which issued a statement from Gromyko lamenting that the meeting did not result in "practical positive changes in the US Administration's foreign policy course" or produce any "visible signs" of progress.[29] Such was to be expected from the dour Soviet, who needed to reassure his Politburo colleagues that he had not been beguiled by the American president. For his part, Reagan felt satisfied that Gromyko was "going home with a pretty clear view of where we stand."[30] Reagan had also whetted his appetite for direct dialogue with the Soviet leadership. He desired more but knew it would not come with the ailing Chernenko in power.

Reagan's belief in the Soviet economy's fragilities continued to differ from his own intelligence community. A few weeks after the Gromyko meeting, the CIA produced a classified analysis revising *upward* its prediction of Soviet economic growth, to a respectable rate of between 2.5 and 3 percent annually for the next five years.[31] Where the CIA's Soviet analysts saw growth and resilience, Reagan perceived decline and weakness.

V

Two episodes three thousand miles apart reinforced the religious stakes in the Cold War. In Ethiopia, the Soviet-backed Mengistu regime escalated its persecution of the country's small community of Jews, tormenting them for practicing their faith while also barring them from seeking refuge in Israel. Known as Beta Israel, they traced their Ethiopian lineage back twenty-five hundred years. Mengistu's brutal policies also fueled a famine that from 1983 to 1985 would cause over one million Ethiopians to die from starvation.

Suffering the twin plagues of famine and communist oppression, the Beta Israel faced the prospect of extinction. Several thousand of them fled across the border into neighboring Sudan, where they languished in the desert.

The CIA station chief in Khartoum was Milt Bearden. One of Casey's favorite officers, the swashbuckling Texan worked with Mossad to set up a covert rescue named Operation Moses. At first, with the quiet consent of Sudanese president Jaafar Nimeiri (and some hefty bribes paid by Mossad to other Sudanese officials), they arranged for buses to shuttle the Jewish refugees to the Khartoum airport for special charter flights. A media leak revealed the operation, leading other Arab governments to pressure Nimeiri to scuttle it. Seeing his hold on power imperiled, Nimeiri shut down the flights, and Sudanese security officials became hostile. Bearden then designed a daring operation involving Delta Force commandos and CIA paramilitaries escorting the Beta Israel at night to a desert airstrip, where a fleet of US Air Force C-130 transports landed, loaded the refugees, and flew them to Israel. After the refugee evacuation, Bearden hid four Mossad agents in his home for a few weeks and then spirited them back to Israel by hiding them in special wooden crates labeled "diplomatic mail" and smuggled onto a US Air Force C-141 cargo plane.[32] When new Israeli prime minister Shimon Peres visited the Oval Office in October, he thanked Reagan for "sav[ing] the lives of 10,000 Ethiopian Jews."[33] This covert rescue did much to restore goodwill between the White House and Israel after the tensions of the past two years over Lebanon. Nor did it mean neglect of the other famine victims. The Reagan administration sent over $400 million in food relief aid to Africa in 1984, primarily to Ethiopia.[34]

Meanwhile, in Poland, a young priest, Father Jerzy Popieluszko, attracted thousands of worshippers each week to mass at Warsaw's Church of St. Stanislaw Kostka. His captivating homilies urged, in George Weigel's words, that "people should live 'as if' they were free, refusing to participate in the continuing culture of lies that was communism." Radio Free Europe amplified his reach by broadcasting his sermons throughout Poland and elsewhere in Eastern Europe. The Jaruzelski regime felt threatened by the young priest's support for Solidarity and message that Christian hope would peacefully eclipse communism.

On October 19, Polish secret police, likely encouraged by the KGB, abducted Popieluszko and beat him to death. They tied rocks to his feet and disposed of his body in the Vistula River. His spirit proved harder to quench. Father Popieluszko's martyrdom captivated the country and backfired on the regime. Hundreds of thousands of mourners congregated for his funeral mass on November 3, inspired by his conviction that "one cannot murder hopes." The CIA helped print and distribute across the country his sermon texts and forty thousand postcards with his picture. Solidarity swelled in numbers and energy, while many Poles and Western governments dismissed Jaruzelski's anemic reforms as contrivances. The Kremlin worried anew about communism's slipping grip on Poland.[35]

VI

The day after Father Popieluszko's funeral, the Iron Curtain suffered another blow when American voters reelected Ronald Reagan in a landslide. He won almost 59 percent of the popular vote and carried forty-nine states. Much of Reagan's electoral appeal came from America's economic turnaround and renewed national spirit, exemplified by his "Morning in America" campaign theme. The White House also viewed the win as a mandate for his foreign policy. A strong endorsement from American voters enhanced Reagan's standing in the eyes of foreign leaders.

However, victory did not salve the bruised egos or close the rifts that plagued the White House staff. Reagan's revelry in his electoral triumph soon got arrested by a cascade of complaints and threatened resignations from his national security team. The Sunday after the election, McFarlane flew with the president from California back to Washington, DC. Aboard Air Force One, he warned Reagan, "I fear that nothing can get accomplished if you don't recognize that you face paralysis within your administration owing to the largely personal animus that exists between Cap and George." McFarlane encouraged Reagan to retain either Weinberger or Shultz and dismiss the other one, and then offered to resign himself "if there is someone you can think of who would be a more effective National Security Advisor than I with regard to this specific problem of the intractability of these two people." In McFarlane's telling, Reagan responded, "I wish they could get along with each other better. But at my age and their age, people don't change very much. And they are both my friends. I don't want to fire either one of them."[36]

Shultz raised the same concerns with Reagan in the Oval Office three days later. Lamenting his differences with Kirkpatrick, Casey, and Weinberger, the secretary delivered a blunt message to the president: "To succeed, we have to have a team; right now there just isn't one. . . . I'm frustrated and I'm ready to step aside so you can put somebody else in at State who can get along with them."[37]

Though Reagan turned down these resignation offers from McFarlane and Shultz, the divisions continued to fester. Two days later, Casey wrote Reagan complaining about another round of media leaks from the White House and urging the president to change the personnel in his senior team, saying, "You need to have much, much stronger support in order to make full use of the historic opportunity provided by your great victory." The CIA director also sought to protect his own job. In recent weeks a series of news stories had reported that Casey planned to resign right after the election—and that Baker would likely replace him. Casey had no intention of stepping down and fingered Baker as the main White House leaker. Casey urged Reagan to dispatch Baker from the West Wing to Turtle Bay to replace Kirkpatrick at the United Nations.[38]

Casey was not alone in using the venerable tactic of urging a president to appoint adversaries to ambassadorships and thus exile them from Washington. For their part, Baker and Shultz tried to get Reagan to send Kirkpatrick to Paris and Weinberger to London as the ambassadors to France and the United Kingdom, respectively.[39] Kirkpatrick and Weinberger both recognized the gambit for the demotion it was and declined the offers.

Not that Kirkpatrick wanted to stay at the UN. While she had been a fierce and eloquent voice for Reagan's policies, the turgid UN bureaucracy and incessant shuttling between New York and Washington wearied her. She also felt embittered toward Shultz—and demoralized at losing policy fights. Just before the election, she unburdened herself to her friend James Theberge, ambassador to Chile. "I don't mind fighting on behalf of my country's interest overseas," she lamented, "but I can't continue worrying about being stabbed in the back by members of the administration." Shultz especially frustrated her. "George turns out to be a traditional liberal businessman whose views coincide with that of the [Washington] Post or [New York] Times. That is why he dislikes the Chilean military regime," she continued, "and he confuses US desires with US interests. . . . It is extraordinary that the second Reagan administration threatens to be more Carter-like than the first."[40]

In castigating Shultz, she failed to appreciate that he spoke for Reagan. The president and secretary of state both realized that dictators such as Chile's Pinochet were wasting assets. Though they had strategic value as anticommunist partners, over time their authoritarianism came at the expense of destabilizing discontent from their citizens and erosion of America's moral capital. Reagan and Shultz believed the better path lay in pressing Pinochet and his ilk to embrace reform, human rights, and democracy.

Kirkpatrick's four years at Turtle Bay made her the longest-serving US ambassador to the UN in the organization's history. She decided to resign. Reagan wrote in his diary that he was "sorry to see her go." He added, "The conservatives who worry that I'll go soft will lose a lot of sleep."[41] A disappointed Kirkpatrick prepared to return to her professorship at Georgetown and a position at the American Enterprise Institute, the conservative think tank. In response to a reporter's query on what she had learned during her time at the UN, she responded, "A great deal. I am in every way a sadder and wiser woman about the world."[42]

Reagan nominated Vernon Walters to replace Kirkpatrick at the UN. The retired general, globe-trotting troubleshooter, and linguist had already served as CIA deputy director, ambassador to Brazil, and presidential envoy for a myriad of sensitive diplomatic missions.[43]

On the feuds fracturing his national security team, Reagan knew where he stood. He wrote in his diary, "It's so out of hand George sounds like he wants out. I can't let that happen. Actually George is carrying out my policy. I'm going to meet with Cap and Bill and lay it out to them. Won't be fun but has to be done."[44] On three of the most important issues—negotiations with the Soviets, reducing nuclear arms, and promoting democracy in authoritarian nations—Reagan sided with Shultz. Or rather, Shultz sided with Reagan, since the secretary of state better understood the president's policies. In those respects, Kirkpatrick, Casey, and Weinberger had fallen out of step with the president they served.

Yet Reagan valued them in the roles to which he had appointed them. He applauded Weinberger's tenacious management of the military buildup, and Casey's enterprising use of covert action to pressure the Soviet empire, and Kirkpatrick's anticommunism and unsparing defenses of American sovereignty at the UN. When he called Weinberger and Casey on the Saturday morning following Shultz's threatened resignation, Reagan told them he appreciated their work even as he reminded them that Shultz was carrying out his Soviet policy.

As for Baker, he was as eager to be rid of the chief of staff job as his rivals were eager to be rid of him. Shortly after the election, he was venting with Treasury Secretary Donald Regan when Regan suddenly proposed that they switch jobs: Regan would become chief of staff, and Baker would become secretary of the Treasury. Baker agreed, and when they pitched it to Reagan he readily approved, without giving it much thought.

The move would prove too cute by half. Baker's tenure at Treasury would be the successful part of the transaction. Regan's sojourn as chief of staff faced unhappier prospects. Baker had been effective in the role because, as he often remarked, the most important part of the title was "staff." The imperious Regan instead relished the "chief" part.[45] Another portent came from a ten-page letter of advice the irrepressible Nixon sent to Regan about his new job. Nixon urged Regan to "make sure that the First Lady is involved in the general course of events," noting, "She has excellent political instincts and, of course, has more influence with the President . . . than anybody else. . . . I'm confident you will find her good to work with, provided you keep her informed and seek her counsel when a decision has to be made which involves the President's schedule."[46] Baker had modeled this insight, carefully cultivating Nancy Reagan's support and trust. Regan would not, with fateful consequences.

VII

The rivalry between Shultz and Weinberger was about much more than bureaucratic turf. The Pentagon and State Department buildings stood just one and a half miles apart across the Potomac River, but their leaders seemed to inhabit different universes. While ego, policy differences, and bureaucratic jealousies fueled their acrimony, the core of their dispute was a conceptual divide over national security.

The biggest fights often start from shared beliefs, and Shultz and Weinberger agreed on much. Both were internationalists, deeply committed to allies, fierce anticommunists, and believers in strong executive branch authority to conduct national security. Both were World War II combat vets. Both supported providing arms to American partners and insurgents fighting against communism. They did not tussle over resources; unusually for a secretary of state, Shultz strongly supported the Pentagon's increased budgets.

Their fight rather was over how those resources should be used. What was the military for? Shultz believed in integrating force and diplomacy; Weinberger sought to keep them separate.

Shultz articulated his view in two 1984 speeches, "Power and Diplo-

The newly sworn in president prepares to deliver his inaugural address on January 20, 1981. His expression captures his sentiments: resolute, hopeful, pensive.

On January 27, 1981, Reagan welcomed to the White House the fifty-two American hostages freed after 444 days in Iranian captivity.

In February 1981, Reagan became the first president in history to read a Congressional Medal of Honor citation when he presented it to Army Green Beret Sergeant Roy Benavidez for combat valor in Vietnam thirteen years earlier. Reagan did so in part to show support for the military in the aftermath of the war. General Colin Powell recalled, "That afternoon marked the changing of the guard for the armed forces. We no longer had to hide in civvies. . . . The military services had been restored to a place of honor."

Reagan and Secretary of State Al Haig meet with French president François Mitterrand at the Ottawa G7 summit. Here Mitterrand told Reagan about the Farewell Dossier, leading to a joint American–French intelligence operation that became one of the Cold War's most effective covert actions against the Soviet Union.

The president and First Lady Nancy Reagan visit Pope John Paul II at the Vatican in 1982. Reagan and the pope, who both survived assassination attempts the year before, shared a spiritual assessment of the Cold War and forged a strong partnership against communism.

On June 11, 1982, Reagan accompanied West German chancellor Helmut Schmidt and West Berlin mayor Richard von Weizsäcker to Checkpoint Charlie dividing East and West Berlin. Five years and a day later, Reagan would return to the partitioned city and demand that the Berlin Wall be torn down.

Reagan delivers his iconic Westminster address, calling for a "crusade for freedom" and condemning Marxism-Leninism to "the ash heap of history."

Reagan and British Prime Minister Margaret Thatcher, his closest friend among allied leaders, stand in front of a portrait of Winston Churchill. The legacy of World War II loomed over Reagan's presidency in many ways.

After firing Al Haig, Reagan asked George Shultz to serve as his new secretary of state. Shultz flew immediately from a business trip in London to meet with Reagan at Camp David over the weekend, where they discussed the world situation on a walk, right after Reagan's horseback ride.

New Japanese Prime Minister Yasuhiro Nakasone visits the White House in January 1983. Reagan often described the US–Japan relationship as "the most important bilateral relationship in the world," and he partnered with Nakasone to transform it from primarily an economic rivalry into a potent, strategic partnership.

Reagan hosts Pakistan's president Muhammad Zia-ul-Haq at the White House. Zia was an indispensable partner in supporting the anti-Soviet insurgency in Afghanistan—yet also duplicitous in pursuing a clandestine nuclear program and promoting Islamist extremism in the region.

After their acrimonious primary election campaign against each other, Reagan and George H. W. Bush overcame their differences to become an effective team. As vice president, Bush undertook a number of sensitive diplomatic missions and policy tasks for Reagan. Bush generally said little in National Security Council meetings, instead sharing his counsel with Reagan in their weekly private lunches.

Secretary of Defense Caspar Weinberger presents Reagan with a copy of the Pentagon's new report on Soviet military power. Weinberger skillfully led the Pentagon buildup and modernization for Reagan, though he did not share the president's interest in negotiating with the Soviets.

A shirtless Afghan mujahideen in the Oval Office, accompanied by CIA case officer Gust Avrakotos, shows Reagan his wounds from Soviet atrocities.

Reagan with National Security Advisor Bill Clark. An affable California rancher and Reagan's former gubernatorial chief of staff, Clark was the most effective of Reagan's six national security advisors, overseeing the development of many strategy directives that put specific policies behind Reagan's overall Cold War vision.

UN Ambassador Jeane Kirkpatrick visits with Reagan. As a conservative intellectual, she gave eloquent voice to many of Reagan's policies. Yet she chafed at the UN's sclerotic bureaucracy and did not fully embrace Reagan's support for democracy promotion in right-wing dictatorships.

An animated CIA director Bill Casey expostulates to Reagan. Brilliant, unorthodox, indefatigable, and often indifferent to rules, Casey rebuilt the CIA from its demoralization under Carter and made it a central instrument in Reagan's fight against Soviet communism.

Reagan with new West German chancellor Helmut Kohl at the Williamsburg G7 summit in May 1983. Kohl would become one of Reagan's most valued friends and partners among allied leaders.

The proverbial "three A.M. phone call" became literal for Reagan when Shultz and National Security Advisor Robert "Bud" McFarlane awakened him on October 23, 1983, with the news that a terrorist bombing had killed 241 marines on a peacekeeping mission in Beirut, Lebanon.

Prime Minister Eugenia Charles of Dominica meets with Reagan in October 1983 about the American invasion of Grenada. Worried that further Soviet- and Cuban-backed communist insurgencies threatened democracies in the region, she appealed to the United States on behalf of several Caribbean leaders to intervene after a Marxist movement seized power in a coup in Grenada.

During his trip to Japan on November 11, 1983, Reagan becomes the first US president to address the Japanese Diet.

Reagan meets with Chinese premier Deng Xiaoping. Reagan eventually managed to craft a China policy that balanced support for Taiwan and cooperation with Beijing against the Soviet Union.

On May 21, 1984, Reagan hosted president-elect of El Salvador José Napoleon Duarte in the Oval Office. Reagan's controversial El Salvador policy sought to support democracy and Duarte's Christian Democrats party against vicious right-wing militias and a communist insurgency. Reagan wrote appreciatively in his diary that Duarte is "outspoken against both the extremists on the right & the [communist] Guerillas."

Angolan rebel leader Jonas Savimbi meets with Reagan in the Oval Office. Along with Nicaragua, Cambodia, and Afghanistan, Angola was a central front in the Reagan Doctrine's support for anticommunist insurgencies.

Reagan hosts new Filipino president Corazon Aquino at the White House after supporting her peaceful democratic revolution that ejected military dictator Ferdinand Marcos.

"My fellow Americans...

We begin bombing in five minutes."

Ronald Wilson Reagan

Insane Anglo Warlord

NUCLEAR FREE AMERICA • 2521 GUILFORD AVENUE • BALTIMORE, MD 21218 • (301) 235-3575

Reagan evoked fierce criticism while president, especially from left-wing groups opposed to his policies. Most of these critics failed to appreciate Reagan's desire to abolish nuclear weapons and bring the Cold War to a peaceful end. This 1984 poster from the Nuclear Free America organization ridicules Reagan's joking comment made during a microphone check and invokes the anagram "Ronald Wilson Reagan = Insane Anglo Warlord." As a teenager during the 1980s, the author hung this poster on his bedroom wall. He has since revised his assessment of Reagan.

Photo from author's collection

New Canadian prime minister Brian Mulroney enjoys a laugh with Reagan. Mulroney became the final member—along with Thatcher, Kohl, and Nakasone—of the quintet of center-right leaders led by Reagan who united around free enterprise reforms at home and anticommunism abroad.

Author and Russia expert Suzanne Massie has lunch with Reagan. She would become an influential yet unofficial advisor on Soviet affairs and taught him the Russian phrase "Trust but verify" that he employed often with Gorbachev.

Reagan meets with Soviet leader Mikhail Gorbachev for the first time in Geneva in November 1985. The two leaders forged a bond of goodwill despite their strong differences over policy and ideology.

In their Reykjavík summit in October 1986, Reagan and Gorbachev came agonizingly close to agreeing to abolish all nuclear weapons, only to have the deal collapse when Reagan held firm against Gorbachev's demands that he confine Strategic Defense Initiative research to the laboratory. Their grim faces as they depart bespeak their mutual disappointment.

Standing at the Brandenburg Gate in Berlin on June 12, 1987, Reagan demands, "Mr. Gorbachev, tear down this wall!"

Reagan discusses policy with his final national security advisor, General Colin Powell. Along with his predecessor, Frank Carlucci, Powell helped rebuild the NSC System and staff after the calamitous Iran-contra scandal.

Reagan welcomes famed Soviet Jewish dissident Natan Shcharansky and his wife, Avital, to the White House after negotiating Shcharansky's release from Soviet imprisonment and securing permission for him to immigrate to Israel.

Reagan hosts a luncheon for more than one hundred Soviet dissidents and human rights activists at Spaso House, the US ambassador's residence, during his 1988 visit to Moscow. Even while building a partnership with Gorbachev to slash nuclear arsenals, Reagan kept up human rights pressure on the Kremlin.

Reagan and Gorbachev celebrate the US Senate's ratification of their epochal Intermediate-Range Nuclear Forces Treaty, the first (and, thus far, only) treaty in history to abolish an entire class of nuclear weapons.

Reagan stands under an imposing bust of Lenin while delivering his address at Moscow State University on May 31, 1988. "Because [Americans] know that liberty, just as life itself, is not earned but a gift from God, they seek to share that gift with the world," proclaimed Reagan in a speech that just three years earlier would have been inconceivable for an American president to be allowed to give in Moscow.

Reagan walks out of the Oval Office on his last day as president, January 20, 1989. "The world is quiet today, Mr. President," Powell told him earlier that morning during his final national security briefing.

macy" and "The Ethics of Power." He declared, "Diplomacy not backed by strength is ineffectual. . . . Leverage, as well as good will, is required." He used arms control negotiations as one example. "Only if the Soviet leaders see the West as determined to modernize its own forces will they see an incentive to negotiate agreements. . . . The lesson is that power and diplomacy are not alternatives. They must go together."[47]

Historian Gail Yoshitani labeled this the "Shultz Doctrine." She describes his belief "that the presence of American forces on the ground was important in demonstrating the nation's resolve and lent credibility and strength to diplomatic efforts."[48] It did not just mean having a large and lethal military in reserve; rather, to bolster diplomacy, sometimes those units needed to be visible and forward deployed. Shultz found vindication in policies ranging from the INF basing in Europe, to the Grenada invasion, to providing arms to the Afghan resistance, all of which strengthened America's credibility and negotiating hand. Political scientist Henry Nau, a former member of the Reagan NSC staff, calls this "armed diplomacy," in which presidents "arm their diplomacy from the beginning, believing that the threat or use of force does not disrupt negotiations but gives them the best chance to succeed."[49]

However, Lebanon displayed the deficiencies in this approach, when troops were sent into the way of harm with an unclear mission, deprived of firepower matched to the threats, bereft of unified political support from their civilian chain of command, and misaligned with diplomatic efforts. Shultz saw these vulnerabilities in his doctrine. In one of the speeches, he struck a defensive tone, averring, "It was precisely our military role in Lebanon that was problematical, not our diplomatic exertions. Our military role was hamstrung by legislative and other inhibitions; the Syrians . . . could judge from our diplomatic debate that our staying power was limited."[50]

Weinberger delivered his riposte at the National Press Club on November 28. His remarks, soon known as the "Weinberger Doctrine," may well be the most influential speech ever given by a secretary of defense. It set the terms of debate on the use of force that continue to this day. The address grew out of America's two most recent military tragedies, the Vietnam War and the Beirut barracks bombing. In trying to avoid further ill-advised interventions, Weinberger sought to bring clarity to when and how force would be used.

He did so with "six major tests to be applied when . . . weighing the use of US combat forces abroad." First, it must be for a "vital interest" of the

United States or its allies. Second, it must be done "wholeheartedly and with the clear intention of winning." Third, it should have "clearly defined political and military objectives." Fourth, "the relationship between our objectives and the forces we have committed . . . must be continually reassessed." Fifth, it must have "the support of the American people and their elected representatives in Congress." Sixth, it should be a "last resort."[51]

At their best, Weinberger's six principles were sensible, prudent, and able to protect the American military from costly foreign misadventures. However, the Weinberger Doctrine treated force and diplomacy as antithetical rather than complementary. The secretary of defense resisted letting the military be used to project power toward strategic goals. He reserved it only for deterring and, if needed, fighting and winning wars. Moreover, the six tests were hard to define and almost impossible to fulfill. They were at once amorphous and constricting, like shackling the president in a marshmallow straitjacket. Such was the view of *New York Times* columnist William Safire, whose tart pen lambasted the speech: "To oversimplify for reasons of space and purposes of demolition, Secretary Weinberger's stunning doctrine suggests that we take a poll before we pull a trigger." The well-sourced Safire also spotted the Pentagon-State feud lurking between the lines. "Secretary Weinberger's purpose in enunciating the doctrine of only-fun-wars is to undermine Secretary of State George Shultz's position in the battle for President Reagan's strategic soul." He concluded, "The new Weinberger 'vital interest' criterion is suitable for Switzerland, but not for a superpower. The Department of Defense does not exist solely for defending a fortress; it is part of America's commitment to preserve order in the world."[52]

The Shultz-Weinberger contretemps was not, as often depicted, a feud between the "moderate" Shultz and the "conservative" Weinberger. By some measures, such as his support for Israel, overall hawkishness, aggressiveness against terrorism, and support for promoting freedom, Shultz was actually more "conservative" than Weinberger. Theirs rather was a debate between two conservatives over what conservatism meant in national security—especially what it meant in Reagan's national security policy.

The conservative in chief had a say too. In the debate over the Shultz and Weinberger doctrines, which side did Reagan take? Both, and neither. In his belief in "peace through strength," Reagan aligned more with Shultz on the need to connect power with diplomacy. The president believed his military buildup and INF deployment would induce the Kremlin to the negotiating table and strengthen his hand to push for Soviet concessions and major arms reductions. Yet he shared Weinberger's reticence about using force. Reagan agonized over the casualties that war wrought and feared getting trapped in escalation spirals when enemies would hit back. The Grenada invasion would be the only time during his eight years in office that Reagan deployed ground troops in combat.

In short, Reagan was pragmatic and ecumenical in his national security catechisms. There was room in his broad church for both the Shultz and Weinberger doctrines. As the commander in chief and diplomat in chief, he would lean one way, then another, as seemed fit in each situation. Sometimes this presidential synthesis succeeded; other times it left his government divided and policies confused.

VIII

The aftershocks of Reagan's landslide extended all the way to Moscow. The Kremlin, realizing that it faced another four years of Reagan, soon reversed and announced it would resume arms control talks on the full spectrum of issues. Shultz and Gromyko agreed to meet in Geneva in January. Meanwhile, between Thanksgiving and Christmas, Reagan welcomed a parade of foreign leaders on official visits to Washington.

Among his visitors was Helmut Kohl. Mindful that West Germany would be hosting the G7 summit in the upcoming year just before May 8, the fortieth anniversary of Nazi Germany's surrender in World War II, the West German chancellor spoke with great emotion about the burden of history. He said, "[May 8] represents the depth of our deepest valley . . . our country was completely vanquished; and we all suffered the great shame brought on the German people by the Nazis." The anniversary would "once again break open old wounds," worried Kohl. Such grief did not spare him. His older brother, he added, had died in the war as a teenage Wehrmacht conscript. Kohl made a special request. Following the Bonn summit, would Reagan be willing to extend his stay and commemorate the war's end, including visiting a military cemetery with Kohl? Declared the chancellor, "It is important that our friends stand by us, especially those who were our enemies 40 years ago." Reagan, devoted to his ally and unable to refuse such a personal appeal, readily agreed.[53] It would prove a foreboding choice.

Reagan also welcomed Margaret Thatcher for her first visit to Camp David. The indefatigable British leader arrived straight from China, where she had signed the treaty that would transfer control of Hong Kong back to Beijing in 1997. Just prior to her Asia trip, she had hosted in London an intriguing Soviet Politburo member named Mikhail Gorbachev, whom Kremlin watchers saw as a potential successor to the ailing Chernenko. Reagan was eager to hear her impressions.

Gorbachev seemed different, reported Thatcher. "He talks readily and, in contrast to the stultified manner of Soviet leaders, does not just stick to prepared statements. He picks up points made in discussion and responds to them. . . . I certainly found him a man one could do business with."

Gorbachev had spent much of their meeting bemoaning SDI. Thatcher told Reagan, "His line was that if you go ahead with the SDI, the Russians would either have to develop their own or, more probably, develop nuclear weapons that would upset your SDI defenses." This struck Thatcher as bluster, yet also revealing of Soviet fright. "The overriding impression left was that the Russians are genuinely fearful of the immense cost of having to keep up with a further American technological advance and are therefore prepared to negotiate seriously on nuclear weapons." Thatcher assured Reagan that she had stressed to Gorbachev her support for SDI, saying, "I warned him of trying to drive wedges between the Allies: we were at one on this issue."

Except they were not. In truth Thatcher had intimated to Gorbachev her skepticism about SDI, which the crafty Soviet detected as an alliance rift that he might exploit.[54] As she and Reagan sat together at Camp David, Thatcher segued from her description of Gorbachev to her concerns about SDI. Like the American critics of the program, Thatcher's views straddled a contradiction. She fretted to Reagan that SDI would undermine deterrence, would be destabilizing in tempting the Soviets to launch a first strike, would erode alliance solidarity—and was technologically infeasible. Put simply, she worried both that it would work and that it would not work.

Reagan, "speaking with notable intensity," in the words of the British notetaker, responded that SDI could work and that it was central to his dream of escaping the insanity of mutual assured destruction. The president quoted an old letter from Eisenhower on the need to guard against mankind's capacity to annihilate itself. "My ultimate goal," he reminded her, "is to eliminate nuclear weapons."

Reagan turned to McFarlane and asked him to describe how SDI countered the Soviet nuclear posture. The NSA excelled at such analyses. McFarlane explained to Thatcher that because the Kremlin had been shifting much of its arsenal to mobile missile systems, offensive deterrence might soon not work. Between the challenges of targeting these movable missiles and congressional reluctance to support the MX, the United States could not rely on maintaining its own retaliatory capability to deter a Soviet surprise attack. Hence Reagan's interest in defensive deterrence. Or as Shultz put it, "We may be moving from . . . mutually assured destruction to mutually assured defense."[55]

Back in Washington, Reagan held a series of NSPG meetings to prepare for the Geneva negotiations. The CIA opened one meeting describing how the new weapons in the Reagan arms buildup—especially the B-1 bomber, stealth technology, cruise missiles, and Pershing IIs—scared the Kremlin. Moreover, "No amount of capital that the Soviet Union can invest would permit them to compete successfully with the United States in terms of SDI, because of their inability to develop modern computers" at the rate and quality level of the United States. Even though the CIA still overestimated the Soviet economy's resilience, Langley recognized that Reagan's military modernization was achieving its purposes.

Reagan reminded his team that SDI was not for sale at the negotiating table. He told Shultz, Weinberger, and McFarlane, "There is no price on SDI and we must be frank with the Soviet Union on the need to go down the path towards defense, to eliminate nuclear weapons, but clearly we are not going to give up SDI."[56] He confided the same sentiment to his diary: "We're convinced [the Soviets] want above all to negotiate away our right to seek a defensive weapon against ballistic missiles. They fear our technology. I believe such a defense could render nuclear weapons obsolete and thus we could rid the world of that threat."[57]

In the next four years he would pursue that dream as far as it could go. And in the next four months, he would see his strategy of pressuring the Kremlin to produce a reformist leader bear fruit.

CHAPTER 10

WAITING FOR GORBACHEV

I

Reagan began the New Year by welcoming Nakasone back to the United States. On January 2, 1985, they met at the Century Plaza Hotel in Los Angeles. By this point, Reagan and Shultz had succeeded in establishing Japan as the cornerstone of America's strategic posture in Asia and enjoyed Japan's commitment to shoulder its share of the defense burden. Soviet Foreign Minister Gromyko himself had inadvertently validated their policy a few months earlier, when he had complained to Shultz that Japan's increasing military budget and security cooperation with the United States felt menacing to Moscow.[1]

Yet as the US-Japan security relationship had improved, economic relations had worsened. America's trade deficit with Japan now stood at $34 billion and climbing. It stemmed in part from a paradox of prosperity. Reagan's economic revival had produced higher employment, wage growth, and more disposable income for Americans. American consumers responded by buying even more Toyota and Datsun vehicles, Sony Walkman cassette players, Panasonic stereos, Nintendo video games, and Mitsubishi kitchen appliances—all made in Japan. The quality of Japanese products made them appealing; the strong dollar made them affordable. However, America's open door to Japanese imports made Japan's closed door to American exports all the more vexing. American public opinion had further soured, and a cantankerous Congress threatened to punish Japan with harsh tariffs. It was not a partisan fight. Some of Capitol Hill's loudest caterwauling against Japan came from Republicans, such as Senator John Danforth of Missouri.

Because he had strengthened the alliance foundations, Reagan now had the latitude to press Nakasone hard on specific measures to open Japan's markets without disrupting vital strategic cooperation. Reagan issued an NSDD before the meeting, declaring that he would tell Nakasone "a severe problem exists" and would demand that Japan take dramatic measures to increase market access in four sectors: telecommunications, electronics, forest products, and medical devices and pharmaceuticals. These sectors represented relative strengths in American production quality, in contrast to the many four-wheeled lemons that rolled off Detroit's assembly lines and induced American drivers to buy Japanese vehicles instead. Gaston Sigur observed, "[In trade] so much of our difficulties have to do with ourselves—let's face it—and have little to do with them."[2]

Reagan and Nakasone enjoyed a warm three-hour meeting. The Japanese leader expressed his strong support for SDI—making him the only allied leader to do so—and agreed to push his government for trade progress in the areas that Reagan had identified. The president warned that pressures from Congress were boiling over and putting his free-trade convictions to the test. Reagan stressed that this was a dispute within the allied family. To a press query about what "arguments" he would employ against Nakasone, he responded, "We don't argue, we're good friends."[3]

Nakasone again proved as good as his word. One year later Shultz reported that Japan "exceeded our expectations" in meeting these benchmarks for opening its markets.[4]

II

A few days later, Shultz traveled to Geneva to meet with Gromyko. The secretary arrived with an entourage of squabbling staff and bruised egos. Over the holidays, the administration's senior arms control officials had bickered over every aspect of the negotiations, including what the Americans would say, who would say it, when it would be said, who would be present in the room when it was said, and how they would respond to what the Soviets said. The American delegation's acrimony became so well known that the press dubbed their plane to Geneva the "Ship of Feuds."

When the interagency process froze into hardened bunkers, the impasse broke only after Shultz appealed to the president. Reagan approved the "central concept" proposed by Shultz:

> Our objective should be a radical reduction in the power of exist-ing and planned offensive nuclear arms as well as stabilizing the relationship between offensive and defensive nuclear arms, whether land-, sea-, air- or space-based. We should even now be looking forward to a period of transition . . . to effective non-nuclear defen-sive forces, including defenses against offensive nuclear arms. This period of transition should lead to the eventual elimination of all nuclear arms, both offensive and defensive.

The president then issued a sixteen-page NSDD giving precise guidance on the American policy positions. Specifically, the United States would seek to protect SDI, keep START and INF negotiations separate (to bolster lever-age for the zero option on INF), and insist on combining offensive and de-fensive systems in the negotiations. This would ensure that SDI's leverage as a defensive system could help pressure the Soviets to make reductions in their offensive systems.[5]

Approaching the Geneva negotiations, Reagan and Shultz made ex-plicit their departure from Nixon and Kissinger on another key concept: linkage. Nixon and Kissinger had woven together the many issues in the US-Soviet relationship so that progress in one area depended on advances in other areas. This "linkage" had made strategic sense in the early 1970s as the United States sought Soviet cooperation on an array of issues, including extricating American forces from Vietnam, recalibrating the Middle East, and controlling the arms race. Now, a decade later, Reagan and Shultz be-lieved that linkage had run its course. The Kremlin had flipped the tables by using it to hold American priorities hostage to other concessions sought by Moscow.

Shortly before his Geneva trip, Shultz detailed the new framework in a speech. Of linkage he warned, "If applied rigidly, it could yield the initiative to the Soviets, letting them set the pace and character of the relationship." Instead, in regaining the initiative, the United States would deal with each issue on its own, pushing the Kremlin for progress on human rights, and arms control, and other areas of concern. Concluded Shultz, "Linkage is a tactical question; the strategic reality of leverage comes from creating facts in support of our overall design."[6]

Fervent media interest greeted the delegation in Geneva, including over eight hundred journalists and the three anchors of the major American television news programs (Dan Rather of CBS, Peter Jennings of ABC, Tom Brokaw of NBC), who would broadcast live from the Swiss city.[7] The negotiations proceeded at first in a torturous loop. The irascible Gromyko— "endowed with a nearly singular ability to repeat the same thing endlessly without shame," in Arms Control and Disarmament Agency director Ken Adelman's words—alternated between blustery monologues and sullen stares during which he only said, "I am silent, like fish."[8] As he would a sturgeon hooked on a thin line, Shultz deftly played Gromyko through a combination of patient arguments, and occasional flashes of temper and threats to walk out. The Soviet finally relented. He agreed to a framework for negotiations, including three negotiation channels on SDI, INF, and START. Shultz and McFarlane phoned Reagan to give him the update. An impressed McFarlane told the president, "You have got an iron-ass Secretary of State. . . . Your victory in the election has made an impression on Moscow, that's for sure." As Adelman recalled, the Geneva agreement gave birth to all future arms control talks: "To be there was to be 'present at the creation'" of the US-Soviet summits that lay ahead.[9]

III

The Geneva agreement started Reagan's new term with a boost. For his second inaugural, he sought to anchor his presidency in the stream of history, asking his nation to "stand as one . . . determined that our future shall be worthy of our past." On a day so cold that the ceremony had to be moved indoors to the Capitol rotunda, Reagan proclaimed his hope that his years in office would be remembered as a time "when America courageously supported the struggle for individual liberty, self-government, and free enterprise throughout the world and turned the tide of history away from totalitarian darkness and into the warm sunlight of human freedom."[10]

If Reagan spoke the poetry for his second term, Shultz provided the prose. The next week, the secretary testified before the Senate Foreign Relations Committee on the state of the world. Shultz described a globe in ferment, saying, "Change is constant." He spotted trends early in their appearing and synthesized them into a bigger strategic picture. Shultz cataloged a series of shifts: the military balance tilting away from Moscow and toward the

United States; America's alliances evolving from mere security pacts to robust diplomatic and economic partnerships; Eastern Europe straining against its Kremlin overlords; East Asian economies powering global growth; democracy ascendant in Latin America; anticommunist insurgencies displacing communist revolutions in the Third World; free markets replacing statism; a technology and communications revolution birthed in Silicon Valley now sweeping the globe. Like Reagan, Shultz also enjoyed turning Marxist agitprop back on the Kremlin. Invoking the Soviets' term for assessing trends in the global balance of power, the secretary concluded, "The 'correlation of forces' is shifting back in *our* favor." This did not mean he counseled complacency. "History won't do our work for us," he cautioned.[11]

Immediately after Shultz vacated the witness seat, Weinberger took the same chair before the Senate committee to make the case for continuing the military buildup. In contrast to Shultz's optimism, the defense secretary described an America still vulnerable and a Pentagon cup half-empty next to the Kremlin's fearsome arsenal. Weinberger appealed for Congress to support the defense budget request of $285 billion, a 13 percent increase.[12] Reagan's defense budget included money for twenty-one additional MX missiles. Under the contorted terms of an earlier deal with Congress, any further MX funding required two separate votes of approval by both the Senate and the House. To congressional critics who doubted the missile's strategic value, Reagan, Shultz, and Kampelman stressed that they needed the MX to bolster their bargaining hand at the upcoming Geneva arms negotiations. As Reagan warned a group of House members, the Soviets "will be looking for evidence of continued US resolve—or for breaks in that resolve."[13]

A president's most valuable assets are his time and his political capital. Measured in those terms, Reagan regarded the MX as the single biggest priority of his legislative agenda for the year. He spent hours each day for the entire month of March calling or meeting with members of Congress, including almost daily cocktail sessions at the White House with small cliques of senators and representatives as he alternatively charmed, cajoled, or threatened them for their votes. The combination of presidential pleas, White House grandeur, and strong martinis did the job, barely. The MX passed the Senate by five votes, and the House by just three votes.[14]

Reagan still faced a fight on his overall defense budget. A skeptical congressional aviary, including Republican deficit hawks and Democrat defense doves, squawked in unison at the Pentagon price tag. Reagan's request for even more military funding came as the United States faced a budget deficit of $180 billion and escalating national debt. The debt threatened America's economic recovery, while the allies still griped about the deficits. The UK, West Germany, and France regularly complained to the White House that America's deficits sucked investment capital away from their countries to finance the United States' spending binge.

Weinberger remonstrated that the quality and types of weapons mattered more than the amount. In a *Newsweek* interview, he pointed out, "You've got to look at what the other side has. . . . If the other side is getting very accurate, very sophisticated things, in which they don't give much of a damn about the cost because of the system they have, it is not a very good idea to make something you know is inferior to that." He also implied that the potential cost of losing in the Cold War eclipsed the costs of the military expansion—which ultimately had an economic and diplomatic purpose.[15]

IV

Reagan continued arming others to fight communism too. On the evening of February 6, standing before a joint session of Congress to deliver his State of the Union address, Reagan warned, "We cannot play innocents abroad in a world that's not innocent; nor can we be passive when freedom is under siege . . . we must not break faith with those who are risking their lives—on every continent from Afghanistan to Nicaragua—to defy Soviet-supported aggression and secure rights which have been ours from birth."[16]

He had just announced the Reagan Doctrine. Yet no one there, not even Reagan himself, realized it at the time. Most of his Cold War presidential predecessors had given speeches announcing their eponymous doctrines—such as the Truman Doctrine, Eisenhower Doctrine, Nixon Doctrine, and Carter Doctrine—as new policies. Reagan instead described what he had been doing already for the past four years. It fell to columnist Charles Krauthammer to put a name to it. Several weeks later he wrote in *Time*, "[Reagan] has produced the Reagan Doctrine. You may not have noticed. . . . President Reagan saw fit to bury his doctrine in his 1985 State of the Union address beneath the balanced budget amendment, school prayer, and the line-item veto." Krauthammer elaborated that the doctrine "proclaims overt and unashamed American support for anti-Communist revolution." For the first time since the Vietnam War, Reagan has "establish[ed] a new, firmer—a doctrinal—foundation for such support by declaring equally worthy all armed resistance to Communism, whether foreign or indigenously imposed." Continued Krauthammer in a follow-up column, "[The Reagan Doctrine] relies on indigenous revolutionaries to challenge (for reasons that parallel, but need to coincide with ours) the Soviet empire at its periphery. It is the American response to the Brezhnev Doctrine. The Brezhnev Doctrine declares: once a Soviet acquisition, always a Soviet acquisition. The Reagan Doctrine means to test that proposition."[17]

Since his debut in office, Reagan had been providing weapons and other support to anticommunist insurgents, first in Afghanistan, then in Nicaragua and Cambodia, now soon in Angola. It was another prong in his campaign to apply pressure on the Kremlin from all sides, especially in its most vulnerable spots. Casey took the lead in putting it into action. Like Reagan himself, the CIA director paid heed to the words of Soviet chieftains. Writing to Richard Nixon, Casey quoted a 1962 statement by Nikita Khrushchev: "Communism will win, not by nuclear war which might destroy the world, not by conventional war which could lead to nuclear war, but by national wars of liberation." Given the stalemate with NATO in a divided Europe in the early 1960s, Khrushchev and his successor Brezhnev had turned their gaze to the Third World, seeing it as fertile soil for the growth of Marxism-Leninism. The Kremlin spent the 1960s and 1970s sponsoring communist revolutionaries in Africa, the Middle East, Asia, and Latin America. Continued Casey, "We should be encouraged that the tide has changed on this. During the '70s people all over the world were flocking into communist insurgent movements. Today people are taking up arms against communist imposed governments, 400,000 of them in Afghanistan, Cambodia, Ethiopia, and Nicaragua."[18] Casey salivated at the prospect of bolstering those revolts and inflicting pain on the Soviet tentacles spreading through the Third World.

The Reagan Doctrine offered several other benefits. It reinforced the White House's economic pressure on the Kremlin. Casey relished pointing out that Moscow spent $5 to 6 billion annually to prop up dictatorships in Cuba, Vietnam, Ethiopia, Angola, and Nicaragua. American support for resistance movements made such subsidies even more painful for Moscow.[19] It imposed costs on the Kremlin without increasing the risk of war between the United States and USSR. Targeting the peripheries of the Soviet empire, instead of a direct showdown between American and Red Army troops across the Fulda Gap, created more space for Reagan to reach out to Moscow while ensuring his diplomacy had teeth. It forged new bilateral partnerships and deepened old ones. China provided vital cooperation on the Cambodia and Afghanistan programs; on the latter, so also did Pakistan and Saudi Arabia.

It even united Reagan's fractious national security team. All of his top principals supported the Reagan Doctrine as a strategy, albeit while bickering over its details. Weinberger appreciated that it had others do the fighting rather than American troops. Shultz believed it strengthened his negotiating hand. Casey prized its covert action programs and militance against communist forces. McFarlane valued its secrecy and efficiency.

For a strategy that advanced American interests, cost little in American blood and treasure, promoted interagency harmony, and imposed disproportionate costs on the Soviet empire, what could go wrong? Plenty, it would turn out. While the Reagan Doctrine contributed to some of Reagan's greatest policy achievements, it would also tarnish America's moral standing and fuel a scandal that nearly broke the presidency.

In practice, three liabilities plagued the doctrine. First, some of the anticommunist insurgents it supported were corrupt and barbarous. Their depredations showed the downside of sponsoring militants outside of traditional command-and-control structures: The United States bore responsibility for their abuses, even if it did not authorize or encourage them. Second, it caused frictions with important allies. European allies regularly griped to the administration about its Central America and southern Africa policies, as did some regional partners, such as Mexico and Costa Rica. Third, it depended on public support and congressional backing in a divided nation. When Congress restricted funds and operations in key theaters, it stuck the White House with a hard choice: Allow more communist advances, or break the law.

V

Afghanistan would be the Reagan Doctrine's signature success. It produced the most results with the fewest liabilities, at least at the time. Congress gave the program bipartisan support, allies and partners helped implement it, and it sparked little domestic controversy. It was the only theater that involved targeting Soviet troops, unlike the dual-proxy wars in Nicaragua, Cambodia, and Angola, where local forces supported by the United States fought other forces (whether local, Vietnamese, or Cuban) sponsored by the Soviets.

In 1985, Reagan upped the ante in Afghanistan. His policy in his first term had focused on bleeding the Soviets; now he decided to try to beat them by driving the Red Army out of the country. Several factors fueled this shift in strategy. First, the Soviets had doubled down on their occupation. To counter the mujahideen's persistent harassment, the Red Army had sent more troops, including deploying elite Spetsnaz special forces backed by Mi-24 Hind helicopter gunships that devastated the Afghan insurgents. The Soviet escalation signaled to the Reagan team that the previous policy of providing the mujahideen with large amounts of low-grade weapons would only result in more dead Afghans. It also provided an opportunity. More Soviet forces meant more Soviet targets.

Second, Soviet atrocities against Afghan civilians fueled international revulsion, and the backlash generated more support for the mujahideen. The Red Army used chemical weapons on civilians, incinerated towns and villages with napalm, poisoned water supplies and food stocks, deployed thirty million land mines in the country, and created booby-trapped toys to maim and kill children. By some estimates, up to one-third of the Afghan population suffered displacement, with five million refugees flooding into camps in Pakistan and Iran. Journalists and aid workers spread word of these fiendish tactics, which mobilized previously hesitant members of Congress to do more.[20]

Third, Pakistani president Zia-ul-Haq made his own shift toward taking the fight to the Soviets. He authorized Pakistani-supported mujahideen to conduct cross-border raids inside the Soviet Union. "Bear-baiting," in the parlance of Pakistani intelligence, these daring intruders launched rocket and mortar attacks on Soviet military bases, blew up Soviet river barges, and tried to incite the restive Muslim populations of Soviet Central Asia to revolt against their atheistic Moscow overlords. Zia also began asking his American and Chinese patrons for more advanced weaponry to funnel to the resistance fighters. He decided that the chance to eject the Soviets from Afghanistan made it worth the increased risk of Soviet retaliation.[21]

Fourth, policy entrepreneurs at the CIA, Pentagon, and State Department fought and won bureaucratic battles to shift to a more aggressive strategy. CIA officers Gust Avrakotos and Mike Vickers showed how equipping the mujahideen with upgraded weapons such as the Swiss Oerlikon antiaircraft cannon could impose punishing costs on the Soviets. Under Secretary of Defense Fred Iklé and his new deputy, Michael Pillsbury, pushed for more and better weapons. To keep the "holy" in the holy warriors, Casey directed the CIA to print and distribute thousands of copies of the Koran in the native languages of the mujahideen. The CIA chief of station in Islamabad, Bill Piekney, put it bluntly. The United States wanted the Afghan fighters "to have the right kinds of weapons and have enough money and food so they could kill as many Russians as they could."[22]

Reagan agreed. The affable president could be ruthless in inflicting pain on the Kremlin. In March he issued NSDD-166, declaring the new goal "to pressure the Soviet Union to withdraw its forces from Afghanistan" and providing all necessary resources to do so. The directive essentially declared that what happened in Afghanistan did not stay in Afghanistan. It urged "firmness of purpose in deterring Soviet aggression in the Third World," especially because "anti-Soviet insurgencies in Central America, Africa, and Asia" watched Afghanistan for signs of American resolve and Soviet weakness—or vice versa. There was an even more important audience inside the Soviet Union itself. NSDD-166 directed efforts to "bring news of the war home to the Soviet people to reduce their confidence in the Soviet military and Soviet external policies."[23] This anodyne bureaucratic language masked a grim truth. If Soviet soldiers started coming home in body bags, as tens of thousands of dead soldiers would over the course of the war (and American information programs amplified this harsh news), then their families would vent outrage at the Kremlin for wasting their lives in a fruitless occupation.[24]

In tandem with NSDD-166, Congress appropriated $250 million to the Afghanistan program. The Saudis again matched it dollar for dollar. In 1985 alone, $500 million to the mujahideen put sharp teeth behind NSDD-166's new ambitions. The United States further provided Pakistan about $1 billion per year in economic and security assistance. Primarily intended to keep Islamabad aligned with Washington, this aid also cemented Pakistan's role as the main patron—both supplier and manager—of the Afghan resistance.

There was a problem. Zia also continued his covert program to develop a nuclear weapon, mainly to deter Pakistan's nuclear-armed archnemesis, India. Two related US laws, the Glenn Amendment and the Pressler Amendment, required terminating US aid to Pakistan if Reagan determined the country was pursuing nuclear weapons. Zia personally assured Reagan that he was not trying to build the bomb, but American intelligence reports indicated otherwise. Shultz, McFarlane, and the State Department lawyers engaged in Solomonic legerdemain to find a way for Reagan to comply with the law while preserving the partnership with Pakistan. Otherwise, warned McFarlane, "the equities involved are so enormous" and "a mistake in judgment would pull the rug out from under Pakistan at a moment when it is coming under tremendous pressure from the Soviets in Afghanistan." Reagan concurred and certified Pakistan's compliance.[25] The aid kept flowing to Islamabad, the arms kept flowing to the mujahideen—and Pakistan kept developing nuclear weapons. It was another hard Cold War trade-off.

VI

Reagan also opened up a new front in Angola, which soon became the Reagan Doctrine's foothold in Africa. A former Portuguese colony, Angola underwent a tumultuous war for independence in the mid-1970s that effectively replaced its Portuguese overlords with Soviet and Cuban imperial control. Havana sent forty thousand Cuban troops, backed by billions of dollars in Soviet arms and economic aid, to prop up the MPLA government that José Eduardo dos Santos led in various roles beginning in 1975. Though educated in the Soviet Union, dos Santos was more a corrupt opportunist than devoted communist. He still welcomed such patronage from Moscow and Havana and placed his country at their disposal as long as he could stay in power.

Though the 1975 Clark Amendment prohibited American support to UNITA, Jonas Savimbi and his rebels had continued their guerilla resistance from the bush for the next decade, supported by South Africa. An erstwhile Maoist turned anticommunist, Savimbi had his own authoritarian inclinations. He and UNITA also received support from other unsavory sources, such as Mobutu Sese Seko, the sadistic kleptocrat ruling neighboring Zaire. As a resilient UNITA's strength grew and renewed its threat to the MPLA government, so did Moscow's alarm. By 1985, as Bob Gates recalls, "the Soviets became deeply involved in combat operations, and directed Angolan-Cuban forces in more than one large engagement. So massive and so threatening was their offensive that the South Africans reentered the conflict in substantial numbers" to bolster the UNITA forces.[26]

The Soviet-backed onslaught in Angola shocked the Democratic-controlled US House of Representatives into repealing the Clark Amendment, as did the GOP Senate. A bipartisan congressional coalition now urged the White House to aid UNITA. Reagan eagerly did so. He signed a finding authorizing a CIA covert action providing weapons and intelligence support to UNITA. This soon included one of America's newest and most effective weapons, the portable Stinger antiaircraft missile, so mobile that it could be carried and fired by a single guerilla. UNITA rebels began downing the MPLA's Soviet-made MiG-21 fighter jets and other aircraft, and turned the tide of the battle.[27] It was the first time the United States shared the Stinger with an insurgent force; it would not be the last.

On the US side, Savimbi's backers ranged from a motley group of Republican members of Congress, conservative activists, think tanks such as the Heritage Foundation, and well-heeled lobbyists, to a CIA case officer dispatched by Casey to live in a grass hut in the Angolan village that served as Savimbi's base of operations. The MPLA attracted its share of influential American support too, starting with the massive energy company Chevron. Angola stood alongside Nigeria in having Africa's largest oil reserves, and Chevron was the country's leading oil producer. The company put significant revenues into the MPLA's coffers, funds that helped support the Soviet and Cuban presence in the country. Chevron in turn became one of the loudest—and most lucrative—voices in Washington, DC, for the MPLA and against UNITA.[28]

South Africa's odious apartheid regime continued to complicate Reagan's strategy in the region. American policy could not live with Pretoria and could not live without it. Though Reagan detested apartheid, he considered his efforts to end it a lower priority than eradicating communism and restoring peace to the entire region. This did not leave him insensate to appeals otherwise. After South Africa's Bishop Desmond Tutu won the Nobel Peace Prize for his antiapartheid leadership, Reagan welcomed him to the Oval Office. Reagan told Tutu he found apartheid "repugnant" and described the progress his policies were making toward regional goals of removing Cuban troops from Angola, Namibian independence, and peace between South Africa and its neighbors, such as Mozambique. The president also explained his reticence about economic sanctions and divestment pressures. "We have learned that in some cases, such as Poland, sanctions actually hurt the common man the worst," Reagan noted. He continued that sanctions would hurt Black South Africans—whose livelihoods and future empowerment depended on economic development—more than their oppressive government.

Tutu agreed with Reagan's aversion to divestment but added that private-sector investment should be used as "leverage to enforce changes" in South African policies. He lamented that four years of Reagan's "carrot" of "constructive engagement . . . had not worked" absent a credible stick. He reminded Reagan that after almost four decades of America's "quiet persuasive tactics," the repression of Black South Africans had only worsened. The eloquent cleric urged the United States to "increase its public pressure" on the South African government.[29]

Tutu's appeal convicted Reagan. Three days later, the president gave a speech for Human Rights Day that included three paragraphs on South Africa (the Soviet Union was the only country to receive longer denunciations). Reagan voiced "our grief over the human and spiritual costs of apartheid" and called on South Africa to take several specific measures, including releasing political prisoners, ending the forced removal of Black people from their communities, and welcoming all Black South Africans into an inclusive democratic government.[30] He also took some stronger public steps, such as recalling US ambassador Herman Nickel to protest a slew of South African iniquities, including violence against Black protestors and military raids against US oil company facilities in Angola.[31]

Virtue was in short supply in southern Africa. Like many other Cold War hot spots, it confronted American policymakers with no good choices, only bad. By this point in the twentieth century, communism had a consistent record: Wherever it took power, it brought dictatorship, repression, poverty, and murder. Reagan focused on his strategic goal of bringing the chief architect of this despotism, the Soviet Union, to a negotiated surrender—even if doing so entailed tactical partnerships with communist regimes in China, Yugoslavia, and Mozambique, and anticommunist authoritarians elsewhere. Ever mindful of World War II, Reagan knew that the United States had made similar choices to partner with the USSR and Nationalist China to defeat Nazi Germany and imperial Japan.[32]

VII

If Afghanistan represented the Reagan Doctrine's strongest fist, Nicaragua remained its Achilles heel. On the battlefield, the contras showed little progress, and in Washington, Congress showed little interest in supporting them. Senate Foreign Relations Committee chairman Richard Lugar, himself a contra supporter, distilled the Nicaragua dilemma as fateful choices Congress refused to make: Americans did not want to deploy their own troops there, did not want to aid the contras, yet did not want to accept the Sandinista regime either.[33]

A contra frenzy consumed Washington, DC, in the spring and summer. The Boland Amendment still barred the CIA and Pentagon from giving military aid to the contras, but a special provision allowed consideration of $14 million for weapons and additional funds in humanitarian supplies. The Reagan administration took flak from all sides. Archconservatives on Capitol Hill flayed Reagan and Shultz for the sins of insufficient support of the contras and not making the overthrow of the Sandinista regime official US policy. Voices from the center-left, such as a group of scholars from the Brookings Institution, wailed that Reagan planned to invade Nicaragua. Speaker Tip O'Neill warned incessantly that Nicaragua was "another Vietnam" and whipped his caucus of Democrats to defeat any contra aid in the House. A grassroots coalition of some 150 peace, human rights, and religious groups mobilized to pressure Congress against contra aid. It became the foreign policy issue that most seized the Left after the nuclear freeze campaign of a few years earlier. And while Washington's opposition to contra aid had strengthened, the contras had weakened. Paltry US support and contra infighting had enfeebled the resistance. Now the question was not whether the contras could defeat the Sandinistas. They could not. The question was whether the contras could even survive.

White House pollster Dick Wirthlin warned Reagan and Shultz that contra aid "was an exceedingly unpopular issue in the country, and the White House could only lose by a high visibility public appeal."[34] Public distaste was easy to fathom. The civil war devastated Nicaragua and ultimately caused the deaths of over thirty thousand, many of them civilians.[35] Yet no options, including American disengagement, promised an end to the suffering. Even if unchallenged by the contras, the Sandinista regime had already shown its brutality to its own people, especially Catholic clergy and the indigenous Miskito living on the country's Atlantic coast. In the region, the Sandinistas destabilized Honduras and fueled the civil war in El Salvador.

Knowing he held a weak hand on contra aid, and having spent much of his political capital on the MX vote, Reagan chose not to make a strong public push with Congress. Instead he made some targeted appeals behind the scenes, while deputizing Shultz and a group of activists and policymakers to argue the public case. The coalition of contra supporters went beyond conservatives; it included Costa Rican president Luis Monge and Jimmy

Carter's national security advisor Zbigniew Brzezinski. Jeane Kirkpatrick, freshly unshackled from her UN fetters, led the charge as a private citizen. She spent much of April advocating for contra aid, giving speeches, congressional testimony, and media interviews, and leading strategy sessions on how to rally public opinion. Contra leader Adolfo Calero flew to Washington to reinforce her efforts. Risking sacrilege, he told a dinner in her honor, "[There are] two great ladies that Nicaraguan freedom fighters hold in great esteem, whom we do not even refer to by name. In the case of the Virgin Mary we call her 'our lady,' in the case of Mrs. Kirkpatrick it is 'the lady.'"[36] Though Shultz differed with Kirkpatrick on much, he agreed with her on contra aid. He warned in one speech against "those who would grant the Sandinistas a peculiar kind of immunity in our legislation—in effect enacting the Brezhnev doctrine into American law" and "consigning Nicaragua to the endless darkness of communist tyranny."[37]

In the midst of the congressional debates, Democratic senators John Kerry and Tom Harkin traveled to Managua for freelance diplomacy with Ortega that undercut US policy by bolstering the Sandinista hand and marginalizing the contras. A furious Shultz denounced the Kerry-Harkin trip: "Members of Congress have every right to travel to Nicaragua to review the situation, but we cannot have a successful policy when they take trips or write 'Dear Commandante' letters with the aim of negotiating as self-appointed emissaries to the communist regime."[38]

As Kerry and Harkin returned to Washington, on April 23 the House narrowly voted down any further contra aid. The same day in Managua, Ortega announced a return trip to Moscow. He traveled the next week to the Kremlin to supplicate for more economic aid. The Soviets, eager to capitalize on the congressional vote and cement Nicaragua in their orbit, agreed to supply some 80–90 percent of Managua's oil needs, in addition to more advanced weapons.[39]

The Ortega pilgrimage sparked a new furor on Capitol Hill. A coalition of moderate and conservative Democrats held the center of political gravity. Many of them had provided the swing votes against contra aid based on the hope that the Sandinistas would not align with Moscow. Now, burned by Ortega's pilgrimage, they reversed course and passed $27 million in humanitarian, nonlethal aid to the contras.[40] Krauthammer made the pungent observation that in April, Reagan "refused to risk his prestige by going on television to support contra aid. It lost in the House by two votes. The only thing that saved it in the end was Daniel Ortega's travel agent."[41] Now the contras had another year of American funding for food, clothing, shelter, and salaries. They continued to rely on Saudi Arabia for weapons, at McFarlane's quiet behest.

This centrist bloc of lukewarm contra supporters also urged Reagan to impose an embargo on Nicaragua. Reagan and Shultz shared an aversion to economic sanctions grounded in their free-market convictions. While they supported targeted restrictions on sensitive technology exports to adversary governments, in general they opposed broad-based trade sanctions on friend and foe alike, whether Japan, South Africa, Nicaragua, or even the Soviet Union, evidenced by Reagan's lifting of the grain embargo. They believed sanctions inflicted pain on ordinary citizens, both in America and in the sanctioned country, while doing little to change the offending government's behavior. Faced with overwhelming congressional pressure, however, a reluctant Reagan agreed to order the termination of all trade between the United States and Nicaragua.[42]

These congressional flip-flops revealed a larger problem. A committee of 535 people, rife with factions and disagreements, cannot make effective foreign policy. The series of congressional reversals only exacerbated the confusions and contradictions in US policy. Beset by its own internal divisions on Nicaragua, the Reagan administration did not need Congress adding to the chaos.

No Cold War controversy would be complete without religion. In the United States, the religious Left condemned Reagan's Central America policies. The US Conference of Catholic Bishops (USCCB) and several liberal Protestant denominations, such as the United Church of Christ, Presbyterian Church (USA), and American Baptist Churches USA, all mobilized their parishioners and lobbied Congress against any contra aid. This brought a remonstrance from a Catholic human rights organization in Nicaragua, which coordinated with Nicaragua's Catholic leadership to write a sharp letter to the USCCB describing Sandinista atrocities against the church and protesting that the USCCB took the wrong side.[43]

Meanwhile, Sandinista minister of culture and renegade priest Ernesto Cardenal created a "people's church" based on liberation theology, a movement that attempted to fuse Marxism with Christianity. Or as Cardenal proclaimed, the "true Kingdom of God is a Communist society."[44] Such heterodoxy attracted the concern of both the Vatican and the White House.[45] Pope John Paul II personally rebuked Cardenal, barred him from administering communion, and issued an encyclical criticizing liberation theology.

As both a Catholic and CIA director, Casey loathed liberation theology. He convened a conference at CIA headquarters for case officers and analysts to learn more about it from Catholic theologians such as Michael Novak, a critic of the movement. Casey himself delivered a keynote address. He described liberation theology's role in driving "political instability in the Third World" and helping "legitimize insurgency movements." Moreover, he said, "It offers unparalleled opportunity for subversive groups to manipulate the doctrine and its adherents among the reformist clergy—and through them a much wider body of public opinion."[46]

The heated disputes over Nicaragua masked the light of democracy's spread elsewhere in the region. In his Human Rights Day address in December 1984, Reagan pointed out, "Over the last 5 years in Argentina, Bolivia, Ecuador, El Salvador, Honduras, Panama, Peru, and most recently, in Uruguay, military juntas have been replaced by elected civilian governments."[47] A few months later, the continent's largest country, Brazil, began its democratic transition with a return to civilian rule and nationwide elections. In all of these cases, the citizens of each country secured their self-government, but they received quiet yet instrumental support from the Reagan administration. Several times, American policy also helped arrest potential authoritarian backsliding in countries including Peru, Argentina, and Bolivia.[48] Reagan did not spare American partners. He dispatched Assistant Secretary of State Tony Motley to Santiago in February to deliver a letter from Reagan to Augusto Pinochet urging the Chilean leader—who was both an anticommunist stalwart and a brutal dictator—to step down and restore democracy.[49]

VIII

Sometime on the evening of March 10, Konstantin Chernenko breathed his last. A four A.M. phone call from McFarlane woke Reagan with the news that yet another Soviet premier had died. Reagan told his diary, "My mind turned to whether I should attend the funeral. My gut instinct said no." Once again he would send Bush instead. This was not from lack of hope over a new start with the Soviets. A state funeral in Moscow, with its congeries of world leaders and lugubrious Soviet ceremonies, was not the right occasion to seek it.[50]

Now in the fifth year of his presidency, Reagan had yet to meet a Soviet counterpart. He would quip that he wanted to but "they kept dying on me."[51] The third Kremlin leader to expire in less than three years symbolized the decay of the entire Soviet edifice.

Within hours of Chernenko's death, Moscow announced his successor as general secretary of the Communist Party—the USSR's supreme position, since the party reigned over the state. To the surprise of almost no one, it was Mikhail Gorbachev. Having just turned fifty-four a week earlier, Gorbachev would be the first Soviet leader of the postwar generation. The Politburo realized that its festering structural rot could not be cured by another geriatric ideologue in the mold of Brezhnev, Andropov, and Chernenko. Even the pertinacious Gromyko backed Gorbachev.

Reagan hoped that Gorbachev would be the Kremlin reformer that since 1981 he had been waiting for—and pressuring the Soviet system to produce. While Gorbachev's accession stemmed primarily from larger dynamics within the Soviet system—as well as his vision and shrewd maneuvering—Reagan's policies also played a role. Even one of Gorbachev's own advisors admitted his selection resulted in part from "internal domestic pressures and Reagan's rigid position," leading to Kremlin fears of "falling behind" the United States.[52]

Gorbachev in turn sensed that his most important international relationship would be with Reagan. On his first day in office, he directed his aide Alexander Yakovlev to assess the American president. "Reagan is trying persistently to capture the initiative in international affairs," Yakovlev observed. "He would like to solve a number of problems in the context of [his] dream about a 'great peace-maker president.'"[53] Ironically, this Kremlin analysis perceived Reagan more accurately than did much of the American media and academia, still stuck on portraying him as a simpleminded warmonger.

But the White House could not yet tell who Gorbachev was, or would be. Reagan received conflicting assessments from his own team. The day after the Kremlin announced Gorbachev as its new leader, NSC staff member John Lenczowski wrote a memo for Reagan expressing doubt that "the generational change in the Soviet leadership will mean significant changes in Soviet policy." His was not a lone voice; Deputy National Security Advisor John Poindexter added in black marker, "Everyone agrees with this analysis," and NSC Soviet specialists Steve Sestanovich and Ty Cobb co-signed it.[54]

Bush had a different take. On board Air Force Two, returning from the

Moscow funeral, the vice president dictated a cable to Reagan with his impression of Gorbachev. At ten P.M. the night before, the new Soviet leader had met with Bush and Shultz for ninety minutes in the gilded St. Catherine Hall inside the Grand Kremlin Palace. Despite the long day and late hour, the energetic Gorbachev had greeted the two Americans with a forty-five-minute monologue. Using few notes, he expounded his views, with a combination of bluster, humor, and hints at a new approach. Much of it was Soviet boilerplate, but delivered with a smile rather than a sneer.

Bush, who over the years had also met the three previous Soviet dictators, reported to Reagan, "Gorbachev will package the Soviet line for Western consumption much more effectively than any (I repeat any) of his predecessors. He has a disarming smile, warm eyes, and an engaging way of making an unpleasant point and then bouncing back to establish real communication with his interlocutors."

In their meeting, Gorbachev told Bush and Shultz that he would pursue "continuity in the domestic and foreign policy of the USSR" and appealed for a return to the détente era in US-Soviet relations. He cheekily disavowed any "territorial claims on the United States," joking, "We would not even like to have Alaska back!"

Gorbachev wanted the Geneva talks to lead to "real reductions" in nuclear arms and "ending the arms race." He pointedly warned against American hopes that "an arms race would weaken the Soviet Union," saying, "These are pipe dreams." Flipping a familiar phrase, he lamented that "the US was lowering an iron curtain to seal itself off from the USSR" with its restrictions on trade and technology exports.

At last given a chance to speak, Bush handed Gorbachev a letter from Reagan inviting the Soviet "to visit me in Washington at your earliest convenient opportunity." It was a big step from Reagan: an offer to meet without preconditions. Gorbachev was noncommittal.

A clock in the room chimed eleven P.M. Rather than try to match Gorbachev on each point, Bush chose to stick to Reagan's strategic priorities. The vice president reminded Gorbachev that Reagan and Gromyko had agreed last fall on the "mutual goal of eliminating all nuclear weapons."

Bush then turned to human rights. This issue "is extremely important to the President and the American people," Bush said. Reagan wanted Gorbachev to know "the important effect that human rights issues have on our overall relations." Bush invoked the Soviet Union's obligations under the Helsinki Accords. He reminded Gorbachev of the need to allow Jewish emigration and mentioned four priority dissidents by name: Anatoly Shcharansky, Andrei Sakharov, Iosif Begun, and Yuri Orlov.

At the words *human rights,* Gorbachev's good humor disappeared. Snarling, he interrupted Bush and denounced America. "The United States violates human rights not only on its own territory but also beyond its borders!" he fumed. "It disregards the human rights not only of individuals but of entire nations and countries, it brutally represses human rights."

The emotional communist then exclaimed, "I thank God for socialism which saves the Soviet Union from the violations regularly committed within a capitalist society!"

Bush and Shultz knew they had hit a nerve. Human rights was not just a sore spot for Gorbachev but another "bleeding wound" (as Gorbachev would also call the Afghanistan War) in the entire Soviet system. Deep down, Gorbachev knew that the imprisonment of Sakharov, Shcharansky, Begun, Orlov, and thousands like them could not be justified. So he did not try. Instead he blustered about "interference in internal affairs" and American hypocrisy.

Shultz then took the floor. He told Gorbachev, "[Before this trip,] the president asked me to look you squarely in the eyes like a man, and to say the following: 'The President believes that this is a very special moment in the history of mankind. Gorbachev is starting his term as General Secretary. The President is starting his second term as president. . . . The President is ready to work with you. . . . The President very much wants to sit down with you and review the overall state of our relations, to discuss arms control, and to find solutions. . . . The President views this as a historic moment.'"

Gorbachev was impressed. Midnight approached; it was time to part ways. Bidding them farewell, Gorbachev told the Americans, "It is a good thing we have not spoken in diplomatic language but in political language. Leave aside, in brackets, 'human rights,' if what I heard from the vice president and secretary of state quoting the president reflects wanting a 'normal road' and if all this reflects a serious side, we cannot but welcome this."

Concluding his report to Reagan, Bush wrote, "The big question will be—will the 'new look man' merely be a more effective spokesman for tired, failed policies or will he have enough self assurance and foresight to 'start new'—a term he himself used in expressing hope for US-Soviet relations. I don't know the answer to this question but strongly urge that we try to find out."

After all, noted Bush, "as the monkey said when he was shot into space, 'it beats the hell out of the cancer research lab.'"[55]

IX

Neither Reagan nor Gorbachev yet knew it, but they would soon form a partnership rare in world history. These two leaders of enemy nations would come to work together for peace. Together their actions would lead to the slashing of nuclear arsenals, the liberation of Eastern Europe, the dismantlement of the Soviet empire, and the Cold War's peaceful end.

That partnership was not yet to be, however, nor would it mean the end of Reagan's efforts to defeat Soviet communism. He remained determined to keep the heat on the Kremlin. His desire to meet with Gorbachev did not entail easing up on human rights, Afghanistan, Angola, INF deployments, the military buildup, economic pressure, and the other measures that were straining the Soviet system. After all, Reagan used the same hand to sign his letter to Gorbachev on March 11 inviting the Soviet leader to meet that he used sixteen days later to sign death warrants for Red Army soldiers with NSDD-166.

Gorbachev knew he took the helm of an imperiled ship, rotting within and buffeted without. A dedicated Leninist, much of his motivation for improving relations with the United States stemmed from desperation to ease American pressure so that he could reform and preserve Soviet communism.[56] Problems festered from every direction. To the near west, the Warsaw Pact satellites gnashed their teeth under Kremlin control, while beyond the Iron Curtain the American Pershing IIs and Gryphons countered the Soviet SS-20s. To the south, Afghanistan continued to produce unrelenting casualties, a demoralized Red Army, and international opprobrium. To the east, China's growing alignment with the United States created a new challenge, while an emboldened Japan shadowboxed the Red Fleet and anchored the American forward presence. Across the globe, "the Main Enemy" sat confident in Washington, DC, presiding over a growing economy and modernized military that threatened to better Gorbachev's own, in quality if not size.

His most immediate concern was at home. Most of his own people regarded the Soviet state as a parasite on their nation, enriching itself while shackling them in bondage and penury. Their discontent manifested in different ways, from dissent to cynicism to despair, which together created a crisis of legitimacy. Gorbachev felt the urgent need to reform the party, the state, and the economy, in hopes of restoring trust in the Kremlin. He wanted the Soviet people to see themselves as citizens rather than subjects.

It would prove an impossible task. Gorbachev hoped to restore legitimacy to a system that by its nature was illegitimate. Soviet communism had taken power in violent revolution six decades earlier and maintained that power at gunpoint ever since. Gorbachev wanted to be both a genuine communist and a genuine reformer. Pursuing the latter would be incompatible with being the former. Reagan would seize and exploit this contradiction. He hoped Gorbachev could be his partner in negotiating an end to nuclear weapons and the Cold War, even as Reagan would also keep pushing to end Soviet communism itself.

On foreign policy, Gorbachev started off with a harder line. Three days after taking office, he gathered the Communist Party's Central Committee and recounted his meetings with world leaders at Chernenko's funeral. He found Bush and Shultz "quite mediocre" and said he would stall on Reagan's invitation to meet. To Mitterrand, he had appealed for France's cooperation on a return to détente. He had told Kohl he was "very concerned" about West Germany's support for SDI. He had complained to Nakasone that Japan "was getting pulled more and more into military cooperation with the United States." He had warned all of the NATO leaders that the United States sought to drag out the Geneva arms control negotiations to "undermin[e] the unity of the peace movement." Gorbachev left unspoken yet unmistakable his view that America's allies were a source of American strength. For that reason, he had tried to drive each allied leader away from the United States.

He then bragged to the Central Committee of the tongue-lashing he gave Zia over Pakistan's support for the Afghan insurgency: "We put quite serious pressure on Zia ul-Haq, and he left the room clearly unhappy."[57] Gorbachev called Afghanistan a "bleeding wound" and made clear to his Politburo colleagues that he wanted to exit. But intent and outcome are two different things. Gorbachev instead oversaw a ferocious escalation in Afghanistan. While he imbibed his own propaganda about the USSR's self-appointed role as protector of the Third World from Western imperialism, he soon made an imperialist move of his own by replacing Afghanistan's communist leader Babrak Karmal with another leader more to Moscow's liking, Mohammad Najibullah. Gorbachev also worried that a withdrawal would hurt Soviet credibility. "We can under no circumstances just clear out of Afghanistan," he told the Politburo, "or we'll spoil our relations with a great many foreign friends," including Cuba, East Germany, and Iraq.[58]

Gorbachev did not even know how much the USSR spent on defense until he became general secretary and learned with horror that the military was devouring at least some 20–30 percent of his country's GDP. Yet as historian Stephen Kotkin records, "initially, he allocated *more* money to defense and sanctioned an offensive to break the stalemate in the Afghanistan War."[59]

Beyond the Soviet Union's internal corrosion and Afghanistan quagmire, Gorbachev also inherited a decaying empire. Many of the Warsaw Pact satellites had grown restive, their citizens resentful of Kremlin control and their governments seeking more latitude in their foreign policies. A State Department intelligence analysis summarized the challenge: "The USSR is encountering serious problems with more countries on its western periphery than at any time since the death of Stalin." In the past, Moscow had sent in the Red Army to crush its rebellious vassals, such as in East Berlin in 1953, Budapest in 1956, and Prague in 1968. Now, noted the State Department analysis, that approach might not work because "the widespread nature of East European resistance is making the traditional response more difficult than ever before."[60]

Reagan continued fomenting such resistance. Sometimes it meant supporting the citizens of Iron Curtain countries in defying their governments; in other cases it entailed wooing Warsaw Pact leaders away from the Kremlin. Either way, Reagan worked to drive cracks into the Iron Curtain and "reinforc[e] Moscow's 'isolation' within the Communist world," in the words of a strategy memo from Shultz.[61]

In Poland, the CIA ramped up its covert support for Solidarity. Besides increasing the printed material and doubling the funding it poured through Polish border cracks, Langley entered the television age. QRHELPFUL expanded to videocassettes, floppy disks, and other electronic contraband in the materials it smuggled to Solidarity. And even hacking. In a Warsaw suburb, viewers of Polish state television news were shocked one evening to see the message "Solidarity lives" flash on the screen above the unwitting anchor's head. It was one of many television and radio hacks that Solidarity activists employed, using devices and training from the CIA.[62]

Romania, ruled by the vile Nicolae Ceauşescu, chafed under Moscow's control. The previous summer, Bucharest had defied the Soviet bloc boycott and sent its athletes to the Los Angeles Olympics. In 1985, it nettled the Kremlin further by dragging its feet on the renewal of the Warsaw Pact treaty. To show his appreciation and, in McFarlane's words, "stimulat[e] Romanian pressure on the Soviets to show flexibility in negotiations with us," Reagan authorized looser export controls on American technology to Romania. He also increased intelligence sharing and policy briefings with senior Romanian officials.[63] For example, after the Geneva talks in January, Shultz dispatched Ken Adelman to Yugoslavia, Hungary, and Romania to brief their leaders. Reagan and Shultz knew that the Soviets often frustrated Iron Curtain nations by keeping them in the dark about negotiations with the United States. Adelman exploited this by sharing the American readout of the Geneva talks with Belgrade, Budapest, and Bucharest. In Budapest, he indulged in some mischief. Knowing that Hungarian intelligence had bugged the US ambassador's residence to intercept conversations for the KGB, Adelman briefed the ambassador with an ear toward his eavesdroppers in Moscow. Gromyko seemed weak, senescent, and gullible, Adelman reported. The Soviet made needless concessions to the Americans, he continued, marveling at the diplomatic gains Shultz had won from the hapless Gromyko. Whether Adelman's chicanery had any effect is unknown—after decades in the job, Gromyko's days were already numbered—but a few months later Gorbachev replaced him with the reform-minded Eduard Shevardnadze.[64]

X

In the north, Reagan found a new friend. Several months earlier, Canadian voters had replaced one of Reagan's most ill-favored counterparts, Pierre Trudeau, with a conservative prime minister, Brian Mulroney, who quickly became one of Reagan's favorites. Like Thatcher, Kohl, and Nakasone, Mulroney combined free-market, anticommunist, and pro-American convictions with a personal chemistry with Reagan that made him a friend as well as an ally. Together the five leaders would seek to enlarge the free world.[65]

Reagan traveled to Canada on March 17. He and Mulroney shared a hail-fellow-well-met affability befitting their common Irish roots, prompting the Canadian press to christen their meeting "the Shamrock Summit." Mulroney told Reagan he chose Quebec City for their gathering site because "in 1943 and 1944, our respective predecessors, President Roosevelt and

Prime Minister King, met there with Prime Minister Churchill to plan the course of the war and of the peace they were working to restore," adding, "My hope is that our Governments can accomplish together something of lasting significance."[66] Mulroney hoped to join Reagan and Thatcher in a renewed Anglosphere triumvirate to counter the Soviet bloc.

Mulroney had just returned from Chernenko's funeral in Moscow, and Reagan was eager to hear his assessment of Gorbachev. While impressed with Gorbachev's dynamism and openness, Mulroney related the Soviet leader's complaints about the American arms buildup and skepticism of Reagan's intentions. Mulroney warned that the allies must resist Gorbachev's efforts to divide them, saying, "He's no altar boy."

Reagan replied, "Strength is the only thing they understand, but I hope they understand I want peace." Mulroney responded that he had assured Gorbachev that Reagan "is a man of peace" and had marshaled the political support to pursue it. Moved, Reagan's eyes welled with tears. That evening he wrote in his diary, "I must say [Mulroney] is truly a friend—he went to bat for me with our Soviet friend in no uncertain way."

Mulroney also told Reagan that another Canadian official had recently met with Fidel Castro in Havana. To the official's surprise, the Cuban leader described Reagan as "the smartest American president in fifty years in his approach to the Soviets." Even allowing for potential trolling from the wily Castro, Reagan appreciated the compliment.[67]

XI

Reagan redoubled his focus on human liberty. Gorbachev's professed commitment to reform could be put to a simple test: Would the Soviet Union stop tormenting its dissidents?

The week after Gorbachev's coronation, Reagan welcomed a group of American rabbis to the White House to discuss the oppression of Soviet Jews. Reagan told them of his commitment to "quiet diplomacy—the need to lean on the Soviets but to do so one on one—not in the papers."[68] Soviet dissidents knew they had a champion in Reagan. Ten Soviet women imprisoned in the gulag, led by the Christian poet Irina Ratushinskaya, sent a smuggled letter to him through Radio Free Europe/Radio Liberty's network of intermediaries that eventually reached the White House. On a paper scrap just one by two and a half inches, in minute script, they congratulated

Reagan on his reelection. Describing their persecution, they included a three-inch paper slip charting their many hunger strikes. Holding it, Reagan exclaimed, "Damn it, it is an evil empire . . . the system is barbarism!" A few months later he shared their message in a speech: "The United States . . . still remains their hope that keeps them going, their hope for the world." Ratushinskaya recalled, "We found out that our message reached Reagan when the KGB came thundering in . . . to berate us about it."[69]

Shultz was Reagan's chief lieutenant in promoting democracy. The secretary continued to wonder at the democratic wave growing around the world. In a February speech, he made clear that American policy should encourage this trend rather than ignore or even resist it: "As we are the strongest democratic nation on earth, the actions we take—or do not take—have both a direct and an indirect impact on those who share our ideals and hopes around the globe." America's authoritarian partners would not be spared. "We have an interest in seeing peaceful progress toward democracy in friendly countries," promised—or rather warned—Shultz, who proceeded to cite South Korea, South Africa, and the Philippines by name.

Shultz concluded with a robust defense of the Reagan Doctrine. He framed it in part as an effort to level the playing field. "The Soviets and their proxies thus proceed on the theory that any country not Marxist-Leninist is not truly independent, and therefore, the supply of money, arms, and training to overthrow the government is legitimate. Again, 'What's mine is mine. What's yours is up for grabs.' This is the Brezhnev doctrine." He also rejected any moral equivalence. "There is a self-evident difference between those fighting to impose tyranny and those fighting to resist it."[70]

Reagan regarded religious freedom as the first freedom, the bedrock undergirding all other human rights. In April, he welcomed religious leaders, activists, and scholars to the White House for a conference on international religious liberty. Organized by the State Department in conjunction with the Institute on Religion and Democracy and a coalition of religious NGOs, the conference brought together an alphabet soup of Baha'is, Buddhists, Catholics, Eastern Orthodox, Hindus, Jews, Muslims, and Protestants from every continent to address global religious persecution. In Reagan's keynote address, he argued that only in a society "which explicitly affirms the independence of God's realm and forbids any infringement by the state on its prerogatives . . . could the idea of individual human rights take root, grow, and eventually flourish." Whereas under communism, "it is often the church which forms the most powerful barrier against a completely totalitarian system. And so, totalitarian regimes always seek either to destroy the church or, when that is impossible, to subvert it."[71]

XII

As Reagan concluded his remarks to the religious freedom conference, he added an awkward footnote about his upcoming trip to West Germany for the G7 summit.

> Now, let me turn to an issue . . . that has provoked a storm of controversy: my decision to visit the war cemetery at Bitburg. . . . My purpose was and remains not to reemphasize the crimes of the Third Reich in 12 years of power, but to celebrate the tremendous accomplishments of the German people in 40 years of liberty, freedom, democracy, and peace. It was to remind the world that since the close of that terrible war, the United States and the Federal Republic have established an historic relationship.[72]

Reagan's promise to Kohl the previous fall had returned to bedevil him. The West German government had selected the Bitburg cemetery for Reagan and Kohl to visit, claiming that it held only the graves of some two thousand regular German army dead. A few days after the White House announced Reagan's itinerary, media reports revealed that Bitburg also contained the graves of over forty Waffen-SS, the military arm of the Nazi secret police. Some of the SS officers buried at Bitburg had murdered Jews, French civilians, and American POWs.

How such a catastrophic oversight happened remains unclear. Some accounts say the West German government assured the American advance team that there were no controversial graves at Bitburg. Other accounts claim that winter snow obscured the graves when the White House advance team visited, hiding the SS etching on the headstones. Regardless, it consumed the White House for a month. Reagan bemoaned the controversy to his diary every night for weeks. Shultz and Deaver each devote an entire chapter to the episode in their respective memoirs. A president's two most important resources—time and credibility—can be squandered by a weeks-long kerfuffle over something such as where to lay a wreath in a foreign country.

As the controversy raged, it seemed everyone had an opinion. American Jewish organizations, who appreciated Reagan's support for Israel and advocacy for Soviet Jews, felt betrayed and flooded the White House switchboard to say so. The new White House communications director, Patrick Buchanan, an ornery right-winger with anti-Semitic proclivities, derided the protests of Jewish groups and urged Reagan to stick with the Bitburg stop. The Senate and House both passed unanimous resolutions condemning the visit. Margaret Thatcher also opposed it. Richard Nixon and Henry Kissinger, in contrast, urged Reagan to follow through with it for the sake of US-German relations.[73]

In Reagan's mind, only if Kohl released him from his commitment would the president change the planned visit. McFarlane even sent a confidential appeal to his West German counterpart urging just that. Instead, Kohl wrote Reagan a wrenching letter imploring him to keep the Bitburg visit, then followed up with a telephone call to the president pleading the case. Besides appealing to the image of German-American reconciliation forty years after the war, Kohl invoked his political fate. If Reagan canceled the visit, Kohl warned, offended Germans would vote him out of office in his upcoming reelection.

Reagan could not resist such appeals to allied unity and personal loyalty. He remembered how Kohl had stood fast with him on the INF deployment two years earlier. Reagan assured Kohl that he would stand with him now—including at the Bitburg cemetery. Reagan did agree to Shultz's insistence that he at least visit the Bergen-Belsen concentration camp too.[74]

The president also received an unexpected offer of aid. One morning, as Deaver sat fretting in his West Wing office, his secretary told him that General Matthew Ridgway was on the line. Now ninety years old, Ridgway was a World War II legend. He had commanded the Eighty-Second Airborne in the invasions of Italy and Normandy, then led American forces through the Battle of the Bulge and conquest of Germany. Ridgway told Deaver, "I am a soldier and I have never done anything political in my life. But it appears to me that my commander-in-chief is in trouble, and I would like to help. I would like to lay that wreath in Bitburg for him. I am the last living four-star general who was involved in the European theater."

Deaver put Ridgway on hold and rushed into the Oval Office to tell Reagan of the offer. The president picked up the line: "General, this is Ron Reagan. Mike Deaver just told me what you want to do and I won't let you. But I will agree to our laying that wreath together."[75]

Visiting Bergen-Belsen and then having Ridgway at his side at Bitburg tempered the outrage but did not repair the damage. Reagan delivered a moving speech at the concentration camp, concluding, "Out of this tragic and nightmarish time, beyond the anguish, the pain and the suffering for all time, we can and must pledge: Never again."[76] Yet those words faded as he flew from Bergen-Belsen to Bitburg and joined Kohl in laying the wreath at the cemetery. Ridgway stood by his commander in chief, creating a poignant moment when he clasped hands with a Luftwaffe general and war veteran accompanying Kohl.

The Bitburg controversy set several of Reagan's convictions at cross purposes. He believed in devotion to allies, the legacy of World War II, support for the rights and dignity of the Jewish people, keeping his word, and honoring the American military. Now his loyalty to Kohl, fidelity to his promise, and commemoration of the war's end had him seeming to pay tribute to war criminals and downplaying anti-Semitism. In his heart he believed that his intentions were pure as the fallen snow. Yet that same fallen snow that allegedly obscured the SS gravestones also blinded Reagan to how his visit would be seen. Kohl did himself no favors either. The German leader looked weak and selfish to the Reagan team, and ham-handed to his own people.[77]

In a final irony, the Bitburg fiasco overshadowed what was otherwise a successful European trip at a time when Reagan had put US-European relations on their best footing in many years. The economic recovery, successful INF deployments, resumed Geneva arms control talks, and allied alignment on Soviet policy, as well as Reagan's friendships with his European counterparts, together engendered a rare level of transatlantic comity.[78]

The G7 summit brought a reminder that the free-world alliance extended beyond the Atlantic community. During one session on economic policy, Mitterrand groused that he found such meetings worthless. Nakasone then asked for the floor. He reminded Mitterrand that France was surrounded by fellow democracies and that Mitterrand enjoyed the luxury of meeting with democratic leaders in his neighborhood any time he wanted. Then, recalling Japan's postwar transformation four decades earlier, Nakasone admonished his peers:

> Look at my situation. What other major country in Asia can you really call a democracy? Remember, Japan is struggling with this Western concept, and we're making it work, but there is no peer

group around us. We have to go all the way to Australia and New Zealand to find a clear-cut democratic counterpart, so these annual economic summits of the major countries that are free and democratic are of tremendous symbolic significance in Japan. They mean a great deal to me and to us. And they should mean a great deal to you, because Japan is a country that is part of this democratic system.[79]

Such orations showed why Reagan and Shultz held Nakasone and his country in such esteem.

XIII

Reagan and Shultz also redoubled their efforts to bring about more democracies in Asia so that Japan would not be so bereft. This meant clarifying to allied dictators that America had made its treaty commitment to their nation—not to the leader himself.

In April, Reagan hosted President Chun of South Korea at the White House. In their joint press conference, Reagan reminded Chun of his commitment to step down at the end of his term in three years. Notably, in his comments Chun did not acknowledge Reagan's words.[80] Many doubted Chun would keep his pledge—including, it seems, Chun himself. At a dinner with reporters in Seoul he had confessed, "In a country like ours, it requires a lot more courage to give up power than to grab it."[81]

Reagan and Shultz sought to bolster Chun's courage by supporting his democratic opposition. Two months earlier, the Reagan administration had negotiated dissident Kim Dae Jung's return to South Korea after his four years of exile in the United States. This included securing a commitment from the Chun regime not to imprison Kim, and sending embassy staff to the Seoul airport to meet Kim at his flight gate. Even with this visible American support, Chun's security goons roughed up Kim and his entourage as they stepped off the plane and then confined the dissident to his home. Nonetheless, the White House message was clear: America stood for democracy in South Korea.[82]

To the south in the Philippines, the military dictator Ferdinand Marcos and his vainglorious wife, Imelda, clung to power with growing panic and growing ferocity. Like South Korea, the Philippines was also an American

treaty ally that hosted a significant US military presence, including Clark
Air Base and Subic Bay Naval Station, bulwarks of American force projection
in Southeast Asia. And like it had with Chun, the Reagan administration
began putting pressure on Marcos.

The previous fall, Reagan had met with Cardinal Jaime Sin, the Catholic leader who led the peaceful opposition to Marcos's misrule. Cardinal Sin
told Reagan that Marcos needed to resign.[83] Two influential State Department officials, Assistant Secretary for East Asia Paul Wolfowitz and Assistant Secretary for Human Rights Elliott Abrams, had soured on Marcos
ever since the dictator's henchmen had assassinated opposition leader Be-
nigno Aquino in 1983. When Wolfowitz took the Asia job, Abrams phoned
him with congratulations and then asked, "How are we going to get rid of
Marcos?"[84] Shultz expressed similar distrust in the dictator, especially when,
on a visit to the Philippines, he saw firsthand Marcos's corruption and in-
dulgent lifestyle, and the poverty that afflicted so many Filipinos. Adding
to the challenge, a festering communist insurgency in the Philippines
seemed to be growing. While the communists had little popular support,
they posed a more potent threat than Marcos admitted. In a congressional
hearing the previous year, Wolfowitz and Richard Armitage had both testified to the seriousness of the communist threat and the need for Marcos to
democratize. Wolfowitz had told Congress, "Democratic reform is essential
to thwart a Communist victory that would end at one stroke both our hopes
for democracy in the Philippines and our access to these vital [military
bases]."[85]

Reagan, however, hesitated to turn on Marcos. Though firmly committed to democracy promotion in principle, the president still viewed some
policies through a personal lens, and at times his appreciation for a leader
loyal to the United States kept Reagan from seeing that the autocrat needed
to go (in this sense, like the dictators, Reagan could also personalize alliances). The legacy of 1979 also haunted the president. Only six years earlier,
Iran and Nicaragua had shown how revolutions against American-backed
authoritarians could replace bad with worse.

Yet as Marcos's health failed and the democracy movement led by Cardinal Sin and Aquino's widow, Corazon, surged, Reagan realized that the
United States needed to act. In October he dispatched Senator Paul Laxalt
to Manila bearing a handwritten letter from Reagan to Marcos. Laxalt carried a special credibility for the mission. As Reagan's closest friend in Congress, he spoke for the president, and as a soldier in World War II he had

fought at Leyte to liberate the Philippines. Welcomed by Marcos at his presidential palace, Laxalt connected with him over their shared combat experiences. Four decades earlier, Marcos had been fighting the Japanese occupiers in the jungle while Laxalt and his troops waded ashore. Laxalt then handed over Reagan's letter and reinforced its message: Marcos needed to make immediate and drastic reforms or risk losing American support. That night Marcos crafted his own seven-page handwritten letter to Reagan, a florid, meandering discourse on the US-Philippines relationship, his esteem for Reagan, dismissal of his problems, and fulminations against his critics. As Laxalt departed, Marcos remained in denial.[86] A few days later, at Laxalt's urging, the Filipino leader reluctantly announced that he would move forward the next presidential election by a year, to February 1986. Marcos intended this gambit to wrong-foot the opposition and ensure he could fix the vote. Instead he set a trap for himself.

Or perhaps it was a trap baited by history. The next four years would see Asia's biggest transformations since the aftermath of World War II four decades earlier.

CHAPTER 11

MAKING HISTORY IN GENEVA,
AND FINDING TROUBLE IN TEHRAN

I

On June 14, 1985, the 135 Americans who boarded Trans World Airlines (TWA) flight 847 in Athens expected a routine two-hour flight to Rome—not the three weeks of horror that lay in wait. Shortly after their Boeing 727 took off, two Hezbollah terrorists charged the cockpit. Brandishing guns and hand grenades, they forced the pilots to change course and fly to Beirut. Over the next several days, the terrorists directed the plane on a bizarre series of Mediterranean peregrinations, including three separate landings in Beirut and two in Algeria. They demanded the release of over seven hundred Lebanese Shia imprisoned in Israel and insisted that the United States pressure Israel to free them.

The irony was that Israel had already planned to release the prisoners. Now the hijacking changed the equation. Freeing the captives could make Israel appear subservient to the United States and obedient to Hezbollah, and make the United States seem to negotiate with terrorists. All of which raised the moral hazard of incentivizing more terrorist attacks and hostage-taking.

On the tarmac at the Beirut airport, the terrorists shot one passenger, US Navy diver Robert Stethem, dumping his body onto the runway. Then more militants boarded the plane, led by Imad Mughniyeh, the mastermind behind the marine barracks bombing and murder of William Buckley. The reinforcements were from both Hezbollah and Amal, its sometime rival, sometime partner, among the menagerie of Lebanese militias. Mughniyeh and his henchmen dragooned seven passengers, including five more American military, and spirited them to an anonymous basement in the bowels of Beirut. Several of the new terrorists stayed on board and ordered the pilots to fly on to Algeria.

The White House deployed a Delta Force team to a forward staging base in Sicily, ready to launch a hostage rescue attempt if the chance arose. But now the crisis was much more forbidding. The hijackers had boosted their numbers on board from two to ten, and the hostages were now dispersed between those on the plane and those held in Beirut. Neither the Beirut nor the Algiers airport was an operating environment in which Delta could stage a viable rescue. The terrorists knew this and determined to prevent the plane from landing anywhere else that might give the Joint Special Operations Command (JSOC) operators a window. Meanwhile, at each stop the peripatetic hijackers released batches of hostages, primarily women and children, while holding the American men. After three days, the plane made its final stop in Beirut and offloaded the remaining thirty-three American men. They now joined their fellow seven passengers as captives in Beirut.

The impasse tormented the White House with fears that this could be Reagan's sequel to Carter's Iran hostage crisis. It dominated the headlines and evening news and traumatized the nation. Once again militant Shia held a similar number of American hostages (fifty-two in Tehran in 1979, forty-seven in the current crisis, counting the seven other Americans who had been captive in Lebanon for the past year). The president canceled his travel to keep vigil in the White House and considered launching a Delta Force rescue mission, and Algeria played a mediation role. The *Wall Street Journal* editorial page, normally in Reagan's corner, lacerated his handling of the crisis in an editorial titled "Jimmy Reagan"—the most cutting insult imaginable in the White House.

Reagan became consumed with the plight of the hostages. He veered between anger, resolve, and conciliation. He was inclined to meet the terrorists' demands but rationalized it with lawyerly nuance. After the Israeli government stated publicly that it would release the Lebanese prisoners only at the direction of the United States, an annoyed Reagan wrote,

> This of course means that we—not [Israel], would be violating our policy of not negotiating with terrorists. To do so of course—negotiate with terrorists—is to encourage more terrorism. . . . I just

told Bud, "why don't we ask Israel by saying you kidnapped and are holding 760 hostages—we ask you to release them in order to free [Amal leader Nabih] Barri's hostages." That way we wouldn't be dealing with terrorists—just asking that hostages be freed by both sides.[1]

Meanwhile, Shultz coordinated with Benjamin Netanyahu, who had since been promoted to Israel's ambassador to the UN, to direct Jerusalem to quit undercutting American policy in public. Soon thereafter, the American and Israeli public positions became more aligned, even as their differences continued behind the scenes.

Reagan's anguish multiplied when he met with the families of some of the hostages on June 21 and other hostage families a week later. He insisted, "America's policy not to negotiate with terrorists cannot be compromised, or we will all face an ever-increasing terrorist threat."[2] Yet it was the words of the families that had more impact. They pled with the president to do whatever he could to bring their loved ones home. McFarlane described Reagan as "visibly shaken" and "softened . . . just as he was always softened by the suffering or plight of an individual."[3] Securing the release of the hostages obsessed the president.

There ensued a series of diplomatic winks, nods, threats, back-channel communications, intimations, and understandings that encapsulated all of the Middle East's complexities in microcosm. Following a secret appeal from Reagan, Syrian dictator Hafez al-Assad, a patron of the Shia Amal militants, arranged for them to transfer the hostages from Beirut to Damascus into Syrian custody, where Assad would then release them to the United States. Reagan promised not to attack Syria or Lebanon. Israel—under intense pressure from Reagan—committed to freeing the Lebanese prisoners. When Hezbollah balked at releasing its share of the hostages, McFarlane directed Oliver North of the NSC staff to reach out to Iranian parliamentary speaker Hashemi Rafsanjani and request his intervention. Rafsanjani cut a side deal with Assad for Syria to provide Scud ballistic missiles to Iran; in exchange Iran directed Hezbollah to set the TWA hostages free. The last forty TWA hostages were soon flying home on a special US Air Force C-141. The seven original American hostages remained captive, held by Hezbollah somewhere in Lebanon.[4]

By the standards of Reagan's professed policies, the episode was a failure. The year before, in NSDD-138, he had adopted a tough counterterrorism policy on paper. In practice it was a different story. TWA 847 brought the first terrorism crisis since NSDD-138, and the White House found itself unable to use its new tools and doctrines. It also contrasted with Reagan's Cold War strategy. Reagan's restoration of American power and dual-track policy of pressure and diplomacy emboldened him to negotiate with Moscow from a position of strength. America's inability to bring pressure on the terrorists left Reagan feeling helpless, relegated to negotiating with them and their state sponsors from a posture of weakness.

It is easy to criticize Reagan's response but harder to say what could have been done instead. The frequent movements of the plane to different countries, especially once the cabal of terrorists on board expanded in number, made staging a rescue almost impossible to plan, let alone execute. The refusal of the Algerian and Lebanese governments to relinquish sovereignty and cooperate with the Americans, even just to ground the plane, made any operations at their airports even more fraught. The willingness of the terrorists to murder hostages gave them all the leverage in negotiations. Observing the problem from the perspective of what other feasible options were available—almost none—lends a little more sympathy to the Reagan administration. Especially considering the outcome. Of the 135 American passengers, all but one came home safely. The main concession was the release of prisoners that Israel intended to release anyway. War or large-scale military operations, and their likely civilian casualties, were averted.

The TWA 847 legacy would loom in two other ways. Reagan, McFarlane, and North discovered that Iran could direct Hezbollah to release hostages, especially if induced by arms sales. And Reagan convinced himself that deals for hostage releases were mere goodwill gestures rather than concessions to terrorists.

II

From the outside, it had seemed that McFarlane had met his moment. Two journalists, admiring how the national security advisor capitalized on his Middle East expertise in managing the TWA 847 crisis, called it "his finest hour."[5] A month earlier, foreign policy eminence Leslie Gelb had extolled McFarlane in *The New York Times Magazine* as "a powerhouse in the formulation of Administration foreign and defense policy" whose "influence is growing—inside and outside the Administration."[6]

Inside, McFarlane felt otherwise. The job continued slowly to crush him. A combination of drive, duty, and ambition fueled his unrelenting work. It became a trap he could not escape: Eighteen-hour days at the office, followed by more work through the new PROFS email system on his home computer network, combined with sleepless nights as his mind raced with worry and fears ranging from work undone, to feuds with Shultz and Weinberger, to the ever-present possibility of nuclear war. Reagan had long worried about his NSA. A few months earlier, he had fretted in his diary, "My main problem right now is what I can do about Bud McFarlane. He's as irreplaceable as anyone could be. He's an 80 hour a week man and I keep trying to get him to spend more time with his family."[7] At the urging of Poindexter and his executive assistant, McFarlane bought a cabin in the Shenandoah Valley in Virginia for weekend respites with his wife, Jonda. McFarlane soon undercut any bucolic repose by having Poindexter install a computer terminal at the cabin. This connected McFarlane to the White House's classified email system—and kept him chained to his work.[8]

The grind and exhaustion did not help McFarlane's acumen. Enamored of intrigue, he kept proposing secret missions to undertake. Shultz successfully scotched most of these gambits—until David Kimche visited the White House.[9] Three days after the release of the TWA 847 hostages, the senior Israeli Foreign Ministry official met with McFarlane in the national security advisor's suite. Kimche had spent his career with Mossad before taking his current position. He floated a tantalizing idea to McFarlane. A small group of moderates in the Iranian government desired better relations with the United States and Israel and hoped to overthrow Ayatollah Khomeini. They would show their credibility by engineering the release of the American hostages held in Lebanon. Kimche then pressed McFarlane about whether the United States would cooperate with Israel in an operation to assassinate Ayatollah Khomeini. McFarlane rebuffed the idea—but should have seen that Kimche's mere suggestion of it revealed a recklessness to be avoided.

Michael Ledeen had helped broker the Kimche proposal. McFarlane had first hired Ledeen as a consultant at the State Department in 1981, where Ledeen carried out murky projects for him and Haig, such as monitoring European socialist parties. A scholar of fascism and Machiavelli with a fetish for secrecy, Ledeen drew on extensive contacts in Italy and the Middle East to dispatch colorful reports back to Washington. When McFarlane became NSA, he brought Ledeen over to the NSC in a similar role. The brilliant and irascible Ledeen's limitless energy masked hidden agendas and poor judgment.[10]

Especially when a few days after the first Kimche meeting, Ledeen came back to McFarlane and said that the Iranians now demanded one hundred antitank TOW missiles from the Americans in exchange for the hostage releases. The missiles, Ledeen contended, would help the Iranian army in its war with Iraq and also show the White House's good faith in the outreach.

McFarlane should have kicked Ledeen out of his office. Instead he gave both Kimche and Ledeen the green light to explore an opening with Iran. After all, McFarlane had been considering the idea for several months. Earlier in June, he had even tried to persuade Shultz and Weinberger to endorse providing weapons to Iran in a bid for rapprochement with the United States. The two secretaries, otherwise rarely in agreement, had emphatically rejected it. Both reminded McFarlane that official US policy, codified the year before in Operation Staunch, entailed pressuring other nations *not* to provide arms to Iran. Operation Staunch would eventually cut the supply of weapons to Iran from $1 billion to just $200 million worth per year. Both Shultz and Weinberger found the notion of reversing this bad in substance and even worse for credibility with allies.[11]

Yet on July 14, as Shultz flew across Australia from Perth to Canberra, an "eyes only" cable from McFarlane clattered through his plane's telefax machine. Over five breathless pages, McFarlane described the overtures from the Israelis and Iranians, and the Iranian demand for TOW missiles in exchange for hostages. Shultz shared the White House's desire to get the hostages released. Though skeptical, he replied to McFarlane with a message of cautious agreement to explore this overture from the Iranians. Notably, the secretary's response did not object to the TOW missile sale.[12]

McFarlane then sought the president's support. As Reagan lay in bed at Bethesda Naval Hospital recovering from a surgery to remove a cancerous polyp, he endured a steady stream of staff meetings and briefing memos. On July 17, he told his diary, "Some strange soundings are coming from the Iranians. Bud M[cFarlane] will be here tomorrow to talk about it. It could be a breakthrough on getting our 7 kidnap victims back." The next day Reagan wrote, "Bud came by—it seems 2 members of the Iranian government want to establish talks with us. I'm sending Bud to meet with them in a neutral country."[13]

McFarlane's first policy job twelve years earlier had been on the NSC staff under Henry Kissinger, where he helped implement Nixon and Kissinger's opening to China. Now McFarlane envisioned his own strategic play of turning an adversary into an ally. What Kissinger had done in Asia, McFarlane hoped to replicate in the Middle East. There were many differences, however, among them this: Kissinger's main Chinese interlocutors were Chairman Mao Zedong and his deputy Zhou Enlai, who together wielded ultimate authority in China. McFarlane's main Iranian interlocutor would be the grifter and fabulist Manucher Ghorbanifar, who held no authority whatsoever in Iran.

McFarlane had told Shultz that Ghorbanifar was "an advisor to the Prime Minister." Shultz, returned to Washington from his Pacific trip, learned that the year prior the CIA had issued a "burn notice" cautioning against any contact with Ghorbanifar, dismissing him as a "talented fabricator" who had failed multiple polygraph tests. Shultz, already skeptical, now sensed danger and warned Reagan and McFarlane against any arms sales to Iran. Learning of the proposed scheme, Weinberger also inveighed against it.[14]

Reagan convened two different meetings in the White House residence with his national security team to hash it out. Given Weinberger and Shultz's fierce disagreement with McFarlane and Casey over trading arms for hostages, Reagan's views, in the words of one scholar, "were opaque. When his aides disagreed, he often did not commit himself right away. As a result, each participant left the meeting with his own reading of where things stood."[15]

McFarlane claims that at some point in early August, Reagan gave him the go-ahead to sell missiles to Iran in exchange for hostage releases. McFarlane then tasked his deputy Poindexter and NSC staffer Oliver North with implementing the operation, in coordination with the Israelis and a motley crew of middlemen in the murky underworld of arms dealers and Middle East chicanery.[16] Behind Reagan's stunning policy reversal lay a simple fact: He was desperate to bring the hostages home. The incipient scandal stemmed from the purest of motives.

Doing the wrong thing for the right reasons is still wrong. American weapons sales to Iran did not just reverse American policy. They also broke the law, which required congressional notification and prohibited providing arms to state sponsors of terrorism; incentivized further hostage-taking; destabilized the Persian Gulf; eroded American credibility; and stuck a finger in the eye of allies.

Nor did it even work. After receiving the delivery of one hundred TOW missiles, Ghorbanifar reported that the Iranians now demanded four hundred more missiles. The Americans and Israelis complied with a second shipment. On September 15, the captors released the Reverend Benjamin Weir in Beirut—the only one of the seven set free. The other six hostages remained in custody, whereabouts unknown, while Iran now possessed five hundred new antitank missiles ready to deploy against Iraqi armor. Tehran had broken the deal.

Instead of walking away, McFarlane would come back for more. The combination of visions of strategic grandeur, fondness for intrigue, gullibility, and debilitating stress would prove his undoing.

III

While the Bitburg controversy and TWA 847 crisis consumed much of his summer, Reagan did not lose sight of the big picture: the USSR. Reagan and Gorbachev had exchanged letters through the spring, with the Soviet leader bobbing and weaving around the question of a summit. Both sides wanted it; neither wanted to be seen as a supplicant for it.

Tough decisions also confronted Reagan on the arms race. He sought to advance three goals at once: continuing his military buildup, pursuing arms control agreements, and making progress on SDI. Each goal incited its own particular opponents, while other critics disparaged the whole package as a bundle of contradictions. Reagan saw them instead as mutually reinforcing pieces of his strategy.

In May, he dispatched Shultz and McFarlane to Vienna to meet with Gromyko. The ostensible purpose was to discuss US-Soviet relations; the real purpose was to seek agreement on a Reagan-Gorbachev summit. Shultz wanted to raise the summit issue first with Gromyko, but McFarlane worried that would concede leverage. Reagan agreed with McFarlane. In a note sent to Shultz and McFarlane just before the meeting, Reagan wrote, "I feel very strongly that we should do *no more* to indicate we are begging for a meeting. We've invited them to a meeting in the US. (It's our turn.) The ball is in *their* court."[17]

Their meeting was scheduled for two to five P.M. at the Soviet embassy. Gromyko, relishing the home-field advantage, spent most of those three hours filibustering, treating Shultz and the American delegation like a captive audience at a Communist Party Congress as he slogged through the

standard parade of Soviet talking points. Gromyko finally ended his monologue at five thirty P.M. and then moved to end the meeting so all could
prepare for a ceremonial dinner that evening. Paul Nitze described what
came next. "Finally Mr. Shultz got the floor and he began to go through his
points one by one, very leisurely, accurately, precisely, and in an unhurried
fashion. . . . By the time he gave the floor to Mr. Gromyko it was 7:30. . . .
Gromyko felt called upon to rebut the various points Mr. Shultz had made,
and so we continued on."[18] Shultz recalled, "I was determined to go through
every scrap of paper I had with me, and to sit there until he broke." Over six
and a quarter hours, neither side gave an inch or said anything new. The
meeting mercifully ended at eight fifteen P.M. Sometimes diplomacy is
merely a test of stamina.

Then, as Shultz prepared to depart and change into his tuxedo for the
dinner, Gromyko pulled him aside.

"Is there anything else you want to talk about?" the Soviet asked.

No, replied Shultz, cagily.

"What about the summit?" queried Gromyko, who then suggested that
Reagan visit Moscow.

Shultz responded that it was the USSR's turn to come to Washington.
He reminded Gromyko that the previous US-Soviet summits, over the last
twelve years and three presidencies, had taken place in Moscow, Vlad-
ivostok, Helsinki, and Vienna.

"Out of the question!" snapped Gromyko, smarting at the fact that he
had capitulated first in asking about the summit. "It should be in Europe,
in a third country."

"Are you suggesting Geneva?" Shultz asked.

Replied the ornery Soviet, "If you say Geneva, I'll have to say Helsinki."

Shultz could tell that Gorbachev had directed Gromyko not to return
from Vienna without a commitment to hold a summit, even if the location
remained unsettled.[19]

Such jockeying over who would ask, when he would ask, and where to
meet may seem puerile. It was not. For both sides, the signals they sent
about the form of the meeting foreshadowed the substance of the negotiations to follow. Both sides also knew that statecraft includes stagecraft. Superpower summits were as much about success in the court of world
opinion as winning deals at the conference table. After another month of
back-and-forth, Gorbachev agreed to a summit in Geneva in November.

Now in the fifth year of his presidency, on his fourth Soviet leader, Reagan at last would meet with his Kremlin counterpart.

Gromyko had fulminated his last. A few days later, Gorbachev "promoted" him to an honorific role as chairman of the Presidium of the Supreme Soviet. Ambassador Hartman cabled Reagan and Shultz describing Gorbachev's ruthless consolidation of power: "He has managed in these short days since his elevation to eliminate his major opponent (Romanov), promote his most loyal and competent aides (Ligachev, Ryzhkov, and Chebrikov), and do what the Central Committee bureaucrats have wanted to do for a long time—i.e. get Gromyko out of the way."[20] Gorbachev selected Eduard Shevardnadze as his new foreign minister. Shevardnadze made up in reformist instincts and loyalty to Gorbachev for what he lacked in foreign policy experience.

A few weeks later, Shevardnadze and Shultz met for the first time in Helsinki, at a conference commemorating the tenth anniversary of the accords. In a show of respect and goodwill, Shultz walked across the auditorium in full view of hundreds of European officials to introduce himself to Shevardnadze. The Soviet responded warmly; a consequential partnership was born.

Shultz did not shy from the hard issues. He started their first meeting by pressing Shevardnadze on human rights, telling him, "Positive Soviet action in this field affects the atmosphere around all our relations. Until the Soviet Union adopts a different policy on [human rights], no aspect of our dealings will be truly satisfactory, nor will your society be able to progress as it can and should." To Shultz's surprise, Shevardnadze jettisoned the rote Kremlin response denouncing "interference in Soviet internal affairs" and instead smiled and said he would discuss those issues as long as he could raise "concerns" about human rights in the United States too. It was a new tone, at least.[21]

Reagan, meanwhile, had to decide whether the United States would abide by the terms of SALT II, even though the Senate had not ratified the treaty and the United States was not bound to it. Nor were the Soviets honoring their SALT II commitments. Moscow's violations included developing a new ICBM and using encryption to defy the treaty's verification provisions. Reagan weighed his ongoing arms buildup against conciliatory gestures to Gorbachev. He summed up the balance sheet: "Our Allies want us to continue observing SALT II. Our [conservative] friends here at home think we look silly doing that in the face of Soviet cheating."[22] After several NSC debates and much time pondering, Reagan went with the allies. He announced that the United States would continue to adhere to the limits, as a goodwill gesture, "as we pursue with renewed vigor our goal of real reductions in the size of existing nuclear arsenals."[23]

Having placated the allies on SALT II, Reagan then appealed for their help on SDI. The stalwart Nakasone had already signaled Japan's support and then quietly lobbied other allies to bring them on board. For example, in a private meeting with Thatcher, Nakasone told her he favored SDI, which helped bring her over to Reagan's side.[24] Reagan wrote letters to allied leaders reassuring them, "We have made no decision to go beyond research," and said that any further steps would only be taken in consultation with them.[25] He and his team also invited the allies to participate in the SDI research program. In addition to Japan and the UK, West Germany, Italy, Belgium, and the Netherlands all agreed to do so, enticed by a combination of alliance solidarity, the allure of American money, the value of technological innovation, and some hope that SDI might actually work. Only France and Canada demurred. Mitterrand opposed SDI for the same reason Reagan supported it: The French president feared it could make nuclear weapons obsolete (and thus erode France's nuclear deterrent).[26] Mulroney, though personally sympathetic, could not overcome skeptical Canadian public opinion.

Reagan continued to deny that SDI would either be used to gain a first-strike advantage on the Soviets or be sacrificed as a bargaining chip. As he told Newsweek, he viewed SDI as the exit door from the MAD maze. It "may be an answer other than just saying 'Well, if they slaughter us, somebody will slaughter them.'" Instead, he said SDI "ought to be internationalized," stating, "There's no intention for this ever to be viewed as giving us a first-strike capacity. I'd be the first one to say if we had such a weapon, we don't need the offensive weapons."[27] In preparing for the Geneva summit, he repeatedly told his team that he "would *not* trade away . . . SDI for a promise of Soviet reduction in nuclear arms."[28] Reagan would maintain that resolve in Geneva and beyond.

IV

Three economic challenges confronted Reagan in 1985. First, while the American economy had been restored to strength and was now well into its third year of recovery (including reduced unemployment, rising wages, and lowered inflation), populist anger—in Congress and among the general public—toward Japan and other "Asian tiger" countries continued to rage over unfair trade practices that hurt American workers. Second, Reagan sought new ways to bring pressure on the Soviet economy, particularly to starve the Kremlin of the hard currency it needed to fuel its military spending and subsidize its satellites. Third, in his quest to win the Cold War battle of ideas by showing the better way of life the free world offered, Reagan looked to promote economic liberty and open trade—especially in the face of persistent protectionist headwinds in Europe and Asia.

These challenges existed in tension with each other. Salving populist grievances meant catering to protectionism. It was hard to find weapons to target the Soviet economy that did not undermine free markets or hurt American workers and alliance relationships more than the Kremlin. The presidency had limited power over economic policy, which primarily resided with Congress. Nonetheless, over the course of the year, Reagan, Shultz, and Treasury Secretary James Baker developed a mix of feints, jabs, and punches that together made 1985 the pivotal year in Reagan's economic strategy.

Reagan the politician could not ignore the domestic uproar against trade. Reagan the free-market advocate would not surrender to the protectionist furies. Though many of his predecessors had supported an open trading order, Reagan became the first president ever to embrace the term *free trade*. He believed in it because of history, conviction, and strategy. He repeatedly warned that the protectionism of the 1930s contributed to the Depression and World War II, whereas he saw the American-led creation of the postwar international economic order, with open trade a cornerstone, as a driver of prosperity and the cement of the free world. Since the 1950s, he had read widely on free enterprise and come to see tariffs as a tax on consumers and perversion of free markets, whereas free trade fueled innovation, global economic growth, and American prosperity. Reagan also believed trade could bind allies and strengthen diplomacy, hence his advocacy of a North American accord and establishment of a free-trade agreement with Israel.

Yet in geopolitical practice, the world trade order was an unwieldy, distorted system, with sometimes unfair allocations of benefits and costs that inflicted disproportionate pain on lower-income American workers. Genuinely free trade depends on reciprocity, on all nations in the exchange keeping their markets open and eschewing the subsidies, regulations, and other government-dispensed favors that many industries and special interests demanded. Few industrialized nations in the 1980s could resist those seductions.

Free trade also found few enthusiasts on Capitol Hill. In 1984 alone, Congress introduced over six hundred trade bills, almost all raising rather than lowering trade barriers. Bowing to these political realities, the Reagan administration enacted its share of protectionist measures—so many that according to White House economic advisor William Niskanen, in 1984, "For the first time since World War II the United States added more trade restraints than it removed." These were mostly tactical retreats to forestall even more severe blows from Capitol Hill. Continued Niskanen, Reagan's strategy was "to build a five-foot trade wall in order to deter a ten-foot wall [that would have been] established by Congress."[29] Thus the paradox that the president most devoted to free trade in modern history presided over a surge in protectionist measures.

American workers, especially in the automotive and textile industries, did suffer severe job losses during the 1970s and 1980s. Foreign competition and closed export markets deserved some blame. Two other factors, however, were more responsible. First, in the pursuit of efficiency and competitiveness, many firms turned to technology to help reduce labor costs and increase outputs. Such automation benefited American consumers and boosted employment in service industries, but at the cost of many lost manufacturing jobs.[30]

The second cause was the strong dollar. From 1980 to 1985, the greenback grew about 40 percent in value against a basket of foreign currencies. The rocketing dollar made foreign goods cheap for American buyers—and made American goods expensive for foreign buyers. To overseas investors, the resilience of the US economy made its currency an attractive safe haven, while America's insatiable need to borrow and finance its growing deficits made the dollar a lucrative investment. During Reagan's first term, the administration had kept its hands off as the greenback appreciated. By 1985, Reagan, Shultz, and new Treasury secretary James Baker all realized that the disproportionate dollar was a main culprit in America's trade deficit and manufacturing job losses.[31]

Shultz, the most economically literate secretary of state in history, returned to his alma mater in April to spell out the administration's international economic priorities for Reagan's second term. In a speech at Princeton, he explored the paradox of America's economic strength and its growing imbalances, especially the federal deficit, trade deficit, and "exceptionally strong dollar." To arrest the lurching import-export disparity between the United States and Japan, he urged a combination of dollar depreciation, changed policies in Japan to encourage consumers to save less and spend more, and the reverse in America of more saving and less spending. Protectionism, Shultz warned, was "an illness" that amounted to "a hidden tax on the consumer": "Any protectionist action here can do enormous harm to the global economic system. So in our own long-term self-interest, we must remain loyal to our long-standing tradition—our proud commitment to free and open trade." To this end, Shultz proposed a "new round of multilateral negotiations early next year to liberalize trade." Launched the next year as the Uruguay Round of the General Agreement on Tariffs and Trade, Reagan and Shultz's global trade vision would lead the next decade to the founding of the World Trade Organization.

The value of trade extended well beyond dollars. "Trade promotes the flow not only of goods and services, but also of ideas," Shultz argued. "A strong and growing global economy will help advance all of America's most fundamental goals: a world of cooperation, peace, stability, and progress, a world where human rights are respected and freedom flourishes."[32] Shultz, Baker, and Reagan hoped this vision of a free world order, founded on open trade, would appeal more than the repression and privation of the Soviet bloc.

Reagan followed up the next month in Bonn at the G7 summit, pushing his counterparts to commit to a new round of multilateral trade negotiations. Nakasone was already on board; Thatcher chimed in with her support. She praised Reagan's leadership in resisting protectionism, admonished the other leaders against free-riding on the United States, and warned that the legacy of the 1930s showed the grim costs of trade wars—a warning that carried extra weight delivered in a conference room in Germany. The other G7 leaders agreed, save Mitterrand, who remained desperate to protect France's farming subsidies.[33]

Back in Washington, Shultz and Baker began weekly breakfast meetings to coordinate on international economic policy. Though jealous of their respective bureaucratic turf and not personally close, the two agreed on policy and respected each other's formidable competence. They decided to prioritize building the multilateral free-trade architecture and weakening the dollar.[34] Shultz may have been the economic theorist, but it would take Baker's dealmaking savvy to get it done.

On September 22, a quiet Sunday afternoon, the finance ministers of Japan, West Germany, France, and Great Britain slipped surreptitiously into the Gold Room of New York's Plaza Hotel. The elegant surroundings contrasted with the rough talk that awaited. Like the Godfather convening the heads of the Five Families, Baker had summoned his G5 counterparts to make them an offer they could not refuse: Either they drive down the dollar, or Congress would impose harsh tariffs and launch a global trade war. The Treasury secretary proposed that the G5 coordinate currency policy by selling their dollar holdings and raising interest rates for their own currencies. The cowed finance ministers agreed on the spot. They drafted a joint statement, the Plaza Accord, and then issued it to a roomful of bewildered reporters who had been summoned from their Sunday afternoon repose after the meeting began.[35]

The Plaza Accord's success depended in part on its secrecy and suddenness. Only Reagan, Paul Volcker, and a few senior Treasury aides knew of Baker's gambit beforehand. Shultz belatedly learned of the deal when it was announced, and "got livid at me," the Treasury secretary remembered. The agreement showed results immediately. When Reagan met with Nakasone the next month, he and the Japanese leader both lauded the progress on their currency valuations. Within a year the dollar plummeted from buying 240 yen to buying just 154 yen. By 1987, the dollar had tumbled 40 percent against a basket of the world's other currencies.[36] More slowly but still surely, Japan began buying more American products, and even American real estate, as the yen ballooned in purchasing power. However, Tokyo still balked at opening its own favored industries.

Even as United States–Japan economic relations remained tense, Reagan leaned into the strategic partnership. He knew that Nakasone was investing ample political capital in the alliance with the United States, including pushing Japan's bureaucracy and entrenched commercial interests as far as he could.[37] Supporting the United States–Japan alliance even brought Shultz and Weinberger together. The defense secretary often told his staff, "It is more important for the United States to get night landing rights for our naval carrier pilots in Japan than it is for us to save the machine tool industry in the United States."[38]

Weinberger also helped engineer a ploy that year that aided the Japanese and European economies, boosted the American economy, and inflicted more pain on the Soviet Union. Along with Casey and other American officials, he urged Saudi Arabia to increase drilling and thus drive down the price of oil. Because the Soviets relied on oil exports to raise hard currency, declining prices would choke off significant revenue to the Kremlin. When Reagan had hosted Saudi Arabia's King Fahd at the White House earlier in the year, the State Department's briefing memo noted that higher Saudi output would "stimulate economic growth, reduce inflation, and ease economic pressure on oil-importing countries" while also "decreas[ing] producer countries' income (including non-OPEC)."[39] The Soviet Union was the largest non-OPEC oil producer in the world.

The Saudis agreed. They had multiple reasons to do so. Facing declining revenues and diminishing market share from competition with other oil exporters, King Fahd saw economic self-interest in tapping the kingdom's almost limitless petroleum reserves to flood the market. Based on the White House's frequent entreaties, he also knew doing so would curry favor with Saudi Arabia's most important partner and hurt the atheistic Soviets he detested. That summer, the Saudis quietly alerted the White House that they planned to open the spigots. Beginning in August, Saudi petroleum output doubled to six million barrels per day, climbing further to nine million by the next year. Oil plunged to $12 per barrel and starved Moscow of an estimated $20 billion a year in hard currency.[40] The Plaza Accord multiplied the pain on the Soviet economy, since the dollars Moscow earned from energy sales also cratered in value.[41] On top of the many other vexations he inherited, Gorbachev now watched the Kremlin's coffers bleeding dry.

V

The Kremlin could still hit back. Moscow had little economic leverage over the United States but could impose costs in an even more valuable domain: human assets. Beginning in June 1985, the KGB began systematically executing the small cohort of agents the CIA had recruited inside the Soviet government. On the evening of June 9, at a checkpoint outside Moscow, KGB officers seized and bound Adolf Tolkachev, throwing him in the back of a van and spiriting him to the dreaded Lubyanka prison in the basement of KGB headquarters. For several years Tolkachev had passed top secret data on Soviet avionics and radar research to his CIA handlers at a rotating series of Moscow dead drops. His disclosures saved the United States untold billions of dollars, while enabling the Pentagon's aircraft and missile designers to stay one step ahead of Soviet radar defenses. As biographer David

Hoffman describes Tolkachev's spying, "the United States was reading the enemy's mail, in real time."[42] Now Tolkachev had shared his last secret. Four days later, the KGB nabbed his CIA handler Paul Stombaugh, interrogated him, and expelled him from the country. It was a significant escalation. In one of the Cold War's unwritten codes, the American and Soviet intelligence services rarely arrested each other's officers.

Nineteen eighty-five became the "year of the spy," to use CIA officer Milt Bearden's phrase. As soon as Bearden became deputy chief of the Directorate of Operations' Soviet and Eastern Europe Division, his Soviet agents began disappearing. Over the next two years, the KGB rolled up almost every other CIA asset inside the Soviet government. In the seven months alone after Tolkachev's arrest, six other Soviet intelligence officers spying for the United States were all arrested, interrogated, and executed.[43] The CIA's window into the Kremlin, already narrow, now shut entirely.

The United States stumbled into a small victory several weeks later when KGB officer Vitaly Yurchenko walked into the US embassy in Rome and announced his hope to defect. The CIA whisked him to the United States and stashed him at a safe house in Northern Virginia, where Yurchenko revealed that two American intelligence professionals, CIA officer Edward Lee Howard and NSA technician Ronald Pelton, were spying for the KGB. The story took a bizarre turn a few months later when, during a dinner with his CIA minder at the Georgetown restaurant Au Pied de Cochon, Yurchenko—manic, fearful, dispirited over media stories about his revelations, and lovelorn over an unrequited romance—went to the bathroom, climbed out the window, and slipped away to the Soviet embassy. There he announced his intention to return to the Soviet Union. The Kremlin, placing propaganda value above retribution, welcomed the prodigal spy home. Yurchenko's return to Moscow probably reflected his personal torments and maladjustments to life in the United States. His original defection likely was genuine, followed by a genuine change of heart. But amid the Cold War's hall of mirrors, the CIA could not be sure whether Yurchenko was just a tortured, fickle soul or had been a KGB plant all along.[44]

Much of what he revealed turned out to be true, including a bizarre KGB practice of using chemical agents on the shoes of American CIA officers in Moscow to track their movements. CIA scientists analyzed the chemical and found it to be carcinogenic, prompting the State Department to deliver a very strong protest to the Kremlin for exposing Americans to the deadly substance.[45] Yurchenko also identified Howard as the likely culprit who had fingered Tolkachev to the KGB. The FBI began following Howard, but the cagey spy duped his FBI surveillance and absconded to the Soviet Union. Howard was not the only mole who had burrowed in at Langley. On June 13, at the same hour that the KGB bushwhacked Stombaugh in Moscow, CIA officer Aldrich Ames slipped into Chadwicks tavern on the Georgetown waterfront carrying a thick stack of documents. The papers revealed the CIA's entire network of Soviet agents; Ames had easy access to these because he oversaw CIA counterintelligence against the Kremlin. Inside the restaurant, he met with his KGB handler and passed him the folder. In return, the KGB paid him a first installment of what would eventually total $4.6 million. Four months later, FBI agent Robert Hanssen also volunteered his services to the KGB, and betrayed even more American sources, including a joint CIA/FBI project to drill a tunnel under the Soviet embassy for electronic surveillance. It would take the CIA nine more years to discover that Ames was the mole. Hanssen's treachery would not be unearthed until 2001. The treasonous troika of Howard, Ames, and Hanssen caused the deaths of at least eleven Soviets spying for the United States.

VI

These intelligence losses came at the worst possible time for Reagan. Just as he began immersing himself in preparation for his Geneva summit with Gorbachev, the CIA's best human sources into the Kremlin's mindset and capabilities went dark.

Fortunately, Reagan had plenty of other avenues of insight. Though the president had well-formed strategic convictions about the Cold War, for his first meeting with a Soviet leader, he would imbibe extensive detail on the Soviet system, personnel, policies, and capabilities. NSC staffer Jack Matlock put together a book of briefing papers on twenty-four subjects numbering around 250 pages, collectively titled *Soviet Union 101,* which Reagan spent evenings and weekends devouring. Matlock also arranged numerous briefings for Reagan with intelligence and policy professionals and outside scholars. Reagan held multiple two-hour sessions each week over a period of months—an extraordinary allocation of presidential time—so that he could hear a broad range of views on almost every aspect of Soviet government, life, and culture.[46] Senior CIA officer Bob Gates attended one lunch Reagan had with six outside Sovietologists and recalled the scholars' "consensus that dramatic changes were under way in the USSR but that none threatened the system itself."[47] Where most expert opinion saw resilience, Reagan saw instead the Soviet system's fault lines—and resolved to push the cracks wider.

Reagan supplemented these memos and briefings with books that could give him windows into the Soviet mind and soul. His reading list included *Breaking with Moscow* by Arkady Shevchenko, the memoir of the highest-ranking Soviet diplomat to defect, and Suzanne Massie's *Land of the Firebird,* about pre-Bolshevik Russia. The president phoned Massie at her home in rural Maine and invited her back to the White House to help him prepare for meeting Gorbachev. Massie had spent two months in the USSR earlier in the summer and brought fresh insights into Soviet attitudes. In the Oval Office, she updated Reagan on how Gorbachev seemed to buoy the hopes of everyday Russians. Massie also described the resurgence of Christian faith among the Russian people; the CIA echoed this point in a separate briefing, to Reagan's great interest.[48]

The indefatigable Nixon shared a steady stream of advice in phone calls and letters. Reagan seized on Nixon's insight, "We want peace. The Soviet Union needs peace," which the president repeated often to distill the pressure that Gorbachev felt from the Kremlin's military burdens and strained economy. Nixon also urged Reagan to surprise Gorbachev with an ambitious arms control proposal because, among other reasons, "you can honestly point out that these proposals will result in your catching hell from the hawks in Congress, the media, and the Defense Department." Such political heat from the conservative base would show the depth of Reagan's commitment "to establish a totally new relationship with Gorbachev."[49] From Moscow, US ambassador Art Hartman sent his observations of the new Soviet leader in a Hollywood idiom: "[Gorbachev] could be played convincingly by George C. Scott but not by Jimmy Stewart. He is intense, self-assured, and assertive . . . he has a rigid cast of mind and can approach arrogance in rejecting ideas that clash with his preconceptions . . . [and] is a true believer in his system and his party's cause."[50]

The weeks leading up to the summit included a flurry of United States–USSR meetings to set the stage. Reagan met with Shevardnadze twice, Shultz met with him three times, and Shultz and McFarlane flew to Moscow to meet with Gorbachev. Both Gorbachev and Shevardnadze railed against Reagan's strategy of economic and military pressure. In their Kremlin meeting, an agitated Gorbachev interrupted Shultz with a diatribe. "You are inspired by illusions," the Soviet leader thundered, and proceeded to catalog:

> First, you believe that the Soviet Union is less economically power-ful and, therefore, it would be weakened by an arms race. Second, that you have the higher technology and, therefore, the SDI would give you superiority over the Soviet Union in weapons. Third, that the Soviet Union is more interested in negotiations in Geneva than you are. Fourth, that the Soviet Union only thinks of damaging US interests in regions around the world. Fifth, that it would be wrong to trade with the Soviet Union because that would just raise its capability. These are all illusions.

It was actually a fair summary of Reagan's strategy. Gorbachev even tried to turn it back on America. "If you want superiority through your SDI, we will not help you," he declared. "We will let you bankrupt yourselves. But also we will not reduce our offensive missiles. We will engage in a build-up that will break your shield."[51]

In protesting that the American pressures on the USSR were failing, Gorbachev's outbursts instead encouraged Reagan and Shultz that their strategy was working. The CIA detected this as well. In a secret analysis for Reagan, the CIA reported, "[Gorbachev is] deeply concerned that the USSR's current economic problems will make it difficult to aggressively compete with the US. . . . The Soviets fear [new American weapons systems] because these programs threaten to force the diversion of significant incremental resources . . . that the Soviet Union can ill afford."[52]

Reagan and Shultz both pressed hard on human rights. After each of their meetings, Reagan pulled Shevardnadze aside and privately urged him to release imprisoned dissidents and allow Jewish emigration.[53] Besides rais-ing prisoner cases, Shultz encouraged Gorbachev to embrace the emerging information age, both for the sake of individual liberties and to rescue the dying Soviet economy. "The successful societies are the open societies," he told the Soviet leader.[54]

The road to Geneva included shadowboxing over arms control. Gor-bachev tried to seize the initiative ahead of the summit with a new proposal. In September he wrote a letter to Reagan that appeared to offer notable con-cessions, including cutting nuclear arsenals by 50 percent.[55] Once the

Americans analyzed the details, however, Shultz told Reagan the Soviet proposal was "one-sided and self-serving" and "obviously designed for public appeal" rather than genuine negotiations.[56] The Kremlin demanded steep cuts in areas of American advantage such as aircraft carriers and strategic bombers, while protecting the Soviet edge in ICBMs. It also called for the United States to eliminate its GLCMs and Pershing IIs in Europe while letting Moscow keep its SS-20s. And for good measure, Gorbachev again demanded that Reagan terminate SDI. Yet Reagan and Shultz found in it a sign of hope; at last the Soviets showed a willingness to reduce nuclear arms. The week before the summit, the White House issued a counterproposal that affirmed the Soviet call for "deep reductions" in offensive weapons but insisted they be "equitably applied."[57]

SDI continued to terrify the Kremlin because Moscow, bedazzled by American technology, believed it could work. A secret GRU (Soviet military intelligence) assessment concluded that SDI could destroy 90 percent of Soviet strategic missiles, whether launched from land or submarines, and that it posed "a serious threat to the Soviet Union," especially because it could give the United States a first-strike capability. The CIA purloined the GRU briefing and shared it with Reagan. The paranoid Soviets misread the American president. Reagan did not prize SDI because he intended to launch an attack on the Soviet Union. Rather he still hoped that, once it became operational, besides protecting America, he could share SDI with Moscow and use it to escape the balance of terror by making nuclear weapons obsolete.[58]

SDI may have spooked the Soviets, but it also split the White House. While by now all of Reagan's senior team had embraced the strategic value of SDI, they differed fiercely over many details—especially whether continued work on SDI, including testing, would violate the ABM Treaty. Ambiguities in the language and negotiating history of the treaty left it unclear. Both the Soviets and NATO allies insisted that it prohibited testing—while the allies were not party to the treaty, they still viewed it as a cornerstone of nuclear deterrence. American policy for the thirteen years since the treaty signing, across four presidencies, had agreed. Then a few weeks before the summit, McFarlane declared on the *Meet the Press* news program that the treaty did in fact allow testing. Unfortunately, McFarlane had not consulted with Shultz, let alone Reagan, before announcing this reversal in US policy.

McFarlane's announcement prompted a media frenzy that made the White House look confused and inept and brought an unwelcome distraction on the eve of Geneva. Shultz wrote that he "was appalled and angry at

this arrogation of power" by the NSA, without State Department consultation or presidential approval. The secretary, who guarded State's prerogatives like a mother bear guarded its brood, tasked the State legal advisor
Abe Sofaer with doing a careful review. Sofaer concluded, with Nitze's concurrence (which mattered because the venerable Nitze had helped craft the
original treaty), that the treaty did in fact permit testing. This may have
resolved the legal matter but not the policy question. Shultz recommended
to Reagan that the United States declare that while legally the ABM Treaty
permitted testing, as a policy the United States would continue to confine
its SDI program to research. The president approved; Shultz announced this
reversal of McFarlane's words in a speech a few days later. This solution
satisfied the allies, pacified the Soviets, and preserved the presidential prerogative to expand SDI at a later point—for now.[59] The seemingly arcane
matter would return a year later at Reykjavík as the hinge on which rested
the nuclear balance of the Cold War.

Not all welcomed Shultz's announcement. It sparked a firestorm among
Senate conservatives. Leading Republican senators such as Malcolm Wal-
lop, Jesse Helms, Orrin Hatch, and Dan Quayle took to the Senate floor to
denounce Reagan's decision to restrict SDI to research as "appeasement"
that made the United States "look like jackasses to the Soviets."[60] The Senate
uproar could have weakened Reagan ahead of the summit but instead played
to his advantage. To Gorbachev, Reagan could show that the pressure he
faced from his right flank limited his room to make concessions, while also,
as Nixon suggested, proving his willingness to take political risks to improve relations with the USSR.

Reagan felt further emboldened by another new weapon that the Pentagon briefed him on just before the summit: the F-117 Nighthawk stealth
jet. The air force showed Reagan a classified film of the F-117 in the Situation
Room, which he described in his diary as "one of the greatest advances in
aircraft in years and years. It is of course most hush hush."[61] The Pentagon
would not publicly reveal the stealth attack jet for three more years, but the
Kremlin knew it existed. The F-117 flew invisible to radar, able to penetrate
Iron Curtain air defenses, giving the United States another qualitative military edge that the Kremlin could not match no matter how much it spent.

To collect his thoughts before the trip, Reagan wrote a four-page reflec-
tion on Gorbachev and his summit goals. The president saw his strategy
bearing fruit: "[If Gorbachev] really seeks an arms control agreement, it will
only be because he wants to reduce the burden of defense spending that is

stagnating the Soviet economy . . . he doesn't want to face the cost of competing with us." Reagan believed the Kremlin's military planning also confined Gorbachev's options: "[The Soviets] would like to win without [fighting a war] and their chances of doing that depend on being so prepared we could be faced with a surrender or die ultimatum. Thus any new move on our part, such as SDI forces them to revamp, and change their plan at great cost." Reagan knew that the Soviet leader would keep trying to fracture the alliance: "His major goal will continue to be weaning our European friends away from us. That means making us look like the threat to peace while he appears to be a reasonable man of peace."

Reagan spent a full page on human rights. He cited Nixon's advice to push quietly, particularly on Jewish emigration, rather than "force Gorbachev to eat crow and embarrass him publicly," noting, "We must always remember our main goal and his need to show his strength to the Soviet gang back in the Kremlin. Let's not limit the area where he can do that to those things that have to do with aggression outside the Soviet Union." Empathizing with the burdens Gorbachev faced, Reagan made a partial nod to linkage with Soviet behavior elsewhere, rejecting the view that "arms control must be the goal as an end in itself with no connection to regional issues." He would not let up the pressure and planned to warn Gorbachev "that failure to come to a solid, verifiable arms reduction agreement will leave no alternative except an arms race and there is no way that we will allow them to win such a race." But nor would he seek to humiliate the Soviet leader: "Let there be no talk of winners and losers. Even if we think we won, to say so would set us back in view of their inherent inferiority complex."[62]

Reagan had one final task before the summit: to tell the world his plans. He did so in two speeches—one directed to the Soviet people, the other to Americans. On November 9, he gave an address broadcast in nine languages to over fifty nations, including the USSR, on Voice of America. He promised Soviet citizens, "Americans are a peace-loving people; we do not threaten your nation and never will." Heralding the past Soviet-American alliance to defeat Nazi Germany, he urged the Soviet people to summon the same spirit and support his quest to abolish nuclear weapons. Five nights later, Reagan spoke to his fellow Americans from the Oval Office. He invoked Eisenhower's "Open Skies" proposal at his summit with Khrushchev three decades earlier and said he returned to Geneva with the same goal of building superpower trust and reducing the risk of nuclear war. "My mission, stated simply, is a mission for peace," Reagan proclaimed. To leave no doubt, the aspiring peacemaker used the word *peace* twenty-seven times in the half-hour address.[63]

VII

As Reagan prepared for Geneva, the Italian cruise ship *Achille Lauro* sailed across the Mediterranean to the coast of Egypt, with hundreds of European and American passengers aboard. Unnoticed among the guests were four members of the Palestine Liberation Front, a terrorist group commanded by Abu Abbas, under the umbrella of the PLO. On October 7, the terrorists stormed the bridge, firing their guns for effect and taking command of the ship. They ordered the captain at gunpoint to set sail for the Syrian port of Tartus.

As soon as word of the crisis hit Washington, the Pentagon ordered JSOC commander General Carl Stiner to deploy with SEAL Team Six and Delta Force units to a British base on Cyprus. Stiner and his special operators would stage for a potential rescue mission. Mindful of the delays that had hindered rescue efforts in the TWA 847 hijacking, Reagan warned Thatcher, "This act cannot become another protracted hostage situation."[64] For the same reason, Shultz urged all countries bordering the Mediterranean to deny port access to the ship. Keeping it in international waters created more rescue options. It also denied the terrorists access to journalists, who otherwise might create an international media frenzy such as the one the TWA 847 hijackers had exploited.

As the *Achille Lauro* sailed toward Syria, Reagan secretly ordered the US Navy to take any action necessary to "prevent the ship from entering a hostile port or anchorage"—such as Tartus. The president also directed JSOC to be ready to storm the ship and rescue the hostages the next night.[65] Nearing the Syrian coast, the terrorists sent a radio message demanding the release of fifty Palestinian prisoners held in Israel and threatened to execute ship passengers. When the deadline passed with no Israeli response, and as the Syrian government denied the ship docking rights, the lead terrorist wrestled passenger Leon Klinghoffer from his wheelchair, shot him point-blank in the head, and dumped his body and his wheelchair overboard. To the terrorists, Klinghoffer was twice guilty: He was an American and a Jew.

At first, few people on the ship, and no one off the ship, knew of Klinghoffer's murder. The terrorists now directed the *Achille Lauro* back toward

Egypt, where President Hosni Mubarak agreed to let it dock. Because the ship now sailed to an ostensibly friendly country, the US Navy chose not to intercept it. Mubarak, anxious to avoid any further agitation from the Egyptian street and Palestinian protestors, who already distrusted him over Egypt's peace treaty with Israel, agreed to let Arafat and Abbas "negotiate" for the release of the passengers and for the four terrorists to disembark. After the Egyptian and Palestinian leaders colluded to escort the terrorists off the ship, US ambassador to Egypt Nick Veliotes went on board to check on the welfare of the American passengers. Only then did Veliotes learn of Klinghoffer's death. From the ship, Veliotes called his deputy chief of mission and directed him to tell the Egyptian foreign minister: "An American ha[s] been murdered, and we must insist that these sons of bitches be prosecuted." Veliotes's epithet soon became international news.[66]

The United States and Egypt had a complicated relationship. The two countries had deepened ties over the past decade, cemented by Egypt's peace with Israel, anti-Soviet stance, cooperation in arming the Afghan resistance, and $2 billion in annual American military and economic aid. However, Mubarak differed with the Reagan administration over issues including his occasional quiet support for Palestinian terrorists. Now he tried to wash his hands of the Achille Lauro crisis. After Egypt supported Arafat and Abbas in ushering the terrorists off the ship, Mubarak told reporters, "[The terrorists] left Egypt already. I don't know where they went but they possibly went to Tunis. When we accepted the hijackers' surrender, we did not have this information [about Klinghoffer's murder]." Mubarak made the same claim privately to the US government.[67]

The Egyptian president lied. The terrorists were still in Egypt, and he knew it. The White House knew it as well. The National Security Agency monitored Mubarak's phone calls, picking up his discussions about his efforts to help the terrorists escape from Egypt and passing along transcripts of those calls to the Situation Room the moment Mubarak hung up. Reagan, Shultz, Poindexter, and the NSC staff heard every word of Mubarak's treachery. In short order, the Reagan team partnered with Israel to assemble a remarkable intelligence operation. Two future Israeli prime ministers—ambassador to the UN Benjamin Netanyahu and military intelligence chief Ehud Barak—played key roles, ranging from providing real-time tactical intelligence to confirming that Abbas and the terrorists answered to Arafat and the PLO. The Americans and Israelis learned that Mubarak was helping the terrorists abscond to the Cairo airport and from there fly on a special

EgyptAir 737 jet to Tunis, site of the PLO headquarters. Mossad used its network of Egyptian agents to discover the airplane tail number and confirm that Abbas was also boarding the plane.[68]

Naval officer Jim Stark of the NSC staff quickly crafted a plan to intercept the Egyptian plane and force it to land at the NATO base in Sigonella, Sicily, then immediately transfer the terrorists to an American plane to be flown back to the United States for prosecution.[69] McFarlane, traveling with Reagan in Chicago for a domestic policy trip, briefed the president on the plan. Reagan authorized it. Weinberger was flying back from Ottawa at the time. The defense secretary, reflexively averse to the use of force, phoned Reagan on Air Force One to argue against the interception plan. Reagan did not buy it. "Cap, it is pretty cut-and-dried," responded the president, "this is a guilty party; we cannot let them go."[70]

The aircraft carrier USS *Saratoga* launched two F-14 Tomcats and an E-2C Hawkeye reconnaissance plane to find and intercept the EgyptAir 737. Poindexter quarterbacked the operation from the Situation Room, showing the tactical precision he excelled at. The navy jets located the 737 and swooped alongside, ordering it to redirect and land at Sigonella. The Egyptian pilot complied at once. But would Italy allow the plane to land? In the late-night chaos, neither the State Department nor Italian officials could locate Prime Minister Craxi to request his approval. It was not every day that an Egyptian plane carrying Palestinian terrorists was forced by American navy jets to land at an Italian airstrip.

Oliver North, helping the NSC coordinate the many operational strands, enlisted Michael Ledeen, an old friend of Craxi, for help. Ledeen quickly tracked down Craxi in a suite at Rome's Hotel Raphaël. When Ledeen described the urgent request for the 737 bearing Abbas and his henchmen to land at Sigonella, Craxi asked, "Why here?" Taking a stab at humor, Ledeen responded, "Because no other place on earth can offer the unique combination of beautiful weather, cultural tradition, and magnificent cuisine that Sicily can provide." Craxi laughed and quickly agreed.[71]

When the 737 landed, the JSOC commandos surrounded it. As the SEALs prepared to board the plane and capture the hijackers, a large Italian force arrived on the tarmac, insistent on taking control of the situation and custody of the terrorists. It was an extraordinary picture. Eighty US Navy SEALs faced three hundred Italian soldiers and police in an armed standoff, while both forces surrounded a plane holding five Palestinian terrorists. A legal morass of contradictory extradition treaties, sovereignty claims, and international law standards created a thicket that could have taken years to untangle. This needed to be resolved within minutes—and without shooting. The hard fact that the plane was on Italian soil prevailed. In Washington, Reagan, Shultz, and Poindexter agreed to stand down and let the Italians take custody of the terrorists. On the tarmac at Sigonella, JSOC commander General Carl Stiner concurred. He felt confident that his SEALs, outnumbered but not outgunned, would prevail in a firefight—but why risk a bloodbath with a NATO ally?[72]

Even with the terrorists in Italian rather than American captivity, the White House saw the operation as a success. The United States had used the full range of counterterrorism tools developed by NSDD-138. A proud Reagan told a White House press briefing that the terrorists "can run, but they can't hide." Italy followed through in prosecuting the four hijackers; three received long prison sentences, while the fourth went free because he was a minor. But Italy would allow the mastermind Abbas to run and hide. Some years earlier, Rome had cut a deal with the PLO not to attack Italian targets in exchange for Italy's supporting the PLO's objectives. Now Arafat warned Craxi that if Italy did not release Abbas, the deal was off. Just two days after detaining him, Craxi quietly directed that Abbas be set free.[73] An angry Shultz believed "the Italians were trying to buy immunity from the PLO." The terrorist leader found refuge first in Yemen and eventually in Iraq, from where he continued to recruit new terrorists and devise new terror plots.

It was a painful realization for the White House that Italian pusillanimity had undercut a remarkable operational success against terrorism. Though angry for a few days, Reagan "cleared the air" with Craxi when they met at the UN two weeks later and forgave the Italian leader.[74] Reagan rarely held grudges—and he remained grateful for Craxi's steadfast support in deploying the Gryphon cruise missiles in Italy two years earlier. Reagan did not want to risk a rift with a friend on the eve of Geneva. All else paled beside allied resolve against the Soviet Union.

VIII

Reagan arrived in Geneva with a strong hand. He stood on a growing economy, a strengthened military, a 65 percent voter approval rating, and full support from the allies. Thatcher wrote to him that "we could not have a better or braver champion" in Geneva.[75] Nakasone, Kohl, and Mulroney offered "their trust, their love, and their prayers," as Reagan noted in his diary.[76] The CIA's Bob Gates summed it up in a note to Casey: "President Reagan goes to Geneva holding better cards than any president meeting his Soviet counterpart since Eisenhower went to Geneva 30 years ago [to meet with Khrushchev]."[77]

Gorbachev landed in Geneva feeling similarly confident. He had consolidated power in the Kremlin, installed his reform-minded lieutenants in key positions, and energized many Soviet citizens with a feeling they had long forgotten: hope. However, he knew that he led a superpower declining by the day. Though he wielded the world's largest nuclear arsenal, maladies including uncontrolled military spending, declining oil revenues, and the endemic dysfunction of a command economy all severely strained the Kremlin's finances. American technological wizardry kept bringing new weapons online that his best scientists could not understand, let alone replicate or defeat. The American INF deployment in Western Europe had neutralized the Soviet Union's SS-20s, Gorbachev's escalation in Afghanistan was only producing more dead Soviet soldiers, and now SDI threatened to bewitch the Kremlin's ICBM force. The peoples of the Warsaw Pact chafed under Moscow's yoke, and each meddlesome Soviet dissident exiled to the gulag only led to more hectoring from Reagan and Shultz, and more humiliation as the world saw how many of the Soviet people detested their government. Gorbachev resolved to protect his weak hand at the bargaining table and try to buy space from Reagan until he could draw better cards.

Placed at the geographic heart of Europe, in neutral Switzerland, Geneva was a natural choice for the Cold War's most anticipated meeting. *Time*'s claim that "a whole world will be anxiously watching every eyelid [Reagan and Gorbachev] lift or lower" was overwrought, but not by much.[78] Three thousand six hundred fourteen journalists registered for summit credentials. Notable figures from across the political spectrum flocked to Geneva, some to advance a cause, others to advance themselves. Irina Grivnina, a recent Soviet prisoner of conscience just exiled from the country three weeks earlier; Avital Shcharansky; and American conservative activist Phyllis Schlafly denounced Soviet oppression at press conferences. In turn, American progressive activists Jesse Jackson and Bella Abzug denounced Reagan at their own press conferences, and in Jackson's case also in his own meeting with Gorbachev.[79]

White House infighting trailed Reagan to Geneva. Back in Washington, Weinberger fumed at being excluded from the American delegation. Just before Reagan's departure, the defense secretary unburdened himself to the president in a letter urging a firm stance on SDI, detailing the Kremlin's history of treaty violations, and complaining, "Our failure over the years to respond promptly to Soviet violations can only encourage them to commit more—and more significant—violations." An unknown Pentagon official, possibly at Weinberger's behest, leaked the letter to *The New York Times* and *The Washington Post,* and it appeared in articles on November 16, just as Reagan and his delegation departed for Geneva.[80]

The leak sparked a media kerfuffle and unwelcome distraction on the summit eve. A furious McFarlane generated another round of headlines when he blasted Weinberger's letter as a "sabotage" of the summit. The Soviets, publicly annoyed and privately gleeful over the American disarray, denounced the Weinberger letter as "an attempt to torpedo the entire arms control process." Reagan disagreed. He called the media flap a "distortion" in his diary and wrote, "I agree with Cap and wanted his factual accounting in writing." Asked by a reporter if he would fire Weinberger over the leak, Reagan responded, "Hell, no." The president instead felt disappointed with McFarlane for escalating the dispute in public.[81]

The Reagans stayed in the Maison de Saussure, an elegant villa lent to them by the Aga Khan, spiritual leader of the world's Ismaili Muslims. The meetings with Gorbachev would take place in the Villa Fleur d'Eau, an eighteenth-century estate on the shores of Lake Geneva. The Gorbachevs would host a dinner one night at the Soviet mission; the Reagans would reciprocate the second night at their abode.

The day before the summit began, Reagan relaxed in front of the fireplace with his aide James Rosebush, who asked the president how he envisioned the Cold War ending. Replied Reagan:

These [communist] systems will crumble by the sheer fact that a growing majority of people living under their rule have a pent-up desire to be free to worship more than the state; and this demand to know and worship God, and to have a free and open relationship with Him, is what will bring totalitarianism and communism down. Of this I am sure. The people will do it themselves. We need to do everything we can to help them accomplish this.[82]

Not only did Reagan believe that religious faith would help bring down Soviet communism, the evangelist in chief would spend the next three years trying to persuade Gorbachev himself to trust in God.

Since 1981, Reagan had marshaled a full spectrum of pressure on the Soviet Union to produce a reformist leader with whom he could negotiate. Now he would see if Gorbachev was that man. Reagan harbored ambitious hopes, in some tension with each other. He wanted to work with Gorbachev to negotiate an end to nuclear weapons, reduce superpower hostility, and bring both the Cold War and the Soviet empire to a peaceful end. Gorbachev shared the goals of reducing weapons and hostility but was desperate to preserve the Soviet Union, not preside over its collapse.

November 19 dawned cloudy and cold. Reagan, official host for the summit's first day, arrived early at the lakeside estate and gathered with his team in the château's atrium. As Gorbachev's motorcade approached the mansion, an anxious Reagan felt the weight of the occasion. It seemed his entire life—as actor, labor negotiator, corporate pitchman, governor, anti-communist, freedom advocate, nuclear abolitionist, Christian, president—was prologue to this moment.

The car stopped. An equally nervous Mikhail Gorbachev, bundled in overcoat and scarf, stepped out. Before he could ascend the steps, a coatless and smiling Reagan came bounding toward him, exuding vitality despite being two decades older. Reagan extended one hand in greeting while putting his other hand on Gorbachev's elbow to usher him up the steps. It created an iconic image, broadcast to the world, contrasting the hale American and the drab Soviet. At once Gorbachev knew he had met his match.[83]

The two leaders stepped inside and sat next to each other in high-backed chairs, flanked by their interpreters. The official schedule allotted just fifteen minutes to exchange pleasantries before their delegations would join them for the substantive negotiations. Instead they talked for one hour. The intuitive Reagan sought first to connect with Gorbachev on a human level. He hoped that by building a personal relationship, they could transcend the structural and ideological divisions that had fueled the Cold War over the past four decades. Reagan began by reflecting on their common backgrounds as offspring of the small-town hinterlands, born to humble beginnings, now ascended to their roles as the globe's two most powerful men who held "the fate of the world in their hands." He continued, "We are the only ones who could start World War III, but also the only two countries that could bring peace to the world." Gorbachev agreed, noting that in the nuclear age, young and old people alike wondered if they would live to see the future.

The president then described his view of the Cold War as a battle of ideas. Competing, and incompatible, beliefs about the world fueled the mistrust between the superpowers. The Kremlin embraced "the Marxist idea of helping socialist revolutions throughout the world" and believed "the Marxist system should prevail," contended Reagan. Whereas the United States held "a very firm belief that people in all countries had the right of self-determination and the right to choose their own form of government." Gorbachev retorted that Reagan "should not think that Moscow was omnipotent and that when he, Gorbachev, woke up every day he thought about which country he would now like to arrange a revolution in."[84] Here Gorbachev distanced himself from his predecessors. Previous Kremlin leaders had promoted communist revolutions abroad, but Gorbachev knew that the nearly insolvent Soviet empire could no longer afford to do so.

From that start, over the next two days, Reagan and Gorbachev sparred in ten exhaustive and exhausting sessions, sometimes flanked by their senior teams, other times alone. Their conversations ranged from congenial to heated. They discovered anew just how deep their divisions were but also found they liked each other and sensed the first flickering of trust. The public affability masked some private acrimony, especially over Gorbachev's bête noire: SDI. The two leaders spent much of the time treading over the same ground. Around and around they repeated their points, now so familiar that each could parrot the other's arguments as well as his own. Gorbachev insisted that SDI would weaponize space, upset the delicate strategic balance by guaranteeing the United States a first-strike capability, cripple any hopes of arms reductions, and launch a new round of the arms race. Reagan replied that SDI was purely defensive, that the United States posed no threat to the USSR, and that SDI could free both sides from the terror of MAD and lead to abolishing all nuclear weapons. Otherwise, "under the current system of deterrence, it would be impossible to tell the winner from the loser in the event of war," Reagan lamented.[85] He aimed to shift the entire strategic frame from deterrence based on offensive weapons to deterrence based on defensive weapons.

Such appeals did not move Gorbachev. Another sharp exchange revealed the depths of the distrust between the two sides. Though each proclaimed that his nation would not attack the other first, neither would budge from his position, with Gorbachev insisting on abolishing SDI and Reagan insisting on keeping it. When an exasperated Gorbachev asked why Reagan did not believe him, the president replied, "I cannot say to the American people that I could take you at your word if *you* don't believe *us*."[86]

Gorbachev became almost unhinged. He warned that the Soviet Union would "smash your shield." Chief of Staff Don Regan, seated at the table, described Gorbachev as "very violent now, loud, many gestures, reddened face, pointing."[87] Gorbachev then made an ominous threat. If the United States continued with SDI, the Kremlin would adopt "automation which [would] place important decisions in the hands of computers and political leaders [would] just be in bunkers with computers making the decisions." Gorbachev warned, "This could unleash an uncontrollable process."[88]

It is not clear whether Reagan and his team appreciated the gravity of what Gorbachev had just said—the Soviet leader did not just warn what the Kremlin might do but what it had already done. Soviet scientists had recently experimented with a computer system known as Dead Hand that would automatically launch all of the USSR's ICBMs upon detecting an American strike—placing the fate of the world in the hands of machines rather than men. Seeking to retain some semblance of human control, the Kremlin instead earlier in the year had deployed a modified "doomsday machine" known as Perimeter. If a Soviet leader feared a decapitating American strike, he could activate Perimeter, which would send a slew of command rockets flying across the Soviet Union issuing launch signals to the entire Soviet ICBM fleet.[89] Perimeter reassured Gorbachev of the Kremlin's certain ability to retaliate against an American attack—and it terrified him that his government would delegate such authority to a computer. His warning to Reagan stemmed in part from his own fear.

Gorbachev also continued to stew over Reagan's strategy. Reprising his complaints to Shultz in Moscow two weeks earlier, Gorbachev dismissed Reagan's "delusions" about Soviet weakness, claimed that American military and economic pressure on the USSR would not work, and blamed Reagan's policies on the nefarious influence of conservative think tanks such as the Hoover Institution and Heritage Foundation.[90]

True to his approach of addressing human rights in private, Reagan waited until his one-on-one with Gorbachev on the morning of November 20 to raise the issue. The two leaders spent the entire meeting arguing over human rights. Reagan explained to Gorbachev that persecuting its own people hurt the Kremlin's image with Congress and the American public, and that if the Soviet Union allowed more freedom of expression, religion, and emigration, it would create more political support in the United States for progress on other issues. Reagan focused especially on Soviet anti-Semitism. Why could the Kremlin not permit more Soviet Jews to emigrate? Reagan asked. He connected the refusenik movement with Soviet restrictions on Jewish practice, such as bans on teaching the Hebrew language. "Perhaps some people would not think of emigrating from the Soviet Union if they were allowed to practice their religion," Reagan pointed out. In response, an annoyed Gorbachev resorted to a filibuster of "whataboutism," lambasting unequal pay for women and other alleged inequities in America.[91]

Frustrated that Gorbachev had rebuffed his human rights entreaties, Reagan complained during a break that the Soviet leader "believes his own propaganda." For Reagan, how a nation treated its own people, especially its religious minorities, revealed much about the character of its leaders. He could not square Gorbachev's affability with the Kremlin's religious perse-cution. After the convivial dinner with the Soviet delegation the first night, Reagan said he needed to "keep reminding myself that these 'nice guys' . . . are the same Soviets banning Jewish emigration."[92]

At dinner the next night Reagan and Shultz brought up religion again with the Gorbachevs. Shultz asked them about reports of a spiritual revival in the Soviet Union. Gorbachev admitted that some of the older generation still believed in Christianity, but he said, "True believers are dying out." Reagan and Shultz knew otherwise; even their CIA and NSC briefings had described a turn to faith among many young Soviets. Over their two days together, Reagan took notice that several times Gorbachev made passing mention of "God" and even quoted the Bible. Most likely, Gorbachev was just using an idiom he knew Reagan would like. If so, it worked—in several letters to friends and colleagues after the summit, including a readout he sent to Nixon, Reagan highlighted the Soviet leader's references to the divine.[93]

Despite their fierce disagreements, Reagan and Gorbachev believed that they had built a genuine rapport and opened a new path in US-Soviet relations. Both took political risks in doing so. At their closing appearance before the media, Reagan joked to Gorbachev, "Your hard liners and my hard liners are going to swallow very hard seeing us up here shaking hands and smiling."

Replied Gorbachev, "You're so right. They won't like it."[94]

Other than a few small aviation and cultural exchanges, the summit produced no significant deals. Of most consequence, Reagan and Gorbachev agreed to meet again. Over after-dinner cordials on the final night, Reagan set the course for the three years ahead. He told Gorbachev he did not think previous US-Soviet summits over the last three decades had accomplished much. So, Reagan urged, "Let's say 'to hell with the past,' we'll do it our way and get something done." Gorbachev agreed.[95]

IX

The relentless pace and pressure continued to grind down Reagan's team. The day after returning from Geneva, Shultz confided that he felt burned out and was considering resigning. Reagan expressed sympathy but also reminded the secretary of his trust in and reliance on him. Shultz agreed to stay. A few days later, an exhausted and frustrated McFarlane submitted his resignation letter to Reagan. The president, who genuinely valued McFarlane, reluctantly accepted. For almost four years—two in the deputy role, two more in the top spot—McFarlane had served faithfully amid the unforgiving grind of one of the most stressful jobs in the world. He could take pride in all that he had done to make the Geneva summit a success and a fitting capstone to his NSC sojourn.

Reagan decided to promote Poindexter, McFarlane's deputy, into the national security advisor role. The capable and experienced Poindexter had earned Reagan's trust through his deft crisis management in the *Achille Lauro* episode.[96] McFarlane shifted to a "consultant" role to the NSC, keeping the classified White House email system connected to his home and his Virginia cabin, and would continue to run the secret channel with Iran.

The arms-for-hostages machinations had not stopped even for the summit with Gorbachev. While in Geneva, McFarlane had continued to field phone calls, orchestrate maneuvers, and brief Reagan on the latest developments. The day after returning from Geneva, Reagan held an NSC meeting to review the operation and recorded in his diary, "We have an undercover thing going by way of an Iranian which could get [the hostages] sprung momentarily."[97]

It was not to be. Instead there ensued a bewildering tragicomedy that should have put the mad affair to rest. Because Iraq had recently acquired advanced fighter jets from France and the USSR, Iran desperately wanted American-made HAWK ground-to-air missiles to neutralize Iraq's new air superiority. McFarlane, North, Ghorbanifar, and Israeli officials cooked up a scheme involving Saudi financing, Portuguese transit rights, Caribbean island St. Lucia's tiny airline under contract with the CIA, and a menagerie of shady international middlemen to ship eighty HAWK missiles from Israel to Iran and then have the United States replenish Israel's missile stocks. All in exchange for Iran's engineering more hostage releases. Instead a combination of bungling, confusion, misunderstandings, and miscues resulted in only eighteen HAWKs arriving in Tehran. Even worse, these HAWKs were not the advanced model the Iranians had demanded—and bore the Star of David, not a popular logo in the Islamic Republic of Iran. No one was surprised when no more hostages got released.

As the HAWK debacle unfolded, CIA deputy director John McMahon realized Langley was out to sea without the lifeline of a presidential finding authorizing these covert activities. He had the CIA general counsel quickly draft a finding for NSC review and Reagan's approval. Reagan signed it on December 5. The finding, providing for weapons "to the Government of Iran which is taking steps to facilitate the release of the American hostages," had several unusual features. It ordered the CIA director "not to brief" Congress on the initiative, and it claimed to ratify "all prior actions taken by US Government officials"—both of which conflicted with the law governing covert action programs. The finding also made no mention of the ostensible goal of strengthening moderates and improving the US-Iran relationship.[98]

The same day that he signed the finding, Reagan held another NSC meeting on the Iran initiative. Reagan confessed to his diary, "It is a complex undertaking with only a few of us in on it. I won't even write in the diary what we're up to." He did just that two days later:

> Had a meeting with Don R., Cap W. and Bud M., John P., Geo. Shultz and [John] Mahan [sic] of C.I.A. This has to do with the complex plan which could return our 5 hostages and help some officials in Iran who want to turn that country from its present course and on to a better relationship with us. It calls for Israel selling some weapons to Iran. As they are delivered in installments by air our hostages will be released. The weapons will go to the moderate leaders in the army who are essential if there's to be a change to a more stable government. We then sell Israel replacements for the delivered weapons. None of this is a gift—the Iranians pay cash for the weapons—so does Israel. George S., Cap and Don are opposed—Cong[ress] has

imposed a law on us that we can't sell Iran weapons or sell any other country weapons for re-sale to Iran. Geo[rge] also thinks this violates our policy of not paying off terrorists. I claim the weapons are for those who want to change the government of Iran and no ransom is being p[aid] for the hostages. No direct sale would be made by us to Iran but we would be replacing the weapons sold by Israel. We're at a stalemate.[99]

Reagan should have listened to Shultz, Weinberger, and Regan. Their objections—based on law, policy, and common sense—would prove prescient. The diary entry reveals Reagan's intention to trade arms for hostages, and his ability to rationalize and convince himself otherwise. While Reagan shared McFarlane's hope for a strategic opening, the president cared foremost about bringing the hostages home.

Following the bungled HAWK shipment, on December 8, McFarlane and North took a secret trip to London to meet with the Israelis and Ghorbanifar and try to salvage the scheme. McFarlane told Ghorbanifar that the United States would not ship any more weapons until Iranian political leaders showed an interest in strategic dialogue. Ghorbanifar erupted that the Iranian government needed more weapons first to prevail in the Iraq war—"Then we think about all this nice political science!" An angry McFarlane ended the meeting and returned to Washington thinking the operation was over.[100] Upon hearing McFarlane's report, a disappointed Reagan wrote, "[Ghorbanifar] turns out to be a devious character. Our plan regarding the hostages is a 'no go.'"[101]

Meanwhile, North discovered $800,000 in funds remaining from the Iranian-Israeli payments for the HAWK shipment. He had the "neat idea," in his words, to send the leftover money to the contras, who were in perpetual need of additional support.[102]

X

Reagan's covert outreach to Iran did not prevent him from criticizing the clerical regime for its oppression. The day after hearing McFarlane's report on the London meeting, Reagan gave a Human Rights Day speech that singled out Iran's "rampant religious persecution, especially against the Baha'is," and welcomed the Baha'i leadership to the White House for his proclamation signing ceremony. In the same address, Reagan denounced South African apartheid as "abhorrent" and called for its end, urged the Philippines and Chile to return to democracy, and lauded Guatemala's recent election of a civilian president after years of brutal military rule. Reagan also highlighted his support for anticommunist forces in Afghanistan, Cambodia, Nicaragua, and Angola as part of his overall human rights policy, since communist regimes accounted for the preponderance of the world's repression.[103]

As the first year of his second term ended, Reagan had set in motion the policies that would define his legacy. The previous two months in particular had brought out two sides to Reagan. The Iran gambit revealed him at his worst: stubborn, naïve, prone to self-delusion. Geneva showed him at his best: strategic, visionary, bold, in command, setting an agenda to transform the Cold War. The coming year would put both of those sides on display.

CHAPTER 12

———◆———

THE CRUCIBLE

I
———

For his first five years in the White House, Reagan built the pieces of his strategy to promote freedom and end the Soviet threat. Along the way, he had learned much, adapted, and confronted numerous crises—some of his own making, others the bitter fruits of a perilous world. Now, as Reagan looked ahead to his last three years in office, he sought to harvest what he had sown, from midwifing new democracies in Asia and Latin America, to building an international free-trade system, to reducing the risk of nuclear war.

The new year would bring a succession of crises with Libya, the Philippines, and Nicaragua. Reagan would also see his presidency crippled and nearly destroyed by scandal. Of most enduring importance, he would test the new Soviet leader and come to see that Gorbachev was indeed the partner for peace Reagan had long sought. The Soviet Union had always stood at center stage in his foreign policy. Now, as the final scenes approached, Reagan focused the spotlight on the Kremlin. Or perhaps it should be said that the spotlight turned to him and Gorbachev, as Reagan now became both the director and a lead actor in the Cold War drama.

Following Geneva, Reagan and Gorbachev exchanged multiple letters, more or less rehashing the same points. Reagan reiterated his benign intentions with SDI, pressed for the Red Army to withdraw from Afghanistan, and urged progress on human rights. Gorbachev responded with his standard criticism of SDI as a "space strike weapon" designed to give the United

States nuclear primacy and blaming the United States for supporting anti-communist insurgencies and blocking a political settlement in Afghanistan.[1] On New Year's Day 1986, by previous agreement, the two leaders broadcast messages to each other's citizens. Reagan told the Soviet people of his "hope that one day we will be able to eliminate these [nuclear] weapons altogether." Gorbachev focused his remarks on his opposition to SDI, hoping to swing more Americans against their president's policy.[2]

Meanwhile the CIA remained skeptical of the new Soviet leader. In January, Langley sent Reagan a lengthy assessment on the Kremlin's strategy for the next three years. Warning that Gorbachev's main goal was to buy time to restore Soviet strength to "better compete" against the United States (similar to Brezhnev's goals with détente fifteen years earlier), the CIA predicted that the Kremlin would "strongly turn on the Administration in 1987, and possibly just before the Congressional elections, if it hasn't gotten what it wants by then, and denounce the President for making the world more dangerous and his policies toward the USSR as having failed." Casey reinforced the point three days later in a letter to Reagan complaining of more Soviet violations of arms control agreements, dismissing the American response as "weak," and cautioning against inking any new deals with the Kremlin given Moscow's breaches of the existing ones.[3]

Then Gorbachev seized the initiative. On the morning of January 15, Soviet ambassador Anatoly Dobrynin called on Shultz to deliver a letter from Gorbachev to Reagan with a new proposal. The Kremlin simultaneously broadcast it to the world as well: Gorbachev called for eliminating all nuclear weapons in the world by the year 2020. His letter detailed the plan, to be implemented in three phases of five-year increments, starting with a 50 percent reduction in warheads and removal of INF missiles in Europe, followed by the elimination of tactical nuclear weapons, and then the agreement of all nuclear powers in the world to destroy their remaining weapons.

Gorbachev's move caught the Reagan administration off guard. Shultz immediately summoned top arms control officials from State, the Pentagon, and the CIA to scrutinize the proposal, and that afternoon Shultz and Nitze joined Poindexter at the White House to brief Reagan. Most of them took a skeptical view. Nitze thought the Kremlin plan equal parts propaganda and seriousness, while Weinberger, Poindexter, Casey, Ken Adelman, Richard Perle, and others objected that it would ban SDI and that its sequencing would lock in the Soviet edge in ICBMs over the next fifteen years. Indeed, some of Gorbachev's top advisors had intended the proposal for public opinion gains rather than serious policy—for that reason they made it public and included terms unfavorable to the United States. Still, Reagan and Shultz decided to focus on the positive: Not only did Gorbachev now seem to endorse Reagan's zero-zero position to eliminate INF missiles, his plan also affirmed Reagan's vision of a nuclear-free world. Reagan issued a statement that afternoon making just that point. Recalling his several previous calls to abolish all nuclear weapons, Reagan said, "I welcome the Soviets' latest response and hope that it represents a helpful further step in that process."[4]

Two weeks later, Reagan convened an NSPG meeting to consider next steps in responding to Gorbachev, especially since the American negotiating team in Geneva awaited guidance as they resumed working-level talks with their Soviet counterparts. Reagan decided to embrace the goals of the Soviet proposal while pushing for specific steps to implement it, with a focus first on INF reductions. He held fast to SDI yet reiterated his intention to share it, once in the development phase, with the Soviets. Reagan added a note of realism, saying, "There is no guarantee we know how to make SDI work yet"—despite the critics then and later who derided him as a fantasist, deluded about the many technical hurdles facing SDI. Mindful of both his commitment to Nakasone and a possible Kremlin ploy to shift SS-20s from Europe to the Far East rather than scrapping them altogether, Reagan added, "If the Soviets try to keep some SS-20s in Asia, perhaps we could counter by putting Pershing II and GLCM systems in Alaska, where they could reach Soviet systems in Asia. The Soviets must know that if there is not complete elimination of INF, we will not eliminate our INF."[5]

Reagan also knew that the allies worried that any United States–USSR nuclear deal might close the American nuclear umbrella and leave them vulnerable to Soviet aggression. The day after the NSPG meeting, Reagan wrote to his counterparts in NATO capitals, Tokyo, Canberra, and Seoul, reassuring them that while pursuing nuclear negotiations, the United States would still "address the conditions that made [nuclear] weapons necessary," citing the problems of the Red Army's conventional superiority, serial Soviet cheating on other treaties, and the Kremlin's ongoing role in fueling regional conflicts.[6] This did not pacify Thatcher, who had become a Gorbachev skeptic. She responded to Reagan, "Under the veneer is the same brand of dedicated Soviet communist that we have known in the past," and worried that "the search for a world without nuclear weapons holds far more problems for the West than for the Soviet Union."[7]

Meanwhile, Gorbachev took more positive steps. At the February Communist Party Congress, he gave a speech calling for "new political thinking" in Soviet doctrine, while replacing some troglodytes in senior positions with reformers less hostile to the United States. And he decided to release Anatoly Shcharansky. After Reagan had pressed Shcharansky's case in Geneva, Gorbachev had authorized a complicated deal negotiated by Shultz, West Germany's Kohl, and East German and Soviet officials that involved exchanging Shcharansky and three imprisoned Warsaw Pact citizens who had spied for the West for four KGB spies held by the United States. Shcharansky, who had nearly starved to death in the gulag, only got a hint of his possible impending freedom when his guards began feeding him to restore his emaciated body. Soon he was put on a flight to East Germany. Shcharansky, disoriented but euphoric, was escorted to the Glienicke Bridge, spanning the Havel River between Potsdam and West Berlin, site of countless East-West prisoner exchanges over the Cold War decades. There US ambassador Richard Burt met him and escorted him to freedom, first in Frankfurt, where Avital awaited him, and then on to his new home in Israel and a welcoming phone call from Reagan.[8]

Gorbachev's words—and some deeds, such as releasing Shcharansky—were significant. Yet did they signal a decisive shift in Soviet policies? At the same time he extended these olive branches, Gorbachev took other, hostile steps, such as increasing Soviet arms shipments to Muammar Qadhafi. Reagan bluntly remonstrated with Gorbachev in a handwritten letter: "What are we to make of your sharply increased military support of a local dictator who has declared a war of terrorism against much of the rest of the world, and against the United States in particular?"[9]

Reagan increased the pressure on Gorbachev on other fronts. The Kremlin had been using the Soviet mission to the UN as a KGB outpost, with over one hundred KGB officers serving disguised as UN "diplomats." This gave the KGB a disproportionate espionage advantage on American territory. On March 7, Reagan expelled one hundred five of those KGB officers from the United States, producing much wailing and gnashing of teeth in Moscow.[10] Reagan also stepped up navy exercises across the seascapes of the Northern Hemisphere. These served to preserve freedom of navigation in the ocean commons, gather intelligence on Soviet capabilities, and remind Moscow of American force projection. A March 13 exercise particularly rattled the Kremlin, when the cruiser *Yorktown* and destroyer *Caron* sailed through the Black Sea into Soviet territorial waters six miles from the Crimean coast, under the "innocent passage" provision of maritime law. The navy did not know (not that it would have mattered) that Gorbachev happened to be vacationing in his Crimean dacha at the time; the Soviets lodged a formal protest with the US embassy.[11]

The Soviets, meanwhile, continued to disregard Reagan's counterproposals on arms control and demur on a date for the next summit that Reagan and Gorbachev had agreed to hold, instead insisting on US arms control concessions as a precondition to meet again. After multiple exchanges with senior Soviet officials, Shultz and Matlock grew frustrated with Moscow's intransigence. Matlock urged sitting tight, saying, "Otherwise we risk encouraging the Soviets to believe that we are so eager to nail it down we might yet pay a price—which would simply add to their incentive to continue their current tactics."[12] The initial trust Reagan and Gorbachev had forged in Geneva seemed to be fast dissipating.

II

Reagan decided to inflict more pain on the Soviets in Afghanistan. Encountering Afghan victims of Red Army atrocities deepened his resolve. In January 1986 he met with five crippled Afghan children. Seeing their wounds and hearing their stories, Reagan's eyes welled with tears. Still shaken that evening, he wrote in his diary, "They were mere babies—but all victims of Soviet bombings. One little girl with her face virtually destroyed. Three with one arm each and one with only one leg. I'd like to send the photos to Gen. Sec. Gorbachev."[13]

That same month, Republican senator Orrin Hatch returned from a trip to Beijing and Islamabad with surprising news. President Zia wanted to escalate the war by supplying Stinger missiles to the Afghan resistance, and China agreed. The delegation accompanying Hatch included two senior CIA officers, NSC staffer Vince Cannistraro, the Defense Department's Michael Pillsbury, and Mort Abramowitz of the State Department. Each of these officials shared Zia's request with his respective department or agency; it did not hurt that several of them, especially Pillsbury and Abramowitz, had for months been Stinger advocates. However, there were risks. Some senior CIA officers continued to oppose introducing American-made weapons into Afghanistan lest they shred the last fig leaf of deniability of US involvement in the war. At the Pentagon, Weinberger and the Joint Chiefs of Staff resisted because of the risk of a Stinger falling into the Red Army's hands and giving the Kremlin access to its advanced technology. A combination of Zia's endorsement; advocacy by Fred Iklé, Pillsbury, and Abramowitz; and Casey's support led Reagan to decide to provide the Stingers to the Afghan resistance. It would be the most potent display yet of the Reagan Doctrine.[14]

A few months later, a mule caravan carried the first batch of Stingers across the border from Pakistan into Afghanistan. Milt Bearden, now the CIA station chief in Islamabad, oversaw Pakistani intelligence officers in training the Afghan resistance on the Stinger, as simple as it was lethal. Within weeks, a mujahideen leader named Engineer Ghaffar stood with his warrior band on a ridge overlooking the Soviet airbase at Jalalabad. As a group of unsuspecting Hind helicopter gunships took off, Ghaffar and his men cried, "Allahu Akbar!" ("God is great!") and fired. Three Stingers found their targets and incinerated three Hinds. One of Ghaffar's men filmed it with a crude video camera; by coincidence, an American spy satellite overhead captured the imagery as well. Within days, the video had made its way through the senior echelons in Washington. Casey even showed it to an enthused Reagan.[15] The CIA estimated that seven out of every ten Stingers fired had shot down a Soviet jet or helicopter. Each Stinger cost about $60,000–70,000, compared with the $20 million or more price tag on a MiG fighter jet. The Stinger soon made the Afghanistan War even more unsustainable for the Kremlin.[16]

Gorbachev felt torn. Earlier in the year he had made clear his desire to exit Afghanistan. However, he had escalated the Soviet campaign because he did not want to end the war in defeat and disgrace. The Kremlin had also ousted Afghan president Babrak Karmal and replaced him with secret-police head Najibullah, whom Moscow hoped would be more ruthless as a ruler and more compliant with Soviet directives. In July, Gorbachev indicated to the visiting François Mitterrand that he felt no hurry to withdraw. He also faced geopolitical pressure from New Delhi. Indian leader Rajiv Gandhi, a close partner to Moscow, counseled against a Soviet exit that would bolster Pakistan, India's longtime nemesis.[17] Instead, the Afghan resistance began imposing new costs on Moscow, just when Gorbachev could least afford it. In a speech in September, Casey gave an apt summary of the Reagan Doctrine: "Far fewer people and weapons are needed to put a government on the defensive than are needed to protect it." Added the DCI knowingly: "External support is almost always a key factor in resistance success."[18]

III

Maintaining such external support was proving much harder in Nicaragua. As the new year began, Reagan faced renewed resistance to funding the contras. The same Congress that marshaled strong bipartisan majorities to appropriate hundreds of millions of dollars for the Afghan freedom fighters blanched at even a minute fraction of that amount to the Nicaraguan freedom fighters.

Ironically, Nicaragua grew in controversy just as the rest of the region showed progress. El Salvador continued to solidify its democracy and weaken the FMLN insurgency. Guatemala's presidential election the year before had led to reduced violence and pointed toward the eventual end of the civil war. Honduras enjoyed another peaceful presidential transition, while Costa Rica remained a stable democracy. On January 3, Reagan visited Mexico for his annual meeting with President de la Madrid, bringing continued improvement in United States–Mexico relations.

Reagan convened an NSC meeting on January 10 to review US policy in the region. The conversation quickly turned to, in Poindexter's words, "the one significant problem area": Nicaragua. Casey and CIA Central America Task Force head Alan Fiers detailed increased Soviet bloc support for the Sandinistas. Weinberger and JCS chairman Admiral Bill Crowe then described the "considerably less favorable" military situation, with the contras weak, divided, and demoralized. Shultz stressed the need for overt economic aid as well as covert security assistance—the latter better kept secret at the behest of partner nations such as Honduras and Costa Rica, who detested the Sandinistas but wanted to maintain deniability of their support for the contras.

Because the contra needs were so dire, and because his team had overcome its earlier policy divisions, Reagan decided to propose $100 million, with $70 million in overt military assistance and $30 million in humanitarian aid. It was an ambitious amount, albeit less than one-fifth of the over $500 million the Soviet Union had supplied to the Ortega regime in recent years. On submitting the request to Congress, Reagan vented to his diary, "[Securing Hill support] isn't going to be easy. The Sandinistas have a disinformation program that has fooled a lot of people—some want to be fooled."[19] Reagan's wariness would prove correct. The aid package may have united his White House team, but it divided Congress. Moderate Democrats saw the military aid as too much too soon, while Speaker Tip O'Neill saw it as an opportunity to deal Reagan a political defeat.

In turn, White House communications director Pat Buchanan saw it as a chance to score partisan points. Buchanan oversaw a stream of pugilistic op-eds accusing Democrats of becoming, "with Moscow, co-guarantor of the Brezhnev Doctrine in Central America." Reagan himself gave a series of aggressive speeches, warning that Central America could become "covered in a sea of red, eventually lapping at our own borders." Just days before the vote, he addressed the nation, warning that "the malignancy in Managua" had to be stopped before it "becomes a mortal threat to the entire New World." For good measure, he accused the Sandinistas of fraternizing with an almost cartoonish cabal of world villainy, including Qadhafi, Ayatollah Khomeini, North Korea, the PLO, and the Red Brigades Italian terrorist group.[20]

The White House went too far. *Time* magazine, in an otherwise sympathetic article that echoed Reagan's strategic case for contra aid, noted drily that "such attacks predictably backfired against members of Congress who saw their patriotism impugned."[21] The wily O'Neill mobilized most Democrats, along with a handful of liberal Republicans, to reject the package by 222–210. Within minutes of the vote, a furious Reagan convened an NSC meeting to decide on next steps. He fumed that Capitol Hill had betrayed the contras: "Think how the young men who are the freedom fighters must feel now." His team felt the same way. Shultz called the vote "devastating" for "our negotiating strategy" and credibility in the region. Reagan viewed it as the latest installment in congressional undermining of anticommunist partners. He recalled congressional votes in 1975 to cut off funding for anticommunist forces in South Vietnam and Angola: "And here we go again."[22] That night Reagan vented to his diary about the vote: "H[ell] of a way to run a country."[23]

The Vietnam legacy also haunted Poindexter. After serving in the war as a young naval officer, Poindexter had been grieved by what he saw as a sellout of America's South Vietnamese allies when Congress terminated funding. Now, over a decade later, the national security advisor swore to himself that he would not let the contras suffer a similar betrayal.[24]

The battle on Capitol Hill was not over. In mobilizing his caucus against the aid, O'Neill had agreed to requests from some moderate Democrats to hold a second vote on the package later in the summer. A chastened Reagan, seizing the second chance, wooed moderates from both parties by making the case in more sober terms, acknowledging past contra human rights abuses, ascribing good faith to political opponents, and heralding anticommunist Democrats going back to Truman.[25]

Reagan's political problems on Nicaragua did not stem only from the Left. While the White House tried to secure votes from reluctant Democrats and liberal Republicans, malcontented NSC staff member Constantine Menges (who had been demoted by McFarlane and soon would be fired by Poindexter) began fomenting heartburn in the conservative media and on Capitol Hill. Menges carped to his congressional allies that a conspiracy of moderates had seized control of the NSC staff, and together with Shultz were "unraveling" Reagan's foreign policy, especially by selling out the contras in the Contadora diplomatic process. Thirty-three conservative Republican senators and representatives wrote Poindexter demanding that he keep Menges and appoint "more Reagan experts to the NSC senior staff."[26] Reagan did not need congressional meddlers to tell him who he should hire or what his own policy was.

In the midst of this fracas, Reagan and Poindexter discussed a contingency plan. If Congress rejected the aid again, Reagan said he wanted "to figure out a way to take action unilaterally to provide assistance." Poindexter told another NSC staffer that Reagan was "ready to confront the Congress on the constitutional question of who controls foreign policy."[27] Reagan's impulse to claw back presidential authority was sound. But Poindexter would prove not the best person to implement it, nor would contra aid be the best hill on which to take a stand. Poindexter summed up his own contempt of Congress a few years later, when he claimed, "It is very hard to come up with anything constructive or useful that the Congress of the United States has ever done."[28]

Sandinista rejection of the draft Contadora agreement; appeals to support democracy from the leaders of Costa Rica, Honduras, El Salvador, and Guatemala; and Reagan's more conciliatory outreach to congressional Democrats combined to swing enough votes in the House that in June the $100 million contra aid package passed by a vote of 221–209. It was a triumph for the White House and a turning point in locking in bipartisan support for the contras. The Senate approved it in August, but the congressional recess and other technical tweaks meant it did not arrive on Reagan's desk for signature until October, and the first tranche of funds did not reach the contras until the end of November. That five-month window left the contras desperate and destitute. Poindexter and NSC staff member Oliver North had already hatched a plan to cover that funding gap—with fateful consequences.[29]

In the midst of the Nicaragua debates, Congress also passed a major immigration reform bill that increased border enforcement while offering a pathway to citizenship for those who had previously entered the country illegally. Reagan supported both principles and happily signed it into law. As a former governor of a border state, he knew firsthand the importance of border security and lamented to his diary, "We've lost control of our borders."[30] A hallmark of any sovereign government is control of its borders and regulation of who is allowed in. Yet he also saw his country as a refuge for people seeking liberty and opportunity. America's appeal to those fleeing oppression contrasted with the Soviet bloc's desperation to keep its citizens locked behind the Iron Curtain.

Reagan viewed immigration policy in part through the lens of his broader Latin America strategy. He continued to worry that the United States, as the "Colossus of the North," needed to stay on the side of liberty and prosperity for the other peoples of the region, even while fighting against communism. In June, he endorsed a bipartisan measure to provide $300 million in development aid to Honduras, Costa Rica, El Salvador, and Guatemala. Reagan knew that people who enjoyed peace, freedom, and opportunity in their home countries would have no cause to flee north to the United States.

He also felt compassion for those caught in the system's inequities. The year before, he had described to his diary how he planned to reverse a pending deportation: "An El Salvador young lady who entered the country illegally but who now has an Am[erican] husband and baby is slated for deportation. I want it stopped. We shouldn't be breaking up families."[31]

IV

Reagan's commitment to the contras would soon converge, in a most peculiar manner, with his Iranian errand to trade arms for hostages. Though in December the Iran project had seemed to die, the new year and new national security advisor gave it new life.

Oliver North sensed the opening. Blaming the HAWK fiasco on Ledeen, Ghorbanifar, and the Israelis, North urged Poindexter to try again. A new Israeli counterterrorism official, Amiram Nir, became involved and traveled to Washington to pitch Poindexter. The national security advisor recalled Israel's vital intelligence cooperation in the *Achille Lauro* hijacking a few months earlier. Appealing in equal parts to Poindexter's strategic creativity, penchant for secrecy, disdain for Congress, and commitment to the US-Israel relationship, not to mention the seductions of improved relations with Iran and hostage releases, North and Nir won him over.

Poindexter and North worked with Casey to draft a new finding reauthorizing the initiative as a covert action. It made explicit the goals of "establishing a more moderate government in Iran" and "furthering the release of the American hostages." Reagan, focused only on the latter, signed it on January 17. He told his diary of "our effort to get our 5 hostages out of Lebanon," saying, "Involves selling TOW anti-tank missiles to Iran. I gave a go ahead." He did so over more vehement objections from Shultz and Weinberger. In one indication of just how farcical the new scheme was, at Casey and Poindexter's behest, Ghorbanifar remained involved—despite that month failing yet another CIA polygraph. This time the Iranian lied on thirteen of the fifteen questions, while registering "inconclusive" on the other two, his name and birthplace.[32]

Over the next month, Poindexter and North arranged two shipments totaling one thousand TOW missiles to Iran. No more hostages were released. North was undeterred, perhaps in part because he had overcharged the Iranians so that, even after paying the middlemen, a $6.3 million profit remained. He still had his "neat idea" on how to use the money. In April, he and Poindexter put together the "diversion" scheme to route it secretly to the contras—who at the time were still barred by law from receiving weapons funded by the US government and were fast depleting their other accounts. North easily diverted the profits because over the past year he had already jerry-rigged a contra support contraption of secret Swiss accounts, shell companies, arms merchants, mercenaries, private airplanes, and multiple Central American officials. North's patchwork of contra funders included foreign governments, such as Saudi Arabia, Taiwan, and Israel; American conservative activists and philanthropists; and for good measure the sultan of Brunei. To implement his scheme, the renegade marine assembled a motley crew, which in one journalist's description included "a one-eyed tax preparer looking for adventure in the off-season. A haunted young man hoping to prove his manhood. A tarnished Air Force two-star. An ex-Iranian bagman. An outré fund-raiser who could persuade right-wing wahoos that by giving money they would stop hearing things that go bump in the night."[33] By this standard, adding a few million dollars to the mix from selling weapons to Iran was comparatively pedestrian.

Meanwhile the Iranians pocketed the TOW missiles and continued to string the White House along. A series of meetings in Frankfurt, Paris, and Washington, DC, between North, CIA and Israeli officials, and other figures connected to the Iranian government eventually led to an invitation brokered by Ghorbanifar for a senior American delegation to visit Tehran. Poindexter and North suggested McFarlane to lead it, and Reagan agreed. Despite McFarlane's earlier disillusionment, Poindexter and North had kept him updated at home via his secure email connection. Now rested and bored, McFarlane missed the action and still believed the elusive opening to Iran might be just around the corner.

On the morning of May 25, an Israeli 707 piloted by the CIA landed in Tehran. Out stepped McFarlane and his delegation, including North, retired CIA officer George Cave, NSC staffer Howard Teicher, and Nir. It was a bizarre picture. Traveling under fake Irish passports, the group bore gifts for their anticipated Iranian interlocutors, including six custom .357 Magnum pistols and a chocolate cake with a frosted key on top—to unlock a new "opening" in the United States–Iran relationship. The Americans realized something was amiss when no Iranian official was there to greet them. Instead, bemused members of the Islamic Revolutionary Guard Corps (IRGC) stationed at the airport—anti-American militants who protected the regime and sponsored terrorism throughout the region—ate the cake.

An hour later a flustered Ghorbanifar arrived, spewing excuses while escorting the delegation to the local Hilton hotel. The next three days unfolded in unrelenting frustration for McFarlane. Instead of meeting with senior Iranian leaders, he endured a parade of midlevel officials, associates of senior leaders, and other go-betweens. The Iranians showed no interest in strategic dialogue on the United States–Iran relationship, instead insisting on more weapons deliveries as a precondition for any further hostage releases. Then they added demands including Israel's withdrawing from the Golan Heights and releasing imprisoned Shia militants. Unbeknownst to McFarlane, parliamentary speaker Akbar Rafsanjani—a member of Ayatollah Khomeini's inner circle who later became Iran's president—was orchestrating the various interlocutors visiting the hotel. Rafsanjani's goal seems only to have been securing more weapons from the gullible Americans, and possibly some concessions from Israel too. McFarlane kept Reagan and

Poindexter apprised of the negotiations. At one point a deal seemed close in which the Americans would send a plane carrying more weapons at the same time the hostages were being turned over, but the Iranians balked and it came to naught.[34]

McFarlane and his delegation flew home demoralized and empty-handed. But he still clung to hope. The next day the group briefed Reagan in the Oval Office. While admitting that the mission had failed, McFarlane told Reagan, "The Iranians are moved by the opportunity to restore ties. . . . A lot may be possible. You have begun to open the door to these people." That did not console the president. A bitter Reagan lamented to his diary, "It seems the rug merchants said the Hisballah would only agree to 2 hostages. Bud told them to shove it, went to the airport and left for Tel Aviv. This was a heartbreaking disappointment for all of us."[35]

V

While Reagan was selling arms and extending diplomatic outreach to one terrorist-sponsoring Middle Eastern country, he was preparing to bomb another terrorist-sponsoring Middle Eastern country. Qadhafi's Libya had escalated its violence with a terrorist attack that killed twenty people at the Rome and Vienna airports two days after Christmas 1985. Five Americans were among the dead, including an eleven-year-old girl.

A few days later Reagan ordered all American companies to exit Libya, and cut off all travel and economic relations with the United States. To his diary he derided Qadhafi as the "mad clown."[36] Reagan ordered his team to begin developing additional means to increase the pressure on Qadhafi. Libya's extensive oil exports to Europe and Asia, and some two thousand Soviet military advisors in the country, constrained their options.

Meanwhile, ambassador to the Vatican William Wilson tried appeasement. In a comically irresponsible act of rogue diplomacy, just before the Rome and Vienna attacks, Wilson had secretly traveled to Tripoli to meet with Qadhafi and recommended "an increase of commercial exchanges leading eventually to better relations" with the United States. Qadhafi, no doubt wary of this peculiar envoy, demurred. After the airport attacks, Wilson then pitched the prime minister of Malta (who enjoyed close relations with Qadhafi) on mediating between the United States and Libya "in direct diplomatic action to ease the tension and possibly to defuse the very dangerous situation that was unfolding." Wilson also tried to send messages to Qadhafi, through the Italian foreign minister, disavowing Reagan's denunciations of the Libyan leader and urging a rapprochement between the United States and Libya. Neither Reagan nor Shultz knew about Wilson's freelancing. When Shultz found out, he was predictably livid. Reagan was unhappy too. The president, though reluctant to dismiss errant envoys and fond of Wilson as a longtime personal friend, agreed with Shultz he should have Wilson resign.[37]

While Wilson tried to woo Qadhafi, Casey and Poindexter led an effort—approved by Reagan—to overthrow him. A few months earlier, Reagan had signed a finding launching a covert action, Operation Tulip, for the CIA to support Libyan exiles training in Algeria, Egypt, and Iraq to filter back into Libya and foment an insurrection against the tyrant. Casey and Poindexter also developed a more fanciful scheme that called for Egypt, backed by US airpower, to invade Libya and depose Qadhafi. It is not clear whether Reagan signed this finding as well, especially since Weinberger and Shultz (understandably) opposed it. As did Egyptian president Mubarak. When Poindexter had traveled to Egypt the previous September to sell it to Mubarak, the Egyptian leader rebuffed him, saying, "Look, Admiral, when we decide to attack Libya, it will be our decision and on our timetable." However, after the Rome and Vienna airport terrorism, Reagan quietly increased support for the Libyan exiles—a decision that became much less quiet when it was leaked and published on the front page of *The Washington Post*.[38]

In March, Reagan ordered the Sixth Fleet to escalate pressure on Qadhafi with another freedom-of-navigation operation in the Gulf of Sidra. The blustery Libyan leader declared his Mediterranean Sea claim "the line of death" and threatened to attack any American ships or planes that transgressed it. Which was exactly what the White House hoped to provoke. When the Sixth Fleet forces crossed the line by sea and air, Qadhafi ordered retaliation from surface-to-air missiles and Libyan navy patrol boats. The navy quickly destroyed the missile launchers and sank the boats.[39]

The next week a bomb tore through a West Berlin disco, killing one American soldier and injuring seventy-eight others, as well as over one hundred civilians. Qadhafi had struck back. British intelligence shared with the White House electronic intercepts of Libyan terrorists bragging to Qadhafi of their plans to bomb the disco at his behest. The NSA had also detected messages from Qadhafi activating other Libyan terrorist cells in

Europe against American targets. The East German Stasi approved in advance the Berlin disco plot.[40]

With this proof of Qadhafi's guilt, Reagan decided to retaliate. It would be the first significant military action he took against terrorism. US Air Force F-111 bombers would hit three targets in Tripoli, including Qadhafi's compound and a terrorist training camp, while navy A-6 jets from Sixth Fleet aircraft carriers would attack an airfield and troop barracks in Benghazi. Counting tankers, communications, backup, and air defense suppression, a sizable armada of around one hundred American aircraft would carry out the mission.

Reagan asked Thatcher for permission to launch from UK air bases. The Iron Lady waffled. British public opinion overwhelmingly opposed the use of force, and Thatcher herself felt discomfort over retaliatory strikes. Reagan wrote her a second appeal, in unusually blunt language: "You should not underestimate the profound effect on the American people if our actions to put a halt to these crimes continue to receive lukewarm support or no support at all from our closest allies whom we have committed ourselves to defend." His words convicted the British leader, who underlined them. After a sleepless night, Thatcher rose early and told a close aide her decision: "We have to support the Americans on this. That's what allies are for."[41] She told Reagan that the F-111s could take off from Royal Air Force base Lakenheath for the raid.

Paris proved a different story. The most direct route from the UK to Libya traversed France, and Reagan made a personal appeal to Mitterrand to grant overflight rights to the American bombers. Describing the proof of Libyan authorship of the bombing and pleading, "American tourists, servicemen, and diplomats are being brutally murdered by terrorists in Europe," Reagan concluded, "The United States feels a special responsibility because we are in a position to act decisively. I need your support to make this possible."[42] Mitterrand refused. He was coy about his reasons, but they seem to have included public sentiment against an attack, French reliance on Libyan oil, worry over making France a target for more terrorism—and his lingering resentment against Reagan for failing to join the French airstrikes in 1983 after the Beirut barracks bombings.[43] Spain also denied overflight rights. The F-111s had to fly around the perimeter of Europe and enter Libya from the west. They would be airborne thirteen hours with four inflight refuelings, a grueling and risky mission.

The attack took Libya by surprise. Swooping in two hundred feet above the desert floor, their terrain-hugging radar guiding them through the darkness, the American planes arrived on target simultaneously. The Tripoli and Benghazi night skies blazed in a cacophony of light, heat, and explosions as American bombs and Libyan antiaircraft fire and surface-to-air missiles all erupted at once. The operational results were mixed. Some bombs hit their targets, others missed, and still other planes had to abort due to equipment failures. Bombs landed inside Qadhafi's compound, destroying some structures but just missing his main building. It remains unknown if he was there at the time or not. Though this was not a targeted assassination attempt, the White House would have felt no regret if Qadhafi had died. All American planes returned safely but one, an F-111 shot down by Libyan air defenses, killing both crewmen.[44]

Strategically, Operation El Dorado Canyon succeeded. The attack put enough of a scare into Qadhafi that he curtailed planning for over thirty terrorist plots under way against American targets in Europe.[45] Many European leaders and editorial pages at first fulminated against the American raid, but then European governments quietly began arresting or expelling more than one hundred Libyan intelligence officers masquerading as diplomats and businessmen. Japan and several Arab countries also reined in or kicked out Libyan operatives in their countries. Not all applauded Reagan's strike. The Kremlin denounced the American attack on their sometime client state, and Shevardnadze canceled his upcoming meeting with Shultz.[46] Three months after the raid, in an article titled "Bombing Gadhafi Worked," *The Washington Post*'s David Ignatius wrote that it "broke the psychology that had allowed Gadhafi to intimidate much of the world and revealed that, far from being an international giant, Gadhafi was weak, isolated and vulnerable. . . . The raid hasn't halted Libyan terrorism, but it certainly has curbed it."[47] Qadhafi, fearing a potential uprising, relocated to a tent compound in the desert.[48]

What explains the difference between Reagan's aggressive response to Libyan terrorism and his simultaneous conciliatory gestures to Iran? Three factors seem paramount. First, a close partner nation, Israel, persistently urged the Iran outreach, whereas Israel held no brief for Qadhafi. Second, three of Reagan's top aides—McFarlane, Casey, and Poindexter—were the three biggest enthusiasts for the Iran outreach, while also being hard-liners on Libya. Third, and most decisive, were the American hostages. Tormented by their plight, Reagan would have tried almost anything to bring them home—including violating his own policies by selling arms to the nation that sponsored their captors.

VI

At the same time that Reagan wrestled with the challenge posed by adversary states Iran and Libya, he encountered a different manner of test from an ally. After the Filipino ruler Ferdinand Marcos had agreed to American demands that he hold a nationwide election, Corazon Aquino ran as his main opponent, with enthusiastic backing from Cardinal Sin and the Philippines' burgeoning People Power democracy movement. Marcos wrote Reagan promising "free, honest, fair, and democratic elections," and audaciously invited Reagan to send election observers or even come visit himself. The embattled dictator remained confident he would win.[49] The reason for his confidence became clear on Election Day, February 7. When the Filipino people cast their ballots, they soon found that—contrary to Marcos's pledge to Reagan—the election was coerced, dishonest, unfair, and autocratic. Marcos engineered a scheme to steal it. The bipartisan American observer delegation, led by Senator Richard Lugar and Congressman Jack Murtha, reported widespread fraud and disputed Marcos's declaration of victory. Lugar and Murtha believed that Aquino actually received between 60 and 70 percent of the vote, an overwhelming win. People Power protests soon consumed the Philippines, as Cardinal Sin and other Catholic leaders led millions of Aquino supporters in peaceful protests calling for Marcos to step aside.[50]

As the protests continued to escalate and Marcos faced growing American pressure to concede defeat, Gorbachev mischievously intervened. He issued a statement congratulating *Marcos* on his victory, making the Soviet Union the only nation in the world to recognize the Filipino dictator. It was a cynical ploy to split Manila from Washington. Meanwhile, Reagan, loyal sometimes to a fault, was not eager to see Marcos ejected from office. At a press conference, the president made the ham-handed claim that "both sides" were guilty of election fraud, and made it seem that the United States cared only about access to its military bases.[51]

Shultz reminded Reagan that America's alliance was with the Philippines as a nation, not its ruler, and that a strongman who loses his people also loses his strength. Reagan agreed but remained concerned, in the words of Gaston Sigur, "that the United States would not in any way be a contributor to bloodshed." The president redoubled his warnings to Marcos not to use force against the protestors. It was a difficult balance. As Wolfowitz told a British diplomat, American policy entailed "trying to let legitimate Philippine political processes take their own course, while acting discreetly to strengthen positive developments." Wolfowitz pointed out that the most successful democratic transitions take place with American support but not intervention, adding wryly, "Our own record of success in dismantling regimes and setting up successor governments is not a good one."[52]

The crisis accelerated when Marcos's defense minister and one of his top generals turned against him. Their coup effort failed, but it showed his slipping grip on power. Reagan now realized that Marcos needed to go. He wrote to the beleaguered dictator urging him to step aside and avoid any violence. Reagan also dispatched Sigur to Tokyo to coordinate with Nakasone. While some senior Japanese officials wanted Marcos to stay in power, Nakasone sided with Reagan and told the Diet that Japan supported a democratic transition in the Philippines—a powerful signal from a nation that was still at the time the only Asian democracy.[53]

Panicked, the Marcoses grasped for any lifeline they could find. The dictatress phoned Nancy Reagan, and the desperate dictator called Paul Laxalt. The First Lady and the senator both consulted with Reagan and then reinforced his message to the duo. As Laxalt told Marcos: "Cut and cut cleanly. The time has come." On February 25, a US Air Force transport plane ferried Marcos and his family from Clark Air Base to exile in Hawaii. The United States became the first country in the world to recognize Cory Aquino as the new president of the Philippines.[54]

On the same day as the Filipino elections, a US Air Force plane flew Haitian dictator "Baby Doc" Duvalier and his family to France. It was a similar story. With Reagan's support, Shultz and Elliott Abrams had conditioned American economic aid on democratic reform and leaned hard on Duvalier—whose brutality was exceeded only by his corruption—to step down, while striking a deal with France to take him into exile. Shultz later called it the end of the era "of unquestioning American support for right-wing dictators who are pro-US and anti-Communist but otherwise odious."[55] Marcos and Duvalier would not be the only despots to be toppled by a combination of popular uprisings and American pressure. Taiwan's Chiang Ching-kuo, South Korea's Chun Doo-Hwan, and Chile's Augusto Pinochet, among others, all took unhappy notice of Marcos's fate. In a democratic version of the domino theory, autocrats were beginning to tumble, one by one.

VII

Shultz illumined these trends of the emerging information age and eco-nomic liberty in a speech the next month in Paris. Heralding innovations such as personal computers, videocassette recorders, and robotics, he con-nected them to the Cold War's battle of ideas:

> The technological and economic successes of the entire free world are direct consequences and incontrovertible proof of the benefits that flow from self-government. The more the West dedicates itself to its freedoms, the stronger it becomes—both politically, as an attractive and viable alternative to statism, and economically, as a dynamic and expanding system of material productivity that brings benefits on a mass scale. . . . [Soviet bloc] regimes face an agonizing choice: they can either open their societies to the freedoms necessary for the pursuit of technological advance, or they can risk falling even farther behind the West.

Optimist though he was, Shultz closed with a warning against protec-tionist sentiments in the West: "None of the opportunities before us will bear fruit unless the free nations can agree to open rather than restrictive trade in these revolutionary products and services."[56]

Brian Mulroney agreed. Just three days earlier, the Canadian prime minister had returned to the White House. Besides his personal rapport with Reagan, geography also bound their countries—not just a shared bor-der but shared oceans. Canada and the United States were both Atlantic and Pacific nations, fellow NATO members who also together looked west to deepen their engagement with Asia. They discussed Reagan's long-standing vision of a North American accord. While statist Mexico remained unen-thused, Canada was eager, and completing the United States–Canada trade agreement would be a promising start.

Mulroney and Reagan continued to puzzle over Gorbachev. Reflecting on their respective meetings with the Soviet leader, they lamented, in Mul-roney's words, Gorbachev's "misperceptions of Western society" and that "he really seems to believe Soviet propaganda." Reagan agreed that Gor-bachev "remains a dedicated communist" but noted, "He may just be the first Soviet leader to really see the need for a reduction of tensions." The president then described his hope to bring Gorbachev to the United States so that he could see "how the American worker really lived," in freedom and prosperity. Reagan also reiterated his desire "to get the General Secretary alone, without translators," to find out whether Gorbachev might secretly believe in God—and persuade him to do so if he did not.[57]

Reagan would see Mulroney again just a few weeks later in Tokyo for the G7 summit. As Air Force One flew west across the Pacific, the strategic triangles of Reagan's Asia policy seemed in alignment. Japan, the key leg of the most important triangles, had just increased its defense budget again and was bearing ever more of the security burden in northeast Asia. Nakasone would soon announce, as he had already told Reagan, that Japan would participate in SDI research—further rattling a Kremlin already fearful of the American and Japanese edge in technology.[58] The US-Japan-China and US–Japan–South Korea triangles both kept their equipoise as Tokyo continued to improve its ties with Beijing and Seoul. All three nations partnered with the United States against the Kremlin, giving the United States and China an edge in their competitive triangle with the Soviet Union. Reagan balanced the US-China-Taiwan triangle by deepening defense cooperation with Beijing "as a deterrent to Soviet expansionism" while maintaining arms sales to Taiwan. Not that Deng Xiaoping gave up his ambitions to reclaim the island. Fresh off bamboozling the British into signing a treaty affirming Hong Kong's democracy that the CCP had no intention of honoring, Deng tried to entice Washington into a similar "one country, two systems" deal for Taiwan. Shultz and Wolfowitz refused to countenance such a betrayal and rebuffed Beijing's lobbying. Reagan also called up Bill Clark from retirement to lead a successful effort to preserve Taiwan's membership in the Asian Development Bank, against Beijing's campaign to expel the island nation.[59]

After the G7, Reagan returned to Washington while Shultz journeyed on to Seoul. The secretary arrived in a South Korea churning with democratic ferment. In equal parts inspired by the success of the People Power revolution in the Philippines and angered with Chun's repression and slow-walking on reforms, student activists launched another round of protests in several major cities. Some turned violent, as protestors hurled Molotov cocktails and bricks, and police responded in force. It posed a precarious balancing act for the Reagan administration: how to support South Korea as an anticommunist ally, prevent violence in either government repression or political revolution, and encourage a peaceful transition to democracy?

Shultz handed Chun a letter from Reagan reminding the Korean leader of his commitment to step down and affirming "the democratic institutions and traditions that all Koreans desire." At a press conference, Shultz denounced violence and urged embracing democracy "in a stable and orderly way." This drew wrath from all sides. Opposition leaders, angered that Shultz did not jettison Chun or show more urgency for their cause, declaimed their "burning resentment" at his "obtuseness on the desperate political needs in Korea," while Chun and his lieutenants seethed at the secretary's public support for democracy.[60]

VIII

At 1:24 A.M. on April 26, 1986, a blast equivalent to sixty tons of TNT jarred awake the residents of the Soviet town of Pripyat in northern Ukraine. A botched test had exploded a reactor at the Chernobyl nuclear power plant. The detonation sent seven tons of uranium fuel and deadly gases—"among the most dangerous substances known to man" in the words of an authoritative account—into the night sky. It ignited a fire in the reactor core that would burn out of control for nine more days, fueling toxic radiation clouds that would soon reach Western Europe and Asia, in amounts much greater than what was emitted by the atomic bomb dropped on Hiroshima. The blast and subsequent exposure forced the removal of 336,000 Soviets and killed at least 30 of them; the true death toll in the months and years ahead would be impossible to determine but much higher. The worst nuclear power crisis in history soon mushroomed into a crisis of credibility for the Soviet system.[61]

Chernobyl displayed the Soviet edifice of deceit. Local authorities hid it from Moscow. The Kremlin, upon learning the scope of the disaster, withheld it from the Soviet people. The Politburo lied to the world. KGB chief Viktor Chebrikov boasted to the Party Central Committee that he had launched "measures to control the activities of foreign diplomats and correspondents, limit their ability to gather information on the accident at the Chernobyl nuclear power plant, and foil attempts to use it for stoking the anti-Soviet propaganda campaign in the West." KGB operatives followed up with an extensive "active measures" campaign to deceive and harass Western journalists while planting false stories and using credulous front groups to deflect Kremlin responsibility.[62]

A CIA report alerted Reagan to the explosion while he was in Hawaii on the first leg of his Asia trip. He immediately sent Gorbachev an offer of humanitarian and technical aid, including a team of American nuclear energy experts who could help contain the burning reactor.[63] The Soviet leader refused any American help. As the fire raged and fallout dispersed through the atmosphere, it caused radioactive rain to fall in Tokyo on May 4, the same day that Reagan and his G7 counterparts assembled for their summit. For Reagan it highlighted the stakes in the Cold War. In his radio address from Tokyo, he described "the contrast between the leaders of free nations meeting at the summit to deal openly with common concerns and the Soviet Government, with its secrecy and stubborn refusal to inform the international community of the common danger from this disaster." He and Thatcher shared these concerns in their private summit meeting. "Gorbachev has been a public relations star," Thatcher observed, "but this accident has shown his true Soviet colors."[64]

Reagan and Thatcher's frustration was understandable, but Gorbachev actually felt more besieged than defiant and doctrinaire. His government had been shamed in the eyes of the world, provoked anger across the entire Eurasian landmass, and failed to even tell him the truth. Biographer William Taubman concludes that the disaster "marked a turning point for Gorbachev and the Soviet regime. . . . For the flaws revealed at Chernobyl and afterward were characteristic of the system as a whole: rampant incompetence, cover-ups at all levels, and self-destructive secrecy at the top."[65] Chernobyl also fueled Gorbachev's growing distrust of nuclear weapons. He later observed that within just one missile there "lurked a hundred Chernobyls."[66]

Reagan remained eager to partner with Gorbachev to eliminate such weapons yet unrelenting in his pressure. That same month, Reagan faced anew the annual decision on whether the United States would continue to adhere voluntarily to the SALT II weapons limits, known as "interim restraint." The year before, he had affirmed interim restraint for another twelve months. Now Reagan felt irked by Soviet transgressions of arms control agreements and Gorbachev's failure to respond to the American counterproposals or even set a summit date. Among his advisors, only Shultz and Nitze favored continuing interim restraint, to hold the political high ground and maintain alliance solidarity. Weinberger, Poindexter, Casey, JCS chairman Crowe, and Adelman all opposed it. Adelman argued, "[While] the Allies will be squeamish, they need leadership. The man on the street will understand." Reagan agreed and decided to jettison interim restraint. He did so in part as a political message to the Kremlin that American good faith would not continue alongside Soviet violations, and in part to continue his military expansion—specifically deploying more state-of-the-art Trident ballistic missile submarines and air-launched cruise missiles (ALCMs) on B-52 bombers, both to offset the Soviet edge in ICBMs.[67]

The allies blanched at Reagan's announcement. Thatcher complained that Reagan had "hand[ed] Gorbachev an enormous propaganda advantage just at the moment when he [was] on the defensive over Chernobyl" and "put the United States rather than the Soviet Union in the wrong." The next day, Shultz met with his NATO counterparts in Halifax and reported back to Reagan, "The Allies are deeply disturbed. Every single minister at Halifax opposed our interim restraint decision."[68] Reagan was willing to endure allied grousing. Frustrated at Gorbachev's unresponsiveness, he wanted to pressure the Soviets back to the negotiating table. This did not mean stopping his outreach. Reagan sent another letter to Gorbachev reiterating his hope to meet and told his advisors, "Chernobyl has altered Gorbachev's outlook on the dangers of nuclear war. The time is right for something dramatic." As the White House puzzled over the Kremlin's reticence, Shultz speculated to Reagan that Gorbachev was "play[ing] for time," tempted "to wait out your presidency and hope that your successor will be less resolute or less popular, and thus be less able to drive a tough bargain." For his part, Gorbachev replied to Reagan's letter with a lengthy screed blaming the United States for the impasse, and castigating the attack on Libya and the abandonment of SALT II constraints as "extremely negative, dangerous" decisions.[69]

A French socialist and a disgraced Republican helped change Gorbachev's mind. For the July 4 holiday, Reagan welcomed François Mitterrand to New York City for the centennial of France's gift of the Statue of Liberty. Knowing that the French president would journey next to Moscow, Reagan detailed for Mitterrand his arms reduction proposals to Gorbachev and his genuine desire to strike a deal with the Soviet leader.[70] A few days later at the Kremlin, Mitterrand beseeched Gorbachev to see that, contrary to Marxist dogma and Gorbachev's accusations, Reagan was not captive to the "US military-industrial complex" and really desired to end the arms race. Mitterrand assured Gorbachev, "Unlike many other American politicians, Reagan is not an automaton. He is a human being."[71]

The next week, Richard Nixon arrived in Moscow. Mindful that Reagan feared Gorbachev might be trying to wait out the American president's term, the shrewd Nixon turned the political calendar around and appealed to history and destiny. Nixon pointed out to Gorbachev that he and Reagan "were both enormously popular and strong leaders of the world's two strongest countries" and told him, "That confluence of circumstances might not occur again for years to come. . . . More than any two post-war leaders of the Soviet Union and United States, you and President Reagan have the unique opportunity to make progress toward reducing that awesome danger [of nuclear war]." "This is the time," Nixon urged, to meet and strike a deal.[72]

Taken together, Mitterrand and Nixon's appeals persuaded Gorbachev to reconsider Reagan. The next week, when another letter from Reagan arrived at the Kremlin, Gorbachev read it with fresh eyes. Reagan made a series of proposals that reset the strategic agenda. Rejecting the previous stalemate in which Gorbachev had conditioned reductions in offensive arms on the United States' relinquishing SDI, Reagan instead proposed that the United States and USSR both pursue research on defensive systems. They would do so in tandem with an agreement for each side to share its successful system with the other while also eliminating "the offensive ballistic missiles of *both* sides." As an intermediate step, Reagan also reiterated his long-standing zero-zero proposal to eliminate all INF. To leave no doubt about his intentions, Reagan repeated three times in the letter his ultimate goal of the "total elimination of all nuclear weapons."[73]

Once again, Reagan had seized the initiative. In short, Gorbachev had called for first rejecting SDI and then eliminating offensive weapons. Reagan flipped this to a new position: First embrace SDI, and at the same time eliminate offensive weapons. For four decades the Cold War arms race had been about both sides competing to be able to destroy each other. Reagan proposed to start a new race in which both sides competed to protect themselves—and shared that protection with each other.

During his August vacation in Crimea, Gorbachev told his top aide, Anatoly Chernyaev, to draft a reply letter to Reagan proposing to meet in late September or early October in London or Reykjavík. When Chernyaev asked why the remote Icelandic capital, Gorbachev replied, "It's a good idea. Halfway between us and them, and none of the big powers will be offended."[74]

Just when Moscow and Washington began moving toward a summit, two arrests derailed the progress. On August 23 in New York, the FBI detained a UN official and Soviet citizen, Gennadi Zakharov, for attempting to steal American defense technology. One week later, the KGB nabbed *U.S. News & World Report* bureau chief Nicholas Daniloff from a Moscow street and accused the journalist of working for the CIA. The Kremlin made clear that it saw Daniloff as a hostage to be exchanged for Zakharov.

The Washington political and media class erupted. In treating an American journalist as equivalent to a Soviet spy, the KGB had demolished one of the Cold War's unwritten rules of espionage. Now that one of their own was in peril, even journalists not normally hawkish toward the Soviet Union or favorable to Reagan demanded that the president take a hard line for press freedom. Reagan, also irate, wrote Gorbachev with his "personal assurance that Mr. Daniloff has no connection whatever with the US Government" and demanded Daniloff's release. Gorbachev replied two days later asserting that Daniloff "had for a long time been engaged in impermissible activities damaging to the state interests of the USSR."[75]

Reagan did not know when he sent the letter that Daniloff actually did have a connection to the CIA, albeit an oblique one. Twice during the previous five years, mysterious envelopes had been given to Daniloff addressed to the US government. Daniloff had turned them over to the US embassy, where the CIA station determined that the envelopes contained top secret documents on Soviet ballistic missiles of very high intelligence value. Paul Stombaugh, the CIA case officer later expelled by the KGB in the Tolkachev case, had contacted a possible Russian source of the documents and in doing so had identified Daniloff as the intermediary—despite strict CIA policy against ever using journalists. The KGB had sent the documents to Daniloff as bait in a slow-developing trap, and the contact Stombaugh approached worked for the KGB. Now the KGB had what it needed: a journalist who had passed classified Soviet documents to American officials, and both a letter and phone call recording from the CIA naming Daniloff. From there, the KGB had waited for an opportune time to spring the trap, when Daniloff's hostage value would be at a premium. Zakharov's arrest in August 1986 was that moment. It was patient, devious tradecraft.[76]

After Reagan wrote Gorbachev, a sheepish Casey confessed to Reagan and Shultz how the CIA's bungling had exposed Daniloff to arrest. This did not change the truth of Reagan's protest that Daniloff was not a spy nor employed by the US government, but Reagan and Shultz now realized their dilemma. The Kremlin's trap had created evidence that could convict Daniloff of espionage, yet the White House could not reveal anything to the public about the CIA's role in the reporter's plight. This left the White House with limited leverage to negotiate with the Soviets for Daniloff's release, while facing a firestorm of domestic outrage for not taking a tougher line with the Kremlin over this cruel abuse of media freedom.[77]

To show the Kremlin his disfavor, Reagan expelled back to Moscow another twenty-five KGB officers masquerading as UN diplomats. He then authorized Shultz to negotiate with the Soviets to release Daniloff, with guidance that Zakharov could be returned to Moscow as well, but not in an explicit one-for-one trade, lest the United States seem to accept the equivalence between a journalist and a spy.

In the midst of this crisis, Reagan and Shultz did not halt their discussions with Moscow on other issues, especially the possible summit. The secretary brought Soviet foreign minister Shevardnadze into the Oval Office to deliver Gorbachev's invitation to meet in Reykjavík. Reagan accepted but recorded in his diary, "[I] made it plain we wanted Daniloff returned to us before anything took place. I let the F.M. know I was angry and that I resented their charges that Daniloff was a spy after I had personally given my word that he wasn't." Shultz had rarely seen the president in such controlled fury: "I knew Ronald Reagan was an accomplished actor, but this was no act."[78]

Now that Reagan had conditioned meeting with Gorbachev on Daniloff's release, the negotiations accelerated. Over the next two weeks, Shultz orchestrated an elaborate deal that entailed the Kremlin's releasing Daniloff and also freeing the imprisoned dissident Yuri Orlov, while the United States remanded Zakharov back to Moscow. All things considered, it was the best feasible outcome, but conservatives still savaged Reagan for caving to the Kremlin. William Safire called it "this generation's Yalta." George Will, though a personal friend of the Reagans, skewered the president: "Having paid ransom to the hostage-taker, the administration is traveling to Iceland as a payment to get Gorbachev to do what he said at the Geneva summit he would do."[79]

IX

In the midst of its negotiations with the Kremlin over Daniloff, the White House also wrangled with Congress over South Africa. It was a mess largely of the administration's own making. Over the past year, furor over Pretoria's growing repression and the evil of apartheid had consumed Congress and fueled many activists. Regional tensions worsened as Soviet and Cuban support for the Angolan regime increased, South Africa reacted with more support for anticommunist militias in the region, and militants affiliated with the African National Congress launched a spate of terrorist attacks. The Reagan administration faced the additional challenge of South Africa's secret nuclear weapons program and growing risks of further proliferation. Worried that Pretoria was developing a small nuclear arsenal, the White House increased pressure on the Botha regime to abandon its efforts and sign the Nuclear Non-Proliferation Treaty.[80]

Poindexter, who cared little about either political sensitivities or Africa, outsourced much of the White House's work on the apartheid issue to Chief of Staff Don Regan and Communications Director Pat Buchanan, the latter of whom trafficked with an odious network of white supremacists and apartheid supporters. A fierce interagency feud erupted, pitting Shultz and Chester Crocker, who favored combining pressure on Pretoria with diplomatic inducements to end apartheid, against Buchanan, Poindexter, and Casey, who argued for embracing the South African regime as an anticommunist ally. An ambivalent and distracted Reagan avoided the conflict instead of resolving it. Ironically, for all of its internal divisions, the administration remained united in opposition to broad-based sanctions. Reagan, Shultz, and Crocker believed that sanctions primarily hurt Black South Africans and constrained diplomatic options. As Reagan complained to his diary, "[Sanctions mean] we'd have no contact or ability to help rid them of apartheid."[81] Meanwhile, Buchanan and his compatriots opposed sanctions for the opposite reason: They could undermine the apartheid government.

In some ways the sanctions debate began trailing new realities in practice. Many American companies, under pressure from consumers and activists, began voluntarily exiting South Africa anyway. Meanwhile the Senate and the House, frustrated with White House dithering and outraged at South Africa's continuing intransigence and escalating racial oppression, in September passed new sanctions legislation by overwhelming bipartisan majorities. Shultz and Crocker encouraged Reagan to veto it, but only if accompanied by further strong executive actions to increase pressure on South Africa. Instead the conniving Buchanan carried the day, as he persuaded Reagan to issue a peremptory veto statement without any new policy measures. Reagan's diary reveals his focus was elsewhere during this time, with each day's entry focused on the Daniloff negotiations and no mention of his half-hearted veto until Congress overrode it; "I expected that," he noted drily.[82]

It was another unforced error, squandering moral and political capital while gaining nothing. Less noticed was Reagan's appointment soon after of Edward Perkins as the first Black American ambassador to South Africa, who would serve with distinction in helping usher in momentous changes. Meanwhile, the congressional sanctions began squeezing Pretoria and creating new opportunities for diplomacy that Shultz and Crocker would exploit the next year.[83]

X

———————

Reagan and Gorbachev scheduled their Reykjavík meeting for October 11–12. Normally, a superpower summit took at least six months of advance staff work in pre-negotiating agreements and protocols. Reykjavík instead would come together in less than three weeks; Reagan and Gorbachev would do the negotiating themselves.

Concern mounted among experts and pundits that Reagan was walking into an Icelandic trap set by the Kremlin. Zbigniew Brzezinski derided it as "a joke," sneering, "A summit on two weeks' notice? Without an agenda?" Henry Kissinger penned a *Newsweek* cover story warning that its haste meant a "grave risk of failure" because of "a quest for agreements almost for their own sake" and "defining progress by what the Soviets have said they would accept."[84] Even Reagan's own staff worried that their president was endangered. NSC staffer Steve Sestanovich wrote to Poindexter, "The early date of the next meeting may imply that the Soviets can extract some concessions."[85]

Gorbachev did plan to offer some bold initiatives, but they would largely mirror previous proposals made by Reagan, including the agenda Reagan set in his July letter to the Soviet leader. For example, just before the trip, Gorbachev told the Politburo he was now ready to embrace the zero-zero option on INF: "We want Europe to be completely free of these weapons because the Pershing II missiles are like a pistol held to our head." Which was exactly what Reagan had intended; that display of force would soon lead to a diplomatic breakthrough. Gorbachev also felt desperate to stop the overall arms race. With remarkable candor, he told his staff that if he could not relieve American military pressure on Soviet defense spending, "we will be pulled into an arms race beyond our power, and we will lose this race . . . the pressure on our economy will be inconceivable." Gorbachev feared that Japan and West Germany, the Soviet Union's World War II foes turned American allies, would further tighten the vise by increasing their defense spending on advanced weapons platforms.[86]

Such was the trap Reagan had set for the Kremlin. He had reaffirmed it in September when he issued a new National Security Decision Directive, NSDD-238, to update NSDD-32 from four years earlier. It recounted the goals of working with allies to "foster restraint in Soviet military spending, discourage Soviet adventurism, and weaken the Soviet alliance system by forcing the USSR to bear the brunt of its economic shortcomings, and to encourage long-term liberalizing and nationalist tendencies within the Soviet Union and allied countries." This meant "US military systems which particularly stress Soviet defenses, or require a disproportionate expenditure of Soviet resources to counter, represent an especially attractive investment."[87]

Before his trip, Reagan welcomed Suzanne Massie back to the White House for another lunch briefing. It was their third meeting since May. With his penchant for biblical prophecy, Reagan was intrigued to learn from her that *chernobyl* means "wormwood" in Ukrainian, which the Book of Revelation describes as a source of bitterness and death in the end of days. Her description of widespread shortages and public despair confirmed Shultz and Reagan's sense that "the Soviet Union was on the road to collapse."[88] Now Massie taught Reagan a Russian proverb: "*Doveryai no proveryai*"— "Trust, but verify"—and encouraged him to invoke it with Gorbachev. The enthused president committed the Russian phrase to memory.[89]

Though nuclear arms would be the main issue, Reagan and Shultz made clear they would not neglect human rights. NSDD-238 declared, "The underlying competition between the United States and the Soviet Union is in the realm of ideas and values. . . . The greatest threat to the Soviet system . . . is the concept of freedom itself."[90] Reagan wanted to accelerate that threat. Earlier in the year he had welcomed Anatoly Shcharansky to the White House, and the dissident had described how Reagan's advocacy emboldened prisoners of conscience. Reagan wrote in his diary, "I learned that I'm a hero in the Soviet Gulag. The prisoners read the attacks on me in TASS and Pravda and learn what I'm saying about the Soviets and they like me."[91] As a goodwill gesture on the eve of Reykjavík, the Kremlin released additional prisoners of conscience, including two Jewish refuseniks and the Christian poet Irina Ratushinskaya.[92]

This was a start but not enough. The day before flying to Reykjavík, Shultz told an audience of Jewish leaders, "Our message to the Soviets is simple: Token gestures for short-term lowering of barriers will not suffice. What the American people want to see is a genuine and lasting improvement in the situation of Soviet Jews." The same day, Reagan met with the just-released Orlov at the White House and told a group of human rights activists, "I will make it amply clear to Mr. Gorbachev that unless there is real Soviet movement on human rights, we will not have the kind of political atmosphere necessary to make lasting progress on other issues."[93] This was not a formal readoption of linkage. Rather it was a signal to Gorbachev that, as with the Siberian Pentecostals four years earlier, Reagan would assess the Kremlin's trustworthiness based in part on its treatment of political and religious dissidents.

XI

When Reagan landed at Iceland's Keflavík Airport, he beheld, in the words of a UPI dispatch, "one of the strangest places on Earth—a windblown, volcanic moonscape populated by sheep, ponies, elves, pagan gods and 241,000 bookish descendants of the Vikings." It was a surreal setting for what would be the Cold War's most surreal summit. Reagan's meetings with Gorbachev would take place on an isolated stretch of Atlantic waterfront in Höfði House, an eerie mansion alleged to be haunted. When asked about such spectral inhabitants on the eve of the summit, the Icelandic Foreign Ministry spokesman replied, "We do not confirm nor deny that the Höfði has a ghost."[94]

Diplomatic protocol had Reagan host the first meeting. As in Geneva, he and Gorbachev would start with a one-on-one session before being joined by their respective foreign ministers. Though they had not seen each other in eleven months, Reagan and Gorbachev just resumed where they left off. Knowing that most of their time would be devoted to nuclear weapons, Reagan made sure to tie human rights to arms control, stressing the issue's personal importance to him and to the American people. "It is easier for the US to reach agreements with the USSR if public opinion is not aroused" by human rights abuses, stressed Reagan.[95]

Turning to arms control, at first the two leaders trod familiar ground, repeating many points that they had traded in Geneva. Reagan reminded Gorbachev of US concerns about Soviet compliance with past agreements and quoted in Russian the phrase Massie had given him: "Trust but verify." Verification provisions would be as important as the agreements themselves, Reagan said. After an hour, Shultz and Shevardnadze joined them, and the discussion continued. As their session drew to a close, Gorbachev presented the Soviet arms control proposals for Reagan to consider. The paper described more or less the same offers that the Soviet leader had made nine months earlier in January. They broke for lunch, each leader to consult with his respective advisors before their afternoon session.

After lunch, something changed. Reagan began the afternoon session by detailing his responses to Gorbachev's proposals. The Kremlin continued to link ending SDI with steep cuts in offensive weapons. Reagan deftly shifted the terms of the negotiation. He both embraced and reversed Gorbachev's proposals. Yes, let's agree to these cuts in offensive weapons, Reagan exclaimed, but let's do it *in tandem with SDI, not instead of SDI*. He reminded Gorbachev of his new strategic concept to shift the Cold War arms race from an offensive to a defensive balance.

Desperate to shoot down SDI, Gorbachev retreated to the ABM Treaty, demanding that Reagan commit to upholding it within the narrow interpretation that would allegedly restrict SDI. Reagan countered by reminding Gorbachev of the repeated Soviet violations of the ABM Treaty and the American view that research on SDI would not violate it. As ACDA director Ken Adelman recalls, "Here ironies abounded. Reagan was pledging to uphold a treaty he clearly despised—'This is not civilized!'—while Gorbachev was pledging to strengthen a treaty he was clearly violating."[96]

This did not prevent them from finding common ground. Line by line, Reagan went through each specific item on the Soviet list—many of which mirrored proposals Reagan himself had first made—and pushed for action. Again and again, he pressed Gorbachev, "Let's agree to this now," on INF cuts, on cutting short-range missiles, on verification measures.

It was an extraordinary moment. In each past Cold War summit for the previous four decades, the US and Soviet leaders had tried to preserve every possible edge for themselves, reluctantly negotiating restraints in armaments only where it seemed the other side could be equally limited. Now the restraints came off as Reagan and Gorbachev sprinted to outdo each other in propositions to slash their own nuclear arsenals. The race to build arms now became a race to cut arms.

Reagan reiterated his intention that if SDI became operational, he would share it with the Soviets. Incredulous, Gorbachev retorted that he "could not take this seriously." After all, American export restrictions prohibited giving the Soviets "oil drilling equipment, automatic machinery, even milk factories. For the US to give the products of high technology would be a second American Revolution, and it would not happen," exclaimed the skeptical Soviet.

Reagan retorted that he meant what he said.[97]

The two leaders broke for dinner and agreed to meet again in the morning. They directed their staff to keep working on the specific arms control and human rights proposals to see if they could develop agreements for Reagan and Gorbachev to address—and hopefully bless—the next day.

The American and Soviet negotiating teams worked all night. A breakthrough came at three forty-five A.M. when the Soviet delegation head, Sergey Akhromeyev, chief of the Soviet General Staff, told Nitze and the Americans that Gorbachev had agreed to 50 percent reductions in strategic arms, down to equal levels of 1,600 delivery vehicles and 6,000 warheads each. The last concession was key; previously the Soviets had insisted on 50 percent relative cuts, which would advantage the Kremlin with its larger overall arsenal. At eight A.M., exhausted and exhilarated, they briefed Shultz and Poindexter on their results, who in turn updated Reagan.[98]

Reagan and Shultz rejoined Gorbachev and Shevardnadze at ten A.M. The mood was intense; both leaders felt history's glare and humanity's hope. Gorbachev tried to lighten it with a nod to the biblical account of the world's creation; they were just on the second day and had a long way to go to the seventh, he quipped. Reagan laughed and said perhaps they should be resting instead since it was Sunday.

Turning serious, Reagan voiced his disappointment that their negotiating teams had not achieved more overnight. While the agreement on strategic arms reductions was notable, they remained at an impasse on INF, specifically the Soviet refusal to remove its SS-20s from Asia. Reagan would not betray his commitment to Nakasone. Nor did he want to leave China exposed to the SS-20 threat. Reagan also reminded Gorbachev that the missiles were mobile; if the United States agreed to let the Soviets maintain its SS-20 force in the Russian Far East, the Kremlin could easily redeploy them to the European theater once the American missiles had been withdrawn from NATO countries. Then Gorbachev made a big concession: He would be willing to reduce INF to one hundred missiles held by each side, to be divided between Europe and Asia. It was not yet the American zero-zero position, but it was much closer.

Both men sensed the moment. Each now saw the other was ready to make bold moves. Reagan pointed out that "if the US and Soviet Union were to start the process of reducing their own nuclear forces to zero, and would stand shoulder-to-shoulder in telling other nations that they must eliminate their own nuclear weapons, it would be hard to think of a country that would not do so."

Agreeing, Gorbachev observed, "I was not in a position a year ago, to say nothing of two or three years ago, to make the kind of proposals I am now making. I might not be in the same position in a year or so. Time passes and things change. Reykjavík will become simply a memory."

SDI snapped this reverie. Gorbachev insisted on keeping the ABM Treaty and ending SDI because he did not trust the United States to not exploit a Soviet window of vulnerability. He told Reagan, "Once one decided to reduce nuclear arms, one had to be certain that one side could not act behind the back of the other."

Reagan grew angry. "What the hell are we defending?" he exclaimed. "[The ABM Treaty] says our only defense is that if someone wants to blow us up, the other will retaliate." He rejected the perverse logic of mutual assured destruction. "Why the hell should the world have to live for another ten years under the threat of nuclear weapons if we have decided to eliminate them?"[99]

Their fierce agreement in eliminating nuclear weapons masked a fundamental difference. It was a vital distinction that would bedevil their negotiations and stymie a final deal. Gorbachev sought to slash nuclear arms in order to preserve Soviet communism; Reagan sought to slash nuclear arms on the way to ending Soviet communism. Reagan realized that a Soviet Union without its nuclear weapons would be a hollow shell, the Soviet system a starving parasite that had sucked its last from its host, bereft of any legitimate claim to power or the means to enforce its rule. Yet to Gorbachev, he disavowed any such designs. Reagan told the Soviet leader, "We harbor no hostile intentions toward the Soviets. We recognize the differences in our systems. We can live as friendly competitors." Such reassurances were a diplomatic necessity—how could Reagan negotiate with Gorbachev while admitting he sought the demise of the Soviet system?—but they were disingenuous.

Gorbachev realized as much. He complained to Reagan that the Soviet

Union had little money to spend on grain because the United States and Saudi Arabia had conspired to lower oil prices, thus starving his country of hard currency. He bemoaned that Reagan had recently reaffirmed his "1981 Westminster speech that referred to the Soviet Union as an evil empire and called for a crusade against socialism in order to relegate it to the ash heap of history." Never mind the wrong date and mash-up that conflated at least three of Reagan's speeches; Gorbachev knew that Reagan believed Soviet communism to be illegitimate and destined to fail. In response Reagan did not disavow his words at all. Instead he reminded Gorbachev that while the United States permitted the American Communist Party to operate and contest elections, the Soviet Union and its communist satellites imposed one-party rule by force everywhere they seized power. He knew that if Soviet communism allowed multiparty elections and tolerated dissent, it would lose its monopoly on power—and would probably get as few votes from Soviet citizens as the American Communist Party received in the United States.

At this Gorbachev had had enough. Turning positive, he suggested that even though he and Reagan disagreed, "a man-to-man relationship between us is possible." Reagan agreed, and joked that if they became friends, he might even persuade Gorbachev to become a Republican.[100]

Shultz brought them back to arms control. Gorbachev insisted that the Soviet proposals be "regarded as a package" and that if the United States would not agree to a ten-year commitment to the ABM Treaty, the other terms were moot. Reagan protested that they seemed to be close to agreements on cutting strategic arms by 50 percent and sharp reductions in INF. Gorbachev disagreed. Their scheduled time was over; he said he was ready to return to Moscow. Then, sensing the moment, Gorbachev changed his mind and agreed to meet again for one final session.

One final session stretched into two. Reagan and Gorbachev met for another hour, took a break, and came back again for eighty more grueling minutes. Throngs of media buzzed and scavenged for any tidbit of information; the world beyond watched and waited anxiously. Around and around Reagan and Gorbachev went. They veered between arcane disputes over the meaning of the ABM Treaty and audacious proposals to slash nuclear arsenals. Discussing whether they should focus on ballistic missiles or all nuclear warheads, Reagan said, "It would be fine with me if we eliminate all nuclear weapons."

Gorbachev responded, "We can do that; we can eliminate them."

Chimed in Shultz: "Let's do it."

But they did not. As they verged on cinching an agreement, one word kept unraveling it: *laboratory*.

As a condition of giving up nuclear weapons, Gorbachev insisted on confining SDI research to the laboratory for the next ten years. Leaving no doubt of its importance, Gorbachev repeated this demand *twenty-eight times* during their Sunday afternoon sessions alone.[101] Reagan refused, wanting to pursue more expansive SDI research and testing. Confining it to a laboratory would stifle it. For Reagan, a functioning SDI was a prerequisite to eliminating nuclear weapons because, as he would explain to the nation the next night, "SDI is America's insurance policy that the Soviet Union would keep the commitments" it made on nuclear missiles.

At this deadlock, Reagan scribbled a note and passed it to Shultz. "Am I wrong?" he asked.

"No, you are right," whispered Shultz.

Feeling the window closing, the two leaders' pleas to each other became intensely personal.

"You are three steps away from becoming a great president," Gorbachev insisted, pressing Reagan to agree to the laboratory restriction.

"I am asking you to change your mind as a favor to me, so that hopefully we can go on and bring peace to the world," entreated Reagan.

Their reciprocal appeals did not avail.

By now the sun had set over the North Atlantic, and with it had slipped away the chance of a historic deal to eliminate all nuclear weapons. Reagan and Gorbachev did not hide their bitterness. Each blamed the other. As they bade farewell in the darkness and stepped into their limos, Gorbachev told Reagan, "I don't know what else I could do."

Replied Reagan, "You could have said yes."[102]

It was not the mere "laboratory" dispute that proved the undoing at Reykjavík, but the more fundamental issue of trust. Though Gorbachev's personal regard for Reagan deepened, there remained a chasm he could not cross, especially knowing that the American president only had two years left in office. Gorbachev could not abide the notion of a United States, under an unknown future president, able to defend itself from Soviet ICBMs and thus able to launch a first strike. Gorbachev put it bluntly in their last session: SDI "would permit the United States to destroy the Soviet Union's offensive nuclear potential." Even if he could accept that possibility, his Politburo would not, and he knew acquiescing to SDI could mean getting ousted by the Kremlin.[103]

Gorbachev's obsession with SDI, to the point of torpedoing the most consequential nuclear agreement in history over it, also belies the notion that he and his advisors thought it would never work. Reagan, for his part, also did not trust the future. He knew that once a technology such as nuclear weapons became known, it could not become unknown, and repeatedly expressed the fear that a future "madman" (he cited Qadhafi as an example) could acquire nuclear missiles and threaten the United States. He told Gorbachev that he had promised the American people he would not relinquish any means to protect them. To Gorbachev's exasperation, Reagan often invoked the example of chemical weapons: Even though the world banned them after World War I, nations did not give up their gas masks.[104]

Three thousand journalists had descended on Reykjavík. The grim countenances of Reagan and Shultz told the story of the summit's end more than any press statement or interview. As the American and Soviet delegations prepared to fly home to their respective capitals, the media recounted to the world what had happened. It portrayed a debacle for Reagan. Typical was Sam Donaldson of ABC News, who described the summit as a "very bad setback for the president" with "the magic of the Reagan persona gone." Continued Donaldson, "Time has just about run out on the Reagan presidency"; he said the Kremlin would "just wait him out."[105] The next week, *Time* and *Newsweek* ran cover stories reinforcing the sense of failure. "No Deal: Star Wars Sinks the Summit," blared *Time*, over a photo of a despondent Reagan and smirking Gorbachev.[106]

Gorbachev returned to Moscow unhappy with the American president. On October 14, he vented to the Politburo that Reagan was a "class enemy, who exhibited extreme primitivism, a caveman outlook, and intellectual impotence," and who believed "that the US might exhaust us economically via [the] arms race." He lamented to a visiting congressional delegation that the White House was "waiting for [the Soviet Union] to drown." But Gorbachev relished, as he told the Politburo, that at least Carter's secretary of state Cyrus Vance and many congressional Democrats blamed Reagan for Reykjavík's failures.[107]

While the media, Democrats, and the Kremlin bemoaned Reagan's refusal to relinquish SDI, some of his own staff and allies remonstrated over the opposite: his eagerness to relinquish nuclear weapons. Four days after the summit, Poindexter sent Reagan a memo titled "Why We Can't Commit to Eliminating All Nuclear Weapons Within 10 Years," which proceeded over six pages to tell the president he was wrong to pursue nuclear abolition and "strongly recommend" that he not even talk about it. "I strongly feel that you should step back—and do so now," concluded Poindexter. The NSA made some important points, including how the Soviet advantage in conventional forces would be even more menacing without the American nuclear deterrent and how the allies would feel betrayed if the United States closed the nuclear umbrellas protecting Europe and Asia. Still, it was an extraordinary dissent by a senior official against his president's declared policy.[108]

Poindexter was right about the allies. The day after the summit, Margaret Thatcher spoke with Reagan by phone and warned him that "Reykjavík looked like a Soviet setup" to split the alliance. She inveighed against nuclear abolition as "extremely dangerous" and "tantamount to surrender," and worried that a nuclear-free world would leave the UK and Western Europe at the mercy of Soviet conventional forces. (Rarely content to make a point just once, Thatcher would repeat these objections at length to Reagan the next month during a visit to Camp David.) The next week, Helmut Kohl visited the White House and expressed the same concerns to Reagan.[109]

That Reagan was willing to cause so much allied heartburn over his vision of a nuclear-free world showed the fervor of his convictions. Part of the reason why he did not fret as much about the Soviet conventional threat was not just because the United States enjoyed the security buffer of two oceans—it was because Reagan also envisioned a world free of Soviet communism. This he pursued in tandem with his nuclear abolitionism. He wanted to be rid of both the instruments of danger and the source of the danger itself.

Ultimately, this is why Reagan refused to give up SDI at Reykjavík. Doing so would have meant relinquishing his entire Cold War strategy.

Though the initial consensus dismissed Reykjavík as a failure, what few beyond Reagan and Shultz realized at the time is the summit showed both sides just how far each was willing to go in taking dramatic steps to transform the Cold War. Once Reagan and Gorbachev saw that in each other, their momentary frustration soon turned to grudging, then open admiration—and trust. Shultz pressed this point on the naysayers. In the days following the summit, he argued that Reykjavík had opened dramatic new potential for agreements on strategic arms, verification, and especially an INF agreement.[110]

Reykjavík also prompted a breakthrough on human rights. The Kremlin at last agreed to include human rights as one of the four agenda items in US-Soviet negotiations. To show his commitment to this new era of glasnost ("openness"), Gorbachev directed several further steps. At the Helsinki review conference in Vienna the next month, the Soviet delegation abandoned its usual obstreperous posture and instead engaged in dialogue with the NGOs and activists present. Shevardnadze shocked the conference hall when he announced that Moscow would host a global conference on human rights.

Perhaps of most significance, on December 16, Gorbachev phoned the physicist Andrei Sakharov at his apartment in the city of Gorky (where the Soviet Union's most eminent dissident had been banished to internal exile for the last six years) and told Sakharov that he was now free. Sakharov and his wife, Elena Bonner, herself a noted Jewish activist, were welcome to return home to Moscow and speak freely. Which they did. As soon as he stepped off the train in Moscow to a welcoming crowd of a couple hundred journalists and friends, Sakharov delivered an extemporaneous denunciation of the Soviet system, especially its war in Afghanistan. He suffered no repercussions and was able to resume his physics research at the Academy of Sciences as well as his political activism.[111]

What few saw in the summit aftermath, including Reagan's critics, staff, and allies, is that within the creaky, windswept walls of Höfði House, on an island nation somewhere between the outer periphery of Europe and the nowhere of the North Atlantic, the Cold War began to end. Though Reagan and Gorbachev parted with acrimony and without a deal, both saw that they had created a new realm of possibilities. Paradoxically, Reykjavík may also have been Gorbachev's last chance to save the Soviet economy from its self-immolation. By refusing Reagan's offers to slash nuclear arsenals, Gorbachev consigned his country to at least another year of running an arms race that it could not win. Reagan knew as much; two weeks after the summit he told his diary, "The Soviets if faced with an arms race would have to negotiate—they can't squeeze their people any more to try and stay even with us."[112]

Reagan also now knew that this Soviet leader was the reformer he had been waiting for, the partner for peace with whom he could negotiate the end of the Cold War—and perhaps even the surrender of the Soviet Union itself.

XII

Two events, separated by one month and seven thousand miles, soon converged to set off a chain reaction that erupted in Washington, consumed the White House, and made Reykjavík seem a distant memory. In Nicaragua, on October 5, a fourteen-year-old Sandinista soldier fired a missile at a C-123 cargo plane overhead. The missile shot down the plane, killing the two pilots. A single crewman survived, Eugene Hasenfus, who parachuted to earth only to be captured by the Sandinistas. Hasenfus quickly confessed that he worked for the CIA and the plane was carrying weapons to resupply contra forces. The shoot-down caused a panic in Washington, especially because the Boland Amendment prohibitions on contra aid were still in effect. Several administration officials scrambled to cover up the CIA connection while issuing denials of any US government involvement that were as emphatic as they were untrue.[113]

Then on November 3, a Lebanese magazine, *Al-Shiraa*, published an article (almost certainly leaked by the Iranian government) revealing that McFarlane and other administration officials had traveled to Tehran earlier in the year to trade arms for hostages. The next day the Iranian government confirmed the story. Through the fall, Poindexter and North had resumed contacts with Iran, even to the point of secreting a small group of Iranian officials to Washington for meetings at the White House. They had also shipped more weapons to Iran. While two hostages had been released, at the same time Hezbollah had abducted three more Americans in Beirut. After eighteen months, the net number of American hostages remained the same, while Iran had gained thousands of advanced missiles, parts, and other weapons. William Safire acidly summarized the record: "One difference between French appeasement and American appeasement is that France pays ransom in cash and gets its hostages back while the US pays ransom in arms and gets additional hostages taken."[114]

As a policy—to secure hostage releases and to improve the United States–Iran relationship—the scheme failed. Now, transformed from ill-advised policy to scandal, it threatened to destroy Reagan's presidency.

The White House descended into a spasm of finger-pointing, backstabbing, ship-jumping, and all other manner of self-preservation. Don Regan immediately began telling journalists that the whole affair was McFarlane's fault—never mind that as chief of staff, Regan had known of the operation and done little to try to stop it. Vice President Bush denied in a television interview that any arms had been traded for hostages, prompting Shultz to remind him that Bush had been briefed on the plan and had not objected. This prompted a heated exchange as Bush defended the deal while disavowing any involvement; "There was considerable tension between us when we parted," recalled Shultz. Meanwhile, Casey resented Shultz for opposing the Iran scheme and then distancing himself once it became public. The CIA director urged Reagan to fire Shultz for not being a team player. Shultz in turn implored Reagan to fire Casey, Poindexter, and Regan. Bush and the First Lady echoed that Reagan should fire the chief of staff but also hinted Shultz should go. For good measure, Regan suggested getting rid of Shultz, while Shultz came close to resigning. The beleaguered president rebuffed these entreaties, insisting, "I'm not firing anybody."[115]

The White House hurt itself further with its clumsy, evasive, and deceptive responses. Reagan addressed the nation on the evening of November 13. From the Oval Office, he spoke to the camera in his most solemn, earnest, and emphatic tone. "The charge has been made that the United States has shipped weapons to Iran as ransom payment for the release of American hostages in Lebanon, that the United States undercut its allies and secretly violated American policy against trafficking with terrorists. Those charges are utterly false."[116] Except those charges were all true; it was Reagan's denial that was false. Reagan made things worse the next week when he held a press conference and uttered several more false or inaccurate statements, such as when he denied that Israel had played any role in the arms shipments. The White House defense amounted to "we did not trade arms for hostages, and if we did it was to improve the relationship with Iran." Almost as bad as the falsehoods was Reagan's appearance at the podium: shaken, confused, diminished.

Three weeks into the scandal, Reagan, McFarlane, Poindexter, and Casey defiantly insisted that the Iran outreach was not only the right thing to do but *should continue as American policy*. McFarlane emailed Poindexter insisting "there really is a circle of sensible people in Iran" that, "if we are to carry this forward," would need to reciprocate with positive gestures. Poindexter wrote an op-ed in *The Wall Street Journal* on November 24 defending the outreach to "pragmatic elements" in Iran as a strategic imperative. That same day, in an NSPG meeting, Poindexter and Casey argued for continuing to engage with Iran. Dumbfounded, Shultz and Weinberger pushed back with vehemence. An angry Reagan pounded on the table and insisted the Iran outreach was the right thing to do.[117]

Then the scandal, already bizarre, took a surreal turn. Ed Meese and Regan pulled Reagan aside after the meeting and told him they had just discovered that Poindexter and North had been diverting profits from the Iran arms sales to fund the contras. Reagan's diary records his reaction: "This was a violation of the law against us giving the Contras money without an authorization by Congress. North didn't tell me about this. Worst of all John P[oindexter] found out about it and didn't tell me. This may call for resignations."[118] The next morning, Poindexter, at Reagan's direction, stepped down. The same day Reagan fired North from the NSC staff. Before vacating their offices, Poindexter and North fed thousands of pages of documents detailing the scheme into their paper shredders.

One of the many lingering puzzles of Iran-contra has been whether Reagan authorized, or even knew of, the diversion of funds to the contras. The best evidence seems to indicate he did not. Unlike his diary entries on the arms-for-hostages transactions—which show clearly his knowledge, intent, and approval—he seems genuinely to have been surprised and baffled to learn of the contra diversion. Poindexter also claims that he never told Reagan about it. However, not knowing does not grant Reagan complete absolution. A president is responsible for the "command climate" he creates and for what his staff do in his name. Reagan had made clear for years his fervent commitment to the contras and his disinterest in many details of governing. Scheming zealots such as North exploited those conditions.

As for Reagan, what at Reykjavík had been a virtue—his resolve, self-confidence, and belief in his vision despite naysayers on all sides—turned now into a vice of self-deception. He willed himself to believe that he had not traded arms for hostages and kept insisting as much to his staff, to the media, to the nation, even to his own diary—despite overwhelming evidence, including many of his own previous diary confessions, that he had in fact done just that.

It took a Democrat to convince Reagan otherwise. On the evening of December 4, Democratic lawyer and elder statesman Bob Strauss joined Bill Rogers, a Republican stalwart who had served as Nixon's secretary of state, in the White House residence for a confidential dinner with Reagan. They came at the behest of the First Lady and Mike Deaver, the former White House aide, who remained close to the Reagans. Both worried that the president's continued refusal to see the truth could destroy his presidency.

Rogers assured Reagan that the controversy would go away. Strauss disagreed. A patriot with bipartisan friendships, he liked Reagan and revered the institution of the presidency, and feared that both were in grave peril. Strauss did not mince words. He told Reagan that he did not believe his account and said, "You are unintentionally mis-stating the facts, because it is inconceivable to me that they could be true." Strauss also urged Reagan to fire Don Regan, warning that the chief of staff was looking out for himself more than the president.

Mrs. Reagan chimed in, telling her husband: "Bob doesn't believe what you are saying is accurate even though you think it is, and neither do I. He is just the first one who said it to you clearly and strongly, beside me."[119] Unfailingly devoted to Reagan, the First Lady was also fiercely protective. In this case, she knew that protecting him from the unfolding scandal meant protecting him from himself. Though it would take more time for the reluctant president to admit that he traded arms for hostages, the blunt words from Strauss and the First Lady would prove a turning point in convincing him of the severity of the problem.

That same week, Reagan had appointed a bipartisan Special Review Board. Led by former senator John Tower, former national security advisor Brent Scowcroft, and former secretary of state Edmund Muskie, Reagan's executive order charged the "Tower Commission" with studying "the future role of the National Security Council staff."[120] This was because the architects of Iran-contra—McFarlane, Poindexter, and North—all worked on the NSC staff, and in their operational schemes had gone rogue from the NSC staff's traditional roles of coordinating policy and advising the president. The Tower Commission's anodyne charter masked another purpose, unwritten yet arguably more important. As commission attorney Stephen Hadley recalls, it focused on an "institutional problem: how to purge the system when the president gets in trouble?" In other words, when the chief executive presides over a scandal that threatens the integrity of the entire executive branch, how can credibility and trust be restored? Tower's theory of the case was blunt: "You need to kick the president in the solar plexus" to get him to admit the problem and his role in it. Only then can a rebuilding of the institution, and trust in it, begin.[121] It was the same message Strauss had delivered.

The Tower Commission would probe policy failures but did not have the authority to explore potential lawbreaking. Four days after its announcement, Attorney General Meese persuaded Reagan to request the appointment of an independent counsel to investigate, and prosecute, any criminal conduct. Former federal judge Lawrence Walsh got selected for the role. Between the Tower Commission, the independent counsel, a special bicameral congressional committee, and almost every journalist in town, to paraphrase H. L. Mencken, one could not throw a bag of shredded documents on a Washington sidewalk without hitting someone involved in Iran-contra, as either an investigator, participant, pundit, or "unindicted co-conspirator."[122]

Most political scandals are fueled by venality, lust for power, concupiscence, or avarice. In contrast, Iran-contra is perhaps the only major scandal in presidential history motivated solely by policy goals—and commendable ones at that. Reagan, McFarlane, Poindexter, and North sought to secure the release of American hostages, improve relations with an adversarial nation, and sustain anticommunist forces in Nicaragua. They did so in the belief that the executive authority of the presidency gave them wide latitude to conduct policy in the national interest. This combination of policy goals and presidential power explains in part why Reagan resisted for so long admitting any error; his motives were right, so how could his actions be wrong?

Reagan's focus on purity of heart blinded him to how his actions toward Iran violated several of his own strategic principles, such as: Negotiate from strength. Keep faith with allies. Incentivize adversaries to engage in good behavior; do not reward bad behavior. Build public support for policies rather than keeping them secret. Even "trust but verify."

Especially since underlying it all, the Iran gambit rested on a series of illusions. Scholar David Crist concludes, "A 'moderate' wing never existed in Iran. . . . For Khomeini, it was never about a strategic opening but rather about beating Iraq and spreading the revolution. He had no compunction about turning America's own weapons on their maker."[123] Such was the strategic flaw at the core of the venture. Even though Reagan, McFarlane, and Poindexter all invoked the precedent of Nixon and Kissinger's secret diplomacy and strategic opening to Beijing, they failed to see that Iran was not China. For rival nations to reconcile, each needs an alignment of interests and top leaders committed to making it happen. In 1972, China and the United States had both; in 1986, Iran and the United States had neither.

Reagan's bad month got worse when he learned that Casey had a malignant brain tumor. For the past few weeks the normally indefatigable and phlegmatic CIA director had been weary, erratic, snappish. Given his deep involvement in both the Iran and Nicaragua legs of the scheme, his family and staff had worried that the stress of the unfurling scandal was undoing him. The mounting investigations indeed rattled Casey, but a violent seizure revealed advanced cancer as the main cause of his torments. He underwent emergency surgery, resigned as CIA director, stayed hospitalized for months, and would die on May 5, 1987. A keeper of secrets throughout his life, the old spymaster kept them still unto death, to the dismay of the congressional investigators and independent counsel. More positive aspects of his legacy would endure in other ways, including the fact that he was the Reagan Doctrine's lead architect and had reinvigorated the CIA. His deputy and eventual successor, Bob Gates, put it best: "Bill Casey was the last of the great buccaneers."[124]

For most of 1986, Reagan had enjoyed overwhelming popularity. Iran-contra decimated his political standing. His Gallup poll approval rating plummeted in November alone from 67 percent to 46 percent, setting an ignominious record for the steepest decline in modern presidential history. Only 28 percent of Americans approved of his handling of foreign policy. Many Americans now doubted his competence and his honesty.[125]

Then on the evening of Saturday, December 6, millions of American television viewers saw a different side of their president. They watched as Reagan walked into the Oval Office and took charge of a meeting of his advisors. The president barked orders, displayed meticulous command of minute details, orchestrated complex financial and diplomatic transactions, even spoke to foreign leaders in fluent Arabic and German. His exhausted staff could only look on in awe.

It was a parody skit on the iconic *Saturday Night Live* comedy show.[126] Hilarious though the sketch was, it also revealed perhaps the greatest risk of the Iran-contra scandal. Reagan's fumbling, confused performance was turning him into an object of ridicule and pity. Such an image could be devastating for a president and corrosive to the institution of the presidency. He had only two years left to recover.

CHAPTER 13

COMEBACK

I

A s the new year of 1987 began, Reagan wished he could leave the Iran-contra scandal behind as just a disagreeable dream, but the accelerating investigations and White House turmoil confronted him with the hard reality that he could not. The fate of his presidency, not least his foreign policy legacy, depended on his response.

Any recovery would rest on a new team. To replace the departed Poindexter as national security advisor, Reagan recruited Frank Carlucci, who had most recently served him as deputy secretary of defense in the first term before a sojourn in the private sector. At Carlucci's recommendation, Reagan tapped General Colin Powell as deputy national security advisor. Powell was a rising star who was the army's highest-ranking Black officer—and who before the year was out would be elevated again by Reagan to be the first Black national security advisor. The president picked FBI director William Webster to lead the CIA. Reagan ushered out Pat Buchanan as communications director. The right-wing gadfly had gone too far too many times with his freelancing in politics and policy, in part because of his own quixotic presidential ambitions.[1] Reagan completed the overhaul by bringing in former Senate Majority Leader Howard Baker as the new chief of staff. Don Regan, already on thin ice, had sealed his demise by hanging up on Nancy Reagan during a heated phone call over the president's schedule.[2]

Bud McFarlane had left the White House over a year ago and then suffered public disgrace when his role as architect of the Iran scheme was exposed. With his strong sense of honor, McFarlane descended into further despair at the shame he had helped bring to the presidency and what now felt like his own irrelevance. On the evening of February 8, he tried to kill himself by swallowing twenty Valium pills. Fortunately, his wife, Jonda, discovered him before he succumbed and summoned medical help that saved his life.[3] His suicide attempt highlighted the scandal's personal toll and further shook the demoralized White House.

The dejection started at the top. During the Tower Commission's two interviews with Reagan, its leaders sat stunned at the president's confused answers, memory lapses, and occasional contradictions, such as when he first confirmed and then later denied authorizing the initial arms transfer to Israel. Several times Reagan just read off cue cards drafted by his anxious lawyers. In hindsight, some of his staff have speculated that this may have been the inchoate signs of the Alzheimer's disease that would later cause his death; more likely it was just a combination of exhaustion, age, and stress. Reagan's disheveled performance also stemmed from his inattention to details, aversion to admitting wrong, and discomfort with personal confrontation. His unsteadiness only furthered the sense that the presidency was in crisis.[4]

Reagan had to first confront his political problems of damaged credibility and diminished approval ratings. The Tower Commission report gave Reagan the chance to lance this boil and begin to turn the corner. Though the congressional investigations would continue into the summer, and the Walsh special counsel investigation would stagger on for six more years (to its growing discredit), the Tower Commission completed its work in three months. Tower, Scowcroft, and Muskie presented their findings to Reagan on February 26, the same day they released their report to the public. It provided just the gut-punch that the stubborn president needed. Over the next four days Reagan read every page of the 304-page report. Bitter tonic though it was, digesting it forced him to confront what had gone wrong and his responsibility for it.[5]

On March 4, Reagan addressed the nation from the Oval Office and gave the speech he should have given three months earlier. He confessed breaking trust with the American people and took "full responsibility for my own actions and for those of my administration." Though still pleading purity of heart, he at last came clean: "A few months ago I told the American people I did not trade arms for hostages. My heart and my best intentions still tell me that's true, but the facts and the evidence tell me it is not.

As the Tower board reported, what began as a strategic opening to Iran deteriorated, in its implementation, into trading arms for hostages."[6] Reagan's contrition did the job. His approval rating crept back above 50 percent, and even *The New York Times* paid him the tribute of a favorable historical comparison: "Not since John F. Kennedy took the blame for the catastrophic Bay of Pigs invasion in 1961 has any president so openly confessed error."[7]

The Tower Commission identified a rogue NSC staff as a primary cause of the scandal, and its recommendations focused on reforming the NSC—but also strengthening and preserving it as a tool of presidential authority. Ollie North's escapades had exemplified the problem of an unaccountable NSC staff trying to run covert operations out of the White House. As an institution, the NSC does not control a large budget, staff, soldiers, or weapons. Whatever power it wields derives entirely from its proximity to the president. Under McFarlane and Poindexter, that power had been abused, most egregiously by North, who engineered many of the Iran-contra schemes just by invoking White House authority.[8]

Though NSC and CIA malfeasance lay at the core of the scandal, other governing institutions also failed. Congress did not acquit itself well. Particularly on the question of contra aid, Congress acted like an institutional Hamlet, changing or outright reversing its Nicaragua legislation five times in less than five years and rendering it impossible for the executive branch to carry out a coherent, consistent policy. As Steve Hayward acidly observes of the Iran-contra investigations, in the wake of yet another congressional reversal and vote to support aid to the contras, "There was something perverse about the fact that, in regard to the diversion of funds to the contras, Congress and an independent counsel were looking to criminalize a policy that Congress now *approved.*"[9]

To fix the NSC, two months before the Tower Commission report, Carlucci had already begun overhauling its entire staff and structure. He and Powell banned the staff from freelancing and conducting operations, and returned the NSC to its traditional roles of coordinating interagency policy, monitoring implementation, and advising the president.[10] Though the Iran-contra taint and ongoing investigations would continue to badger the White House for the next several months, Carlucci and Powell's reset helped Reagan regain the initiative for his final two years. Often the best cure for political problems is policy success. Such is what would at last free Reagan from the Iran-contra morass.

II

There was still a Cold War to wage. Iran-contra had arrested any strategic momentum that might have come from Reykjavík. The summit at least revealed some potential openings for deals on INF, reducing strategic forces, and human rights. Yet now, despite two meetings and a deepened rapport with Gorbachev, Reagan still had not concluded a single arms control agreement with the Soviet Union after over six years in office. This burdened Reagan less than it irked his critics. He believed that a bad deal was worse than no deal and remained determined to hold out instead for a good deal.

This meant maintaining pressure on Moscow. In February, Reagan decided to move forward with a "phased deployment" of SDI—rather than confining research to the laboratory, he ordered SDI component systems to be tested and put into operation as soon as feasible, beginning with the Space-Based Kinetic Kill Vehicle (SBKKV). A rather fantastical system designed to take out ballistic missiles in their boost phase from outer space, it would prove its value in the worry it induced in Moscow more than any operational success. Impatient with the Kremlin's caviling, Reagan told his diary: "The problem is how to continue arms reduction dialog with the Soviets and at same time eliminate any compromise on SDI. I have proposed a plan to seek an agreement that we will . . . put it in hands of an international force as a defense against any and all nuclear missiles from wherever they are launched in the world." In short, Reagan wanted to call Moscow's bluff by taking SDI off the United States–USSR bargaining table and instead making it available to the whole world, so that no nation would have a strategic edge and every nation would be protected.[11]

Reagan continued to impose costs on the Kremlin on other fronts. On Afghanistan, in February he directed an NSC task force to develop new measures to enhance "the real possibility that the Soviets could lose."[12] Downrange, as the Soviets adapted to the Stinger threat by having their aircraft fly at higher altitudes, the CIA began supplying more lethal antitank weapons so that the resistance fighters could destroy more Soviet armor. In March, the mujahideen took their aggressiveness too far—literally—when they crossed the border into the Soviet Union itself and attacked an industrial site. It rattled both Moscow and Washington—the former to have its vulnerability exposed, the latter because the White House assuredly did not want to risk such escalation. The CIA's Milt Bearden delivered a stern message to Pakistani intelligence and its mujahideen allies forbidding any more cross-border operations. Meanwhile, Gorbachev continued to tell the Politburo he wanted to withdraw from the Afghan quagmire, but not in too much haste lest it hurt the Soviet Union's international credibility and its relationship with India.[13] Reagan, Shultz, Carlucci, and Powell met again on Afghanistan in May. Carlucci's terse notes summarize their conclusion: "Soviets stepping up pressure in Afghan[istan]. We the same. Nearing end game and both sides putting more chips on table." A few weeks later, Carlucci's talking points for his meeting with Soviet official Georgi Arbatov contained the blunt message the NSA delivered: "You say you want to get out. But we simply do not believe you. . . . Until you show real seriousness," the United States would expand its support for the insurgency.[14]

Staying aggressive in the battle of ideas, Reagan escalated the CIA covert action flooding the Iron Curtain with contraband media to undermine communism. The CIA summarized the program as "designed to exploit the current Soviet policy of 'glasnost' and the revolution in electronic communications, two phenomena which offer an unprecedented opportunity for our covert action program to impact on Soviet audiences," noting, "Last year, some 500,000 books, periodicals, audio cassettes, and video cassettes were distributed inside the Soviet Union and Eastern Europe"[15] Complementing this covert psychological warfare, USIA director Charlie Wick increased the overt bombardment of the Iron Curtain with radio waves from Voice of America, Radio Free Europe, Radio Liberty, and other broadcasting measures. Many Soviet and Eastern European citizens relished their growing access to information and ideas—even sermons—contrary to the stale propaganda their dictators had long inflicted on them.

The Reagan military modernization also continued to bring strategic benefits, even as the Democratic Congress curtailed further growth in the Pentagon budget. Reagan visited the Pentagon in April to meet with the Joint Chiefs of Staff. JCS chairman Crowe said, "The goal of Competitive Strategy is to enhance traditional US strengths and capitalize on the Soviets' weaknesses by making their weapons and tactics obsolete and their major military investments ineffective." The Joint Chiefs then briefed their commander in chief on several new weapons platforms either in development or recently deployed, including stealth aircraft, drones, and the Multiple Launch Rocket System, each of which was designed to neutralize Soviet advantages in areas such as air defense and tanks. Reagan summarized to his diary that night: "We can't match the Soviets Tank for Tank so we use our technology and come up with a weapon that nullifies their superior numbers. There was much top secret and brand new in aircraft."[16]

The Pentagon briefing reinforced Reagan's long-held belief that American innovation and technology could outsmart the Red Army and outmatch Soviet industrial output, while forcing the Kremlin into a hard choice between bankruptcy and surrender. But he encountered strong dissent from his own intelligence community. In March 1987, the CIA and DIA reported that 1986 "turned out to be a very good year for the [Soviet] economy" and alleged that it grew more than 4 percent, its highest rate in ten years. In April, Carlucci tasked the CIA with producing a special assessment for Reagan on the USSR's economic capacity for the arms race with the United States. The CIA concluded that the Kremlin could keep pace with the United States for as long as needed: "The Soviet economy . . . is vested with great crude strength from its enormous base, and remains a viable system, capable of producing huge quantities of goods and services annually especially for industrial and military applications."[17] Wrong as this assessment would turn out to be, at least the CIA did not tailor its views to align with its First Customer's beliefs. Moreover, many Soviet experts outside of government generally shared the CIA's view. Though hindsight reveals the Soviet Union's utter decrepitude, at the time the Kremlin's fragility was by no means so evident. Reagan's convictions otherwise went against the prevailing expert consensus.

III

Shultz remained Reagan's indispensable partner on Soviet policy. While sharing his president's views on Soviet vulnerabilities, Shultz continued the diplomacy prong of Reagan's dual-track strategy of outreach and pressure. He did so amid much criticism, and not just from the Right. In January, historian Ronald Steel wrote a *New York Times Magazine* profile that disparaged Shultz as "unprepared" at Reykjavík; stated, "Chances for a breakthrough arms accord with the Russians seem slim"; and sneered, "Shultz has made no real mark of his own on foreign policy and, judging by the record, is unlikely to leave a lasting legacy."[18]

Three months later Shultz traveled to Moscow and secured Soviet agreement on what would become the INF Treaty, the most significant nuclear arms agreement in history.

Signs of a breakthrough had first emerged in March. The Soviet delegation at the Geneva talks had signaled to Max Kampelman that Gorbachev might now be willing to delink an INF accord from his previous demands to abolish SDI, and to accept Reagan's long-standing zero option to eliminate all INF missiles in Europe. The CIA sent Reagan an assessment on "Soviet motives" that suggested Gorbachev now sought to turn the tables by embracing the INF deal and thus split the United States from its European allies while increasing political demands on Reagan to cut defense spending and SDI. After reading the CIA analysis, a cheeky Reagan told his team, "We should take advantage of the Soviet eagerness to put something over on us."[19]

Arriving in Moscow, Shultz learned from Shevardnadze that the signals were true: Gorbachev wanted to strike a deal on INF. Gorbachev confirmed as much in his four-and-a-half-hour meeting with Shultz. Gorbachev's strategic calculation was straightforward. He likened the American missiles to "a pistol held to our head" and wanted them gone. Over three days of marathon meetings that sometimes stretched until midnight, Shultz, Shevardnadze, and their staffs worked over the details. Some particulars would need to be resolved over the next several months—such as on verification procedures, the precise range of missiles to be classified under "intermediate," the elimination of Soviet SS-20s in the Russian Far East, and the disposition of Pershing 1a missiles that were owned by West Germany but tipped with nuclear warheads controlled by the United States—but the foundations of the treaty were in place. Gorbachev also told Shultz that the Kremlin would now agree to most American positions on reducing strategic arms by 50 percent. The Soviet leader still blanched at SDI but had dropped his insistence that abolishing it be linked to any deal on arms reductions. Reagan's resolve at Reykjavík had paid off.[20]

Though it would be the INF agreement that grabbed the headlines, Shultz put human rights and democracy at the center of his trip. Over several hours in meetings with both Gorbachev and Shevardnadze, Shultz made his usual appeals for the release of imprisoned dissidents. He focused on religious freedom in particular, since fully one-third of Soviet prisoners of conscience were incarcerated for their faith.[21] Shultz added a new dimension when he showed charts to Gorbachev and Shevardnadze displaying projections of the global economy up to the year 2000. Shultz described the "outline of the future taking shape," noting, "The central feature is the great growth of the global economy: a general rise in GNP, gigantic expansion in goods and services, a huge increase in trade flows. As the world's output expands overall, the distribution of that output is more and more dispersed." Knowing that Gorbachev still held fast to Marxist dogma, Shultz pointed out that the dichotomy between capital and labor—a distinction held by both communism and industrial capitalism—"is becoming obsolete because we have entered a world in which the truly important capital is human capital, what people know, how freely they exchange information and knowledge, and the intellectually creative product that emerges." Regimes that oppressed their citizens and restricted human freedom, he concluded, would find themselves left far behind by the information age.[22]

Once again, this was a rare moment in the annals of diplomacy. Rather than the usual negotiating practice of bargaining over competing claims in their respective national interests, the earnest yet canny Shultz tried to teach the Soviets a better way to define their own national interests. Reagan would deliver a similar message himself the next year in Moscow. While indeed it would have been to Moscow's advantage to embrace an open society and information-age market economy, Reagan and Shultz both knew that if the Kremlin actually took these steps, the Soviet system of totalitarian communism would cease to exist. Such a prospect did not trouble them.

Shultz made another gesture that may have done more for religious freedom than all of his appeals to Gorbachev and Shevardnadze. His trip coincided with the Jewish Passover, and the secretary donned a yarmulke and participated in the Passover Seder dinner held annually at Spaso House, the US ambassador's residence. Such solidarity—rife with the holiday's symbolism commemorating God's deliverance of the Israelites from slavery in ancient Egypt—left the Kremlin in no doubt about the American commitment to religious freedom.

At Shultz's behest, the embassy included about 130 Jewish refuseniks, all of whom by attending put themselves at increased risk of further persecution. Foreign Service Officer Michael Einik, who organized and led the Seder each year, recalls, "[Shultz] spent about an hour walking through the crowd, he seemed to know everyone and their stories. I think only a poet, probably one writing in Russian, could convey the electricity in the room. . . . It was clear to the Russians that [Shultz] was not just going through the motions, but this . . . meant something to him in a way that transcended diplomacy or politics."[23] One guest, a young Soviet mathematician just off a twenty-day hunger strike protesting the Kremlin's oppression, handed Shultz a letter for Reagan and implored, "Keep it up. Just keep it up. You're the only thing going for us in this world." ACDA director Ken Adelman writes, "Shultz, the seemingly immovable Buddha, looked down misty-eyed while the rest of us were reduced to tears. The Secretary then took the podium to tell the dinner guests . . . that they in turn should 'keep it up.'"[24]

Before departing Moscow, Shultz made a stop south of the city at the Peredelkino village, a colony for writers and artists. He and his wife, Obie, worshipped at an Orthodox Church service, and he reported to Reagan how "the old ladies chanting along with bearded priests were vivid reminders that there is still some vestige of religious intensity inside the Soviet Union." They visited the dacha where Boris Pasternak wrote *Doctor Zhivago* and lunched with a group of Russian intellectuals who related their gratitude to the United States for being "a beacon of strength to those struggling to speak and write freely [in the USSR]." Shultz saw in the bucolic Peredelkino a glimpse into the Russian soul, which "provided a striking and revealing contrast to the bland, faceless character of Communist Moscow."[25] It reinforced the view he shared with Reagan of Soviet communism as an alien imposition on Russia, leaching away the country's history, culture, and faith.

From Moscow, Shultz journeyed first to Brussels to brief NATO leaders on his negotiations. Several NATO allies, led by the British and West Germans, balked at the INF agreement because they feared eliminating the Pershing IIs and GLCMs would erode the United States' commitment to alliance security. Gorbachev "boxed us in," griped one NATO official. Retorted Shultz, "It's a wonderful box. It's the box we've been trying to get into."[26] Then Shultz flew straight to California to brief Reagan at Rancho del Cielo. The president was gratified to learn of the success of his stance on INF—and that Gorbachev had agreed to visit Washington, DC, later in the year for a summit.

Reagan and Shultz's diplomatic triumph on INF provoked an unhappy response from many of their fellow Republicans, starting with Richard Nixon and Henry Kissinger. In an extraordinary public criticism, the former president and secretary of state wrote a seventeen-hundred-word broadside published concurrently in *The Washington Post,* the *Los Angeles Times,* and other nationwide periodicals. They took a barbed shot at Reagan's ambitions for peace: "Every president has an understandable desire to ensure his place in history as a peacemaker. But he must always remember that however he may be hailed in today's headlines, the judgment of tomorrow's history would severely condemn a false peace." Continuing, they warned that the INF deal could "create the most profound crisis of the NATO alliance in its 40-year history" and that "any Western leader who indulges in the Soviets' disingenuous fantasies of a nuclear-free world courts unimaginable perils." The substance of their critique boiled down to gripes familiar to the White House: The INF deal worried the allies and did not account for the Soviet edge in conventional forces.[27]

It was not what was said but who said it that most bothered Reagan. The irked president nonetheless agreed to Carlucci's suggestion that he invite Nixon for a private talk. It was an act of grace by Reagan to welcome Nixon for his first visit back to the White House since departing in Watergate's ignominy thirteen years earlier. Greeting Nixon in the second-floor study of the residence, Reagan had the two of them sit in soft-backed chairs, joined only by Carlucci and Chief of Staff Howard Baker. After some awkward banter, Nixon elaborated on his criticisms of the INF deal. Nixon protested, unconvincingly, that he sought not to scuttle the INF accord but merely hoped to strengthen it. Continuing, Nixon scorned Shultz as a weak secretary, beholden to the State Department's career Foreign Service, who had "never negotiated with communists," and damned him with the faint praise that he was better suited as a domestic negotiator with labor unions. Nixon also repeated his usual warnings about Gorbachev's alleged deviousness in trying to fleece Reagan. Tired and annoyed, Reagan defended his budding partnership with Gorbachev, telling Nixon he believed Chernobyl had made the Soviet leader more serious about reducing the nuclear threat.[28]

For all of Nixon's geopolitical acumen, his critique was yawningly conventional. It was nothing Reagan had not heard already, including from some of his allies and his own staff. Nixon remained stuck in the stale Cold War logic that Reagan sought to transcend. As for Reagan, the fragile camaraderie he and Nixon had rebuilt over the course of his presidency was not quite shattered, but it was damaged. The problem was not Nixon's disagreement with the INF deal. It was that he made it so public. In Nixon's effort to sink what would become one of Reagan's landmark accomplishments, he broke Reagan's trust and violated the norm that ex-presidents should not try to undermine their successors' policies. Not to mention that of all people, Nixon—who in 1972 had shown how a staunch anticommunist could open the door with China—should have appreciated that it took a fierce Cold Warrior like Reagan to abolish an entire class of nuclear weapons.

Nixon was not alone in his objections. The conservative *National*

Review, arguably Reagan's favorite magazine, founded and run by his long-time friend William F. Buckley Jr., flayed him from the right. Its May 22 cover story lambasted the proposed INF Treaty as "Reagan's suicide pact," and in a private letter to Reagan, Buckley further remonstrated against the president's hope to abolish nuclear weapons. Reagan wrote back to Buckley reminding him that his original zero-zero proposal had been "blasted far and wide" for being unrealistically tough on the Soviets, yet now the Kremlin had conceded Reagan's position. "I have not changed my belief that we are dealing with an 'evil empire,'" Reagan assured Buckley, "in fact, I warned [Gorbachev] in Reykjavik that his choice was to join in arms reduction or face an arms race he couldn't win." Unpersuaded, Buckley responded, "We must agree to disagree—and hope that you are correct in your vaticinations."[29]

Reagan's conservative critics missed the point. In the four-year nuclear standoff in Europe, the Kremlin had just blinked. For almost a decade, Soviet SS-20s had held Western Europe hostage, threatening to blackmail NATO members if not incinerate them with less than ten minutes' warning. Now, as Helmut Kohl told Reagan in a phone call, by deploying American missiles, holding firm on SDI, and applying the full spectrum of pressure on the Kremlin, Reagan had forced the hostage-taker to drop the gun.[30]

IV

The region where Iran-contra most harmed American interests was the place of the scandal's nativity: the Middle East. Hal Brands summarizes the costs: "The scandal jeopardized everything America had worked for in the Gulf since 1979, by damaging the credibility and relationships that Carter and Reagan had built. Gulf governments had taken great risks in opposing Iran and facilitating the buildup of US military infrastructure; they now discovered that Reagan was secretly arming the country that most threatened them."[31]

After six years in the White House, Reagan still had not developed a strategic vision for the Middle East. He had not once set foot there as president, in contrast to his multiple trips to Europe, Asia, and Latin America. He had not built a close relationship with any Middle Eastern leader who could help interpret local dynamics for him, in contrast to his friendships with Nakasone, Kohl, and Thatcher. He had not identified a positive agenda to promote for the region, such as his support for democracy and free markets in Asia and Latin America, or his efforts to rid Europe of nuclear missiles and the Iron Curtain. Instead the Middle East seemed only to present a ceaseless cascade of headaches, and his clumsy efforts to solve one problem, such as hostage-taking, had just created further problems.

Now a new challenge had manifested. Iran had seized the momentum in its war with Iraq with an offensive that threatened the southern Iraqi city of Basra and its abundant oil fields. To press its gains and starve Iraq of revenue from its regional supporters, Tehran began mining the Persian Gulf and attacking Kuwaiti oil tankers. The emir of Kuwait cleverly made a joint appeal to Washington and Moscow to protect its oil ships. The Kremlin quickly agreed and began putting five Kuwaiti tankers under the Soviet flag. Gorbachev's focus on internal reforms in the Soviet Union did not preclude him from exploiting opportunities in the Middle East to gain an advantage on the United States.

The Kuwaiti request prompted Carlucci to encourage Reagan to review—and reset—US policy in the region overall. Reagan convened an NSPG meeting on February 12. Dennis Ross and Robert Oakley of the NSC staff described the weakened American posture and the need to reaffirm the United States' "strategic cooperation with Israel" because of "the stake that both the United States and Israel have in strengthening the forces of moderation and weakening those of radicalism in the region." Reagan conceded, "Some Arab governments are concerned that the US is weak and unable or unwilling to help our friends because of the Iran problem." Treasury Secretary Baker, just returned from the region, reported a basis for hope: "[The Saudi leadership,] although scared about Iran and disappointed in us, are still with us." He said they remained committed to keeping oil output high and prices low.[32]

The State Department and the Pentagon deadlocked over whether to reflag the Kuwaiti tankers and deploy US Navy warships to escort them. Reversing their usual positions on the use of force, Shultz opposed the reflagging and Weinberger supported it. The secretary of defense faced additional resistance from the navy, which worried that the mission would divert naval assets from their core mission of countering the Soviets. His new secretary of the navy, James Webb, even protested that the gulf operation violated the Weinberger Doctrine's standard of only using force with clear objectives and strong public support (the Democratic Congress was already threatening to invoke the War Powers Resolution to curtail any naval deployments). Weinberger responded that the safe passage of oil tankers was both unambiguous and important. Carlucci joined Weinberger in worrying that Iran's gulf mischief threatened to drive up oil prices, hurting economies of American allies in Europe and Asia—and undercutting the American campaign to use high Saudi output to starve the Soviets of oil revenues. Rich Armitage, an influential proponent of granting the Kuwaiti request, recalls an additional reason: "This presented a golden opportunity to assist the moderate Arabs and restore US credibility after Iran-Contra, having devastated [the Gulf Arabs] by lying" about selling arms to Iran.[33]

Reagan sided with Weinberger and Carlucci. "Mark this point well," the president declared, "the use of the vital sea-lanes of the Persian Gulf will not be dictated by the Iranians. These lanes will not be allowed to come under the control of the Soviet Union." Reagan believed that maintaining the navy's forward presence was a historic pillar of American maritime power. He reminded the NSC, "Our Naval Strategy since W[orld] W[ar] I has been to base elements of the fleet all over the world where our nat[ional] interests are involved. We've based ships and planes there in the Gulf and the Arabian sea for 38 years." Shultz set aside his misgivings and saluted, and the State Department scored a diplomatic victory when it persuaded the Kuwaitis to halt the Soviet reflagging of their five ships and instead put all Kuwaiti tankers under American protection, with American flags on their masts and American warships at their sides. Some gulf and European allies at first expressed reluctance to join, fearful of risking a war with Iran and doubtful about American resolve after the 1984 Lebanon pullout and the Iran-contra imbroglio. As the navy warships began their work, and following further entreaties from Reagan, Weinberger, and Shultz, the allies came along. Saudi AWACS planes provided surveillance; the British Royal Navy, France, Italy, the Netherlands, and Belgium deployed minesweepers; and Japan contributed advanced technical support.[34]

The teeter-tottering American posture in the Iran-Iraq War now tilted back toward Iraq. The United States increased its economic support to Baghdad to over $1 billion, loosened export controls of dual-use technology, and deployed sixty Defense Intelligence Agency analysts to Iraq to provide intelligence and targeting support on Iranian positions to the Iraqi army. Reagan renewed Operation Staunch to pressure other nations against supplying arms to Tehran (prompting some eye-rolling in foreign capitals at the American chutzpah in telling them not to do what the United States had just been doing). Not that the United States wanted Iraq to win; it just

wanted to restore a stalemate so that both sides would see little gain in further fighting. The show of force in the Persian Gulf strengthened diplomatic
efforts in Turtle Bay, as the United States even partnered with the Kremlin
to pass a UN Security Council resolution demanding a cease-fire in the Iran-
Iraq War. Shultz reveled, "Nothing like this unanimous vote on an issue of
real importance and difficulty had ever happened before in the history of
the United Nations. A thaw in the cold war was clearly underway."[35]

V

Just weeks after helping Japan's economy by protecting gulf oil shipments,
Reagan took a different step to hurt Japan's economy. In April 1987, he lev-
eled a 100 percent tariff on $300 million worth of Japanese computers, tele-
visions, and electric tools, in retaliation for Japan's unrepentant violations
on semiconductors. Despite an agreement the prior year, Japanese firms had
continued "dumping" (selling for lower prices than their manufacturing
cost) these microchips in an effort to seize American market share. It was a
major escalation. "TRADE WARS: The U.S. Gets Tough with Japan" blared
the cover of *Time*. The Plaza Accord had fueled a 60 percent rise in the yen's
value since September 1985, but that had not been enough to curtail the
trade deficit, given Japan's other market-distorting practices.

Why did Reagan choose now to punish Japan, after having resisted protectionist measures for over six years? Four reasons stand out. First, he and
Nakasone had put the United States–Japan partnership on such firm ground
that it could withstand increased trade frictions without losing its strategic
punch. Second, Japan's infractions on semiconductors were egregious and
long-standing; after all other options had been tried, it was a last resort.
Third, the national security community supported the tariffs. Unlike other
trade disputes, where defense hawks prioritized strategic cooperation with
Japan over punitive measures, in this case semiconductors were essential to
many American weapons platforms, such as missile guidance systems and
aircraft avionics.[36] Fourth, Reagan's political standing was still weak at
home. When he had enjoyed 70 percent approval ratings, he would withstand pressure to impose tariffs on Japan. Now, with his approval rating
around 50 percent, he had less political capital to spend resisting public
sentiment for protectionism.

Three weeks after announcing the tariffs, Reagan welcomed Nakasone to the White House for another state visit. The Japanese leader brought his own travails with him, suffering from legislative setbacks and diminished political support in Tokyo—which hindered his ability to get his own government to make further trade concessions to the United States. Reagan's NSC briefing emphasized the "force and depth" of the United States–Japan partnership despite the trade frictions, and Reagan told his team he wanted to continue other measures to "strengthen the relationship." In their meeting, Nakasone appealed for easing the trade sanctions before they would meet again in June at the G7 summit. Three months later, Reagan would do just that for his friend, lifting 20 percent of the tariffs.[37] Between the Plaza Accord and the microchip tariffs, the Reagan administration had delivered two populist blows to Japan's market distortions while still holding fast to its strategic commitment to free trade.

While leaning on Japan to open its economy, the Reagan administration increased its pressure on South Korea to open its government to democracy. Gaston Sigur, who had succeeded Wolfowitz as assistant secretary of state for East Asia, put the Chun dictatorship on notice in a February 6, 1987, speech when he called for a new system to ensure that "peaceful transfers of power continue into the future" and a new constitution to "create a more open and legitimate political system." Reagan and Shultz made clear that Sigur spoke for the administration; Weinberger quietly signaled to the South Korean military that he too supported Sigur's message. None of this sat well with the recalcitrant Chun, who announced two months later the suspension of several of the constitutional reforms he had promised. His backsliding sparked a new wave of protests by students and other activists, some of which turned violent.[38]

Several forces now converged and started to crack the Chun dictatorship. South Korea was scheduled to host the Summer Olympic Games in 1988, bringing the international spotlight to Seoul and raising the reputational costs of any government crackdown. The Philippines' peaceful transition the previous year had inspired many Koreans about the prospects for democracy in Asia. South Korea's economic boom over the last two decades had created a middle class eager for self-government. American funding from the National Endowment for Democracy (NED) provided the democratic opposition with resources to organize and spread its messages. However, threats to a smooth transition loomed on all sides. Besides the risk of Chun ordering the military to crush the demonstrations, the Reagan team worried that North Korea might exploit the chaos by engaging in subterfuge or even launching a surprise attack on the south. To deter any such mischief, the White House sent private messages to Pyongyang warning of a strong American response.

In many ways, pushing an autocratic ally to democratize is even harder than promoting democracy in an adversary state. Because the United States depends on the ally for security and economic cooperation—such as basing rights, intelligence sharing, joint military operations, supply chains and shared markets, and other benefits of partnership—there is more at stake, and more to be lost, if the ally resists American efforts to support human rights and political reform, or if those efforts so destabilize the country that rival states exploit it from without or violent revolution ensues within. Reagan and Shultz took no small risks in supporting these democratic transitions.

Of course, what matters more than American policies are conditions inside the country in question, especially the will of its people. The White House did well to recognize and align—albeit sometimes hesitantly—with popular currents in nations such as the Philippines, South Korea, and Taiwan. And as Michael Green points out, American security partnerships can also aid democratic transitions. "What Reagan did was to fuse interests and ideals; to focus on strengthening the institutions of freedom rather than just weakening the hold of authoritarian leaders; to ensure that allies were better governed at home so that they would be more resilient against imperialism from abroad. . . . Carter's strong credentials on human rights did not sway authoritarian leaders in Asia—Reagan's strong credentials on national security did."[39]

Reagan put those credentials to work in June when he wrote to Chun urging him to release political prisoners, allow media freedom, eschew the use of force, and honor his commitment to step down and hold free elections. Reagan directed Ambassador Jim Lilley, recently arrived in Seoul as the new US envoy, to deliver the letter in person to Chun. The embattled dictator balked at first but then agreed to receive Lilley, in part because the deft ambassador had kept ties to Chun even as the United States encouraged democracy. The timing was fortuitous. Lilley arrived at Chun's office on the afternoon of June 19, not knowing that Chun was preparing to impose martial law early the next morning. When Lilley handed Chun the letter, he told the dictator that the Defense and State Departments stood united behind Reagan's message, lest Chun entertain any hopes of siphoning support from the large US military presence in Korea. Reagan's letter, combined with Lilley's blunt warnings, pulled Chun back. Drawing on the playbook he had used during the 1980 presidential transition to spare Kim Dae Jung's life, Reagan also offered Chun a valedictory visit to the White House in 1988 if he would leave office.

Meanwhile the protests swelled to two hundred thousand or even three hundred thousand people, capturing global headlines and captivating audiences in the United States. As Chun continued to waffle, a few days later Reagan dispatched Sigur as a presidential emissary to reinforce American policy. To make sure the Korean people knew that the White House supported their efforts to bring change to the Blue House (the Korean presidential mansion), Sigur also met with opposition leaders such as Kim Dae Jung and Kim Young-Sam, and Cardinal Stephen Kim Sou-hwan, Korea's Catholic leader whose Seoul cathedral served as a refuge for dissidents. That month, when police tried to arrest student activists hiding in the cathedral, Cardinal Kim blocked their way. "You can step on me, then the priests and nuns behind me, before you can take away the students," he declared. Sigur's pilgrimage to the cathedral, along with strong warnings from Lilley against any police use of force, made it clear that the cardinal enjoyed Reagan's support too.[40]

The voices of the Korean people, amplified and supported by the United States, carried the day. On June 29, the ruling party issued a statement affirming the transition to democracy, led by an open presidential election in December. The United States–Korea alliance held firm even as the dictatorship crumbled. As Sigur recalled, Reagan and his team wanted to show that "security and democracy go hand in hand."[41]

Taiwan provided another test of this principle. In June 1987, the same month that South Korea embraced democracy, the ailing autocrat of Taiwan, Chiang Ching-kuo, summoned his vice president Lee Teng-hui and several other close advisors for a talk about their country's future. "If Taiwan wants to survive it must have democracy," he declared.[42] Six months later, Chiang died of a heart attack. In the years since the 1982 settlement with China that solidified continued American arms sales along with Reagan's "Six Assurances" reinforcing America's commitment to Taiwan, voices for democracy on the island had grown in volume and energy. The relative security afforded by the American defense umbrella gave Taiwanese activists the space to advocate for more freedom, while quiet funding from the NED gave them the resources. In 1986, dissidents had formed the Democratic Progressive Party (DPP) to challenge the ruling KMT. Under pressure, the next year the KMT ended martial law. Upon Chiang's death, Lee succeeded him as president, and the devout Christian felt a spiritual imperative to begin accelerating Taiwan's embrace of democracy.[43]

Supporting these democratic transitions bolstered Reagan's broader strategy in the Cold War's battle of ideas. By supporting self-determination, he sought to expand the perimeters of the free world and display the benefits of accountable governments as a positive alternative to communist despotism. The White House also believed that self-government further cemented alliance bonds. Shultz told Congress in 1985, "It is no accident . . . that America's closest and most lasting relationships are its alliances with its fellow democracies."[44]

The unfolding democratic transitions in South Korea and Taiwan brought new dimensions to Reagan's strategic triangles in Asia. Now the United States–Japan–South Korea alliance triangle would consist of three democracies with shared values along with shared security commitments. In contrast, the United States–China–Taiwan triangle would see increased tension as Taiwan's democracy belied Beijing's claim that Chinese people could not govern themselves. On the other hand, the United States–China–Soviet Union great-power triangle approached more equipoise. When Shultz visited Beijing in March 1987, Deng Xiaoping and other CCP leaders described their belief that "Gorbachev really is on the path to reform" and "will seek to reduce tensions with China and the US in the interest of economic reform at home." The year before, Gorbachev had even proposed Moscow's own "triangle in Asia" of the USSR, India, and China, as he sought to check American influence and reposition the Soviet presence in the region with more friends and fewer foes. Deng also repeated to Shultz his suspicion: "Gorbachev may be moving too fast."[45]

VI

The democratic wave crested across the Pacific too. In his State of the Union address, Reagan reveled in the fact that "90% of the people of Latin America live in democracy." To support that hemispheric trend, he convened the NSC to discuss South American democracy. Opening the meeting, Reagan lamented past American arrogance and interventions that had fueled resentments in the region toward "the Colossus of the North" and reiterated his vision of free nations "from the Tierra del Fuego to the North Pole." Carlucci urged a "democratic alliance" to be a "mirror image of the Brezhnev

Doctrine that insures the irreversibility of democratic gains." Worry over the mounting debt burdens besetting several countries, especially Brazil and Argentina, tempered the democratic optimism. Nor had the fear of Soviet influence abated, as acting CIA director Gates warned that Gorbachev planned "an unprecedented visit" within the next year to seven Latin American countries. The Kremlin stood to "reap major benefits," he continued, including "the chipping away of the Monroe Doctrine," "increasing their political access," and showing "the legitimacy of a Soviet role in the Western hemisphere." Shultz responded, "Democracy is the best insurance we can have [against Soviet meddling]," and worried that a contra defeat in Nicaragua would "be a big loss." The secretary distilled the dilemma facing the United States: "The South Americans have two big fears: one is a US military intervention in [Nicaragua] . . . [the other is] that we might pull the plug and walk away and let Gorbachev walk in." Shultz also urged continued attention to the "problem countries" of Chile and Paraguay, both still right-wing dictatorships.[46]

Two years earlier, Reagan had begun withdrawing support from Paraguay's anticommunist strongman Alfredo Stroessner. Reagan suspended Paraguay's access to preferential trade and directed US ambassador Clyde Taylor to support the democratic opposition, while the NED poured in funding as well. Even the Pentagon and the Pope joined the effort. In 1988, General Frederick Woerner, commander of US Southern Command, met with his counterparts in the Paraguayan military to encourage their support for a democratic transition. The same year, Pope John Paul II visited, met with democracy activists, and called for a "moral cleansing" from Stroessner's repression and "authentic democracy" for the country. The pressure worked. Just two weeks after Reagan left office, Stroessner's generals ousted him, and Paraguay held open elections a few months later.[47]

In Chile, the Reagan administration had been gradually escalating pressure on Pinochet since 1983. By 1986, promoting a democratic transition became the explicit policy, when Reagan convened an NSC meeting on "how we can persuade Pinochet to move toward a democratic form of government." Reagan noted in his diary, "We're agreed we must try."[48] Reagan waffled at times, valuing Pinochet's free-market economic policies and stalwart anticommunism. But the president came to heed the voices of Shultz, Elliott Abrams, and many in Congress, who highlighted Pinochet's brutal repression and broken promises. In 1986, the White House put the tyrant on notice by passing a resolution in the UN Commission on Human

Rights condemning his regime's manifest abuses. The NED poured in funding for Chilean opposition groups, and US ambassador to Chile Harry Barnes became a visible supporter of democracy activists, Catholic human rights groups, and Pinochet's victims. Once again, John Paul II proved a valuable partner. On a 1987 visit to Chile, he had what Shultz called a "showdown" with Pinochet, when the Pope pressed the dictator on democracy and human rights and persisted with a beatification mass for a Chilean nun before a million worshippers despite the regime's efforts to disrupt it.[49]

A further turning point came that year for the White House when a secret CIA assessment concluded that Pinochet (aided by Paraguay's Stroessner) had personally ordered the assassination of Chilean dissident Orlando Letelier in a ghastly Washington, DC, bombing in 1976—at the time "the only clear case of state-supported terrorism that ha[d] occurred in Washington DC," in Shultz's words. The secretary continued, "The consequences of [Pinochet's] staying in office would be highly dangerous for Chile and the region as a whole." Reagan put strong American support behind a 1988 plebiscite that Pinochet intended to bolster his rule. Instead the Chilean people voted him out by 54 percent, leading to the restoration of democracy.[50] Six years after Reagan had called for the "gradual growth of freedom and democratic ideals" in his Westminster address, democracy was expanding in Asia and Latin America—not gradually, but rapidly.

In Nicaragua, ironically in the wake of Iran-contra, the contras improved their standing. Even while a special congressional committee investigated the scandal, Congress voted to increase aid to the contras, who made a series of battlefield advances against the Sandinistas as the economy began to collapse. Then Moscow stepped in. In October, a Sandinista defector revealed Managua's plans to grow its army to six hundred thousand troops, funded by a new five-year agreement with the Kremlin that included advanced weapons such as surface-to-air missiles, helicopter gunships, and MiG-21 fighter jets. Moscow also provided an additional one hundred thousand tons of oil, bringing the combined value of Soviet and Cuban aid to the Sandinistas to $1 billion in 1987 alone (US assistance to the contras was paltry in comparison, totaling around $250 million over eight years). Reagan seized on this disclosure to warn that a diplomatic settlement could only be found if the contras kept pressure on the Sandinistas. "The Freedom Fighters brought the Sandinistas to the negotiating table," he declared, and "only the Freedom Fighters can keep them there." It turned out that much of this Soviet support stemmed more from Politburo hard-liners than

Gorbachev himself, who worried about the added drain on the Kremlin's coffers. When Reagan met with Gorbachev in December, he took the Soviet leader for a walk on the South Lawn and pressed him to halt arms to the Sandinistas. To Reagan's pleasant surprise, Gorbachev agreed, and followed through in the next year. Meanwhile, into 1988, a fickle Congress vacillated on further contra aid, while in Nicaragua the rebels and their Sandinista opponents fought to a rough stalemate both on the battlefield and in the negotiating room, signing a cease-fire agreement in March.[51]

The Cold War, meanwhile, was beginning to leave Nicaragua behind and enter its endgame back where it began, in a divided Europe.

VII

The most famous four words of the Cold War almost went unsaid.[52] As Reagan prepared to travel to Europe for the G7 summit and a speech in Berlin, he and his speechwriters skirmished with the NSC and State Department over a line in his remarks: "Tear down this wall!" For weeks leading up to the trip, Shultz, Powell, and their respective staffs kept expunging the words from multiple speech drafts, while speechwriters Tony Dolan and Peter Robinson kept reinserting them.

Robinson originally penned the offending phrase. Several weeks before Reagan's visit, the speechwriter had taken an advance trip to Berlin. Local friends hosted a dinner party for him with a cross section of citizens of Berlin. All spoke with passion about their loathing of the wall. One man described how his walk to work each morning went past a guard tower at the wall, where an East German sentry looked down at him through binoculars. "That soldier and I speak the same language. We share the same history. But one of us is a zookeeper and the other is an animal, and I am never certain which is which." Another woman grew impassioned and declared, "If the Russians are willing to open up, then the wall must go."[53]

Back at the White House, Reagan welcomed hurling an imprecation against the wall. Its demise had been his goal since he first beheld it in 1978. In a staff meeting to review a speech draft that his national security team had cleansed of the phrase, Reagan was asked what message he wanted to deliver. Replied the president, "Well, that passage about tearing down the wall. That's what I want to say to the people on the other side."[54]

The State Department and NSC staff continued to resist. Their comments on early drafts give the flavor of their criticism. This "won't fly with Germ[ans]. Not sentimental people." "Seems silly as edited." "This *must* come out. West Germans do *not* want to see East Germans insulted." "Weak." Needs "concrete ideas [instead of] sentimental fluff." Too much "emphasis on good guys/bad guys."[55] These objections were more than aesthetic. Behind them lay the concerns of many foreign policy experts, not entirely without warrant, that Reagan should not challenge Gorbachev too directly and thus risk alienating or weakening the Soviet leader; that the speech could damage relations with allies, especially West Germany; that it could raise false hopes and thus hurt America's credibility; even that it could destabilize the delicate new reform equilibrium emerging in the Cold War.

The Berlin Wall address did not cause the only speechwriting kerfuffle. Before Berlin, Reagan would see Pope John Paul II, and speechwriter Josh Gilder worked on the president's remarks at the Vatican. Knowing that afterward the pontiff would be traveling to Poland, in an Oval Office meeting ahead of time Reagan dictated for Gilder how he wanted to bless the Pope's return to his native land:

> Our prayers will go with you in profound hope that soon the hand of God will lighten the terrible burden of brave people everywhere who yearn for freedom, even as all men and women yearn for the freedom that God gave us all when he gave us a free will. . . . Perhaps it's not too much to hope that true change will come to all countries that now deny or hinder the freedom to worship God. And perhaps we'll see that change comes through the reemergence of faith.

State Department officials deleted the spiritual language, telling Gilder, "It's inappropriate to have so much language about God."

Replied Gilder, "So much language about God? The President will be talking to the *Pope.*"

Not to mention, Gilder added, that the language was Reagan's own.

The president got his way. On June 6, Reagan proclaimed his words to the pontiff in the Papal Library.[56] Bearing this presidential blessing, the Pope journeyed to Poland, where his week included an open-air mass in Gdańsk with one million faithful, striking further tremors from Jaruzelski's office all the way to the Kremlin. Reagan went to Venice for a relatively placid G7 summit, where the main dispute came in a staff meeting when he fended off one last State Department bid to strike out the notorious four words from his upcoming Berlin speech.[57]

The morning of June 12, the two headlines of *The Washington Post* heralded Margaret Thatcher's landslide reelection in the UK and announced, "Pope Extols Solidarity in Poland/Papal Endorsement Among Strongest Yet for Opposition," alongside a picture of John Paul II embracing Lech Walesa.[58] That same day, Reagan arrived at the Brandenburg Gate.

Though his speech was occasioned by Berlin's 750th anniversary, Reagan had more recent history in mind. His predecessor John F. Kennedy had spoken at this same spot a quarter century earlier and proclaimed American solidarity with the people of the partitioned city. Standing in front of the gate, gashed by the Berlin Wall on either side, Reagan began by honoring Kennedy's visit, even as he sought to fulfill Kennedy's unfinished hopes. He paid tribute to the Marshall Plan and the progress of the free world in the four decades since.

Turning to the present moment, he connected the concrete-and-barbed-wire edifice encircling Berlin to the global contest for liberty. "As long as this gate is closed, as long as this scar of a wall is permitted to stand, it is not the German question alone that remains open, but the question of freedom for all mankind."

Now his appeal—not a plea, but a demand directed to the one man who could fulfill it:

"General Secretary Gorbachev, if you seek peace, if you seek prosperity for the Soviet Union and Eastern Europe, if you seek liberalization: Come here to this gate! Mr. Gorbachev, open this gate! Mr. Gorbachev, tear down this wall!"

The crowd erupted, as Reagan took the private wish of a West German woman and turned it into a public cry, uttered by one of the world's two most powerful men to the other.

He did so to test the Soviet leader's sincerity and credibility. Did Gorbachev, who had visited East Berlin just two weeks earlier, really mean to pursue reform, openness, and peace? Then let him prove it by dismantling this abomination that divided Berlin and pierced the heart of Europe.[59]

There was another divide, even more profound. Concluding his speech, Reagan turned from the strategic to the spiritual. The wall was but a symbol of "the most fundamental distinction of all between East and West. The totalitarian world produces backwardness because it does such violence to the spirit, thwarting the human impulse to create, to enjoy, to worship. The totalitarian world finds even symbols of love and of worship an affront." He described a luminescent cross that appeared in the sunlight on an East Berlin tower, despite the communist government's efforts to extinguish it. The metaphor was clear. Decades of state-enforced atheism had not quenched the religious faith of multitudes in the Soviet bloc. Reagan, and America, stood with them.[60]

Reagan's demand to destroy the wall was not a one-off applause line. He enshrined it as official US policy and would repeat his call in public at least fourteen more times over the duration of his presidency.[61]

Not everyone appreciated Reagan's words. The Soviet news agency TASS fumed that it was "an openly provocative, war-mongering speech." Henry Kissinger praised the speech as "very effective" but then dismissed the heart of its message. The Soviets "won't tear down the Wall," he declared. *Washington Post* columnist Jim Hoagland huffed, "History is likely to record the challenge to tear down the wall as a meaningless taunt."[62]

History, and the people of Berlin, would do otherwise.

CHAPTER 14

ENDGAME

I

Though Reagan's Europe trip was a policy success, he remained beleaguered at home and in allied eyes. In July 1987, Thatcher, emboldened by her landslide reelection, paid another visit to Washington. Her advisor Charles Powell delivered a caustic assessment ahead of her trip: "The President is besieged. His authority is weakened by Irangate from which he is unable so far to break free. . . . There are insistent reports of encroaching senility and declining comprehension. . . . There is a real risk of a vacuum in the leadership of the West at the very moment when the Soviet system has thrown up an articulate and appealing leader." The despondent Powell then gave his boss an extraordinary charge: "Your role is to rally the West and provide a sense of purpose and direction. . . . The task is at least to disguise the weakness of American leadership. . . . It is also an opportunity to remind the American people more widely that the United States' leadership role in the world is as vital as ever."[1]

Ironically, just prior to Thatcher's arrival, Reagan received a boost from an unlikely source: Oliver North. The erstwhile NSC staffer had captivated the nation the previous week with his testimony before the Iran-contra congressional committee. Liar and lawbreaker though he was, North changed the terms of the national debate by delivering impassioned defenses of the importance of covert action, supporting anticommunist fighters who depended on the United States, and the presidential prerogative to direct national security policy. He sparred with posturing congressional Democrats and came out ahead, both in the hearing room and in the court of public opinion. Admitting without apology that he had lied and destroyed evidence, North went on offense: "Congress is to blame because of the fickle, vacillating, unpredictable, on-again off-again policy toward the Nicaraguan Democratic Resistance. . . . [By cutting off funds,] the Congress of the United States left soldiers in the field unsupported and vulnerable to their Communist enemies. . . . Our adversaries laugh at us, and our friends recoil in horror."

North succeeded in changing the story. By this point, almost eight months since the scandal first broke, most Americans had taken account of the Reagan administration's misconduct. Now, with North's fusillades, delivered over seven days of riveting testimony, the public heard for the first time that perhaps Congress bore some guilt too. Two senators otherwise critical of the White House, liberal Republican Bill Cohen and Democrat George Mitchell, conceded afterward that "one Marine against twenty-six lawyer-politicians wasn't even close. North held a Gatling gun while [the committee members] sat like ducks in a shooting gallery. The American people loved it." One poll that week found that by 43 to 30 percent, Americans now blamed Congress more than Reagan for the scandal.[2]

Despite Charles Powell's grim predictions, it was a chipper Reagan who greeted his friend Thatcher at the White House on July 17. Even more important than her private encouragement was the public boost she provided. On the CBS Sunday show *Face the Nation,* Thatcher rebuked host Lesley Stahl's querulous pessimism: "Now why are all you media taking a downbeat view? Cheer up! America is a strong country with a great president, a great people and a great future! . . . I beg of you, you should have as much faith in America as I have!" A grateful Reagan told his diary she "was absolutely magnificent and left Lesly [sic] Stahl a little limp."[3]

As Reagan regained his political standing and saw his policies in Asia and the Middle East beginning to bear fruit, other critics continued to carp. On September 2, readers of *The New York Times, The Washington Post,* and *The Boston Globe* opened their newspapers to find a full-page "open letter" from a flamboyant New York City real estate developer named Donald J. Trump. Addressed "To the American People" and titled "There's nothing wrong with America's Foreign Defense Policy that a little backbone can't cure," it was a broadside against Reagan. Trump whined, "For decades, Japan and other nations have been taking advantage of the United States." He continued, "The saga continues unabated as we defend the Persian Gulf, an area of only marginal significance to the United States for its oil supplies, but one upon which Japan and others are almost totally dependent. . . . The world is laughing at America's politicians as we protect ships we don't own, carrying oil we don't need, destined for allies who won't help."[4]

Reagan paid little mind to such sniping; he had no brief for protectionism or isolationism. He did care, however, when allies felt disregarded, and such was the case that same month with Canada and his friend Mulroney. Despite Reagan's support for a free-trade accord with Canada, a series of technicalities threatened to torpedo the agreement that he and Mulroney had long championed. The impasse between their respective trade staffs grew so acrimonious that the Canadian delegation walked out of negotiations with their American counterparts less than two weeks before the congressionally mandated deadline.

When negotiations resumed only to fall apart again just five hours before the deadline, an exasperated Mulroney told Treasury Secretary Jim Baker that he planned to phone Reagan at Camp David and ask, "Ron, how is it that the United States can agree to a nuclear reduction deal with their worst enemy, the Soviet Union, and they can't agree to a free trade agreement with their best friend, the Canadians?"

Baker knew the president would not want such a call. Instead the Treasury secretary phoned Reagan at Camp David; the president authorized the final compromise, and Baker concluded the deal. Following the earlier agreement with Israel, it was only the second bilateral free-trade agreement in American history, and one step closer to Reagan's vision of a North American accord.[5]

II

At seven P.M. on May 28, in the twilight of a late spring evening, Muscovites walking through Red Square were startled to see a small Cessna circling overhead. The buzzing plane soon swooped down and landed on the Bolshoy Moskvoretsky Bridge next to St. Basil's Cathedral. Out stepped a gangly West German teenager, eighteen-year-old Mathias Rust, who claimed to be on a "mission for peace" bearing a plan for Gorbachev for a nuclear-free world. Whatever Rust's intention, the effect was to expose the USSR's security vulnerabilities to the world and to provoke an irate Gorbachev to dismiss defense minister Sergey Sokolov and about one hundred senior Red

Army officers. It was the largest purge of general officers since Stalin, though in this case Gorbachev merely sent them to early retirement, rather than the firing squad. The Soviet leader found Rust's jaunt a welcome excuse to replace military hard-liners with supporters of his reform agenda.[6]

Following up on his Brandenburg Gate speech, Reagan kept probing for cracks in the Soviet empire, especially any splits between the Kremlin and its Warsaw Pact satellites. General John Galvin, supreme allied commander Europe (SACEUR), briefed Reagan on the Red Army's forward deployments in Eastern Europe and highlighted the "significant strain" they put on the Soviet economy. Reagan asked if the Kremlin's command-and-control could "order Warsaw Pact forces to attack without approval of [their] Eastern European governments." Galvin confirmed it could. Control of the military is a cornerstone of a sovereign government; Moscow's seizure of this authority from Warsaw, East Berlin, Budapest, Prague, and other capitals was in Reagan's mind a particularly ugly example of Soviet imperialism. It was also a vulnerability. Reagan saw that the Kremlin had trapped itself in an unsustainable exchange: Moscow's resources flowed out to fund its troops in Eastern Europe, while Eastern European resentments flowed back to Moscow over its occupation of their countries—and its control of their own sons under arms.[7] Gorbachev recognized this too. Though the White House did not know it, earlier in the year, Gorbachev had told the Politburo that the Soviet Union needed to come clean about its occupation of Eastern Europe and draw down its military footprint. He just did not yet have the political support of his Politburo comrades to do so.[8]

Meanwhile at the White House, though the details of the INF Treaty were coming together and a summit with Gorbachev in Washington seemed likely, neither was yet finalized. Even once intermediate-range missiles were banned, the larger and more destructive arsenals of long-range multiwarhead ICBMs and SLBMs would remain. It was these strategic arms that could annihilate the planet, and that the Soviet and American delegations continued to negotiate in the Strategic Arms Reduction Talks (START) in Geneva. Reagan and Gorbachev still agreed on the principle of cutting those arms by 50 percent; whether they could come to terms on the specifics and codify them in a treaty remained to be seen.

As his advisors debated the details, Reagan reminded them of his ultimate goal, and the stakes: "You've got to remember that the [START negotiations were] born of the idea that the world needs to get rid of nuclear weapons. We've got to remember that we can't win a nuclear war and we can't fight one." He then described the carnage that a nuclear exchange would inflict on the planet. Reagan concluded the meeting on an apocalyptic note, quite literally: "Some day people are going to ask why we didn't do something now about getting rid of nuclear weapons. You know, I've been reading my Bible and the description of Armageddon talks about destruction, I believe, of many cities and we absolutely need to avoid that. We have to do something now."[9]

It bears remembering just how uncertain the future looked to Reagan and his advisors. Progress with the Soviets seemed to be accelerating, but no one really knew if it would be enduring or ephemeral. The arms race continued. Neither nation had yet cut a single nuclear weapon from its massive arsenal, with each side just a launch code or miscalculation away from annihilating the other. Though Gorbachev said he wanted to leave Afghanistan and curb Soviet adventurism elsewhere, he had not yet withdrawn any soldiers or reduced Soviet support for communist forces in Nicaragua, Angola, and Cambodia. Nor had he pulled back any Red Army units from their occupation of Eastern Europe. In short, Reagan's fear of Armageddon was not just an idiosyncratic scriptural reference—it was a plausible threat assessment of the world in the fall of 1987.

But September also brought signs of hope. Shevardnadze's visit to Washington entailed productive meetings with both Shultz and Reagan, including firming up the final details of the INF Treaty and preparing for the anticipated summit. Then, a setback. Reagan was not the only superpower leader dealing with a fractious team; Gorbachev faced even more severe internal divisions. When Shultz flew to Moscow in October to finalize plans for the summit, a dyspeptic Gorbachev blindsided him with a rant about all manner of alleged American misdeeds over the previous three decades. Of more concern, Gorbachev seemed to return to his condition (previously dropped) that the United States end SDI and walked back his commitment to set a date for the Washington summit.[10]

Shultz had endured tough sessions before with Gorbachev, but now "something distinctly different" had taken place. Gorbachev seemed wounded and weakened. The secretary told his staff, "He no longer looks to me like a boxer who has never been hit. This boxer has been hit." The person who had hit Gorbachev, Shultz soon learned, was his Politburo rival Boris Yeltsin. Two days before, at a Central Committee meeting, Yeltsin had resigned in protest while denouncing Gorbachev's reforms as anemic and ineffective. Gorbachev was used to enduring criticism from Soviet troglodytes, but this attack from a fellow reformer hurt, frightened, and infuriated him all at once. As soon as Shultz departed for Washington, a sheepish Gorbachev realized his indiscretion. He sent his foreign minister right back to Washington bearing a letter to Reagan accepting summit dates in December.[11]

III

In October, Weinberger told Reagan he planned to resign. Exhausted from almost seven years of unrelenting stress and anxious about his wife's ailing health, the defense secretary was also tired of fighting with, and losing to, Shultz. It seemed an irreparable breach. Rich Armitage, who although on Weinberger's staff had collaborated well with Shultz on Asia policy, at one point tried to broker a truce between the two cabinet adversaries.

At a reception, Armitage went up to Shultz and suggested, "Mr. Secretary, why don't you and Secretary Weinberger take a six-pack of beer, go out in a row boat in the middle of the lake and talk this thing through?"

Replied Shultz, "He wouldn't come."

The next day, after the Pentagon morning staff meeting, Armitage relayed the conversation to Weinberger, including Shultz's claim that Weinberger would refuse the gesture.

Weinberger responded, "He's right."

Weinberger also had seen for some time that his resistance to negotiations with the Soviets put him at growing odds with Reagan. Weinberger's rigidity in his positions, at times an asset, turned into a liability when he failed to keep pace with the Cold War's shifting terrain, including his commander in chief's desire to negotiate steep arms cuts with the Soviets. In Armitage's words, Weinberger "never changed the tape"—in 1987 he kept repeating his same positions from 1981.[12] Yet Weinberger also could take pride in much. He had served faithfully in the main task Reagan had entrusted to him: modernizing and expanding the force, and restoring its fighting spirit. Few if any of Reagan's diplomatic successes would have been possible absent the formidable military that Weinberger rebuilt and modernized. It is a legacy that has benefited every president and defense secretary since.

Reagan picked Carlucci to be the new secretary of defense and promoted Powell in his place, making Powell the first Black national security advisor in history. Together Shultz, Powell, and Carlucci forged a bureaucratic entente and ensured that Reagan's final year in office would enjoy an interagency cooperation that had been miserably absent the first seven years.

As Gorbachev's White House visit approached, Reagan redoubled his pressure on the Soviet Union's atheistic underbelly. On November 12, he hosted six Afghan resistance leaders at the White House. In the accompanying press conference, Reagan promised America's "continued strong support" for their holy war against the Soviet occupation and criticized Gorbachev's refusal to withdraw Soviet forces.[13] The Kremlin's "bleeding wound" would continue to hemorrhage. Two weeks later, Reagan gave a speech at the Heritage Foundation that offered his test for Gorbachev's reforms: "One of the truest measures of glasnost will be the degree of religious freedom the Soviet rulers allow their people." Specifically, Reagan urged Gorbachev to legalize the Ukrainian Catholic Church. The Reagan administration had long covertly supported the Ukrainian Catholics amid harsh persecution; now Reagan made his concern public. The church posed two potent threats to the Kremlin's imperial authority: It represented spiritual loyalty to the Vatican and the national identity of Ukraine.[14]

Reagan felt confident as the summit approached. He delivered a special Voice of America broadcast throughout Europe, reassuring Europeans of his continued solidarity even with the elimination of INF missiles. Proclaiming that "freedom and peace go hand in hand," he called for the liberation of Eastern Europe and said he hoped "someday General Secretary Gorbachev and I could meet in Berlin and together take down the first bricks of that wall—and we could continue taking down walls until the distrust between our peoples and the scars of the past are forgotten."[15]

Two weeks later in Geneva, to finalize the summit preparations, the American delegation led by Shultz and Powell had dinner with their Soviet counterparts, including Marshal Sergey Akhromeyev, the Kremlin's top defense official. The Americans felt an extra measure of regard for Akhromeyev—for both his stature as the last World War II combat veteran in a senior Soviet leadership position and his comparative reasonableness in their negotiations. At the dinner, one of the Americans asked Akhromeyev about his wartime service, as an eighteen-year-old sergeant during the Nazi siege of Leningrad, in which one and a half million city residents died. His answer transfixed the room. "For eighteen months, I never set foot inside a building, even when the temperature went to fifty below zero. I was out of doors through two winters, never knew a warm day, always fighting, always hungry. And such loss of life. Eight out of ten boys my age died during the war. Only I and one other from my high school class of thirty-two survived."[16]

For much of that time his unit had guarded a key road into the city. When Shultz closed the dinner by commending Akhromeyev's patriotism and grit in holding his position, the Soviet replied, "But we all knew, Mr. Secretary, that Stalin would have had us shot if we left the road." Two weeks later at the Washington summit, Akhromeyev and Shultz again sat together at dinner. Returning to his wartime service, the Soviet told the secretary, "My country is in trouble, and I am fighting alongside [Gorbachev] to save it. That is why we made such a lopsided deal on INF, and that is why we want to get along with you. We want to restructure ourselves and to be part of the modern world."[17]

Even the CIA began making unprecedented connections with its main foe. Powell arranged for CIA deputy director Bob Gates to have dinner with his KGB counterpart, Vladimir Kryuchkov, visiting from Moscow as part of the Soviet delegation. It would be the highest-level meeting between the KGB and CIA in the entire Cold War. Dining in the elegant French restaurant Maison Blanche with their nervous security details looking on, the two crafty spymasters alternated between wary banter and serious discussion. Kryuchkov caught Gates's attention when he commented repeatedly on America's wealth and might—saying he could "feel the power" in the United States. The KGB official then told Gates that he hoped the CIA "was telling the US leadership that the Soviet Union was not a weak, poor country that could be pushed around."

They sparred at length over Afghanistan. Kryuchkov confirmed that Moscow wanted an exit but only if a "political solution" (that did not appear as a US victory) could be found. In a prophetic note, the meeting transcript records that the KGB officer "expressed particular concern about the possibility of a rise to power in Afghanistan of another fundamentalist Islamic state. He noted that neither the Soviet Union nor the United States needed a second fundamentalist state like Iran. He observed in passing that the United States seemed to be fully occupied trying to deal with just one fundamentalist Islamic state."[18]

The CIA remained skeptical of Gorbachev's intentions. Gates sent Reagan a summit briefing that argued, "Gorbachev's gameplan potentially can be played out over a prolonged period—thus giving him and the USSR a significant advantage. His long range strategy is an important backdrop for the summit." Reagan disagreed. In the margins he wrote, "Our course [is] much steadier," and "Don't give [Gorbachev] too much credit for total fore-sight."[19] Even though Reagan had only one year left in office, he believed that America's strengths positioned it better to win the Cold War. He also had spent enough time with Gorbachev to detect that the Soviet leader was im-provising, adapting, feeling his way forward on an uncertain path. Reagan wanted to steer that path toward peace.

Meanwhile, American and Soviet negotiators haggled in the days lead-ing up to the summit on every last detail, ranging from the verification pro-visions in the INF Treaty to the number of Soviet staff for which the White House would pay travel costs. The imbibing habits of the Soviet advance team irked Reagan, who complained to his diary, "At [the] Madison Hotel they empty the mini-bars in their rooms into their suitcases every morning in addition to running up big bar bills—all of which we have to pay." After the White House got stiffed with a $1,400 alcohol tab for the Soviets' first night, Powell ordered the hotel to stop restocking the bar.[20] Such were the hidden costs of the Cold War.

IV

Reagan and Gorbachev's summit discussions would lack the depth of their previous sessions in Geneva and Reykjavík, but as Gorbachev biographer William Taubman points out, "almost everything else about it seemed ex-traordinary, both to Gorbachev and to Americans." The Reagans welcomed Gorbachev with all the state-visit pageantry normally granted only to the closest allies: a South Lawn arrival ceremony, a twenty-one-gun salute, a state dinner featuring pianist Van Cliburn playing iconic Russian songs, Soviet and American flags bedecking Pennsylvania Avenue. Gorbachev fur-ther burnished the celebrity atmosphere by hosting a dinner the next night at the Soviet embassy, with eclectic guests including Paul Newman, Robert De Niro, Henry Kissinger, Gregory Peck, Meryl Streep, Yoko Ono, Arthur Miller, John Kenneth Galbraith, George Kennan, John Denver, and Joyce Carol Oates.

The next morning, en route to the White House for his final meeting with Reagan, Gorbachev suddenly ordered his limousine to stop at the cor-ner of Connecticut Avenue and L Street. To the consternation of his joint US-Soviet security detail, he got out and waded into the throng of fans and onlookers, smiling, shaking hands, and reveling in the adulation.[21] He arrived at the White House ninety minutes late for his meeting with Reagan. It was a stunning breach of protocol, yet the affable president could not muster much annoyance. Reagan appreciated a deft theatrical display himself and had wanted Gorbachev to see the vibrancy of America. Now Gorbachev had shown the American people his own vibrancy. Many Americans were now seeing firsthand what Reagan had previously recognized. This was a different kind of Soviet altogether.

The summit discussions between Reagan and Gorbachev were more perfunctory. Both repeated many of their now-familiar positions on human rights, strategic arms reductions, and SDI. Gorbachev continued to oppose the latter, but having conceded on INF, he now linked halting SDI to progress on START. The Soviet leader displayed his usual verve, command of the issues, and verbosity. Reagan's posture was more taciturn, detached, yet punctuated by moments of passion. At one point when Gorbachev accused the United States of being "foggy" on its adherence to the ABM Treaty, Reagan erupted with some rare profanities: "I am not making things foggy. I want to make things clear . . . let's talk about how the hell our two sides are to eliminate half our nuclear weapons. I want to talk about how we can sign an agreement like the one we signed yesterday. . . . Let's get started with it!" Reagan also pressed Gorbachev to remove all Soviet troops from Afghanistan and get Vietnam to withdraw from Cambodia, and reminded the Soviet leader he "could and should tear down the [Berlin] wall today." Gorbachev retorted that a Soviet retreat from Afghanistan depended on the United States ending its weapons supply to the mujahideen. In response, Reagan noted that the Afghan resistance deserved "a voice in their own government," which the puppet regime installed by Moscow sought to deny them.[22] Of most consequence, Reagan accepted Gorbachev's invitation to visit Moscow in May.

The summit's apotheosis came with the signing of the INF Treaty. At one forty-five P.M.—a time later revealed to have been dictated by the First Lady's astrologer—the two leaders entered the White House East Room and inscribed their signatures on a document unprecedented in the annals of the Cold War. Reagan remarked on what it meant: "It was over 6 years ago, November 18, 1981, that I first proposed what would come to be called the zero option. It was a simple proposal—one might say, disarmingly simple. . . . For the first time in history, the language of 'arms control' was replaced by 'arms reduction'—in this case, the complete elimination of an entire class of US and Soviet nuclear missiles." Gorbachev added that at last they were on "the road leading away from the threat of catastrophe . . . and mov[ing] together toward a nuclear-free world."[23]

Not all shared this hope. Some conservatives and realists continued to criticize the INF Treaty. Brent Scowcroft derided it as "a bad idea whose time has come." University of Chicago professor John Mearsheimer worried that it hurt "the credibility of [the US] defense commitment" to NATO. George Will complained that Reagan was "drunk on détente." Henry Kissinger lamented that Reagan "seemed bent on ending his term by dismantling the concepts and practices that have shaped Western strategy for four decades."[24] Nixon, though more artful in expressing it, shared these concerns. In a phone call with Reagan three days after Gorbachev's departure, the former president said that now that the INF Treaty had been signed, with reluctance he would support its Senate ratification—but then added he hoped the Senate would amend it with provisions that would in effect kill the treaty. Nixon's summary of the call noted that Reagan "did not respond one way or another"—a sure sign that he did not appreciate Nixon's advice.[25]

Because the critics viewed the Cold War as a static standoff between two great powers, they failed again to see Reagan's efforts to transform the conflict. Like SDI, the INF Treaty represented another way Reagan rejected the illusory "stability" created by the balance of terror in which thousands of nuclear warheads stood minutes away from destroying every European city from Lisbon to Moscow (not to mention Tokyo, Beijing, and Seoul from the SS-20s in the Russian Far East). Instead, Reagan showed he could partner with Gorbachev to reverse the arms race and build trust and cooperation between two enemy superpowers. Yet this trust only went so far. At the signing ceremony, Reagan invoked his "trust but verify" mantra—"You repeat that at every meeting," jabbed Gorbachev; "I like it," responded Reagan—and he reassured nervous NATO allies that the United States maintained some four thousand tactical and short-range nuclear weapons in Europe to deter the Red Army.[26]

V

As Reagan's last year in office unfolded, his eponymous doctrine led to diplomatic successes in Afghanistan and southern Africa. He also regained his footing in the Middle East with a display of force in the Persian Gulf that was noticed in Moscow and beyond.

On February 8, 1988, the Kremlin made a surprise announcement: The Red Army would withdraw from Afghanistan within the year. Gorbachev had decided to cut his losses. The Soviet decision jump-started negotiations in Geneva with the Americans, Afghans, and Pakistanis over the terms of the withdrawal and future political order. Not wanting to abandon the mujahideen to retribution from the Moscow-backed Najibullah government, Reagan insisted on the right to keep supporting the insurgents during and after the Soviet exit—though in fact American funding would dry up not long afterward. The Geneva accords also obligated Pakistan to end its sponsorship of the holy warriors. However, Zia phoned Reagan and told him that Pakistan intended to keep providing a safe haven for training and equipping the mujahideen. If asked, Zia continued, he would "just lie about it": "We've been denying our activities there for eight years," he said. "Muslims have the right to lie in a good cause."[27] Shultz summed up the strategic consequences for the Cold War: "The Reagan Doctrine of support for people who fight for freedom had won out over the Brezhnev Doctrine of perpetual control by the Soviets of territory they had seized."[28]

Meanwhile, January brought a breakthrough in southern Africa. A combination of UNITA battlefield successes, dwindling Kremlin support for the MPLA, South African isolation, and creative and indefatigable diplomacy by Chet Crocker induced Havana to announce that it would withdraw Cuban troops if allowed to participate in a negotiated settlement. Soon thereafter, South Africa agreed to end its occupation of Namibia and also withdraw its forces from Angola. Several more months of shuttle diplomacy ensued, culminating in the signing of the interlocking agreements at the United Nations in December. In one State Department official's vivid description, "Diplomats and generals from Angola, Cuba, South Africa, the Soviet Union, the South West African People's Organization and the neighboring African states raised their glasses to the historic achievements of an American mediation effort that they had spent nearly a decade denigrating and obstructing." Even Congress played a constructive role. Strong bipartisan congressional majorities had maintained funding for UNITA and backed Savimbi's participation in the diplomatic process. Reagan's support for UNITA generated little of the partisan acrimony that beset Nicaragua policy; notably, senators ranging from archconservative Jesse Helms to centrist Democrat Dennis DeConcini to liberal Chris Dodd all endorsed Savimbi.[29] In removing one of the primary regional threats to South Africa, the agreement also deflated much of the apartheid government's paranoia and rationale for militancy, and contributed to the eventual demise of apartheid and transition to South African democracy over the next several years.

The Reagan Doctrine also left some bitter fruits. Statecraft entails hard trade-offs, managing risk, and choosing from among unpalatable options. The Reagan Doctrine was no exception. While solving some problems, it created or exacerbated others. It helped free Nicaragua, Angola, Afghanistan, and Cambodia from communist misrule but left behind divided, impoverished countries awash in armed factions, instability, and corruption. In the Cold War's aftermath, each nation would face decades of continued strife and struggle. Yet from the vantage point of 1981, or even 1986, the option of neglecting these insurgencies would have meant leaving them to Soviet predation—and the record of countries swallowed in the Soviet orbit is a grim catalog of oppression and regional instability. In turning back those outcomes, and weakening the Kremlin, the Reagan Doctrine succeeded on its own terms—and did so without risking American troops. It reached its limits, and even contributed to other problems, on the hard questions of what came next.

The Middle East remained bereft of any good options. Nonetheless, a combination of force and diplomacy also brought some progress, particularly in the Persian Gulf. Iran had continued to test American protection for oil shipping. Through the fall of 1987, US forces retaliated several times for Iranian provocations, including sinking an Iranian minelayer and several gunboats and destroying a gunboat base. Tehran persisted in mining the gulf. On April 14, 1988, an Iranian mine detonated and nearly sank the navy frigate USS *Samuel B. Roberts*. To strike back, Reagan ordered Operation Praying Mantis. He tried to calibrate the use of force, directing that before commencing fire, the navy first warn the Iranians to abandon their platforms and ships. "We seek no killing—just the destruction of targets," Reagan wrote. On April 18, three US Navy surface action groups, backed by aircraft from the carrier *Enterprise*, destroyed two Iranian oil-platforms-turned-naval-bases and sank six Iranian navy ships—fully half of the Iranian navy. Around sixty Iranian servicemembers were killed in action. The United States lost two sailors when their helicopter crashed into the sea in a night operation. It was the largest US naval surface warfare action since World War II and remains to this day the most high-intensity combat the US has engaged in with Iran.[30]

The operation's greatest consequence came at the negotiating table. The American use of force, along with Iraq's battlefield advances (aided by

chemical weapons) in its war with Iran, caused Tehran to "reluctantly conclude that it could not sustain a continuing war with Baghdad *and* an in-
tensifying conflict with Washington," as Hal Brands points out. Within a
few months, Iran agreed to sign a cease-fire with Iraq, on the terms set by
UN resolution 598, negotiated by Shultz the previous year. The net effect of
the more assertive US posture in the gulf produced several successes, including an end to the Iran-Iraq War, a curtailment of Iran's malign activities, and stability to oil and gas supply chains flowing from the region to
fuel the global economy. Problems simmered, however, that would resurface after Reagan left office, beginning with a Saddam Hussein who felt empowered by Iraq's performance in the war, resentful about America's erratic
support, and desperate for money to pay down his massive debt.[31]

Two days after Operation Praying Mantis, Reagan signed a memorandum of understanding with Israel, deepening United States–Israel security
cooperation. Dennis Ross, the Middle East expert who served on Reagan's
NSC staff, points out that Reagan and Shultz "viewed Israel through a lens
of shared values. . . . Reagan did not see a contradiction between cooperating with Israel on matters of security interest to [the United States] and
having good relations with the Arabs." Unlike prior administrations who
viewed US relations with Israel and Arab states as zero-sum trade-offs,
where pursuing one came at the direct expense of the other, "Reagan and
Shultz would prove otherwise and create a baseline for all succeeding administrations."[32]

VI

With developments breaking America's way in Asia, Africa, Latin America,
and the Middle East, Reagan prepared for a step he had never taken in his
seventy-seven years: setting foot in the Soviet Union. He would travel there
in May for another summit with Gorbachev. The trip would culminate his
presidency. For seven and a half years, he had combined pressure and outreach toward the Kremlin, seeking to bring it to a negotiated surrender. His
trip would coincide with the millennium of Christianity's arrival in Russia,
and he would come bearing his own call to repentance and faith.

To prepare, Reagan and Shultz both read a book Gorbachev had just
written titled *Perestroika*, in which the Soviet leader laid out his thinking
on domestic and foreign policy.[33] Reagan wanted to focus as much as pos-

sible on human rights and religious freedom, especially after Shultz and the American negotiators in Geneva failed to come to terms with the Soviet delegation on the hoped-for START treaty to cut strategic arms. While Moscow had made progress on human rights, Jewish emigration had plateaued, and over two hundred religious believers remained imprisoned for their faith.[34] In the weeks before his Moscow departure, Reagan held at least five White House meetings with religious freedom activists, including evangelical Protestants, Ukrainian Catholics, Jews, and dissidents late of the gulag, such as the Christian poet Irina Ratushinskaya.[35] Such encounters helped generate ideas for how best he could persuade Gorbachev of the importance of religious freedom. Even more, captivated as he was by personal stories, hearing firsthand from victims of religious persecution anguished, infuriated, and inspired Reagan ahead of his Moscow summit.

Shortly before his trip, Reagan issued NSDD-302, setting out his strategic agenda: "My visit to the Soviet Union should not be seen as a dialogue only with the Soviet government, but also as a way of communicating with the Soviet people. I want to emphasize throughout my trip that the democratic values that make our country great are those toward which much of the world—including, we hope, the Soviet Union—is moving."[36]

Notwithstanding the positive trends in US-Soviet relations, both sides remained locked in a security competition. Ahead of the annual NATO summit in March, Powell wrote to Thatcher's top advisor, "We cannot allow Soviet rhetoric and clever diplomacy to obscure the reality of their concerted effort to expand and modernize their armed forces." Thatcher had become a Gorbachev skeptic, warning a gathering of NATO leaders, "The Soviets are the more dangerous the more sweetly they talk; they continue to aim at undermining and dividing NATO [and] maintaining military superiority for themselves."[37] Reagan, though much more optimistic about the Soviet leader, agreed that the alliance needed to maintain the pressure. He told his national security team, "Our [summit] objective must be to convince our Allies to keep up their defense expenditures. . . . I do not think Gorbachev wants to engage in an arms race with the United States, but our task is to convince him not to try."[38]

The Pentagon did its part. In April, the Air Force unveiled a picture of its newest stealth bomber, the B-2 Spirit, an unvarnished message to the Kremlin ahead of the Moscow summit. When asked about the timing of the announcement, Reagan confessed, "I don't think it will hurt at the summit." Senate Armed Services Committee chairman Sam Nunn, an influential backer of the aircraft, claimed the B-2 would "render obsolete billions of dollars of Soviet investment in their current air defense."[39] This bat-winged, nuclear-armed wraith, invisible to Soviet radar, exemplified the competitive strategies framework of using America's technological edge to levy unsustainable costs on Moscow. No matter how many more surface-to-air missiles the Kremlin might buy, they could not hit what they could not see.

The day after revealing the B-2, Reagan gave a speech in Massachusetts that provoked more heartburn in Moscow. Recalling the foundation of his Cold War strategy, that "containment was not enough . . . the expansion of human freedom was our goal," he set his terms for the upcoming summit: "[A] Soviet Union that oppresses its own people, that violates the Helsinki accords on human rights . . . that continues to suppress free expression and religious worship and the right to travel . . . can never truly have normal relations with the United States and the rest of the free world."[40] The next day, by coincidence, Shultz and Powell met with Gorbachev at the Kremlin for final preparations for the summit. The irked Soviet leader harangued the Americans for forty-five minutes about Reagan's speech, asking, "Is this summit going to be a catfight?" Having vented his frustrations, Gorbachev downshifted to a more congenial tone and completed his summit preview with Powell and Shultz.[41]

Reagan shared Gorbachev's worry about the fate of the INF Treaty. Having survived one year of US-Soviet negotiations, the treaty then faced the gauntlet of the "world's greatest deliberative body." After its December signing, six months of torturous US Senate hearings and ratification debate ensued. Republican hawks such as Dan Quayle and Jesse Helms led opposition to the treaty, though conservative Democrats such as Nunn also subjected it to exacting scrutiny. Finally, as Reagan prepared to depart for the Soviet Union, he and Shultz appealed to the Senate opponents to unblock it, lest the president arrive at the Kremlin appearing weak and hamstrung by his own party. Two days before Reagan landed in Moscow, the Senate approved the treaty ninety-three to five.[42]

The day prior to his first meeting with Gorbachev, Reagan confided to his diary, "I'm going to tackle him on religious freedom—not as a deal with us but as a suggestion to him as an answer to some of his problems."[43] Here again was a quiet diplomatic revolution. In their negotiations with Gorbachev, Reagan and Shultz made a further break with the approach that all of their predecessors had taken toward Soviet leaders. For the past four decades, American presidents had relied on a combination of leverage and national interests in their diplomacy with the Kremlin. They would describe American interests on issues such as the arms race, Third World conflicts, access to Berlin, Jewish emigration, and others, and then probe their Soviet counterparts for areas of compromise, concession, or agreement. Reagan and Shultz jettisoned that playbook. Instead they tried to persuade Gorbachev to embrace their views because *they were in his country's best interests*. It was audacious, even brazen. Reagan—the evangelist for abolishing nuclear weapons, ending Soviet imperialism, respecting human rights, believing in God—sought to convince Gorbachev to believe in those too.

All of the strands of Reagan's Cold War strategy converged in Moscow. By outcompeting the Soviets in the military and economic domains, American pressure had contributed to the USSR's financial exhaustion and ideological bankruptcy. The Kremlin could no longer fund itself, let alone its control of its Warsaw Pact satrapies or its Third World adventurism. Few people living under communism believed in it anymore. In short, Reagan's military modernization and economic expansion earned him the right to be heard in Moscow, by both the Soviet people and their leader. The Cold War had come to this. Two mortal adversaries now faced off in a final clash—not of arms but over what makes a good society.

Almost every aspect of the Moscow visit would display these questions. At the Kremlin welcome ceremony, Reagan concluded his remarks with a simple "Thank you and God bless you." Gorbachev's interpreter recalls that the salutation sounded "like blasphemy to some of the ears of the Soviet officials present" as "the heretofore impregnable edifice of communist atheism was being assaulted before their very eyes."[44]

Reagan continued the assault, gently, in his initial one-on-one with Gorbachev. After exchanging felicitations, the Soviet leader sought to preempt the human rights issue by lecturing Reagan about racism and economic inequality in the United States. Reagan listened politely, acknowledging America's problems but also defending its openness and progress. Then the president said that in confidence he wanted to raise "a personal dream" of his, which would benefit Gorbachev and the Soviet Union. Reagan asked Gorbachev, "What if you ruled that religious freedom was part of the people's rights, that people of any religion"—including Muslims, Jews, Protestants, Ukrainian Catholics—could worship freely? Continuing, Reagan suggested, "This could go a long way to solving the Soviet emigration problem. Potential emigrants often want to go because of their limited ability to worship the God they believed in."

Reagan's appeal struck a nerve with Gorbachev. Growing defensive, the Soviet leader blustered that atheists did not have the same rights as believers in the United States.

Not so, responded Reagan. Then he took an intensely personal turn. "My own son is an atheist," Reagan revealed, referring to his namesake, Ron Jr., and making clear that he enjoyed equality with all other Americans.

Reagan then tried another angle, appealing to Gorbachev's vanity and desire to improve the USSR's image in the world. If Gorbachev were to protect religious freedom, Reagan continued, "I feel very strongly that you will be a hero, and that much of the prevailing feeling against the Soviet Union will disappear like water in hot sun."

Reagan did not just want Gorbachev to embrace religious freedom; he wanted him to believe in God. The president closed their meeting with two anecdotes about the impossibilities of atheism. One (probably apocryphal) described a Soviet soldier in World War II who beheld the celestial majesty of the night sky and trusted in God just before dying in combat.

The other was about his son. "One thing I have long yearned to do is serve my son the perfect gourmet dinner, to have him enjoy the meal, and then to ask him if he believed there was a cook. I wonder how he would answer?"

Replied Gorbachev, "The only possible answer is 'yes.'"

The meeting ended.[45]

Reagan's evangelistic seeds fell on rocky soil; Gorbachev would persist in his atheism. But the conversation deepened their personal bond. The Soviet leader saw Reagan's genuine care for him as a human being—to the point of concern over his soul—and appreciated the president's candor in sharing his anguish over his son's unbelief.

The next day Reagan took his message to the Soviet people. At Suzanne Massie's recommendation, he visited the Danilovsky Monastery. One of Moscow's most sacred places, under Stalin it had been perverted into a prison for the children of political opponents, until Brezhnev on his deathbed returned it to the Orthodox Church and Gorbachev allowed it to be restored. In remarks to the assembled monks, Reagan hoped "for a new age of religious freedom in the Soviet Union . . . a new policy of religious tolerance that will extend to all peoples of all faiths." He then rather subversively quoted Russia's greatest living writer and one of the Kremlin's fiercest critics, Alexander Solzhenitsyn. "When you travel the byroads of central Russia, you begin to understand the secret of the pacifying Russian countryside.

It is in the churches . . . reminding men that they must abandon trivial concerns of this world and give time and thought to eternity."[46] From the monastery, Reagan went to the US ambassador's residence to host a lunch for ninety-eight Soviet dissidents. He made clear that the United States stood with them in their struggle. He also told them, "I came here hoping to do what I could to give you strength. Yet I already know it is you who have strengthened me."[47]

The actual negotiating sessions between Reagan and Gorbachev covered the usual ground: haggling on details over strategic arms reductions, verification provisions, SDI and the ABM Treaty, regional conflicts. Each leader generally stuck to familiar talking points and themes. As it had been in their Washington summit six months earlier, so again in Moscow: The most interesting and consequential events took place outside the negotiating room.

For example, following their morning meeting on May 31, Reagan and Gorbachev went for a stroll in Red Square, abutting the Kremlin. As the two leaders beheld the grandeur of one of the world's iconic settings, the irrepressible Sam Donaldson of ABC News shouted a question: "Do you still think you're in an evil empire, Mr. President?"

"No," replied Reagan, "I was talking about another time and another era."

As with many media interactions with political leaders, the exchange was not entirely spontaneous. The Kremlin had seethed over the imprecation in the five years since Reagan first uttered it, and during the previous few months, Soviet diplomats had sent quiet requests to the White House for the president to update his views. Reagan elaborated at a press conference the next day, saying that *evil empire* no longer pertained largely because of Gorbachev, "who I have found different than previous Soviet leaders." The general secretary cherished this vote of confidence from his main adversary—and now friend.[48]

Over dinner following a Bolshoi Ballet performance, the two leaders swapped jokes with the easy bonhomie that Reagan otherwise enjoyed only with his closest allies, such as Thatcher, Nakasone, Kohl, and Mulroney. The conversation turned serious when Reagan brought up his fear of nuclear apocalypse and asked Gorbachev about Chernobyl and the "wormwood" prophesy in the Book of Revelation. Shultz, also at the table, noticed that a "deeply affected" Gorbachev responded by describing "with seemingly genuine horror the devastation that would occur" in a nuclear war.[49]

The zenith came when Reagan stepped inside the capacious lecture hall at Moscow State University to speak to its students. A mural heralding the 1917 revolution and a massive statue of Lenin overlooked the podium where he would speak—rather apt in that Reagan's message would challenge all that the patrimonial Bolshevik believed.[50] Reagan later recalled, "I tried in a few minutes . . . to summarize a philosophy that had guided me most of my life."[51] Reagan began by saying he wanted to speak

> about a very different revolution that is taking place right now, quietly sweeping the globe without bloodshed or conflict. . . . It's been called the technological or information revolution, and as its emblem, one might take the tiny silicon chip, no bigger than a fingerprint. One of these chips has more computing power than a roomful of old-style computers.

It was a remarkable contrast between the two systems of government. Here stood the seventy-seven-year-old American president serving as an apostle of the future, to his Soviet counterpart two decades his junior and even to the Soviet students in the room some six decades his junior.

Reagan continued, "We're emerging from the economy of the Industrial Revolution . . . into, as one economist titled his book, 'The Economy in Mind,' in which there are no bounds on human imagination and the freedom to create is the most precious natural resource. . . . But progress is not foreordained. The key is freedom—freedom of thought, freedom of information, freedom of communication."

For all of his optimism about human liberty and the information age, Reagan was not a materialist techno-utopian extolling a libertarian ambition for radical autonomy. His vision was for ordered liberty, for freedom anchored in the organic traditions of community, history, and faith. He turned to this next: "Freedom, it has been said, makes people selfish and materialistic, but Americans are one of the most religious peoples on Earth. Because they know that liberty, just as life itself, is not earned but a gift from God, they seek to share that gift with the world. . . . Positive change must be rooted in traditional values—in the land, in culture, in family and community—and it must take its life from the eternal things, from the source of all life, which is faith."

He concluded with his hope for peace and reminded his audience of America's history of turning enemies into friends.

People do not make wars; governments do. And no mother would ever willingly sacrifice her sons for territorial gain, for economic advantage, for ideology. A people free to choose will always choose peace. Americans seek always to make friends of old antagonists. After a colonial revolution with Britain, we have cemented for all ages the ties of kinship between our nations. . . . We fought two world wars in my lifetime against Germany and one with Japan, but now the Federal Republic of Germany and Japan are two of our closest allies and friends.[52]

Perhaps, the peacemaker suggested, Russia and the United States could enjoy a similar future.

Reagan's speech captivated the city. Eric Edelman, an American diplomat serving in Moscow, describes it as "the single most discussed issue of the day in Moscow after the Summit, both among diplomats and the Soviet citizens with whom I met in the aftermath." The young scholar Svetlana Savranskaya was also in the audience that day. "For those of us in attendance . . . the Cold War ended on May 31, 1988. For us, the graduating class, it was a kind of commencement address, and we understood that the smiling man who spoke about things close to our heart, like human rights, would not push the button."[53]

The Moscow summit helps illumine one of the mysteries of Reagan's Cold War policy: What exactly did he intend for the Soviet Union? Did he purpose to negotiate better behavior while leaving the Soviet regime intact, or to collapse it altogether? Judging by his words leaves some ambiguity. At times he spoke of creating more peaceful relations between the two nations—implying a willingness to coexist with a better-behaved version of the USSR. Other times he spoke of ending communism entirely, consigned to the "ash-heap of history."

Judging by his deeds brings more clarity. If one focuses only on Reagan's efforts to negotiate with Gorbachev for the end of nuclear weapons and reduced US-Soviet tensions, it could appear Reagan might have been content to leave the Kremlin otherwise as it was. However, at the Moscow summit and throughout his presidency, Reagan pursued other policies that struck at the core of the Soviet system. He urged Gorbachev and all Soviet citizens to believe in God. He pushed for the Soviet Union to respect human rights and allow freedom of emigration, religious freedom, freedom of expression. He tried to persuade Gorbachev to adopt free markets and let private enterprise and the knowledge economy flourish. He lured the Soviet military and economy into an arms race it could not sustain. He worked to liberate the Warsaw Pact satellites from Soviet imperial control.

Such a Soviet Union, one that believed in God, free markets, and individual liberty and defunded its military and relinquished its empire, would be a "Union of Soviet Socialist Republics" in name only—it would otherwise cease to exist.

This is why Reagan's strategic goal toward the Soviet Union is best understood as a negotiated surrender. He pursued diplomacy with Gorbachev in genuine efforts to eliminate nuclear weapons, end proxy conflicts around the world, and bring peace between the two nations—but also to bring Soviet communism to a peaceful death.

VII

From Moscow, Reagan traveled first to London to brief Thatcher and visiting Japanese prime minister Noboru Takeshita (who had succeeded Nakasone), then onward, home to the United States. The Moscow trip bolstered Reagan's political standing and completed his recovery from the Iran-contra scandal. Even many of his usual media critics applauded his performance; *Time* called it "Reagan's finest hour."[54]

Back at the White House, Reagan had to confront simmering tensions with a surprising source: his own vice president. Ever the faithful lieutenant while at Reagan's right hand, Bush had recently taken on a new role that entailed some distance. He had won the Republican nomination for the presidency. Now the old navy pilot had to pull off a complicated maneuver: distancing himself from Reagan and embracing him at the same time. Bush needed to show voters he was his own man while still basking in Reagan's popularity. Politics aside, as a seasoned statesman Bush also had his own beliefs about the right course of action—and wanted to do what he could to shape the world that he hoped to inherit on Inauguration Day in 1989.

The main issues where Bush parted ways with Reagan were in many ways dissimilar, though both involved how to deal with two complicated heads of state: Gorbachev and Panama's Manuel Noriega. On the Soviet leader, Bush did not echo Reagan's optimism. A few days after the Moscow summit, Bush told reporters that he did not share Reagan's view that Gorbachev was bringing "fundamental change" to the Soviet Union. In response to a question from George Will, the vice president admitted "maybe [there is] a difference" between him and his president on Soviet policy. Bush continued to voice these doubts throughout the summer and fall, though he did not try to change Reagan's policies.[55]

This was not the case on Panama. In deliberations on what to do about the Panamanian dictator Noriega, Bush actively opposed Reagan's policy preference. The Panama crisis escalated at the start of the year when the Justice Department indicted Noriega for drug trafficking and racketeering. Many Panamanians, disaffected by his corruption and oppressive rule, took to the streets to protest against him. The dictator reacted by cracking down on the opposition and closing the banks, putting the country on the verge of collapse.

There was a certain historical irony to Panama emerging as a test for the White House. Opposition to the Panama Canal treaties had boosted Reagan's national prominence a decade earlier; now this small Central American country returned to vex him in the closing days of his presidency. At the start of the year, he had dispatched Rich Armitage to Panama to try to persuade Noriega to step down. Armitage stayed up late draining a bottle of scotch with Noriega, but the dictator, both when sober and when drunk, repeatedly refused to go.[56] A few months later, as the crisis escalated, Reagan and Shultz sent another emissary to Panama, the able State Department lawyer Mike Kozak. "Our man Kozak," as Reagan called him, had helped negotiate the Panama Canal treaties in 1977. Now Kozak returned to try to negotiate Noriega's departure. Kozak arrived in Panama City bearing the stick of the indictment and the carrot of an offer to drop all criminal charges if Noriega would go into exile in Spain.

Yet while Kozak cajoled Noriega in Panama City, back at the White House, Bush argued vehemently against the deal, complaining that it would appear soft on crime and undercut the Justice Department. Treasury Secretary Jim Baker and Attorney General Ed Meese agreed with Bush. They found surprising allies in Nancy and Maureen Reagan. The president's wife and daughter complained to Reagan it looked like he was "giving in to a drug dealer." An annoyed Reagan vented to his diary that critics of the deal didn't "seem to realize the only alternative would be a military invasion of Panama." Shultz and Powell agreed and supported Reagan's effort. Ultimately, Noriega himself resolved the White House dispute. He first accepted the deal, then backpedaled and turned it down. Reagan's concern proved prophetic. Noriega stayed in power until December 1989, when then-president Bush resorted to an invasion of Panama to oust the dictator.[57]

VIII

On November 8, voters elected George H. W. Bush as the forty-first president. Though Bush had turned into a solid candidate, he benefited from Reagan's popularity and a hapless opponent in Michael Dukakis. Bush's election presented its own validation of Reagan's legacy. It was only the third time in US history, and the first time in almost 150 years, that a sitting vice president won election to the presidency. It was also the first time in over a century that voters had selected a member of the same party to succeed a two-term president.[58] For good reason, many described Bush's election as "Reagan's third term."

For Reagan, November and December brought a last round of farewells. Helmut Kohl visited the White House, followed the next day by Margaret Thatcher, for whom the Reagans hosted their final state dinner. Then came word from Moscow that Gorbachev would be coming to New York to address the UN General Assembly and wanted to meet with Reagan and Bush. Bush did not favor the meeting but felt unable to decline it. Amid the political netherworld of a presidential transition, he worried that he would be seen as responsible for the US-Soviet relationship, even though he did not yet have the authority to manage it. Bush also fretted that Gorbachev might use the meeting to wheedle some final concessions from Reagan. Yet it turned out that Gorbachev was the one bearing concessions. On the morning of December 7, the Soviet leader told the UN that he planned to cut his conventional forces by five hundred thousand troops, ten thousand tanks, and eight hundred aircraft, effectively reducing the Soviet arsenal by 10 percent. He also called for "freedom of choice" in international politics, and for good measure, a "new world order."[59]

Gorbachev's announcement electrified the hall and captured international headlines. It also vindicated Reagan's faith that his friend was a transformative leader. From Turtle Bay, Gorbachev made the short jaunt to Governors Island, where he met Reagan and Bush. The president-elect's worries were assuaged as Gorbachev and Reagan kept the mood light. Reagan presented Gorbachev a signed, framed photo of their first encounter in

Geneva; the president's inscription read, "We have walked a long way to-gether to clear a path for peace." They spent most of their time reminiscing about past summits and joking about Reagan's retirement plans. There was a final gesture of quiet human rights diplomacy: Reagan gave Gorbachev a list of six more Soviet prisoners of conscience he hoped to see released.[60]

As he prepared to leave office, Reagan's approval ratings stood at 63 percent in the Gallup poll and 68 percent in the *New York Times*/CBS poll. Eighty-one percent of Americans approved of his handling of US-Soviet relations in particular. He would end his presidency enjoying the highest regard of any president since Franklin Roosevelt.[61] It is perhaps no coinci-dence that Roosevelt was the other twentieth-century president to lead the nation to victory over a totalitarian foe—though for both Roosevelt and Rea-gan, it would fall to their successors to see the conflict through to its end.

On January 11, 1989, Reagan delivered his farewell address from the Oval Office. He spoke more of his country than himself:

> I've been reflecting on what the past 8 years have meant and mean. And the image that comes to mind like a refrain is a nautical one— a small story about a big ship, and a refugee, and a sailor. It was back in the early eighties, at the height of the boat people. And the sailor was hard at work on the carrier *Midway,* which was patrol-ling the South China Sea. . . . The crew spied on the horizon a leaky little boat. And crammed inside were refugees from Indochina hoping to get to America. The *Midway* sent a small launch to bring them to the ship and safety. As the refugees made their way through the choppy seas, one spied the sailor on deck, and stood up, and called out to him. He yelled, "Hello, American sailor. Hello, free-dom man." . . . Because that's what it was to be an American in the 1980s. We stood, again, for freedom.

He invoked a favorite image, America as a "shining city on a hill," and continued, "If there had to be city walls, the walls had doors and the doors were open to anyone with the will and the heart to get here."

He closed with his hope:

> And how stands the city on this winter night? More prosperous, more secure, and happier than it was 8 years ago. But more than that: After 200 years, two centuries, she still stands strong and true

on the granite ridge, and her glow has held steady no matter what storm. And she's still a beacon, still a magnet for all who must have freedom, for all the pilgrims from all the lost places who are hurtling through the darkness, toward home."[62]

Nine days later, on the morning of January 20, 1989, Colin Powell arrived in the Oval Office to give Reagan his final national security briefing. It was short: "The world is quiet today, Mr. President."[63]

EPILOGUE

Hushed whispers in the stillness of the US Capitol rotunda passed word of a new arrival. "Is that Gorbachev? Is Gorbachev here?" The aged Soviet leader walked slowly, solemnly, forward, past the velvet rope lines and to the center of the cavernous hall. Flanked by the honor guard, he mournfully rubbed his hand over the flag-enveloped casket and bowed his head in silence. It was the tenth of June 2004; it was his farewell to Ronald Reagan.

"I gave him a pat," Gorbachev said affectionately of his deceased rival and friend. "He was an extraordinary political leader" who decided at the right moment "to be a peacemaker."[1]

Ten years earlier, Reagan had announced to the world his diagnosis of Alzheimer's disease and his retreat from public life. Even then he had already seen much of his legacy unfold. As president, Reagan had transformed the art of the possible. Things inconceivable in 1980 became reality by 1989. A Soviet leader committed to reform at home and repudiating imperialism abroad. The elimination of an entire class of nuclear weapons. Steep reductions in Soviet conventional forces and the Red Army withdrawing from Afghanistan. Democracy dawning in South Korea, the Philippines, Taiwan, El Salvador, Chile, Brazil, Argentina, and other once-authoritarian nations. South African forces withdrawing from Namibia and Cuban forces departing Angola.

All of these changes had taken place by January 20, 1989, as the Reagans boarded the steps of the plane they knew as Air Force One and flew, following the setting sun, to their California home.

The Cold War was not yet over. The Soviet Union still possessed a fearsome arsenal of nuclear weapons targeted at the United States. The Red Army still stood ready to flood through the Fulda Gap. The Iron Curtain and Berlin Wall both still divided Europe. But the conflict had been transformed. Reagan could at least declare victory in the battle of ideas. The Iron Curtain and Berlin Wall may have appeared to the naked eye to still be standing, but the forces that would bring them down were already boring away within. Marxism-Leninism stood discredited, and free societies were ascendant.

In general, presidents are judged by events that take place while they are in office. The most consequential presidents also shape what comes after them. Just as Franklin Roosevelt did not live to see World War II end with the surrenders of Nazi Germany and imperial Japan, Reagan would be retired to private life when the Berlin Wall crumbled, the Iron Curtain came down, and the Soviet Union gave up its many ghosts. Yet just as Roosevelt rightly is regarded as the architect of American strategy in World War II, Reagan oversaw the American strategy for the successful end of the Cold War. He brought the Soviet Union to the brink of a negotiated surrender.

As Hal Brands concludes, "Reagan and his advisers facilitated a veritable strategic renaissance." They "developed ambitious strategic frameworks that put the force of American power behind the vital tectonic shifts" under way in the world.[2] Many of those geopolitical currents were already swirling when Reagan took office, leaving him to help steer them. Other trends he inspired and accelerated. In 1980, history's ineluctable tides and Reagan's resolve and vision came together. It was a moment, in Derek Leebaert's words, "of the man and the hour meeting."[3]

The biggest changes simmered just months away from Reagan's retirement. June 1989 would bring a massive Solidarity victory in Poland's first free elections. In November the people of Berlin would tear down the wall that divided their city, and with it, the rest of the Iron Curtain would be torn asunder as Eastern Europe became free. Two years later, on Christmas Day 1991, the Soviet Union itself would cease to exist.

President George H. W. Bush and his team exercised a deft hand in managing these transformations. Cautious at first, they soon saw that the world was being convulsed and in need of steady statecraft and strategic vision from the United States. They answered the call: Germany reunited, Russia and its former states welcomed into the community of nations, arsenals slashed—in short, "a world transformed," as Bush titled his memoir. Reagan's legacy became Bush's legacy too, of the Cold War's peaceful end.

II

The Reagan legacy is not without its bitter fruits. His policies at times included providing support to China, Saddam Hussein's Iraq, Iran, and jihadists in Afghanistan—all of whom would become America's adversaries in the ensuing years. Such were the hard choices of geopolitics at the time. Strategic successes sometimes contain the seeds of future threats. Just as the United States armed the Soviet Union during World War II against the common foe of Nazi Germany, only for Washington and Moscow to become adversaries afterward, so the Reagan administration's support for China and the mujahideen may have sprung from an anti-Soviet imperative but also had considerable downstream costs.

Over time, his international economic policies may look different too. Free trade has fallen into disfavor of late, as populisms of both the Left and the Right criticize trade's inequities and embrace protectionism. Meanwhile, deficit spending and national debt fueled by bipartisan spending binges have become in vogue again, making the deficits and debt of the Reagan era seem paltry by comparison. This should not obscure the fact that when Reagan won election in 1980, protectionism was exacerbating the unemployment, inflation, and stagnation afflicting the American and world economies. Reagan's economic policies, including trade liberalization, restored the American economy and fueled global growth that extended for over two decades. As political and economic cycles go, it should not surprise that at some point the inequities and dislocations that can accompany free trade would reappear and inspire a populist backlash. But it would be an error of both history and policy to impose a hindsight verdict that Reagan should have indulged protectionism instead.

Though the Cold War never turned into a third world war, its regional conflicts left many dead, among them far too many civilians. Asia, Africa, the Middle East, and Latin America all suffered from civil wars and other conflicts, some fueled by weapons provided by the Reagan administration and leaders supported by Reagan. Instability and strife, and poor governance and corruption, continue to plague some of these countries to this day, as collateral damage from the Cold War.

III

Time's passage calibrates history's scale. Weighed in that balance, the Reagan legacy measures well.

Like Franklin Roosevelt, he led his nation and its allies in vanquishing a totalitarian empire. Like Eisenhower, he left his nation stronger, more secure, more hopeful and united. Like Kennedy, he inspired America and summoned it to a higher purpose. Like Nixon, he reduced tensions between the Soviet Union and the United States and transformed America's strategic posture in Asia.

And like Truman, he strengthened America's national security institutions. The Pentagon, CIA, and State Department in particular all enjoyed a renaissance under Reagan. When he took office, each had been demoralized and hollowed out. Under him and his lieutenants, each became rebuilt, modernized, and expanded. Well into the twenty-first century, much of the Pentagon's force projection still depends on weapons platforms developed or acquired under Reagan, just as much of the intelligence community's continuing tools and tradecraft date to his presidency. The State Department still takes pride in the 1980s as a heyday of diplomacy.

America's alliances also underwent a renewal. Arguably no president before or since has been more devoted to allies than Reagan. Though he spent much time cultivating personal relationships with his alliance counterparts, he also oversaw the strengthening of the institutional sinews of those alliances, giving them a resilience that endured once he left office. Reagan's vision of a nuclear-free world has not come to pass, but the combined nuclear arsenals of the United States and Soviet Union are approximately one-tenth the size they were when Reagan left office.

In statecraft, he leaves a legacy on the integration of power and diplomacy. Reagan balanced restraint about deploying the military in combat with two other effective uses of force to achieve political goals: the Reagan Doctrine's support for others to do the fighting, and a modernization of the American military that could be wielded at the diplomatic table. Reagan showed that democracy and security need not be seen in antinomy but rather can be partners—and that the United States can promote human rights and democracy by providing resources and political support to those voices in other countries laboring for their freedom and self-government.

At home, Reagan helped restore the institution of the presidency. He became the first president since Eisenhower to win reelection and serve two full terms. After two decades of failed presidencies, many Americans, and many world leaders, had begun to fear that the office itself was broken. Though Reagan did his own harm to the institution through the Iran-contra scandal, he overcame that and demonstrated the resilience of the American presidency in leading the nation and the free world.

It is often said that Reagan restored America's self-confidence, and indeed he did. The long decade of the 1970s afflicted the United States with a prolonged crisis of faith. The Vietnam War and its aftershocks chastened the nation with a sense of its limits. But that needful awareness of limits turned into self-doubt about whether the United States had much to offer the world at all, and a belief that America's presence abroad was cause more for ill than for good. In this way, Reagan did not just restore the country's faith in itself, he also restored the world's belief in America—not as a perfect nation, but as a strong and good nation.

Reagan did not believe that his country could remedy all that ailed the world. He was a dreamer and visionary but not a utopian. He knew the earth was fallen, as were the men and women who walked it and ruled it. What he did believe is that American leadership could make that flawed world a better place.

Reagan delivered one of his last public addresses to the Oxford Union on December 4, 1992. He titled his speech "Democracy's Next Battle." Surveying the peaceful end of the Cold War, he warned against the isolationism and complacency that he now saw encroaching.

> Ironically, the end of communist tyranny has robbed much of the west of its uplifting, common purpose. In the aftermath of victory, we search, not for new enemies but for a renewed sense of mission. With the Soviet empire defeated, will we fall into petty, self-absorbed economic rivalries? Will we squander the moral capital of half a century? Will we turn inward, lulled by a dangerous complacency and the short-sighted view that the end of one Evil Empire means the permanent banishment of evil in all its forms?

The elder statesman hoped not. After all, he declared, "the work of freedom is never done and the task of the peacemaker is never complete."[4]

ACKNOWLEDGMENTS

I am one of those people who, on picking up a new book, always turns first to the acknowledgments. I enjoy seeing whom the author relied on for research, editing help, feedback, intellectual community, encouragement, friendship, and succor along the way. One of the paradoxes of writing is that it is an intensely solitary process that nonetheless depends on the help of others. This book is no exception.

Several of my students at the University of Texas at Austin provided able assistance with the research. These include Anna Miller, Michael Stanley, Jade Monk, Kelsey Ritchie, Sean Salome, Ashlyn Hand, Alexandra Vermooten, Trey Curran, Anita Durairaj, and Milad Pournik. A special thanks to Diana Bolsinger for taking time out from her own research on Reagan's foreign policy to track down some missing archival documents.

Many archivists and librarians at numerous universities and presidential libraries lent indispensable help. The idyllic environs of the Ronald Reagan Presidential Library, in particular, became almost a second home for a few years. The entire staff of the library were very welcoming. I should make special thanks to archival specialists Ray Wilson, Kelly Barton, Steve Branch, and Jennifer Mandel, and, of course, to the singular director of the Reagan Foundation, John Heubusch.

My editor, Brent Howard, has been a great support and guide throughout the entire process. From the outset, Brent grasped the vision for the book and helped me bring it to fruition. Grace Layer ably oversaw the production process, and Aja Pollock performed invaluable copyediting and fact-checking.

This book would not have happened without my literary agent, the late Jim Hornfischer. Jim believed in it from the beginning, helped shape and structure it, and championed it with a zeal that every author should envy. I will always cherish being able to share the completed manuscript with him just a few weeks before he succumbed to cancer in 2021. Thank you, Jim—you are missed. I also thank Sharon Hornfischer for her indispensable help in the book's final stages, as she ably carries forward her beloved husband's legacy.

Special thanks are owed to a few friends who made special contributions to this endeavor. Andrew Coffin, for a memorable tour of Rancho del Cielo; the literal vistas are incomparable, as were the intellectual vistas opened by this new vantage on the private Reagan. Kuropatkin Tawil, an enterprising sleuth who tracked down a vintage copy of a memorable Reagan poster and generously sent it to his professor. Trent Tate and Elizabeth Doughtie for creative advice and help on cover design. Jennifer Lind for the author photo.

The proper locale can make all the difference between flowing prose and a blank screen. Several families generously provided the use of their vacation homes for writing retreats. For this I am grateful to George and Gretchen Seay, Pauline and Austin Neuhoff, Nancy Seay, Kathy and Harlan Crow, Les and Amy Ware, Marlee and Bud Payne, and Gerardo and Marabel Salazar.

Tom Farr and Timothy Samuel Shah gave encouragement and generous support to this book in its earliest stages, especially through their leadership of the erstwhile Religious Freedom Project at Georgetown University. I also benefited from the feedback I received when presenting the book's themes or chapter drafts in workshops at Yale, Harvard, University of Michigan, University of Missouri, Stanford's Hoover Institution, the Ronald Reagan Institute, the Vandenberg Coalition, the Tikvah Fund, and my home institution, the University of Texas at Austin.

I owe undying appreciation to those fellow scholars and friends who lent their expertise in countless ways, including endless discussions and responses to my queries, reading significant portions of the manuscript, and help in excising mistakes, refining interpretations, smoothing prose, and all other manner of improvements. These include Paul Lettow, Henry Nau, Frank Gavin, Mark Pomar, Simon Miles, Alexandra Evans, Evan McCormick, James Graham Wilson, Elizabeth Charles, Peter Feaver, Bob Zoellick, Hal Brands, Jeremi Suri, Mike Green, Catherine Evans, Jonathan Hunt, George Seay, and Eric Edelman.

Others who contributed helpful ideas, served as sounding boards, or lent voices of encouragement are Bobby Chesney, Mark Lawrence, Jim Steinberg, Philip Bobbitt, Mark Updegrove, Admiral Bob Inman, Joshua Shifrinson, Andrew Preston, Philip Zelikow, Dan Twining, Kristen Silverberg,

Jamie Galbraith, the late Bob Jervis, Bill Brands, Steve Hayward, John Yoo, John Ciorciari, Larry Silberman, Jeffrey Engel, Matt Waxman, Colin Kahl, Derek Chollet, Thomas Mallon, Cherie Harder, Pete Wehner, Mike Gerson, Yuval Levin, Dany Pletka, Bob Beschel, James Jay Carafano, Kim Holmes, Nadia Schadlow, Michael Allen, Kiron Skinner, Mel Leffler, Charlie Laderman, Paul Miller, Roger Zakheim, Rachel Hoff, Randy Schriver, Bridge Colby, Wess Mitchell, Marin Strmecki, Seth Center, Justin Dyer, Cindy Ewing, Mac Thornberry, Mike Gallagher, Steve Hadley, Meghan O'Sullivan, Brendan and Randan Steinhauser, Aaron O'Connell, Will Tobey, Elliott Abrams, Ray Takeyh, Sheena Chestnut Greitens, Tim Morrison, Aaron Maclean, Gabe Scheinmann, Jenna Lifhits, John and Laura Hanford, Jim Langdon, Karl Rove, Amy Zegart, Steve Slick, Paul Pope, Vince Brooks, Bob Neller, Nick Rasmussen, Michele Malvesti, Bill McRaven, Tom Reed, Lou Marchetti, Jamie Fly, Colin Dueck, Jeff Gedmin, John Bew, Ken deGraffenreid, Richard Allen, Charlie Laderman, Eliot Cohen, Daron Shaw, Michael Rainsborough, Mike Magan, Ryan Evans, Doyle Hodges, Megan Oprea, Jim Golby, Theo Milonopoulos, Jaehan Park, Tommy Jamison, Alexandra Sukalo, William Chou, Joseph Ledford, Zoltan Feher, Emily Whalen, Elena Wicker, Adam Klein, Carrie Filipetti, Amanda Rothschild, Brett Fetterly, and Emily Clise.

The staff of the Clements Center for National Security deserve an extra measure of thanks for bearing additional burdens in keeping things running while my time was focused on writing. Besides those mentioned above, I also thank Paul Edgar, Alexandra Foggett, Amber Howard, Emily Burch, and Caroline Nicholson.

In addition to those already named, these other Clements Center board members offered steadfast encouragement and support: Joel Robuck, Pat Oles, Pam Willeford, Bob Rowling, Ross Perot Jr., Tom Luce, Ray Nixon, Barbara Moroney, Bonnie Smith, Scott Caven, Alan Tully, and Ann Huff Stevens.

Friends in Austin provided steady encouragement, refreshing breaks, and even occasional playdates with our kids so Dad could have time to write. These include: Graeme and Meg Rein, Joel and Melissa Pardue, Evan and Tobi Young, John and Amy Wages, Barton and Jennie Prideaux, Kristen Burks, Barry and Susanna McBee, Cliff and Jill Angelo, Adam Blum, John and Carolyn Ahrens, Suzy Weatherford, Christa Carlton, Steph Carlton, and Emily Anne Skinner.

I owe a special thanks to the University of Texas leadership, including Jay Hartzell, J. B. Milliken, Nancy Oakley, Sharon Wood, Scott Rabenold,

Jim Davis, Amanda Cochran-McCall, JR DeShazo, and former president Greg Fenves.

My academic training in history is now measured in decades gone by, but the passing of time only enhances my gratitude for my undergraduate and graduate mentors: David Kennedy, John Lewis Gaddis, Paul Kennedy, Jon Butler, and Harry Stout. They trained me in the craft of history and remain valued friends. Nonetheless, they bear no fault for my scholarly judgments, some of which they may not share.

Completion of a project like this highlights the gift of friends who have walked so many steps of life's journey with me. They include Sebastian Traeger, Alan Philp, Matt Aiello, Duncan Rein, Kevin Prestwich, Alan Hanson, Paul Vinogradov, Keith Carlson, Andrew Cuneo, Terry Taylor, Matt Woelbern, Bailey White, Brian Lee, Ben Sasse, Dan Bryant, Derek Lewis, Mike Horton, Rod Macleod, Hartwell Brown, Eric Gregory, Timothy Jackson, Hunter Powell, and Ryan Streeter. I have also been blessed by the pastors of our churches in Washington, DC, Dubai, London, and Austin: Eric Landry, Bryce Waller (who also read much of the manuscript), John Folmar, Mark Dever, Michael Lawrence, Hugh Palmer, Rico Tice, Juan Sanchez, and Ben Wright.

My family provided a steady reservoir of encouragement and support. I thank my siblings, Brian and Jennifer; and my Hawaii *ohana*, including Cyrus and Phyllis Siu, Audrey Ii, and Kiri Siu.

This book is dedicated to my parents, Bill and Connie Inboden. From a very young age they encouraged my love of history and, in the decades since, have been perpetual sources of wisdom, inspiration, help, and perspective.

Closest to home and closest to my heart are my wife, Rana Siu Inboden, and our sons, Liam and CJ. Some of our boys' earliest memories will be of their dad's work on this book; now at least writing time will no longer delay playing catch in the backyard. Rana's contributions are impossible to measure. From joining me for months of research trips to taking our boys on countless outings so that "Daddy can keep writing" to helping me think through themes and characters to reading—and improving—the entire manuscript to faithful encouragement at every stage, it would not have been finished without her.

Soli Deo Gloria.

Austin, Texas

March 14, 2022

SOURCES AND BIBLIOGRAPHY

ARCHIVES

George H. W. Bush Presidential Library

Jimmy Carter Presidential Library

Churchill Archives Centre

Georgetown University Archives

Hoover Institution, Stanford University

Library of Congress

The National Archives, United Kingdom

Princeton University Archives

Ronald Reagan Presidential Library

University of Washington Special Collections

Yale University Archives

INTERVIEWS

Elliott Abrams

Kenneth Adelman

Richard Armitage

Milt Bearden

Frank Carlucci

Paula Dobriansky

Robert Gates

Stephen Hadley

Charles Hill

Bob Inman

Jack Matlock

Bud McFarlane

Edwin Meese

Henry Nau

John Poindexter

Mark Pomar

Colin Powell

Thomas Reed

Peter Robinson

Roger Robinson

Dennis Ross

George Shultz

Laurence Silberman

Paul Wolfowitz

BOOKS

Abrams, Elliott. *Undue Process: A Story of How Political Differences Are Turned into Crimes.* New York: Free Press, 1993.

———. *Realism and Democracy: American Foreign Policy After the Arab Spring.* New York: Cambridge University Press, 2017.

Absher, Kenneth Michael, Michael C. Desch, and Roman Popadiuk, eds. *Privileged and Confidential: The Secret History of the President's Intelligence Advisory Board.* Lexington, KY: University Press of Kentucky, 2012.

Abshire, David M. *Saving the Reagan Presidency: Trust Is the Coin of the Realm.* College Station, TX: Texas A&M University Press, 2005.

———. *The Statesman: Reflections on a Life Guided by Civility, Strategic Leadership, and the Lessons of History.* Lanham, MD: Rowman & Littlefield, 2018.

Adamishin, Anatoly, and Richard Schifter. *Human Rights, Perestroika, and the End of the Cold War.* Washington, DC: United States Institute of Peace, 2009.

Adelman, Kenneth L. *The Great Universal Embrace: Arms Summitry—A Skeptic's Account.* New York: Simon & Schuster, 1989.

———. *Reagan at Reykjavik: Forty-Eight Hours That Ended the Cold War.* New York: Broadside Books, 2014.

Adkin, Mark. *Urgent Fury: The Battle for Grenada.* Lexington, MA: Lexington Books, 1989.

Aldous, Richard. *Reagan and Thatcher: The Difficult Relationship.* New York: W. W. Norton, 2012.

Ambinder, Marc. *The Brink: President Reagan and the Nuclear War Scare of 1983.* New York: Simon & Schuster, 2018.

Amstutz, J. Bruce. *Afghanistan: The First Five Years of Soviet Occupation.* Honolulu, HI: University Press of the Pacific, 2002.

Anderson, Martin. *Revolution: The Reagan Legacy.* Stanford, CA: Hoover Institution Press, 1990.

Anderson, Martin, and Annelise Anderson. *Reagan's Secret War: The Untold Story of His Fight to Save the World from Nuclear Disaster.* New York: Crown Publishers, 2009.

———. *Ronald Reagan: Decisions of Greatness.* Stanford, CA: Hoover Institution Press, 2009.

Andrew, Christopher, and Vasili Mitrokhin. *The Sword and the Shield: The Mitrokhin Archive and the Secret History of the KGB.* New York: Basic Books, 1999.

———. *The World Was Going Our Way: The KGB and the Battle for the Third World.* New York: Basic Books, 2005.

Applebaum, Anne. *Gulag: A History.* New York: Anchor Books, 2003.

Baier, Bret, with Catherine Whitney. *Three Days in Moscow: Ronald Reagan and the Fall of the Soviet Empire.* New York: William Morrow, 2018.

Baker, James A., III. *"Work Hard, Study . . . and Keep Out of Politics!" Adventures and Lessons from an Unexpected Public Life.* New York: G. P. Putnam's Sons, 2006.

Baker, Peter, and Susan Glasser. *The Man Who Ran Washington: The Life and Times of James A. Baker III.* New York: Doubleday, 2020.

Barletta, John R. *Riding with Reagan: From the White House to the Ranch.* New York: Citadel Press, 2005.

Baucom, Donald R. *The Origins of SDI, 1944–1983.* Lawrence, KS: University Press of Kansas, 1992.

Bearden, Milt, and James Risen. *The Main Enemy: The Inside Story of the CIA's Final Showdown with the KGB.* New York: Ballantine Books, 2003.

Beckerman, Gal. *When They Come for Us, We'll Be Gone: The Epic Struggle to Save Soviet Jewry.* New York: Houghton Mifflin Harcourt, 2010.

Bergman, Ronen. *Rise and Kill First: The Secret History of Israel's Targeted Assassinations.* New York: Random House, 2018.

Bird, Kai. *The Good Spy: The Life and Death of Robert Ames.* New York: Broadway Books, 2014.

———. *The Outlier: The Unfinished Presidency of Jimmy Carter.* New York: Crown, 2021.

Blinken, Antony J. *Ally vs. Ally: America, Europe, and the Siberian Pipeline Crisis.* New York: Praeger, 1987.

Blumenthal, Sidney, and Thomas Byrne Edsall, eds. *The Reagan Legacy.* New York: Pantheon Books, 1988.

Bohn, Michael K. *The Achille Lauro Hijacking: Lessons in the Politics and Prejudice of Terrorism.* Dulles, VA: Potomac Books, 2004.

Boot, Max. *Invisible Armies: An Epic History of Guerilla Warfare from Ancient Times to the Present.* New York: Liveright, 2013.

Boykin, John. *Cursed Is the Peacemaker: The American Diplomat Versus the Israeli General, Beirut 1982.* Belmont, CA: Applegate Press, 2002.

Braithwaite, Rodric. *Afgantsy: The Russians in Afghanistan 1979–89.* New York: Oxford University Press, 2011.

Brands, H. W. *Reagan: The Life.* New York: Doubleday, 2015.

Brands, Hal. *Latin America's Cold War.* Cambridge, MA: Harvard University Press, 2010.

———. *What Good Is Grand Strategy? Power and Purpose in American Statecraft from Harry S. Truman to George W. Bush.* Ithaca, NY: Cornell University Press, 2014.

———. *Making the Unipolar Moment: US Foreign Policy and the Rise of the Post–Cold War Order.* Ithaca, NY: Cornell University Press, 2016.

———. *The Twilight Struggle: What the Cold War Teaches Us About Great-Power Struggle Today.* New Haven, CT: Yale University Press, 2022.

Brands, Hal, and Jeremi Suri, eds. *The Power of the Past: History and Statecraft.* Washington, DC: Brookings Institution Press, 2016.

Braw, Elisabeth. *God's Spies: The Stasi's Cold War Espionage Campaign Inside the Church.* Grand Rapids, MI: Eerdmans, 2019.

Brinkley, Douglas, ed. *The Reagan Diaries Unabridged*. 2 vols. New York: HarperCollins, 2009.

———. *The Notes: Ronald Reagan's Private Collection of Stories and Wisdom*. New York: Harper Perennial, 2011.

Brown, Archie. *The Human Factor: Gorbachev, Reagan, and Thatcher, and the End of the Cold War*. New York: Oxford University Press, 2020.

Buckley, William F., Jr. *In Search of Anti-Semitism*. New York: Continuum, 1992.

———. *The Reagan I Knew*. New York: Basic Books, 2008.

Burke, John P. *Honest Broker? The National Security Advisor and Presidential Decision Making*. College Station, TX: Texas A&M University Press, 2009.

Burns, William J. *The Back Channel: A Memoir of American Diplomacy and the Case for Its Renewal*. New York: Random House, 2019.

Burton, Fred, and Samuel M. Katz. *Beirut Rules: The Murder of a CIA Station Chief and Hezbollah's War Against America*. New York: Berkley, 2018.

Byrne, David T. *Ronald Reagan: An Intellectual Biography*. Lincoln, NE: Potomac Books, 2018.

Byrne, Malcolm. *Iran-Contra: Reagan's Scandal and the Unchecked Abuse of Presidential Power*. Lawrence, KS: University of Kansas Press, 2014.

Campbell, Kurt M., and James B. Steinberg. *Difficult Transitions: Foreign Policy Troubles at the Outset of Presidential Power*. Washington, DC: Brookings Institution Press, 2008.

Cannon, Lou. *President Reagan: The Role of a Lifetime*. New York: Simon & Schuster, 1991.

Carter, Ash. *Inside the Five-Sided Box: Lessons from a Lifetime of Leadership in the Pentagon*. New York: Dutton, 2019.

Caryl, Christian. *Strange Rebels: 1979 and the Birth of the 21st Century*. New York: Basic Books, 2014.

Cha, Victor. *The Impossible State: North Korea Past and Future*. New York: HarperCollins, 2012.

Chamberlin, Paul Thomas. *The Cold War's Killing Fields: Rethinking the Long Peace*. New York: Harper, 2018.

Charles, Elizabeth C., ed. *Foreign Relations of the United States, 1981–1988*. Vol. 5, *Soviet Union, March 1985–October 1986*. Washington, DC: Government Printing Office, 2020.

———. *Foreign Relations of the United States, 1981–1988*. Vol. 4, *Soviet Union, January 1983–March 1985*. Washington, DC: Government Printing Office, 2021.

Claire, Rodger W. *Raid on the Sun: Inside Israel's Secret Campaign That Denied Saddam the Bomb*. New York: Broadway Books, 2004.

Clarridge, Duane R. *A Spy for All Seasons: My Life in the CIA*. New York: Scribner, 1997.

Cohen, Eliot. *The Big Stick: The Limits of Soft Power and the Necessity of Military Force*. New York: Basic Books, 2016.

Cohen, Warren I. *The Cambridge History of American Foreign Relations*. Vol. 4, *America in the Age of Soviet Power, 1945–1991*. New York: Cambridge University Press, 1995.

Coleman, Bradley Lynn, and Kyle Longley, eds. *Reagan and the World: Leadership and National Security, 1981–1989*. Lexington, KY: The University Press of Kentucky, 2017.

Coll, Alberto, and Anthony Arend, eds. *The Falklands War: Lessons for Strategy, Diplomacy, and International Law*. Boston: George Allen & Unwin, 1985.

Coll, Steve. *Ghost Wars: The Secret History of the CIA, Afghanistan, and bin Laden, from the Soviet Invasion to September 10, 2001*. New York: Penguin, 2004.

Collier, Peter. *Political Woman: The Big Little Life of Jeane Kirkpatrick*. New York: Encounter Books, 2012.

Craig, Campbell, and Fredrik Logevall. *America's Cold War: The Politics of Insecurity*. Cambridge, MA: Harvard University Press, 2009.

Crandall, Russell. *The Salvador Option: The United States in El Salvador, 1977–1992*. New York: Cambridge University Press, 2016.

Crile, George. *Charlie Wilson's War*. New York: Grove Press, 2003.

Crist, David. *The Twilight War: The Secret History of America's Thirty-Year Conflict with Iran*. New York: Penguin Press, 2012.

Crocker, Chester. *High Noon in Southern Africa: Making Peace in a Rough Neighborhood*. New York: W. W. Norton, 1992.

Cull, Nicholas J. *The Cold War and the United States Information Agency: American Propaganda and Public Diplomacy, 1945–1989*. New York: Cambridge University Press, 2008.

Curry, Dean C., ed. *Evangelicals and the Bishops' Pastoral Letter*. Grand Rapids, MI: Eerdmans, 1984.

Daalder, Ivo H., and I. M. Destler. *In the Shadow of the Oval Office: Profiles of the National Security Advisers and the Presidents They Served—from JFK to George W. Bush*. New York: Simon & Schuster, 2009.

Dallek, Matthew. *The Right Moment: Ronald Reagan's First Victory and the Decisive Turning Point in American Politics*. New York: Oxford University Press, 2000.

Deaver, Michael K. *Behind the Scenes*. New York: William Morrow, 1987.

De Wolf, Koenraad. *Dissident for Life: Alexander Ogorodnikov and the Struggle for Religious Freedom in Russia*. Grand Rapids, MI: Eerdmans, 2013.

Diggins, John Patrick. *Ronald Reagan: Fate, Freedom, and the Meaning of History*. New York: W. W. Norton, 2007.

Dobrynin, Anatoly. *In Confidence: Moscow's Ambassador to America's Six Cold War Presidents*. New York: Times Books, 1995.

Domber, Gregory. *Empowering Revolution: America, Poland, and the End of the Cold War*. Chapel Hill, NC: University of North Carolina Press, 2014.

Downing, Taylor. *1983: Reagan, Andropov, and a World on the Brink*. New York: Da Capo Press, 2018.

Dueck, Colin. *Hard Line: The Republican Party and US Foreign Policy Since World War II*. Princeton, NJ: Princeton University Press, 2010.

Dunn, Charles W., ed. *The Enduring Reagan*. Lexington, KY: The University Press of Kentucky, 2009.

Edwards, Anne. *Early Reagan: The Rise to Power*. New York: William Morrow, 1987.

Edwards, Lee. *The Essential Ronald Reagan*. Lanham, MD: Rowman & Littlefield, 2005.

Ehrman, John. *Neoconservatism: Intellectuals and Foreign Affairs, 1945–1994*. New Haven, CT: Yale University Press, 1995.

———. *The Eighties: America in the Age of Reagan*. New Haven, CT: Yale University Press, 2005.

Ehrman, John, and Michael W. Flamm. *Debating the Reagan Presidency*. Lanham, MD: Rowman & Littlefield, 2009.

Engel, Jeffrey A. *When the World Seemed New: George H. W. Bush and the End of the Cold War*. New York: Houghton Mifflin Harcourt, 2017.

Engerman, David. *Know Your Enemy: The Rise and Fall of America's Soviet Experts*. New York: Oxford University Press, 2009.

Evans, Thomas W. *The Education of Ronald Reagan: The General Electric Years and the Untold Story of His Conversion to Conservatism*. New York: Columbia University Press, 2006.

Farr, Thomas. *World of Faith and Freedom: Why International Religious Freedom Is Vital to American National Security*. New York: Oxford University Press, 2008.

Fehrman, Craig. *Author in Chief: The Untold Story of Our Presidents and the Books They Wrote*. New York: Avid Reader Press, 2020.

Felzenberg, Alvin S. *A Man and His Presidents: The Political Odyssey of William F. Buckley Jr.* New Haven, CT: Yale University Press, 2017.

Firth, Noel, and James Noren. *Soviet Defense Spending: A History of CIA Estimates, 1950–1990*. College Station, TX: Texas A&M University Press, 1998.

Fischer, Beth A. *The Reagan Reversal: Foreign Policy and the End of the Cold War*. Columbia, MO: University of Missouri Press, 2000.

———. *The Myth of Triumphalism: Rethinking President Reagan's Cold War Legacy*. Lexington, KY: University Press of Kentucky, 2019.

Fosdick, Dorothy, ed. *Staying the Course: Henry M. Jackson and National Security*. Seattle, WA: University of Washington Press, 1987.

———. *Henry M. Jackson and World Affairs: Selected Speeches, 1953–1983*. Seattle, WA: University of Washington Press, 1990.

Funabashi, Yoichi. *Managing the Dollar: From the Plaza to the Louvre*. Washington, DC: Institute for International Economics, 1988.

Funderburk, David B. *Pinstripes and Reds: An American Ambassador Caught Between the State Department and the Romanian Communists, 1981–1985*. Washington, DC: Selous Foundation Press, 1989.

Gaddis, John Lewis. *Russia, the Soviet Union, and the United States: An Interpretive History*. New York: McGraw-Hill, 1990.

———. *The United States and the End of the Cold War: Implications, Reconsiderations, Provocations*. New York: Oxford University Press, 1992.

———. *The Cold War: A New History*. New York: Penguin Press, 2005.

———. *Strategies of Containment: A Critical Appraisal of American National Security Policy During the Cold War*. New York: Oxford University Press, 2005.

———. *George F. Kennan: An American Life*. New York: Penguin Press, 2011.

Gans, John. *White House Warriors: How the National Security Council Transformed the American Way of War*. New York: Liveright Publishing, 2019.

Garthoff, Raymond L. *Détente and Confrontation: American-Soviet Relations from Nixon to Reagan*. Washington, DC: Brookings Institution Press, 1993.

Gates, Robert M. *From the Shadows: The Ultimate Insider's Story of Five Presidents and How They Won the Cold War*. New York: Simon & Schuster, 1996.

Geraghty, Timothy J. *Peacekeepers at War*. Washington, DC: Potomac Books, 2009.

Gibbs, Nancy, and Michael Duffy. *The Preacher and the Presidents: Billy Graham in the White House*. New York: Center Street, 2007.

Gilkey, Langdon. *Shantung Compound: A Story of Men and Women Under Pressure*. New York: Harper and Row, 1975.

Glad, Betty. *An Outsider in the White House: Jimmy Carter, His Advisors, and the Making of American Foreign Policy*. Ithaca, NY: Cornell University Press, 2009.

Gorbachev, Mikhail. *Memoirs*. New York: Doubleday, 1995.

Graff, Garrett. *Raven Rock: The Story of the US Government's Secret Plan to Save Itself—While the Rest of Us Die*. New York: Simon & Schuster, 2017.

Grandin, Greg. *Empire's Workshop: Latin America, the United States, and the Rise of the New Imperialism*. New York: Picador, 2021.

Green, Michael J. *By More Than Providence: Grand Strategy and American Power in the Asia Pacific Since 1783*. New York: Columbia University Press, 2017.

Gregg, Donald P. *Pot Shards: Fragments of a Life Lived in CIA, the White House, and the Two Koreas*. Washington, DC: New Academia Publishing, 2014.

Greitens, Sheena Chestnut. *Dictators and Their Secret Police: Coercive Institutions and State Violence*. New York: Cambridge University Press, 2016.

Grimes, Sandra, and Jeanne Vertefeuille. *Circle of Treason: A CIA Account of Traitor Aldrich Ames and the Men He Betrayed*. Annapolis, MD: Naval Institute Press, 2012.

Gromyko, Andrei. *Memoirs*. New York: Doubleday, 1989.

Gustafson, Thane. *The Bridge: Natural Gas in a Redivided Europe*. Cambridge, MA: Harvard University Press, 2020.

Haig, Alexander M., Jr. *Caveat: Realism, Reagan, and Foreign Policy*. New York: Macmillan, 1984.

Hannaford, Peter. *The Reagans: A Political Portrait*. New York: Coward-McCann, 1983.

Harris, Shane. *The Watchers: The Rise of America's Surveillance State*. New York: Penguin, 2010.

Haynes, John Earl, and Harvey Klehr. *In Denial: Historians, Communism, and Espionage*. San Francisco: Encounter Books, 2005.

Hayward, Steven F. *The Age of Reagan: The Fall of the Old Liberal Order, 1964–1980*. New York: Three Rivers Press, 2001.

———. *The Age of Reagan: The Conservative Counterrevolution, 1980–1989*. New York: Crown Forum, 2009.

Helgerson, John L. *Getting to Know the President: Intelligence Briefings of Presidential Candidates, 1952–2004*. Washington, DC: Center for the Study of Intelligence, 2012.

Herring, George C. *From Colony to Superpower: US Foreign Relations Since 1776*. New York: Oxford University Press, 2008.

Heymann, Philip B. *Living the Policy Process*. New York: Oxford University Press, 2008.

Higginbotham, Adam. *Midnight in Chernobyl: The Untold Story of the World's Greatest Nuclear Disaster*. New York: Simon & Schuster, 2019.

Hinton, Deane Roesch. *Economics and Diplomacy: A Life in the Foreign Service of the United States*. Washington, DC: New Academia Publishing, 2015.

Hoffman, David E. *The Dead Hand: The Untold Story of the Cold War Arms Race and Its Dangerous Legacy*. New York: Anchor Press, 2009.

———. *The Billion Dollar Spy*. New York: Anchor Books, 2015.

Hunt, Jonathan, and Simon Miles, eds. *The Reagan Moment: America and the World in the 1980s*. Ithaca, NY: Cornell University Press, 2021.

Inderfurth, Karl F., and Loch K. Johnson. *Fateful Decisions: Inside the National Security Council*. New York: Oxford University Press, 1994.

Irwin, Douglas A. *Clashing over Commerce: A History of US Trade Policy*. Chicago: University of Chicago Press, 2017.

Jentleson, Bruce W. *Pipeline Politics: The Complex Political Economy of East-West Energy Trade*. Ithaca, NY: Cornell University Press, 1986.

Jones, Frank Leith. *Sam Nunn: Statesman of the Nuclear Age*. Lawrence, KS: University Press of Kansas, 2020.

Jones, Nate, ed. *Able Archer: The Secret History of the NATO Exercise That Almost Triggered Nuclear War*. New York: New Press, 2016.

Jones, Seth G. *A Covert Action: Reagan, the CIA, and the Cold War Struggle in Poland*. New York: W. W. Norton, 2018.

Judt, Tony. *Postwar: A History of Europe Since 1945*. New York: Penguin Books, 2005.

Jurdem, Laurence R. *Paving the Way for Reagan: The Influence of Conservative Media on US Foreign Policy*. Lexington, KY: University Press of Kentucky, 2017.

Kagan, Richard C. *Taiwan's Statesman: Lee Teng-hui and Democracy in Asia*. Annapolis, MD: Naval Institute Press, 2007.

Kagan, Robert. *A Twilight Struggle: American Power and Nicaragua, 1977–1990*. New York: Free Press, 1996.

Kalinovsky, Artemy M. *A Long Goodbye: The Soviet Withdrawal from Afghanistan*. Cambridge, MA: Harvard University Press, 2011.

Kaplan, Fred. *The Bomb: Presidents, Generals, and the Secret History of Nuclear War*. New York: Simon & Schuster, 2020.

Kaplan, Robert D. *The Good American: The Epic Life of Bob Gersony, the US Government's Greatest Humanitarian*. New York: Random House, 2021.

Kaufman, Robert G. *Henry M. Jackson: A Life in Politics*. Seattle, WA: University of Washington Press, 2000.

Keeley, Theresa. *Reagan's Gun-Toting Nuns: The Catholic Conflict over Cold War Human Rights Policy in Central America*. Ithaca, NY: Cornell University Press, 2020.

Kengor, Paul. *God and Ronald Reagan: A Spiritual Life*. New York: ReganBooks, 2004.

———. *A Pope and a President: John Paul II, Ronald Reagan, and the Extraordinary Untold Story of the 20th Century*. Wilmington, DE: ISI Books, 2017.

Kengor, Paul, and Patricia Clark Doerner. *The Judge: William P. Clark, Ronald Reagan's Top Hand*. San Francisco: Ignatius Press, 2007.

Kengor, Paul, and Robert Orlando. *The Divine Plan: John Paul II, Ronald Reagan, and the Dramatic End of the Cold War*. Wilmington, DE: ISI Books, 2019.

Kimmage, Michael. *The Abandonment of the West: The History of an Idea in American Foreign Policy*. New York: Basic Books, 2020.

Kopelson, Gene. *Reagan's 1968 Dress Rehearsal: Ike, RFK, and Reagan's Emergence as a World Statesman*. Los Angeles: Figueroa Press, 2016.

Kostin, Sergei, and Eric Raynaud. *Farewell: The Greatest Spy Story of the Twentieth Century*. Las Vegas, NV: Amazon Crossing, 2011.

Kotkin, Stephen. *Armageddon Averted: The Soviet Collapse 1970–2000*. Updated edition. New York: Oxford University Press, 2008.

Kramer, Mark, ed. *The Black Book of Communism: Crimes, Terror, Repression*. Cambridge, MA: Harvard University Press, 1999.

Kraemer, Sven F. *Inside the Cold War: From Marx to Reagan*. Lanham, MD: University Press of America, 2015.

Krepinevich, Andrew, and Barry Watts. *The Last Warrior: Andrew Marshall and the Shaping of Modern American Defense Strategy*. New York: Basic Books, 2015.

Kristol, Irving. *Neo-Conservatism: The Autobiography of an Idea.* New York: Free Press, 1995.

Kuhn, Jim. *Ronald Reagan in Private: A Memoir of My Years in the White House.* New York: Sentinel, 2004.

LaFeber, Walter. *The Clash: US-Japan Relations Throughout History.* New York: W. W. Norton, 1997.

Laxalt, Paul. *Nevada's Paul Laxalt: A Memoir.* Reno, NV: Jack Bacon and Company, 2000.

Ledeen, Michael A. *Perilous Statecraft: An Insider's Account of the Iran-Contra Affair.* New York: Charles Scribner's Sons, 1988.

Leebaert, Derek. *The Fifty-Year Wound: The True Price of America's Cold War Victory.* New York: Little, Brown, 2002.

Leffler, Melvyn P. *For the Soul of Mankind: The United States, the Soviet Union, and the Cold War.* New York: Hill and Wang, 2007.

Lehman, John. *Oceans Ventured: Winning the Cold War at Sea.* New York: W. W. Norton, 2018.

LeoGrande, William M. *Our Own Backyard: The United States in Central America, 1977–1992.* Chapel Hill, NC: University of North Carolina Press, 1998.

Lettow, Paul. *Ronald Reagan and His Quest to Abolish Nuclear Weapons.* New York: Random House, 2006.

Lilley, James. *China Hands: Nine Decades of Adventure, Espionage, and Diplomacy in Asia.* New York: Public Affairs, 2004.

Locher, James R., III. *Victory on the Potomac: The Goldwater-Nichols Act Unifies the Pentagon.* College Station, TX: Texas A&M University Press, 2002.

Lohbeck, Kurt. *Holy War, Unholy Victory: Eyewitness to the CIA's Secret War in Afghanistan.* Washington, DC: Regnery Gateway, 1993.

Longley, Kyle. *In the Eagle's Shadow: The United States and Latin America.* Wheeling, IL: Harlan Davidson, 2009.

Lord, Carnes. *The Presidency and the Management of National Security.* New York: Free Press, 1988.

Luthi, Lorenz. *Cold Wars: Asia, the Middle East, Europe.* New York: Cambridge University Press, 2020.

Lynch, Edward A. *The Cold War's Last Battlefield: Reagan, the Soviets, and Central America.* Albany, NY: State University of New York Press, 2011.

Macintyre, Ben. *The Spy and the Traitor: The Greatest Espionage Story of the Cold War.* New York: Crown, 2018.

Mahnken, Thomas, ed. *Competitive Strategies for the Twenty-First Century: Theory, History, and Practice.* Stanford, CA: Stanford University Press, 2012.

———. *Net Assessment and Military Strategy: Retrospective and Prospective Essays.* Amherst, NY: Cambria Press, 2020.

Mallon, Thomas. *Finale: A Novel of the Reagan Years.* New York: Vintage, 2016.

Mann, James. *About Face: A History of America's Curious Relationship with China, from Nixon to Clinton.* New York: Vintage Books, 2000.

———. *The Rise of the Vulcans: The History of Bush's War Cabinet.* New York: Penguin Books, 2004.

———. *The Rebellion of Ronald Reagan: A History of the End of the Cold War.* New York: Viking, 2009.

———. *The Great Rift: Dick Cheney, Colin Powell, and the Broken Friendship That Defined an Era.* New York: Henry Holt, 2020.

Marlo, Francis H. *Planning Reagan's War: Conservative Strategists and America's Cold War Victory.* Washington, DC: Potomac Books, 2012.

Martin, David, and John Walcott. *Best Laid Plans: The Inside Story of America's War Against Terrorism.* New York: Touchstone, 1988.

Massie, Suzanne. *Land of the Firebird: The Beauty of Old Russia.* Blue Hill, ME: HeartTree Press, 1980.

———. *Trust but Verify: Reagan, Russia, and Me.* Rockland, ME: Maine Authors Publishing, 2013.

Matlock, Jack F., Jr. *Reagan and Gorbachev: How the Cold War Ended.* New York: Random House, 2004.

McAlister, Melani. *Epic Encounters: Culture, Media, and US Interests in the Middle East Since 1945.* Berkeley, CA: University of California Press, 2005.

McCarry, Charles. *Second Sight.* New York: Overlook Press, 2009.

McCartin, Joseph A. *Collision Course: Ronald Reagan, the Air Traffic Controllers, and the Strike That Changed America.* New York: Oxford University Press, 2013.

McDougall, Walter A. *Promised Land, Crusader State: The American Encounter with the World Since 1776.* New York: Mariner Books, 1997.

McFarlane, Robert C. *Special Trust.* New York: Cadell & Davies, 1994.

McGarr, Kathryn J. *The Whole Damn Deal: Robert Strauss and the Art of Politics.* New York: Public Affairs, 2011.

McGregor, Richard. *Asia's Reckoning: China, Japan, and the Fate of US Power in the Pacific Century.* New York: Viking, 2017.

McPherson, Alan. *Ghosts of Sheridan Circle: How a Washington Assassination Brought Pinochet's Terror State to Justice.* Chapel Hill, NC: University of North Carolina Press, 2019.

Meacham, Jon. *Destiny and Power: The American Odyssey of George Herbert Walker Bush.* New York: Random House, 2015.

Meese, Edwin. *Reagan: The Inside Story.* Washington, DC: Regnery History, 1992.

Melady, Thomas Patrick. *The Ambassador's Story: The United States and the Vatican in World Affairs.* Huntington, IN: Our Sunday Visitor, 1994.

Menges, Constantine C. *Inside the National Security Council: The True Story of the Making and Unmaking of Reagan's Foreign Policy.* New York: Touchstone, 1988.

Middendorf, J. William, II. *Potomac Fever: A Memoir of Politics and Public Service.* Annapolis, MD: Naval Institute Press, 2011.

Middlebrook, Martin. *The Falklands War.* Barnsley, UK: Pen and Sword Military, 2014.

Miles, Simon. *Engaging the Evil Empire: Washington, Moscow, and the Beginning of the End of the Cold War.* Ithaca, NY: Cornell University Press, 2020.

Miller, Chris. *We Shall Be Masters: Russian Pivots to East Asia from Peter the Great to Putin.* Cambridge, MA: Harvard University Press, 2021.

Moore, Charles. *Margaret Thatcher: The Authorized Biography; From Grantham to the Falklands.* New York: Vintage, 2013.

———. *Margaret Thatcher: The Authorized Biography; At Her Zenith: In London, Washington, and Moscow.* New York: Vintage, 2015.

———. *Margaret Thatcher: The Authorized Biography; Herself Alone.* New York: Alfred A. Knopf, 2019.

Morgan, Iwan. *Reagan: American Icon.* New York: I. B. Tauris, 2016.

Morgan, Michael Cotey. *The Final Act: The Helsinki Accords and the Transformation of the Cold War*. Princeton, NJ: Princeton University Press, 2018.

Morris, Edmund. *Dutch: A Memoir of Ronald Reagan*. New York: HarperCollins, 1999.

Moyar, Mark. *Oppose Any Foe: The Rise of America's Special Operations Forces*. New York: Basic Books, 2017.

Mulroney, Brian. *Memoirs: 1939–1993*. Toronto: McClelland & Stewart, 2007.

Naftali, Timothy. *Blind Spot: The Secret History of American Counterterrorism*. New York: Basic Books, 2005.

Nash, George H. *The Conservative Intellectual Movement in America Since 1945*. Wilmington, DE: ISI Books, 2006.

Nash, Ronald H., ed. *Liberation Theology*. Grand Rapids, MI: Baker Books, 1988.

Nau, Henry. *The Myth of America's Decline: Leading the World Economy into the 1990s*. New York: Oxford University Press, 1990.

———. *Conservative Internationalism: Armed Diplomacy Under Jefferson, Polk, Truman, and Reagan*. Princeton, NJ: Princeton University Press, 2013.

Netanyahu, Benjamin, ed. *Terrorism: How the West Can Win*. New York: Farrar, Straus and Giroux, 1986.

Neustadt, Richard E. *Presidential Power and the Modern Presidents: The Politics of Leadership from Roosevelt to Reagan*. New York: Free Press, 1990.

Nitze, Paul. *From Hiroshima to Glasnost: At the Center of Decision—A Memoir*. New York: Grove Weidenfeld, 1989.

Noonan, Peggy. *When Character Was King: A Story of Ronald Reagan*. New York: Viking, 2001.

———. *What I Saw at the Revolution: A Political Life in the Reagan Era*. New York: Random House, 2010.

Novak, Michael. *Will It Liberate? Questions About Liberation Theology*. New York: Paulist Press, 1986.

Novak, Robert D. *The Prince of Darkness: 50 Years Reporting in Washington*. New York: Crown Forum, 2007.

Nye, Joseph S., Jr. *Presidential Leadership and the Creation of the American Era*. Princeton, NJ: Princeton University Press, 2013.

Oberdorfer, Don. *From the Cold War to a New Era: The United States and the Soviet Union, 1983–1991*. Baltimore, MD: Johns Hopkins University Press, 1998.

———. *Senator Mansfield: The Extraordinary Life of a Great American Statesman and Diplomat*. Washington, DC: Smithsonian Books, 2003.

Oberdorfer, Don, and Robert Carlin. *The Two Koreas: A Contemporary History*. New York: Basic Books, 2014.

O'Neill, Tip, with William Novak. *Man of the House*. New York: Random House, 1987.

O'Sullivan, John. *The President, the Pope, and the Prime Minister: Three Who Changed the World*. Washington, DC: Regnery, 2006.

Owens, Bill. *Lifting the Fog of War*. New York: Farrar, Straus and Giroux, 2000.

Perlstein, Rick. *The Invisible Bridge: The Fall of Nixon and the Rise of Reagan*. New York: Simon & Schuster, 2014.

———. *Reaganland: America's Right Turn, 1976–1980*. New York: Simon & Schuster, 2020.

Persico, Joseph. *Casey: From the OSS to the CIA*. New York: Viking, 1990.

Pipes, Kasey S. *After the Fall: The Remarkable Comeback of Richard Nixon.* Washington, DC: Regnery, 2019.

Pipes, Richard. *Vixi: Memoirs of a Non-Belonger.* New Haven, CT: Yale University Press, 2003.

Plokhy, Serhii. *Chernobyl: The History of a Nuclear Catastrophe.* New York: Basic Books, 2018.

Pollock, John. *The Siberian Seven.* London: Hodder & Stoughton, 1979.

Pomfret, John. *The Beautiful Country and the Middle Kingdom: America and China, 1776 to the Present.* New York: Henry Holt, 2016.

Powell, Colin. *My American Journey.* New York: Ballantine Books, 1995.

Prados, John. *Keepers of the Keys: A History of the National Security Council from Truman to Bush.* New York: William Morrow, 1991.

Preston, Andrew. *Sword of the Spirit, Shield of Faith: Religion in American War and Diplomacy.* New York: Alfred A. Knopf, 2012.

Priess, David. *The President's Book of Secrets: The Untold Story of Intelligence Briefings to America's Presidents from Kennedy to Obama.* New York: Public Affairs, 2016.

Radchenko, Sergey. *Unwanted Visionaries: The Soviet Failure in Asia at the End of the Cold War.* New York: Oxford University Press, 2014.

Rapp-Hooper, Mira. *Shields of the Republic: The Triumph and Peril of America's Alliances.* Cambridge, MA: Harvard University Press, 2020.

Ratnesar, Romesh. *Tear Down This Wall: A City, a President, and the Speech That Ended the Cold War.* New York: Simon & Schuster, 2009.

Ratushinskaya, Irina. *Grey Is the Colour of Hope.* London: Sceptre, 2016.

Reagan, Nancy. *My Turn: The Memoirs of Nancy Reagan.* New York: Random House, 1989.

Reagan, Ronald. *An American Life.* New York: Threshold Editions, 1990.

Reed, Thomas C. *At the Abyss: An Insider's History of the Cold War.* New York: Presidio Press, 2005.

———. *The Reagan Enigma, 1964–1980.* Los Angeles: Figueroa Press, 2014.

Reeves, Richard. *President Reagan: The Triumph of Imagination.* New York: Simon & Schuster, 2005.

Regan, Donald T. *For the Record: From Wall Street to Washington.* New York: Harcourt Brace Jovanovich, 1988.

Renouard, Joe. *Human Rights in American Foreign Policy: From the 1960s to the Soviet Collapse.* Philadelphia, PA: University of Pennsylvania Press, 2016.

Reynolds, David. *Summits: Six Meetings That Shaped the Twentieth Century.* New York: Basic Books, 2007.

Rid, Thomas. *Active Measures: The Secret History of Disinformation and Political Warfare.* New York: Farrar, Straus and Giroux, 2020.

Riedel, Bruce. *What We Won: America's Secret War in Afghanistan, 1979–1989.* Washington, DC: Brookings Institution Press, 2014.

Robinson, Gilbert A. *Reagan Remembered.* New York: Beaufort Books, 2016.

Robinson, Peter. *How Ronald Reagan Changed My Life.* New York: Harper, 2003.

Rodman, Peter. *More Precious Than Peace: The Cold War and the Struggle for the Third World.* New York: Charles Scribner's Sons, 1994.

———. *Presidential Command: Power, Leadership, and the Making of Foreign Policy from Richard Nixon to George W. Bush.* New York: Alfred A. Knopf, 2009.

Rooney, Francis. *The Global Vatican.* Lanham, MD: Rowman & Littlefield, 2013.

Rosebush, James. *True Reagan: What Made Ronald Reagan Great and Why It Matters.* New York: Hachette Book Group, 2016.

Rosenau, William. *Tonight We Bombed the Capitol: The Explosive Story of M19, America's First Female Terrorist Group.* New York: Atria Books, 2019.

Ross, Dennis. *Doomed to Succeed: The US-Israel Relationship from Truman to Obama.* New York: Farrar, Straus and Giroux, 2015.

Rothkopf, David. *Running the World: The Inside Story of the National Security Council and the Architects of American Power.* New York: Public Affairs, 2005.

Rowland, Robert, and John M. Jones. *Reagan at Westminster: Foreshadowing the End of the Cold War.* College Station, TX: Texas A&M University Press, 2010.

Salamon, Julie. *An Innocent Bystander: The Killing of Leon Klinghoffer.* New York: Little, Brown, 2019.

Saltoun-Ebin, Jason. *The Reagan Files: Inside the National Security Council.* 2nd ed. Santa Barbara, CA: Seabec Books, 2014.

Sargent, Daniel J. *A Superpower Transformed: The Remaking of American Foreign Relations in the 1970s.* New York: Oxford University Press, 2015.

Satter, David. *Age of Delirium: The Decline and Fall of the Soviet Union.* New Haven, CT: Yale University Press, 2001.

Sayle, Timothy Andrews. *Enduring Alliance: A History of NATO and the Postwar Global Order.* Ithaca, NY: Cornell University Press, 2019.

Schaeffer, Howard B., and Teresita C. Schaeffer. *How Pakistan Negotiates with the United States: Riding the Roller Coaster.* Washington, DC: United States Institute of Peace, 2011.

Schlosser, Eric. *Command and Control: Nuclear Weapons, the Damascus Accident, and the Illusion of Safety.* New York: Penguin Press, 2013.

Schrecker, Ellen, ed. *Cold War Triumphalism: The Misuse of History After the Fall of Communism.* New York: New Press, 2004.

Schweikart, Larry. *Reagan: The American President.* New York: Post Hill Press, 2019.

Schweizer, Peter. *Victory: The Reagan Administration's Secret Strategy That Hastened the Collapse of the Soviet Union.* New York: Atlantic Monthly Press, 1994.

———. *Reagan's War: The Epic Story of His Forty-Year Struggle and Final Triumph over Communism.* New York: Anchor Books, 2002.

Scott, James M. *Deciding to Intervene: The Reagan Doctrine and American Foreign Policy.* Durham, NC: Duke University Press, 1996.

Serina, Guillaume. *An Impossible Dream: Reagan, Gorbachev, and a World Without the Bomb.* New York: Pegasus Books, 2019.

Service, Robert. *The End of the Cold War, 1985–1991.* New York: Public Affairs, 2015.

Sestanovich, Stephen. *Maximalist: America in the World from Truman to Obama.* New York: Alfred A. Knopf, 2014.

Sharansky, Natan. *Fear No Evil.* New York: Random House, 1988.

Shattan, Joseph. *Architects of Victory: Six Heroes of the Cold War.* Washington, DC: Heritage Foundation, 1999.

Shimer, David. *Rigged: America, Russia, and One Hundred Years of Covert Election Interference.* New York: Alfred A. Knopf, 2020.

Shimron, Gad. *Mossad Exodus: The Daring Undercover Rescue of the Lost Jewish Tribe.* Jerusalem: Gefen Publishing House, 2007.

Shirley, Craig. *Reagan's Revolution: The Untold Story of the Campaign That Started It All.* Nashville, TN: Thomas Nelson, 2005.

——. *Rendezvous with Destiny: Ronald Reagan and the Campaign That Changed America.* Wilmington, DE: ISI Books, 2009.

——. *Reagan Rising: The Decisive Years, 1976–1980.* New York: Broadside Books, 2017.

Shultz, George. *Turmoil and Triumph: My Years as Secretary of State.* New York: Charles Scribner's Sons, 1993.

Sikkink, Kathryn. *Mixed Signals: US Human Rights Policy and Latin America.* Ithaca, NY: Cornell University Press, 2007.

Skinner, Kiron K., Annelise Anderson, and Martin Anderson, eds. *Reagan, in His Own Hand: The Writings of Ronald Reagan That Reveal His Revolutionary Vision for America.* New York: Touchstone, 2001.

——. *Reagan: A Life in Letters.* New York: Free Press, 2003.

——. *Reagan's Path to Victory: The Shaping of Ronald Reagan's Vision; Selected Writings.* New York: Free Press, 2004.

Snyder, Sarah B. *Human Rights Activism and the End of the Cold War: A Transnational History of the Helsinki Network.* New York: Cambridge University Press, 2011.

Solzhenitsyn, Aleksandr. *Between Two Millstones.* Book 2, *Exile in America, 1978–1994.* Notre Dame, IN: University of Notre Dame Press, 2020.

Sparrow, Bartholomew. *The Strategist: Brent Scowcroft and the Call of National Security.* New York: Public Affairs, 2015.

Spitz, Bob. *Reagan: An American Journey.* New York: Penguin Press, 2018.

Stanik, Joseph T. *El Dorado Canyon: Reagan's Undeclared War with Qaddafi.* Annapolis, MD: Naval Institute Press, 2003.

Stone, Norman. *The Atlantic and Its Enemies: A History of the Cold War.* New York: Basic Books, 2010.

Streusand, Douglas E., ed. *The Grand Strategy That Won the Cold War: Architecture of Triumph.* Lanham, MD: Lexington Books, 2016.

Strober, Deborah Hart, and Gerald S. Strober. *The Reagan Presidency: An Oral History of the Era.* Washington, DC: Brassey's, 2003.

Suri, Jeremi. *The Impossible Presidency: The Rise and Fall of America's Highest Office.* New York: Basic Books, 2017.

Talbott, Strobe. *Deadly Gambits: The Reagan Administration and the Stalemate in Arms Control.* New York: Vintage, 1985.

Taubman, Philip. *The Partnership: Five Cold Warriors and Their Quest to Ban the Bomb.* New York: Harper, 2012.

Taubman, William. *Gorbachev: His Life and Times.* New York: W. W. Norton, 2017.

Teicher, Howard, and Gayle Radley Teicher. *Twin Pillars to Desert Storm: America's Flawed Vison in the Middle East from Nixon to Bush.* New York: William Morrow, 1993.

Teng-hui, Lee. *The Road to Democracy: Taiwan's Pursuit of Identity.* Tokyo: PHP Institute, 1999.

Thatcher, Margaret. *Margaret Thatcher: The Autobiography.* New York: Harper Perennial, 2010.

Thompson, Kenneth W., ed. *Foreign Policy in the Reagan Presidency: Nine Intimate Perspectives.* Lanham, MD: University Press of America, 1993.

Thompson, Nicholas. *The Hawk and the Dove: Paul Nitze, George Kennan, and the History of the Cold War.* New York: Henry Holt, 2009.

Thornton, Richard C. *The Reagan Revolution*. Vol. 1, *The Politics of US Foreign Policy*. Victoria, BC: Trafford, 2003.

———. *The Reagan Revolution*. Vol. 2, *Rebuilding the Western Alliance*. Victoria, BC: Trafford, 2005.

———. *The Reagan Revolution*. Vol. 3, *Defeating the Soviet Challenge*. Victoria, BC: Trafford, 2009.

———. *The Reagan Revolution*. Vol. 4, *From Victory to the New World Order*. Victoria, BC: Trafford, 2013.

Timberg, Robert. *The Nightingale's Song*. New York: Touchstone, 1995.

Tower, John G. *Consequences: A Personal and Political Memoir*. New York: Little, Brown, 1991.

Troy, Gil. *Morning in America: How Ronald Reagan Invented the 1980s*. Princeton, NJ: Princeton University Press, 2005.

Troy, Tevi. *Intellectuals and the American Presidency: Philosophers, Jesters, or Technicians?* Lanham, MD: Rowman & Littlefield, 2002.

———. *The Fight House: Rivalries in the White House from Truman to Trump*. Washington, DC: Regnery History, 2020.

Tumulty, Karen. *The Triumph of Nancy Reagan*. New York: Simon & Schuster, 2021.

Turek, Lauren. *To Bring the Good News to All Nations: Evangelical Influence on Human Rights and US Foreign Policy*. Ithaca, NY: Cornell University Press, 2020.

Tyler, Patrick. *A World of Trouble: The White House and the Middle East—from the Cold War to the War on Terror*. New York: Farrar, Straus and Giroux, 2009.

Vins, Georgi. *The Gospel in Bonds*. Eureka, MT: Lighthouse Trails Publishing, 2014.

Von Damm, Helene. *At Reagan's Side: Twenty Years in the Political Mainstream*. New York: Doubleday, 1989.

Wacker, Grant. *America's Pastor: Billy Graham and the Shaping of a Nation*. Cambridge, MA: Harvard University Press, 2014.

Waller, Douglas. *Disciples: The World War II Missions of the CIA Directors Who Fought for Wild Bill Donovan*. New York: Simon & Schuster, 2015.

Wallison, Peter J. *Ronald Reagan: The Power of Conviction and the Success of His Presidency*. Boulder, CO: Westview Press, 2004.

Walsh, Lawrence E. *Firewall: The Iran-Contra Conspiracy and Cover-up*. New York: W. W. Norton, 1997.

Walters, Vernon A. *The Mighty and the Meek: Dispatches from the Front Line of Diplomacy*. London: St Ermin's Press, 2001.

Ward, Jon. *Camelot's End: Kennedy vs. Carter and the Fight That Broke the Democratic Party*. New York: Twelve, 2019.

Weigel, George. *Witness to Hope: The Biography of Pope John Paul II*. New York: Harper Perennial, 2001.

———. *The End and the Beginning: Pope John Paul II—The Victory of Freedom, the Last Years, the Legacy*. New York: Doubleday, 2010.

Weinberger, Caspar. *Fighting for Peace: Seven Critical Years in the Pentagon*. New York: Warner Books, 1990.

———. *In the Arena: A Memoir of the 20th Century*. Washington, DC: Regnery, 2001.

Weiner, Tim. *Legacy of Ashes: The History of the CIA*. New York: Doubleday, 2007.

Westad, Odd Arne. *The Global Cold War: Third World Interventions and the Making of Our Times*. New York: Cambridge University Press, 2007.

——. *The Cold War: A World History.* New York: Basic Books, 2017.

Whipple, Chris. *The Gatekeepers: How the White House Chiefs of Staff Define Every Presidency.* New York: Crown, 2017.

——. *The Spymasters: How the CIA Directors Shape History and the Future.* New York: Scribner, 2020.

Wilber, Del Quentin. *Rawhide Down: The Near Assassination of Ronald Reagan.* New York: Picador, 2011.

Wilentz, Sean. *The Age of Reagan: A History, 1974–2008.* New York: Harper, 2008.

Wills, David C. *The First War on Terrorism: Counter-terrorism Policy During the Reagan Administration.* Lanham, MD: Rowman & Littlefield, 2003.

Wilson, James Graham. *The Triumph of Improvisation: Gorbachev's Adaptability, Reagan's Engagement, and the End of the Cold War.* Ithaca, NY: Cornell University Press, 2014.

——, ed. *Foreign Relations of the United States, 1981–1988.* Vol. 6, *Soviet Union, October 1986–January 1989.* Washington, DC: Government Printing Office, 2016.

Winik, Jay. *On the Brink: The Dramatic, Behind-the-Scenes Saga of the Reagan Era and the Men and Women Who Won the Cold War.* New York: Simon & Schuster, 1996.

Witcher, Marcus M. *Getting Right with Reagan: The Struggle for True Conservatism, 1980–2016.* Lawrence, KS: University Press of Kansas, 2019.

Woodward, Bob. *Veil: The Secret Wars of the CIA, 1981–1987.* New York: Simon & Schuster, 1987.

Worthen, Molly. *The Man on Whom Nothing Was Lost: The Grand Strategy of Charles Hill.* New York: Houghton Mifflin, 2005.

Wroe, Ann. *Lives, Lies & the Iran-Contra Affair.* New York: I. B. Tauris, 1992.

Yoshitani, Gail E. S. *Reagan on War: A Reappraisal of the Weinberger Doctrine, 1980–1984.* College Station, TX: Texas A&M University Press, 2012.

Yousaf, Mohammed, and Mark Adkin. *Afghanistan: The Bear Trap.* Havertown, PA: Casemate, 1992.

Zelikow, Philip, and Condoleezza Rice. *To Build a Better World: Choices to End the Cold War and Create a Global Commonwealth.* New York: Twelve, 2012.

Zelizer, Julian E. *Arsenal of Democracy: The Politics of National Security—from World War II to the War on Terrorism.* New York: Basic Books, 2010.

Zoellick, Robert. *America in the World: A History of US Diplomacy and Foreign Policy.* New York: Twelve, 2020.

Zubok, Vladislov M. *A Failed Empire: The Soviet Union in the Cold War from Stalin to Gorbachev.* Chapel Hill, NC: University of North Carolina Press, 2009.

——. *Collapse: The Fall of the Soviet Union.* New Haven, CT: Yale University Press, 2021.

NOTES

INTRODUCTION

1. Telegram 1978, June 1, 1982, from Thatcher Manuscripts, THCR 1/10/33, Churchill Archives Centre (hereinafter cited as CAC).

2. Robert Rowland and John M. Jones, *Reagan at Westminster: Foreshadowing the End of the Cold War* (College Station: Texas A&M University Press, 2010), 60–64.

3. *The Tower Commission Report: The Full Text of the President's Special Review Board* (New York: Bantam Books, 1987), x.

4. Francis Gavin, "Thinking Historically: A Guide for Strategy and Statecraft," War on the Rocks, November 19, 2019. Available at: https://warontherocks.com/2019/11/thinking -historically-a-guide-for-strategy-and-statecraft/.

5. Hal Brands, *Making the Unipolar Moment: US Foreign Policy and the Rise of the Post–Cold War Order* (Ithaca, NY: Cornell University Press, 2016), 5–6.

6. George Shultz, *Turmoil and Triumph: My Years as Secretary of State* (New York: Charles Scribner's Sons, 1993), xii.

7. Colin Powell, *My American Journey* (New York: Ballantine, 1996), 257.

8. The contrast with his successor President George H. W. Bush is stark. Despite a largely deserved reputation for restraint and caution, Bush actually deployed American troops into combat twice, in Operation Just Cause's invasion of Panama and Operation Desert Storm in the Persian Gulf, even though he served as president for only half the length of time Reagan did.

9. The same obtains for Reagan's successors, who have continued US support for authoritarian regimes, of late in the name of counterterrorism.

10. The number of deaths caused by communist regimes can never be known with certainty. Historian Stephen Kotkin cites a figure of sixty-five million, while the team of European scholars who produced the landmark *Black Book of Communism* place their estimate at one hundred million. See Stephen Kotkin, "The Communist Century," *Wall Street Journal*, November 4–5, 2017, C1, and Mark Kramer, ed., *The Black Book of Communism: Crimes, Terror, Repression* (Cambridge, MA: Harvard University Press, 1999).

11. Portions of this section draw on the author's previously published essay for the Ronald Reagan Institute, "The President Who Tore Down That Wall," and are used here by permission. Available at: https://www.reaganfoundation.org/media/357270/inboden_berlin -wall-address_reagan-institute.pdf.

12. Henry Nau, *Conservative Internationalism: Armed Diplomacy Under Jefferson, Polk, Truman, and Reagan* (Princeton, NJ: Princeton University Press, 2013), 172.

13. I've borrowed a phrase from Langdon Gilkey's classic account of life in a Japanese intern-ment camp in China during World War II: *Shantung Compound: The Story of Men and Women Under Pressure* (New York: Harper and Row, 1975).

CHAPTER 1: EAST OF CALIFORNIA

1. Details of this event drawn from Craig Shirley, *Rendezvous with Destiny: Ronald Reagan and the Campaign That Changed America* (Wilmington, DE: ISI Books, 2009), 72–74.

2. Reagan, "Remarks Announcing Candidacy for the Republican Presidential Nomination," November 13, 1979. Available at: https://www.reaganlibrary.gov/archives/speech/ronald -reagans-announcement-presidential-candidacy-1979.

3. "Conservative Hopes Buoyed by Reagan Candidacy," *Human Events*, November 24, 1979 (this also cites the *WSJ* editorial).

4. Reagan, "A Time for Choosing," October 27, 1964. Available at: https://www.presidency .ucsb.edu/documents/address-behalf-senator-barry-goldwater-time-for-choosing.

5. Kiron K. Skinner, Annelise Anderson, and Martin Anderson, eds., *Reagan, in His Own Hand: The Writings of Ronald Reagan That Reveal His Revolutionary Vision for America* (New York: Touchstone, 2001), 441–42.

6. Gene Kopelson, *Reagan's 1968 Dress Rehearsal: Ike, RFK, and Reagan's Emergence as a World Statesman* (Los Angeles: Figueroa Press, 2016), 80–81.

7. Thomas C. Reed, *The Reagan Enigma, 1964–1980* (Los Angeles: Figueroa Press, 2014), 46–47; David Broder, "Eisenhower Meets Reagan and Backs Him for Governor," *New York Times*, June 16, 1966; author interview with Thomas Reed, March 7, 2019.

8. Reed, *Reagan Enigma*, 49; Kopelson, *Reagan's 1968 Dress Rehearsal*, 449–52.

9. Either Nixon or Reagan ran in or at least strongly influenced every single presidential election from 1952 through 1988. In 1952 and 1956, Nixon ran as Eisenhower's vice presi-dential candidate. In 1960, Nixon ran as the GOP presidential nominee, narrowly losing to Kennedy. In 1964, Nixon staged a covert campaign to deny Goldwater the nomination, while Reagan's "A Time for Choosing" speech virtually eclipsed Goldwater's campaign and marked Reagan's national political debut. In 1968, Reagan made his first presidential bid, as Nixon earned the nomination and won the presidency. In 1972, Nixon won reelec-tion as president. In 1976, Reagan challenged incumbent Gerald Ford for the nomination, narrowly losing. In 1980 and 1984, Reagan won the presidency and reelection. In 1988, all GOP candidates competed for the mantle of Reagan's heir, with Reagan's vice president, George Bush, eventually capturing the nomination and then the White House.

10. John Lewis Gaddis, *Strategies of Containment: A Critical Appraisal of American National Security Policy During the Cold War* (New York: Oxford University Press, 2005), 287, 319.

11. Brands, *Making the Unipolar Moment*, 26.

12. Author interview with Reed, April 11, 2017.

13. Quoted in James Mann, *The Rebellion of Ronald Reagan: A History of the End of the Cold War* (New York: Viking, 2009), 21.

14. Skinner et al., *Reagan, in His Own Hand*, 15.

15. Walter Isaacson, *Kissinger: A Biography* (New York: Touchstone, 1992), 698–99.

16. This account and the Morris quote come from Steven F. Hayward, *The Age of Reagan: The Fall of the Old Liberal Order, 1964–1980* (New York: Three Rivers Press, 2001), 477–81.

17. Richard Allen interview, March 28, 2002, Ronald Reagan Oral History Project, University

of Virginia Miller Center (hereinafter RROHP). Available at: https://millercenter.org/the
-presidency/presidential-oral-histories/richard-allen-oral-history-assistant-president
-national.

18. Reagan CPAC remarks, box 29, Richard V. Allen Papers, Hoover Institution Archives (hereinafter HIA).

19. Here Reagan anticipated the argument that Georgetown professor Jeane Kirkpatrick would develop two years later in her seminal "Dictatorships and Double Standards" article (Jeane Kirkpatrick, "Dictatorships and Double Standards," *Commentary*, November 1979), which he would read with appreciation.

20. Ronald Reagan, "United States Foreign Policy and World Realities," 1977, box 10, Fred Iklé Papers, HIA.

21. Craig Shirley, *Reagan Rising: The Decisive Years, 1976–1980* (New York: Broadside Books, 2017), 113.

22. Skinner et al., *Reagan, in His Own Hand*, 103–4.

23. See ibid., 121–25, and Ronald Reagan, "Intelligence Capability Impaired," September 5, 1978, box 11, Fred Iklé Papers, HIA.

24. Reagan, Tokyo speech, April 17, 1978, box 29, Richard V. Allen Papers, HIA.

25. Reagan, Taipei speech, April 21, 1978, box 29, Richard V. Allen Papers, HIA.

26. Skinner et al., *Reagan, in His Own Hand*, 113–14.

27. Memo from Allen to Reagan, August 25, 1978, box 27, Richard V. Allen Papers, HIA.

28. Richard Aldous, *Reagan and Thatcher: The Difficult Relationship* (New York: W. W. Norton, 2012), 16.

29. Hannaford interview, January 10, 2003, RROHP. Available at: https://millercenter.org
/the-presidency/presidential-oral-histories/peter-hannaford-oral-history.

30. Hannaford, "Listening and Learning: Ronald Reagan's First Visit to Berlin, 1978," box 7, Jim Mann Papers, HIA.

31. Quoted in Peter Hannaford, *The Reagans: A Political Portrait* (New York: Coward-McCann, 1983), 191–92.

32. George Weigel, *The End and the Beginning: Pope John Paul II—The Victory of Freedom, the Last Years, the Legacy* (New York: Doubleday, 2010), 100–113.

33. Skinner et al., *Reagan, in His Own Hand*, 174–77.

34. Ibid., 177–78. Note that in Reagan's original script he erroneously wrote "Chernogorsk" rather than "Chmykhalov," confusing the city with the family. See also "The Siberian Seven: Escaping Religious Persecution in the USSR," in ADST Oral History Collection, available at: https://adst.org/2016/11/siberian-seven-escaping-religious-persecution-u-s-s-r/.

35. Martin Anderson, *Revolution: The Reagan Legacy* (Stanford, CA: Hoover Institution Press, 1990), 80–83.

36. Skinner et al., *Reagan, in His Own Hand*, 79.

37. "SALT and the Search for Peace" speech, September 15, 1979, box 10, Fred Iklé Papers, HIA.

38. Memo to Reagan from Roger Fontaine, August 2, 1979, box 28, Richard V. Allen Papers, HIA.

39. "Remarks Announcing Candidacy for the Republican Presidential Nomination," November 13, 1979. Available at: https://www.reaganlibrary.gov/archives/speech/ronald-reagans
-announcement-presidential-candidacy-1979.

40. Joseph Persico, *Casey: From the OSS to the CIA* (New York: Viking, 1990), ix.

41. Norman Podhoretz, "The Present Danger," *Commentary,* March 1980.

42. Reagan, "Peace and Security in the 1980s," March 17, 1980, address to Chicago Council on Foreign Relations, and Lou Cannon, "Reagan Is Conciliatory in Foreign Policy Statement," *Washington Post,* March 18, 1980, both in box 10, Fred Iklé Papers, HIA.

43. Elizabeth Drew, "A Reporter at Large; 1980: Reagan," *New Yorker,* March 24, 1980. Article in box 11, Fred Iklé Papers, HIA.

44. Kirkpatrick, "Dictatorships and Double Standards."

45. Hayward, *Age of Reagan: Fall of the Old,* 567.

46. Jay Winik, *On the Brink: The Dramatic, Behind-the-Scenes Saga of the Reagan Era and the Men and Women Who Won the Cold War* (New York: Simon & Schuster, 1996), 86–103.

47. Quoted in Douglas Feith and Richard Perle, "Fred Iklé: Champion of Missile Defense," *Wall Street Journal,* November 8, 2011.

48. List of Foreign Policy Advisors, April 20, 1980, box 11, Fred Iklé Papers, HIA.

49. Thomas C. Reed, *At the Abyss: An Insider's History of the Cold War* (New York: Presidio Press, 2005), 234–35.

50. For a thoughtful exploration of this question, see Melvyn Leffler, "Ronald Reagan and the Cold War: What Mattered Most," *Texas National Security Review* 1, no. 3 (May 2018).

51. "Republican National Convention Acceptance Speech, 1980," July 17, 1980. Available at: https://www.reaganlibrary.gov/archives/speech/republican-national-convention -acceptance-speech-1980.

52. Hayward, *Age of Reagan: Fall of the Old,* 676.

53. "Remarks of Governor Reagan's August 16 Press Conference on Government to Government Relations with Taiwan," box 30, Allen Papers, HIA.

54. James Mann, *About Face: A History of America's Curious Relationship with China, from Nixon to Clinton* (New York: Vintage Books, 2000), 116–18; James Lilley, *China Hands: Nine Decades of Adventure, Espionage, and Diplomacy in Asia* (New York: Public Affairs, 2004), 218–22; statement by Ronald Reagan, August 25, 1980, box 30, Allen Papers, HIA.

55. Hannaford, *Reagans,* 288.

56. Reagan speech and *Washington Post* article cited in Hayward, *Age of Reagan: Fall of the Old,* 678–80.

57. "The Iranian Hostage Crisis: The Next Seven Weeks," box 14, Fred Iklé Papers, HIA.

58. Darker allegations have long circulated that Casey tried to engage in subterfuge by dissuading the Iranians from releasing the hostages until after Election Day, even to the point of traveling to Madrid in July and Paris in October to meet with Iranian emissaries and promise them Israeli arms sales in exchange for holding the hostages. The charge, if true, would be tantamount to treason. But after decades of investigations by scholars, journalists, and separate US Senate and House committees, no credible evidence emerged proving that Casey attempted this stunt. One senior American official, who was deeply involved in the Iran hostage negotiations and had firsthand access to the most sensitive intelligence, offered his succinct verdict in the language of intelligence analysis: He judged "with the highest possible confidence" that Casey did not try to cut a hostage deal with the Iranians. That this official knew Casey well and otherwise held him in very low regard adds to the credibility of his conclusion. Author interview with former senior official, July 8, 2019. For a balanced treatment of the overall allegations, see H. W. Brands,

Reagan: The Life (New York: Doubleday, 2015), 232–37. For the case against Casey, see Kai Bird, *The Outlier: The Unfinished Presidency of Jimmy Carter* (New York: Crown, 2021), 551–63.

59. Shirley, *Reagan Rising,* 480, 510.

60. "A Strategy of Peace for the '80s," October 19, 1980, box 10, Fred Iklé Papers, HIA.

61. Quoted in Hayward, *Age of Reagan: Fall of the Old,* 706–7.

62. Eric S. Edelman, "The Great Communicator and the Beginning of the End of the Cold War," Ronald Reagan Institute. Available at: https://www.reaganfoundation.org/media /354711/amb_edelman_moscow_state_university.pdf.

63. Robert M. Gates, *From the Shadows: The Ultimate Insider's Story of Five Presidents and How They Won the Cold War* (New York: Simon & Schuster, 1996), 178.

64. James A. Baker III, *"Work Hard, Study . . . and Keep Out of Politics!" Adventures and Lessons from an Unexpected Public Life* (New York: G. P. Putnam's Sons, 2006), 122–31.

65. "Memorandum to Members of the Interim Foreign Policy Advisory Board," November 14, 1980, box 15, Fred Iklé Papers, HIA.

66. The formal title of the position is "assistant to the president for national security affairs" (APNSA), but for simplicity's sake this book will refer to the role as "NSA."

67. Baker, *"Work Hard, Study,"* 139; Meese describes his meeting with Haig in Deborah Hart Strober and Gerald S. Strober, *The Reagan Presidency: An Oral History of the Era* (Washington, DC: Brassey's, 2003), 65.

68. Memo from Nixon to Reagan, November 17, 1980, box 55, Jim Mann Papers, HIA.

69. Rowland Evans and Robert Novak, "'Secret' Diplomacy with the South Koreans," *Washington Post,* February 4, 1981.

70. Don Oberdorfer and Robert Carlin, *The Two Koreas: A Contemporary History,* 3rd ed. (New York: Basic Books, 2014), 105–7.

71. Anatoly Dobrynin, *In Confidence: Moscow's Ambassador to America's Six Cold War Presidents* (New York: Times Books, 1995), 472, 501.

72. Nau, note to author, April 21, 2018, with attached memorandum of conversation, November 25, 1980, and memorandum of conversation, December 4, 1980.

73. Steven R. Weisman, "Mexican President and Reagan Pledge Close Relationship," *New York Times,* January 6, 1981.

74. Memo from Allen to Reagan re: "The Hostage Negotiations," January 16, 1980, box 14, Fred Iklé Papers, HIA.

CHAPTER 2: TAKING THE STAGE

1. Author interview with Inman, May 13, 2019.

2. Inaugural address, January 20, 1980. Available at: https://www.reaganfoundation.org /media/128614/inaguration.pdf.

3. "Talking Points for Meeting Between President-Elect Reagan and Secretary-Designate Haig," January 6, 1981, folder 21, box 130, Alexander M. Haig Papers, Library of Congress (hereinafter LOC). As a devout Catholic whose brother was a priest, Haig was fond of religious imagery.

4. Alexander M. Haig Jr., *Caveat: Realism, Reagan, and Foreign Policy* (New York: Macmillan, 1984), 56–58.

5. Baker, *"Work Hard, Study,"* 140–41.

6. Memo to Jim Baker from Frank Hodsoll re: "Cabinet Organization on International Issues," January 31, 1981, folder: "Cabinet Organization/International Issues CFOA 28," box 1, Edwin Meese Papers, Ronald Reagan Presidential Library (hereinafter RPL); Martin Schram and Michael Getler, "Organization Table for Foreign Policy Limits Haig's Role," *Washington Post*, February 26, 1981, in folder 3, box 215, Haig Papers, LOC.

7. Gates, *From the Shadows,* 193.

8. Transcript of January 29, 1981, press conference. Available at: https://www.presidency.ucsb.edu/documents/the-presidents-news-conference-992.

9. Douglas Brinkley, ed., *The Reagan Diaries Unabridged* (New York: HarperCollins, 2009) (hereinafter RRD), February 4, 1981, entry.

10. Christopher Andrew and Vasili Mitrokhin, *The Sword and the Shield: The Mitrokhin Archive and the Secret History of the KGB* (New York: Basic Books, 1999), 242–43.

11. RRD, January 28, 1981.

12. Memo from Allen to president re: "Your Meeting with President Chun of Korea," February 6, 1981, folder: "Chun visit—February 1981 (1 of 2)," box 10, Donald P. Gregg Files, RPL.

13. Donald P. Gregg, *Pot Shards: Fragments of a Life Lived in CIA, the White House, and the Two Koreas* (Washington, DC: New Academia Publishing, 2014), 168.

14. Memorandum of conversation of president's meeting with President Chun Doo-Hwan, February 2, 1981, folder: "Memo of Conf. Pres Reagan [February 2, 1981]: Pres Chun of Korea Box 48," box 13, Executive Secretariat: NSC, Subject File, RPL.

15. RRD, January 29, 1981.

16. Memo from Allen to President on "Amb Mansfield's Cable to You," January 28, 1981; memo from Allen to the Cabinet, February 2, 1981, Mansfield cable, January 26, 1981, folder: "Japan (1/20/81) (1) Box 8," box 14, Executive Secretariat, NSC: Country File, Asia [Far East], RPL.

17. Japan may have even been the world's second-largest economy by this point. While most global GDP rankings put the USSR ahead of Japan as the second-largest economy, the Kremlin's suspect economic figures made an accurate accounting almost impossible.

18. Armitage, interview with author, March 5, 2019.

19. Margaret Thatcher, *The Autobiography* (New York: Harper Perennial, 2010), 335–36.

20. "Highly Confidential" memo of 8/9 February 1981, THCR 1/10/19 f3, Margaret Thatcher Foundation Archive. Available at: https://www.margaretthatcher.org/document/114255.

21. Charles Moore, *Margaret Thatcher: The Authorized Biography; From Grantham to the Falklands* (New York: Vintage Books, 2015), 566.

22. Memorandum of conversation of president's meeting with Prime Minister Margaret Thatcher, February 26, 1981, Margaret Thatcher Foundation Archive. Available at: https://www.margaretthatcher.org/document/205923.

23. RRD, February 27, 1981.

24. Caspar Weinberger, *Fighting for Peace: Seven Critical Years in the Pentagon* (New York: Warner Books, 1991), 7–9.

25. Caspar Weinberger interview, November 19, 2002, RROHP. Available at: https://miller-center.org/the-presidency/presidential-oral-histories/caspar-weinberger-oral-history-secretary-defense.

26. "Comparison of NATO and Warsaw Pact Land Forces in Europe," NATO. Available at: https://www.nato.int/cps/fr/natohq/declassified_138256.htm.

27. These numbers include older models of both Soviet and NATO tanks.

28. Memo from Weinberger to Carlucci, January 17, 1981, with attached memo from Tower, "Restoring the Military Balance," folder 4: "Confirmation Materials Notebook," box 572, Caspar Weinberger Papers, LOC.

29. "Total Strategic Missiles and Bombers," NATO, https://www.nato.int/nato_static_fl2014/assets/pictures/e2-cold-war-def-det-force-comp/20161206_dd-cw-comp-007.jpg.

30. James Mann, *The Great Rift: Dick Cheney, Colin Powell, and the Broken Friendship That Defined an Era* (New York: Henry Holt, 2020), 48.

31. David Crist, *The Twilight War: The Secret History of America's Thirty-Year Conflict with Iran* (New York: Penguin Press, 2012), 53.

32. Weinberger testimony before Senate Armed Services Committee, January 28, 1981, folder 5: "Confirmation Materials Notebook," box 572, Caspar Weinberger Papers, LOC.

33. Minutes of March 19, 1981, NSC meeting, folder: "NSC 00005 (Sinai Peacekeeping and Pakistan)," Executive Secretariat, NSC: NSC Meeting Files, RPL.

34. Andrew Krepinevich and Barry Watts, *The Last Warrior: Andrew Marshall and the Shaping of Modern American Defense Strategy* (New York: Basic Books, 2015), 150–51.

35. Memo from Bremer to group re: "April 1 Interagency Review Group Meeting on NSSD 1-82," "The Role of Allies and Others" draft, section G: "Force Integration," March 31, 1982, folder: "NSSD 1-82 (3 of 8)," box 1, Executive Secretariat, NSC: National Security Study Directives: Records, RPL.

36. Krepinevich and Watts, *Last Warrior,* 130, 154–55.

37. Ibid., x, 162–63.

38. Cited in February 24, 1981, notes, folder: "White House Notes 2/18/81–2/28/81," box 1, Sara Fritz Papers, RPL.

39. Powell, *My American Journey,* 258.

40. As a member of the NSC staff from 2005 to 2007, the author participated in many meetings in the Sit Room, both its cramped Reagan-era version and then its upgraded current version following its 2006 renovation.

41. NSC meeting minutes, February 6, 1981, folder: "NSC 00001 6 Feb 1981 [Caribbean Basin and Poland] (12)," box 91282, Executive Secretariat, NSC: NSC Meeting Files, RPL.

42. Russell Crandall, *The Salvador Option: The United States in El Salvador, 1977–1992* (New York: Cambridge University Press, 2016), 131.

43. Ibid., 140–48, 160–66.

44. RRD, February 11, 1981. Reagan diary entries are generally included verbatim as they appeared, though shorthand punctuation is spelled out, misspellings are corrected, and other punctuation lapses are amended. Where needed, abbreviations are lengthened in brackets to show their original meaning.

45. Memo from Richard Allen to Reagan, February 6, 1981, folder: "Memos to the President (02/06/1981–09/21/1981) Box 53," box 17, Executive Secretariat: NSC, Subject File, RPL.

46. NSC meeting minutes, February 11, 1981, folder: "NSC 00002 11 Feb 1981," box 91282, Executive Secretariat: NSC, NSC Meeting Files, RPL.

47. There are numerous possible spellings of Qadhafi's name in its English transliteration from Arabic; this book will use the same spelling as Reagan administration official documents: "Qadhafi."

48. Hal Brands, *Latin America's Cold War* (Cambridge, MA: Harvard University Press, 2010), 196.

49. NSC meeting minutes, February 18, 1981, in Jason Saltoun-Ebin, *The Reagan Files: Inside the National Security Council*, 2nd ed. (Seabec Books, 2014), 9–12.

50. Memorandum of conversation of president's meeting with Prime Minister Margaret Thatcher, February 26, 1981. Available at: https://www.margaretthatcher.org/document /205923.

51. Summary of conclusions from February 27, 1981, NSC meeting, February 28, 1981, folder: "NSC 00004 27 Feb 1981 [Poland, Caribbean Basin, F-15, El Salvador] (3/4)," box 91282, Executive Secretariat: NSC, NSC Meeting Files, RPL.

52. State 127757, cable, folder: "Prime Minister Suzuki's Visit May 7–8, 1981 (1 of 4)," box 10, Donald P. Gregg Files, RPL.

53. RRD, April 17, 1981.

54. See Andrew and Mitrokhin, *Sword and the Shield*, 486–507.

55. Transcript of January 29, 1981, press conference, American Presidency Project. Available at: https://www.presidency.ucsb.edu/documents/the-presidents-news-conference-992.

56. Memorandum of conversation with Foreign Minister Hans-Dietrich Genscher, March 9, 1981, folder: "Memorandums of Conversation, President Reagan [March 9–19, 1981] (6) Box 48," and memorandum of conversation with Chancellor Helmut Schmidt, March 30, 1981, folder: "Memorandums of Conversation, President Reagan [March 20–30, 1981] (7) Box 48," both in Executive Secretariat: NSC, Subject File, Box 13; memorandum of conversation with Helmut Schmidt, May 21, 1981, folder: "MemCons—President Reagan, 5-21-81," and memorandum of conversation with Reagan and French Minister Claude Cheysson, June 5, 1981, folder: "Memorandums of Conversation, President Reagan [June, 1981] (9)," both in box 14, Executive Secretariat: NSC, Subject File, RPL.

57. Memorandum of conversation with Prime Minister Fukuda, March 20, 1981, folder: "Chrono—March 1981 (5 of 6)," box 3, Donald P. Gregg Files, RPL.

58. Memo to the president from Allen, May 2, 1981; memorandum of conversation with Prime Minister Zenko Suzuki, Department of State, May 7, 1981; memorandum of conversation with Prime Minister Suzuki, NSC, May 7, 1981; and memorandum of conversation with Prime Minister Suzuki, NSC, May 8, 1981, all from folder: "Chrono—May 1981 (3 of 7)," RPL.

59. Part of the controversy emanated from Suzuki's use of a Japanese term for "alliance" that was last used to describe imperial Japan's partnership with Nazi Germany during World War II; in the postwar era, Japan customarily used a term translated as "treaty" to describe its relationship with the United States. Weinberger, *Fighting for Peace*, 226–28; memo from Donald Gregg to Richard Allen re: "The Situation in Japan," May 18, 1981, folder: "Chrono—May 1981 (5 of 7)," box 3, Donald P. Gregg Files, RPL.

60. Michael J. Green, *By More Than Providence: Grand Strategy and American Power in the Asia Pacific Since 1783* (New York: Columbia University Press, 2017), 405.

61. Memorandum of conversation, March 19, 1981, folder: "Memo of Con., President Reagan [March 9–19, 1981] (6) Box 48," box 13, Executive Secretariat: NSC, Subject File, RPL.

62. Minutes of NSC meeting, March 26, 1981, folder: "NSC 00006 28 Mar 1981," box 91282, Executive Secretariat: NSC, NSC Meeting Files, RPL.

63. These NSC meeting examples are found in Saltoun-Ebin, *Reagan Files*, 9–25.

64. RRD, March 19 and 24, 1981.

65. Letter from Nixon to Reagan, March 26, 1981, box 55, Jim Mann Papers, HIA.

66. Memo to Allen from Bremer re: "Letter from Soviet President Brezhnev," with attached translation of letter, March 7, 1981. Available at: http://www.thereaganfiles.com/19810306.pdf.

67. Martin and Annelise Anderson, *Reagan's Secret War: The Untold Story of His Fight to Save the World from Nuclear Disaster* (New York: Crown Publishers, 2009), 44–45.

68. Translated transcript of Andropov speech to KGB caucus meeting, March 25, 1981. Available at: https://nsarchive2.gwu.edu//dc.html?doc=5028353-Document-01-KGB-Chairman-Yuri-Andropov-to-KGB.

69. RRD, March 30, 1981.

70. Del Quentin Wilber, *Rawhide Down: The Near Assassination of Ronald Reagan* (New York: Picador, 2011), 171–77; Weinberger, *Fighting for Peace,* 86–88. The thought that the Kremlin was behind the shooting occurred to Reagan too. The morning after he was shot, as he lay in the hospital bed, Baker, Deaver, and Meese visited and informed him that Hinckley was the assailant. Reagan responded, "I had hoped it was a KGB agent. On second thought, he wouldn't have missed then." Wilber, *Rawhide Down,* 215.

71. Wilber, *Rawhide Down,* 166–68, 171–77.

72. Quoted in Wilber, *Rawhide Down,* 220.

73. RRD, March 30, 1981.

74. Ronald Reagan, *An American Life* (New York: Threshold Editions, 1990), 269.

75. RRD, April 21, 1981. "Striped pants set" refers to the caricature of State Department diplomats as dandies fond of pin-striped suits.

76. Anderson and Anderson, *Reagan's Secret War,* 50.

77. RRD, April 23, 1981.

78. Letters from Reagan to Brezhnev, April 24, 1981. Available at: http://www.thereaganfiles.com/19810424-2.pdf. See https://history.state.gov/historicaldocuments/frus1981-88v03/d46 for more background on the multiple letters.

79. Memorandum of conversation with Prime Minister Zenko Suzuki, Department of State, May 7, 1981, folder: "Chrono—May 1981 (3 of 7)," box 3, Donald P. Gregg Files, RPL.

80. RRD, April 24, 1981.

81. Reagan, *An American Life,* 273.

82. Dobrynin, *In Confidence,* 499.

CHAPTER 3: THE GLOBAL CHESSBOARD

1. George Weigel, *The End and the Beginning: Pope John Paul II; The Victory of Freedom, the Last Years, the Legacy* (New York: Doubleday, 2010), 131–33.

2. Cited in Paul Kengor, *A Pope and a President: John Paul II, Ronald Reagan, and the Extraordinary Untold Story of the 20th Century* (Wilmington, DE: ISI Books, 2017), 257.

3. Quoted in James Graham Wilson, *The Triumph of Improvisation: Gorbachev's Adaptability, Reagan's Engagement, and the End of the Cold War* (Ithaca, NY: Cornell University Press, 2014), 30.

4. Carter, address at University of Notre Dame, May 22, 1977. Available at: https://millercenter.org/the-presidency/presidential-speeches/may-22-1977-university-notre-dame-commencement.

5. Address at University of Notre Dame, May 17, 1981. Available at: https://www.presidency.ucsb.edu/documents/address-commencement-exercises-the-university-notre-dame-0.

6. Joseph Persico, *Casey: From the OSS to the CIA* (New York: Viking, 1990), 217.

7. Gates, *From the Shadows,* 198.

8. Letter from Casey to Reagan, May 6, 1981, folder 3, box 1, Presidential Handwriting File, RPL.

9. Gates, *From the Shadows*, 213.

10. "The CIA: Can Casey Survive?," *Newsweek*, August 3, 1981, copy in folder: "The Hon. William J. Casey (2) OA 11832," box 50, Edwin Meese Files, RPL.

11. Persico, *Casey*, 257–61.

12. Ibid., 72.

13. Ibid., 81–82.

14. Gates, *From the Shadows*, 199.

15. Persico, *Casey*, 225–26; author interview with Inman, September 30, 2019.

16. George J. Church, "Arming for the '80s," *Time*, July 27, 1981, 6–21.

17. "First Presidency Statement on Basing of MX Missile," May 5, 1981. Available at: https://www.churchofjesuschrist.org/study/ensign/1981/06/news-of-the-church/first-presidency-statement-on-basing-of-mx-missile?lang=eng.

18. Church, "Arming for the '80s."

19. Reed, *At the Abyss*, 267.

20. Gus Weiss, "The Farewell Dossier," *Studies in Intelligence* 39, no. 5 (1996); Sergei Kostin and Eric Raynaud, *Farewell: The Greatest Spy Story of the Twentieth Century* (Las Vegas, NV: Amazon Crossing, 2011), 166–72.

21. Rodger W. Claire, *Raid on the Sun: Inside Israel's Secret Campaign That Denied Saddam the Bomb* (New York: Broadway Books, 2004), 164–99; John T. Correll, "Air Strike at Osirak," *Air Force Magazine*, April 2012, 58–62.

22. RRD, June 7, 1981.

23. RRD, April 23, 1981.

24. Author interview with George Shultz, May 17, 2017; Shultz, *Turmoil and Triumph*, 550–51.

25. Ambassador Samuel Lewis interview, Foreign Affairs Oral History Collection, Association for Diplomatic Studies and Training, Arlington, VA; RRD, May 5, 1981; Richard Allen, "Memorandum for the File," May 5, 1981, folder: "Mem of Conv. President Reagan [May 1981] (8) Box 48," box 13, Executive Secretariat: NSC, Subject File, RPL.

26. Memorandum of conversation with Reagan and five Arab ambassadors, June 11, 1981, and memorandum of conversation with Reagan and Ambassador Ephraim Evron of Israel, June 11, 1981, both in folder: "Memorandums of Conversation, President Reagan [June, 1981] (9) Box 48," box 14, Executive Secretariat: NSC, Subject File, RPL.

27. RRD, June 9 and 11, 1981.

28. Dennis Ross, *Doomed to Succeed: The US-Israel Relationship from Truman to Obama* (New York: Farrar, Straus and Giroux, 2015), 182.

29. Author interview with Abrams, December 14, 2017.

30. Interagency intelligence assessment on "Implications of Israeli Attack on Iraq," July 1, 1981, folder: "NSPG 0017 30 June 1981 Box 91305," box 1, NSPG, NSC Executive Secretariat, RPL.

31. Memorandum of conversation of July 27 meeting with Habib, July 28, 1981, folder: "Memorandums of Conversation, President Reagan [July, 1981] Box 49," box 14, Executive Secretariat: NSC, Subject File, RPL; memo from Richard Nixon to Haig re: "Conversation Between President Sadat and Former President Richard Nixon," August 11, 1981, folder 5, box 216, Haig Papers, LOC.

32. The United States had also agreed to sell AWACS planes to Iran in 1977 but scuttled that deal in 1979 following the Islamic Revolution.

33. Reagan, *An American Life,* 411.

34. James Mann, *About Face: A History of America's Curious Relationship with China, from Nixon to Clinton* (New York: Vintage Books, 2000), 120–22.

35. Ibid., 122; James Lilley, *China Hands: Nine Decades of Adventure, Espionage, and Diplomacy in Asia* (New York: Public Affairs, 2004), 228–29; author interview with Richard Armitage, March 5, 2019.

36. Mann, *About Face,* 122–23.

37. Memo to president from Allen re: "U.S. Military Sales to China," August 24, 1981, and memo from Haig/Weinberger to president re: "Military Sales to China," August 21, 1981, folder: "China-General 08/24/1981–09/30/81 CF 0160," box 2, Edwin Meese Files, RPL.

38. Minutes of NSC meeting on theater nuclear forces, April 30, 1981, folder: "NSC 00008 30 Apr 1981 (2/3) Box 91282," Executive Secretariat, NSC: NSC Meeting Files, RPL.

39. Memo to Richard Pipes from Keith Gardiner with attached CIA memorandum "Strategic Implications of the Proposed Soviet–West European Natural Gas Arrangement," March 4, 1981, folder: "USSR—Pipeline (1/6)," box 30, Jack F. Matlock Files, RPL; memo to Pipes from Maurice Ernst with attached CIA assessment "Soviet Oil Prospects," May 29, 1981, folder: "Soviet Union—Energy (2/2)," box 25, Jack F. Matlock Files, RPL; memo from Pipes to Norman Bailey re: "Siberian Gas Pipeline Project," July 7, 1981, folder: "USSR—Pipeline (2/6)," box 30, Jack F. Matlock Files, RPL.

40. CIA, "Possible Allied Responses to US Strategy on the Yamal Pipeline," folder: "USSR—Pipeline (4/6)," box 30, Jack F. Matlock Files, RPL.

41. "Minutes of NSC Meeting on East-West Trade Controls," July 9, 1981, in Saltoun-Ebin, *Reagan Files,* 54–63.

42. Ibid.

43. RRD, October 16, 1981.

44. Seth G. Jones, *A Covert Action: Reagan, the CIA, and the Cold War Struggle in Poland* (New York: W. W. Norton, 2018), 117. For good background on Solidarity and the Poland crisis, see 92–115.

45. "Economic Aid to Poland," NSC briefing memorandum, July 14, 1981, folder: "NSPG 0019 14 July 1981 Box 91305," box 1, National Security Council: Executive Secretariat NSPG, RPL.

46. RRD, July 14, 1981.

47. "Minutes of NSC Meeting on Further Economic Aid to Poland," September 15, 1981, in Saltoun-Ebin, *Reagan Files,* 73–76.

48. RRD, February 6–12, 1984.

49. This description comes from the author's observations during a visit to the ranch in 2018, with special thanks for the tour to Andrew Coffin of Young America's Foundation.

50. Steven F. Hayward, *The Age of Reagan: The Conservative Counterrevolution, 1980–1989* (New York: Crown Forum, 2009), 169–70.

51. RRD, August 3, 1981.

52. Hayward, *Age of Reagan: Conservative Counterrevolution,* 172–73.

53. Peggy Noonan, *When Character Was King: A Story of Ronald Reagan* (New York: Viking, 2001), 226.

54. NSC meeting minutes, July 31, 1981. Available at: http://www.thereaganfiles.com/document -collections/the-libyan-files.html.

55. Weinberger, *Fighting for Peace,* 177–78.

56. John Lehman, *Oceans Ventured: Winning the Cold War at Sea* (New York: W. W. Norton, 2018), 74–82.

57. Author interview with Inman, November 21, 2019.

58. Lehman, *Oceans Ventured,* xii.

59. Draft "Dear Colleague" letter with cover note from "Dickie" to "Scoop," folder 12, box 308, Accession No. 3560-5, Henry M. Jackson Papers, University of Washington Archives.

60. RRD, September 14, 1981.

61. George J. Church, "AWACS: He Does It Again," *Time,* November 9, 1981, 12–18.

62. Peter Collier, *Political Woman: The Big Little Life of Jeane Kirkpatrick* (New York: Encounter Books, 2012), 124–27.

63. Ibid., 120.

64. Memorandum of conversation, March 17, 1981, meeting with Argentine president-designate General Roberto O. Viola, folder: "Memorandums of Conversation, President Reagan [March 9–19 1981] Box 48," box 13, Executive Secretariat: NSC, Subject File, Presidential Daily Brief, Argentina: President-Designate Viola, March 17, 1981, RPL, available at: https://www.reaganlibrary.gov/sites/default/files/digitallibrary/argentina/argentina-reaganpdb.pdf.

65. Russell Crandall, *The Salvador Option: The United States in El Salvador, 1977–1992* (New York: Cambridge University Press, 2016), 223–30.

66. Memo for the president from Allen re: "Your Meeting with Avital Shcharansky and Iosif Mendelovich," May 26, 1981, folder: "Dissidents (2 of 23)," box 23, Jack F. Matlock Files, RPL; RRD, May 28, 1981. Reagan refused to write out the full script of curse words in his diary, instead using dashes.

67. Author interview with Abrams, December 14, 2017.

68. Memo from Wolfowitz and Eagleburger to Haig re: "Human Rights Policy," October 2, 1981, in Alexander O. Poster, ed., *Foreign Relations of the United States, 1981–1988,* vol. 41, *Global Issues II,* document 53. Available at: https://history.state.gov/historicaldocuments/frus1981-88v41/d53.

69. Memo from Clark and Kennedy to Haig re: "Reinvigoration of Human Rights Policy," October 26, 1981, in Poster, *Foreign Relations of the United States,* document 54. Available at: https://history.state.gov/historicaldocuments/frus1981-88v41/d54. While Under Secretary Richard Kennedy is listed as a coauthor, Abrams was the main architect of the memo, along with Charles Fairbanks.

70. RRD, September 28, 1981.

71. National Security Decision Directive 12, "Strategic Forces Modernization Program," October 1, 1981. Available at: https://fas.org/irp/offdocs/nsdd/nsdd-12.pdf.

72. National Security Decision Directive 13, "Nuclear Weapons Employment Policy," October 19, 1981. Available at: https://www.archives.gov/files/declassification/iscap/pdf/2013-104-doc01.pdf.

73. Letter from Reagan to Thatcher, October 1, 1981, PREM 19/417, National Archives, United Kingdom.

74. Garrett Graff, *Raven Rock: The Story of the US Government's Secret Plan to Save Itself—While the Rest of Us Die* (New York: Simon & Schuster, 2017), 242–46; RRD, 84.

75. Minutes of NSC meeting on civil defense, December 3, 1981, in Saltoun-Ebin, *Reagan Files,* 98–103; RRD, December 3, 1981.

76. Memo from Chris Shoemaker to Richard Allen re: "SIOP Briefing," November 10, 1981, folder: "SIOP Briefing (Nov 1981–Nov 1983)," box 97, Executive Secretariat: NSC, Subject File, RPL.

77. "Reagan's Peace Offensive," *Newsweek,* November 30, 1981.

78. Minutes of NSC meeting on "Theater Nuclear Forces," November 12, 1981, in Saltoun-Ebin, *Reagan Files,* 92–98. See also Paul Lettow, *Ronald Reagan and His Quest to Abolish Nuclear Weapons* (New York: Random House, 2006), 59–61.

79. "Reagan's Peace Offensive," and Michael Getler, "Speech Could Change Tone of Administration," *Washington Post,* November 19, 1981.

80. "Memorandum of Telephone Conversation Between Reagan and Schmidt," November 21, 1981, folder: "Memorandums of Conversation, President Reagan [11/15/1981–11/30/1981] Box 49," box 14, Executive Secretariat: NSC, Subject File, RPL.

81. "Reagan's Peace Offensive," and Henry Muller, "Disarming Threat to Stability," *Time,* November 30, 1981.

82. "Remarks to Members of the National Press Club on Arms Reduction and Nuclear Weapons," November 18, 1981. Available at: https://www.reaganlibrary.gov/research/speeches/111881a.

83. "Remarks at the Annual Meeting of the Boards of Governors of the World Bank Group and International Monetary Fund," September 29, 1981. Available at: https://www.reaganlibrary.gov/research/speeches/92981a.

84. Memo from Casey to Reagan re: "The State of the Soviet Economy and the Role of East-West Trade," October 29, 1981, with attached October 26, 1981, CIA report, folder: "USSR—Economy (2/10)," box 25, Jack F. Matlock Files, RPL.

85. Emphasis original. Note that for a brief period from 1978 to 1982, USIA was known as the "United States International Communication Agency" before reverting back to USIA. Memo from John Hughes to Director Wick re: "Project Truth," October 15, 1981, folder: "Project Truth (October 1981 (1) Box 86)," box 24, Executive Secretariat: NSC, Subject File, RPL; author interview with Dr. Mark Pomar, August 21, 2018; letter from Wick to Casey, July 30, 1982, with attached July 20, 1982, report on Project Truth. Available at: https://ia800205.us.archive.org/10/items/ProjectTRUTH/Project%20TRUTH_text.pdf.

86. Allen's ignominious record would be eclipsed in 2017 by Michael Flynn, fired after just twenty-four days as President Trump's NSA.

87. Jones, *A Covert Action,* 5; Gregory Domber, *Empowering Revolution: America, Poland, and the End of the Cold War* (Chapel Hill, NC: University of North Carolina Press, 2014), 41.

88. Author interview with Inman, November 21, 2019.

89. Domber, *Empowering Revolution,* 42.

90. Letter from Reagan to Thatcher, December 19, 1981, THCR 3/1/17 f86 (T179/81), Thatcher MSS, CAC, available at: https://www.margaretthatcher.org/document/121561; "Record of Conversation Between Thatcher and Carrington," December 20, 1981, PREM 19/1871, National Archives, United Kingdom. See also Domber, *Empowering Revolution,* 38.

91. "Excerpts from a Telephone Conversation with Pope John Paul II About the Situation in Poland," December 14, 1981. Available at: https://www.reaganlibrary.gov/research/speeches/121481b.

92. Memorandum of conversation between President Reagan and Agostino Cardinal Casaroli, December 15, 1981, folder: "MemCons—President Reagan, 12-15-81," box 49, Executive Secretariat: NSC, Subject File, RPL.

93. Michael K. Deaver, *Behind the Scenes* (New York: William Morrow, 1987), 142.

94. Minutes of NSC meeting on Poland, December 21, 1981, in Saltoun-Ebin, *Reagan Files*, 114–22. Note that FDR actually delivered his "quarantine" speech in 1937.

95. Ibid.

96. "Address to the Nation About Christmas and the Situation in Poland," December 23, 1981. Available at: https://www.reaganlibrary.gov/research/speeches/122381e.

97. Letter from Reagan to Brezhnev, December 23, 1981. Available at: http://www.thereagan files.com/19811223.pdf.

98. Letter from Brezhnev to Reagan, December 25, 1981, and Reagan handwritten note. Emphasis original. Available at: http://www.thereaganfiles.com/19811225.pdf.

99. Telegram 3950 from British embassy to FCO, December 29, 1981, PREM 19/872, National Archives, United Kingdom.

100. Cable State 342580, December 30, 1981, folder: "Vatican 1983–1984 (10 of 13) RAC Box 7," box 5, European and Soviet Affairs Directorate, NSC: Records, RPL. Richard Pipes, *Vixi: Memoirs of a Non-Belonger* (New Haven, CT: Yale University Press, 2003), 175.

CHAPTER 4: THE BATTLE IS JOINED

1. Paul Kengor and Patricia Clark Doerner, *The Judge: William P. Clark, Reagan's Top Hand* (San Francisco: Ignatius Press, 2007), 108–16.

2. Memorandum of conversation, January 2, 1982, folder 1, box 73, William Clark Papers, HIA.

3. Letter and memo from Nixon to Clark, January 14, 1982, folder 16, box 54, William Clark Papers, HIA.

4. "A Mandate for Leadership Report: The First Year," draft, November 1981, folder 2, box 222, Alexander M. Haig Papers, LOC.

5. Memorandum for clients re: "The Concerns of Conservatives," folder 14, box 54, William Clark Papers, HIA.

6. Letter to Reagan from forty-three members of Congress, February 25, 1982, folder 13, box 56, William Clark Papers, HIA.

7. Norman Podhoretz, "The Neo-Conservative Anguish over Reagan's Foreign Policy," *New York Times Magazine,* May 2, 1982, in folder 6, box 25, Accession 3560-6, Henry M. Jackson Papers, University of Washington Archives.

8. Letter from Reagan to Brezhnev, January 15, 1982, and memo from Pipes to Clark, January 26, 1982, with attached January 22, 1982, letter from Brezhnev to Reagan, both in folder: "USSR—Pentecostals (1/4)," box 30, Jack F. Matlock Files, RPL.

9. RRD, January 30, 1982; "One of the Siberian Seven Goes Home," UPI, February 12, 1982.

10. Reed, *At the Abyss,* 267–69.

11. Weiss, "Farewell Dossier," 121–26.

12. Memo from Norman Bailey to William Clark re: "Soviet Bloc Economic and Financial Condition, Update No. 5," January 18, 1982, and "USSR: Hard Currency Outlook," CIA special analysis, February 2, 1982, both in folder: "USSR—Economy (3/10)," box 25, Jack F. Matlock Files, RPL.

13. Telnos 25 and 26, Schmidt/Reagan Meeting: Poland, January 7, 1982, PREM 19/872, National Archives, United Kingdom; notes re: "Schmidt visit," January 5, 1982, folder: "White House Notes 1/01/82–1/14/82," box 2, Sara Fritz Papers, RPL.

14. "Summary Record of a Telephone Conversation Between the Prime Minister and the Chancellor of the Federal Republic of Germany at 2100 Hours on 14 January 1982," PREM 19/762, National Archives, United Kingdom.

15. Cable from Haig to Reagan, January 29, 1982. Available at: https://www.margaretthatcher .org/document/109312.

16. Letter from Thatcher to Reagan, January 29, 1982, PREM 19/724, National Archives, United Kingdom.

17. RRD, January 30, 1982.

18. William P. Clark interview, August 17, 2003, RROHP. Available at: https://millercenter .org/the-presidency/presidential-oral-histories/william-p-clark-oral-history.

19. Memo from Clark to Reagan, January 15, 1982, with attached December 28, 1981, letter to Reagan from Independent Students' Association Committee on Human Rights in Poland, folder 7, box 73, William Clark Papers, HIA.

20. Memo to president from James Nance re: "Aircraft Sales to Taiwan—CIA Analysis," December 22, 1981, folder: "China—Dec 1981 (4 of 4)," box 7, Donald P. Gregg Files; minutes of National Security Planning Group meeting re: "Sale of Advanced Aircraft to Taiwan," January 7, 1982, folder: "NSPG 0033 07 Jan 1982 Box 91305," box 1, Executive Secretariat: NSPG, RPL.

21. Lilley, *China Hands,* 232–33; Mann, *About Face,* 123–24.

22. Memo from Lilley to Allen re: "Memorandum of Conversation—President's Meeting with Vice Premier Huang Hua, 29 October 1981," November 2, 1981, folder: "China—Historical—Brown Briefing Book #2/MemCons—1980—present [July 1982] (5 of 11) RAC Box 21," box 13, David Laux Files, RPL.

23. Lilley, *China Hands,* 235, 238.

24. Memorandum of conversation between Weinberger and Huang, November 3, 1981, folder: "China—Historical—Brown Briefing Book #2/MemCons—1980—present [July 1982] (6 of 11) RAC Box 21," box 13, David Laux Files, RPL.

25. "Reagan's Memo and Its Prequel on Arms Sales to Taiwan," Global Taiwan Institute, October 20, 2019, available at: http://www.ketagalanmedia.com/2019/10/20/reagans-memo-and -its-prequel-on-arms-sales-to-taiwan/; Reagan handwritten note, March 1, 1982, available at: https://shirleykannet.files.wordpress.com/2019/10/reagan-note-march-1982.pdf.

26. RRD, March 26 and March 29, 1982.

27. Memorandum of conversation between president and Abu Ghazala, March 29, 1982, folder: "Memorandums of Conversation, President Reagan (March 1982) Box 50," box 15, Executive Secretariat: NSC, Subject File, RPL.

28. Ross, *Doomed to Succeed,* 190–91.

29. Ambassador Samuel Lewis interview, Foreign Affairs Oral History Collection, Association for Diplomatic Studies and Training, Arlington, VA.

30. RRD, February 6, 1982.

31. Note from Clark to Haig, March 27, 1982, folder 13, box 51, William Clark Papers, HIA.

32. RRD, November 16, 1981.

33. Minutes of National Security Council meeting on strategy toward Cuba and Central America, November 10, 1981, folder: "NSC 00024, 10 November 1981 [Strategy towards Cuba and Central America]," Executive Secretariat: NSC, NSC Meeting File, RPL.

34. Memorandum of conversation between Reagan and Herrera, November 17, 1981, folder: "Memorandums of Conversation, President Reagan [11/19/1981–11/27/1981] Box 49," box 14, Executive Secretariat: NSC, Subject File, RPL.

35. Memorandum of conversation between Reagan and Monge, June 22, 1982, folder: "Memorandums of Conversation, President Reagan (June 1982) Box 15," box 50, Executive Secretariat: NSC, Subject File, RPL.

36. Hal Brands, *Latin America's Cold War* (Cambridge, MA: Harvard University Press, 2010), 202.

37. "The Fire Next Door," *Newsweek,* March 1, 1982, 16–24.

38. "Remarks to the Permanent Council of the Organization of American States on the Caribbean Basin Initiative," February 24, 1982, available at: https://www.reaganlibrary.gov /research/speeches/22482a; press briefing, February 24, 1982, folder: "White House Notes February 1982 (2)," box 2, Sara Fritz Papers, RPL.

39. Walter Isaacson, "El Salvador: A Lot of Show, but No Tell," *Time,* March 22, 1982, 18–22.

40. Bob Woodward and Patrick Tyler, "US Approves Covert Plan in Nicaragua," *Washington Post,* March 10, 1982.

41. Isaacson, "El Salvador."

42. Crandall, *Salvador Option,* 266–70, and https://en.wikipedia.org/wiki/1982_Salvadoran _Constitutional_Assembly_election.

43. RRD, March 31, 1982.

44. Memorandum of conversation, January 2, 1982, folder 1, box 73, William Clark Papers, HIA.

45. Gaddis, *Strategies of Containment,* 354.

46. Author interview with Thomas Reed, April 11, 2017.

47. Quoted in Hal Brands, *What Good Is Grand Strategy? Power and Purpose in American Statecraft from Harry S. Truman to George W. Bush* (Ithaca, NY: Cornell University Press, 2014), 109.

48. Author interview with Thomas Reed, April 11, 2017.

49. Emphasis original. Skinner et al., *Reagan, in His Own Hand,* 110–13.

50. Author interview with Thomas Reed, April 11, 2017.

51. Rowen himself later estimated Soviet military expenditures to be 20–23 percent of GDP, still a gigantic share. See Noel Firth and James Noren, *Soviet Defense Spending: A History of CIA Estimates, 1950–1990* (College Station, TX: Texas A&M University Press, 1998), 72. For an overview of recent scholarship, see Austin Long, "Rubles, Dollars, and Power: US Intelligence on the Soviet Economy and Long-Term Competition," *Texas National Security Review* 1, no. 4 (August 2018).

52. Quoted in Hayward, *Age of Reagan: Conservative Counterrevolution,* 115.

53. Seweryn Bialer and Joan Afferica, "Reagan and Russia," *Foreign Affairs,* Winter 1982/1983.

54. Graff, *Raven Rock,* 287–88; Reed, *At the Abyss,* 243–45.

55. Emphasis added. Minutes of National Security Council meeting on National Security Study Directive 1-82, April 16, 1982, folder: "NSC 00045 16 Apr 1982 (1/3) Box 91284"; minutes of National Security Council meeting on National Security Study Directive 1-82, April 27, 1982, folder: "NSC 00047 27 Apr 1982 (3/3) Box 91284," both in Executive Secretariat, NSC: NSC Meeting Files, RPL. Reed made similar declarations in a subsequent NSC meeting with Reagan two weeks later, predicting again that "the decade of the 80's

[would] be the decade of resolution" and reaffirming the goal of "the dissolution of the Soviet empire." No one present disagreed.

56. Minutes of National Security Council Meeting on National Security Study Directive 1-82, April 16, 1982, folder: "NSC 00045 16 Apr 1982 (1/3) Box 91284"; minutes of National Security Council meeting on National Security Study Directive 1-82, April 27, 1982, folder: "NSC 00047 27 Apr 1982 (3/3) Box 91284," Executive Secretariat, NSC: NSC Meeting Files, RPL.

57. National Security Decision Directive 32, "US National Security Strategy," May 20, 1982. Available at: https://fas.org/irp/offdocs/nsdd/nsdd-32.pdf.

58. Memo to Clark from Pipes re: "Your Georgetown Speech," May 27, 1982, with attached TASS article "Clark Speech on New US Strategy Viewed," May 25, 1982, folder: "Chron Memos to Clark, William P (3)," box 16, Richard Pipes Files, RPL. Emphasis original.

59. Richard Pipes, "A Reagan Soviet Policy," revised October 1981, folder: "Miscellaneous Papers [Reagan Soviet Policy—Working Draft—October 1981]," box 3, Richard Pipes Files, RPL; Richard Pipes, *Vixi: Memoirs of a Non-Belonger* (New Haven, CT: Yale University Press, 2003), 193–97. Emphasis original.

60. Memo from Pipes to Clark re: "Statement of US Strategy Toward Soviet Union," March 5, 1982, folder: "National Security Study Directive 11-82 (18)," box 1, Executive Secretariat, NSC: National Security Study Directives: Records, RPL.

61. Pipes, *Vixi*, 198.

62. The arrival of a new secretary of state, George Shultz (on whom more in the next chapter), helped at first in smoothing NSC-State relations, at least for the completion of National Security Decision Directive 75.

63. National Security Decision Directive 75, "US Relations with the USSR," January 17, 1983. Available at: https://fas.org/irp/offdocs/nsdd/nsdd-75.pdf.

64. The authoritative overview of each president's Cold War strategy remains Gaddis, *Strategies of Containment*.

65. Melvyn Leffler, "Ronald Reagan and the Cold War: What Mattered Most," *Texas National Security Review* 1, no. 3 (May 2018).

66. "Terms of Reference for High-Level USG Mission to Europe on Soviet Sanctions," February 22, 1982, folder: "USSR—Pipeline (4/6)," box 30, Jack F. Matlock Files, RPL.

67. Roger W. Robinson Jr., "Why and How the US Should Stop Financing China's Bad Actors," *Imprimis* 48, no. 10 (October 2019).

68. Minutes of NSC meeting, "Debrief of Under Secretary Buckley's Trip to Europe," March 25, 1982, available at: http://www.thereaganfiles.com/19820325-nsc-44.pdf; Tyler Esno, "Reagan's Economic War on the Soviet Union," *Diplomatic History* 42, no. 2 (April 2018): 281–304.

69. Minutes of NSC meeting, "Debrief of Under Secretary Buckley's Trip to Europe," March 25, 1982, available at: http://www.thereaganfiles.com/19820325-nsc-44.pdf; "Report on Interagency Mission to Europe," folder: "NSC Meetings: NSC 03/25/1982 Sanctions," box 3, Richard Pipes Files, RPL.

70. Memorandum of conversation with Shintaro Abe, January 18, 1982, folder: "Chrono—January 1982 (2 of 5)," box 5, Donald P. Gregg Files; memorandum of conversation with Masumi Esaki, February 23, 1982, and memorandum from Gregg to Clark re: "Ed Meese's Thursday Meeting with Masumi Esaki," February 24, 1982, both in folder: "Chrono—February 1982 (4 of 4)," box 5, Donald P. Gregg Files, RPL; memorandum of conversation with Yoshio Sakurauchi, March 22, 1982, folder: "Chrono—March 1982 (13 of 14)," box 6, Donald P. Gregg Files, RPL.

71. Weinberger, remarks at Japan Press Center, March 26, 1982, folder: "Chrono—March 1982 (8 of 14)," box 6, Donald P. Gregg Files, RPL; Green, *By More Than Providence*, 404.

72. Seoul 3160, cable, March 31, 1982, and Seoul 13204, cable, October 29, 1981, folder: "ROK (3 of 4)," box 10, Donald P. Gregg Files, RPL.

73. Gregg, *Pot Shards*, 169.

74. Seoul 4408, cable, May 3, 1982, folder: "ROK (2 of 4)," box 10, Donald P. Gregg Files, RPL; "The Right Signal in Seoul," *New York Times*, April 30, 1982, in folder: "China Foreign Relations—US Vice President Bush's 1982 Trip (5 of 8) RAC Box 18," box 10, David Laux Files, RPL.

75. Gregg, *Pot Shards*, 169.

76. Letter from Suzuki to Reagan, April 13, 1982; Tokyo 5468, cable, April 1, 1982, folder: "Chrono—April 1982 (1 of 8)," box 6, Donald P. Gregg Files, RPL.

77. State 127036, cable, folder: "Taiwan [12/31/1986] Box 6," box 5, James Kelly Files; "China: Limited Room to Maneuver on US Arms Sales," CIA assessment, May 26, 1982, folder: "Taiwan Arms Sales—Vol. II 1982 (1 of 13)," box 10, Donald P. Gregg Files, RPL; Mann, *About Face*, 125.

78. Lilley, *China Hands*, 243–45; Taipei 2720, cable, folder: "Taiwan Arms Sales—Vol. II 1982 (1 of 13)," box 10, Donald P. Gregg Files, RPL.

79. Martin Middlebrook, *The Falklands War* (Barnsley, UK: Pen and Sword Books, 2014), 16–17.

80. "James Rentschler's Falklands Diary, 1 April–25 June 1982," available at: https://www.margaretthatcher.org/document/114320; Moore, *Margaret Thatcher: From Grantham*, 668.

81. Lawrence D. Freedman, "The Special Relationship Then and Now," *Foreign Affairs*, May/June 2006, 61–73; Don Oberdorfer, "A Diplomatic Dilemma: US Has Pacts with Feuding Nations," *Washington Post*, April 4, 1982.

82. Freedman, "The Special Relationship Then and Now," 61–73.

83. Miller Center Presidential Oral History Program, "The Falklands Roundtable," May 15–16, 2003. Available at: http://web1.millercenter.org/poh/falklands/transcripts/falklands_2003_0515.pdf.

84. The National Security Planning Group was a smaller gathering of the national security principals, often to assess covert action programs and other sensitive matters. It otherwise closely resembled the NSC, with many overlapping functions and participants.

85. Notes from press conference, April 5, 1982, folder: "White House Notes—April 1982," box 2, Sara Fritz Papers, RPL.

86. Weinberger, *Fighting for Peace*, 214–15.

87. Lou Cannon, *President Reagan: The Role of a Lifetime* (New York: Simon & Schuster, 1991), 160.

88. Aldous, *Reagan and Thatcher*, 87–88. Haig's characterization in his memoir that he supported the UK in the Falklands crisis does not align with the historical record.

89. Archconservative Republican senator Jesse Helms, an enthusiastic supporter of Latin American anticommunist dictatorships, cast the only nay vote.

90. Minutes of April 30, 1982, NSC meeting on South Atlantic Crisis, in Saltoun-Ebin, *Reagan Files*, 174–77; Moore, *Margaret Thatcher: From Grantham*, 708.

91. Moore, *Margaret Thatcher: From Grantham*, 717.

92. Memorandum of conversation between Thatcher and Reagan, May 13, 1982, folder: "Mem-

orandums of Conversation, President Reagan (May 1982) Box 50," box 15, Executive Secretariat: NSC, Subject File, RPL.

93. Memorandum of conversation between Thatcher and Reagan, May 31, 1982, folder: "Memorandums of Conversation, President Reagan (May 1982) Box 50," box 15, Executive Secretariat: NSC, Subject File, RPL.

CHAPTER 5: SUMMER OF FREEDOM

1. Walter Isaacson, "Ready for the Grand Tour," *Time,* June 7, 1982, 6–9.

2. Address at Eureka College, May 9, 1982, folder 25, box 49, Accession 3560-006, Henry M. Jackson Papers, University of Washington Archives.

3. Department of State Bureau of Public Affairs, "US Arms Control Policy," July 1982, folder 25, box 49, Accession 3560-006, Henry M. Jackson Papers, University of Washington Archives.

4. Memo to president from Clark re: "White House Invitation for Solzhenitsyn," March 20, 1982, with attached March 5, 1982, memo from Pipes to Clark re: "Proposed White House Invitation for Solzhenitsyn," folder: "Dissident Lunch—White House May 11, 1982 (1 of 2)," box 22, Jack F. Matlock Files, RPL. Mindful of political pressures and Reagan's personal interest in meeting Solzhenitsyn, Pipes and other White House staff realized they could not block the invitation outright. Instead, they recommended that Reagan broaden the meeting by inviting a group of Soviet dissidents in addition to Solzhenitsyn. Pipes also had a long-running intellectual feud with Solzhenitsyn and had been on the receiving end of much print criticism by the Soviet dissident, which no doubt contributed to Pipes's resistance to bringing him to the White House.

5. Pipes, *Vixi,* 185–86.

6. Memo from Pipes to Clark re: "May 11 Luncheon," May 6, 1982, folder: "Dissident Lunch—White House May 11, 1982 (2 of 2)," box 22, Jack F. Matlock Files, RPL.

7. Pipes, *Vixi,* 187.

8. "Remarks for Luncheon with Soviet Emigres and Exiles," May 11, 1982, folder: "Dissident Lunch—White House May 11, 1982 (2 of 2)," box 22, Jack F. Matlock Files, RPL.

9. Robert G. Kaiser, "Solzhenitsyn Refuses Invitation to White House," *Washington Post,* May 11, 1982; Pipes, *Vixi,* 187.

10. Memo to Clark from Nau re: "Versailles Summit: East-West Export Credits," June 11, 1982, folder: "USSR—Sanctions (1/2)," box 34, Jack F. Matlock Files, RPL.

11. Background briefing with Cheysson, June 3, 1982, folder: "White House Notes June 1982 (1)," box 2, Sara Fritz Papers, RPL.

12. Peter Schweizer, *Victory: The Reagan Administration's Secret Strategy That Hastened the Collapse of the Soviet Union* (New York: Atlantic Monthly Press, 1994), 107; Kengor and Doerner, *The Judge,* 172–73; "Remarks of the President and His Holiness the Pope," June 7, 1982, folder: "Vatican 1983–1984 (9 of 13) RAC Box 7," box 5, European and Soviet Affairs Directorate, NSC: Records, RPL.

13. Kengor, *A Pope and a President,* 298–300.

14. RRD, June 11, 1982.

15. Telegram 1978, June 1, 1982, from Thatcher Manuscripts, THCR 1/10/33, CAC.

16. Quoted in Peter Robinson, *How Ronald Reagan Changed My Life* (New York: Harper, 2003), 207.

17. Rowland and Jones, *Reagan at Westminster*, 49.

18. Hayward, *Age of Reagan: Conservative Counterrevolution*, 254.

19. Robert Zoellick, *America in the World: A History of U.S. Diplomacy and Foreign Policy* (New York: Twelve, 2020), 392.

20. Brands, *Making the Unipolar Moment*, 124.

21. As Bismarck is often quoted, "The statesman's task is to hear God's footsteps marching through history, and to try and catch on to His coattails as He marches past."

22. Address to members of the British Parliament, June 8, 1982. Available at: https://www.reaganlibrary.gov/research/speeches/60882a.

23. Lou Cannon, "Soviets Assail Reagan's European Trip; TASS Says US Scuttling Détente," *Washington Post*, June 13, 1982.

24. Rowland and Jones, *Reagan at Westminster*, 92.

25. "Ronald Reagan's Flower Power," *New York Times*, June 9, 1982.

26. Rowland and Jones, *Reagan at Westminster*, 96.

27. Quoted in Robinson, *How Ronald Reagan Changed My Life*, 70–71.

28. "Record of a Meeting Between the Prime Minister and the President of the United States of America," June 9, 1982, PREM 19/943, National Archives, United Kingdom.

29. Lou Cannon, "Reagan Urges Deterrence Through Strength," *Washington Post*, June 10, 1982.

30. Steven R. Weisman, "Reagan, in Berlin, Bids Soviet Work for a Safe Europe," *New York Times*, June 12, 1982; Cannon, *President Reagan*, 471–72.

31. Memo to president from Clark re: "NSC Meeting of June 18, 1982," June 17, 1982, folder: "NSC Meetings: NSC 06/18/1982 Sanctions," box 3, Richard Pipes Files, RPL.

32. Address to United Nations General Assembly Special Session Devoted to Disarmament, June 17, 1982. Available at: https://www.reaganlibrary.gov/research/speeches/61782a.

33. President's concluding remarks at the National Security Council meeting, June 18, 1982, folder: "NSC Meetings: NSC 06/18/1982 Sanctions," box 3, Richard Pipes Files, RPL.

34. RRD, June 18, 1982. Emphasis original.

35. President's concluding remarks at the National Security Council meeting, June 18, 1982, folder: "NSC Meetings: NSC 06/18/1982 Sanctions," box 3, Richard Pipes Files, RPL.

36. Cannon, *President Reagan*, 201.

37. RRD, June 25, 1982; Bob Woodward, "Haig Reportedly Believes He Was 'Set Up,'" *Washington Post*, June 30, 1982.

38. Shultz, *Turmoil and Triumph*, 3–4.

39. Cited in Hayward, *Age of Reagan: Conservative Counterrevolution*, 253.

40. Shultz, *Turmoil and Triumph*, 38–39.

41. Ibid., 21.

42. In a curious confluence of pop culture and statecraft, the same day that Shultz was sworn in, rock musician Warren Zevon released his new album *The Envoy*, dedicated to Habib. Habib, shuttling between Beirut and Jerusalem as Israel upped its attacks and Arafat reneged on his promises to withdraw the PLO, had little time to enjoy his moment of musical acclaim. Though, as Zevon recalls, Habib later wrote him a letter of gratitude. See: https://www.warrenzevon.com/TheEnvoy/#open-modal.

43. Kai Bird, *The Good Spy: The Life and Death of Robert Ames* (New York: Broadway Books, 2014), 207–21, and Ronen Bergman, *Rise and Kill First: The Secret History of Israel's*

Targeted Assassinations (New York: Random House, 2018), 214–24. Ames's PLO connections included a close relationship with Ali Hassan Salameh, the sometime operational leader of the Black September terrorist unit, which was responsible for murdering many Israelis, such as the eleven Olympic athletes killed in Munich in 1972. Ruthless though he was, Salameh provided valuable information to the CIA and helped implement a PLO pledge not to kill Americans. That did not stop the Mossad from assassinating him in 1979, which grieved Ames and provoked tensions between the CIA and Mossad. Note that Bird and Bergman differ over Salameh's involvement in the Munich operation.

44. Shultz, *Turmoil and Triumph,* 48–50.

45. Memo to Reagan from Clark re: "NSPG Meeting on Middle East Policy," June 14, 1982, folder: "NSPG 0039 14 June 1982 Box 91305," NSPG box 1, Executive Secretariat: NSC, RPL.

46. Memorandum of conversation with Foreign Minister Yitzhak Shamir, August 2, 1982, folder: "Memorandums of Conversation, President Reagan (8/09/82) Box 50," box 15, Executive Secretariat: NSC, Subject File, RPL.

47. Ambassador Samuel Lewis interview, Foreign Affairs Oral History Collection, Association for Diplomatic Studies and Training, Arlington, VA.

48. "Minutes of NSC Meeting on Lebanon Situation," August 4, 1982, in Saltoun-Ebin, *Reagan Files,* 192–96. Dennis Ross recalls, "It mattered little that UPI admitted several weeks later that the photo had been doctored and the baby had not lost her arms; the truth was that a baby was suffering and the image of brutality stuck with Reagan." Ross, *Doomed to Succeed,* 195.

49. Habib had warned Begin against targeting Arafat, which the United States worried would further inflame the region. As the PLO leader accompanied his fighters boarding their evacuation ships at the Beirut port, several Israeli snipers drew a clear bead on Arafat. With one trigger pull he would have been dead. But the Israeli government, internally divided and under American pressure, did not authorize the killing. Arafat boarded the ship, unscathed and unaware. The next day, Begin presented Habib with a photo of Arafat in the crosshairs, taken by one of the snipers the day before as proof of Israel's restraint. Bergman, *Rise and Kill First,* 254–55, 261.

50. Ambassador Samuel Lewis interview, Foreign Affairs Oral History Collection, Association for Diplomatic Studies and Training, Arlington, VA.

51. Reagan consulted with Congress but did not seek formal authorization. He remarked wistfully to an NSC staff member that the only previous time a US president had deployed marines to Lebanon, "Ike didn't have to worry about being impeached under the War Powers Resolution." Quoted in John Gans, *White House Warriors: How the National Security Council Transformed the American Way of War* (New York: Liveright Publishing, 2019), 73. Twenty-four years earlier, Eisenhower had deployed a marine battalion to Lebanon to protect the government of President Camille Chamoun from potential overthrow by Arab nationalists reportedly in league with communists. Murky though the threat was, Eisenhower's mission had succeeded. The US troops, backed by deft diplomacy, helped stabilize the government, with just one American life lost. Reagan's marine mission would not end as well.

52. Shultz, *Turmoil and Triumph,* 100.

53. Ross, *Doomed to Succeed,* 200.

54. Bird, *Good Spy,* 280–84.

55. RRD, September 19, 1982.

56. Memo from Clark to president re: "Meeting with Joint Chiefs of Staff," December 22, 1982, folder 8291013, box 15, Executive Secretariat: NSC System File, RPL.

57. Shultz, *Turmoil and Triumph,* 107–9.

58. Memo from Oliver North to Clark re: "Item on Role of Multi-National Force in Lebanon," September 22, 1982, folder: "Shultz, Weinberger, Clark Thursday Group 9/22/1982–9/29/1982," box 96, Executive Secretariat: NSC, Subject File, RPL.

59. Memo from William Clark to Robert McFarlane with attached memo to president from Clark re: "Taiwan Arms Sales," July 2, 1982, and attached June 29, 1982, memo to Reagan from Haig re: "Taiwan Arms Issue," folder: "Taiwan Arms Sales—Vol. II 1982 (10 of 13)," box 11, Donald P. Gregg Files, RPL.

60. United States–China Joint Communiqué, August 17, 1982, box 13, Fred Iklé Papers, HIA. The First Communiqué was the agreement that Nixon signed with Zhou Enlai in 1972 consolidating the new United States–China partnership; the Second Communiqué was Carter's 1979 agreement establishing United States–PRC diplomatic relations.

61. Lilley, *China Hands,* 247.

62. Memo from Reagan to Shultz and Weinberger re: "Arms Sales to Taiwan," August 17, 1982. Available at: https://www.ait.org.tw/wp-content/uploads/sites/269/08171982-Reagan-Memo-DECLASSIFIED.pdf.

63. Green, *By More Than Providence,* 398.

64. RRD, August 17, 1982.

65. Mann, *About Face,* 127.

66. Paul Nitze, *From Hiroshima to Glasnost: At the Center of Decision—a Memoir* (New York: Grove Weidenfeld, 1989), 375–85.

67. Nicholas Thompson, *The Hawk and the Dove: Paul Nitze, George Kennan, and the History of the Cold War* (New York: Henry Holt, 2009), 287.

68. Memo re: "Rostow/Nitze Initiative on INF Talks," July 29, 1982, folder: "INF: Nitze Mtg 'Walk in the Woods' (07/29/1982–07/31/1982) Box 3," box 3, William P. Clark Files, RPL.

69. Winik, *On the Brink,* 196–203.

70. Thompson, *Hawk and the Dove,* 289.

71. National Security Decision Directive 56, "Private INF Exchange," September 15, 1982. Available at: https://fas.org/irp/offdocs/nsdd/nsdd-56.pdf.

72. Interview with Nitze by Harold Evans, Steve Rearden, and Ann Smith, June 24, 1986. Transcript shared with author by James Graham Wilson.

73. Paul L. Montgomery, "Throngs Fill Manhattan to Protest Nuclear Weapons," *New York Times,* June 13, 1982.

74. "USSR: Invigorating the Peace Movement," analysis from Bureau of Intelligence and Research, November 15, 1982, folder: "USSR—General [1981–1983] (4/5)," box 26, Jack F. Matlock Files, RPL.

75. Andrew and Mitrokhin, *Sword and the Shield,* 484.

76. Letter from Clark to Luce, July 30, 1982, folder 3, box 53, William Clark Papers, HIA.

77. SECTO 17097, cable, folder: "Vatican 1983–1984 (9 of 13) RAC Box 7," box 5, European and Soviet Affairs Directorate, NSC: Records, RPL.

78. "Approval Rating for Reagan Is Lowest Ever in Gallup Poll," *New York Times,* August 17, 1982.

79. Cited in Bob Spitz, *Reagan: An American Journey* (New York: Penguin Press, 2018), 535.

80. RRD, August 8, August 18, August 19, 1982; Karen Tumulty, "Ronald Reagan's Letter to His Dying Father-in-Law," *Washington Post,* September 14, 2019, available at: https://www

.washingtonpost.com/news/opinions/wp/2018/09/14/ronald-reagans-letter-to-his-dying-father-in-law-annotated/.

81. Thatcher interview with BBC Television, September 1, 1982. Available at: https://www.margaretthatcher.org/document/104815.

82. Minutes of National Security Council meeting on pipeline sanctions, September 22, 1982, in Saltoun-Ebin, *Reagan Files,* 197–99.

83. Shultz, *Turmoil and Triumph,* 135–45.

84. For an overview of the program as well as skeptical assessment of its most hyped claim, see Alex French, "The Secret History of a Cold War Mastermind," *Wired,* March 11, 2020. Available at: https://www.wired.com/story/the-secret-history-of-a-cold-war-mastermind/.

85. Roger W. Robinson Jr., "Reagan's Soviet Economic Take-Down Strategy," in Douglas E. Streusand, ed., *The Grand Strategy That Won the Cold War: Architecture of Triumph* (Lanham, MD: Lexington Books, 2016), 169.

86. John Lewis Gaddis, *George F. Kennan: An American Life* (New York: Penguin Press, 2011), 259–61, 278; George Kennan, "The Sources of Soviet Conduct," *Foreign Affairs* 25 (July 1947), 566–82.

87. National Security Decision Directive 54, "United States Policy Toward Eastern Europe," September 2, 1982. Available at: https://fas.org/irp/offdocs/nsdd/nsdd-54.pdf.

88. Jones, *A Covert Action,* 138–39.

89. Notes from European trip, June 10, 1982, folder: "White House Notes June 1982 (1)," box 2, Sara Fritz Papers, RPL.

90. William Inboden, "Grand Strategy and Petty Squabbles: The Paradox and Lessons of the Reagan NSC," in Hal Brands and Jeremi Suri, eds., *The Power of the Past: History and Statecraft* (Washington, DC: Brookings Institution Press, 2016), 166–68.

91. RRD, November 4, 1982.

92. Remarks to a White House luncheon for delegates to the Conference on Free Elections, November 4, 1982. Available at: https://www.reaganlibrary.gov/research/speeches/110482b.

93. Letter from Reagan to Brezhnev, October 20, 1982, and letter from Brezhnev to Reagan, October 30, 1982, both in folder: "USSR: General Secretary Brezhnev (8290742, 8290870)," box 38, Executive Secretariat, NSC: Head of State File: Records, 1981–1989, RPL; Sergey Radchenko, *Unwanted Visionaries: The Soviet Failure in Asia at the End of the Cold War* (New York: Oxford University Press, 2014), 23. See also Natan Sharansky, *Fear No Evil* (New York: Random House, 1988), 339–52.

94. RRD, November 11, 1982.

95. Robinson, *How Ronald Reagan Changed My Life,* 187.

96. Ben Macintyre, *The Spy and the Traitor: The Greatest Espionage Story of the Cold War* (New York: Crown, 2018), 142–48.

97. Simon Miles, "Engaging the 'Evil Empire': East-West Relations in the Second Cold War," unpublished dissertation, University of Texas at Austin, May 2017, 137–38.

98. Ibid., 138–39.

99. Memorandum of conversation between Reagan and FRG Chancellor Kohl, November 15, 1982, folder: "Memorandums of Conversation, President Reagan (11/01/82–12/06/82) Box 50," box 15, Executive Secretariat: NSC, Subject File, RPL.

100. Memo from Clark to Reagan re: "Telephone Call to New Japanese Prime Minister," November 24, 1982, folder: "Memorandums of Conversation, President Reagan (11/01/82–12/06/82) Box 50," box 15, Executive Secretariat: NSC, Subject File, RPL.

101. National Security Decision Directive 62, "National Security Decision Directive on United States–Japan Relations," October 25, 1982. Available at: https://fas.org/irp/offdocs/nsdd/nsdd-62.pdf.

102. Minutes of NSC meeting, November 23, 1982, in Saltoun-Ebin, *Reagan Files,* 209–13; National Security Decision Directive 71, "US Policy Toward Latin America in the Wake of the Falklands Crisis," November 30, 1982, available at: https://fas.org/irp/offdocs/nsdd/nsdd-71.pdf.

103. "Summary of the President's Meeting with Dr. Roberto Suazo Cordova, President of Honduras," July 14, 1982, folder: "Memorandums of Conversation, President Reagan (July 1982) Box 50," box 15, Executive Secretariat: NSC, Subject File; memorandum of conversation with President Ricardo de la Espriella of Panama, October 1, 1982, folder: "Memorandums of Conversation, President Reagan (October 1982) Box 50," box 15, Executive Secretariat: NSC, Subject File, RPL.

104. RRD, December 1, 1982.

105. "A Hemisphere of Democracy," folder 8, box 40, William Clark Papers, HIA.

106. RRD, December 3–4, 1982.

107. RRD, November 15, 1982. Available at: https://fas.org/irp/offdocs/nsdd/nsdd-69.pdf.

108. "Background Only with David Gergen," December 15, 1982, folder: "White House Notes, December 1982 (1/2)," box 3, Sara Fritz Papers, RPL.

109. Robert Kagan, *A Twilight Struggle: American Power and Nicaragua, 1977–1990* (New York: Free Press, 1996), 243–44.

110. Duane R. Clarridge, *A Spy for All Seasons: My Life in the CIA* (New York: Scribner, 1997), 209.

111. "USSR: Aid to the Third World in 1982," special analysis, folder: "USSR—Third World," box 36, Jack F. Matlock Files, RPL.

CHAPTER 6: RAISING THE STAKES

1. RRD, January 7, 1983; notes from background lunch with Bob Sims, February 16, 1983, and notes from call with Bob Sims, February 23, 1982, both in folder: "White House Notes, February 1983," box 3, Sara Fritz Papers, RPL.

2. Quoted in Hayward, *Age of Reagan: Conservative Counterrevolution,* 283.

3. "Remarks at the Annual Convention of the National Association of Religious Broadcasters," January 31, 1983. Available at: https://www.reaganlibrary.gov/research/speeches/13183b.

4. RRD, January 31, 1983.

5. RRD, January 17, 1983.

6. RRD, January 16 and 17, 1983.

7. State 08477, cable, January 12, 1983, folder: "Japan (1/6/83–1/14/83) Box 8," box 16, Executive Secretariat, NSC: Country File, Japan, RPL.

8. Memorandum of conversation re: "President's Tete-a-Tete with PM Nakasone," January 18, 1983, and memorandum of conversation of meeting between President Reagan and PM Nakasone, January 18, 1983, both in folder: "Memorandums of Conversation,

President Reagan (12/27/82–01/31/83) Box 51," box 16, Executive Secretariat: NSC, Subject File, RPL.

9. Green, *By More Than Providence,* 405. Note that Nakasone originally referred to Japan as "a big ship" but the overzealous interpreter translated it as "unsinkable aircraft carrier." However, Nakasone embraced the latter term when the translation mistake was pointed out to him.

10. Memo from Sigur to Clark re: "Background Material for Your 6:30 p.m. Meeting," January 19, 1983, folder: "Japan (1/19/83) Box 8," box 16, Executive Secretariat: NSC, Country File, Japan, RPL. See also Richard McGregor, *Asia's Reckoning: China, Japan, and the Fate of US Power in the Pacific Century* (New York: Viking, 2017), 85, 106.

11. Radchenko, *Unwanted Visionaries,* 56–57.

12. Toast by Vice President Bush at dinner for Prime Minister Nakasone, January 18, 1983, folder: "Meetings with Foreigners—January 1983: Japanese Prime Minister Nakasone, January 18, 1983," box 13, Meetings with Foreigners Files, Donald Gregg Files, Office of National Security Affairs, Office of Vice President George Bush, George H. W. Bush Presidential Library.

13. Green, *By More Than Providence,* 390, and Shultz, *Turmoil and Triumph,* 172.

14. Green, *By More Than Providence,* 390.

15. Memorandum of conversation, president's meeting with Prime Minister Fraser, June 30, 1981, folder: "Memorandums of Conversation, President Reagan [July, 1981] Box 49," box 14, Executive Secretariat: NSC, Subject File, RPL.

16. See, for example, Bureau of Intelligence and Research Analysis, "The Chinese Role in the Strategic Triangle," June 30, 1983, folder: "Soviet Union: Sino-Soviet Relations (3/3)," box 34, Jack F. Matlock Files, RPL.

17. Author interview with Wolfowitz, June 14, 2019.

18. Shultz, *Turmoil and Triumph,* 183.

19. SECTO 1031, cable, folder: "Japan (2/1/83) Box 8," box 16, Executive Secretariat: NSC, Country File, Japan, RPL.

20. Beijing 220, cable, folder: "China Foreign Relations—US Sec. Shultz 1983 Trip (16 of 25) RAC Box 18," box 8, David Laux Files, RPL.

21. Memo from Wolfowitz to Shultz re: "Your Meeting with Deng Xiaoping," January 26, 1983, folder: "China Foreign Relations—US Sec. Shultz 1983 Trip (20 of 25) RAC Box 18," box 8, David Laux Files, RPL.

22. Gates, *From the Shadows,* 255–56.

23. Peter Rodman, *More Precious Than Peace: The Cold War and the Struggle for the Third World* (New York: Charles Scribner's Sons, 1994), 192.

24. Shultz, *Turmoil and Triumph,* 389–92.

25. SECTO 1059, cable, transcript of remarks to American business community, February 3, 1983, folder: "China Foreign Relations—US Sec. Shultz 1983 Trip (12 of 25) RAC Box 18," box 8, David Laux Files, RPL.

26. Memo from Sigur to Clark re: "Secretary Shultz's speech on East Asian Affairs on March 5," March 4, 1983, folder: "Far East—General (3/4/83–6/12/83) Box 8," box 14, Executive Secretariat, NSC: Country File, Asia, RPL.

27. Karen Tumulty, *The Triumph of Nancy Reagan* (New York: Simon & Schuster, 2021), 2.

28. Memo from Clark to president re: "The Prospects for Progress in US-Soviet Relations," February 4, 1983, folder: "Sensitive Chron File [1/07/1983–3/02/1983] RAC Box 7," Robert C. "Bud" McFarlane Files, RPL. In his memoir, Shultz inexplicably portrays Clark as

opposed to Reagan's meeting with Dobrynin, but this is belied by Clark's memo. See Shultz, *Turmoil and Triumph,* 164.

29. RRD, February 15, 1983.

30. Memorandum of conversation on US-Soviet Relations, February 15, 1983, folder: "Memorandums of Conversation, President Reagan (2/15/83–3/31/83) Box 51," box 16, Executive Secretariat: NSC, Subject File, RPL.

31. Shultz, *Turmoil and Triumph,* 165.

32. Dobrynin, *In Confidence,* 526–27.

33. Max M. Kampelman, "The Ronald Reagan I Knew," *Weekly Standard,* November 24, 2003.

34. Shultz, *Turmoil and Triumph,* 171.

35. Thomas Miller oral history, Association for Diplomatic Studies and Training. Available at: https://adst.org/oral-history/fascinating-figures/George-shultz-country-united-states/.

36. Shultz, *Turmoil and Triumph,* 167, 267.

37. Nancy Gibbs and Michael Duffy, *The Preacher and the Presidents: Billy Graham in the White House* (New York: Center Street, 2007), 268–74.

38. Remarks at the Annual Convention of the National Association of Evangelicals in Orlando, FL, March 8, 1983. Available at: https://www.reaganlibrary.gov/research/speeches/30883b. On Reagan's role in the speech, see Martin J. Medhurst, "Writing Speeches for Ronald Reagan: An Interview with Tony Dolan," *Rhetoric and Public Affairs* 1, no. 2 (1998): 245–56.

39. Anthony Lewis, "Onward Christian Soldiers," *New York Times,* March 10, 1983; Paul Kengor, "Hot Words in the Cold War," *Christian History* 99 (2008), available at: https://christianhistoryinstitute.org/magazine/article/hot-words-in-the-cold-war.

40. Serge Schmemann, "Soviet Says Reagan Has 'Pathological Hatred,'" *New York Times,* March 10, 1983; John F. Burns, "Soviet Official Rebuts 'Focus of Evil' Speech," *New York Times,* March 18, 1983.

41. Charles McCarry, *Second Sight* (New York: Overlook Press, 2009), 265.

42. Interview with Shcharansky, "The View from the Gulag," *Weekly Standard,* June 21, 2004.

43. Memo to president from Keyworth re: "Letter from Edward Teller," July 29, 1982, folder 13, box 58, William P. Clark Papers, HIA. Reagan's reference to the United States' having once rejected the submarine may be apocryphal, but his larger point about the military's sometimes resisting new innovations was true.

44. RRD, February 11, 1983.

45. Lettow, *Ronald Reagan and His Quest,* 107.

46. Draft memo re: "Staff Reservations About Your Initiative in the Speech," March 22, 1983, folder 15, box 73, William P. Clark Papers, HIA.

47. "Address to the Nation on Defense and National Security," March 23, 1983. Available at: https://www.reaganlibrary.gov/research/speeches/32383d.

48. MO 11/9/4 President Reagan's Speech on Defensive Technology, March 29, 1983, PREM 19/1188, National Archives, United Kingdom.

49. Dusko Doder, "Andropov Accuses Reagan of Lying About Soviet Arms," *Washington Post,* March 27, 1983.

50. Transcript of meeting with reporters, March 29, 1983. Available at: https://www.reaganlibrary.gov/research/speeches/32983a.

51. Ash Carter, *Inside the Five-Sided Box: Lessons from a Lifetime of Leadership in the Pentagon* (New York: Dutton, 2019), 69–70. Carter later served as secretary of defense under President Barack Obama.

52. "Facts and Figures About the Reagan Administration Defense Program," folder 10, box 41, William P. Clark Papers, HIA.

53. Quoted in Brands, *What Good Is Grand Strategy?*, 112.

54. RRD, April 6, 1983. Emphasis original.

55. Leslie Gelb, "Moscow Angrily Settles Back to Await End of Reagan Era," *New York Times,* March 30, 1983.

56. Thomas R. Johnson, *American Cryptology During the Cold War, 1945–1989,* book 4: *Cryptologic Rebirth 1981–1989* (Center for Cryptologic History, National Security Agency, 1999), 318. Available at: https://nsarchive2.gwu.edu/NSAEBB/NSAEBB426/docs/2.American%20Cryptology%20During%20the%20Cold%20War%201945-1989%20Book%20IV%20Cryptologic%20Rebirth%201981-1989-1999.pdf.

57. State 178528, cable, re: "The Northwest Pacific: Airspace Violations and Territoriality." In author's possession, downloaded from State Department FOIA website. See also Marc Ambinder, *The Brink: President Reagan and the Nuclear War Scare of 1983* (New York: Simon & Schuster, 2018), 131–35.

58. Quoted in David E. Hoffman, *The Dead Hand: The Untold Story of the Cold War Arms Race and Its Dangerous Legacy* (New York: Anchor Books, 2009), 65–66.

59. Ibid., 66–68.

60. Gates, *From the Shadows,* 250–51.

61. William Casey, "Regroup to Check the Soviet Thrust," *Wall Street Journal,* April 22, 1983, in folder 2, box 317, William J. Casey Papers, HIA.

62. Rodman, *More Precious Than Peace,* 265. Emphasis original.

63. Kurt Lohbeck, *Holy War, Unholy Victory: Eyewitness to the CIA's Secret War in Afghanistan* (Washington, DC: Regnery Gateway, 1993), 88.

64. George Crile, *Charlie Wilson's War* (New York: Grove Press, 2003), 256.

65. Gates, *From the Shadows,* 252.

66. RRD, December 7, 1982; memorandum of conversation between Reagan and Pakistani President Zia, December 7, 1982, folder: "Memorandums of Conversation, President Reagan (12/11/82–12/23/82) Box 50," box 15, Executive Secretariat: NSC, Subject File, RPL.

67. "Toasts of President Reagan and President Mohammad Zia-ul-Haq of Pakistan at the State Dinner," December 7, 1982. Available at: https://www.reaganlibrary.gov/research/speeches/120782f. While Zia's use of the word *peacemaker* came in the immediate context of Reagan's Israeli-Palestinian peace plan, later in his toast Zia applied the concept to Afghanistan, Pakistan, and the Cold War.

68. RRD, February 2, 1983. See also Reagan's description of the meeting to Thatcher several months later in memorandum of conversation between Reagan and Thatcher, September 29, 1983, folder: "Memorandums of Conversation, President Reagan (9/28/83–09/30/83) Box 51," box 16, Executive Secretariat: NSC, Subject File, RPL.

69. Crile, *Charlie Wilson's War,* 174–269.

70. Memo to Clark from Sapia-Bosch re: "Central America," January 29, 1983, folder: "Central America—General (1/28/83–1/29/83) Box 27," box 40, Executive Secretariat, NSC: Country File, Latin America, RPL.

71. "Remarks on Central America and El Salvador at the Annual Meeting of the National Association of Manufacturers," March 10, 1983. Available at: https://www.reaganlibrary .gov/research/speeches/31083a.

72. George Weigel, *Witness to Hope: The Biography of Pope John Paul II* (New York: Harper Perennial, 2001), 455–56.

73. Quoted in Joseph Persico, *Casey: From the OSS to the CIA* (New York: Viking, 1990), 305.

74. Winik, *On the Brink,* 254–57.

75. RRD, February 17, 1983.

76. "The White House and El Salvador" (notes), March 3, 1983, folder: "White House Notes March 1983 (1/2)," box 3, Sara Fritz Papers, RPL.

77. Tip O'Neill with William Novak, *Man of the House* (New York: Random House, 1987), 370–71.

78. Christopher Andrew and Vasili Mitrokhin, *The World Was Going Our Way: The KGB and the Battle for the Third World* (New York: Basic Books, 2005), 128–29.

79. Note from Nixon to Clark with attached op-ed draft, April 25, 1983, folder 19, box 67, William P. Clark Papers, HIA.

80. Letter from Reagan to Nixon, June 1, 1983, box 55, Jim Mann Papers, HIA.

81. Memo from Tony Dolan to Bill Clark, April 25, 1983, folder: "Central America Speech April 25, 1983 Box 2," box 2, William P. Clark File, RPL.

82. "Address Before a Joint Session of Congress on Central America," April 27, 1983. Available at: https://www.reaganlibrary.gov/research/speeches/42783d.

83. Memorandum of Telephone Conversation with President Magana, April 5 1983, folder: "Memorandums of Conversation, President Reagan (April 83) Box 51," box 16, Executive Secretariat: NSC, Subject File, RPL.

84. Quoted in Persico, *Casey,* 324.

85. Deane Roesch Hinton, *Economics and Diplomacy: A Life in the Foreign Service of the United States* (Washington, DC: New Academia Publishing, 2015), 357.

86. Notes from media Q & A with Reagan re: "El Salvador," March 4, 1983, folder: "White House Notes March 1983 (1/2)," box 3, Sara Fritz Papers, RPL. Available at: https://www .reaganlibrary.gov/sites/default/files/digitallibrary/personalpapers/fritz/box-003/40-414 -003-014-2018.pdf.

87. "Remarks on Central America and El Salvador at the Annual Meeting of the National Association of Manufacturers," March 10, 1983. Available at: https://www.reaganlibrary .gov/research/speeches/31083a.

88. Kengor and Doerner, *The Judge,* 206–7.

89. RRD, January 4, 1983.

90. William P. Clark interview, August 17, 2003, RROHP, Miller Center, University of Virginia. Available at: https://millercenter.org/the-presidency/presidential-oral-histories /william-p-clark-oral-history. See also Kengor and Doerner, *The Judge,* 214–18.

91. Spitz, *Reagan,* 112–13.

92. RRD, May 3, 1982.

93. Tim Naftali, "Ronald Reagan's Long-Hidden Racist Conversation with Richard Nixon," *Atlantic,* July 30, 2019. Available at: https://www.theatlantic.com/ideas/archive/2019/07 /ronald-reagans-racist-conversation-richard-nixon/595102/.

94. Rick Perlstein, *Reaganland: America's Right Turn, 1976–1980* (New York: Simon & Schuster, 2020), 829–35.

95. Lou Cannon, "Reagan's Southern Stumble," *New York Times,* November 18, 2007.

96. Odd Arne Westad, *The Global Cold War: Third World Interventions and the Making of Our Times* (New York: Cambridge University Press, 2007), 241, 251–52, 279.

97. Chester Crocker interview, Foreign Affairs Oral History Collection, Association for Diplomatic Studies and Training, Arlington, VA. See also Chester Crocker, *High Noon in Southern Africa: Making Peace in a Rough Neighborhood* (New York: W. W. Norton, 1992), 86–92.

98. KGB funding of the ANC continued into the 1980s, while KGB "active measures" disinformation campaigns spread fabrications about American support for the apartheid regime. See Andrew and Mitrokhin, *World Was Going Our Way,* 464–67.

99. RRD, March 30, 1983.

100. Herman Nickel interview, Foreign Affairs Oral History Collection, Association for Diplomatic Studies and Training, Arlington, VA.

101. "Angola-USSR-South Africa: Growing Conflict," special analysis, December 5, 1983, folder: "Soviet Project (2)," box 90763, Donald Fortier Papers, RPL.

102. Bird, *Good Spy,* 301–15.

103. Persico, *Casey,* 314–17.

104. Casey felt especially burned by Iran's role. Six months earlier, in the spycraft version of a peace offering, he had tipped off Ayatollah Khomeini to the presence of a hundred Soviet spies operating in Iran. The gesture had not mitigated Tehran's enmity toward the United States. Persico, *Casey,* 316.

105. Patrick Tyler, *A World of Trouble: The White House and the Middle East—from the Cold War to the War on Terror* (New York: Farrar, Straus and Giroux, 2009), 292.

106. Memorandum of conversation between Reagan and Prince Bandar, June 24, 1983, folder: "Memorandums of Conversation, President Reagan (6/23/83–07/25/83) Box 51," box 16, Executive Secretariat: NSC, Subject File, RPL.

107. RRD, May 4, 1983.

108. John Boykin, *Cursed Is the Peacemaker: The American Diplomat Versus the Israeli General, Beirut 1982* (Belmont, CA: Applegate Press, 2002), 307.

109. Memorandum from Clark to Reagan re: "National Security Planning Group Meeting," June 21, 1983, folder: "NSPG 0064 21 June 1983, Box 91306," box 2, Executive Secretariat, NSPG, RPL.

110. Memo from Clark to Reagan re: "The Middle East," February 4, 1982, folder: "Sensitive Chron File [1/07/1983–3/02/1983]," RAC box 7, Robert C. "Bud" McFarlane Files, RPL; memo from Clark to Reagan re: "A Long Look Ahead," July 9, 1983, folder 13, box 3, Don Oberdorfer Papers, Princeton University Archives (hereinafter PUA).

111. *Report of the President's Commission on Strategic Forces,* April 7, 1983. Available at: http://web.mit.edu/chemistry/deutch/policy/1983-ReportPresCommStrategic.pdf.

112. National Conference of Catholic Bishops, *The Challenge of Peace: God's Promise and Our Response.* Available at: http://www.usccb.org/upload/challenge-peace-gods-promise -our-response-1983.pdf.

113. Kenneth A. Briggs, "Bishops' Letter on Nuclear Arms Is Revised to 'More Flexible' View," *New York Times,* April 6, 1983.

114. Letter to Reverend Stephen Majoros, March 15, 1983, in Kiron K. Skinner, Annelise Anderson, and Martin Anderson, eds., *Reagan: A Life in Letters* (New York: Free Press, 2003), 378.

115. Memo from Clark to Reagan re: "The Middle East," February 4, 1982, folder: "Sensitive Chron File [1/07/1983-3/02/1983]," RAC box 7, Robert C. "Bud" McFarlane Files, RPL.

116. State 097325, cable, folder: "Japan (4/7/83–5/31/83) Box 8," box 16, Executive Secretariat, NSC: Country File, Japan, RPL.

117. Memorandum of conversation between Nakasone and Reagan, May 27, 1983, folder: "Japan (4/7/83–5/31/83) Box 8," box 16, Executive Secretariat, NSC: Country File, Japan, RPL.

118. RRD, May 27–31, 1983.

119. Radchenko, *Unwanted Visionaries,* 59.

120. Quoted in Derek Leebaert, *The Fifty-Year Wound: The True Price of America's Cold War Victory* (New York: Little, Brown, 2002), 589.

121. "Record of Conversation Between Thatcher and Kohl," May 28, 1983, PREM19/1009, National Archives, United Kingdom.

122. "Reagan as diplomat" (notes), May 31, 1983, folder: "White House Notes May 1983 (2/2)," box 4, Sara Fritz Papers, RPL.

123. Brian Mulroney, *Memoirs* (Toronto: McClelland & Stewart, 2007), 357. In substance, Mitterrand supported the missile deployment; on a visit to Bonn in January he had famously warned the Bundestag, *"Les missiles sont à l'est, les pacifistes sont à l'ouest,"* meaning "Missiles are in the east, peace campaigners in the west." Kohl appreciated this public reminder from his French counterpart that without a comparable deterrent, Western Europe was vulnerable to the Soviet missiles. See Dr. Jamie Shea, "1979: The Soviet Union Deploys Its SS220 Missiles and NATO Responds," North Atlantic Treaty Organization, March 4, 2009. Available at: https://www.nato.int/cps/en/natohq/opinions_139274.htm.

124. Author interview with Henry Nau, March 7, 2018, Washington, DC.

125. UK Delegation Williamsburg Telegram Number 14, to FCO, May 30, 1983, PREM 19/1009f113, National Archives, United Kingdom. See also Charles Moore, *Margaret Thatcher: The Authorized Biography; At Her Zenith: In London, Washington, and Moscow* (New York: Vintage Books, 2015), 57–58.

126. RRD, May 27–31, 1983; "From the Archives: 25 Years Ago," *Globe and Mail,* May 30, 2008, available at: https://www.theglobeandmail.com/news/national/from-the-archives/article673422/.

127. "Williamsburg Economic Summit Conference Statement on Security Issues," May 29, 1983. Available at: https://www.reaganlibrary.gov/research/speeches/52983a. The White House staff leaked to the media, duplicitously, that Trudeau had enthusiastically supported the INF statement. Why they did so is unclear. Perhaps it was to paint a more idyllic picture of alliance solidarity. Or perhaps it was to make political mischief in Canada by fomenting the premier's left-wing base against him ahead of his reelection campaign the next year. See also notes, June 1, 1983, folder: "White House Notes June 1983 (1/2)," box 4, Sara Fritz Papers, RPL.

128. Quoted in Shultz, *Turmoil and Triumph,* 357.

129. George Weigel, *The End and the Beginning: Pope John Paul II; The Victory of Freedom, the Last Years, the Legacy* (New York: Doubleday, 2010), 161; Jones, *A Covert Action,* 218–19.

130. Memorandum of conversation of Reagan's meeting with West German foreign minister Genscher, July 11, 1983, folder: "Memorandums of Conversation, President Reagan (6/23/83–07/25/83) Box 51," box 16, Executive Secretariat: NSC, Subject File, RPL.

131. Later that month Max Kampelman raised the stakes in Madrid. After months of cajoling the European allies and tussling with the Soviet bloc, he succeeded in what human rights scholar Sarah Snyder calls "a notable negotiating achievement for the West." The Soviets and their satellite states agreed to a formal series of follow-on meetings to address human

rights violations. Given the Kremlin's previous intransigence in even acknowledging the subject, an agreement to continue talks on human rights was not nothing. But Kampelman knew that it was not enough either. After the deal was announced, Kampelman made a statement that generated international headlines, annoyed the Soviets, and featured in his obituary thirty years later: "We cannot in good conscience permit a limited negotiating success, important as we believe it to be, to make us forget . . . that signatures on a document do not necessarily produce compliance with its provisions." Sarah B. Snyder, *Human Rights Activism and the End of the Cold War: A Transnational History of the Helsinki Network* (New York: Cambridge University Press, 2011), 156; William Yardley, "Max Kampelman, Who Led Arms Talks, Dies at 92," *New York Times,* January 28, 2013.

132. RRD, May 18, 1983.

CHAPTER 7: THE MAELSTROM

1. "1 September 1983—Korean Air 007," cockpit recording transcript, Tailstrike.com. Available at: http://www.tailstrike.com/010983.htm. Other details drawn from Ambinder, *The Brink,* 167–70, and Hoffman, *Dead Hand,* 72–79.

2. RRD, September 2, 1983.

3. "USSR: Economic Performance in 1982," CIA special analysis, March 16, 1983; "USSR Economic Performance," CIA special analysis, June 28, 1983; and "USSR Economic Gains Beginning to Fade," Bureau of Intelligence and Research Analysis, June 29, 1983. All in folder: "USSR—Economy (6/10)," box 25, Jack F. Matlock Files, RPL.

4. Note from Norman Bailey to Lenczkowski/Dobriansky/Robinson, April 15, 1983, with attached April 11, 1983, letter to Bailey from Igor Birman and attached article "The Soviet Economy Is the Only Threat to Comrade Andropov," folder: "USSR—Economy (6/10)," box 25, Jack F. Matlock Files, RPL.

5. Memo from McFarlane to Matlock re: "Summitry," June 16, 1983; memo from Clark to Reagan re: "Summitry," n.d. (June); memo from Casey to Clark re: "Summitry," June 27, 1983; and memo from Matlock to Clark re: "Summitry: Casey's Memo of June 27," July 7, 1983, all in folder: "USSR—Summitry (2/2)," box 36, Jack F. Matlock Files, RPL.

6. Letters cited in Anderson and Anderson, *Reagan's Secret War,* 137–40.

7. Ibid. See also memo from Clark to Reagan re: "Andropov's Reply to Your Letter," n.d., folder 13, box 3, Don Oberdorfer Papers, PUA.

8. Steven R. Weisman, "The Influence of William Clark," *New York Times Magazine,* August 14, 1983.

9. Shultz, *Turmoil and Triumph,* 311–13.

10. "The Big Stick Approach," *Time,* August 8, 1983; Steven R. Weisman, "The Influence of William Clark," *New York Times Magazine,* August 14, 1983; Shultz, *Turmoil and Triumph,* 317–18.

11. Cannon, *President Reagan,* 423–28.

12. Quoted in John Gans, *White House Warriors: How the National Security Council Transformed the American Way of War* (New York: Liveright Publishing, 2019), 74.

13. Talking points for NSC meeting, June 21, 1983, in Saltoun-Ebin, *Reagan Files,* 248–49.

14. Nothing illustrated the region's Byzantine politics more than the question of the Israeli military presence in Lebanon. Up through the spring, Israel sought to keep its forces in Lebanon while the Reagan administration pressured it to withdraw. Now, with summer, the roles seemed to reverse. Israel worried that Lebanon's fragility and escalating violence fueled by Syria put the IDF at risk and wanted to exit the country, or at least withdraw its

forces from the Beirut cauldron to southern Lebanon. The White House saw the IDF as a stabilizing presence against the sectarian strife and pressured Israel to keep its forces in place until conditions improved and a full withdrawal of all foreign forces could be negotiated. The beleaguered Lebanese government also wanted the Israelis to stay in place for the time being, fearing that otherwise the country could be sliced into a three-way partition. See memorandum from Clark to Reagan, July 14, 1983, folder: "NSPG 0065 15 July 1983 Box 91306," NSPG box 2, NSC: Executive Secretariat, RPL.

15. RRD, September 6 and 10, 1983.

16. Memorandum of conversation between Reagan and King Hassan, September 26, 1983, folder: "Memorandums of Conversation, President Reagan (9/28/83–09/30/83) Box 51," box 16, Executive Secretariat: NSC, Subject File, RPL.

17. Ed Magnuson and William R. Doerner, "Atrocity in the Skies," *Time*, September 12, 1983.

18. Memo from Clark to Reagan re: "NSPG Meeting: Soviet Shoot-Down of KAL Airliner," September 2, 1983, folder: "NSPG 0068 and 0068A 3 Sept 1983 (3), Box 91306," NSPG box 2, National Security Council: Executive Secretariat, RPL.

19. "Address to the Nation on the Soviet Attack on a Korean Civilian Airliner," September 5, 1983. Available at: https://www.reaganlibrary.gov/research/speeches/90583a.

20. George J. Church, "Turning on the Heat," *Time*, September 19, 1983.

21. "Address Before the 38th Session of the United Nations General Assembly in New York, New York," September 26, 1983. Available at: https://www.reaganlibrary.gov/research/speeches/92683a.

22. So important was this dimension that Washington and Moscow incorporated it into arms control negotiations, such as the 1972 ABM Treaty's restrictions on certain types of radar.

23. This account drawn from Ambinder, *The Brink*, 178–84, and Hoffman, *Dead Hand*, 6–11.

24. Memorandum of conversation between Reagan and Thatcher, September 29, 1983, folder: "Memorandums of Conversation, President Reagan (9/28/83–09/30/83) Box 51," box 16, Executive Secretariat: NSC, Subject File, RPL.

25. RRD, September 29, 1983.

26. RRD, October 10, 1983.

27. Tyler Rogoway, "The Movie *War Games* Inspired Ronald Reagan to Take Cybersecurity Seriously," TheDrive.com, June 13, 2019, available at: https://www.thedrive.com/the-war-zone/28352/war-games-the-film-that-inspired-reagan-to-take-cybersecurity-seriously-turns-36-today; National Security Decision Directive 145, "National Policy on Telecommunications and Automated Information Systems Security," September 17, 1984, available at: https://fas.org/irp/offdocs/nsdd/nsdd-145.pdf.

28. The dispute that led to McFarlane's appointment is recounted in many places. Virtually all Reagan administration memoirs and histories agree on the basic facts of the episode, as do Reagan's diary entries. The most thorough and balanced description comes from Cannon, *President Reagan*, 427–36; the most colorful description comes from Edmund Morris, *Dutch: A Memoir of Ronald Reagan* (New York: HarperCollins, 1999), 499–500.

29. Coard had joined the Communist Party while a student at Brandeis University in the United States twenty years earlier and had become even more militant on his return to Grenada.

30. This account is largely drawn from McFarlane's memoir, *Special Trust* (New York: Cadell & Davies, 1994), 260–63.

31. David Kennedy and Leslie Brunetta, "Lebanon and the Intelligence Community," Center for the Study of Intelligence. Available at: https://www.hsdl.org/?abstract&did=3615.

32. October 21, 1983, entry, folder: "United States Department of State Diary, Volume 1, 1982–1983," box 1, Kenneth Dam Papers, HIA.

33. RRD, October 18, 1983.

34. Robert Timberg, *The Nightingale's Song* (New York: Touchstone, 1995), 337.

35. Anthony Motley interview, Foreign Affairs Oral History Collection, Association for Diplomatic Studies and Training, Arlington, VA.

36. Ronald H. Cole, *Operation Urgent Fury,* Joint History Office, Office of the Chairman of the Joint Chiefs of Staff, 1997.

37. Moore, *Margaret Thatcher: At Her Zenith,* 117–18.

38. RRD, October 24, 1983.

39. "Remarks of the President and Prime Minister Eugenia Charles of Dominica Announcing the Deployment of United States Forces in Grenada," October 25, 1983. Available at: https://www.reaganlibrary.gov/research/speeches/102583a.

40. Quoted in Deborah Hart Strober and Gerald S. Strober, *The Reagan Presidency: An Oral History of the Era* (Washington, DC: Brasseys Inc., 2003), 281.

41. Moore, *Margaret Thatcher: At Her Zenith,* 128–35.

42. Hayward, *Age of Reagan: Conservative Counterrevolution,* 319–23.

43. Robert D. McFadden, "From Rescued Students, Gratitude and Praise," *New York Times,* October 28, 1983. Such testimonials did not persuade a small band of American women. The next week, on the evening of November 7, the May 19th Communist Organization planted a bomb in the Senate cloakroom at the United States Capitol to protest the Grenada invasion, and denounce Reagan's policies in El Salvador and Nicaragua for good measure. Abbreviated as "M19," the group was America's first terrorist organization founded and led by women, taking their name from the shared birth date of their lodestars Ho Chi Minh and Malcolm X. Their bomb ripped a fifteen-foot-wide crater in the Senate wall and destroyed doors, windows, and portraits. At the late hour it caused no deaths. It was part of a string of bombs M19 detonated over a two-year period against targets such as the National War College, the Washington Navy Yard Officers Club, and an FBI field office. See William Rosenau, *Tonight We Bombed the Capitol: The Explosive Story of M19, America's First Female Terrorist Group* (New York: Atria Books, 2019), 183–87.

44. Constantine C. Menges, *Inside the National Security Council: The True Story of the Making and Unmaking of Reagan's Foreign Policy* (New York: Touchstone, 1988), 88–89.

45. Interagency intelligence assessment, October 30, 1983, folder: "Chron File (Official) [10/28/1983–11/07/1983]," RAC box 6, Robert C. "Bud" McFarlane Files, RPL.

46. Quoted in Strober and Strober, *Reagan Presidency,* 290; author interview with Shultz, May 17, 2017.

47. "Memorandum of Telephone Conversation Between Reagan and Mitterrand," October 24, 1983, folder: "Memorandums of Conversation, President Reagan (October 1983) Box 52," box 17, Executive Secretariat: NSC, Subject File, RPL.

48. Memo from McFarlane to Geoff Kemp and Allan Myer with attached cable Paris 171, October 25, 1983, folder: "Chron File (Official) [9/26/1983–10/27/1983]," RAC box 6, Robert C. "Bud" McFarlane Files, RPL.

49. National Security Decision Directive 111, "Next Steps Toward Progress in Lebanon and the Middle East," October 28, 1983. Available at: https://fas.org/irp/offdocs/nsdd/nsdd-111.pdf.

50. David Crist, *The Twilight War: The Secret History of America's Thirty-Year Conflict with Iran* (New York: Penguin Press, 2012), 132–38.

51. Memo to McFarlane from Diane Dornan re: "Weekly Report," October 21, 1983; memo to McFarlane from Christopher Lehman and Paul Thompson re: "Weekly Report," October 21, 1983; memo to McFarlane from Peter Sommer re: "Weekly Report: Western Europe" (2 pages), October 21, 1983; memo to McFarlane from Walt Raymond re: "Weekly Report," October 21, 1983; memo to McFarlane from Richard Childress re: "Weekly Report," October 21, 1983; memo to McFarlane from Bob Helm re: "Weekly Report," October 21, 1983; memo to McFarlane from Norman Bailey re: "Weekly Report," October 21, 1983; memo to McFarlane from Douglas McMinn re: "Weekly Report," October 21, 1983; memo to McFarlane from William F. Martin re: "Weekly Report," October 21, 1983; and memo to McFarlane from Kenneth deGraffenreid, October 21, 1983, all from folder: "Chron File (Official) [9/26/1983–10/27/1983]," RAC box 6, Robert C. "Bud" McFarlane Files, RPL.

52. Mikhail Gorbachev, *Memoirs* (New York: Doubleday, 1995), 150–52.

53. Note from Matlock to McFarlane, November 5, 1983, with attached memo "US-Soviet Relations: Immediate Prospects," folder: "Soviet Union—Sensitive File 1983 (10/21/1983–11/07/1983)," RAC box 2, Robert C. "Bud" McFarlane Files, RPL.

54. Nate Jones, ed., *Able Archer: The Secret History of the NATO Exercise That Almost Triggered Nuclear War* (New York: New Press, 2016), 1–2.

55. Ambinder, *The Brink*, 194–97.

56. Fred Kaplan, *The Bomb: Presidents, Generals, and the Secret History of Nuclear War* (New York: Simon & Schuster, 2020), 160.

57. Hoffman, *Dead Hand*, 94–95.

58. Ambinder, *The Brink*, 212.

59. Steven F. Hayward, "Back from the Brink," *National Review*, March 11, 2019. Such is the irony that one of the Cold War's intelligence successes—the reduced risk of accidental war during Able Archer—stemmed from mutual intelligence failures: the inability of NATO and the KGB to prevent their respective penetrations by adversary services.

60. Simon Miles, "The War Scare That Wasn't: Able Archer 83 and the Myths of the Second Cold War," *Journal of Cold War Studies* 22, no. 3 (2020): 86–118. See also Gordon Barrass, "Able Archer 83: What Were the Soviets Thinking?," *Survival* 58, no. 6 (2016): 7–30.

61. Simon Miles, *Engaging the Evil Empire: Washington, Moscow, and the Beginning of the End of the Cold War* (Ithaca, NY: Cornell University Press, 2020), 80.

62. Weinberger, *Fighting for Peace*, 18–20.

63. Clare Boothe Luce introduction and William Casey speech "What We Face," October 29, 1983, folder 1, box 306, and "Hottest Cold Warrior Assails Soviets," *Columbia Daily Tribune*, October 30, 1983, in folder 4, box 306, both in William Casey Papers, HIA. Luce, still a wit at eighty years old, told Casey as he stepped down from the podium, "Bill, you must give me a copy of your speech so I can crib and quote from it. You know, the older I get the fewer 'isms' I have. Catholicism and plagiarism are about all that's left." Persico, *Casey*, 357.

64. Memorandum from Herbert Meyer to director of Central Intelligence re: "Why Is the World So Dangerous?," November 30, 1983. In author's possession, downloaded from CIA Electronic Reading Room.

65. Memo from Hal Ford to director of Central Intelligence re: "Why Is the World So Dangerous? An Alternative View," December 6, 1983, in author's possession, downloaded from CIA Electronic Reading Room. See also Steven F. Hayward, "CIA Contrarian Herbert E.

Meyer, RIP," *National Review,* June 27, 2019, available at: https://www.nationalreview
.com/2019/06/remembering-herbert-meyer-cia-contrarian/. There is no record of whether
Casey sent Ford's memo to Reagan.

66. Memo from Clark to Reagan re: "A Long Look Ahead," July 9, 1983, folder 13, box 3, Don
     Oberdorfer Papers, PUA.

67. Memorandum of conversation between Reagan and Wu Xueqian, October 11, 1983, folder:
     "Memorandums of Conversation, President Reagan (October 1983) Box 52," box 17, Ex-
     ecutive Secretariat: NSC, Subject File, RPL.

68. Memorandum from Charles Tyson to William Clark re: "Your Meeting with Japanese
     Ambassador Okawara," October 11, 1983, folder: "Japan (9/24/83–10/19/83) Box 8," box 16,
     Executive Secretariat, NSC: Country File, Japan, RPL.

69. RRD, October 25, 1983.

70. Tokyo 1314 and Tokyo 0860, cables, folder: "Japan (10/21/83–11/7/83) Box 8," box 16, Execu-
     tive Secretariat, NSC: Country File, Japan, RPL. Nakasone's concerns were genuine; in
     the December elections his party lost seats in the Diet, and Nakasone himself had to en-
     gage in deft political maneuvering to keep his premiership.

71. State 341398 and State 341399, cables, folder: "Memorandums of Conversation, President
     Reagan (11/21/1983–12/01/1983) Box 52," box 17, Executive Secretariat: NSC, Subject
     File, RPL.

72. Lettow, *Ronald Reagan and His Quest,* 3–6.

73. "Address Before the Japanese Diet in Tokyo," November 11, 1983. Available at: https://www
     .reaganlibrary.gov/research/speeches/111183a.

74. Shultz, *Turmoil and Triumph,* 193.

75. "Radio Address to the Nation on the President's Trip to Japan and the Republic of Ko-
     rea," November 12, 1983. Available at: https://www.reaganlibrary.gov/research/speeches
     /111283e.

76. See, for example, 1983 Chicago Council Survey "American Public Opinion and US Foreign
     Policy 1983," available at: https://www.thechicagocouncil.org/sites/default/files/2020-11/1982
     -Chicago-Council-Survey-PDF-Report.pdf. See also Louis Harris, "Americans Want Free,
     Balanced Trade," Harris Survey, March 1983, response of 67 percent support for "If Ameri-
     can workers' jobs are going to be protected, then the U.S. government must raise the tariffs
     on competitive products coming in from abroad," available at: https://theharrispoll.com
     /wp-content/uploads/2017/12/Harris-Interactive-Poll-Research-AMERICANS-WANT
     -FREE-BALANCED-TRADE-1983-03.pdf.

77. State 338447, cable, folder: "Memorandums of Conversation, President Reagan (11/21/
     1983–12/01/1983) Box 52," box 17, Executive Secretariat: NSC, Subject File, RPL.

78. "Address Before the Korean National Assembly in Seoul," November 12, 1983. Available
     at: https://www.reaganlibrary.gov/research/speeches/111283b.

79. Memorandum of conversation between Reagan and Casaroli, November 22, 1983, folder:
     "Memorandums of Conversation, President Reagan (11/01/1983–11/17/1983) Box 52," box
     17, Executive Secretariat: NSC, Subject File, RPL.

80. State 341396, cable, folder: "Memorandums of Conversation, President Reagan (11/21/
     1983–12/01/1983) Box 52," box 17, Executive Secretariat: NSC, Subject File, RPL.

81. National Security Planning Group meeting cover memo and supporting documents, No-
     vember 14, 1983, folder: "NSPG 0077 14 November 1983, Box 91306," box 2, Executive
     Secretariat: NSPG, RPL.

82. Crist, *Twilight War,* 144–45.

83. McFarlane, *Special Trust,* 270–71.

84. Weinberger, *Fighting for Peace,* 161–62.

85. RRD, November 14 and November 16, 1983.

86. Crist, *Twilight War,* 146.

87. Poindexter oral history, interview conducted by Robert Timberg. In author's possession.

88. Crist, *Twilight War,* 147.

89. RRD, November 17, 1983. Shultz, whose differences with Weinberger were legion and who rarely missed an opportunity to air those differences, also makes no mention of this episode in his exhaustive memoir—yet if Weinberger had in fact defied a presidential order, Shultz would almost certainly have recounted it.

90. Crist, *Twilight War,* 148. See also David Martin and John Walcott, *Best Laid Plans: The Inside Story of America's War Against Terrorism* (New York: Touchstone, 1988), 138–39.

91. McFarlane, *Special Trust,* 271.

92. Osama bin Laden would later cite America's failure to retaliate, and eventual withdrawal from Beirut a few months later, as evidence of American pusillanimity that encouraged him to orchestrate the September 11, 2001, terrorist attacks.

93. RRD, October 24, 1983.

94. RRD, November 18, 1983.

95. George Russell, "A Soviet Walkout," *Time,* December 5, 1983.

96. George J. Church, "Men of the Year," *Time,* January 2, 1984.

97. "Remarks and a Question-and-Answer Session with Reporters on Strategic Arms Reduction Talks," December 8, 1983. Available at: https://www.reaganlibrary.gov/research/speeches/120883a.

98. "Question-and-Answer Session with Reporters on Domestic and Foreign Policy Issues," December 14, 1983. Available at: https://www.reaganlibrary.gov/research/speeches/121483a.

99. State 365387, cable, folder: "Memorandums of Conversation, President Reagan (12/06/1983–2/03/1984) Box 52," box 17, Executive Secretariat: NSC, Subject File, RPL.

CHAPTER 8: TOIL AND TROUBLE

1. Memorandum from Jack Matlock to Robert Kimmitt re: "Soviet Anecdotes," September 27, 1983, folder: "USSR—General [1981–1983 (5/5)]," box 26, Jack F. Matlock Files, RPL.

2. George J. Church, "Men of the Year: Ronald Reagan and Yuri Andropov," *Time,* January 2, 1984.

3. "An Interview with President Reagan," *Time,* January 2, 1984.

4. Memorandum of conversation between President Reagan and Neil Kinnock, February 14, 1984, folder: "Memorandums of Conversation, President Reagan (02/08/1984–03/23/1984) Box 52," box 17, Executive Secretariat: NSC, Subject File, RPL.

5. Don Oberdorfer, *From the Cold War to a New Era: The United States and the Soviet Union, 1983–1991* (Baltimore, MD: Johns Hopkins University Press, 1998), 70–71.

6. RRD, January 6, 1984.

7. "Address to the Nation and Other Countries on United States–Soviet Relations," January 16, 1984. Available at: https://www.reaganlibrary.gov/research/speeches/11684a.

8. John Lewis Gaddis, *The Cold War: A New History* (New York: Penguin Press, 2005), 228.

9. Dusko Doder, "Times Are Tough for Jim and Sally, but They Can't Tell Ivan and Anya," *Washington Post*, January 22, 1984, in folder 1, box 4, Don Oberdorfer Papers, PUA.

10. Suzanne Massie, *Trust but Verify: Reagan, Russia, and Me* (Rockland, ME: Maine Authors Publishing, 2013), 90–102. Massie was more perceptive of Russians than she was of Reagan. She later wrote of her shock that Reagan "did not know how important religion" (pp. 134–35) was to the Russian people and seemed so unaware of the Russian Orthodox Church. She mistook Reagan's politeness and unassuming deference to her expertise for ignorance. The president had long been fascinated by religious life in the Soviet Union and sought out insights on it whenever he could. But reliable information was hard to come by from the closed society and its atheistic government. This is why Reagan asked Massie about it and valued her insights.

11. RRD, January 16, 1984.

12. See, for example, memorandum of conversation between President Reagan and Neil Kinnock, February 14, 1984, folder: "Memorandums of Conversation, President Reagan (02/08/1984–03/23/1984) Box 52," box 17, Executive Secretariat: NSC, Subject File, RPL, and "An Interview with President Reagan," *Time*, January 2, 1984.

13. Statement by Andrei Gromyko, January 18, 1984, folder 17, box 3, Don Oberdorfer Papers, PUA.

14. Shultz, *Turmoil and Triumph*, 468–71.

15. Note from Abrams to Clark, July 12, 1982, folder: "Vatican 1983–1984 (12 of 13) RAC Box 7," box 6, European and Soviet Affairs Directorate, NSC: Records, RPL.

16. Letter from Billy Graham to Bill Clark, April 25, 1983, folder: "8391492," box 4, Assistant to the President for National Security Affairs: Chron File; memo to Clark from Dennis Blair re: "Establishing Formal Diplomatic Relations with the Holy See," February 22, 1983, folder: "Vatican 1983–1984 (3 of 13) RAC Box 7," box 5, European and Soviet Affairs Directorate, NSC: Records, RPL.

17. Memo from Faith Ryan Whittlesey to McFarlane re: "Recognition of the Vatican," January 13, 1984, folder: "Vatican 1983–1984 (4 of 13) RAC Box 7," box 5, European and Soviet Affairs Directorate, NSC: Records, and memo from Tyrus Cobb and Peter Sommer to McFarlane re: "Meeting with Religious Leaders on Vatican Recognition," January 17, 1984, folder: "Vatican 1983–1984 (2 of 13) RAC Box 7," box 5, European and Soviet Affairs Directorate, NSC: Records, RPL.

18. Weigel, *End and the Beginning*, 163.

19. WHO 1622, cable, folder: "Vatican, RAC Box 16," box 10, European and Soviet Affairs Directorate, NSC: Records, RPL.

20. Letter from Reagan to Pope, February 22, 1984, folder: "Vatican, RAC Box 16," box 10, European and Soviet Affairs Directorate, NSC: Records, RPL.

21. Domber, *Empowering Revolution*, 118–23.

22. Memorandum from McFarlane to Reagan re: "Response to Papal Letter," February 9, 1984, folder: "Vatican 1983–1984 (2 of 13) RAC Box 7," box 5, European and Soviet Affairs Directorate, NSC: Records, and WHO 1622, cable, folder: "Vatican, RAC Box 16," box 10, European and Soviet Affairs Directorate, NSC: Records, RPL.

23. "Address Before a Joint Session of the Congress on the State of the Union—January 1984," January 25, 1984. Available at: https://www.reaganlibrary.gov/research/speeches/12584e.

24. "Radio Address to the Nation on the Budget Deficit, Central America, and Lebanon," February 4, 1984. Available at: https://www.reaganlibrary.gov/research/speeches/20484a.

25. Letter from Reagan to Thatcher, February 6, 1984, THCR 3/1/36, Margaret Thatcher Foundation Archive.

26. February 8, 1984, entry, folder: "United States Department of State Diary, Volume II, 1984–1985," box 1, Kenneth Dam Papers, HIA.

27. Alexandra Evans and A. Bradley Potter, "When Do Leaders Change Course? Theories of Success and the American Withdrawal from Lebanon, 1983–1984," *Texas National Security Review* 2, no. 2 (February 2019).

28. "Confusion, Anger Rise in Congress," *Washington Post,* February 10, 1984; Don Oberdorfer, "Making of a Diplomatic Debacle," *Washington Post,* February 12, 1984.

29. March 7, 1984, entry, folder: "United States Department of State Diary, Volume II, 1984–1985," box 1, Kenneth Dam Papers, HIA.

30. Tyler, *A World of Trouble,* 307.

31. Jack F. Matlock Jr., *Reagan and Gorbachev: How the Cold War Ended* (New York: Random House, 2004), 87.

32. RRD, February 22, 1984.

33. Letter from Reagan to Chernenko, February 11, 1984. Available at: http://www.thereagan files.com/19840211.pdf.

34. Memo to McFarlane from NSC Situation Room re: "Vice President's Meeting with Chernenko," February 14, 1984, folder: "Soviet Union—Sensitive File 1984 (2/14/1984–2/23/1984)," RAC box 3, Robert C. "Bud" McFarlane Files, RPL.

35. Rome 0491, cable, folder: "Soviet Union—Sensitive File 1984 (2/14/1984–2/23/1984)," RAC box 3, Robert C. "Bud" McFarlane Files, RPL.

36. Massie, *Trust but Verify,* 154–55.

37. Ibid., 115–17; James Mann, *The Rebellion of Ronald Reagan: A History of the End of the Cold War* (New York: Viking, 2009), 85–89.

38. Casey speech at Hoover Institution, April 3, 1984, folder 11, box 307, William J. Casey Papers, HIA.

39. Letter from Reagan to Chernenko, April 16, 1984. Available at: http://www.thereaganfiles .com/19840416-2.pdf.

40. Letter from Nixon to McFarlane, March 29, 1984, folder: "Soviet Union—Sensitive File 1984 (3/09/1984–6/20/1984)," RAC box 3, Robert C. "Bud" McFarlane Files, RPL.

41. Seth Jones, "Russian Meddling in the United States: The Historical Context of the Mueller Report," CSIS Issue Brief, March 27, 2019. Available at: https://www.csis.org/analysis /russian-meddling-united-states-historical-context-mueller-report.

42. Andrew and Mitrokhin, *Sword and the Shield,* 242–43.

43. "Summary of NSPG Meeting on Combatting Terrorism," March 2, 1984, folder: "NSPG 0086 02 March 1984, Box 91307," NSPG box 3, Executive Secretariat: NSC, RPL.

44. National Security Decision Directive 138, "Combatting Terrorism," April 3, 1984. Available at: https://fas.org/irp/offdocs/nsdd/nsdd-138.pdf.

45. Accounts vary on the details of his abduction, including whether he was nabbed in his parking garage or from his car outside his building. The details may never be known. This account drawn from sources including Fred Burton and Samuel M. Katz, *Beirut Rules: The Murder of a CIA Station Chief and Hezbollah's War Against America* (New York: Berkley, 2018); Gordon Thomas, "William Buckley: The Spy Who Never Came in from the Cold," *Canada Free Press,* October 25, 2006, available at: https://canadafreepress.com /2006/thomas102506.htm; Martin and Walcott, *Best Laid Plans,* 153–55; and Persico, *Casey,* 316–17.

46. The CIA then removed all of its officers from Lebanon. It was a prudent step. Langley worried that the terrorists might torture Buckley into revealing names, locations, and

methods. But the station evacuation also may have sealed Buckley's fate. Those same CIA operatives would have been best placed to tap their network of sources and agents in the search for their chief.

47. Memo from North to Poindexter re: "TIWG Meeting Regarding Buckley Kidnapping," March 21, 1984, folder: "8490371," box 15, Executive Secretariat: NSC System File, RPL.

48. Gordon Thomas, "William Buckley: The Spy Who Never Came in from the Cold," *Canada Free Press,* October 25, 2006. Available at: https://canadafreepress.com/2006/thomas 102506.htm.

49. Robert Oakley interview, Foreign Affairs Oral History Collection, Association for Diplomatic Studies and Training, Arlington, VA. At one point the CIA thought it had located him in a Paris hotel and asked French intelligence to seize him. When French security forces stormed the room, they found a startled fifty-year-old Spanish tourist rather than the twenty-five-year-old Lebanese terrorist.

50. Adam Goldman and Ellen Nakashima, "CIA and Mossad Killed Senior Hezbollah Figure in Car Bombing," *Washington Post,* January 30, 2015.

51. Shultz, *Turmoil and Triumph,* 646; Shultz, "Terrorism: The Challenge to the Democracies," speech, June 24, 1984; and Shultz, "Terrorism and the Modern World," speech, October 25, 1984, both speeches in folder: "President Chron 1/31/1985 (2) Box 34," Situation Room: White House Records, RPL. Shultz found an ally in an ambitious young diplomat at the Israeli embassy in Washington, DC. Deputy Chief of Mission Benjamin Netanyahu, later to become the longest-serving prime minister in Israel's history, clamored for the United States to recognize terrorism as a first-order threat and to deepen cooperation with Israel against it. Several years earlier, Netanyahu had founded the Jonathan Institute—named after his brother who died leading Israeli commandos on a hostage rescue mission in Entebbe, Uganda, in 1976—as perhaps the world's first think tank devoted to studying terrorism. Shultz conferred regularly with Netanyahu on terrorism and agreed to give keynote remarks at a Jonathan Institute conference that the Israeli diplomat convened in Washington, DC, in June. The Reagan administration was well represented; other speakers included Ed Meese, Jeane Kirkpatrick, and FBI director William Webster, as well as intellectuals such as Senator Daniel Patrick Moynihan, Princeton historian Bernard Lewis, and columnists George Will and Charles Krauthammer. Netanyahu published the conference papers in a book titled *Terrorism: How the West Can Win;* Reagan read it when it came out in 1986. Benjamin Netanyahu, ed., *Terrorism: How the West Can Win* (New York: Farrar, Straus and Giroux, 1986); Shultz, *Turmoil and Triumph,* 790.

52. Brands, *Making the Unipolar Moment,* 250–51.

53. See, for example, memorandum of conversation between Reagan and Craxi, June 7, 1984, and memorandum of conversation between Reagan and Mitterrand, June 7, 1984, folder: "Memorandums of Conversation, President Reagan (06/13/1984–06/14/1984) Box 52," box 17, Executive Secretariat: NSC, Subject File, RPL.

54. Memo from Charles Hill to McFarlane re: "US Policy Towards the Iran-Iraq War," December 19, 1983, folder: "NSPG 0082 22 Dec 1983, Box 91306," NSPG box 2, NSC: Executive Secretariat, RPL.

55. Quoted in Brands, *Making the Unipolar Moment,* 240.

56. Quoted in Crist, *Twilight War,* 97.

57. Memo to McFarlane from Charles Hill re: "Iran-Iraq War," October 27, 1983, folder: "NSPG 0076 07 Nov 1983 (1 of 2), Box 91306," NSPG box 2, NSC: Executive Secretariat, RPL.

58. "Minutes of National Security Planning Group Meeting," March 30, 1984, folder: "NSC 00087, 10 Mar 1984 [Iran-Iraq War]," Executive Secretariat, NSC: NSPG Meeting File,

RPL. Rumsfeld's call for regime change unknowingly foreshadowed his return role as secretary of defense in the George W. Bush administration almost two decades later, when he would oversee the invasions of Afghanistan and Iraq to oust terrorism-sponsoring governments.

59. National Security Decision Directive 141, "Responding to Escalation in the Iran-Iraq War," May 25, 1984. Available at: https://fas.org/irp/offdocs/nsdd/nsdd-141.pdf.

60. Memorandum to Reagan from Shultz and Weinberger re: "NSDD-99 Conclusion Paper with attached 'US Strategy for the Near East and South Asia,'" July 5, 1984, folder: "NSPG 0094 31 Aug 1984 (2 of 3), Box 91307," box 3, Executive Secretariat: NSPG, RPL. Emphasis original.

61. Memorandum from Richard Wirthlin to Michael Deaver re: "Themes and Issues of the President's China Visit," January 9, 1984, folder: "China Foreign Relations President Reagan's Trip to China (5) RAC Box 14," box 3, David Laux Files, RPL.

62. Mann, *About Face*, 134.

63. RRD, April 26–27, 1984.

64. "Remarks to Chinese Community Leaders in Beijing, China," April 27, 1984. Available at: https://www.reaganlibrary.gov/research/speeches/42784a.

65. "Remarks at Fudan University in Shanghai, China," April 30, 1984. Available at: https://www.reaganlibrary.gov/research/speeches/43084e.

66. Mann, *About Face*, 146.

67. "Background for Raising Church Issue with Chinese," Situation Room checklist, April 19, 1984; SECTO 04048, cable, folder: "Vatican 1983–1984 (6 of 13) RAC Box 7," box 5, European and Soviet Affairs Directorate, NSC: Records; and memorandum from Sigur to McFarlane re: "Chinese Relations with the Vatican," May 2, 1984, folder: "China 1984 (7 of 11), RAC Box 5," box 3, Gaston Sigur Files, RPL.

68. Crile, *Charlie Wilson's War*, 268–69; Mann, *About Face*, 136–37; and John Pomfret, *The Beautiful Country and the Middle Kingdom: America and China, 1776 to the Present* (New York: Henry Holt, 2016), 501.

69. Weinberger, *Fighting for Peace*, 282–83; memorandum from David Laux to Robert Kimmitt re: "Accomplishments of the President's Trip to China," May 2, 1984, folder: "China Foreign Relations President Reagan's Trip to China—Accomplishments, RAC Box 14," box 3, David Laux Files, RPL.

70. "Reagan Trip Seen Helping US, China," *Washington Post*, May 2, 1984.

71. Lilley, *China Hands*, 256–63.

72. This account drawn from Anthony Motley and Thomas Pickering interviews, Foreign Affairs Oral History Collection, Association for Diplomatic Studies and Training, Arlington, VA; Gregg, *Pot Shards*, 178–79; Crandall, *Salvador Option*, 293–94; and Kathryn Sikkink, *Mixed Signals: US Human Rights Policy and Latin America* (Ithaca, NY: Cornell University Press, 2007), 172–73.

73. *The Report of the President's National Bipartisan Commission on Central America* (New York: Macmillan, 1984), 4.

74. Shultz, *Turmoil and Triumph*, 403–4.

75. Memorandum from Oliver North and Constantine Menges to McFarlane re: "Shultz/Weinberger/McFarlane Breakfast Item: Emergency Funding for El Salvador," March 7, 1984, folder: "Shultz, Weinberger, McFarlane Breakfast Items (March 1984)," box 97, Executive Secretariat, NSC: Subject File, RPL.

76. Crandall, *Salvador Option*, 317–22.

77. March 26, 1984, entry, folder: "United States Department of State Diary, Volume II, 1984–1985," box 1, Kenneth Dam Papers, HIA, and RRD, March 26, 1984.

78. Crandall, *Salvador Option*, 326–27.

79. "Address to the Nation on United States Policy in Central America," May 9, 1984. Available at: https://www.reaganlibrary.gov/archives/speech/address-nation-united-states-policy-central-america.

80. Duane R. Clarridge, *A Spy for All Seasons: My Life in the CIA* (New York: Scribner, 1997), 269–73.

81. Anthony Motley interview, Foreign Affairs Oral History Collection, Association for Diplomatic Studies and Training, Arlington, VA.

82. Persico, *Casey*, 373–75.

83. *Congressional Record* 134, no. 24 (March 3, 1988).

84. Hayward, *Age of Reagan: Conservative Counterrevolution*, 356–57, and "That 'Dear Comandante' Letter," *Washington Post*, May 3, 1984.

85. Kagan, *A Twilight Struggle*, 321–22.

86. Memorandum of conversation between Shultz and Miguel de la Madrid, May 16, 1984, folder: "Memorandums of Conversation, President Reagan (06/13/1984–06/14/1984) Box 52," box 17, Executive Secretariat: NSC, Subject File, RPL.

87. Minutes of NSPG meeting on Central America, June 25, 1984, folder: "NSC 00091, 25 June 1984 [Central America]," Executive Secretariat, NSC: NSPG Meeting File, RPL.

88. Kagan, *A Twilight Struggle*, 299–302.

89. Minutes of NSPG meeting on Central America, June 25, 1984. Available at: https://nsarchive2.gwu.edu/NSAEBB/NSAEBB483/docs/1984-06-25%20NSPG%20-%20Central%20America.pdf.

90. "Memorandum of Telephone Conversation Between Reagan and Alfonsín," April 5, 1984, folder: "Memorandums of Conversation, President Reagan (03/07/1984–04/04/1984) Box 52," box 17, Executive Secretariat: NSC, Subject File, RPL.

CHAPTER 9: MORNING IN AMERICA, TWILIGHT IN THE COLD WAR?

1. Dusko Doder, "Soviets Withdraw from Los Angeles Olympics," *Washington Post*, May 9, 1984.

2. Andrew and Mitrokhin, *Sword and the Shield*, 238–39.

3. Thomas Rid, *Active Measures: The Secret History of Disinformation and Political Warfare* (New York: Farrar, Straus and Giroux, 2020), 298–311, and Alexander Poster, "The Russian 'Fake News' Campaign That Damaged the United States—in the 1980s," *Washington Post*, March 12, 2018.

4. The KGB's disinformation campaign on AIDS also anticipated the Chinese Communist Party's disinformation campaign almost four decades later that falsely claimed that the COVID-19 virus had been created in an American military lab.

5. Memorandum of conversation between Reagan and Kohl, March 5, 1984, folder: "Memorandums of Conversation, President Reagan (03/07/1984–04/04/1984) Box 52," box 17, Executive Secretariat: NSC, Subject File, RPL.

6. Memorandum of conversation between Mitterrand and Reagan, March 22, 1984, folder: "Memorandums of Conversation, President Reagan (04/06/1984–04/24/1984) Box 52," box 17, Executive Secretariat: NSC, Subject File, RPL.

7. Memorandum from Robert Kimmitt to Charles Hill re: "Presidential Mission: Consultations on Soviet Human Rights Performance," July 16, 1984, and letter from Reagan to Prime Minister Poul Schluter, July 16, 1984, both in folder: "Human Rights 05/1984-07/1984 Box 35," Executive Secretariat, NSC: Subject File, box 11, RPL; State 250404, cable, folder: "Human Rights 08/1984-12/1984 Box 35," Executive Secretariat, NSC: Subject File, box 11, RPL.

8. Max Kampelman interview, June 24, 2003, Foreign Affairs Oral History Collection, Association for Diplomatic Studies and Training, Arlington, VA. Available at: https://www.adst.org/OH%20TOCs/Kampelman,%20Max.toc.pdf.

9. Sharansky, *Fear No Evil,* 366–67.

10. Memorandum of conversation with NATO foreign ministers, May 31, 1984, folder: "Memorandums of Conversation, President Reagan (05/08/1984–06/12/1984) Box 52," box 17, Executive Secretariat: NSC, Subject File, RPL.

11. "Address Before a Joint Session of the Irish National Parliament," June 4, 1984. Available at: https://www.reaganlibrary.gov/archives/speech/address-joint-session-irish-national-parliament. While Reagan promoted the idea of the West, he also expanded it from the transatlantic confines of North America and Western Europe to a more universal aspiration. Three of the anticommunist insurgencies he highlighted were nonwhite, and the fourth—the Polish Catholics leading Solidarity—represented a religious faith and region of Eastern Europe that many Western thinkers had long regarded as inimical to free societies. Reagan self-consciously distinguished his inclusive vision of the West from the vision of the nativists of the Right, who saw "Western values" as the exclusive preserve of white Protestant European civilization, and the relativists of the Left, who saw the United States and Soviet Union as moral equivalents. Historian Michael Kimmage describes Reagan as "anomalous" in both his universalism and his optimism about the West. See Michael Kimmage, *The Abandonment of the West: The History of an Idea in American Foreign Policy* (New York: Basic Books, 2020), 203.

12. Memorandum from Gaston Sigur to McFarlane re: "Further on Japan Mission of January 13–17, 1984," January 20, 1984, folder: "Japan (11/9/83–1/26/84) Box 8," box 16, Executive Secretariat, NSC: Country File, Japan, RPL.

13. Memorandum from Sigur to McFarlane re: "Memorandum from Secretary of State to the President on US-Japan Relations," April 4, 1984, with attached memorandum to Reagan from Shultz re: "US-Japan Relations and the Follow-up," April 3, 1984, folder: "Japan (4/3/84–4/28/84)," box 9, Executive Secretariat, NSC: Country File, Japan, RPL.

14. Memorandum from vice president to president re: "Our Relations with Japan," April 27, 1984, folder: "Japan (4/3/84–4/28/84)," box 9, Executive Secretariat, NSC: Country File, Japan; recommended telephone call memorandum to Reagan from McFarlane, May 29, 1984, folder: "Japan (5/29/84–9/7/84)," box 9, Executive Secretariat, NSC: Country File, Japan, RPL; and letter from Donald Gregg to Scott Pierce, July 27, 1984, folder: "Japan 1984," box 25, Country Files, Donald Gregg Files, Office of National Security Affairs, Office of Vice President George Bush, George H. W. Bush Presidential Library. The White House hoped the currency measures would strengthen the yen in international monetary markets and help reduce America's massive $37 billion trade deficit with Japan. While these particular steps would not end up putting much of a dent in the deficit, it marked a watershed in Tokyo's willingness to adjust its currency policies and set a precedent for more dramatic changes in the next year.

15. "Remarks at a Ceremony Commemorating the 40th Anniversary of the Normandy Invasion, D-day," June 6, 1984. Available at: https://www.reaganlibrary.gov/research/speeches/60684a.

16. William Galston, "How Ronald Reagan Taught Me My Most Unforgettable Political Lesson," Brookings, June 6, 2013. Available at: https://www.brookings.edu/blog/up-front/2013/06/06/how-ronald-reagan-taught-me-my-most-unforgettable-political-lesson/. Galston also came to see that Reagan returned to this memory not for nostalgia but "to shore up the unity of the West against the Soviet Union and to maintain public support for the sacrifices needed to end the Cold War on terms favorable to the cause of liberty."

17. Memorandum of conversation between Reagan and Manfred Woerner, July 13, 1984, folder: "Memorandums of Conversation, President Reagan (06/20/1984–08/16/1984) Box 52," box 17, Executive Secretariat: NSC, Subject File, RPL; Wayne Biddle, "Senate Bars Move to Reduce Troops with NATO Forces," *New York Times,* June 21, 1984; and David M. Abshire, *The Statesman: Reflections on a Life Guided by Civility, Strategic Leadership, and the Lessons of History* (Lanham, MD: Rowan and Littlefield, 2018), 107–13.

18. Memorandum from Kenneth Dam to Reagan re: "Chernenko's Response to Your July 2 Letter on the Vienna Talks," July 7, 1984, folder: "Soviet Union—Sensitive File 1984 (6/21/1984–7/26/1984)," RAC box 3, Robert C. "Bud" McFarlane Files; memorandum from Ed Rowny to McFarlane re: "Strategy for the Talks in Vienna," July 13, 1984, folder 8490785, box 15, Executive Secretariat: NSC System File; and memorandum from McFarlane to Reagan re: "Meeting with the National Security Planning Group," September 18, 1984, folder: "NSPG 0096 18 Sept 1984 [2 of 2], Box 91307," NSPG box 3, Executive Secretariat, NSC, RPL.

19. Memorandum of conversation between Reagan and Hans-Dietrich Genscher, May 7, 1984, folder: "Memorandums of Conversation, President Reagan (05/08/1984–06/12/1984) Box 52," box 17, Executive Secretariat: NSC, Subject File, RPL.

20. Author interview with McFarlane, October 24, 2017.

21. Dobrynin, *In Confidence,* 534.

22. Minutes of NSC meeting on next steps in Vienna process, September 18, 1984, folder: "NSPG 0096 18 Sept 1984 [1 of 2], Box 91307," NSPG box 3, Executive Secretariat: NSC, RPL.

23. Dobrynin, *In Confidence,* 553. Carter's effort to undercut Reagan's strategy toward America's main adversary was a stunning display of bad faith. For two centuries, ex-presidents had generally upheld the norm of not meddling in their successors' conduct of American foreign policy. Carter honored this norm in the breach.

24. Memorandum to Reagan from Nixon re: "The Gromyko Meeting," box 55, Jim Mann Papers, HIA.

25. "Mr. Minister," notes, September 23, 1984, in Skinner et al., *Reagan, in His Own Hand,* 496–98.

26. Andrei Gromyko, *Memoirs* (New York: Doubleday, 1989), 306–9.

27. Shultz, *Turmoil and Triumph,* 484, and Dobrynin, *In Confidence,* 562.

28. Lou Cannon, "Reagan, Gromyko Meet in 'Exchange of Views,'" *Washington Post,* September 29, 1984.

29. "Press Statement by A. A. Gromyko," September 28, 1984, folder 3, box 4, Don Oberdorfer Papers, PUA.

30. RRD, September 28, 1984.

31. "Recent Soviet Economic Performance and Longer Term Growth Prospects," October 29, 1984, folder: "USSR—Economy (8/10)," box 25, Jack F. Matlock Files, RPL.

32. Author interview with Bearden, August 2, 2018; Vernon Loeb, "Undercover to Hardcover," *Washington Post,* December 12, 1998; and Gad Shimron, *Mossad Exodus: The*

Daring Undercover Rescue of the Lost Jewish Tribe (Jerusalem: Gefen Publishing House, 2007), 199–215.

33. Memorandum of conversation between Reagan and Shimon Peres, October 9, 1984, folder: "Memorandums of Conversation, President Reagan (09/12/1984—October 1984) Box 53," box 17, Executive Secretariat: NSC, Subject File, RPL.

34. "Remarks Announcing Additional United States Food Assistance to Africa," December 5, 1984. Available at: https://www.reaganlibrary.gov/archives/speech/remarks -announcing-additional-united-states-food-assistance-africa.

35. Weigel, *End and the Beginning*, 164–67; Jones, *A Covert Action*, 224–29; Rod Dreher, "Fr. Jerzy Popieluzsko's Long Road," *American Conservative*, July 10, 2019, available at: https://www.theamericanconservative.com/dreher/fr-jerzy-popieluzsko-poland-long -road/.

36. McFarlane, *Special Trust*, 286–87.

37. Shultz, *Turmoil and Triumph*, 497–98.

38. Note from Casey to Reagan et al., September 4, 1984, folder 11, box 317, and letter from Casey to Reagan, November 16, 1984, folder 11, box 318, both in William J. Casey Papers, HIA.

39. Shultz, *Turmoil and Triumph*, 498.

40. Notes from Theberge conversation with Kirkpatrick, October 9, 1984, Theberge Papers, HIA, copy shared with the author by Evan McCormick.

41. RRD, January 30, 1985.

42. Collier, *Political Woman*, 167–69.

43. RRD, January 31, 1985.

44. RRD, November 14, 1984.

45. Peter Baker and Susan Glasser, *The Man Who Ran Washington: The Life and Times of James A. Baker III* (New York: Doubleday, 2020), 246–48.

46. Letter from Nixon to Donald Regan, January 28, 1985, folder 10, "Transition," box 215, Donald T. Regan Papers, LOC.

47. Shultz, "Power and Diplomacy in the 1980s," address, April 3, 1984, folder 5, box 3, Don Oberdorfer Papers, PUA; Shultz, "The Ethics of Power," address, December 9, 1984, folder: "President Chron 1/31/1985 (2) Box 34," Situation Room: White House Records, RPL.

48. Gail E. S. Yoshitani, *Reagan on War: A Reappraisal of the Weinberger Doctrine, 1980–1984* (College Station, TX: Texas A&M University Press, 2012), 131.

49. Nau, *Conservative Internationalism*, 6. Emphasis original.

50. Shultz, "Power and Diplomacy in the 1980s," address, April 3, 1984, folder 5, box 3, Don Oberdorfer Papers, PUA.

51. Weinberger, "The Uses of Military Power," address, November 28, 1984, folder 1: "Speeches 1984–1987," box III: 533, Caspar Weinberger Papers, LOC.

52. William Safire, "Only the 'Fun' Wars," *New York Times*, December 3, 1984.

53. Memorandum of conversation between Reagan and Kohl, November 30, 1984, folder: "Memorandums of Conversation, President Reagan (12/04/1984–12/14/1984) Box 53," box 17, Executive Secretariat: NSC, Subject File, RPL.

54. Thatcher, "Meeting with President Reagan: Gorbachev," notes, PREM 19/1394, National Archives, United Kingdom, and Moore, *Margaret Thatcher: At Her Zenith*, 238–48.

55. "Record of a Meeting Between the Prime Minister and President Reagan," December 22, 1984, PREM 19/1656, National Archives, United Kingdom; memorandum of conversation

between Reagan and Thatcher, December 22, 1984, folder: "Thatcher Visit December 1984 (2 of 7), RAC Box 15," box 9, European and Soviet Affairs Directorate, NSC: Records, RPL.

56. Minutes of NSPG meeting re: "Soviet Defense and Arms Control Objectives," November 30, 1984, folder: "NSPG 0100 30 Nov 1984, Box 91307," NSPG box 3, Executive Secretariat, NSC, and minutes of NSPG meeting re: "Substantive Issues for Geneva," December 17, 1984, folder: "NSPG 0104 17 Dec 1984, Box 91307," NSPG box 3, Executive Secretariat, NSC, RPL.

57. RRD, December 7, 1984.

CHAPTER 10: WAITING FOR GORBACHEV

1. Shultz, *Turmoil and Triumph*, 485.

2. National Security Decision Directive 154, "US-Japan Trade Policy Relations," December 31, 1984, available at: https://fas.org/irp/offdocs/nsdd/nsdd-154.pdf, and Gaston Sigur interview, Foreign Affairs Oral History Collection, Association for Diplomatic Studies and Training, Arlington, VA.

3. Gerald M. Boyd, "Reagan and Nakasone to Arrange High-Level Talks on Trade Issues," *New York Times,* January 3, 1985, and RRD, December 27, 1984–January 2, 1985.

4. Memorandum to McFarlane from Gaston Sigur, Roger Robinson, and William Martin re: "US-Japan Talking Points for SIG-IEP," January 3, 1985, folder: "Japan (11/9/84–1/3/85)," box 9, Executive Secretariat, NSC: Country File, Japan, RPL, and Shultz, *Turmoil and Triumph,* 190.

5. Memorandum from Shultz to Reagan re: "Strategy for Geneva," December 27, 1984, in Elizabeth C. Charles, ed., *Foreign Relations of the United States, 1981–1988,* vol. 4, *Soviet Union, January 1983–March 1985* (hereinafter *FRUS,* vol. 4) (Washington, DC: Government Printing Office, 2021), and National Security Decision Directive 153, "Instructions for the Shultz-Gromyko Meeting in Geneva," January 1, 1985, folder: "NSDD and Talking Points [Shultz-Gromyko Meetings in Geneva] (2/2)," box 29, Jack F. Matlock Files, RPL.

6. Shultz, *Turmoil and Triumph,* 487–89.

7. Oberdorfer, *From the Cold War to a New Era,* 102–3.

8. Gromyko's strange expression made more sense in Russian, as he seems to have invoked a Russian saying, "Silent like a fish on ice," referring to a fish caught by ice fishermen, flailing in vain to free itself from the snare of the anglers. I am indebted to Alexandra Sukalo for this insight.

9. Memorandum of conversation, January 8, 1985, in *FRUS,* vol. 4; Kenneth L. Adelman, *The Great Universal Embrace: Arms Summitry—A Skeptic's Account* (New York: Simon & Schuster, 1989), 89, 93; and Shultz, *Turmoil and Triumph,* 515–16.

10. "Inaugural Address, 1985," January 20, 1985. Available at: https://www.reaganlibrary.gov/archives/speech/inaugural-address-1985.

11. George Shultz, "The Future of American Foreign Policy: New Realities and New Ways of Thinking," testimony to Senate Foreign Relations Committee, January 31, 1985, folder: "President Chron 1/31/1985 (1) Box 34," Situation Room: White House Records, RPL.

12. David Hoffman, "Reagan Leads Drive for Hill Support of MX," *Washington Post,* February 1, 1985, and "A Battle over Defense," *Newsweek,* February 11, 1985.

13. David Hoffman, "Reagan Leads Drive for Hill Support of MX," *Washington Post,* February 1, 1985.

14. RRD, multiple entries in March 1985, and Steven V. Roberts, "House Vote Gives Final Approval for Purchase of 21 MX Missiles," *New York Times,* March 29, 1985.

15. "A Talk with Weinberger," *Newsweek*, February 11, 1985.

16. "Address Before a Joint Session of the Congress on the State of the Union—February 1985," February 6, 1985. Available at: https://www.reaganlibrary.gov/archives/speech /address-joint-session-congress-state-union-february-1985.

17. Charles Krauthammer, "The Reagan Doctrine," *Time*, April 1, 1985, and Charles Krauthammer, "The Reagan Doctrine," *Washington Post*, July 19, 1985.

18. Letter from Casey to Nixon, March 8, 1985, folder 5, box 318, William J. Casey Papers, HIA.

19. Remarks by Casey to the Union League Club, January 9, 1985, folder: "President Chron 1/ 22/1985–1/25/1985," box 34, Situation Room: White House Records, RPL.

20. "Memorandum to Congressional Task Force on Afghanistan from Chris Williams," January 14, 1985, shared with author by Diana Bolsinger; "Soviets Said to Use Starvation as Weapon in Afghanistan," Reuters, February 25, 1985, folder: "Afghanistan [12/07/1984– 03/21/1985]," box 1, Vincent Cannistraro Files, RPL; Bruce Riedel, *What We Won: America's Secret War in Afghanistan, 1979–1989* (Washington, DC: Brookings Institution Press, 2014), 30–32; and J. Bruce Amstutz, *Afghanistan: The First Five Years of Soviet Occupation* (Honolulu: University Press of the Pacific, 2002), 172–77.

21. Riedel, *What We Won*, 64–66.

22. *Politics of a Covert Action: The US, the Mujahideen, and the Stinger Missile*, Kennedy School of Government Case Program C15-99-1546.0, and Steve Coll, *Ghost Wars: The Secret History of the CIA, Afghanistan, and bin Laden, from the Soviet Invasion to September 10, 2001* (New York: Penguin, 2004), 104–5.

23. National Security Decision Directive 166, "US Policy, Programs and Strategy in Afghanistan," March 27, 1985. Available at: https://fas.org/irp/offdocs/nsdd/nsdd-166.pdf.

24. The official Soviet casualty figure is 13,833 dead; the real number is almost certainly higher, with estimates up to 50,000. See Riedel, *What We Won*, 161.

25. On Zia's denials, see RRD, December 7, 1982, and August 31, 1984, and memorandum from McFarlane to Reagan re: "Nuclear Certification for Pakistan," November 22, 1985, folder 8591182, box 17, Executive Secretariat: NSC System File, RPL.

26. Gates, *From the Shadows*, 336.

27. Ibid., 347.

28. Rodman, *More Precious Than Peace*, 385. The Gulf Oil company had also long been active in Angola and similarly supported the MPLA. In 1984, Chevron acquired Gulf Oil and the newly merged company continued to support the MPLA. For more on this, see Austin Angel, "Cabinda and the Company: Chevron-Gulf, the CIA, and the Angolan Civil War," *CLA Journal*, no. 6 (2018). Available at: https://uca.edu/cahss/files/2020/07/Angel-CLA -2018.pdf.

29. Memorandum of conversation between Reagan and Desmond Tutu, December 7, 1984, folder: "Memorandums of Conversation, President Reagan (12/04/1984–12/14/1984) Box 53," box 17, Executive Secretariat: NSC, Subject File, RPL.

30. "Remarks on Signing the International Human Rights Day Proclamation," December 10, 1984. Available at: https://www.reaganlibrary.gov/archives/speech/remarks-signing -international-human-rights-day-proclamation.

31. Minutes of National Security Council meeting on South Africa, July 26, 1985, folder: "NSC 00119, 26 July 1985 [South Africa]," Executive Secretariat, NSC: NSC Meeting Files, RPL. This was Nickel's second involuntary departure from the country; twenty-three years earlier, when he was a *Time* magazine journalist based in Johannesburg, the South African government had expelled Nickel for interviewing Black leader Nelson Mandela.

32. Apartheid and communism shared perverse similarities. Both denied human liberty, both denied human equality, both were antidemocratic, both invoked a tendentious view of history to justify their existence, and both relied on state coercion and oppression to maintain power. Each found the other anathema. The Soviet Union used its opposition to apartheid to attract sympathizers in Africa, while the South African government trumpeted its militant anticommunism to deflect criticism from the West.

33. "Forces Are Shifting in Favor of the US, Shultz Tells Senate," *Washington Post,* February 1, 1985.

34. Kenneth Dam, diary entries of April 8, 1985; April 17, 1985; April 22, 1985; June 7, 1985; and June 13, 1985, folder: "United States Department of State Diary, Volume 2, 1984–1985," box 1, Kenneth W. Dam Papers, HIA.

35. Brands, *Making the Unipolar Moment,* 139.

36. Shirley Christian, "Nicaragua Week in the Capital," *New York Times,* April 19, 1985.

37. George Shultz, "America and the Struggle for Freedom," speech, February 22, 1985, folder 5, box 3, Don Oberdorfer Papers, PUA.

38. Bernard Weinraub, "US Rejects Nicaraguan Offer of a Conditional Truce," *New York Times,* April 22, 1985, and Bernard Gwertzman, "Shultz in Warning on Combat Troops for Latin Region," *New York Times,* May 24, 1985.

39. Kagan, *A Twilight Struggle,* 373–76.

40. Sara Fritz, "House Approves Funds for Contras: Aid Bill Passes Easily in Major Reagan Victory," *Los Angeles Times,* June 13, 1985, and Kagan, *A Twilight Struggle,* 377–84.

41. Charles Krauthammer, "The Reagan Doctrine," *Washington Post,* July 19, 1985.

42. Kagan, *A Twilight Struggle,* 376–77.

43. Letter from Human Rights Permanent Commission of Nicaragua to USCCB, November 12, 1985, folder 9, box 4, William Wilson Papers, Georgetown University Archives.

44. Mario Vargas Llosa, "In Nicaragua," *New York Times Magazine,* April 28, 1985, folder: "8506513–8506528 Box 39," box 7, Executive Secretariat: NSC System File, RPL.

45. When Reagan and Bush hosted Vatican secretary of state Casaroli in the Oval Office, they asked the Vatican's thoughts on Catholic priests' joining "radical movements" in Latin America. Casaroli replied that liberation theology "worrie[d the church] since it is not theology but mere wishful thinking." Memorandum of conversation between Reagan and Casaroli, November 22, 1983, folder: "Memorandums of Conversation, President Reagan (11/01/1983–11/17/1983) Box 52," box 17, Executive Secretariat: NSC, Subject File, RPL.

46. Casey remarks at CIA conference on liberation theology, September 19, 1985, folder 15, box 310, William J. Casey Papers, HIA.

47. "Remarks on Signing the International Human Rights Day Proclamation," December 10, 1984. Available at: https://www.reaganlibrary.gov/archives/speech/remarks-signing -international-human-rights-day-proclamation.

48. Brands, *Making the Unipolar Moment,* 144.

49. "Memorandum to Reagan from Shultz," February 20, 1985, folder: "President Chron 2/20/ 1985–2/21/1985," box 34, Situation Room: White House Record, RPL.

50. RRD, March 11 and March 13, 1985.

51. "Remarks and Question-and-Answer Session with Regional Editors and Broadcasters," September 16, 1985. Available at: https://www.reaganlibrary.gov/archives/speech /remarks-and-question-and-answer-session-regional-editors-and-broadcasters.

52. Peter Schweizer, *Reagan's War: The Epic Story of His Forty-Year Struggle and Final Triumph over Communism* (New York: Anchor Books, 2002), 245.

53. Alexander Yakovlev, "About Reagan," memo, March 12, 1985. Available at: https://nsar chive2.gwu.edu//NSAEBB/NSAEBB168/yakovlev01.pdf.

54. "Memorandum from John Lenczowski of the National Security Council Staff to the President's Assistant for National Security Affairs (McFarlane)," March 12, 1985, in Elizabeth C. Charles, ed., *Foreign Relations of the United States, 1981–1988,* vol. 5, *Soviet Union, March 1985—October 1986* (hereinafter *FRUS,* vol. 5) (Washington, DC: Government Printing Office, 2020). Available at: https://history.state.gov/historicaldocuments /frus1981-88v05/d3. NSC senior director for Soviet affairs Jack Matlock did not sign the Lenczowski memo because he was in Moscow with Bush and Shultz when it was written. It also did not reflect his views, which were more optimistic about Gorbachev.

55. Letter from Reagan to Gorbachev, March 11, 1985, box 56, Jim Mann Papers, HIA; memorandum of conversation between Gorbachev, Bush, and Shultz, March 13, 1985, in *FRUS,* vol. 5, available at: https://history.state.gov/historicaldocuments/frus1981-88v05 /d5; State 76521, cable, March 14, 1985; and memorandum from Bush to Reagan from aboard Air Force Two, folder: "President Chron 3/14/1985," box 34, Situation Room: White House Record, RPL.

56. On Gorbachev's reverence for Lenin, see Vladislav M. Zubok, *Collapse: The Fall of the Soviet Union* (New Haven, CT: Yale University Press, 2021), 21, and William Taubman, *Gorbachev: His Life and Times* (New York: W. W. Norton, 2017), 215–16.

57. Minutes of conference of Communist Party Central Committee, March 15, 1985. Available at: https://nsarchive2.gwu.edu/NSAEBB/NSAEBB172/Doc5.pdf.

58. Taubman, *Gorbachev,* 272–74.

59. Stephen Kotkin, *Armageddon Averted: The Soviet Collapse 1970–2000* (updated edition; New York: Oxford University Press, 2008), 61.

60. Bureau of Intelligence and Research Analysis, "The USSR's Relations with Its East European Allies," January 11, 1985, folder: "USSR—Eastern Europe General," box 25, Jack F. Matlock Files, RPL.

61. Memorandum to Shultz from Peter Rodman, July 26, 1984; memorandum of conversation, January 8, 1985, in *FRUS,* vol. 4.

62. Jones, *A Covert Action,* 239–49.

63. Memorandum from McFarlane to Reagan re: "Proposed Letter from the President to Romanian President Ceausescu," January 23, 1985, and letter from Reagan to Ceaușescu, January 24, 1985, both in folder: "8500564–8500599 Box 2," box 2, Executive Secretariat: NSC System File, RPL.

64. Adelman, *Great Universal Embrace,* 117.

65. The other allies did not miss Trudeau either. When Thatcher and her foreign minister Geoffrey Howe first met with Mulroney, Howe inquired after Trudeau's post-government endeavors. Mulroney reported that his predecessor was practicing law and had also just received a peace prize in Washington. Came Thatcher's acid reply: "It must have been the Lenin Peace Prize." Brian Mulroney, *Memoirs: 1939–1993* (Toronto: McLellan and Stewart, 2007), 360.

66. Letter from Mulroney to Reagan, December 19, 1984, folder: "8500394–8500440 Box 2," box 1, Executive Secretariat: NSC System File, RPL.

67. Mulroney, *Memoirs,* 365–71; memoranda of conversation between Mulroney and Reagan, March 17 and March 18, 1985, Folder: "8502240 Box 15," box 5, Executive Secretariat: NSC System File, RPL; and RRD, March 17, 1985.

68. RRD, March 20, 1985.

69. Richard Reeves, *President Reagan: The Triumph of Imagination* (New York: Simon & Schuster, 2005), xv; "Remarks at the Annual Convention of the American Bar Association," July 8, 1985, available at: https://www.reaganlibrary.gov/archives/speech/remarks-annual-convention-american-bar-association; and Irina Ratushinskaya, *Grey Is the Colour of Hope* (London: Sceptre, 2016), 291.

70. Shultz in part repudiated Kirkpatrick's famed "Dictatorships and Double Standards" argument. Unlike Kirkpatrick, Shultz embraced a consistent standard of promoting human rights in communist totalitarian and anticommunist authoritarian states alike. Yet in part he affirmed Kirkpatrick's insight of the fundamental distinction between the two types of dictatorships. In Shultz's words, "There are no examples of a communist system, once consolidated, evolving into a democracy." Shultz, "America and the Struggle for Freedom," speech, February 22, 1985, folder 5, box 3, Don Oberdorfer Papers, PUA.

71. "Remarks at a Conference on Religious Liberty," April 16, 1985, available at: https://www.reaganlibrary.gov/archives/speech/remarks-conference-religious-liberty, and State 71821, cable, in author's possession, downloaded from State Department FOIA website.

72. "Remarks at a Conference on Religious Liberty," April 16, 1985. Available at: https://www.reaganlibrary.gov/archives/speech/remarks-conference-religious-liberty.

73. In a fluke of timing, Reagan hosted Holocaust survivor Elie Wiesel (who would be awarded the Nobel Peace Prize the next year) at the White House for an award ceremony. Before the live television broadcast, Wiesel pleaded with Reagan not to visit the cemetery. "That place, Mr. President, is not your place. Your place is with the victims of the SS." On Buchanan's anti-Semitism, see William F. Buckley Jr., *In Search of Anti-Semitism* (New York: Continuum, 1992).

74. Shultz, *Turmoil and Triumph*, 539–60.

75. Deaver, *Behind the Scenes*, 179–85.

76. "Remarks at a Commemorative Ceremony at Bergen-Belsen Concentration Camp in the Federal Republic of Germany," May 5, 1985. Available at: https://www.reaganlibrary.gov/archives/speech/remarks-commemorative-ceremony-bergen-belsen-concentration-camp-federal-republic.

77. Bureau of Intelligence and Research Assessment, "Bitburg: A Look Back and Ahead," June 7, 1985, in author's possession, downloaded from State Department FOIA website.

78. Ever the alliance man, Reagan spent four days of his trip on an Iberian sojourn. NATO's newest member, Spain, and founding member Portugal both welcomed him for state visits. Reagan also lauded the two countries as Europe's youngest democracies. Each had shed its dictatorship just a decade earlier and led an emerging wave of Catholic countries, inspired by Vatican II's reforms and John Paul II's teachings, embracing self-government.

79. Shultz, *Turmoil and Triumph*, 186; "Record of Plenary Session, Bonn Economic Summit," May 4, 1985, PREM 19/1468, Margaret Thatcher Foundation.

80. "Remarks Following Discussions with President Chun Doo Hwan of the Republic of Korea," April 26, 1985. Available at: https://www.reaganlibrary.gov/archives/speech/remarks-following-discussions-president-chun-doo-hwan-republic-korea. The White House hosted Chun for an official visit, less prestigious than a "state visit" because it did not include a state dinner or arrival ceremony.

81. Don Oberdorfer and Robert Carlin, *The Two Koreas: A Contemporary History* (New York: Basic Books, 2014), 177.

82. Memoranda from Shultz to Reagan, January 22 and January 24, 1985, folder: "President Chron 1/22/1985–1/25/1985," box 34, Situation Room: White House Records; memorandum from Shultz to Reagan, February 6, 1985, folder: "President Chron 2/6/1985–2/7/

1985," box 34, Situation Room: White House Record; memoranda from Shultz to Reagan, February 11, 1985, folder: "President Chron 2/12/1985," box 34, Situation Room: White House Record, RPL; Seoul 01762 and Seoul 01728, cables, in author's possession, downloaded from National Archives ISCAP website.

83. RRD, September 23, 1984.

84. Elliott Abrams, *Realism and Democracy: American Foreign Policy After the Arab Spring* (New York: Cambridge University Press, 2017), 57.

85. Quoted in Green, *By More Than Providence*, 418.

86. Manila 32254 and Manila 32307, cables, letter from Marcos to Reagan, October 16, 1985, folder: "Marcos, Ferdinand—1986 [14 of 14], Box 5," box 5, James Kelly Files, RPL, and Paul Laxalt, *Nevada's Paul Laxalt: A Memoir* (Reno, NV: Jack Bacon and Company, 2000), 274–76.

CHAPTER 11: MAKING HISTORY IN GENEVA, AND FINDING TROUBLE IN TEHRAN

1. RRD, June 17, 1985.

2. "Talking Points for the President's Meeting," June 21, 1985, folder 8504994, box 6, Executive Secretariat: NSC System File, RPL.

3. McFarlane, *Special Trust*, 22.

4. This account drawn from Martin and Walcott, *Best Laid Plans*, 161–202; David C. Wills, *The First War on Terrorism: Counter-terrorism Policy During the Reagan Administration* (Lanham, MD: Rowman & Littlefield, 2003), 89–138; and Shultz, *Turmoil and Triumph*, 653–68. When the White House Situation Room patched through the phone call to McFarlane informing him that the TWA hostages would be released, the national security advisor was in the White House theater watching the new hit movie *Rambo* with his wife, Jonda, and the Reagans. The contrast was jarring. On-screen the celluloid Sylvester Stallone character entered Vietnam and killed hundreds of Vietnamese soldiers by himself to rescue American prisoners of war still held captive. In real life the Reagan White House, helpless to rescue the TWA hostages, had resorted instead to the negotiations and concessions to terrorists that it supposedly deplored.

5. Martin and Walcott, *Best Laid Plans*, 186.

6. Leslie Gelb, "Taking Charge," *New York Times Magazine*, May 26, 1985. Fawning *New York Times Magazine* stories on Reagan's national security advisors came to resemble the dreaded *Sports Illustrated* cover jinx; both Clark and McFarlane exited the job within a few months of being so featured.

7. RRD, December 3, 1984.

8. James Graham Wilson, email to author, August 19, 2020.

9. Shultz, *Turmoil and Triumph*, 561–62.

10. Ledeen's "consultant" role by itself invited problems. Exploiting the position's ambiguity, Ledeen could present himself as alternatively speaking for official US policy or not. This often left Israelis, Iranians, arms dealers, and rogue merchants, not to mention McFarlane's own staff, perplexed as to who Ledeen represented—the US government, or himself, or something else altogether.

11. Shultz, *Turmoil and Triumph*, 785–94; Weinberger, *Fighting for Peace*, 362–64; Brands, *Making the Unipolar Moment*, 239; telegram number 601, February 21, 1985, PREM 19/1658 PM's Visit to Washington February 1985: Part 4, National Archives, United Kingdom.

12. Memo from McFarlane to secretary of state's aircraft, July 13, 1985, folder 4: "Iran-Contra Affair Briefing Book," box 205, Donald T. Regan Papers, LOC, and McFarlane, *Special Trust*, 26.

13. RRD, July 17–18, 1985.

14. Shultz, *Turmoil and Triumph*, 795.

15. Malcolm Byrne, *Iran-Contra: Reagan's Scandal and the Unchecked Abuse of Presidential Power* (Lawrence, KS: University of Kansas Press, 2014), 71. Not in doubt was Reagan's desire to free the hostages. He would try any angle he could. In the midst of these disputes, Reagan phoned Nakasone to enlist Japan's help. "[Nakasone] is sending an emissary (very hush hush) to Iran to put the squeeze on for return of our 7 kidnap [victims] in Lebanon," Reagan wrote. "Japan has considerable clout with Iran because of trade. I thanked him and told him how important it was to us." But nothing came from the Tokyo connection. RRD, July 27–28, 1985.

16. McFarlane, *Special Trust*, 31–36.

17. "Memorandum from the President's Assistant for National Security Affairs (McFarlane) to President Reagan," re: "Shultz-Gromyko Meeting: Unresolved Issues," May 13, 1985, in *FRUS*, vol. 5. Available at: https://history.state.gov/historicaldocuments/frus1981-88v05/d27. Reagan, Shultz, and McFarlane all knew that Vienna had a particularly inauspicious history for US-Soviet negotiations. Six years prior, Carter had traveled to Vienna to meet with Brezhnev and sign the SALT II treaty—then six months later the Soviets, energized in part by American concessions on arms control, invaded Afghanistan. Twenty-four years earlier, Vienna had hosted the Kennedy and Khrushchev summit, when the callow American president's fumbling performance had emboldened the Soviet leader to build the Berlin Wall and deploy nuclear missiles in Cuba, precipitating two of the Cold War's worst crises. The Reagan team resolved to avoid a similar Viennese trap.

18. Interview with Paul Nitze by Steve Rearden and Ann Smith, June 4, 1985, shared with author by James Graham Wilson.

19. Memorandum of conversation between Shultz and Gromyko, in *FRUS*, vol. 5, available at: https://history.state.gov/historicaldocuments/frus1981-88v05/d28, and Shultz, *Turmoil and Triumph*, 563–64.

20. Moscow 8857, cable, July 2, 1985, in *FRUS*, vol. 5. Available at: https://history.state.gov/historicaldocuments/frus1981-88v05/d53.

21. Philip Taubman, "He Helped End the Cold War with Kindness," *New York Times*, February 8, 2021, and Shultz, *Turmoil and Triumph*, 573–74.

22. RRD, June 3–4, 1985.

23. "Statement by the President," June 10, 1985, folder 13, box 4, Don Oberdorfer Papers, PUA.

24. "Record of Conversation Between Thatcher and Nakasone," PREM 19/1468 f130, Margaret Thatcher Foundation.

25. Memorandum from McFarlane to Reagan re: "Letters to Prime Ministers Martens, Lubbers, and Craxi on SDI," June 21, 1985, and letter from Reagan to Prime Minister Bettino Craxi, June 21, 1985, folder 8504357, box 5, Executive Secretariat: NSC System File, RPL.

26. Cable from Van Galbraith to Ron Lehman re: "Draft Record of McFarlane-Mitterrand Meeting," January 12, 1985, folder: "8500473–8500499 Box 2," box 2, Executive Secretariat: NSC System File, RPL. Mitterrand remained steadfast in other ways. An NSC memo applauded the French leader as "one of the staunchest colleagues" on Soviet policy, with his "strong support for the INF deployments, heavy pressure on Moscow on compliance with international agreements and human rights, criticism of Moscow's expansionism in the Third World, etc." Memorandum to McFarlane from Peter Sommer re: "Your

Meetings with Thatcher and Mitterrand," September 27, 1985, folder: "8507647–8507669 Box 46," box 7, Executive Secretariat: NSC System File, RPL.

27. "The President's View," *Newsweek,* March 18, 1985.

28. RRD, September 10, 1985. Emphasis Reagan's.

29. Douglas A. Irwin, *Clashing over Commerce: A History of US Trade Policy* (Chicago: University of Chicago Press, 2017), 573–74.

30. Ibid., 569–71.

31. Ibid., 566–68.

32. "National Policies and Global Prosperity," speech, April 11, 1985, folder 5, box 3, Don Oberdorfer Papers, PUA.

33. "Record of Conversation, Bonn Economic Summit Heads of Delegation Morning Meeting," May 3, 1985, and "Record of Conversation, Plenary Session," May 4, 1985, PREM19/1468, Margaret Thatcher Foundation.

34. Memorandum from Shultz to Baker, February 15, 1985, folder: "President Chron 2/15/1985–2/17/1985," box 34, Situation Room: White House Record, RPL.

35. Peter Baker and Susan Glasser, *The Man Who Ran Washington: The Life and Times of James A. Baker III* (New York: Doubleday, 2020), 255–57. Japanese finance minister Noboru Takeshita had left his home in golf shoes and played a round of golf on the front nine to fool any watching reporters, before slipping away to the airport.

36. James A. Baker III, *"Work Hard, Study . . . and Keep Out of Politics!" Adventures and Lessons from an Unexpected Public Life* (New York: G. P. Putnam's Sons, 2006), 427–31; Peter Landers, "The Old US Trade War with Japan Looms over Today's Dispute with China," *Wall Street Journal,* December 13, 2018; and memorandum from Baker to Reagan re: "Your Meeting with Prime Minister Nakasone," October 22, 1985, folder: "8508474–8508482 Box 52," box 8, Executive Secretariat: NSC System File, RPL.

37. Memorandum from John Svahn to Reagan re: "Prime Minister Nakasone's Press Conference," August 2, 1985, folder: "Japan 1985 (28 of 41), RAC Box 9," box 5, Gaston Sigur Files, RPL.

38. Quoted in McGregor, *Asia's Reckoning,* 99.

39. Memorandum to McFarlane from Nicholas Platt re: "Revised Oil Market Fact Sheet for King Fahd Visit," February 1, 1985, folder: "8500700–8500704 Box 3," box 2, Executive Secretariat: NSC System File, RPL. The White House had pitched Riyadh on a similar plan four years earlier to squeeze Libya, also dependent on oil exports. In 1981, Al Haig had proposed to the Saudis that they "[drive] even lower the price of oil, thereby further reducing Qadhafi's resources, by increased Saudi production." Riyadh demurred at the time, given its focus on keeping oil prices high to ensure profit margins. Memorandum of conversation with President Nimeiri, November 20, 1981, folder: "Memorandums of Conversation, President Reagan [11/19/1981–11/27/1981] Box 49," box 14, Executive Secretariat: NSC, Subject File. See also Haig's similar comments in minutes of NSC meeting on Libya and global negotiations, December 8, 1981, folder: "NSC 00029, 08 December 1981 [Libya and Global Negotiations]," Executive Secretariat, NSC: NSC Meeting File, RPL.

40. Hoffman, *Dead Hand,* 227, and Norman Stone, *The Atlantic and Its Enemies: A History of the Cold War* (New York: Basic Books, 2010), 546.

41. Schweizer, *Victory,* 236–37, and Schweizer, *Reagan's War,* 238–41.

42. David E. Hoffman, *The Billion Dollar Spy* (New York: Anchor Books, 2015), 329.

43. Sandra Grimes and Jeanne Vertefeuille, *Circle of Treason: A CIA Account of Traitor Aldrich Ames and the Men He Betrayed* (Annapolis, MD: Naval Institute Press, 2012).

44. Milt Bearden and James Risen, *The Main Enemy: The Inside Story of the CIA's Final Showdown with the KGB* (New York: Ballantine Books, 2003), 115–43, and Shultz, *Turmoil and Triumph*, 595.

45. "Memorandum from the President's Assistant for National Security Affairs (McFarlane) to President Reagan," re: "Soviet Use of Chemical Agents to Track US Officials," August 19, 1985, in *FRUS*, vol. 5. Available at: https://history.state.gov/historicaldocuments /frus1981-88v05/d78.

46. Matlock, *Reagan and Gorbachev*, 133–35, and Taubman, *Gorbachev*, 283.

47. Gates, *From the Shadows*, 343.

48. Massie, *Trust but Verify*, 160–73, and RRD, November 13, 1985.

49. George de Lama, "Nixon Giving Reagan Advice," *Chicago Tribune*, September 17, 1985, and letter from Nixon to Reagan, November 14, 1985, box 55, Jim Mann Papers, HIA.

50. Moscow 16035, cable, folder: "Briefing Material for President Reagan–Gorbachev Meeting 11/27/1985 [*sic*] (3)," box 47, Jack F. Matlock Files, RPL.

51. Moscow 15987, cable, November 6, 1985, in *FRUS*, vol. 5, available at: https://history.state .gov/historicaldocuments/frus1981-88v05/d138; Shultz, *Triumph and Turmoil*, 592–93; and RRD, October 24, 1985. Gorbachev also told Shultz, "I have special information about what was said in the meeting of the Six." Gorbachev seemed to be referencing Reagan's private dinner with Thatcher, Nakasone, Mulroney, Kohl, and Italian prime minister Bettino Craxi at the United Nations ten days earlier, where Reagan had previewed his negotiating plans in Geneva. Presumably the KGB had bugged the room or had some other source eavesdropping on the conversation. Gorbachev conspiratorially labeled this group "the Six," though his outburst may have been prompted by jealousy more than anything. "The Six" represented America's closest allies and Reagan's close friends. The Soviet Union, in contrast, had coerced satellites rather than real allies, and among world leaders Gorbachev was bereft of real friends.

52. CIA analysis, "Gorbachev's Prospective Course," September 9, 1985. Available at: https:// www.cia.gov/readingroom/docs/CIA-RDP90G01359R000200020023-1.pdf.

53. Memorandum of conversation re: "The President's Meeting with Foreign Minister Eduard Shevardnadze of the Soviet Union," September 27, 1985, in *FRUS*, vol. 5, available at: https://history.state.gov/historicaldocuments/frus1981-88v05/d105, and memorandum of conversation re: "The President's Meeting with Soviet Foreign Minister Shevardnadze," October 24, 1985, in *FRUS*, vol. 5, available at: https://history.state.gov/historicaldocu ments/frus1981-88v05/d121.

54. Shultz, *Turmoil and Triumph*, 586–87.

55. Letter from Gorbachev to Reagan, September 12, 1985, folder: "E.1 Pres/Gorbachev Correspondence," box 47, Jack F. Matlock Files, RPL.

56. Memorandum from Shultz to Reagan re: "Response to Soviet Arms Proposals," October 3, 1985, folder 8591041, box 17, Executive Secretariat: NSC System File, RPL.

57. White House, "New US Proposals for Nuclear Arms Reductions," fact sheet, November 13, 1985, folder 16, box 4, Don Oberdorfer Papers, PUA.

58. "Memorandum from the Deputy Director for Operations, Central Intelligence Agency (George) to President Reagan, Vice President Bush, Secretary of State Shultz, Secretary of Defense Weinberger, and the President's Assistant for National Security Affairs (McFarlane)," re: "Discussions by Soviet Officials of the SDI and Other Arms Control Issues," September 25, 1985, in *FRUS*, vol. 5, available at: https://history.state.gov/historicaldocu ments/frus1981-88v05/d98, and "Minutes of a National Security Council Meeting," re: "Soviet Foreign Minister Shevardnadze's Visit," September 20, 1985, in *FRUS*, vol. 5,

available at: https://history.state.gov/historicaldocuments/frus1981-88v05/d94. Reagan told an NSC meeting in September, "[I am] prepared, once any of our SDI programs proved out, to then announce to the world that integrating these weapons in our respective arsenals would put international relations on a more stable footing. In fact, this could even lead to a complete elimination of nuclear weapons."

59. Shultz, *Turmoil and Triumph,* 578–82.

60. "Conservatives Outraged by Reagan's Decision on Treaty," Associated Press, October 17, 1985, in box 52, Jim Mann Papers, HIA.

61. RRD, November 5, 1985.

62. Reagan, "Gorbachev," note, October 13, 1985, folder 4: "Summits, Geneva Switzerland Nov. 1985," box 215, Donald T. Regan Papers, LOC.

63. RRD, November 9, 1985; "Radio Address to the Nation and the World on the Upcoming Soviet–United States Summit Meeting in Geneva," November 9, 1985, available at: https://www.reaganlibrary.gov/archives/speech/radio-address-nation-and-world-upcoming-soviet-united-states-summit-meeting-geneva; and "Address to the Nation on the Upcoming Soviet–United States Summit Meeting in Geneva," November, 14, 1985, available at: https://www.reaganlibrary.gov/archives/speech/address-nation-upcoming-soviet-united-states-summit-meeting-geneva.

64. Letter from Reagan to Thatcher, October 8, 1985, folder 8591046, box 17, Executive Secretariat: NSC System File, RPL.

65. Memorandum from Oliver North to McFarlane re: "Cabinet Office Cable to Prime Minister Thatcher re Hijacking of ACHILLE LAURO," October 8, 1985, folder 8591052, box 17, Executive Secretariat: NSC System File, RPL.

66. Nicholas Veliotes interview, Foreign Affairs Oral History Collection, Association for Diplomatic Studies and Training, Arlington, VA.

67. Wills, *First War on Terrorism,* 150–51.

68. Poindexter interview conducted by Robert Timberg. In author's possession.

69. NSC staff member Oliver North, who was already demonstrating a casual relationship with the truth, falsely claimed to many journalists that he devised the plan.

70. Wills, *First War on Terrorism,* 154–55. The frazzled defense secretary, also in flight at the time, failed to use a secure telephone, which allowed an amateur ham radio operator to monitor his conversation with Reagan and then share it with the media. It was not Weinberger's finest hour.

71. Michael A. Ledeen, *Perilous Statecraft: An Insider's Account of the Iran-Contra Affair* (New York: Charles Scribner's Sons, 1988), 174–82.

72. Julie Salamon, *An Innocent Bystander: The Killing of Leon Klinghoffer* (New York: Little, Brown, 2019), 111–15.

73. Michael K. Bohn, *The Achille Lauro Hijacking: Lessons in the Politics and Prejudice of Terrorism* (Dulles, VA: Potomac Books, 2004), 35–43, and Shultz, *Turmoil and Triumph,* 675.

74. RRD, October 24, 1985.

75. Letter from Thatcher to Reagan, September 12, 1985, PREM 19/1660 f227, Margaret Thatcher Foundation Archive. Available at: https://www.margaretthatcher.org/document/143042.

76. RRD, October 24, 1985.

77. Gates, *From the Shadows,* 342.

78. George J. Church, "Geneva: The Whole World Will Be Watching," *Time,* November 18, 1985.

79. Hoffman, *Dead Hand,* 228, and Hugh Sidey, "On a Free Stage," *Time,* December 2, 1985.

80. "Weinberger Letter to Reagan on Arms Control," *New York Times,* November 16, 1985.

81. RRD, November 17, 1985; "Summit Notes," folder 3: "Summits, Geneva Switzerland November 1985," box 215, Donald T. Regan Papers, LOC; and R. W. Apple Jr., "Weinberger Note Seen as Opposing Softness at Talks," *New York Times,* November 18, 1985. Shultz shared McFarlane's fury and retaliated with mockery. Speaking at a Kennedy Center gala after the summit, the secretary joked that in Geneva he received a cable from Weinberger that read: "Wish you were here, and vice versa." James F. Clarity and Warren Weaver Jr., "Briefing; A Weinberger Lament," *New York Times,* December 10, 1985.

82. James Rosebush, *True Reagan: What Made Ronald Reagan Great and Why It Matters* (New York: Hachette Book Group, 2016), 177.

83. Jim Kuhn, *Ronald Reagan in Private: A Memoir of My Years in the White House* (New York: Sentinel, 2004), 163–72, and notes from dinner with Andrei Grachev, May 27, 1990, folder 16, box 4, Don Oberdorfer Papers, PUA.

84. Memorandum of conversation between Reagan and Gorbachev, first private meeting, November 19, 1985, folder: "851041 (1 of 4)," box 8, Executive Secretariat: NSC System File, RPL.

85. Memorandum of conversation between Reagan and Gorbachev, Third Plenary Meeting, November 20, 1985, folder: "851041 (2 of 4)," box 8, Executive Secretariat: NSC System File, RPL.

86. Evan Thomas, "Fencing at the Fireside Summit," *Time,* December 2, 1985.

87. "Summit Afternoon Session Notes 11/19/85," folder 3: "Summits, Geneva Switzerland November 1985," box 215, Donald T. Regan Papers, LOC, and memorandum of conversation between Reagan and Gorbachev, Third Plenary Meeting, November 20, 1985, folder: "851041 (2 of 4)," box 8, Executive Secretariat: NSC System File, RPL.

88. Memorandum of conversation between Reagan and Gorbachev, Second Plenary Meeting, November 19, 1985, folder: "851041 (1 of 4)," box 8, Executive Secretariat: NSC System File, RPL.

89. Hoffman, *Dead Hand,* 22–23, 151–54, 421–23.

90. Memorandum of conversation between Reagan and Gorbachev, First Plenary Meeting, November 19, 1985, folder: "851041 (1 of 4)," box 8, Executive Secretariat: NSC System File, RPL.

91. Memorandum of conversation between Reagan and Gorbachev, Third Private Meeting, November 20, 1985, in *FRUS,* vol. 5. Available at: https://history.state.gov/historicaldocuments/frus1981-88v05/d156.

92. "Summit Notes—11/20/85—second day—afternoon," folder 4: "Summits, Geneva Switzerland November 1985," box 215, Donald T. Regan Papers, LOC.

93. RRD, November 13, 1985; Lauren Turek, *To Bring the Good News to All Nations: Evangelical Influence on Human Rights and US Foreign Policy* (Ithaca, NY: Cornell University Press, 2020), 95–97; Mann, *Rebellion of Ronald Reagan,* 93; and letter from Nixon to Reagan, December 20, 1985, box 51, Jim Mann Papers, HIA.

94. Summit notes, folder 3: "Summits, Geneva Switzerland November 1985," box 215, Donald T. Regan Papers, LOC. In fact, American conservative media generally applauded Reagan's performance at Geneva.

95. Memorandum of conversation between Reagan and Gorbachev, after-dinner conversation, folder: "851041 (2 of 4)," box 8, Executive Secretariat: NSC System File; RPL.

96. RRD, November 30–December 1, 1985.

97. RRD, November 22, 1985.

98. Memorandum from Casey to Poindexter re: "Presidential Finding on Middle East, with Attached Finding," November 26, 1985, folder 5, "Iran-Contra Affair Briefing Book," box 205, Donald T. Regan Papers, LOC, and Malcolm Byrne, *Iran-Contra: Reagan's Scandal and the Unchecked Abuse of Presidential Power* (Lawrence, KS: University of Kansas Press, 2014), 94–108.

99. RRD, December 5 and 7, 1985.

100. McFarlane, *Special Trust,* 48–51.

101. RRD, December 10, 1985.

102. Hayward, *Age of Reagan: Conservative Counterrevolution,* 446.

103. "Remarks on Signing the Bill of Rights Day and the Human Rights Day and Week Proclamation," December 10, 1985. Available at: https://www.reaganlibrary.gov/archives /speech/remarks-signing-bill-rights-day-and-human-rights-day-and-week -proclamation-0.

CHAPTER 12: THE CRUCIBLE

1. Letter from Reagan to Gorbachev, November 28, 1985; letter from Reagan to Gorbachev, December 7, 1985; and letter from Gorbachev to Reagan, December 24, 1985, all in *FRUS,* vol. 5.

2. Lettow, *Ronald Reagan and His Quest,* 190–91.

3. "Soviet Strategy Toward the US in 1986–88," January 7, 1986, folder: "Intelligence Reports [pre-1980, May 85—Jan 86] (1/6)," box 28, Jack F. Matlock Files, and letter from Casey to Reagan, January 10, 1986, folder: "8591202 (1 of 2)," box 17, Executive Secretariat: NSC System File, RPL.

4. Memorandum from Shultz to Reagan, January 15, 1986; Paul Nitze, "Memorandum for the Record," January 15, 1986, in *FRUS,* vol. 5; note from Poindexter to Bush and Regan with attached draft statement from Reagan, January 15, 1986, folder: "Chron January 1986," box 1, John Poindexter Files, RPL; and Taubman, *Gorbachev,* 291–92.

5. "Minutes of NSPG Meeting on Arms Control—Responding to Gorbachev," February 3, 1986, folder: "NSPG 0127 02/03/1986 (2 of 2), Box 91308," box 4, Executive Secretariat, NSC: NSPG, RPL.

6. Memorandum from Bill Wright/Bob Linhard to Poindexter re: "Letter to Allied Heads of State on Responding to Gorbachev," February 4, 1986, folder 8690091, box 18, Executive Secretariat: NSC System File, RPL.

7. Letter from Thatcher to Reagan, February 11, 1986, PREM 19/1693, National Archives, United Kingdom.

8. Telegram from Burt to Reagan and Shultz, February 11, 1986, in *FRUS,* vol. 5, and Gal Beckerman, *When They Come for Us, We'll Be Gone: The Epic Struggle to Save Soviet Jewry* (New York: Houghton Mifflin Harcourt, 2010), 478–85. Upon his release and immigration to Israel, the dissident revised his name to become "Natan Sharansky," as he has been known ever since.

9. Letter from Reagan to Gorbachev, February 16, 1986, folder: "Chron Feb. 1986," box 1, John Poindexter Files, RPL.

10. Shultz, *Turmoil and Triumph,* 712–13.

11. Lehman, *Oceans Ventured,* 180–83.

12. Memorandum from Matlock to Poindexter, March 17, 1985, in *FRUS*, vol. 5.

13. RRD, January 24, 1985, and Matlock, *Reagan and Gorbachev*, 181–82.

14. *Politics of a Covert Action: The US, the Mujahideen, and the Stinger Missile*, Kennedy School of Government Case Program C15-99-1546.0, and author interview with Milt Bearden, August 2, 2018. Some influential senators, such as Sam Nunn, voiced similar concerns about Stingers falling into Soviet hands. However, other CIA officials pointed out that Soviet military intelligence had already purloined the Stinger blueprints from a NATO source. Soon thereafter, Reagan welcomed a group of five mujahideen leaders to the White House. Referencing the Stingers, he reinforced his commitment to providing "the most effective weapons" available and assured them that he would not negotiate a separate deal with the Soviets that did not have the involvement and support of Afghan leaders. Reagan also urged the resistance leaders, notoriously fractious and divided, to set aside their feuds, telling them, "[Better cooperation] will help you to defeat the Soviets politically as you fight them militarily." "Talking Points for the President's Meeting with Afghan Resistance Leaders," June 16, 1986, folder: "Afghanistan Resistance, Working Group (5)," box 91555, Vincent Cannistraro Files, RPL.

15. Bearden and Risen, *Main Enemy*, 236–48.

16. Crile, *Charlie Wilson's War*, 437.

17. Westad, *Global Cold War*, 374; letter from Mitterrand to Thatcher, August 2, 1986, PREM 19/1760, National Archives, United Kingdom; and Riedel, *What We Won*, 122–24.

18. Remarks to the OSS/Donovan Symposium, September 19, 1986, folder 18, box 312, William J. Casey Papers, HIA.

19. RRD, February 18, 1986.

20. Kagan, *A Twilight Struggle*, 423–27, and "Address to the Nation on the Situation in Nicaragua," March 16, 1986, available at: https://www.reaganlibrary.gov/archives/speech/address-nation-situation-nicaragua.

21. Evan Thomas, "Tough Tug of War," *Time*, March 31, 1986.

22. Minutes of NSC meeting re: "Aid to the Nicaraguan Democratic Resistance," March 20, 1986. Available at: https://www.thereaganfiles.com/19860320-nscl29a-2010-decla.pdf.

23. RRD, March 20, 1986.

24. Author interview with Poindexter, October 24, 2017. Poindexter became visibly emotional when making this point.

25. "Address to the Nation on United States Assistance for the Nicaraguan Democratic Resistance," June 24, 1986. Available at: https://www.reaganlibrary.gov/archives/speech/address-nation-united-states-assistance-nicaraguan-democratic-resistance.

26. Letter from Menges to Ambassador Bill Wilson with attachments, May 18, 1986, folder 71, box 2, William Wilson Papers, Georgetown University Archives, and letter from members of Congress to Poindexter, April 30, 1986, folder: "Chron 5/01/1986 to 5/11/1986," box 1, John Poindexter Files, RPL.

27. Poindexter email re: "Contra Project," May 2, 1986, folder 4: "Iran-Contra Affair Briefing Book," box 205, Donald T. Regan Papers, LOC.

28. Poindexter interview conducted by Robert Timberg, May 18, 1992. In author's possession.

29. Kagan, *A Twilight Struggle*, 431–62.

30. RRD, October 9, 1984.

31. RRD, January 28, 1985.

32. Memorandum from Poindexter to Reagan re: "Covert Action Finding Regarding Iran," January 17, 1986, folder 4, Iran-Contra Briefing Book, box 205, Donald T. Regan Papers, LOC; RRD, January 17, 1986; and Byrne, *Iran-Contra*, 144–67.

33. Timberg, *Nightingale's Song*, 434.

34. Byrne, *Iran-Contra*, 186–207, and Crist, *Twilight War*, 190–95.

35. Memorandum of conversation on US–Iran dialogue, May 29, 1986, and RRD, May 28, 1986.

36. RRD, December 29, 1985–January 2, 1986.

37. "Aide Memoire," folder 15, box 4, William Wilson Papers, Georgetown University Archives, and Shultz, *Turmoil and Triumph*, 678–79.

38. Timothy Naftali, *Blind Spot: The Secret History of American Counterterrorism* (New York: Basic Books, 2005), 167–69; Bob Woodward, *Veil: The Secret Wars of the CIA, 1981–1987* (New York: Simon & Schuster, 1987), 415–16; Bob Woodward, "US Decided to Give Libya Firm Message," *Washington Post*, March 26, 1986, in folder: "Chron 3/17/1986 to 3/31/1986," box 1; and note from Poindexter to Rodney McDaniel, April 2, 1986, folder: "Chron April 1986," box 1, John Poindexter, Files, RPL.

39. Minutes of NSPG meeting on Libya, March 14, 1986, folder: "NSPG 129 14 March 1986, Box 91308," box 4, Executive Secretariat, NSC: NSPG, RPL.

40. Joseph T. Stanik, *El Dorado Canyon: Reagan's Undeclared War with Qaddafi* (Annapolis, MD: Naval Institute Press, 2003), 142–45.

41. Moore, *Margaret Thatcher: At Her Zenith*, 508–9.

42. Letter from Poindexter to Jean-Louis Bianco with attached message from Reagan to Mitterrand, April 12, 1986, folder: "Libya—El Dorado Canyon [7 of 10]," box 91747, James Stark Files, RPL.

43. Crist, *Twilight War*, 148.

44. Stanik, *El Dorado Canyon*, 146–205.

45. Moore, *Margaret Thatcher: At Her Zenith*, 517.

46. Memorandum to Reagan from Shultz re: "Soviet Reaction to US Actions in Libya," April 15, 1986, folder: "Soviet Reaction to US Actions in Libya," box 35, Jack F. Matlock Files, RPL.

47. David Ignatius, "Bombing Gadhafi Worked," *Washington Post*, July 13, 1986.

48. Minutes of NSPG meeting on Libya, August 14, 1986, folder: "NSPG 0137, 14 Aug 1986 [Libya]," Executive Secretariat, NSC: NSPG Meeting File, RPL.

49. Letter from Marcos to Reagan, January 16, 1986, folder: "Marcos, Ferdinand—1986 [3 of 14], Box 5," box 5, James Kelly Files, RPL.

50. Marcos fell afoul of what scholar Sheena Chestnut Greitens calls the "coercive dilemma" facing autocrats: In setting up their personal security forces, dictators face a choice. They can keep their henchmen unified under one command, which makes the secret police more effective in detecting and suppressing dissent but also makes them a more potent threat if they decide to turn against the dictator in a coup. Or the dictator can engage in "coup-proofing" by dispersing his security forces into multiple, rival units, which hinders them in detecting and suppressing dissent but also renders them less of a potential rival to the dictator. The paranoid Marcos had chosen the latter. His internal security forces, divided and rivalrous, failed to see the widespread popular resentment against him, let alone the emerging People Power wave that crested over the country. Sheena Chestnut Greitens, *Dictators and Their Secret Police: Coercive Institutions and State Violence* (New York: Cambridge University Press, 2016).

51. Brands, *Making the Unipolar Moment*, 154.

52. State 363553, cable, in author's possession, downloaded from State Department FOIA website. The irony with the 2003 Iraq War is self-evident.

53. Gaston Sigur interview, Foreign Affairs Oral History Collection, Association for Diplomatic Studies and Training, Arlington, VA, and Shultz, *Turmoil and Triumph*, 624–41.

54. RRD, February 22–26, 1986, and Laxalt, *Nevada's Paul Laxalt*, 278–80.

55. Shultz, *Turmoil and Triumph*, 620–23.

56. George Shultz, "The Shape, Scope, and Consequences of the Age of Information," address, March 21, 1986, folder 5, box 3, Don Oberdorfer Papers, PUA.

57. Memorandum of conversation between Reagan and Mulroney, March 18, 1986, folder: "8602469–8602479 Box 73," and memorandum of conversation between Reagan and Mulroney, March 19, 1986, folder: "8602430–8602439 Box 72," both in box 9, Executive Secretariat: NSC System File, RPL. Mulroney visited Beijing soon after his White House meeting. He asked Deng Xiaoping his assessment of the Soviet chieftain. "Gorbachev is not going to last long as leader," responded Deng. "His ambitions for political reform are going to overtake any possibility of the economy sustaining the Soviet people, and they will throw him out." Deng averred that the Kremlin should instead follow China's path of liberalizing its economy while preserving the Communist Party's monopoly on power. Mulroney, *Memoirs*, 438–39.

58. Letter from Nakasone to Reagan, and attached documents, September 9, 1986, folder 8606480, box 10, Executive Secretariat: NSC System File, RPL.

59. Memorandum to Poindexter from Kenneth Kissell and David Laux re: "Establishment of an IG on US Military Cooperation with the PRC," August 27, 1986, folder: "China—Military 1986," box 1, James Kelly Files, RPL; undated note to Sigur from David Laux re: "ADB Package for the Judge," folder: "Taiwan—1986 (1), Box 6," box 5, James Kelly Files, RPL; and Mann, *About Face*, 150–54.

60. Letter from Reagan to Chun, April 24, 1986, folder: "Korea (04/16/1986–05/15/1986), Box 3," box 1, James Kelly Files, RPL; letter from ROK assembly members to Reagan, May 22, 1986, folder: "Korea (05/16/1986–06/30/1986), Box 3," box 1, James Kelly Files, RPL; and Shultz, *Turmoil and Triumph*, 979–80.

61. Adam Higginbotham, *Midnight in Chernobyl: The Untold Story of the World's Greatest Nuclear Disaster* (New York: Simon & Schuster, 2019), 88.

62. Quoted in ibid., 179; Calder Walton, "The Deadly Fallout of Disinformation," *Washington Post*, July 8, 2020.

63. Telegram from Department of State to Embassy Moscow re: "Presidential Message on Reactor Accident," April 29, 1986, in *FRUS*, vol. 5.

64. "Radio Address to the Nation on the President's Trip to Indonesia and Japan," May 4, 1986, available at: https://www.reaganlibrary.gov/archives/speech/radio-address-nation -presidents-trip-indonesia-and-japan; memorandum of conversation between Reagan and Thatcher, May 4, 1986, folder 8603593, box 9, Executive Secretariat: NSC System File, RPL; and Higginbotham, *Midnight in Chernobyl*, 200–201.

65. Taubman, *Gorbachev*, 240–41.

66. Archie Brown, *The Human Factor: Gorbachev, Reagan, and Thatcher, and the End of the Cold War* (New York: Oxford University Press, 2020), 164–65.

67. Minutes of NSPG meeting on options in responding to Soviet violations, April 16, 1986, folder: "NSPG 0131 04/16/1986, Box 2," box 4, Executive Secretariat, NSC: NSPG, RPL, and letter from Reagan to Thatcher, May 23, 1986, PREM 19/1694, National Archives, United Kingdom.

68. Letter from Thatcher to Reagan, May 26, 1986, PREM 19/1694, National Archives, United Kingdom, and memorandum from Shultz to Reagan re: "US-Soviet Relations," June 3, 1986, in *FRUS*, vol. 5.

69. Letter from Reagan to Gorbachev, May 23, 1986; memorandum from Shultz to Reagan re: "US-Soviet Relations," June 3, 1986, in *FRUS*, vol. 5; minutes of NSPG meeting on US-Soviet Relations, June 12, 1986, folder: "NSPG 0135 12 June 1986, Box 91308," box 4, Executive Secretariat, NSC: NSPG; and letter from Gorbachev to Reagan, June 19, 1986, folder: 8690474, box 7, Chron File: Assistant to the President for National Security Affairs, RPL.

70. RRD, July 4, 1986.

71. Taubman, *Gorbachev*, 293, and Brown, *Human Factor*, 170.

72. Memorandum of conversation between Nixon and Gorbachev, July 18, 1986, box 55, Jim Mann Papers, HIA. Nixon sent the transcript of his discussion with Gorbachev to Reagan, Shultz, and other senior administration officials. It had been Nixon's first time meeting Gorbachev, who was the third Soviet leader Nixon had spent time with, after Khrushchev and Brezhnev. Ever enamored of strength, Nixon added his observation, "Gorbachev is as tough as Brezhnev, but better educated, more skillful, more subtle. . . . Brezhnev used a meat axe in his negotiations, Gorbachev uses a stiletto. But beyond the velvet glove he always wears, there is a steel fist . . . he is the most affable of all the Soviet leaders I have met, but at the same time without question the most formidable because his goals are the same as theirs and he will be more effective in attempting to achieve them." Nixon was correct that Gorbachev was no pushover. But the former president, otherwise so seasoned in Soviet policy, missed what Reagan and Shultz had detected in Geneva and since: Gorbachev did *not* share all the same goals as his predecessors. He was a different kind of Soviet leader. Mann, *Rebellion of Ronald Reagan*, 36–37.

73. Letter from Reagan to Gorbachev, July 25, 1986, in *FRUS*, vol. 5.

74. Taubman, *Gorbachev*, 294.

75. Letter from Reagan to Gorbachev, September 4, 1986, available at: https://www.therea ganfiles.com/19860904.pdf, and letter from Gorbachev to Reagan, September 6, 1986, available at: https://www.thereaganfiles.com/19860906.pdf.

76. Bearden and Risen, *Main Enemy*, 50–58, 182–85, and Shultz, *Turmoil and Triumph*, 728–39.

77. Shultz, *Turmoil and Triumph*, 733–37.

78. RRD, September 19, 1986, and Shultz, *Turmoil and Triumph*, 742–43.

79. RRD, September 25, 1986; George Will, "Reagan Botched the Daniloff Affair," *Washington Post*, September 18, 1986; and George Will, "Reeling Toward Reykjavik," *Washington Post*, October 3, 1986. Both Will articles in box 55, Jim Mann Papers, HIA. In the latter column, Will also accused Reagan of delusion about the very nature of the Soviet Union: "President Reagan has been sold a soothing theory that explains the dynamic of the Soviet state in terms of anxieties and paranoia rather than an ideologically driven pursuit of power. . . . Reagan wants a summit in order to practice therapeutic policy. Gorbachev wants a summit because he dines on people who think like that."

80. Memorandum to Poindexter from Philip Ringdahl re: "South Africa—Nuclear Matters," April 29, 1986, folder 8603438, box 9, Executive Secretariat: NSC System File, RPL.

81. RRD, June 11, 1986.

82. RRD, September 29, 1986.

83. Crocker, *High Noon in Southern Africa*, 316–32.

84. Taubman, *Gorbachev*, 294, and Henry Kissinger, "Danger at the Summit?" *Newsweek*, October 13, 1986.

85. Memorandum to Poindexter from Steve Sestanovich re: "The Iceland Pre-Summit," September 30, 1986, folder: "Reykjavik (1 of 4) RAC Box 12," box 2, European and Soviet Affairs Directorate: Records, RPL.

86. Matlock, *Reagan and Gorbachev,* 212–13, and Anatoly Chernyaev, notes, October 4, 1986, National Security Archive Electronic Briefing Book no. 203, available at: https://nsarchive2.gwu.edu/NSAEBB/NSAEBB203/Document05.pdf.

87. National Security Decision Directive 238, "Basic National Security Strategy," September 2, 1986. Available at: https://fas.org/irp/offdocs/nsdd/nsdd-238.pdf.

88. RRD, May 20, 1986, and Shultz, *Turmoil and Triumph,* 724.

89. Massie, *Trust but Verify,* 280–83.

90. National Security Decision Directive 238, "Basic National Security Strategy," September 2, 1986. Available at: https://fas.org/irp/offdocs/nsdd/nsdd-238.pdf.

91. RRD, May 13, 1986.

92. Sam Roberts, "Irina Ratushinskaya, Soviet Dissident and Writer, Dies at 63," *New York Times,* July 13, 2017.

93. Cited in Fred A. Lazin, "The Role of Ethnic Politics in US Immigration and Refugee Policy: The Case of Soviet Jewry," Center for Comparative Immigration Studies Working Paper 175, February 2009, and Bernard Weinraub, "President Links Rights in Soviet to Summit Success," *New York Times,* October 8, 1986.

94. Cited in Kenneth L. Adelman, *Reagan at Reykjavik: Forty-Eight Hours That Ended the Cold War* (New York: Broadside Books, 2014), 41, 51–54.

95. Memorandum of conversation between Reagan and Gorbachev, October 11, 1986, 10:40 a.m. to 12:30 p.m., folder: "8690725 (1 of 3)," box 19, Executive Secretariat: NSC System File, RPL.

96. Adelman, *Reagan at Reykjavik,* 108.

97. Memorandum of conversation between Reagan and Gorbachev, October 11, 1986, 3:30 p.m. to 5:40 p.m., folder: "8690725 (1 of 3)," box 19, Executive Secretariat: NSC System File, RPL.

98. Adelman, *Reagan at Reykjavik,* 123–24, and Memorandum for the record re: "Reykjavik Chronology," in *FRUS,* vol. 5.

99. Memorandum of conversation between Reagan and Gorbachev, October 12, 1986, 10:00 a.m. to 1:35 p.m., folder: "8690725 (2 of 3)," box 19, Executive Secretariat: NSC System File, RPL.

100. Memorandum of conversation between Reagan and Gorbachev, October 12, 1986, 10:00 a.m. to 1:35 p.m., folder: "8690725 (2 of 3)," box 19, Executive Secretariat: NSC System File, RPL.

101. Adelman, *Reagan at Reykjavik,* 153.

102. Memorandum of conversation between Reagan and Gorbachev, October 12, 1986, 3:30 p.m. to 6:50 p.m., folder: "8690725 (2 of 3)," box 19, Executive Secretariat: NSC System File, RPL.

103. Ibid.

104. "Address to the Nation on the Meetings with Soviet General Secretary Gorbachev in Iceland," October 13, 1986, available at: https://www.reaganlibrary.gov/archives/speech/address-nation-meetings-soviet-general-secretary-gorbachev-iceland; Shultz, *Turmoil and Triumph,* 773–74; and memorandum of conversation between Reagan and Gorbachev, October 12, 1986, 3:30 p.m. to 6:50 p.m., folder: "8690725 (2 of 3)," box 19, Executive Secretariat: NSC System File, RPL.

105. Quoted in Adelman, *Reagan at Reykjavik,* 182–83.

106. Johanna McGeary, "Sunk by Star Wars," *Time*, October 20, 1986, and "Deadlock in Iceland," *Newsweek*, October 20, 1986.

107. Politburo meeting minutes, October 14, 1986, National Security Archive Electronic Briefing Book no. 203, available at: https://nsarchive2.gwu.edu/NSAEBB/NSAEBB203/Document21.pdf, and Stephen Sestanovich, *Maximalist: America in the World from Truman to Obama* (New York: Alfred A. Knopf, 2014), 236. Congressional Democrats lambasted Reagan. Senator Ted Kennedy declared, "It is difficult to believe that any other president since World War II would have ignored the opportunity that knocked at Reykjavik." Senator Patrick Leahy blamed the failed negotiations on "the administration's commitment to a non-existent system," saying, "They seem to ignore the fact that the Soviet warheads are real. I must admit I find difficulty with the logic." Representative Ed Markey piled on: "This weekend we had a chance to cash in Star Wars for the best deal the Russians have offered an American president since they sold Alaska for $7 million, and Ronald Reagan turned it down cold." Memorandum to the president from Pat Buchanan, October 16, 1986, folder 7: "Summits, Reykjavik, Iceland Oct. 1986," box 215, Donald T. Regan Papers, LOC.

108. Memorandum to Reagan from Poindexter, October 16, 1986, folder: "Reykjavik Briefings Memo re: 'Eliminating Nuclear Weapons' (3 of 3)," box 91636, Alton Keel File, RPL.

109. Summary of telephone conversation between Reagan and Thatcher, October 13, 1986, folder 8607413, box 10, Executive Secretariat: NSC System File; memorandum from Peter Sommer to Poindexter re: "Your Meeting with Ambassador Acland," October 27, 1986, folder: "Thatcher Visit 11/151986 (5 of 7), RAC Box 15," box 10, European and Soviet Affairs Directorate, NSC: Records, RPL; and Robert J. McCartney, "Kohl, Reagan to Meet Here Today," *Washington Post*, October 21, 1986, in box 51, Jim Mann Papers, HIA.

110. TELNO 283, re: "Reykjavik Summit: NAC Briefing by Shultz," October 13, 1986, PREM 19/1759, National Archives, United Kingdom.

111. Beckerman, *When They Come for Us*, 495–500.

112. RRD, October 27, 1986.

113. Byrne, *Iran-Contra*, 234–35. It would later come to light that the plane belonged to the same CIA airline, Southern Air Transport, that had flown some of the missile shipments to Iran.

114. Crist, *Twilight War*, 196–98; Safire quoted in Shultz, *Turmoil and Triumph*, 829.

115. Note from McFarlane to Poindexter, November 8, 1986, folder 4, "Iran-Contra Affair Briefing Book," box 205, Donald T. Regan Papers, LOC; Shultz, *Turmoil and Triumph*, 808–9; Persico, *Casey*, 541–42; and Spitz, *Reagan*, 672–73.

116. "Address to the Nation on the Iran Arms and Contra Aid Controversy," November 13, 1986. Available at: https://www.reaganlibrary.gov/archives/speech/address-nation-iran-arms-and-contra-aid-controversy-november-13-1986.

117. Note from McFarlane to Poindexter re: "Perspective," November 15, 1986, folder 4, "Iran-Contra Affair Briefing Book," box 205, Donald T. Regan Papers, LOC; John Poindexter, "The Prudent Option in Iran," *Wall Street Journal*, November 24, 1986; Shultz, *Turmoil and Triumph*, 838; and Byrne, *Iran-Contra*, 276–77.

118. RRD, November 24, 1986.

119. Kathryn McGarr, *The Whole Damn Deal: Robert Strauss and the Art of Politics* (New York: Public Affairs, 2011), 298–300.

120. Executive Order 12575, in *The Tower Commission Report* (New York: Bantam Books, 1987).

121. Author interview with Stephen J. Hadley, September 25, 2020. Hadley would later serve as national security advisor to President George W. Bush; the author worked for him on the NSC staff.

122. Bob Strauss had also quietly brokered the deal with Congress to create a single bicameral investigative committee rather than separate Senate and House investigative committees, thus sparing the White House the burden of competing congressional inquiries.

123. Crist, *Twilight War,* 183.

124. Persico, *Casey,* 575.

125. Hayward, *Age of Reagan: Conservative Counterrevolution,* 528, and Spitz, *Reagan,* 681.

126. "President Reagan, Mastermind," *Saturday Night Live,* December 6, 1986. Available at: https://www.youtube.com/watch?v=b5wfPlgKFh8&t=1s.

CHAPTER 13: COMEBACK

1. Though Buchanan would decide not to run in 1988, his GOP primary challenge to Bush in 1992 would contribute to the incumbent's eventual defeat.

2. Chris Whipple, *The Gatekeepers: How the White House Chiefs of Staff Define Every Presidency* (New York: Crown, 2017), 145–46, emphasis original; Donald T. Regan, *For the Record: From Wall Street to Washington* (New York: Harcourt Brace Jovanovich, 1988); and Tumulty, *Triumph of Nancy Reagan,* 478–89. When James Baker heard of his successor's transgression, he marveled: "He hung up on the First Lady! That's not just a firing offense. That may be a *hanging* offense!" Some of Regan's frustrations became more understandable when he revealed that the First Lady had been letting her astrologer dictate parts of the president's schedule.

3. McFarlane, *Special Trust,* 1–16, and John G. Tower, *Consequences: A Personal and Political Memoir* (New York: Little, Brown, 1991), 276–77.

4. Byrne, *Iran-Contra,* 286–87.

5. RRD, February 26–March 1, 1987, and Tumulty, *Triumph of Nancy Reagan,* 491–92.

6. "Address to the Nation on the Iran Arms and Contra Aid Controversy," March 4, 1987. Available at: https://www.reaganlibrary.gov/archives/speech/address-nation-iran-arms-and-contra-aid-controversy-0.

7. Hayward, *Age of Reagan: Conservative Counterrevolution,* 535.

8. *The Tower Commission Report* (New York: Bantam Books, 1987), and Bartholomew Sparrow, *The Strategist: Brent Scowcroft and the Call of National Security* (New York: Public Affairs, 2015), 244–61. The Tower Commission's recommendations on the NSC structure were primarily shaped by Brent Scowcroft, the only Tower Commission member with significant executive branch experience, as a former assistant to the president for national security affairs under President Ford who would go on to hold the same position under Bush. In coauthoring the Tower Report, Scowcroft in effect wrote his new job description.

9. Hayward, *Age of Reagan: Conservative Counterrevolution,* 535.

10. Memorandum from Carlucci to Reagan re: "NSC Activities," December 24, 1986, folder: "The President (12/24/1986–02/11/1987) Box 92462," box 3, Frank Carlucci Files, RPL.

11. Minutes of senior presidential advisor meeting on SDI, February 3, 1987, folder: "NSPG 0143A 02/03/1987 (1 of 2), Box 91308," box 5, Executive Secretariat, NSC: NSPG; minutes of NSPG meeting on arms control and SDI, February 10, 1987, folder: "NSPG 143, 3 Feb 1987 [SDI]," Executive Secretariat, NSC: NSPG Meeting File, RPL; and RRD, February 10, 1987.

12. Memorandum from Fritz Ermath to Robert Oakley re: "Increasing Time Pressure on Soviets in Afghanistan," February 4, 1987, folder: "Afghan Resistance, Working Group (7)," box 91555, Vincent Cannistraro Files, RPL.

13. Bearden and Risen, *Main Enemy,* 267–68, 282–89.

14. "Notes from Meeting with the President," May 6, 1987, folder: "The President (4/29/1987–06/30/1987)," box 3, Frank C. Carlucci Files; memorandum from Ermath re: "FCC TPs for Arbatov," May 22, 1987, folder: "Soviet Union—1987–19877, Memos, Etc (5)," in Nelson Ledsky Files, RPL.

15. CIA paper, November 13, 1987, in James Graham Wilson, ed., *Foreign Relations of the United States, 1981–1988,* volume 6, *Soviet Union, October 1986–January 1989* (hereinafter *FRUS,* vol. 6) (Washington, DC: Government Printing Office, 2016).

16. Minutes of meeting with the Joint Chiefs of Staff, April 8, 1987, folder 8790363, box 19, Executive Secretariat: NSC System File, RPL, and RRD, April 8, 1987.

17. Michael R. Gordon, "CIA's Report Revives Soviet-Growth Debates," *New York Times,* March 29, 1987, in box 52, Jim Mann Papers, HIA, and note from Carlucci to president, April 24, 1987, with attachment "The State of the Soviet Economy," April 22, 1987, folder: "The President (2/12/1987–04/28/1987)," box 3, Frank C. Carlucci Files, RPL.

18. Ronald Steel, "Shultz's Way," *New York Times Magazine,* January 11, 1987.

19. RRD, March 6, 1987, and memorandum from Carlucci with attached paper "Soviet Motives," March 16, 1987, folder: "The President (2/12/1987–04/28/1987)," box 3, Frank C. Carlucci Files, RPL. This progress took place amid the eruption of another spy scandal. The KGB had snared two US Marine guards at Embassy Moscow in "honey traps." Russian women working for the KGB had seduced the lascivious marines and enticed them to share access to the embassy's most sensitive secrets. "The Soviets have scored a major intelligence success . . . our national security has been severely damaged," concluded an NSC assessment. "The mood in [Washington] became boiling mad" toward the Soviets, recalled Shultz, so poisonous that seventy US senators passed a resolution demanding that he cancel his Moscow trip. As with previous crises such as the KAL 007 shoot-down, Reagan and Shultz remained committed to delinking issues so that they could pursue progress in specific areas without letting other frictions derail the entire USA-USSR relationship. Later investigations would reveal that the intelligence damage caused by the marine indiscretions was not as extensive as feared (and the Ames and Hanssen treason continued undetected at this time), but the NSC assessment captures the prevailing attitude at the time of Shultz's trip. Memorandum from Barry Kelly to Carlucci re: "Moscow Embassy in Context," April 6, 1987, in *FRUS,* vol. 6, and Shultz, *Turmoil and Triumph,* 881–85.

20. Memorandum of conversation between Shultz and Gorbachev, April 14, 1987, in *FRUS,* vol 6, and Gorbachev, *Memoirs,* 444.

21. "Notes of a Meeting," March 18, 1987, and memorandum of conversation between Shultz and Shevardnadze, April 13, 1987, in *FRUS,* vol 6.

22. Shultz, *Triumph and Turmoil,* 891–93. Shultz also brought with him Assistant Secretary of State for Human Rights Richard Schifter. Holders of this position rarely travel with the secretary, especially for meetings in the capitals of rival great powers. By including Schifter on his delegation, Shultz empowered him and sent another signal to the Kremlin about the priority of human rights.

23. Michael Einik, email to author, February 11, 2021; cited with permission.

24. Adelman, *Great Universal Embrace,* 95–96.

25. Telegram from Shultz to Reagan re: "My Last Day in Moscow," April 15, 1987, in *FRUS,* vol. 6, and Shultz, *Triumph and Turmoil,* 896–97.

26. "Dealing at Last," *Newsweek,* April 17, 1987, in box 53, Jim Mann Papers, HIA.

27. Quoted in Kasey S. Pipes, *After the Fall: The Remarkable Comeback of Richard Nixon* (Washington, DC: Regnery, 2019), 190, and Mann, *Rebellion of Ronald Reagan,* 49–50.

28. Frank Carlucci, "Notes from Reagan Meeting with Kirkpatrick," February 24, 1987, in *FRUS,* vol. 6; Frank Carlucci, "Notes of Reagan Meeting with Nixon," April 28, 1987, folder: "The President (2/12/1987–04/28/1987)," box 3, Frank C. Carlucci Files, RPL; and "Nixon Memorandum to the File," April 28, 1987, box 51, Jim Mann Papers, HIA. As Reagan explained Gorbachev to Nixon, the president was mindful that Gorbachev had defended him two months earlier in a Moscow meeting with Kissinger. When the former secretary of state had disparaged Reagan as "unprepared" at Reykjavík, Gorbachev retorted that he found Reagan a worthy partner committed to continuing dialogue to solve problems.

29. Letter from Buckley to Reagan, April 5, 1987; letter from Reagan to Buckley, May 5, 1987; and letter from Buckley to Reagan, June 28, 1987, all in William F. Buckley Jr., *The Reagan I Knew* (New York: Basic Books, 2008), 198–204.

30. Memorandum of conversation between Reagan and Kohl, May 12, 1987, folder: "0930 Meetings Box 92462," box 2, Frank Carlucci Files, RPL.

31. Brands, *Making the Unipolar Moment,* 265.

32. Minutes of NSPG meeting on US policy in the Middle East, February 12, 1987, folder: "NSPG 0144 12 Feb 1987, Box 91306," box 5, Executive Secretariat, NSC: NSPG, RPL.

33. Crist, *Twilight War,* 212–14, and Weinberger, *Fighting for Peace,* 401–2. Oddly, in his memoir Shultz claims to have supported reflagging from the start, but the documentary record indicates otherwise. See Shultz, *Turmoil and Triumph,* 925–27.

34. Crist, *Twilight War,* 213–28; RRD, June 17, 1987; Weinberger, *Fighting for Peace,* 404–8; and Shultz, *Turmoil and Triumph,* 928–35.

35. Shultz, *Turmoil and Triumph,* 932.

36. George Russell, "Trade Face-Off," *Time,* April 13, 1987, and McGregor, *Asia's Reckoning,* 110–11.

37. NSC meeting memo with attachments, April 28, 1987, folder 8790429-8790431, box 7, Assistant to the President for National Security Affairs, Chron File, RPL, and RRD, June 8, 1987.

38. Gaston Sigur, "Korean Politics in Transition," address, February 6, 1987; schedule proposal to Ryan from Green re: "Courtesy Call on President Reagan by Korean Minister of National Defense Lee Ki Baek," with attached memo for assistant to the president for national security affairs re: "Courtesy Call on President Reagan by the ROK Minister of National Defense," March 19, 1987, folder: "Korea 03/16/1987–04/30/1987, Box 3," box 2, James Kelly Files, RPL.

39. Green, *By More Than Providence,* 420.

40. Choe Sang-Hun, "Stephen Kim Sou-hwan, Cardinal, Dies at 86," *New York Times,* February 16, 2009; Gaston Sigur interview, Foreign Affairs Oral History Collection, Association for Diplomatic Studies and Training, Arlington, VA; Lilley, *China Hands,* 274–78; and Oberdorfer and Carlin, *Two Koreas,* 129–34.

41. Gaston Sigur interview, Foreign Affairs Oral History Collection, Association for Diplomatic Studies and Training, Arlington, VA.

42. Richard C. Kagan, *Taiwan's Statesman: Lee Teng-hui and Democracy in Asia* (Annapolis, MD: Naval Institute Press, 2007), 100.

43. Jonathan Kandell, "Lee Teng-hui, 97, Who Led Taiwan's Turn to Democracy, Dies," *New York Times,* July 30, 2020.

44. Green, *By More Than Providence,* 420, and Chris Miller, *We Shall Be Masters: Russian Pivots to East Asia from Peter the Great to Putin* (Cambridge, MA: Harvard University Press, 2021), 261.

45. Cable from Douglas Paal to James Kelly re: "Secretary Shultz's China Trip," March 7, 1987, folder: "China 1987 (2)," box 1, James Kelly Files, RPL.

46. "Address Before a Joint Session of Congress on the State of the Union—1987," January 27, 1987, available at: https://www.reaganlibrary.gov/archives/speech/address-joint-session-congress-state-union-1987, and minutes of NSC meeting on South American democracy, March 13, 1987, folder 8602018, box 9, Executive Secretariat: NSC System File, RPL.

47. Brands, *Making the Unipolar Moment,* 145–46, and Weigel, *Witness to Hope,* 560–62.

48. RRD, November 18, 1986.

49. Minutes of NSC meeting on the president's trip to Europe, May 21, 1987, folder: "NSC 00147, 21 May 1987 [Political Issues for the President's Trip to Europe]," Executive Secretariat, NSC: NSC Meeting Files, RPL, and Weigel, *Witness to Hope,* 532–35.

50. Memorandum from Shultz to Reagan re: "Pinochet and the Letelier-Moffitt Murders: Implications for US Policy," October 15, 1987; CIA assessment, "Pinochet's Role in the Letelier Assassination and Subsequent Coverup," May 1, 1987, available at: https://www.reaganlibrary.gov/archives/chile-documents; Shultz, *Turmoil and Triumph,* 969–75; and Brands, *Making the Unipolar Moment,* 146–49. For more on the Letelier assassination, see Alan McPherson, *Ghosts of Sheridan Circle: How a Washington Assassination Brought Pinochet's Terror State to Justice* (Chapel Hill, NC: University of North Carolina Press, 2019).

51. Kagan, *A Twilight Struggle,* 564–96; RRD, December 10 and 15, 1987; and "Radio Address to the Nation on Foreign Issues and the Budget," December 19, 1987, available at: https://www.reaganlibrary.gov/archives/speech/radio-address-nation-foreign-issues-and-budget. Passions over Central America left no corner of American life untouched—even funerals. Earlier in the year the president and First Lady traveled to Long Island to attend Bill Casey's funeral mass at his home parish, St. Mary's Church, along with other mourners, including Richard Nixon, Weinberger, Carlucci, Meese, and new CIA director Bill Webster. The Reagans and other guests shuffled awkwardly in the pews while waiting for the presiding bishop, John McGann, who arrived twenty-five minutes late—and proceeded to deliver a homily lambasting American nuclear policy and "the violence wrought in Central America by support of the contras." McGann continued, "I cannot conceal or disguise my fundamental disagreement on these matters [with Casey]," though the bishop added his gratitude for Casey's generosity to the church. Casey's widow, Sophia, had asked Jeane Kirkpatrick to give a eulogy. Taking the pulpit, the former UN ambassador rebuked the sanctimonious bishop. Kirkpatrick observed, "Some mean-spirited, ill-informed comments have been written and spoken in the last days . . . [but] Casey could take the guff required to support unpopular ideas." As for Central America, she said, "Supporting the Nicaraguan freedom fighters had a special priority for him, no question about it, but that had no more priority than law." The bishop's drive-by denunciation of his dead parishioner made national news, including the front page of *The New York Times.* Noting McGann's criticism in his diary, Reagan wrote, "Jeane Kirkpatrick took care of that in her Eulogy and got a big hand. First time I've ever heard [that] at a funeral." Persico, *Casey,* 573–74; Steven V. Roberts, "Contra Controversy Raised at Casey Funeral," *New York Times,* May 10, 1987; and RRD, May 10, 1987.

52. Portions of this section draw on the author's previously published essay for the Ronald Reagan Institute, "The President Who Tore Down That Wall," and are used here by permission. Available at: https://www.reaganfoundation.org/media/357270/inboden_berlin-wall-address_reagan-institute.pdf.

53. Peter Robinson, "Notes from Dinner at the Home of Herr Dieter Elz," folder: "Notes on Berlin from Pre-Advance," box 9, Peter M. Robinson Files, 1983–88, RPL, and Robinson, *How Ronald Reagan Changed My Life*, 97–98.

54. Interview with Ken Duberstein by Peter Robinson, May 30, 3002, box 55, Jim Mann Papers, HIA.

55. Robert Rowland and John M. Jones, "Reagan at the Brandenburg Gate: Moral Clarity Tempered by Pragmatism," *Rhetoric and Public Affairs* 9, no. 1 (Spring 2006): 21–50.

56. Robinson, *How Ronald Reagan Changed My Life*, 191–93, and "Remarks Following Discussions with Pope John Paul II in Vatican City," June 6, 1987, available at: https://www.reaganlibrary.gov/archives/speech/remarks-following-discussions-pope-john-paul-ii-vatican-city.

57. Interview with Ken Duberstein by Peter Robinson, May 30, 2002, box 55, Jim Mann Papers, HIA.

58. "Headlines in the Washington Post front page for June 12 1987," note, box 53, Jim Mann Papers, HIA.

59. Mann, *Rebellion of Ronald Reagan*, 160.

60. "Remarks on East-West Relations at the Brandenburg Gate in West Berlin," June 12, 1987. Available at: https://www.reaganlibrary.gov/archives/speech/remarks-east-west-relations-brandenburg-gate-west-berlin.

61. Hayward, *Age of Reagan: Conservative Counterrevolution*, 594.

62. Romesh Ratnesar, *Tear Down This Wall: A City, a President, and the Speech That Ended the Cold War* (New York: Simon & Schuster, 2009), 151, and Mann, *Rebellion of Ronald Reagan*, 213. Even Shultz does not mention the speech in his 1,138-page memoir.

CHAPTER 14: ENDGAME

1. Memorandum from Powell to Thatcher re: "Visit to Washington," July 10, 1987, THCR 1/9/18A/8 f67, CAC. Available at: https://www.margaretthatcher.org/document/205268.

2. Cited in Hayward, *Age of Reagan: Conservative Counterrevolution*, 544–47.

3. RRD, July 17 and 19, 1987, and Charles Moore, *Margaret Thatcher: The Authorized Biography; Herself Alone* (New York: Knopf, 2019), 159.

4. Ilan Ben-Meir, "That Time Trump Spent Nearly $100,000 on an Ad Criticizing US Foreign Policy in 1987," BuzzFeed News, July 10, 2015. Available at: https://www.buzzfeednews.com/article/ilanbenmeir/that-time-trump-spent-nearly-100000-on-an-ad-criticizing-us.

5. RRD, October 3–4, 1987, and Baker and Glasser, *Man Who Ran Washington*, 281–83.

6. Taubman, *Gorbachev*, 396–97, and Brown, *Human Factor*, 206–7. One of the original Cold Warriors had taken notice of that agenda. That same month, the State Department commemorated the fortieth anniversary of its strategy office, the Policy Planning Staff (known as S/P), by convening every former S/P director for an off-the-record roundtable. Participants included George Kennan, the first S/P director, who had founded the office the same year he published his iconic *Foreign Affairs* article "The Sources of Soviet Conduct," establishing the doctrine of containment for American Cold War strategy. Since then the brilliant yet erratic Kennan had alternately revised and repudiated containment while becoming a critic of Reagan administration policy—and of his sometime friend and longtime rival (and S/P successor in the Truman administration) Paul Nitze. True to form, the mournful Kennan began the conference by recalling the origins of the Cold War and then dismissed containment as "almost entirely irrelevant to the problems [the

United States] and the rest of the civilized world face[d]." Declaring, "A new wind is blowing from the East," he praised Gorbachev's reforms and "wish to see tensions reduced" but worried the United States would fail to "take the lead in finding a way out of this present Cold War impasse." Later that summer, Reagan spoke to a town hall meeting in Los Angeles. Like Kennan, he reviewed the four decades of the Cold War from its origins at Yalta to the present day; like Kennan, Reagan spoke of "break[ing] out of the stalemate of the Cold War, to push forward with new initiatives that might help the world evolve beyond the postwar era," and highlighted the emerging agreement to abolish intermediate-range nuclear missiles. Kennan failed to see that Reagan had both embraced containment and, crucially, improved on it. Reagan's pressure track sought to accelerate containment's original insight that Soviet communism contained the seeds of its own demise, while his negotiating track sought to partner with Gorbachev in reducing nuclear weapons and beckoning peace closer. As John Lewis Gaddis sums up, the agonized Kennan "[left] it to Reagan to bring his strategy to its successful conclusion." Transcript of State Department Open Forum, May 11, 1987, shared with author by James Graham Wilson; "Remarks on Soviet–United States Relations at the Town Hall of California Meeting in Los Angeles," August 26, 1987, available at: https://www.reaganlibrary.gov/archives /speech/remarks-soviet-united-states-relations-town-hall-california-meeting-los-angeles; and John Lewis Gaddis, *George F. Kennan: An American Life* (New York: Penguin Press, 2011), 670–71.

7. Minutes of Reagan's meeting with the Joint Chiefs of Staff, August 11, 1987, folder 8790824, box 19, Executive Secretariat: NSC System File, RPL.

8. Matlock, *Reagan and Gorbachev,* 253–54.

9. Minutes of NSPG meeting on review of United States arms control positions, September 8, 1987, folder: "NSPG 0165, 8 September 1987 [Review of United States Arms Control Positions]," Executive Secretariat, NSC: NSPG Meeting File, RPL.

10. Memorandum of conversation between Shultz and Gorbachev, October 23, 1987, in *FRUS,* vol. 6.

11. Shultz, *Turmoil and Triumph,* 1001–3, and Taubman, *Gorbachev,* 325–36, 399.

12. Author interview with Armitage, March 5, 2019.

13. "Remarks by the President in Meeting with Afghan Resistance Leaders," November 12, 1987, folder: "Meeting with Afghan Resistance Leaders," box 10, Peter M. Robinson Files, 1983–88, RPL.

14. Memo from Dobriansky to McFarlane re: "Letter from Amb Wilson re Ukrainian Catholic Church," November 26, 1985, with attached note to "Bill"; letter to McFarlane from Wilson, October 18, 1985, with attachment "Situation of the Ukrainian Catholic Church in the Ukraine," November 19, 1985, folder: "USSR—General [1984-1986] (4/5)," box 26, Jack F. Matlock Files, RPL; and Kengor, *A Pope and a President,* 426–27.

15. "Address to the People of Western Europe on Soviet–United States Relations," November 4, 1987. Available at: https://www.reaganlibrary.gov/archives/speech/address-people -western-europe-soviet-united-states-relations.

16. Powell, *My American Journey,* 354–55.

17. Adelman, *Reagan at Reykjavik,* 244–45, and Shultz, *Turmoil and Triumph,* 1011–12. Akhromeyev's loyalty to Gorbachev and reform commitments ended in August 1991, when Akhromeyev and other generals disillusioned with Gorbachev's reforms participated in a failed coup attempt against the Soviet leader. Akhromeyev then died by his own hand.

18. Memorandum of conversation, December 4, 1987, in *FRUS,* vol. 6, and Gates, *From the Shadows,* 423–26. Gates also recalls the shame of later realizing that "at this first high-level CIA-KGB meeting, Kryuchkov smugly knew that he had a spy—Aldrich Ames—in

the heart of CIA, and that he knew quite well what [the CIA was] saying to the President and others about the Soviet Union."

19. Memorandum re: "Gorbachev's Gameplan: The Long View," November 24, 1987. Available at: https://nsarchive2.gwu.edu/NSAEBB/NSAEBB238/usdocs/Doc%2011%20(Memo%20from%20Webster%2011.24.87).pdf.

20. RRD, December 3, 1987, and Powell, *My American Journey,* 358.

21. Taubman, *Gorbachev,* 403–6.

22. Memorandum of conversation between Reagan and Gorbachev, December 9, 1987, 10:55 a.m. to 12:35 p.m.; memorandum of conversation between Reagan and Gorbachev, December 9, 1987, 12:40 p.m. to 2:10 p.m.; memorandum of conversation between Reagan and Gorbachev, December 10, 1987, 12:00 p.m. to 12:15 p.m., all in folder: "8791377 (1 of 2)," box 20, Executive Secretariat: NSC System File; and memorandum from Powell to Reagan re: "The Washington Summit and SDI," December 31, 1987, folder: "Chron—Official 1987 (14)," box 1, Colin Powell Files, RPL.

23. "Remarks on Signing the Intermediate-Range Nuclear Forces Treaty," December 8, 1987. Available at: https://www.reaganlibrary.gov/archives/speech/remarks-signing -intermediate-range-nuclear-forces-treaty.

24. "Breakfast with Scowcroft," *Christian Science Monitor,* November 20, 1987; George Will, "Drunk on Détente," *Washington Post,* December 13, 1987; and Henry Kissinger, "The Dangers Ahead," *Newsweek,* December 21, 1987, in box 52, Jim Mann Papers, HIA.

25. Nixon notes on conversation with Reagan, December 14, 1987, box 55, Jim Mann Papers, HIA.

26. "Remarks on Signing the Intermediate-Range Nuclear Forces Treaty," December 8, 1987. Available at: https://www.reaganlibrary.gov/archives/speech/remarks-signing -intermediate-range-nuclear-forces-treaty.

27. Rodman, *More Precious Than Peace,* 344–49; Shultz, *Turmoil and Triumph,* 1090–91; and Robert Oakley interview, Foreign Affairs Oral History Collection, Association for Diplomatic Studies and Training, Arlington, VA.

28. Shultz, *Turmoil and Triumph,* 1094.

29. The only significant political heat Reagan's Angola policy generated came from his own right flank, as some conservatives griped that he—and Shultz and Crocker—were insufficiently devoted to Savimbi. After right-wing activist Paul Weyrich brought a group of, in Reagan's words, "hard core Conservative leaders" to the White House in April, Reagan vented to his diary: "Half hour meeting became an hour. As usual they had us on the wrong side in Afghanistan settlement, Mozambique, Chile and Angola. It's amazing how certain they can be when they know so d——n little of what we're really doing." RRD, April 12, 1988; Gates, *From the Shadows,* 433–34; and Rodman, *More Precious Than Peace,* 384–90; Chas. W. Freeman Jr., "The Angola/Namibia Accords," *Foreign Affairs,* Summer 1989, 126–141.

30. RRD, April 17, 1988, and Crist, *Twilight War,* 334–57.

31. Brands, *Making the Unipolar Moment,* 268–72.

32. Ross, *Doomed to Succeed,* 215–16. Reagan's lifelong aversion to anti-Semitism shaped a related decision in his final year in office. Honoring a campaign pledge to B'nai B'rith, he secured Senate ratification of the Genocide Convention, committing signatory nations to take action against genocide. Reagan's support also overturned a three-decade precedent in the US Senate that had blocked approval of human rights treaties, paving the way for future American engagement with multilateral human rights measures. Sikkink, *Mixed Signals,* 179.

33. RRD, January 15–17, 1988.

34. "Soviet Jewry/Emigration" and "Religion in the Soviet Union," Department of State briefing papers, folder: "DOS Background Book: Visit of Soviet Foreign Minister Shevardnadze (3 of 3)," RAC box 2, Lisa Jameson Files, RPL.

35. RRD, April 25 and May 3, 12, and 17, 1988.

36. National Security Decision Directive 305, "Objectives at the Moscow Summit," April 26, 1988. Available at: https://fas.org/irp/offdocs/nsdd/nsdd-305.htm.

37. Memorandum from Fritz Ermath to Colin Powell re: "Message to Charles Powell," February 26, 1988, folder 8890181; memorandum from Ermath to Powell re: "Issues for London," February 22, 1988, folder 8890177, both in box 20, Executive Secretariat: NSC System File, RPL.

38. Minutes of NSPG meeting re: "NATO Summit," February 26, 1988, folder: "NSPG 0177, 26 February 1988 [NATO Summit]," Executive Secretariat, NSC: NSPG Meeting File, RPL.

39. "Remarks to the World Affairs Council," April 21, 1988, box 52, Jim Mann Papers, HIA; Richard Halloran, "Stealth Bomber Takes Shape: A Flying Wing and Crew of 2," *New York Times,* May 16, 1988; and Malcolm Browne, "Will the Stealth Bomber Work?," *New York Times Magazine,* July 17, 1988.

40. "Remarks to the World Affairs Council," April 21, 1988, box 52, Jim Mann Papers, HIA.

41. Shultz, *Turmoil and Triumph,* 1096–97. Gorbachev also complained about Nixon's recent criticism of the INF Treaty. "Nixon has taken a break from the labor of writing his memoirs to take part in political debates," said a sarcastic Gorbachev. "The dead should not be allowed to take the living by the coattails and drag them back to the past. We should not let old politicians prevent us from building up better relations."

42. RRD, May 24 and 27, 1987, and Shultz, *Turmoil and Triumph,* 1081–85.

43. RRD, May 28, 1987.

44. Massie, *Trust but Verify,* 334.

45. Memorandum of conversation between Reagan and Gorbachev, May 29, 1988, folder 8890497, box 20, Executive Secretariat: NSC System File, RPL.

46. Massie, *Trust but Verify,* 330, and "Remarks to Religious Leaders at the Danilov Monastery in Moscow," May 30, 1988, available at: https://www.reaganlibrary.gov/archives/speech/remarks-religious-leaders-danilov-monastery-moscow.

47. "Remarks to Soviet Dissidents at Spaso House in Moscow," May 30, 1988. Available at: https://www.reaganlibrary.gov/archives/speech/remarks-soviet-dissidents-spaso-house-moscow.

48. Mann, *Rebellion of Ronald Reagan,* 304–6.

49. Memorandum of conversation at dinner between Reagan and Gorbachev, June 1, 1988, and memorandum from Shultz to Reagan re: "Your June 1 Dinner with General Secretary Gorbachev" (no date), in *FRUS,* vol. 6.

50. Bret Baier with Catherine Whitney, *Three Days in Moscow: Ronald Reagan and the Fall of the Soviet Empire* (New York: William Morrow, 2018), 253–54.

51. Ronald Reagan, *An American Life* (New York: Threshold Editions, 1990), 713.

52. "Remarks and a Question-and-Answer Session with the Students and Faculty at Moscow State University," May 31, 1988. Available at: https://www.reaganlibrary.gov/archives/speech/remarks-and-question-and-answer-session-students-and-faculty-moscow-state.

53. Eric S. Edelman, "The Great Communicator and the Beginning of the End of the Cold War" (no date), Ronald Reagan Institute. Available at: https://www.reaganfoundation.org/media/354711/amb_edelman_moscow_state_university.pdf.

54. Hugh Sidey, "Good Chemistry," *Time,* June 13, 1988.

55. Mann, *Rebellion of Ronald Reagan,* 307–10.

56. Author interview with Armitage, March 5, 2019, and RRD, January 4, 1988.

57. RRD, April 27 and May 13, 19, 20, 21, and 22, 1988, and Shultz, *Turmoil and Triumph,* 1051–79.

58. Harry Truman had first ascended to the presidency following Franklin Roosevelt's death in 1945, before Truman won reelection in 1948.

59. Taubman, *Gorbachev,* 422, and James Graham Wilson, *The Triumph of Improvisation: Gorbachev's Adaptability, Reagan's Engagement, and the End of the Cold War* (Ithaca, NY: Cornell University Press, 2014), 143.

60. Memorandum of conversation in Reagan's private meeting with Gorbachev, December 7, 1988, folder 8890944, box 21, Executive Secretariat: NSC System File, RPL.

61. David M. Abshire, *Saving the Reagan Presidency: Trust Is the Coin of the Realm* (College Station, TX: Texas A&M Press, 2005), 197.

62. "Farewell Address to the Nation," January 11, 1989. Available at: https://www.reagan library.gov/archives/speech/farewell-address-nation. Americans watching Reagan's speech also saw on the newsstands that week *Time* magazine's January 16, 1989, cover featuring New York real estate developer Donald J. Trump. Little could Reagan or anyone else imagine that twenty-eight years later, to the week, Trump would be inaugurated as a Republican president of a very different sort.

63. Kuhn, *Ronald Reagan in Private,* 268.

EPILOGUE

1. Robert G. Kaiser, "Gorbachev: We All Lost Cold War," *Washington Post,* June 11, 2004.

2. Brands, *Making the Unipolar Moment,* 342.

3. Leebaert, *Fifty-Year Wound,* 587.

4. Address at the Oxford Union, December 4, 1992. Available at: https://www.c-span.org /video/?35586-1/arising-ashes-world-order#.

INDEX

ABOUT THE AUTHOR

William Inboden is executive director and William Powers Jr. chair at the William P. Clements Jr. Center for National Security and associate professor at the LBJ School of Public Affairs, both at the University of Texas at Austin. Prior to academia, he worked for fifteen years as a policymaker in Washington, DC, and overseas, including senior positions with the State Department and the National Security Council in the George W. Bush administration. A graduate of Stanford University, he earned his doctorate at Yale. He is a life member of the Council on Foreign Relations and editor in chief of the *Texas National Security Review*. His commentary has appeared in numerous outlets, including *The Wall Street Journal, The New York Times, The Washington Post,* the *Los Angeles Times, World,* Politico, NPR, CNN, Sky News, and the BBC. He is the author of *Religion and American Foreign Policy, 1945–1960: The Soul of Containment.*